VIEW OF THE ATTIC PLAINS, WITH A GLIMPSE OF THE ACROPOLIS OF ATHENS. — Frontispiece.

A

GENERAL HISTORY

FOR

COLLEGES AND HIGH SCHOOLS,

BY

P. V. N. MYERS, A.M.

AUTHOR OF "ANCIENT HISTORY," "MEDIÆVAL AND
MODERN HISTORY," ETC.

BOSTON, U.S.A., AND LONDON

GINN & COMPANY, PUBLISHERS

1904

TYPOGRAPHY BY J. S. CUSHING & CO., BOSTON, U.S.A.

PRESSWORK BY GINN & CO., BOSTON, U.S.A.

PREFACE.

THIS volume is based upon my *Ancient History* and *Mediæval and Modern History*. In some instances I have changed the perspective and the proportions of the narrative ; but in the main, the book is constructed upon the same lines as those drawn for the earlier works. In dealing with so wide a range of facts, and tracing so many historic movements, I cannot hope that I have always avoided falling into error. I have, however, taken the greatest care to verify statements of fact, and to give the latest results of discovery and criticism.

Considering the very general character of the present work, an enumeration of the books that have contributed facts to my narration, or have helped to mould my views on this or that subject, would hardly be looked for ; yet I wish here to acknowledge my special indebtedness, in the earlier parts of the history, to the works of George Rawlinson, Sayce, Wilkinson, Brugsch, Grote, Curtius, Mommsen, Merivale, and Leighton ; and in the later parts, and on special periods, to the writings of Hodgkin, Emerton, Ranke, Freeman, Michaud, Bryce, Symonds, Green (J. R.), Motley, Hallam, Thiers, Lecky, Baird, and Müller.

Several of the colored maps, with which the book will be found liberally provided, were engraved especially for my *Ancient History;* but the larger number are authorized reproductions of charts accompanying Professor Freeman's *Historical Geography of Europe*. The Roman maps were prepared for Professor William

F. Allen's *History of Rome*, which is to be issued soon, and it is to his courtesy that I am indebted for their use.

The illustrations have been carefully selected with reference to their authenticity and historical truthfulness. Many of those in the Oriental and Greek part of the work are taken from Oscar Jäger's *Weltgeschichte;* while most of those in the Roman portion are from Professor Allen's forthcoming work on Rome, to which I have just referred, the author having most generously granted me the privilege of using them in my work, notwithstanding it is to appear in advance of his.

Further acknowledgments of indebtedness are also due from me to many friends who have aided me with their scholarly suggestions and criticism. My warmest thanks are particularly due to Professor W. F. Allen, of the University of Wisconsin; to Dr. E. W. Coy, Principal of Hughes High School, Cincinnati; to Professor William A. Merrill, of Miami University; and to Mr. D. H. Montgomery, author of *The Leading Facts of History* series.

P. V. N. M.

COLLEGE HILL, OHIO,
July, 1889.

TABLE OF CONTENTS.

PART I.

ANCIENT HISTORY.

SECTION I. — THE EASTERN NATIONS.

SECTION II. — GRECIAN HISTORY.

Part II.

MEDIÆVAL AND MODERN HISTORY.

LIST OF MAPS.

———◆◇◆———

[1] For the use of this map I am indebted to the courtesy of Mr. D. H. Montgomery, author of "Leading Facts of French History."

GENERAL HISTORY.

—oo〰oo—

GENERAL INTRODUCTION.

THE RACES AND THEIR EARLY MIGRATIONS.[1]

Divisions of History. — History is usually divided into three periods, — Ancient, Mediæval, and Modern. Ancient History begins with the earliest nations of which we can gain any certain knowledge, and extends to the fall of the Roman Empire in the West, A.D. 476. Mediæval History embraces the period, about one thousand years in length, lying between the fall of Rome and the discovery of the New World by Columbus, A.D. 1492. Modern History commences with the close of the Mediæval period and extends to the present time.[2]

Antiquity of Man. — We do not know when man first came into possession of the earth. We only know that, in ages vastly remote, when both the climate and the outline of Europe were very different from what they are at present, man lived on that continent with animals now extinct; and that as early as 4000 or 3000 B.C., — when the curtain first rises on the stage of history,

[1] For the present (1903) impression of this work, this introductory chapter has been revised and the relevant results of ethnological research since it was first written have been incorporated in the text.

[2] It is thought preferable by some scholars to let the beginning of the great Teutonic migration (A.D. 375) or the restoration of the Empire by Charlemagne (A.D. 800) mark the end of the period of ancient history. Some also prefer to date the beginning of the modern period from the capture of Constantinople by the Turks, A.D. 1453; while still others speak of it in a general way as commencing about the close of the 15th century, at which time there were many inventions and discoveries, and a great stir in the intellectual world.

— in some favored regions, as in the valley of the Nile, there were nations and civilizations already venerable with age, and possessing languages, arts, and institutions that bear evidence of slow growth through long periods of time before history begins.

The Races of Mankind. — Distinctions in form, color, and physiognomy divide the human species into three types or races, known as the Black or Ethiopian Race, the Yellow or Mongolian Race, and the White or European Race (formerly called the Caucasian).[1]   But we must not suppose each of these three types to be sharply marked off from the others ; they shade into one another by insensible gradations.

NEGRO CAPTIVES.
From the Monuments of Thebes.
(Illustrating the permanence of race characteristics.)

There has been no perceptible change in the great types during historic times. The paintings upon the oldest Egyptian monuments show us that at the dawn of history, about five or six thousand years ago, the principal races were as distinctly marked as now, each bearing its racial badge of color and physiognomy. As early as the times of Jeremiah, the permanency of physical characteristics had passed into the proverb, " Can the Ethiopian change his skin? "

The Black Race. — Africa south of the Sahara is the home of the peoples of the Black Race, but we find them on all the other continents and on many of the islands of the seas, whither they have migrated or been carried as slaves by the stronger races ; for since time immemorial they have been " hewers of wood and drawers of water " for their more favored brethren.

The Yellow or Mongolian Race. — Eastern and Northern Asia is the central seat of the Mongolian Race.   Many of the Mongolian tribes are pastoral nomads, who roam over the vast Asian

[1] Some ethnologists reckon a greater number of types or races.   The classification given is simply a convenient and practical one.

plains north of the great ranges of the Himalayas; their leading part in history has been to harass peoples of settled habits. But the most important people of this type are the Chinese, who constitute probably a fifth or more of the entire population of the earth. Already in times very remote this people had developed a civilization quite advanced on various lines; but having reached a certain stage in culture, they strangely ceased to make any further progress. Not until recent times did they become a factor of any significance in world history.

The White Race and its Three Groups. — The so-called White Race embraces the historic nations. The chief peoples of this division of mankind fall into three groups, — the Hamitic, the Semitic, and the Aryan[1] or Indo-European. The members forming any one of these groups must not be looked upon as kindred in blood; the only certain bond uniting the peoples of each group is the bond of language.[2]

The ancient Egyptians were the chief people of the Hamitic *Ham* branch. In the gray dawn of history we discover them already *Egyptia* settled in the valley of the Nile, and there erecting great monuments so faultless in construction as to render it certain that those who planned them had had long previous training in the art of building. Real history begins with these master builders.

---

[1] Ethnologists have ceased to use this name, as well as its equivalents, Indo-European and Indo-Germanic, as an ethnic term; but there is no reason why it should be given up by the historian. It should be carefully noted, however, that where the term Aryan is applied to a people it simply means that the people thus designated use an Aryan speech, and that it does not mean that they are ethnically related to any other Aryan-speaking people. Physical or racial relationships cannot be determined by the test of language; think of the millions of English-speaking African negroes in the United States! For a masterly discussion of the question of the ethnic types or races making up the population of Europe, see Ripley's *The Races of Europe* (New York, 1899).

[2] In the case of the Semites and Hamites, it is probable that the most of the peoples forming each group are in the main actually of the same ethnic stock; in the case of the Aryans, however, we certainly have to do with peoples belonging to several distinct ethnic subvarieties or types.

The Semitic family includes among its chief peoples the ancient Babylonians and Assyrians, the Hebrews, the Phœnicians, and the Arabians. We are not certain what region was the original abode of this family. We only know that by the dawn of history its various clans and tribes, whencesoever they may have come, had spread over the greater part of Southwestern Asia, and in the rich river plains of the Tigris and Euphrates had built great cities and established powerful monarchies.

It is interesting to note that the three great historic religions of the world, — the Hebrew, the Christian, and the Mohammedan, — the three religions which alone (if we except that of Zoroaster) teach a belief in one God, arose among peoples belonging to the Semitic family.

The Aryan-speaking peoples form the most widely dispersed group of the White Race. They include the ancient Greeks and Romans, all the peoples of modern Europe (save the Basques, the Finns and Lapps, the Magyars or Hungarians, and the Ottoman Turks), together with the Persians and Hindus and some other Asian peoples.

The Aryan Dispersion. — Long before the dawn of history the clans and tribes of the hitherto undivided Aryan family,[1] moving in just what way and in what order and under what impulses it is impossible to tell, began to break up and to scatter.

Some of these tribes in the course of their wanderings found their way into the great river plains of India and out upon the table-lands of Iran. They fought fiercely with the aborigines whom they encountered, subjugated them, and communicated to them their language. These peoples thus Aryanized in speech, and probably somewhat changed in blood, became the progenitors of the Persians and the Hindus of history.[2]

[1] Some scholars seek the early home of the primitive Aryan folk in Asia, others look for it in Europe, while still others declare the search to be wholly futile.

[2] It is very important to note that in every case where a non-Aryan people gave up their own language and adopted that of their Aryan conquerors,

Although these migrations of the Aryan clans began in the darkness of the prehistoric ages, still we should not think of them as something past and ended. When the historic age opened in Europe these movements were still going on. Upon the settled Aryan-speaking communities in Italy and in Greece descended from the north wave after wave of Aryan barbarian invaders.[1] Checked in the west by Julius Cæsar, four centuries later these movements began anew in the great Teutonic migration — the "Wandering of the Nations," which signaled the downfall of ancient civilization and the opening of a new age in history. Then ceasing again for a time, in the sixteenth century they recommenced. The overflow in modern times of the crowded population of Europe into the vast sparsely peopled regions of the New World, is simply a continuation of the prehistoric migrations of the clans of the primitive Aryan family.

Thus we see what leading parts, after what we may call the Semitic age, Aryan-speaking peoples have borne in the great drama of history.

Culture of the Primitive Aryans. — One of the most fascinating chapters in the history of civilization is that which tells of the customs, beliefs, and mode of life of the early Aryans, while they were still living together as an undivided people. Our knowledge of this primeval Aryan period, gained chiefly through the study and comparison of the words common to the different

Portuguese. During the modern age, these Romanized nations, through conquest and colonization, have spread their Latin speech and civilization over a great part of the New World. Thus it has come about that to-day the language of the ancient Romans, differentiated into many dialects, is spoken by peoples spread over the earth from Roumania in Eastern Europe to Chile in South America. All these peoples we call Latins, not because they are all descended from the ancient Romans, — in fact they belong to many different ethnic stocks, — but because they all speak languages derived from the old Roman speech. Just as we use the term Latin here, so do we use the term Aryan in connection with the Aryan-speaking peoples.

[1] In the year 390 B.C. Rome was sacked by the Gauls; in 279 B.C. Greece was overrun and devastated by hordes of the same or kindred people; in 102 B.C. took place the invasion of Italy by the Cimbri and Teutones.

Other clans and tribes pushed into the penin...
and Italy and, mingling with the peoples already...
founded the Greek and Italian city-states, and from...
culture which they carried with them, or which...
among the native populations or afterwards receive...
oriental lands, developed what is known as the classical c...

Yet other tribes of the family, either through peacefu...
sion or by conquest, had, long before our era, made A...
speech almost all the remaining regions of Europe. Whe...
first appeared in history the Aryan-speaking peoples of...
parts, representing doubtless a variety of racial elements, w...
grouped in this order : forming a sort of fringe on the weste...
edge of the continent (in Gaul, in Spain, and out upon th...
British Isles) were the Celts, — a hard-pressed race represented
to-day by the Highland Scots, the Irish, the Welsh, and the
Bretons in Brittany. Eastward of these Celtic folk, and pushing
hard against them, was a great crowd of Teutonic tribes, filling
middle Europe and the Scandinavian peninsulas, — lands in
which their lineal descendants are centrally at home to-day. To
the east of these Teutons were the Slavic folk, crowding hard
against them even as they were crowding upon the Celts in their
front. These Slavs were the ancestors of the Russians and other
kindred peoples.[1]

there must have taken place at the same time almost necessarily a mingling
of the blood of the two races. "Thus it will be correct to say that an Aryan
strain permeates all or most of the groups now speaking Aryan tongues."—
Keane, *Ethnology*, p. 396 (Cambridge Geographical Series, 1896).

[1] This prehistoric Aryan expansion can best be made plain by the use of
an historical parallel, — the Roman expansion. From their cradle city on
the Tiber, the ancient Romans — a folk Aryan in speech if not in race —
went out as conquerors and colonizers of the Mediterranean world. Wherever they went they carried their language and their civilization with them.
Many of the peoples whom they subjected gave up their own speech, and
along with the civilization of their conquerors adopted also their language.
In this way a large part of the ancient world became Romanized in speech
and culture. When the Roman Empire broke up, there arose a number of Latin-speaking nations, among these the French, Spaniards, and

Aryan languages, and from the weapons, utensils, and other remains of the early Aryans found in caves, graves, and the heaps of refuse that accumulated near their villages, may be summed up as follows : [1]The primitive Aryans were in the polished stone age of culture ; they were unacquainted with the metals, save perhaps copper in a native state, of which they made ornaments, but not weapons. All their implements were made of wood, bone, horn, and stone. They were herdsmen, and perhaps occasional farmers. They had domesticated the cow, the sheep, the goat, and the dog. The horse they seem to have known only in its wild state ; there is nothing which indicates that they ever used this animal for riding or driving. They had clumsy wagons, drawn by cattle. They made rude earthenware. Their garments were usually the skins of animals, but they were acquainted with the arts of spinning and weaving, and to some extent used woven cloth. During the winter they lived in subterranean dwellings ; when on the move, their wagons served them also as houses. They navigated the rivers and lakes of their homeland with rude "dug-outs." The primitive forms of marriage by purchase and by capture prevailed among them. It is certain that they offered human sacrifices, and that the widow was burned with the body of her husband.

Importance of Aryan Studies. — This picture of life in the early Aryan period, the elements of which are gathered in so novel a way, is of the greatest historical value and interest. In these customs, beliefs, and practices of the early Aryans, we discover the germs of many of the institutions of the Hindus and Persians, of the classical Greeks and Romans, and of other peoples who either sprang from the Aryan stock or received from some Aryan people their language and their culture.

---

[1] The foremost authority in this field is Dr. O. Schrader, in his notable work entitled, in the English translation, *The Prehistoric Antiquities of the Aryan Peoples.*

PART I.

ANCIENT HISTORY.

—•◦•—

SECTION I.—THE EASTERN NATIONS.

—•◦•—

CHAPTER I.

INDIA AND CHINA.

1. INDIA.

The Aryan Invasion. — At the time of the great Aryan migration (see p. 4), some Aryan bands, journeying from the northwest, settled first the plains of the Indus and then occupied the valley of the Ganges. They reached the banks of the latter river as early probably as 1500 B.C.

These fair-skinned invaders found the land occupied by a dark-skinned, non-Aryan race, whom they either subjugated and reduced to serfdom, or drove out of the great river valleys into the mountains and the half-desert plains of the peninsula.

The Origin of Castes. — The conflict of races in Northern India gave rise to what is known as the system of castes; that is, society became divided into a number of rigid hereditary classes. There arose gradually four chief castes: (1) Brahmans, or priests; (2) warriors; (3) agriculturists and traders; and (4) serfs, or Sudras. The Brahmans were those of pure Aryan blood, while the Sudras were the despised and oppressed non-Aryan aborigines. The two middle classes, the warriors and the cultivators of the soil, were of mixed Aryan and non-Aryan blood. Below these several castes were the Pariahs, or outcasts, the most degraded of the degraded natives.[1]

The system of castes, modified however by various influences, particularly by the later system of Buddhism (see p. 11), has characterized Hindu society from the time the system originated down to the present, and is one of the most important facts of Indian history.

The Vedas. — The most important of the sacred books of the Hindus are called the Vedas. They are written in the Sanscrit language, which is believed to be the oldest form of Aryan speech. The Rig-Veda, the most ancient of the books, is made up of hymns which were composed chiefly during the long period, perhaps a thousand years or more, while the Aryans were slowly working their way from the mountains on the northwest of India across the peninsula to the Ganges. These hymns are filled with memories of the long conflict of the fair-faced Aryans with the dark-faced aborigines. The Himalayas, through whose gloomy passes the early emigrants journeyed, must have deeply impressed the wanderers, for the poets often refer to the great dark mountains.

Brahmanism. — The religion of the Indian Aryans is known as Brahmanism. This system gradually developed from the same germs as those out of which grew the Greek and Roman religions. It was at first a pure nature-worship, that is, the worship of the most striking phenomena of the physical world as intelligent and moral beings. The chief god was Dyaus-Pitar, the Heaven-Father. As this system characterized the early period when the oldest Vedic hymns were composed, it is known as the Vedic religion.

---

[1] At a later period, the Brahmans, in order to perpetuate their own ascendancy and to secure increased reverence for their order, incorporated among the sacred hymns an account of creation which gave a sort of divine sanction to the system of castes by representing the different classes of society to have had different origins. The Brahmans, the sacred books are made to say, came forth from the mouth of Brahma, the soldier from his arms, the farmer from his thighs, and the Sudra from his feet.

In course of time this nature-worship of the Vedic period developed into a sort of pantheism, that is, a system which identifies God with the universe. This form of the Indian religion is known as Brahmanism. Brahma, an impersonal essence, is conceived as the primal existence. Forth from Brahma emanated, as heat and light emanate from the sun, all things and all life. Banish a personal God from the universe, as some modern scientists would do, leaving nothing but nature with her original nebula, her endless cycles, her unconscious evolutions, and we have something very like Brahmanism.

A second fundamental conception of Brahmanism is that all life, apart from Brahma, is evil, is travail and sorrow. We can make this idea intelligible to ourselves by remembering what are our own ideas of this earthly life. We call it a feverish dream, a journey through a vale of sorrow. Now the Hindu regards *all* conscious existence in the same light. He has no hope in a better future ; so long as the soul is conscious, so long must it endure sorrow and pain.

This conception of all conscious existence as necessarily and always evil, leads naturally to the doctrine that it is the part of wisdom and of duty for man to get rid of consciousness, to annihilate himself, in a word, to commit soul-suicide. Brahmanism teaches that the only way to extinguish self and thus get rid of the burden of existence, is by re-absorption into Brahma. But this return to Brahma is dependent upon the soul's purification, for no impure soul can be re-absorbed into the primal essence. The necessary freedom from passion and the required purity of soul can best be attained by self-torture, by a severe mortification of the flesh ; hence the asceticism of the Hindu devotee.

As only a few in each generation reach the goal, it follows that the great majority of men must be born again, and yet again, until all evil has been purged away from the soul and eternal repose found in Brahma. He who lives a virtuous life is at death born into some higher caste, and thus he advances towards the longed-for end. The evil man, however, is born into a lower caste, or perhaps his soul enters some unclean animal. This doctrine of re-birth is known as the transmigration of souls (metempsychosis).

Only the first three classes are admitted to the benefits of religion. The Sudras and the outcasts are forbidden to read the sacred books, and for any one of the upper classes to teach a serf how to expiate sin is a crime.

Buddhism. — In the fifth century before our era, a great teacher and reformer, known as Buddha, or Gautama (died about 470 B.C.), arose in India. He was a prince, whom legend represents as being so touched by the universal misery of mankind, that he voluntarily abandoned the luxury of his home, and spent his life in seeking out and making known to men a new and better way of salvation. He condemned the severe penances and the self-torture of the Brahmans, yet commended poverty and retirement from active life as the best means of getting rid of desire and of attaining *Nirvana*, that is, the repose of unconsciousness.

STATUE OF BUDDHA.

Buddha admitted all classes to the benefits of religion, the poor outcast as well as the high-born Brahman, and thus Buddhism was a revolt against the earlier harsh and exclusive system of Brahmanism. It holds somewhat the same relation to Brahmanism that Christianity bears to Judaism.

Buddhism gradually gained the ascendancy over Brahmanism; but after some centuries the Brahmans regained their power, and by the eighth century after Christ, the faith of Buddha was driven out of almost every part of India. But Buddhism has a profound missionary spirit, like that of Christianity, Buddha having commanded his disciples to make known to all men the way to Nirvana; and consequently during the very period when India was being lost, the missionaries of the reformed creed were spreading the teachings of their master among the peoples of all the countries of Eastern Asia, so that to-day Buddhism is the religion of almost one third of the human race. Buddha has probably nearly as many followers as both Christ and Mohammed together.

During its long conflict with Buddhism, Brahmanism was greatly modified, and caught much of the gentler spirit of the new faith, so that modern Brahmanism is a very different religion from that of the ancient system; hence it is usually given a new name, being known as Hinduism.[1]

Alexander's Invasion of India (327 B.C.). — Although we find obscure notices of India in the records of the early historic peoples of Western Asia, yet it is not until the invasion of the peninsula by Alexander the Great in 327 B.C. that the history of the Indian Aryans comes in significant contact with that of the progressive nations of the West. From that day to our own its systems of philosophy, its wealth, and its commerce have been more or less important factors in universal history. Greece carried on an intellectual commerce with this country; Rome, and the Italian republics of the Middle Ages, a more material but not less important trade. Columbus was seeking a short all-sea route to this country when he found the New World. And in the upbuilding of the imperial greatness of the England of to-day, the wealth and trade of India have played no inconsiderable part.

2. CHINA.

General Remarks: the Beginning. — China is the seat of a very old civilization, older perhaps than that of any other land save Egypt; yet Chinese affairs have not until recently exerted any appreciable influence upon the general current of history.

---

[1] Among the customs introduced into Brahmanism during this period was the rite of Suttee, or the voluntary burning of the widow on the funeral pyre of her husband.

All through ancient and mediæval times the country lay, vague and mysterious, in the haze of the world's horizon. During the Middle Ages the land was known to Europe under the name of Cathay.

The beginning of the Chinese nation was a band of Turanian wanderers who came into the basin of the Yellow River, from the West, probably prior to 3000 B.C. These immigrants gradually pushed out the aborigines whom they found in the land, and laid the basis of institutions that have endured to the present day.

Dynastic History. — The government of China since the remotest times has been a parental monarchy. The Emperor is the father of his people. But though an absolute prince, still he dare not rule tyrannically : he must rule justly, and in accordance with the ancient customs and laws.

The Chinese have books that purport to give the history of the different dynasties that have ruled in the land from a vast antiquity ; but these records are largely mythical and legendary. Everything is confused and uncertain until we reach the eighth or seventh century before our era ; and even then we meet with little of interest in the dynastic history of the country until we come to the reign of Che Hwang-te (246–210 B.C.). This energetic ruler strengthened and consolidated the imperial power, and executed great works of internal improvement, such as roads and canals. As a barrier against the incursions of the Huns, he began the erection of the celebrated Chinese Wall, a great rampart extending for about 1500 miles along the northern frontier of the country.[1]

From the strong reign of Che Hwang-te to the end of the period

---

[1] The Great Wall is one of the most remarkable works of man. " It is," says Dr. Williams, " the only artificial structure which would arrest attention in a hasty survey of the globe." It has been estimated that there is more than seventy times as much material in the wall as there is in the Great Pyramid of Cheops, and that it represents more labor than 100,000 miles of ordinary railroad. It was begun in 214(?) and finished in 204(?) B.C. It is twenty-five feet wide at base, and from fifteen to thirty feet high. Towers forty feet high rise at irregular intervals. In some places it is a mere earthen rampart; in others it is faced with brick ; and then again it is composed of stone throughout.

covered by ancient history, Chinese dynastic records present no matters of universal interest that need here occupy our attention.

Chinese Writing. — It is nearly certain that the art of writing was known among the Chinese as early as 2000 B.C. The system employed is curiously cumbrous. In the absence of an alphabet, each word of the language is represented upon the written page by means of a symbol, or combination of symbols ; this, of course, requires that there be as many symbols, or characters, as there are words in the language. The number sanctioned by good use is about 25,000 ; but counting obsolete characters, the number amounts to over 50,000. A knowledge of 5000 or 6000 characters, however, enables one to read and write without difficulty. The task of learning even this number might well be hopeless, were it not that many of the characters bear a remote resemblance to the objects for which they stand, and when once explained, readily suggest the thing or idea represented. The nature of the characters shows conclusively that the Chinese system of writing, like that of all others with which we are acquainted, was at first purely hieroglyphical, that is, the characters were originally simply rude outline pictures of material objects. Time and use have worn them to their present form.

This Chinese system of representing thought, cumbrous and inconvenient as it is, is employed at the present time by one third of the human race.

Printing from blocks was practised in China as early as the sixth century of our era, and printing from movable types as early as the tenth or eleventh century, that is to say, about four hundred years before the same art was invented in Europe.

Chinese Literature : Confucius and Mencius. — The most highly prized portion of Chinese literature is embraced in what is known as the Five Classics and the Four Books, called collectively the *Nine Classics.* The Five Classics are among the oldest books in the world. For some of the books an antiquity of 3000 years is claimed. The books embrace chronicles, political and ethical maxims, and numerous odes. One of the most important of the

Classics is the so-called Book of Rites, said to date from 1200 B.C.

The Four Books are of later origin than the Five Classics, having been written about the fifth and fourth centuries before the Christian era; yet they hardly yield to them in sacredness in the eyes of the Chinese. The first three of the series are by the pupils of the great sage and moralist Confucius (551–478 B.C.), and the fourth is by Mencius (371–288 B.C.), a disciple of Confucius, and a scarcely less revered philosopher and ethical teacher. The teachings of the Four Books may be summed up in the simple precept, "Walk in the Trodden Paths." Confucius was not a prophet, or revealer; he laid no claims to a supernatural knowledge of God or of the hereafter; he said nothing of an Infinite Spirit, and but little of a future life. His cardinal precepts were obedience to superiors, reverence for the ancients, and imitation of their virtues. He himself walked in the old paths, and thus added the force of example to that of precept. He gave the Chinese the Golden Rule, stated negatively: "What you do not want done to yourself, do not do to others."

During the reign of Che Hwang-te (see p. 13), Chinese literature suffered a great disaster. That despot, for the reason that the teachers in their opposition to him were constantly quoting the ancient writings against his innovations, ordered the chief historical books to be destroyed, and sentenced to death any one who should presume to talk about the proscribed writings, or even allude to the virtues of the ancients in such a way as to reflect upon his reforms. The contumacious he sent to work upon the Great Wall. But the people concealed the books in the walls of their houses, or better still hid them away in their memories; and in this way the priceless inheritance of antiquity was preserved until the storm had passed.

Influence of this Literature and of the Sage Confucius. — It would be impossible to exaggerate the influence which the Nine Classics have had upon the Chinese nation. For more than 2000 years these writings have been the Chinese Bible. And as all of the

Four Books, though they were not written by Confucius, yet bear the impress of his mind and thought, just as the Gospels teach the mind of Christ, a large part of this influence must be attributed to the life and teachings of that great Sage. His influence has been greater than that of any other teacher, excepting Christ and perhaps Buddha. His precepts, implicitly followed by his countrymen, have shaped their lives from his day to the present.

The moral system of Confucius, making, as it does, filial obedience and a conformity to ancient customs primary virtues, has exalted the family life among the Chinese and given a wonderful stability to Chinese society. Chinese children are the most obedient and reverential to parents of any children in the world, and the Chinese Empire is the only one in all history that has prolonged its existence from ancient times to the present.

But along with much good, one great evil has resulted from this blind, servile following of the past. The Chinese in strictly obeying the injunction to walk in the old ways, to conform to the customs of the ancients, have failed to mark out any new footpaths for themselves. Hence their lack of originality, their habit of imitation : hence the unchanging, unprogressive character of Chinese civilization.

Education and Civil Service Competitive Examinations. — China has a very ancient educational system. The land was filled with schools, academies, and colleges more than a thousand years before our era, and education is to-day more general among the Chinese than among any other pagan people. A knowledge of the sacred books is the sole passport to civil office and public employment. All candidates for places in the government must pass a competitive examination in the Nine Classics. This system is practically the same in principle as that which we, with great difficulty, are trying to establish in connection with our own civil service.

The Three Religions, — Confucianism, Taoism, and Buddhism. — There are three leading religions in China, — Confucianism, Taoism, and Buddhism. The great Sage Confucius is reverenced and worshipped throughout the Empire. He holds somewhat the same relation to the system that bears his name that Christ holds to that of Christianity. Taoism takes its name from Tao, which is made, like Brahma in Brahmanism, the beginning of all things. It is a very curious system of mystical ideas and superstitious practices. Buddhism was introduced into China about the opening of the Christian era, and soon became widely spread.

There is one element common to all these religions, and that is the worship of ancestors. Every Chinese, whether he be a Confucianist, a Taoist, or a Buddhist, reverences his ancestors, and prays and makes offerings to their spirits.

Policy of Non-Intercourse. — The Chinese have always been a very self-satisfied and exclusive people. They have jealously excluded foreigners and outside influence from their country. The Great Wall with which they have hedged in their country on the north, is the symbol of their policy of isolation. Doubtless this characteristic of the Chinese has been fostered by their geographical isolation ; for great mountain barriers and wide deserts cut the country off from communication with the rest of the Asiatic continent. And then their reverence for antiquity has rendered them intolerant of innovation and change. Hence, in part, the unwillingness of the Chinese to admit into their country railroads, telegraphs, and other modern improvements. For them to adopt these new-fangled inventions, would be like our adopting a new religion. Such a departure from the ways and customs of the past has in it, to their way of thinking, something akin to disrespect and irreverence for ancestors.

CHAPTER II.

EGYPT.

I. POLITICAL HISTORY.

Egypt and the Nile. — Egypt comprises the delta of the Nile and the flood-plains of its lower course. The whole land is formed of the deposits of the river; hence Herodotus, in happy phrase, called the country "the gift of the Nile." The delta country was known to the ancients as Lower Egypt; while the valley proper, reaching from the head of the delta to the First Cataract, a distance of six hundred miles, was called Upper Egypt.[1]

Through the same means by which Egypt was originally created, is the land each year still renewed and fertilized. The Nile, swollen by the heavy tropical rains about its sources, begins to rise in its lower parts late in June, and by October, when the inundation has attained its greatest height, the country presents the appearance of an inland sea.

By the end of November the river has returned to its bed, and the fields, over which has been spread a film of rich earth,[2] present the appearance of black mud-flats. Usually the plow is run lightly over the soft surface, but in some cases the grain is sown upon the undisturbed deposit, and simply trampled in by flocks of

---

[1] About seven hundred miles from the Mediterranean a low ledge of rocks, stretching across the Nile, forms the first obstruction to navigation in passing up the river. The rapids found at this point are termed the First Cataract. Six other cataracts occur in the next seven hundred miles of the river's course.

[2] The rate of the fluviatile deposit is from three to five inches in a century. The surface of the valley at Thebes, as shown by the accumulations about the monuments, has been raised seven feet during the last seventeen hundred years.

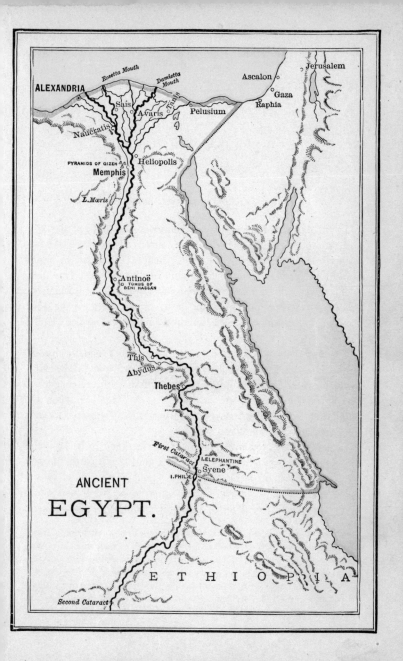

Rosetta Mouth

Damietta Mouth

Jerusalem

Ascalon

ALEXANDRIA

Tanis

Gaza
Raphia

Sais

Avaris

Pelusium

Naucratis

PYRAMIDS OF GIZEH

Heliopolis

Memphis

L. Mœris

Antinoë
D TOMBS OF
BENI HASSAN

This

Abydus

Thebes

First Cataract

I. ELEPHANTINE

Syene

I. PHILÆ

ANCIENT

EGYPT.

E T H I O P I A

Second Cataract

sheep and goats driven over it. In a few weeks the entire land, so recently a flooded plain, is overspread with a sea of verdure, which forms a striking contrast to the desert sands and barren hills that rim the valley.

Climate. — In Lower Egypt, near the sea, the rainfall in the winter is abundant; but the climate of Upper Egypt is all but rainless, only a few slight showers falling throughout the year. This dryness of the Egyptian air is what has preserved through so many thousand years, in such wonderful freshness of color and with such sharpness of outline, the numerous paintings and sculptures of the monuments of the Pharaohs.

The southern line of Egypt only just touches the tropics; still the climate, influenced by the wide and hot deserts that hem the valley, is semi-tropical in character. The fruits of the tropics and the cereals of the temperate zone grow luxuriantly. Thus favored in climate as well as in the matter of irrigation, Egypt became in early times the granary of the East. To it less favored countries, when stricken by famine, — a calamity so common in the East in regions dependent upon the rainfall, — looked for food, as did the families of Israel during drought and failure of crops in Palestine.

Dynasties and Chronology. — The kings, or Pharaohs, that reigned in Egypt from the earliest times till the conquest of the country by Alexander the Great (332 B.C.), are grouped into thirty-one dynasties. Thirty of these we find in the lists of Manetho, an Egyptian priest who lived in the third century B.C., and who compiled a chronicle of the kings of the country from the manuscripts kept in the Egyptian temples.

We cannot assign a positive date to the beginning of the First Dynasty, chiefly because Egyptologists are at a loss to know whether to consider all the dynasties of Manetho's list as successive or in part contemporaneous. Thus, it is held by some scholars that several of these families were reigning at the same time in the different cities of Upper and Lower Egypt; while others think that they all reigned at different epochs, and that the sum of the lengths of the several dynasties gives us the true date of the beginning of the political history of the country. Accordingly, some place the beginning of the First Dynasty at about 5000 B.C., while others put it at about 3000 B.C. The constantly growing evidence of the monuments is in favor of the higher figures.

Menes, the First of the Pharaohs. — Menes is the first kingly personage, shadowy and indistinct in form, that we discover in the early dawn of Egyptian history. Tradition makes him the founder of Memphis, near the head of the Delta, the site of which capital he secured against the inundations of the Nile by vast dikes and various engineering works. To him is ascribed the achievement of first consolidating the numerous petty principalities of Lower Egypt into a single state.

The Fourth Dynasty: the Pyramid Kings (about 2700 B.C.). — The kings of the Fourth Dynasty, who reigned at Memphis, are called the Pyramid builders. Kufu I., the Cheops of the Greeks, was the first great builder. To him we can now positively ascribe the building of the Great Pyramid, the largest of the Gizeh group, near Cairo ; for his name has been found upon some of the stones, — painted on them by his workmen before the blocks were taken from the quarries.

The mountains of stone heaped together by the Pyramid kings are proof that they were cruel oppressors of their people, and burdened them with useless labor upon these monuments of their ambition. Tradition tells how the very memory of these monarchs was hated by the people. Herodotus says that the Egyptians did not like even to speak the names of the builders of the two largest pyramids.

The Twelfth Dynasty (about 2300 B.C.). — After the Sixth Dynasty, Egypt, for several centuries, is almost lost from view. When finally the valley emerges from the obscurity of this period, the old capital Memphis has receded into the background, and the city of Thebes has taken its place as the seat of the royal power.

The period of the Twelfth Dynasty, a line of Theban kings, is one of the brightest in Egyptian history. Many monuments scat-

tered throughout the country perpetuate the fame of the sovereigns
of this illustrious house. Egyptian civilization is regarded by
many as having during this period reached the highest perfection
to which it ever attained.

The Hyksos, or Shepherd Kings (from about 2100 to 1650 B.C.).
— Soon after the bright period of the Twelfth Dynasty, Egypt
again suffered a great eclipse. Nomadic tribes from Syria crossed
the eastern frontier of Egypt, took possession of the inviting pas-
ture-lands of the Delta, and established there the empire of the
Shepherd Kings.

These Asiatic intruders were violent and barbarous, and destroyed or mutilated the monuments of the country. But gradually they were transformed by the civilization with which they
were in contact, and in time they adopted the manners and culture of the Egyptians. It was probably during the supremacy of
the Hyksos that the families of Israel found a refuge in Lower
Egypt. They received a kind reception from the Shepherd Kings,
not only because they had the same pastoral habits, but also,
probably, because of near kinship in race.

At last these intruders, after they had ruled in the valley four or
five hundred years, were expelled by the Theban kings, and driven
back into Asia. This occurred about 1650 B.C. The episode of
the Shepherd Kings in Egypt derives great importance from the
fact that these Asiatic conquerors were one of the mediums
through which Egyptian civilization was transmitted to the Phœnicians, who, through their wide commercial relations, spread the
same among all the early nations of the Mediterranean area.

And further, the Hyksos conquest was an advantage to Egypt
itself. The conquerors possessed political capacity, and gave the
country a strong centralized government. They made Egypt in
fact a great monarchy, and laid the basis of the power and glory
of the mighty Pharaohs of the Eighteenth and Nineteenth Dynasties.

The Eighteenth Dynasty (about 1650–1400 B.C.). — The revolt
which drove the Hyksos from the country was led by Amosis, or

Ahmes, a descendant of the Theban kings. He was the first king of what is known as the Eighteenth Dynasty, probably the greatest race of kings, it has been said, that ever reigned upon the earth.

The most eventful period of Egyptian history, covered by what is called the New Empire, now opens. Architecture and learning seem to have recovered at a bound from their long depression under the domination of the Shepherd Kings. To free his empire from the danger of another invasion from Asia, Amosis determined to subdue the Syrian and Mesopotamian tribes. This foreign policy, followed out by his successors, shaped many of the events of their reigns.

Thothmes III., one of the greatest kings of this Eighteenth Dynasty, has been called "the Alexander of Egyptian history." During his reign the frontiers of the empire reached their greatest expansion. His authority extended from the oases of the Libyan desert to the Tigris and the Euphrates.

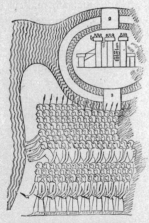

PHALANX OF THE KHITA:

In the background, town protected by walls and moats.

Thothmes was also a magnificent builder. His architectural works in the valley of the Nile were almost numberless. He built a great part of the temple of Karnak, at Thebes, the remains of which form the most majestic ruin in the world. His obelisks stand to-day in Constantinople, in Rome, in London, and in New York.

The name of Amunoph III. stands next after that of Thothmes III. as one of the great rulers and builders of the Eighteenth Dynasty.

The Nineteenth Dynasty (about 1400-1280 B.C.). — The Pharaohs of the Nineteenth Dynasty rival those of the Eighteenth in their fame as conquerors and builders. It is their deeds and works, in connection with those of the preceding dynasty, that have given Egypt such a name and place in history. The two great names of the house are Seti I. and Rameses II.

One of the most important of Seti's wars was that against the Hittites (*Khita,* in the inscriptions) and their allies. The Hittites were a powerful non-Semitic people, whose capital was Carchemish, on the Euphrates, and whose strength and influence were now so great as to be a threat to Egypt.

But Seti's deeds as a warrior are eclipsed by his achievements as a builder. He constructed the main part of what is perhaps the most impressive edifice ever raised by man, — the world-renowned "Hall of Columns," in the Temple of Karnak, at Thebes (see illustration, p. 32). He also cut for himself in the Valley of the Tombs of the Kings, at the same place, the most beautiful and elaborate of all the rock-sepulchres of the Pharaohs (see p. 31). In addition to these and numerous other works, he began a canal to unite the Red Sea and the Nile, — an undertaking which was completed by his son and successor, Rameses II.

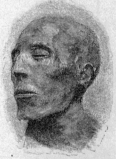

SETI I. (From a photograph of the mummy.)

Rameses II., surnamed the Great, was the Sesostris of the Greeks. His is the most prominent name of the Nineteenth Dynasty. Ancient writers, in fact, accorded him the first place among all the Egyptian sovereigns, and made him the hero of innumerable stories. His long reign, embracing sixty-seven years, was, in truth, well occupied with military expeditions and the superintendence of great architectural works.

His chief wars were those against the Hittites. Time and again is Rameses found with his host of war-chariots in their country, but he evidently fails to break their power; for we find him at last concluding with them a celebrated treaty, in which the chief of the Hittites is called "The Great King of the Khita" (Hittites), and is formally recognized as in every respect the equal of the king of Egypt. Later, Rameses marries a daughter of the Hittite king. All this means that the Pharaohs had met their peers in the princes of the Hittites, and that they could no longer hope to become masters of Western Asia.

It was probably the fear of an invasion by the tribes of Syria that led Rameses to reduce to a position of grinding servitude the Semitic peoples that under former dynasties had been permitted to settle in Lower Egypt; for this Nineteenth Dynasty, to which Rameses II. belongs, was the new king (dynasty) that arose "which knew not Joseph" (Ex. i. 8), and oppressed the children

RAMESES II. RETURNING IN TRIUMPH FROM SYRIA, with his chariot garnished with the heads of his enemies. (From the monuments of Karnak.)

of Israel. It was during the reign of his son Menephtha that the Exodus took place (about 1300 B.C.).

The Twenty-sixth Dynasty (666–527 B.C.). — We pass without comment a long period of several centuries, marked, indeed, by great vicissitudes in the fortunes of the Egyptian monarchs, yet characterized throughout by a sure and rapid decline in the power and splendor of their empire.

During the latter part of this period Egypt was tributary to Assyria. But about 666 B.C., a native prince, Psammetichus I. (666–612 B.C.), with the aid of Greek mercenaries from Asia Minor, succeeded in expelling the Assyrian garrisons. Psammetichus thus became the founder of the Twenty-sixth Dynasty.

The reign of this monarch marks a new era in Egyptian history. Hitherto Egypt had secluded herself from the world, behind barriers of jealousy, race, and pride. But Psammetichus being himself, it seems, of non-Egyptian origin, and owing his throne chiefly to the swords of Greek soldiers, was led to reverse the policy of the past, and to throw the valley open to the commerce and influences of the world. His capital, Saïs, on the Canopic branch of the Nile, forty miles from the Mediterranean, was filled with Greek citizens; and Greek mercenaries were employed in his armies.

This change of policy, occurring at just the period when the rising states of Greece and Rome were shaping their institutions, was a most significant event. Egypt became the University of the Mediterranean nations. From this time forward Greek philosophers, as in the case of Pythagoras and of Plato, are represented as becoming pupils of the Egyptian priests; and without question the learning and philosophy of the ancient Egyptians exerted a profound influence upon the quick, susceptible mind of the Hellenic race, that was, in its turn, to become the teacher of the world.

The liberal policy of Psammetichus, while resulting in a great advantage to foreign nations, brought a heavy misfortune upon his own. Displeased with the position assigned Greek mercenaries in the army, the native Egyptian soldiers revolted, and two hundred thousand of the troops seceding in a body, emigrated to Ethiopia, whence no inducement that Psammetichus offered could persuade them to return.

The son of Psammetichus, Necho II. (612–596 B.C.), the Pharaoh-Necho of the Bible, followed the liberal policy marked out by his father. To facilitate commerce, he attempted to reopen the old canal dug by Seti I. and his son, which had become unnavigable. After the loss of one hundred and twenty thousand workmen in the prosecution of the undertaking, Necho was constrained to abandon it; Herodotus says, on account of an unfavorable oracle.

Necho then fitted out an exploring expedition for the circumnavigation of Africa, in hope of finding a possible passage for his fleets from the Red Sea to the Nile by a water channel already opened by nature, and to which the priests and oracles could interpose no objections. The expedition, we have reason to believe, actually accomplished the feat of sailing around the continent; for Herodotus, in his account of the enterprise, says that the voyagers upon their return reported that, when they were rounding the cape, the sun was on their right hand (to the north). This feature of the report, which led Herodotus to disbelieve it, is to us the very strongest evidence possible that the voyage was really performed.

The Last of the Pharaohs. — Before the close of his reign, Necho had come into collision with the king of Babylon, and was forced to acknowledge his supremacy. A little later, Babylon having yielded to the rising power of Persia, Egypt also passed under Persian authority (see p. 77). The Egyptians, however, were restive under this foreign yoke, and, after a little more than a century, succeeded in throwing it off; but the country was again subjugated by the Persian king Artaxerxes III. (about 340 B.C.), and from that time until our own day no native prince has ever sat upon the throne of the Pharaohs. Long before the Persian conquest, the Prophet Ezekiel, foretelling the debasement of Egypt, had declared, "There shall be no more a prince of the land of Egypt." [1]

Upon the extension of the power of the Macedonians over the East (333 B.C.), Egypt willingly exchanged masters; and for three centuries the valley was the seat of the renowned Græco-Egyptian Empire of the Ptolemies, which lasted until the Romans annexed the region to their all-absorbing empire (30 B.C.).

"The mission of Egypt among the nations was fulfilled; it had lit the torch of civilization in ages inconceivably remote, and had passed it on to other peoples of the West."

---

[1] Ezek. xxx. 13.

2. Religion, Arts, and General Culture.

Classes of Society. — Egyptian society was divided into three great classes, or orders, — priests, soldiers, and common people; the last embracing shepherds, husbandmen, and artisans.

The sacerdotal order consisted of high-priests, prophets, scribes, keepers of the sacred robes and animals, sacred sculptors, masons, and embalmers. They enjoyed freedom from taxation, and met the expenses of the temple services with the income of the sacred lands, which embraced one third of the soil of the country.

The priests were extremely scrupulous in the care of their persons. They bathed twice by day and twice by night, and shaved the entire body every third day. Their inner clothing was linen, woollen garments being thought unclean; their diet was plain and even abstemious, in order that, as Plutarch says, "their bodies might sit light as possible about their souls."

Next to the priesthood in rank and honor stood the military order. Like the priests, the soldiers formed a landed class. They held one third of the soil of Egypt. To each soldier was given a tract of about eight acres, exempt from all taxes. They were carefully trained in their profession, and there was no more effective soldiery in ancient times than that which marched beneath the standard of the Pharaohs.

The Chief Deities. — Attached to the chief temples of the Egyptians were colleges for the training of the sacerdotal order. These institutions were the repositories of the wisdom of the Egyptians. This learning was open only to the initiated few.

The unity of God was the central doctrine in this private system. They gave to this Supreme Being the very same name by which he was known to the Hebrews — *Nuk Pu Nuk*, "I am that I am."[1] The sacred manuscripts say, "He is the one living and

[1] "It is evident what a new light this discovery throws on the sublime passage in Exodus iii. 14; where Moses, whom we may suppose to have been initiated into this formula, is sent both to his people and to Pharaoh to proclaim the true God by this very title, and to declare that the God of the

true God, . . . who has made all things, and was not himself made."

The Egyptian divinities of the popular mythology were frequently grouped in triads. First in importance among these groups was that formed by Osiris, Isis (his wife and sister), and Horus, their son. The members of this triad were worshipped throughout Egypt.

The god Set (called Typhon by the Greek writers), the principle of evil, was the Satan of Egyptian mythology. While the good and beneficent Osiris was symbolized by the life-giving Nile, the malignant Typhon was emblemized by the terrors and barrenness of the desert.

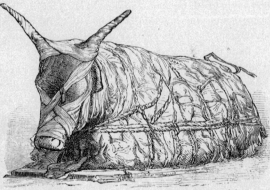

MUMMY OF A SACRED BULL. (From a photograph.)

Animal-Worship. — The Egyptians regarded certain animals as emblems of the gods, and hence worshipped them. To kill one of these sacred animals was adjudged the greatest impiety. Persons so unfortunate as to harm one through accident were sometimes murdered by the infuriated people. The destruction of a cat in a burning building was lamented more than the loss

highest Egyptian theology was also the God of Abraham, of Isaac, and of Jacob. The case is parallel to that of Paul at Athens." — Smith's *Ancient History of the East*, p. 196, note.

of the property. Upon the death of a dog, every member of the family shaved his head. The scarabæus, or beetle, was especially sacred, being considered an emblem of the sun, or of life.

Not only were various animals held sacred, as being the emblems of certain deities, but some were thought to be real gods. Thus the soul of Osiris, it was imagined, animated the body of some bull, which might be known from certain spots and markings.

Upon the death of the sacred bull, or Apis, as he was called, a great search, accompanied with loud lamentation, was made throughout the land for his successor : for, the moment the soul of Osiris departed from the dying bull, it entered a calf that moment born. The calf was always found with the proper markings ; but, as Wilkinson says, the young animal had probably been put to " much inconvenience and pain to make the marks and hair conform to his description."

The body of the deceased Apis was carefully embalmed, and, amid funeral ceremonies of great expense and magnificence, deposited in the tomb of his predecessors. In 1851, Mariette discovered this sepulchral chamber of the sacred bulls. It is a narrow gallery, two thousand feet in length, cut in the limestone cliffs just opposite the site of ancient Memphis. A large number of the immense granite coffins, fifteen feet long and eight wide and high, have been brought to light.

Many explanations have been given to account for the existence of such a debased form of worship among so cultured a people as were the ancient Egyptians. Probably the sacred animals in the later worship represent an earlier stage of the Egyptian religion, just as many superstitious beliefs and observances among ourselves are simply survivals from earlier and ruder times.

Judgment of the Dead. — Death was a great equalizer among the Egyptians. King and peasant alike must stand before the judgment-seat of Osiris and his forty-two assessors.

This judgment of the soul in the other world was prefigured by a peculiar ordeal to which the body was subjected here. Between each chief city and the burial-place on the western edge of the

valley was a sacred lake, across which the body was borne in a
barge. But, before admittance to the boat, it must pass the
ordeal called "the judgment of the dead." This was a trial before
a tribunal of forty-two judges, assembled upon the shore of the
lake. Any person could bring accusations against the deceased,
false charges being guarded against by the most dreadful penalties.
If it appeared that the life of the deceased had been evil, passage
to the boat was denied; and the body was either carried home in
dishonor, or, in case of the poor who could not afford to care for
the mummy, was interred on the shores of the lake. Many mummies of those refused admission to the tombs of their fathers have
been dug up along these "Stygian banks."

JUDGMENT OF THE DEAD: above, an ape-assessor scourges an evil soul,
that has been changed into an unclean animal.

But this ordeal of the body was only a faint symbol of the dread
tribunal of Osiris before which the soul must appear in the lower
world. In one scale of a balance was placed the heart of the
deceased; in the other scale, an image of Justice, or Truth. The
soul stands by watching the result, and, as the beam inclines, is
either welcomed to the companionship of the good Osiris, or
consigned to oblivion in the jaws of a frightful hippopotamus-
headed monster, "the devourer of evil souls." This annihilation,
however, is only the fate of those inveterately wicked. Those
respecting whom hopes of reformation may be entertained are

condemned to return to earth and do penance in long cycles of lives in the bodies of various animals. This is what is known as the transmigration of souls. The kind of animals the soul should animate, and the length of its transmigrations, were determined by the nature of its sins.

Tombs. — The Egyptians bestowed little care upon the temporary residences of the living, but the "eternal homes" of the dead were fitted up with the most lavish expenditure of labor. These were chambers, sometimes built of brick or stone, but more usually cut in the limestone cliffs that form the western rim of the Nile valley; for that, as the land of the sunset, was conceived to be the realm of darkness and of death. The cliffs opposite the ancient Egyptian capitals are honeycombed with sepulchral cells.

BRICK-MAKING IN ANCIENT EGYPT. *(From Thebes.)*

In the hills back of Thebes is the so-called Valley of the Tombs of the Kings, the "Westminster Abbey of Egypt." Here are twenty-five magnificent sepulchres. These consist of extensive rock-cut passages and chambers richly sculptured and painted.

The subjects of the decorations of many of the tombs, particularly of the oldest, are drawn from the life and manners of the times. Thus the artist has converted for us the Egyptian necropolis into a city of the living, where the Egypt of four thousand years ago seems to pass before our eyes.

The Pyramids. — The Egyptian pyramids, the tombs of the earlier Pharaohs, are the most venerable monuments that have been preserved to us from the early world. They were almost all erected before the Twelfth Dynasty. Although thus standing away back in the earliest twilight of the historic morning, nevertheless they mark, not the beginning, but the perfection of Egyptian art. They speak of long periods of growth in art and science lying beyond the era they represent. It is this vast and mysterious background that astonishes us even more than these giant forms cast up against it.

THE GREAT HALL OF COLUMNS AT KARNAK.

Being sepulchral monuments, the pyramids are confined to the western side of the Nile valley (see p. 31). There are over thirty still standing, with traces of about forty more.

The Pyramid of Cheops, the largest of the Gizeh group, near Cairo, rises from a base covering thirteen acres, to a height of four hundred and fifty feet. According to Herodotus, Cheops employed one hundred thousand men for twenty years in its erection.

Palaces and Temples. — The earlier Memphian kings built great unadorned pyramids, but the later Theban monarchs constructed splendid palaces and temples. Two of the most prominent masses of buildings on the site of Thebes are called, the one the Palace of Karnak, and the other the Temple of Luxor, from the names of two native villages built near or within the ruined enclosures. The former was more than five hundred years in building. As an adjunct of the Palace at Karnak was a Hall of Columns, which consisted of a phalanx of one hundred and sixty-four gigantic pillars. Some of these columns measure over seventy feet in height, with capitals sixty-five feet in circumference.

In Nubia, beyond the First Cataract, is the renowned rock-hewn temple of Ipsambul, the front of which is adorned with four gigantic portrait-statues of Rameses II., seventy feet in height.

STATUES OF MEMNON AT THEBES.

This temple has been pronounced the greatest and grandest achievement of Egyptian art.

Sculpture : Sphinxes and Colossi. — A strange immobility, due to the influence of religion, attached itself, at an early period, to Egyptian art. The artist, in the portrayal of the figures of the gods, was not allowed to change a single line in the conventional form. Hence the impossibility of improvement in sacred sculpture. Wilkinson says that Menes would have recognized the statue of Osiris in the Temple of Amasis. Plato complained that the pictures and statues in the temples in his day were no better than those made " ten thousand years" before.

The heroic, or colossal size of many of the Egyptian statues excites our admiration. The two colosii at Thebes, known as the "Statues of Memnon," are forty-seven feet high, and are hewn each from a single block of granite. The appearance of these time-worn, gigantic figures, upon the solitary plain, is singularly impressive. "There they sit together, yet apart, in the midst of the plain, serene and vigilant, still keeping their untired watch over the lapse of ages and the eclipse of Egypt."

One of these statues acquired a wide reputation among the Greeks and Romans, under the name of the "Vocal Memnon." When the rays of the rising sun fell upon the colossus, it emitted low musical tones, which the Egyptians believed to be the greeting of the statue to the mother-sun.[1]

The Egyptian sphinxes were figures having a human head and the body of a lion, symbolizing intelligence and power. The most famous of the sphinxes of Egypt is the colossal figure at the base of the Great Pyramid, at Gizeh, sculptured, some think, by Menes, and others, by one of the kings of the Fourth Dynasty. The immense statue, cut out of the native rock, save the fore-legs, which are built of masonry, is ninety feet long and seventy feet high. "This huge, mutilated figure has an astonishing effect; it seems like an eternal spectre. The stone phantom seems attentive; one would say that it hears and sees. Its great ear appears to collect the sounds of the past; its eyes, directed to the east, gaze, as it were, into the future; its aspect has a depth, a truth of expression, irresistibly fascinating to the spectator. In this figure — half statue, half mountain — we see a wonderful majesty, a grand serenity, and even a sort of sweetness of expression."

---

[1] It is probable that the musical notes were produced by the action of the sun upon the surface of the rock while wet with dew. The phenomenon was observed only while the upper part of the colossus, which was broken off by an earthquake, remained upon the ground. When the statue was restored, the music ceased.

The Greeks accounted for the early rise of the science of geometry among the Egyptians by reference to the necessity they were under each year of re-establishing the boundaries of their fields — the inundation obliterating old landmarks and divisions. The science thus forced upon their attention was cultivated with zeal and success. A single papyrus has been discovered that holds twelve geometrical theorems.

Arithmetic was necessarily brought into requisition in solving astronomical and geometrical problems. We ourselves are debtors to the ancient Egyptians for much of our mathematical knowledge, which has come to us from the banks of the Nile, through the Greeks and the Saracens.

Medicine and the Art of Embalming. — The custom of embalming the dead, affording opportunities for the examination of the body, without doubt had a great influence upon the development of the sciences of anatomy and medicine among the Egyptians. That the embalmers were physicians, we know from various testimonies. Thus we are told in the Bible that Joseph " commanded the *physicians* to embalm his father." The Egyptian doctors had a very great reputation among the ancients.

Every doctor was a specialist, and was not allowed to take charge of cases outside of his own branch. As the artist was forbidden to change the lines of the sacred statues, so the physician was not permitted to treat cases save in the manner prescribed by the customs of the past ; and if he were so presumptuous as to depart from the established mode of treatment, and the patient died, he was adjudged guilty of murder. Many drugs and medicines were used ; the ciphers, or characters, employed by modern apothecaries to designate grains and drams are of Egyptian invention.

The Egyptians believed that after a long lapse of time, several thousand years, the departed soul would return to earth and reanimate its former body ; hence their custom of preserving the body by means of embalmment. In the processes of embalming, the physicians made use of oils, resin, bitumen, and various aromatic

gums. The body was swathed in bandages of linen, while the
face was sometimes gilded, or covered with a gold mask. As this,
which was the "most approved method" of embalming, was very
costly, the expense being equivalent probably to $1000 of our
money, the bodies of the poorer classes were simply "salted and
dried," wrapped in coarse mats, and laid in tiers in great trenches
in the desert sands.

PROFILE OF RAMESES II. (From a photograph of the mummy.)

Only a few years ago (in 1881) the mummies of Thothmes III.,
Seti I., and Rameses II., together with those of nearly all of the
other Pharaohs of the Eighteenth, Nineteenth, Twentieth, and
Twenty-first Dynasties, were found in a secret cave near Thebes.

It seems that, some time in the 12th century B.C., a sudden alarm caused these bodies to be taken hastily from the royal tombs of which we have spoken (see p. 31), and secreted in this hidden chamber. When the danger had passed, the place of concealment had evidently been forgotten; so the bodies were never restored to their ancient tombs, but remained in this secret cavern to be discovered in our own day.

The mummies were taken to the Boulak Museum, at Cairo, where they were identified by means of the inscriptions upon the cases and wrappings. Among others the body of Seti I. and that of Rameses II. were unbandaged (1886), so that now we may look upon the faces of the greatest and most renowned of the Pharaohs. The faces of both Seti and Rameses are so remarkably preserved, that "were their subjects to return to earth to-day they could not fail to recognize their old sovereigns." Both are strong faces, of Semitic cast, that of Rameses bearing a striking resemblance to that of his father Seti, and both closely resembling their portrait statues and profiles. Professor Maspero, the director-general of the excavations and antiquities of Egypt, in his official report of the uncovering of the mummies, writes as follows of the appearance of the face of Rameses: "The face of the mummy gives a fair idea of the face of the living king. The expression is unintellectual, perhaps slightly animal; but even under the somewhat grotesque disguise of mummification, there is plainly to be seen an air of sovereign majesty, of resolve, and of pride." [1]

[1] On the finding and identification of the Pharaohs, consult two excellent articles in *The Century Magazine* for May, 1887.

CHAPTER III.

CHALDÆA.

1. POLITICAL HISTORY.

Basin of the Tigris and Euphrates. — The northern part of the Tigris and Euphrates valley, the portion that comprised ancient Assyria, consists of undulating plains, broken in places by considerable mountain ridges.

But all the southern portion of the basin, the part known as Chaldæa, or Babylonia, having been formed by the gradual encroachment of the deposits of the Tigris and Euphrates upon the waters of the Persian Gulf, is as level as the sea. During a large part of the year, rains are infrequent; hence agriculture is dependent mainly upon artificial irrigation. The distribution of the waters of the Tigris and the Euphrates was secured, in ancient times, by a stupendous system of canals and irrigants, which, at the present day, in a sand-choked and ruined condition, spread like a perfect network over the face of the country (see cut, p. 41).

The productions of Babylonia are very like those of the Nile valley. The luxuriant growth of grain upon these alluvial flats excited the wonder of all the Greek travellers who visited the East. Herodotus will not tell the whole truth, for fear his veracity may be doubted. The soil is as fertile now as in the time of the historian; but owing to the neglect of the ancient canals, the greater part of this once populous district has been converted into alternating areas of marsh and desert.

The Three Great Monarchies. — Within the Tigris-Euphrates basin, three great empires — the Chaldæan, the Assyrian, and the Babylonian — successively rose to prominence and dominion. Each, in turn, not only extended its authority over the valley, but also made the power of its arms felt throughout the adjoining regions. We shall now trace the rise and the varied fortunes of these empires, and the slow growth of the arts and sciences from rude beginnings among the early Chaldæans to their fuller and richer development under the Assyrian and Babylonian monarchies.

The Chaldæans a Mixed People. — In the earliest times Lower Chaldæa was known as Shumir, the Shinar of the Bible, while Upper Chaldæa bore the name of Accad. The original inhabitants were conjecturally of Turanian race, and are called Accadians.

ANCIENT BABYLONIAN CANALS.

These people laid the basis of civilization in the Euphrates valley, so that with them the history of Asian culture begins. They brought with them into the valley the art of hieroglyphical writing, which later developed into the well-known cuneiform system. They also had quite an extensive literature, and had made considerable advance in the art of building.

The civilization of the Accadians was given a great impulse by the arrival of a Semitic people. These foreigners were nomadic in habits, and altogether much less cultured than the Accadians.

Gradually, however, they adopted the arts and literature of the people among whom they had settled; yet they retained their own language, which in the course of time superseded the less perfect Turanian speech of the original inhabitants; consequently the mixed people, known later as Chaldæans, that arose from the blending of the two races, spoke a language essentially the same as that used by their northern neighbors, the Semitic Assyrians.

Sargon (Sharrukin) I. (3800? B.C.). — We know scarcely anything about the political affairs of the Accadians until after the arrival of the Semites. Then, powerful kings, sometimes of Semitic and then again of Turanian, or Accadian origin, appear ruling in the cities of Accad and Shumir, and the political history of Chaldæa begins.

The first prominent monarch is called Sargon I. (Sharrukin), a Semitic king of Agadê, one of the great early cities. An inscription recently deciphered makes this king to have reigned as early as 3800 B.C. He appears to have been the first great organizer of the peoples of the Chaldæan plains.

Yet not as a warrior, but as a patron and protector of letters, is Sargon's name destined to a sure place in history. He classified and translated into the Semitic, or Assyrian tongue the religious, mythological, and astronomical literature of the Accadians, and deposited the books in great libraries, which he established or enlarged, — the oldest and most valuable libraries of the ancient world. The scholar Sayce calls him the Chaldæan Solomon.

Conquest of Chaldæa by the Elamites (2286 B.C.). — While the Chaldæan kings were ruling in the great cities of Lower Babylonia, the princes of the Elamites, a people of Turanian race, were setting up a rival kingdom to the northeast, just at the foot of the hills of Persia.

In the year 2286 B.C., a king of Elam, Kudur-Nakhunta by name, overran Chaldæa, took all the cities founded by Sargon and his successors, and from the temples bore off in triumph to his capital, Susa, the statues of the Chaldæan gods, and set up in these lowland regions what is known as the Elamite Dynasty.

More than sixteen hundred years after this despoiling of the Chaldæan sanctuaries, a king of Nineveh captured the city of Susa, and finding there these stolen statues, caused them to be restored to their original temples.

The Chedorlaomer of Genesis, whose contact with the history of the Jewish patriarch Abraham has caused his name to be handed down to our own times in the records of the Hebrew people, is believed to have been the son and successor of Kudur-Nakhunta.

Chaldæa eclipsed by Assyria. — After the Elamite princes had maintained a more or less perfect dominion over the cities of Chaldæa for two or three centuries, their power seems to have declined; and then for several centuries longer, down to about 1300 B.C., dynasties and kings of which we know very little as yet, ruled the country.

During this period, Babylon, gradually rising into prominence, overshadowed the more ancient Accadian cities, and became the leading city of the land. From it the whole country was destined, later, to draw the name by which it is best known — Babylonia.

Meanwhile a Semitic power had been slowly developing in the north. This was the Assyrian empire, the later heart and centre of which was the great city of Nineveh. For a long time Assyria was simply a province or dependency of the lower kingdom; but about 1300 B.C., the Assyrian monarch Tiglathi-nin conquered Babylonia, and Assyria assumed the place that had been so long held by Chaldæa. From this time on to the fall of Nineveh in 606 B.C., the monarchs of this country virtually controlled the affairs of Western Asia.

2. ARTS AND GENERAL CULTURE.

Tower-Temples. — In the art of building, the Chaldæans, though their edifices fall far short of attaining the perfection exhibited by the earliest Egyptian structures, displayed no inconsiderable architectural knowledge and skill.

The most important of their constructions were their tower-temples. These were simple in plan, consisting of two or three terraces, or stages, placed one upon another so as to form a sort of rude pyramid. The material used in their construction was chiefly sun-dried brick. The edifice was sometimes protected by outer courses of burnt brick. The temple proper surmounted the upper platform.

All these tower-temples have crumbled into vast mounds, with only here and there a projecting mass of masonry to distinguish them from natural hills, for which they were at first mistaken.

Cuneiform Writing. — We have already mentioned the fact that the Accadians, when they entered the Euphrates valley, were in possession of a system of writing. This was a simple pictorial, or hieroglyphical system, which they gradually developed into the cuneiform.

In the cuneiform system, the characters, instead of being formed of unbroken lines, are composed of wedge-like marks ; hence the name (from *cuneus*, a wedge). This form, according to the scholar Sayce, arose when the Accadians, having entered the low country, substituted 'ablets of clay for the papyrus or other similar material which they had formerly used. The characters were impressed upon the soft tablet by means of a triangular writing-instrument, which gave them their peculiar wedge-shaped form.

The cuneiform mode of writing, improved and simplified by the Assyrians and the Persians, was in use about two thousand years, being employed by the nations in and near the Euphrates basin, down to the time of the conquest of the East by the Macedonians.

Books and Libraries. — The books of the Chaldæans were in general clay tablets, varying in length from one inch to twelve inches, and being about one inch thick. Those holding records of special importance, after having been once written over and baked, were covered with a thin coating of clay, and then the matter was written in duplicate and the tablets again baked. If the outer writing were defaced by accident or altered by design, the removal of the outer coating would at once show the true text.

The tablets were carefully preserved in great public libraries. Even during the Turanian period, before the Semites had entered the land, one or more of these collections existed in each of the chief cities of Accad and Shumir. "Accad," says Sayce, "was the China of Western Asia. Almost every one could read and write." Erech was especially renowned for its great library, and was known as "the City of Books."

The Religion. — The Accadian religion, as revealed by the tablets, was essentially the same as that held to-day by the nomadic Turanian tribes of Northern Asia — what is known as Shamanism. It consisted in a belief in good and evil spirits, of which the latter held by far the most prominent place. To avert the malign influence of these wicked spirits, the Accadians had resort

CHALDÆAN TABLET.

to charms and magic rites. The religion of the Semites was a form of Sabæanism, — that is, a worship of the heavenly bodies, — in which the sun was naturally the central object of adoration.

When the Accadians and the Semites intermingled, their religious systems blended to form one of the most influential religions of the world — one which spread far and wide under the form of Baal worship. There were in the perfected system twelve primary gods, at whose head stood Il, or Ra. Besides these great divinities, there were numerous lesser and local deities.

There were features of this old Chaldæan religion which were destined to exert a wide-spread and potent influence upon the minds of men. Out of the Sabæan Semitic element grew astrology, the pretended art of forecasting events by the aspect of the stars, which was most elaborately and ingeniously developed, until the fame of the Chaldæan astrologers was spread throughout the ancient world, while the spell of that art held in thraldom the mind of mediæval Europe.

Out of the Shamanistic element contributed by the Turanian Accadians, grew a system of magic and divination which had a most profound influence not only upon all the Eastern nations, including the Jews, but also upon the later peoples of the West. Mediæval magic and witchcraft were, in large part, an unchanged inheritance from Chaldæa.

The Chaldæan Genesis. — The cosmological myths of the Chaldæans, that is, their stories of the origin of things, are remarkably like the first chapters of Genesis.

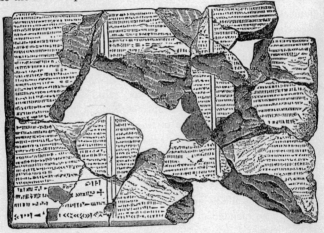

ASSYRIAN TABLET WITH PARTS OF THE DELUGE LEGEND.

The discoveries and patient labors of various scholars have reproduced, in a more or less perfect form, from the legendary tablets, the Chaldæan account of the Creation of the World, of an ancestral Paradise and the Tree of Life with its angel guardians, of the Deluge, and of the Tower of Babel.[1]

The Chaldæan Epic of Izdubar. — Beside their cosmological

[1] Consult especially George Smith's *The Chaldæan Account of Genesis;* see also *Records of the Past,* Vol. VII. pp. 127, 131.

and gold, which were carried away to Babylon, and the temple itself with the adjoining palace was given to the flames; the people, save a miserable remnant, were also borne away into the "Great Captivity" (586 B.C.).

With Jerusalem subdued, Nebuchadnezzar pushed with all his forces the siege of the Phœnician city of Tyre, whose investment had been commenced several years before. In striking language the prophet Ezekiel (ch. xxix. 18) describes the length and hardness of the siege : "Every head was made bald, and every shoulder was peeled." After a siege of thirteen years, the city seems to have fallen into the hands of the Babylonian king, and his authority was now undisputed from the Zagros Mountains to the Mediterranean.

The numerous captives of his many wars, embracing peoples of almost every nation in Western Asia, enabled Nebuchadnezzar to rival even the Pharaohs in the execution of enormous works requiring an immense expenditure of human labor. Among his works were the Great Palace in the royal quarter of the city; the celebrated Hanging Gardens; and gigantic reservoirs, canals, and various engineering works, embracing a vast system of irrigation that reached every part of Babylonia.

In addition to all these works, the indefatigable monarch seems to have either rebuilt or repaired almost every city and temple throughout the entire country. There are said to be at least a hundred sites in the tract immediately about Babylon which give evidence, by inscribed bricks bearing his legend, of the marvellous activity and energy of this monarch.

In the midst of all these gigantic undertakings, surrounded by a brilliant court of councillors and flatterers, the reason of the king was suddenly and mysteriously clouded.[1] After a period the cloud

---

[1] "Nebuchadnezzar fell a victim to that mental aberration which has often proved the penalty of despotism, but in the strange and degrading form to which physicians have given the name of lycanthropy; in which the patient, fancying himself a beast, rejects clothing and ordinary food, and even (as in this case) the shelter of a roof, ceases to use articulate speech, and sometimes persists in going on all-fours." — Smith's *Ancient History of the East,* p. 357.

passed away, "the glory of his kingdom, his honor, and bright-
ness returned unto him." But it was the splendor of the evening;
for the old monarch soon after died at the age of eighty, worn out
by the toils and cares of a reign of forty-three years, the longest,
most memorable, and instructive in the annals of the Babylonian
or Assyrian kings.

The Fall of Babylon. — In 555 B.C., Nabonadius, the last king
of Babylon, began his reign. He seems to have associated with
himself in the government his son Belshazzar, who shared with his
father the duties and honors of royalty, apparently on terms of
equal co-sovereignty.

To the east of the valley of the Tigris and the Euphrates, beyond
the ranges of the Zagros, there had been growing up an Aryan
kingdom, the Medo-Persian, which, at the time now reached by
us, had excited by its aggressive spirit the alarm of all the nations
of Western Asia. For purposes of mutual defence, the king of
Babylon, and Crœsus, the well-known monarch of Lydia, a state
of Asia Minor, formed an alliance against Cyrus, the strong and
ambitious sovereign of the Medes and Persians. This league
awakened the resentment of Cyrus, and, after punishing Crœsus
and depriving him of his kingdom (see p. 75), he collected his
forces to chastise the Babylonian king.

Anticipating the attack, Nabonadius had strengthened the defences of Babylon, and stationed around it supporting armies. But
he was able to avert the fatal blow for only a few years. Risking
a battle in the open field, his army was defeated, and the gates of
the capital were thrown open to the Persians (538 B.C.).[1]

With the fall of Babylon, the sceptre of dominion, borne for so
many years by Semitic princes, was given into the hands of the
Aryan peoples, who were destined, from this time forward, to
shape the course of events, and control the affairs of civilization.

---

[1] The device of turning the Euphrates, which Herodotus makes an incident
of the siege, was not resorted to by Cyrus; but it seems that a little later (in
521–519 B.C.), the city, having revolted, was actually taken in this way by the
Persian king Darius. Herodotus confused the two events.

The Great Edifices of Babylon. — The deep impression which
Babylon produced upon the early Greek travellers was made
chiefly by her vast architectural works, — her temples, palaces,
elevated gardens, and great walls. The Hanging Gardens of Nebuchadnezzar and the walls of the city were reckoned among the
wonders of the world.

The Babylonians, like their predecessors the Chaldæans, accorded to the sacred edifice the place of pre-eminence among
their architec-
tural works.
Sacred archi-
tecture in the
time of Neb-
uchadnezzar
had changed
but little from
the early Chal-
dæan models
(see p. 44) ;
save that the
temples were
now larger and
more splen-
did, being

BIRS-NIMRUD.   (Ruins of the great Temple of the Seven Spheres,
near Babylon.)

made, in the language of the inscriptions, "to shine like the
sun." The celebrated Temple of the Seven Spheres, at Bor-
sippa, a suburb of Babylon, may serve as a representative of
the later Babylonian temples. This structure was a vast pyramid, rising in seven consecutive stages, or platforms, to a height
of over one hundred and fifty feet. Each of the stages was
dedicated to one of the seven planets, or spheres. (The sun
and moon were reckoned as planets.) The stages sacred to the
sun and moon were covered respectively with plates of gold and
silver. The chapel, or shrine proper, surmounted the uppermost
stage. An inscribed cylinder discovered under the corner of one

of the stages (the Babylonians always buried records beneath the corners of their public edifices), informs us that this temple was a restoration by Nebuchadnezzar of a very ancient one, which in his day had become, from " extreme old age," a heap of rubbish. This edifice in its decay has left one of the grandest and most impressive ruins in all the East.

The Babylonian palaces and palace-mounds, in all essential features, were like those of the Assyrians, already described.

The so-called Hanging Gardens excited the greatest admiration of the ancient Greek visitors to Babylon. They were constructed by Nebuchadnezzar, to please his wife Amytis, who, tired of the monotony of the Babylonian plains, longed for the mountain scenery of her native Media. The gardens were probably built somewhat in the form of the tower-temples, the successive stages being covered with earth, and beautified with rare plants and trees, so as to simulate the appearance of a mountain rising in cultivated terraces towards the sky.

Under the later kings, Babylon was surrounded with stupendous walls. Herodotus affirms that these defences enclosed an area just fourteen miles square. A recently discovered inscription corroborates the statement of the historian. The object in enclosing such an enormous district seems to have been to bring sufficient arable ground within the defences to support the inhabitants in case of a protracted siege. No certain traces of these great ramparts can now be found.

literature with them was simply a medium for the conveyance of religious instruction and the awakening of devotional feeling.

The Hebrew religion, a pure monotheism, the teachings of a long line of holy men — patriarchs, lawgivers, prophets, and priests — stretching from Abraham down to the fifth century B.C., is contained in the sacred books of the Old Testament Scriptures. In these ancient writings, patriarchal traditions, histories, dramas, poems, prophecies, and personal narratives blend in a wonderful mosaic, which pictures with vivid and grand effect the various migrations, the deliverances, the calamities — all the events and religious experiences in the checkered life of the Chosen People.

Out of this old exclusive, formal Hebrew religion, transformed and spiritualized by the Great Teacher, grew the Christian faith. Out of the Old Testament arose the New, which we should think of as a part of Hebrew literature : for although written in the Greek language, and long after the close of the political life of the Jewish nation, still it is essentially Hebrew in thought and doctrine, and the supplement and crown of the Hebrew Scriptures.

Besides the Sacred Scriptures, called collectively, by way of pre-eminence, the Bible (The Book), it remains to mention especially the Apocrypha, embracing a number of books that were composed after the decline of the prophetic spirit, and which show traces, as indeed do several of the later books of the Bible, of the influence of Persian and Greek thought. These books are generally regarded by the Jews and Protestants as uncanonical, but in the main are considered by the Roman Catholics as possessing equal authority with the other books of the Bible.

Neither should we fail to mention the Talmud, a collection of Hebrew customs and traditions, with the comments thereupon of the rabbis, a work held by most Jews next in sacredness to the Holy Book ; the writings of Philo, an illustrious rabbi who lived at Alexandria just before the birth of Christ ; and the *Antiquities of the Jews* and the *Jewish Wars* by the historian Josephus, who lived and wrote about the time of the taking of Jerusalem by Titus ; that is, during the latter part of the first century after Christ.

CHAPTER VII.

THE PHŒNICIANS.

The Land and the People. — Ancient Phœnicia embraced a little strip of broken sea-coast lying between the Mediterranean and the ranges of Mount Lebanon. One of the most noted productions of the country was the fine fir-timber cut from the forests that crowned the lofty ranges of the Lebanon Mountains. The "cedar of Lebanon" holds a prominent place both in the history and the poetry of the East.

Another celebrated product of the country was the Tyrian purple, which was obtained from several varieties of the murex, a species of shell-fish, secured at first along the Phœnician coast, but later sought in distant waters, especially in the Grecian seas.

The Phœnicians were of Semitic race, and of close kin to most of the so-called Canaanitish tribes. They were a maritime and trading people.

Tyre and Sidon. — The various Phœnician cities never coalesced to form a true nation. They simply constituted a sort of league, or confederacy, the petty states of which generally acknowledged the leadership of Tyre or of Sidon, the two chief cities. The place of supremacy in the confederation was at first held by Sidon, but later by Tyre.

From the 11th to the 4th century B.C., Tyre controlled, almost without dispute on the part of Sidon, the affairs of Phœnicia. During this time the maritime enterprise and energy of her merchants spread the fame of the little island-capital throughout the world. She was queen and mistress of the Mediterranean.

During all the last centuries of her existence, Phœnicia was, for the most part, tributary to one or another of the great monarchies about her. She acknowledged in turn the suzerainty of the Assyr-

by any ruler before his time. It stretched from the Indus to the farthest limits of Asia Minor, and from the Caspian Sea to the Persian Gulf, thus embracing not only the territories of the Median kingdom, but also those of the allied kingdoms of Lydia and Babylonia. The subjugation of Babylonia to the Persian authority has already been narrated (see p. 60). We will now tell how Cyrus gained the kingdom of Lydia.

Lydia was a country in the western part of Asia Minor. It was a land highly favored by nature. It embraced two rich river valleys, — the plains of the Hermus and the Cayster, — which, from the mountains inland, slope gently to the island-dotted Ægean. The Pactolus, and other tributaries of the streams we have named, rolled down "golden sands," while the mountains were rich in the precious metals. The coast region did not at first belong to Lydia ; it was held by the Greeks, who had fringed it with cities. The capital of the country was Sardis, whose citadel was set on a lofty and precipitous rock.

The Lydians were a mixed people, formed, it is thought, by the mingling, in prehistoric times, of Aryan tribes that crossed the Ægean from Europe, with the original non-Aryan population of the country.

The last and most renowned of the Lydian kings was Crœsus. Under him the Lydian empire attained its greatest extension, embracing all the states of Asia Minor west of the Halys, save Lycia. The tribute Crœsus collected from the Greek cities, which he subjugated, and the revenues he derived from his gold mines, rendered him the richest monarch of his times, so that his name has passed into the proverb "Rich as Crœsus."

Now Astyages, whom Cyrus had just overthrown, was the brother-in-law of this Crœsus. When Crœsus heard of his relative's misfortune, he resolved to avenge his wrongs. The Delphian oracle (see p. 104), to which he sent to learn the issue of a war upon Cyrus, told him that he "would destroy a great kingdom." Interpreting this favorably, he sent again to inquire whether the empire he should establish would prove permanent, and received this oracle : "Flee and tarry not when a mule [1] shall be king of the Medes." Deeming the accession of a mule to the Persian throne altogether impossible, he inferred the oracle to mean that his empire should last forever.

Thus encouraged in his purpose, Crœsus prepared to make war upon Persia. But he had miscalculated the strength and activity of his enemy. Cyrus marched across the Halys, defeated the Lydian army in the field, and after a short siege captured Sardis ; and Lydia became a province of the new Persian empire.

There is a story which tells how Cyrus had caused a pyre to be erected on which to burn Crœsus, but at the last moment was struck by hearing the unfortunate monarch repeatedly call the name of Solon. Seeking the meaning of this, he was told that Crœsus in his prosperous years was visited by the Greek sage Solon, who, in answer to the inquiry of Crœsus as to whether he did not deem him a happy man, replied, "Count no man happy until he is dead." Cyrus was so impressed with the story, so the legend tells, that he released the captive king, and treated him with the greatest kindness.

TOMB OF CYRUS THE GREAT.

This war between Crœsus and Cyrus derives a special importance from the fact that it brought the Persian empire into con-

[1] The allusion is to the (traditional) mixed Persian and Median descent of Cyrus.

tact with the Greek cities of Asia, and thus led on directly to that memorable struggle between Greece and Persia known as the Græco-Persian War.

Tradition says that Cyrus lost his life while leading an expedition against some Scythian tribes in the north. He was buried at Pasargadæ, the old Persian capital, and there his tomb stands to-day, surrounded by the ruins of the magnificent buildings with which he adorned that city. The following cuneiform inscription may still be read upon a pillar near the sepulchre : " I am Cyrus, the king, the Akhæmenian."

Cyrus, notwithstanding his seeming love for war and conquest, possessed a kindly and generous disposition. Almost universal testimony has ascribed to him the purest and most beneficent character of any Eastern monarch.

Reign of Cambyses (529–522 B.C.). — Cyrus the Great left two sons, Cambyses and Smerdis : the former, as the oldest, inherited the sceptre, and the title of king. He began a despotic and unfortunate reign by causing his brother, whose influence he feared, to be secretly put to death.

With far less ability than his father for their execution, Cambyses conceived even vaster projects of conquest and dominion. Asia had hitherto usually afforded a sufficient field for the ambition of Oriental despots. Cambyses determined to add the country of Africa to the vast inheritance received from his father. Upon some slight pretext, he invaded Egypt, captured Memphis, and ascended the Nile to Thebes. From here he sent an army of fifty thousand men to subdue the oasis of Ammon, in the Libyan desert. Of the vast host not a man returned from the expedition. It is thought that the army was overwhelmed and buried by one of those fatal storms, called simooms, that so frequently sweep over those dreary wastes of sand.

After a short, unsatisfactory stay in Egypt, Cambyses set out on his return to Persia. While on his way home, news was brought to him that his brother Smerdis had usurped the throne. A

Magian[1] impostor, Gomates by name, who resembled the murdered Smerdis, had personated him, and actually grasped the sceptre. Entirely disheartened by this startling intelligence, Cambyses in despair took his own life.

Reign of Darius I. (521–486 B.C.). — The Persian nobles soon rescued the sceptre from the grasp of the false Smerdis, and their leader, Darius, took the throne. The first act of Darius was to punish, by a general massacre, the Magian priests for the part they had taken in the usurpation of Smerdis.

CAPTIVE INSURGENTS BROUGHT BEFORE DARIUS. Beneath his foot is the Magus Gomates, the false Smerdis. (From the great Behistun Rock.)

With quiet and submission secured throughout the empire, Darius gave himself, for a time, to the arts of peace. He built a palace at Susa, and erected magnificent structures at Persepolis;

[1] There were at this time two opposing religions in Persia: Zoroastrianism, which taught the simple worship of God under the name of Ormazd; and Magianism, a less pure faith, whose professors were fire-worshippers. The former was the religion of the Aryans; the latter, that of the non-Aryan portion of the population. The usurpation which placed Smerdis on the throne was planned by the Magi, Smerdis himself being a fire-priest.

reformed the administration of the government (see p. 82), making such wise and lasting changes that he has been called "the second founder of the Persian empire"; established post-roads, instituted a coinage for the realm, and upon the great rock of Behistun, a lofty smooth-faced cliff on the western frontier of Persia, caused to be inscribed a record of all his achievements.[1] And now the Great King, Lord of Western Asia and of Egypt, conceived and entered upon the execution of vast designs of conquest, the far-reaching effects of which were destined to live long after he had passed away. Inhospitable steppes on the north, and burning deserts on the south, whose shifting sands within a period yet fresh in memory had been the grave of a Persian army, seemed to be the barriers which Nature herself had set for the limits of empire in these directions. But on the eastern flank of the kingdom the rich and crowded plains of India invited the conqueror with promises of endless spoils and revenues; while on the west a new continent, full of unknown mysteries, presented virgin fields never yet traversed by the army of an Eastern despot. Darius determined to extend the frontiers of his empire in both these directions.

At one blow the region of northwestern India known as the Punjab, was brought under Persian authority; and thus with a single effort were the eastern limits of the empire pushed out so as to include one of the richest countries of Asia — on which henceforth returned to the Great King an annual revenue vastly larger than that of any other province hitherto acquired, not even excepting the rich district of Babylonia.

With an army numbering, it is said, more than 700,000 men, Darius now crossed the Bosphorus by means of a sort of pontoon bridge, constructed by Grecian architects, and passing the Danube by means of a similar bridge, penetrated far into what is now Rus-

[1] This important inscription is written in the cuneiform characters, and in three languages, Aryan, Turanian, and Semitic. It is the Rosetta Stone of the cuneiform writings, the key to their treasures having been obtained from its parallel columns.

sia, which was then occupied by Scythian hordes. The results of the expedition were the addition of Thrace to the Persian empire, and the making of Macedonia a tributary kingdom. Thus the Persian kings secured their first foothold upon the European continent.

The most significant campaign in Europe was yet to follow. In 500 B.C., the Ionian cities in Asia Minor subject to the Persian authority revolted. The Greeks of Europe lent aid to their sister states. Sardis was sacked and burned by the insurgents. With the revolt crushed and punished with great severity, Darius determined to chastise the European Greeks, and particularly the Athenians, for their insolence in giving aid to his rebellious subjects. Herodotus tells us that he appointed a person whose sole duty it was daily to stir up the purpose of the king with the words, "Master, remember the Athenians."

A large land and naval armament was fitted out and placed under the command of Mardonius, a son-in-law of Darius. The land forces suffered severe losses at the hands of the barbarians of Thrace, and the fleet was wrecked by a violent storm off Mount Athos, three hundred ships being lost (492 B.C.).

Two years after this disaster, another expedition, consisting of 120,000 men, was borne by ships across the Ægean to the plains of Marathon. The details of the significant encounter that there took place between the Persians and the Athenians will be given when we come to narrate the history of Greece. We need now simply note the result, — the complete overthrow of the Persian forces by the Greeks under Miltiades (490 B.C.).

Darius, angered beyond measure by the failure of the expedition, stirred up all the provinces of his vast empire, and called for new levies from far and near, resolved upon leading in person such an army into Greece that the insolent Athenians should be crushed at a single blow, and the tarnished glory of the Persian arms restored. In the midst of these preparations, with the Egyptians in revolt, the king suddenly died, in the year 486 B.C.

Reign of Xerxes I. (486–465 B.C.). — The successor of Darius, his son Xerxes, though more inclined to indulge in the ease and luxury of the palace than to subject himself to the hardship and discipline of the camp, was urged by those about him to an active prosecution of the plans of his father.

After crushing the Egyptian revolt and another insurrection in Babylonia, the Great King was free to devote his attention to the distant Greeks. Mustering the contingents of the different provinces of his empire, Xerxes led his vast army over the bridges he had caused to be thrown across the Hellespont, crushed the Spartan guards at the Pass of Thermopylæ, pushed on into Attica, and laid Athens in ruins. But there fortune forsook him. At the naval battle of Salamis, his fleet was cut to pieces by the Grecian ships; and the king, making a precipitate retreat into Asia, hastened to his capital, Susa. Here, in the pleasures of the harem, he sought solace for his wounded pride and broken hopes. He at last fell a victim to palace intrigue, being slain in his own chamber (465 B.C.).

End of the Persian Empire. — The power and supremacy of the Persian monarchy passed away with the reign of Xerxes. The last one hundred and forty years of the existence of the empire was a time of weakness and anarchy. This period was spanned by the reigns of eight kings. It was in the reign of Artaxerxes II., called Mnemon for his remarkable memory, that took place the well-known expedition of the Ten Thousand Greeks under Cyrus, the brother of Artaxerxes, an account of which will be given in connection with Grecian history (see chap. xv.).

The march of the Ten Thousand through the very heart of the dominions of the Great King demonstrated the amazing internal weakness of the empire. Marathon and Salamis had shown the immense superiority of the free soldiery of Greece over the splendid but servile armies of Persia, that were often driven to battle with the lash. These disclosures invited the Macedonians to the invasion and conquest of the empire.

In the year 334 B.C., Alexander the Great, king of Macedonia, led a small army of thirty-five thousand Greeks and Macedonians across the Hellespont. Three great battles — that of the Granicus, that of Issus, and that of Arbela — decided the fate of the Persian Empire. Darius III., the last of the Persian kings, fled from the field of Arbela, on the plains of Assyria, only to be treacherously assassinated by one of his own generals.

The succeeding movements of Alexander, and the establishment by him of the short-lived Macedonian monarchy upon the ruins of the Persian state, are matters that properly belong to Grecian history, and will be related in a following chapter.

2. Government, Religion, and Arts.

The Government. — Before the reign of Darius I., the government of the Persian Empire was like that of all the great monarchies that had preceded it ; that is, it consisted of a great number of subject states, which were allowed to retain their own kings and manage their own affairs, only paying tribute and homage, and furnishing contingents in time of war, to the Great King.

We have seen how weak was this rude and primitive type of government. Darius I., who possessed rare ability as an organizer, remodelled the system of his predecessors, and actually realized for the Persian monarchy what Tiglath-Pileser II. had long before attempted, but only with partial and temporary success, to accomplish for the Assyrian.

The system of government which Darius I. thus first made a real fact in the world, is known as the *satrapal*, a form represented to-day by the government of the Turkish Sultan. The entire kingdom was divided into twenty or more provinces, over each of which was placed a governor, called a satrap, appointed by the king. These officials held their position at the pleasure of the sovereign, and were thus rendered his subservient creatures. Each province contributed to the income of the king a stated revenue. There were provisions in the system by which the king might be apprised of the disloyalty of his satraps. Thus the whole dominion was firmly cemented together, and the facility with which almost sovereign states — which was the real character of the different parts of the empire under the old system — could plan and execute revolt, was removed.

Literature and Religion: Zoroastrianism. — The literature of the ancient Persians was mostly religious. Their sacred book is called the Zenda-vesta. The oldest part is named the Vendidad. This consists of laws, incantations, and mythical tales.

The religious system of the Persians, as taught in the Zend-avesta, is known as Zoroastrianism, from Zoroaster, its founder. This great reformer and teacher is now generally supposed to have lived and taught about 1000 B.C.

Zoroastrianism was a system of belief known as dualism. Opposed to the "good spirit," Ormazd (Ahura Mazda), there was a

THE KING IN COMBAT WITH A MONSTER.
(From Persepolis.)

"dark spirit," Ahriman (Angro-Mainyus), who was constantly striving to destroy the good creations of Ormazd by creating all evil things — storm, drought, pestilence, noxious animals, weeds and thorns in the world without, and evil in the heart of man within. From all eternity these two powers had been contending for the mastery; in the present neither had the decided advantage; but in the near future Ormazd would triumph over Ahriman, and evil be forever destroyed.

The duty of man was to aid Ormazd by working with him against the evil-loving Ahriman. He must labor to eradicate every evil and vice in his own bosom; to reclaim the earth from barrenness; and to kill all bad animals — frogs, toads, snakes, lizards — which Ahriman had created. Herodotus saw with amazement the Magian priests armed with weapons and engaged in slaying these animals as a "pious pastime." Agriculture was a sacred calling, for the husbandman was reclaiming the ground from the curse of the Dark Spirit. Thus men might become co-workers with Ormazd in the mighty work of overthrowing and destroying the kingdom of the wicked Ahriman.

The evil man was he who allowed vice and degrading passions to find a place in his own soul, and neglected to exterminate noxious animals and weeds, and to help redeem the earth from the barrenness and sterility created by the enemy of Ormazd.[1]

After death the souls of the good and the bad alike must pass over a narrow bridge: the good soul crosses in safety, and is admitted to the presence of Ahura Mazda; while the evil soul is sure to fall from the path, sharp as the edge of a scimitar, into a pit of woe, the dwelling-place of Ahriman.

Architecture. — The simple religious faith of the Persians discouraged, though it did not prohibit, the erection of temples: their sacred architecture scarcely included more than an altar and

---

[1] The belief of the Zoroastrians in the sacredness of the elements, — earth, water, fire, and air, — created a difficulty in regard to the disposal of dead bodies. They could neither be burned, buried, thrown into the water, nor left to decay in a sepulchral chamber or in the open air, without polluting one or another of the sacred elements. So they were given to the birds and wild beasts, being exposed on lofty towers or in desert places. Those whose feelings would not allow them thus to dispose of their dead, were permitted to bury them, provided they first encased the body in wax, to preserve the ground from contamination. The modern Parsees, or Fire-Worshippers, give their dead to the birds.

pedestal. The palace of the monarch was the structure that absorbed the best efforts of the Persian artist.

In imitation of the inhabitants of the valley of the Euphrates, the Persian kings raised their palaces upon lofty terraces, or platforms. But upon the table-lands they used stone instead of adobe or brick, and at Persepolis, raised, for the substruction of their palaces, an immense platform of massive masonry, which is one of the most wonderful monuments of the world's ancient builders. This terrace, which is uninjured by the 2300 years that have passed since its erection, is about 1500 feet long, 1000 feet wide, and

THE RUINS OF PERSEPOLIS.

40 feet high. The summit is reached by broad stairways of stone, pronounced by competent judges the finest work of the kind that the ancient or even the modern world can boast.

Surmounting this platform are the ruins of the palaces of several of the Persian monarchs, from Cyrus the Great to Artaxerxes Ochus. These ruins consist chiefly of walls, columns, and great monolithic door- and window-frames. Colossal winged bulls, copied from the Assyrians, stand as wardens at the gateway of the ruined palaces.

Numerous sculptures in bas-relief decorate the faces of the walls, and these throw much light upon the manners and customs of the ancient Persian kings. The successive palaces increase, not only in size, but in sumptuousness of adornment, thus registering those changes which we have been tracing in the national history. The residence of Cyrus was small and modest, while that of Artaxerxes Ochus equalled in size the great palace of the Assyrian Sargon.

TABLE OF KINGS OF MEDIA AND PERSIA.

Kings of Media	Phraortes	? –625
	Cyaxares	625–585
	Astyages	585–558
Kings of Persia	Cyrus	558–529
	Cambyses	529–522
	Pseudo-Smerdis	522–521
	Darius I.	521–486
	Xerxes I.	486–465
	Artaxerxes I. (Longimanus)	465–425
	Xerxes II.	425
	Sogdianus	425–424
	Darius II. (Nothus)	424–405
	Artaxerxes II. (Mnemon)	405–359
	Artaxerxes III. (Ochus)	359–338
	Arses	338–336
	Darius III. (Codomannus)	336–330

CHAPTER IX.

THE LAND AND THE PEOPLE.

Divisions of Greece. — Long arms of the sea divide the Grecian peninsula into three parts, called Northern, Central, and Southern Greece.

Northern Greece included the ancient districts of Thessaly and Epirus. Thessaly consists mainly of a large and beautiful valley, walled in on all sides by rugged mountains. It was celebrated far and wide for the variety and beauty of its scenery. On its northern edge, lay a beautiful glen, called the Vale of Tempe, the only pass by which the plain of Thessaly could be entered from the north. The district of Epirus stretched along the Ionian Sea on the west. In the gloomy recesses of its forests of oak was situated the renowned Dodonean oracle of Zeus.

Central Greece was divided into eleven districts, among which were Phocis, Bœotia, and Attica. In Phocis was the city of Delphi, famous for its oracle and temple ; in Bœotia, the city of Thebes ; and in Attica, the brilliant Athens.

Southern Greece, or the Peloponnesus, was also divided into eleven provinces, of which the more important were Arcadia, embracing the central part of the peninsula ; Achaia, the northern part ; Argolis, the eastern ; and Messenia and Laconia, the southern. The last district was ruled by the city of Sparta, the great rival of Athens.

Mountains. — The Cambunian Mountains form a lofty wall along a considerable reach of the northern frontier of Greece,

shutting out at once the cold winds and hostile races from the
north. Branching off at right angles to these mountains is the
Pindus range, which runs south into Central Greece.

In Northern Thessaly is Mount Olympus, the most celebrated
mountain of the peninsula. The ancient Greeks thought it the
highest mountain in the world (it is 9700 feet in height), and
believed that its cloudy summit was the abode of the celestials.

South of Olympus, close by the sea, are Ossa and Pelion, celebrated in fable as the mountains which the giants, in their war
against the gods, piled one upon another, in order to scale
Olympus.

Parnassus and Helicon, in Central Greece, — beautiful mountains clad with trees and vines and filled with fountains, — were
believed to be the favorite haunts of the Muses. Near Athens are
Hymettus, praised for its honey, and Pentelicus, renowned for its
marbles.

The Peloponnesus is rugged with mountains that radiate in all
directions from the central country of Arcadia, — " the Switzerland
of Greece."

Islands about Greece. — Very much of the history of Greece
is intertwined with the islands that lie about the mainland. On
the east, in the Ægean Sea, are the Cyclades, so called because
they form an irregular circle about the sacred isle of Delos, where
was a very celebrated shrine of Apollo. Between the Cyclades and
Asia Minor lie the Sporades, which islands, as the name implies,
are sown irregularly over that portion of the Ægean.

Just off the coast of Attica is a large island called by the
ancients Eubœa, but known to us as Negropont. Close to the
Asian shores are the large islands of Lesbos, Chios, Samos, and
Rhodes.

To the west of Greece lie the Ionian Islands, the largest of which
was called Corcyra, now Corfu. The rugged island of Ithaca was
the birthplace of Odysseus, or Ulysses, the hero of the *Odyssey*.
Cythera, just south of the Peloponnesus, was sacred to Aphrodite
(Venus), as it was here fable said she rose from the sea-foam.

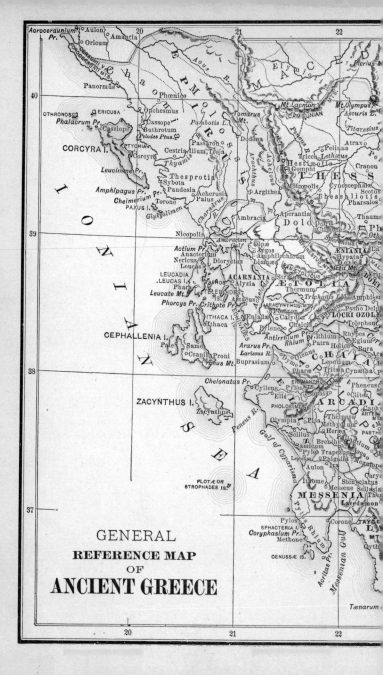

GENERAL
REFERENCE MAP
OF
ANCIENT GREECE

Beyond Cythera, in the Mediterranean, midway between Greece and Egypt, is the large island of Crete, noted in legend for its labyrinth and its legislator Minos.

Influence of Country. — The physical features of a country have much to do with the moulding of the character and the shaping of the history of its people. Mountains, isolating neighboring communities and shutting out conquering races, foster the spirit of local patriotism and preserve freedom ; the sea, inviting abroad, and rendering intercourse with distant countries easy, awakens the spirit of adventure and develops commercial enterprise.

Now, Greece is at once a mountainous and a maritime country. Abrupt mountain-walls fence it off into a great number of isolated districts, each of which in ancient times became the seat of a distinct community, or state. Hence the fragmentary character of its political history. The Hellenic states never coalesced to form a single nation.

The peninsula is, moreover, by deep arms and bays of the sea, converted into what is in effect an archipelago. Few spots in Greece are forty miles from the sea. Hence its people were early tempted to a sea-faring life. The shores of the Mediterranean and the Euxine were dotted with Hellenic colonies. Intercourse with the old civilizations of Egypt and Phœnicia stirred the naturally quick and versatile Greek intellect to early and vigorous thought. The islands strewn with seeming carelessness through the Ægean Sea were " stepping-stones," which invited the earliest settlers of Greece to the delightful coast countries of Asia Minor, and thus blended the life and history of the opposite shores.

Again, the beauty of Grecian scenery inspired many of the most striking passages of her poets ; and it is thought that the exhilarating atmosphere and brilliant skies of Attica were not unrelated to the lofty achievements of the Athenian intellect.

The Pelasgians. — The historic inhabitants of the land we have described were called by the Romans Greeks, but they called themselves Hellenes, from their fabled ancestor Hellen.

But the Hellenes, according to their own account, were not the original inhabitants of the country. They were preceded by a people whom they called Pelasgians. Who these folk were is a matter of debate. Some think that the Pelasgians and Hellenes were kindred tribes, but that the Hellenes, possessing superior qualities, gradually acquired ascendency over the Pelasgians and finally absorbed them.

PREHISTORIC WALLS AT MYCENÆ. (The Lions' Gate.)

The Pelasgians were somewhat advanced beyond the savage state. They cultivated the ground, and protected their cities with walls. Remnants of their rude but massive masonry still encumber in places the soil of Greece.

The Hellenes. — The Hellenes were divided into four tribes; namely, the Ionians, the Dorians, the Achæans, and the Æolians.

The Ionians were a many-sided, imaginative people. They developed every part of their nature, and attained unsurpassed excellence in art, literature, and philosophy. The most noted Ionian city was Athens, whose story is a large part of the history of Hellas.

The Dorians were a practical, unimaginative race. Their speech and their art were both alike without ornament. They developed the body rather than the mind. Their education was almost wholly gymnastic and military. They were unexcelled as warriors. The most important city founded by them was Sparta, the rival of Athens.

These two great Hellenic families divided Hellas[1] into two rival parties, which through their mutual jealousies and contentions finally brought all the bright hopes and promises of the Hellenic race to utter ruin.

The Achæans are represented by the Greek legends as being the predominant race in the Peloponnesus during the Heroic Age. The Æolians formed a rather ill-defined division. In historic times the name is often made to include all Hellenes not enumerated as Ionians or Dorians.

These several tribes, united by bonds of language and religion, always regarded themselves as members of a single family. They were proud of their ancestry, and as exclusive almost as the Hebrews. All non-Hellenic people they called *Barbarians.*[2]

When the mists of antiquity are first lifted from Greece, about the beginning of the eighth century B.C., we discover the several families of the Hellenic race in possession of Greece proper, of the islands of the Ægean, and of the western coasts of Asia Minor. Respecting their prehistoric migrations and settlements, we have little or no certain knowledge.

[1] Under the name Hellas the ancient Greeks included not only Greece proper and the islands of the adjoining seas, but also the Hellenic cities in Asia Minor, Southern Italy, Sicily, and elsewhere. "Wherever were Hellenes, there was Hellas."

[2] At first, this term meant scarcely more than "unintelligible folk"; but later, it came to express aversion and contempt.

Oriental Immigrants. — According to their own traditions the early growth of civilization among the European Hellenes was promoted by the settlement among them of Oriental immigrants, who brought with them the arts and culture of the different countries of the East.

From Egypt, legend affirms, came Cecrops, bringing with him the arts, learning, and priestly wisdom of the Nile valley. He is represented as the builder of the citadel (the *Cecropia*) of what was afterwards the illustrious city of Athens. From Phœnicia Cadmus brought the letters of the alphabet, and founded the city of Thebes. The Phrygian Pelops, the progenitor of the renowned heroes Agamemnon and Menelaus, settled in the southern peninsula, which was called after him the Peloponnesus (the Island of Pelops).

The nucleus of fact in all these legends is probably this, — that the European Greeks received the primary elements of their culture from the East through their Asiatic kinsmen.

Local Patriotism of the Greeks : the City the Political Unit. — The narrow political sympathies of the ancient Greeks prevented their ever uniting to form a single nation. The city was with them the political unit. It was regarded as a distinct, self-governing state, just like a modern nation. A citizen of one city was an alien in any other : he could not marry a woman of a city not his own, nor hold property in houses or lands within its territory.

A Greek city-state usually embraced, besides the walled town, a more or less extensive border of gardens and farms, a strip of sea-coast, or perhaps a considerable mountain-hemmed valley or plain. The *model* city (or *state*, as we should say) must not be over large. In this, as in everything else, the ancient Greeks applied the Delphian rule — " Measure in all things." " A small city," says one of their poets, " set upon a rock and well governed, is better than all foolish Nineveh." Aristotle thought that the ideal city should not have more than ten thousand citizens.

CHAPTER X.

THE LEGENDARY, OR HEROIC AGE.

(From the earliest times to 776 B.C.)

Character of the Legendary Age. — The real history of the Greeks does not begin before the eighth century B.C. All that lies back of that date is an inseparable mixture of myth, legend, and fact. Yet this shadowy period forms the background of Grecian history, and we cannot understand the ideas and acts of the Greeks of historic times without at least some knowledge of what they believed their ancestors did and experienced in those prehistoric ages.

So, as a sort of prelude to the story we have to tell, we shall repeat some of the legends of the Greeks respecting their national heroes and their great labors and undertakings. But it must be carefully borne in mind that these legends are not history, though some of them may be confused remembrances of actual events.

The Heroes: Heracles, Theseus, and Minos. — The Greeks believed that their ancestors were a race of heroes of divine or semi-divine lineage. Every tribe, district, city, and village even, preserved traditions of its heroes, whose wonderful exploits were commemorated in song and story. Many of these personages acquired national renown, and became the revered heroes of the whole Greek race.

Heracles was the greatest of the national heroes of the Greeks. He is represented as performing, besides various other exploits, twelve superhuman labors, and as being at last translated from a blazing pyre to a place among the immortal gods. The myth of Heracles, who was at first a solar divinity, is made up mainly of the very same fables that were told of the Chaldæan solar hero

Izdubar (see p. 46). Through the Phœnicians, these stories found their way to the Greeks, who ascribed to their own Heracles the deeds of the Chaldæan sun-god.

Theseus, a descendant of Cecrops, was the favorite hero of the Athenians, being one of their legendary kings. Among his great exploits was the slaying of the Minotaur, — a monster which Minos, king of Crete, kept in a labyrinth, and fed upon youths and maidens sent from Athens as a forced tribute.

Minos, king of Crete, was one of the greatest tribal heroes of the Dorians. Legend makes him a legislator of divine wisdom, the suppressor of piracy in the Grecian seas, and the founder of the first great maritime state of Hellas.

The Argonautic Expedition. — Besides the labors and exploits of single heroes, the legends of the Greeks tell of several memorable enterprises conducted by bands of heroes. Among these were the Argonautic Expedition and the Siege of Troy.

The tale of the Argonautic Expedition is told with many variations in the legends of the Greeks. Jason, a prince of Thessaly, with fifty companion heroes, among whom were Heracles, Theseus, and Orpheus, the latter a musician of superhuman skill, the music of whose lyre moved brutes and stones, set sail in " a fifty-oared galley," called the *Argo* (hence the name *Argonauts,* given to the heroes), in search of a "golden fleece" which was fabled to be nailed to a tree and watched by a dragon, in the Grove of Ares, on the eastern shores of the Euxine, an inhospitable region of unknown terrors. The expedition is successful, and, after many wonderful adventures, the heroes return in triumph with the sacred relic.

Different meanings have been given to this tale. In its primitive form it was doubtless a pure myth of the rain-clouds; but in its later forms we may believe it to symbolize the maritime explorations in the eastern seas, of some of the tribes of Pelasgian Greece.

The Trojan War (legendary date 1194–1184 B.C.). — The Trojan War was an event about which gathered a great circle of tales and poems, all full of an undying interest and fascination.

Ilios, or Troy, was the capital of a strong empire, represented as Grecian in race and language, which had grown up in Asia Minor, along the shores of the Hellespont. The traditions tell how Paris, son of Priam, king of Troy, visited the Spartan king Menelaus, and ungenerously requited his hospitality by secretly bearing away to Troy his wife Helen, famous for her rare beauty.

All the heroes of Greece flew to arms to avenge the wrong. A host of one hundred thousand warriors was speedily gathered. Agamemnon, brother of Menelaus and "king of men," was chosen leader of the expedition. Under him were the "lion-hearted Achilles," of Thessaly, the "crafty Ulysses" (Odysseus), king of Ithaca, Ajax, "the swift son of Oïleus," the Telamonian Ajax, the aged Nestor, and many more — the most valiant heroes of all Hellas. Twelve hundred galleys bore the gathered clans from Aulis in Greece, across the Ægean to the Trojan shores.

For ten years the Greeks and their allies hold in close siege the city of Priam. On the plains beneath the walls of the capital, the warriors of the two armies fight in general battle, or contend in single encounter. At first, Achilles is foremost in every fight; but a fair-faced maiden, who fell to him as a prize, having been taken from him by his chief, Agamemnon, he is filled with wrath, and sulks in his tent. Though the Greeks are often sorely pressed, still the angered hero refuses them his aid. At last, however, his friend Patroclus is killed by Hector, eldest son of Priam, and then Achilles goes forth to avenge his death. In a fierce combat he slays Hector, fastens his body to his chariot wheels, and drags it thrice around the walls of Troy.

The city is at last taken through a device of the "crafty Ulysses." Upon the plain in sight of the walls is built a wooden statue of a horse, in the body of which are hidden several Grecian warriors. Then the Greeks retire to their ships, as though about to abandon the siege. The Trojans issue from the gates and gather in wondering crowds about the image. They believe it to be an offering sacred to Athena, and so dare not destroy it; but, on the other hand, misled by certain omens and by a lying Greek named

Sinon, they level a place in the walls of their city, and drag the statue within. At night the concealed warriors issue from the horse, open the gates of the city to the Grecians, and Troy is sacked, and burned to the ground. The aged Priam is slain, after having seen his sons and many of his warriors perish before his face. Æneas, with his aged father, Anchises, and a few devoted followers, escapes, and, after long wanderings, becomes the fabled founder of the Roman race in Italy.

It is a matter of difficulty to point out the nucleus of fact in this the most elaborate and interesting of the Grecian legends. Some believe it to be the dim recollection of a prehistoric conflict between the Greeks and the natives of Asia Minor, arising from the attempt of the former to secure a foothold upon the coast. That there really existed in prehistoric times such a city as Troy, has been placed beyond doubt by the excavations and discoveries of Dr. Schliemann.

Return of the Grecian Chieftains. — After the fall of Troy, the Grecian chieftains and princes returned home. The poets represent the gods as withdrawing their protection from the hitherto favored heroes, because they had not respected the altars of the Trojans. So, many of them were driven in endless wanderings over sea and land. Homer's *Odyssey* portrays the sufferings of the " much-enduring " Odysseus (Ulysses), impelled by divine wrath to long journeyings through strange seas.

In some cases, according to the tradition, advantage had been taken of the absence of the princes, and their thrones had been usurped. Thus at Argos, Ægisthus had won the unholy love of Clytemnestra, wife and queen of Agamemnon, who on his return was murdered by the guilty couple. In pleasing contrast with this we have exhibited to us the constancy of Penelope, although sought by many suitors during the absence of her husband Ulysses.

The Dorian Invasion, or the Return of the Heraclidæ (legendary date 1104 B.C.). — We set the tradition of the return of the Heraclidæ apart from the legends of the enterprises just detailed, for the reason that it undoubtedly contains quite a large historical element. The legend tells how Heracles, an Achæan, in the times before the Trojan War, ruled over the Peloponnesian Achæans. Just before that event his children were driven from the land. Eighty years after the war, the hundred years of exile appointed by the Fates having expired, the descendants of the hero, at the head of the Dorians from Northern Greece, returned, and with their aid effected the conquest of the greater part of the Peloponnesus, and established themselves as conquerors and masters in the land that had formerly been ruled by their semi-divine ancestor.

This legend seems to be a dim remembrance of a prehistoric invasion of the Peloponnesus by the Dorians from the north of Greece, and the expulsion or subjugation of the native inhabitants of the peninsula.

Some of the dispossessed Achæans, crowding towards the north of the Peloponnesus, drove out the Ionians who occupied the southern shore of the Corinthian Gulf, and settling there, gave the name *Achaia* to all that region.

Arcadia, in the centre of the Peloponnesus, was another district which did not fall into the hands of the Dorians. The people here, even down to the latest times, retained their primitive customs and country mode of life ; hence *Arcadian* came to mean rustic and artless.

Migrations to Asia Minor. — The Greek legends represent that the Dorian invasion of the Peloponnesus resulted in three distinct migrations from the mother-land to the shores of Asia Minor and the adjoining islands.

The northwestern shore of Asia Minor was settled, mainly, by Æolian emigrants from Bœotia. The neighboring island of Lesbos became the home and centre of Æolian culture in poetry and music.

The coast to the south of the Æolians was occupied by Ionian emigrants, who, uniting with their Ionian kinsmen already settled upon that shore, built up twelve splendid cities (Ephesus, Miletus, etc.), which finally united to form the celebrated Ionian confederacy.

South of the Ionians, all along the southwestern shore of Asia Minor, the Dorians established their colonies. They also settled the important islands of Cos and Rhodes, and conquered and colonized Crete.

The traditions of these various settlements represent them as having been effected in a very short period ; but it is probable that the movement embraced several centuries, — possibly a longer time than has been occupied by the English race in colonizing the different lands of the Western World.

With these migrations to the Asiatic shores, the Legendary Age of Greece comes to an end. From this time forward we tread upon fairly firm historic ground.

Society in the Heroic Age. — In Homeric times the Greeks were ruled by hereditary kings, who were believed to be of divine or superhuman lineage. The king was at once the lawgiver, the judge, and the military leader of his people. He was expected to prove his divine right to rule, by his courage, strength, wisdom, and eloquence. When he ceased to display these qualities, " the sceptre departed from him."

The king was surrounded by an advisory council of chiefs or nobles. The king listened to what the nobles had to say upon any measure he might propose, and then acted according to his own will or judgment, restrained only by the time-honored customs of the community.

Next to the council of chiefs, there was a general assembly, called the *Agora*, made up of all the common freemen. The members of this body could not take part in any debate, nor could they vote upon any question. This body, so devoid seemingly of all authority in the Homeric age, was destined to become the all-powerful popular assembly in the democratic cities of historic Greece.

Of the condition of the common freemen we know but little ; the legendary tales were concerned chiefly with the kings and nobles. Slavery existed, but the slaves did not constitute as numerous a class as they became in historic times.

In the family, the wife held a much more honored position than she occupied in later times. The charming story of the constant Penelope, which we find in the *Odyssey*, assures us that the Homeric age cherished a chivalric feeling for woman.

In all ranks of society, life was marked by a sort of patriarchal simplicity. Manual labor was not yet thought to be degrading. Ulysses constructs his own house and raft, and boasts of his skill in swinging the scythe and guiding the plow. Spinning and weaving were the chief occupations of the women of all classes.

One pleasing and prominent virtue of the age was hospitality. There were no public inns in those times, hence a sort of gentle necessity compelled the entertainment of wayfarers. The hospitality accorded was the same free and impulsive welcome that the Arab sheik of to-day extends to the traveller whom chance brings to his tent. But while hospitable, the nobles of the heroic age were often cruel, violent, and treacherous. Homer represents his heroes as committing without a blush all sorts of fraud and villanies. Piracy was considered an honorable occupation.

FORTY-OARED GREEK BOAT. (After a Vase Painting.)

Art and architecture were in a rudimentary state. Yet some advance had been made. The cities were walled, and the palaces of the kings possessed a certain barbaric splendor. Coined money was unknown; wealth was reckoned chiefly in flocks and herds, and in uncoined metals. The art of writing was probably unknown, at least there is no certain mention of it; and sculpture could not have been in an advanced state, as the Homeric poems make no mention of statues. The state of literature is shown by the poems of the *Iliad* and *Odyssey:* before the close of the age, epic poetry had reached a perfection beyond which it has never been carried.

Commerce was yet in its infancy.   Although the Greeks were to become a great maritime people, still in the Homeric age they had evidently explored the sea but little.   The Phœnicians then ruled the waves.   The Greeks in those early times knew scarcely anything of the world beyond Greece proper and the neighboring islands and shores.   Scarcely an echo of the din of life from the then ancient and mighty cities of Egypt and Chaldæa seems to have reached their ears.

CHAPTER XI.

RELIGION OF THE GREEKS.

Introductory. — Without at least some little knowledge of the religious ideas and institutions of the ancient Greeks, we should find very many passages of their history wholly unintelligible. Hence a few remarks upon these matters will be in place here.

Cosmography of the Greeks. — The Greeks supposed the earth to be, as it appears, a plane, circular in form like a shield. Around it flowed the "mighty strength of the ocean river," a stream broad and deep, beyond which on all sides lay realms of Cimmerian darkness and terror. The heavens were a solid vault, or dome, whose edge shut down close upon the earth. Beneath the earth, reached by subterranean passages, was Hades, a vast region, the realm of departed souls. Still beneath this was the prison Tartarus, a pit deep and dark, made fast by strong gates of brass and iron. Sometimes the poets represent the gloomy regions beyond the ocean stream as the cheerless abode of the dead.

The sun was an archer-god, borne in a fiery chariot up and down the steep pathway of the skies. Naturally it was imagined that the regions in the extreme east and west, which were bathed in the near splendors of the sunrise and sunset, were lands of delight and plenty. The eastern was the favored country of the Ethiopians,[1] a land which even Zeus himself so loved to visit that often he was found absent from Olympus when sought by suppliants. The western region, adjoining the ocean stream, formed the Elysian Fields, the abodes of the souls of heroes and of poets.[2]

[1] There was also a western division of these people.
[2] These conceptions, it will be understood, belong to the early period of Greek mythology. As the geographical knowledge of the Greeks became more

The Olympian Council. — There were twelve members of the celestial council, six gods and as many goddesses. The male deities were Zeus, the father of gods and men; Poseidon, ruler of the sea; Apollo, or Phœbus, the god of light, of music, and of prophecy; Ares, the god of war; Hephæstus, the deformed god of fire, and the forger of the thunderbolts of Zeus; Hermes, the wing-footed herald of the celestials, the god of invention and commerce, himself a thief and the patron of thieves.

THE WORLD ACCORDING TO HOMER.

The female divinities were Hera, the proud and jealous queen of Zeus; Athena, or Pallas, — who sprang full-grown from the forehead of Zeus, — the goddess of wisdom, and the patroness of the domestic arts; Artemis, the goddess of the chase; Aphrodite, the goddess of love and beauty, born of the sea-foam; Hestia, the

extended, they modified considerably the topography not only of the upper-world, but also of the nether-world.

goddess of the hearth; Demeter, the earth-mother, the goddess of grains and harvests.[1]

These great deities were simply magnified human beings, possessing all their virtues, and often their weaknesses. They give way to fits of anger and jealousy. "Zeus deceives, and Hera is constantly practising her wiles." All the celestial council, at the sight of Hephæstus limping across the palace floor, burst into "inextinguishable laughter"; and Aphrodite, weeping, moves all to tears. They surpass mortals rather in power, than in size of body. They can render themselves visible or invisible to human eyes. Their food is ambrosia and nectar; their movements are swift as light. They may suffer pain; but death can never come to them, for they are immortal. Their abode is Mount Olympus and the airy regions above the earth.

Lesser Deities and Monsters. — Besides the great gods and goddesses that constituted the Olympian council there was an almost infinite number of other deities, celestial personages, and monsters neither human nor divine.

Hades (Pluto) ruled over the lower realms; Dionysus (Bacchus) was the god of wine; the goddess Nemesis was the punisher of crime, and particularly the queller of the proud and arrogant; Æolus was the ruler of the winds, which he confined in a cave secured by mighty gates.

There were nine Muses, inspirers of art and song. The Nymphs were beautiful maidens, who peopled the woods, the fields, the rivers, the lakes, and the ocean. Three Fates allotted life and death, and three Furies (Eumenides or Erinnyes) avenged crime,

---

[1] The Latin names of these divinities are as follows: Zeus = Jupiter; Poseidon = Neptune; Apollo = Apollo; Ares = Mars; Hephæstus = Vulcan; Hermes = Mercury; Hera = Juno; Athena = Minerva; Artemis = Diana; Aphrodite = Venus; Hestia = Vesta; Demeter = Ceres.

These Latin names, however, are not the equivalents of the Greek names, and should not be used as such. The mythologies of the Hellenes and Romans were as distinct as their languages. Consult Rawlinson's *Religions of the Ancient World*.

especially murder and unnatural crimes. The Gorgons were three sisters, with hair entwined with serpents. A single gaze upon them chilled the beholder to stone. Besides these there were Scylla and Charybdis, sea-monsters that made perilous the passage of the Sicilian Straits, the Centaurs, the Cyclops, Cerberus, the watch-dog of Hades, and a thousand others.

Many at least of these monsters were simply personifications of the human passions or of the malign and destructive forces of nature. Thus, the Furies were the embodiment of an aroused and accusing conscience; the Gorgons were tempests, which lash the sea into a fury that paralyzes the affrighted sailor; Scylla and Charybdis were dangerous whirlpools off the coast of Sicily. To the common people at least, however, they were real creatures, with all the parts and habits given them by the poets.

Modes of Divine Communication. — In the early ages the gods were wont, it was believed, to visit the earth and mingle with men. But even in Homer's time this familiar intercourse was a thing of the past — a tradition of a golden age that had passed away. Their forms were no longer seen, their voices no longer heard. In these later and more degenerate times the recognized modes of divine communication with men were by oracles, and by casual and unusual sights and sounds, as thunder and lightning, a sudden tempest, an eclipse, a flight of birds, — particularly of birds that mount to a great height, as these were supposed to know the secrets of the heavens, — the appearance or action of the sacrificial victims, or any strange coincidence. The art of interpreting these signs or omens was called the art of divination.

Oracles. — But though the gods might reveal their will and intentions through signs and portents, still they granted a more special communication of counsel through what were known as *oracles*. These communications, it was believed, were made by Zeus, and especially by Apollo, who was the god of prophecy, the Revealer.

Not everywhere, but only in chosen places, did these gods manifest their presence and communicate the divine will. These favored spots were called oracles, as were also the responses there received. There were twenty-two oracles of Apollo in different parts of the Grecian world, but a much smaller number of those of Zeus. These were usually situated in wild and desolate spots — in dark forests or among gloomy mountains.

The most renowned of the oracles was that of the Pelasgian Zeus at Dodona, in Epirus, and that of Apollo at Delphi, in Phocis. At Dodona the priests listened in the dark forests for the voice of Zeus in the rustling leaves of the sacred oak. At Delphi there was a deep fissure in the ground, which emitted stupefying vapors, that were thought to be the inspiring breath of Apollo. Over the spot was erected a splendid temple, in honor of the oracle. The revelation was generally received by the Pythia, or priestess, seated upon a tripod placed over the orifice. As she became overpowered by the influence of the prophetic exhalations, she uttered the message of the god. These mutterings of the Pythia were taken down by attendant priests, interpreted, and written in hexameter verse. Sometimes the will of Zeus was communicated to the pious seeker by dreams and visions granted to him while sleeping in the temple of the oracle.

The oracle of Delphi gained a celebrity wide as the world : it was often consulted by the monarchs of Asia and the people of Rome in times of extreme danger and perplexity. Among the Greeks scarcely any undertaking was entered upon without the will and sanction of the oracle being first sought.

Especially true was this in the founding of colonies. Apollo was believed " to take delight in the foundation of new cities." No colony could prosper that had not been established under the superintendence of the Delphian god.

Some of the responses of the oracle contained plain and wholesome advice ; but very many of them, particularly those that implied a knowledge of the future, were obscure and ingeniously ambiguous, so that they might correspond with the event however affairs should turn. Thus, Crœsus is told that, if he undertake an expedition against Persia, he will destroy a great empire. He did, indeed ; — but the empire was his own.

The Delphian oracle was at the height of its fame before the Persian War ; in that crisis it did not take a bold or patriotic stand, and its reputation was sensibly impaired.

Ideas of the Future. — To the Greeks life was so bright and joyous a thing that they looked upon death as a great calamity. They therefore pictured life after death, except in the case of a favored few, as being hopeless and aimless.[1] The Elysian Fields, away in the land of sunset, were, indeed, filled with every delight ; but these were the abode only of the great heroes and benefactors of the race. So long as the body remained unburied, the soul wandered restless in Hades ; hence the sacredness of the rites of sepulture.

The Sacred Games. — The celebrated games of the Greeks had their origin in the belief of their Aryan ancestors that the souls of the dead were gratified by such spectacles as delighted them during their earthly life. During the Heroic Age these festivals were simply sacrifices or games performed at the tomb, or about the pyre of the dead. Gradually these grew into religious festivals observed by an entire city or community, and were celebrated near the oracle or shrine of the god in whose honor they were instituted ; the idea now being that the gods were present at the festival, and took delight in the various contests and exercises.

Among these festivals, four acquired a world-wide celebrity. These were the Olympian, celebrated in honor of Zeus, at Olympia, in the Peloponnesus ; the Pythian, in honor of Apollo, near his shrine and oracle at Delphi ; the Nemean, in honor of Zeus, at Nemea ; and the Isthmian, held in honor of Poseidon, on the isthmus of Corinth.

The Olympian Games. — Of these four festivals the Olympian secured the greatest renown. In 776 B.C. Corœbus was victor in

---

[1] Homer makes the shade of the great Achilles in Hades to say : —

> " I would be
> A laborer on earth, and serve for hire
> Some man of mean estate, who makes scant cheer,
> Rather than reign o'er all who have gone down
> To death." — *Od.* XI. 489–90 [Bryant's Trans.].

the foot-race at Olympia, and as from that time the names of the victors were carefully registered, that year came to be used by the Greeks as the starting-point in their chronology. The games were held every fourth year, and the interval between two successive festivals was known as an Olympiad.

The contests consisted of foot-races, boxing, wrestling, and other athletic games. Later, chariot-racing was introduced, and became the most popular of all the contests. The competitors must be of the Hellenic race ; and must, moreover, be unblemished by any crime against the state or sin against the gods. Spectators from all parts of the world crowded to the festival.

The victor was crowned with a garland of wild olive ; heralds proclaimed his name abroad ; his native city received him as a conqueror, sometimes through a breach made in the city walls ; his statues, executed by eminent artists, were erected at Olympia and in his own city ; sometimes even divine honor and worship were accorded to him ; and poets and orators vied with the artist in perpetuating the name and deeds of him who had reflected undying honor upon his native state.

Influence of the Grecian Games. — For more than a thousand years these national festivals exerted an immense influence upon the literary, social, and religious life of Hellas. They enkindled among the widely scattered Hellenic states and colonies a common literary taste and enthusiasm ; for into all the four great festivals, excepting the Olympian, were introduced, sooner or later, contests in poetry, oratory, and history. During the festivals, poets and historians read their choicest productions, and artists exhibited their masterpieces. The extraordinary honors accorded to the victors stimulated the contestants to the utmost, and strung to the highest tension every power of body and mind. To this fact we owe some of the grandest productions of the Greek race.

They moreover promoted intercourse and trade ; for the festivals became great centres of traffic and exchange during the continuance of the games. They softened, too, the manners of the people, turning their thoughts from martial exploits and giving the states respite from war ; for during the month in which the religious games were held it was sacrilegious to engage in military expeditions. In all these ways, though they never drew the states into a common political union, still they did impress a common character upon their social, intellectual, and religious life.

The Amphictyonic Council. — Closely connected with the religious festivals were the so-called Amphictyonies, or " leagues of neighbors." These were associations of a number of cities or tribes for the celebration of religious rites at some shrine, or for the protection of some particular temple.

Pre-eminent among all such unions was that known as the Delphic Amphictyony, or simply The Amphictyony. This was a league of twelve of the sub-tribes of Hellas, whose main object was the protection of the Temple of Apollo at Delphi. Another of its purposes was, by humane regulations, to mitigate the cruelties of war.

The so-called First Sacred War (600–590 B.C.) was a crusade of ten years carried on by the Amphictyons against the cities of Crissa and Cirrha for their robbery of the treasures of the Delphian temple. The cities were finally taken, levelled to the ground, and the wrath of the gods invoked upon any one who should dare to rebuild them. The spoils of the war were devoted to the establishment of musical contests in honor of the Delphian Apollo. Thus originated the renowned Pythian festivals, to which allusion has just been made.

CHAPTER XII.

AGE OF THE TYRANTS AND OF COLONIZATION: THE EARLY GROWTH OF SPARTA AND OF ATHENS.

(776–500 B.C.)

1. AGE OF THE TYRANTS AND OF COLONIZATION.

The Tyrants. — In the Heroic Age the preferred form of government was a patriarchal monarchy. The *Iliad* says, "The rule of many is not a good thing : let us have one ruler only, — one king, — him to whom Zeus has given the sceptre." But by the dawn of the historic period, the patriarchal monarchies of the Achæan age had given place, in almost all the Grecian cities, to oligarchies or aristocracies.

The Oligarchies give Way to Tyrannies. — The nobles into whose hands the ancient royal authority thus passed were often divided among themselves, and invariably opposed by the common freemen, who, as they grew in intelligence and wealth, naturally aspired to a place in the government. The issue of long contentions was the overthrow almost everywhere of oligarchical government and the establishment of the rule of a single person.

Usually this person was one of the nobility, who held himself out as the champion of the people, and who with their help usurped the government. One who had thus seized the government was called a tyrant. By this term the Greeks did not mean one who rules harshly, but simply one who holds the supreme authority in the state illegally. Some of the Greek Tyrants were mild and beneficent rulers, though too often they were all that the name implies among us.

But the Greeks always had an inextinguishable hatred of arbitrary rule ; consequently the Tyrannies were, as a rule, short-lived, rarely lasting longer than three generations. They were usually violently overthrown, and the old oligarchies re-established, or democracies set up in their place. As a rule, the Dorian cities preferred oligarchical, and the Ionian cities democratical, government. The so-called Age of the Tyrants lasted from 650 to 500 B.C.

Among the most noted of the Tyrants were the Pisistratidæ, at Athens, of whom we shall speak hereafter; Periander at Corinth (625–585 B.C.), who was a most cruel ruler, yet so generous a patron of artists and literary men that he was thought worthy of a place among the Seven Sages; and Polycrates, Tyrant of Samos (535-522 B.C.), who, with that island as a stronghold, and with a fleet of a hundred war-galleys, built up a sort of maritime kingdom in the Ægean, and for the space of more than a decade enjoyed such astonishing and uninterrupted prosperity, that it was believed his sudden downfall and death — he was allured to the Asian shore by a Persian satrap, and crucified — were brought about by the envy of the gods,[1] who the Greeks thought were apt to be jealous of over-prosperous mortals.

The Founding of Colonies. — The Age of the Tyrants coincides very nearly with the era of greatest activity in the founding of new colonies. Thousands, driven from their homes, like the Puritans in the time of the Stuart tyranny in England, fled over the seas, and, under the direction of the Delphian Apollo, laid upon remote and widely separated shores the basis of " Dispersed Hellas." The overcrowding of population and the Greek love of adventure also contributed to swell the number of emigrants. During this

---

[1] Herodotus tells how Amasis of Egypt, the friend and ally of the Tyrant, becoming alarmed at his extraordinary course of good fortune, wrote him, begging him to interrupt it and disarm the envy of the gods, by sacrificing his most valued possession. Polycrates, acting upon the advice, threw into the sea a precious ring, which he highly prized; but soon afterwards the jewel was found by his servants in a fish that a fisherman had brought to the palace as a present for Polycrates. When Amasis heard of this, he at once broke off his alliance with the Tyrant, feeling sure that he was fated to suffer some terrible reverse of fortune. The event justified his worst fears.

GREECE
and the
GREEK COLONIES.

Ionian...............

Dorian...............

Other Greek Races...

Phœnician...............

colonizing era Southern Italy became so thickly set with Greek cities as to become known as *Magna Græcia*, "Great Greece." Here were founded during the latter part of the eighth century B.C. the important Dorian city of Tarentum; the wealthy and luxurious Achæan city of Sybaris (whence the term *Sybarite*, meaning a voluptuary); the Great Crotona, distinguished for its schools of philosophy and its victors in the Olympian games.

Upon the island of Sicily was planted, by the Dorian Corinth, the city of Syracuse (734 B.C.), which, before Rome had become great, waged war on equal terms with Carthage.

In the Gulf of Lyons was established about 600 B.C. the important Ionian city of Massalia (Marseilles), the radiating point of long routes of travel and trade.

On the African coast was founded the great Dorian city of Cyrene (630 B.C.), and probably about the same time was established in the Nile delta the city of Naucratis, through which the civilization of Egypt flowed into Greece.

The tide of emigration flowed not only to the west and south, but to the north as well. The northern shores of the Ægean and those of the Hellespont and the Propontis were fringed with colonies. The Argonautic terrors of the Black Sea were forgotten or unheeded, and even those remote shores received their emigrants. Many of the settlements in that quarter were established by the Ionian city of Miletus, which, swarming like a hive, became the mother of more than eighty colonies.

Through this wonderful colonizing movement, Greece came to hold somewhat the same place in the ancient Mediterranean world that England as a colonizer occupies in the world of to-day. Many of these colonies not only reflected honor upon the mother land through the just renown of their citizens, but through their singularly free, active, and progressive life, they exerted upon her a most healthful and stimulating influence.

2. THE GROWTH OF SPARTA.

Situation of Sparta. — Sparta was one of the cities of the Peloponnesus which owed their origin or importance to the Dorian Invasion (see p. 96). It was situated in the deep valley of the Eurotas, in Laconia, and took its name Sparta (sown land) from the circumstance that it was built upon tillable ground, whereas the heart and centre of most Greek cities consisted of a lofty rock (the citadel, or acropolis). It was also called Lacedæmon, after an early legendary king.

Classes in the Spartan State. — In order to understand the social and political institutions of the Spartans, we must first notice the three classes — Spartans (Spartiatæ), Periœci, and Helots — into which the population of Laconia was divided.

The Spartans proper were the descendants of the Dorian conquerors of the country. They composed but a small fraction of the entire population. Their relations to the conquered people were those of an army of occupation. Sparta, their capital, was simply a vast camp, unprotected by any walls until later and degenerate times. The martial valor of its citizens was thought its only proper defence.

The Periœci (dwellers-around), who constituted the second class, were the subjugated Achæans. They were allowed to retain possession of their lands, but were forced to pay tribute, and, in times of war, to fight for the glory and interest of their Spartan masters.

The third and lowest class was composed of slaves, or serfs, called Helots. The larger number of these were laborers upon the estates of the Spartans. They were the property of the state, and not of the individual Spartan lords, among whom they were distributed by lot. Practically they had no rights which their Spartan masters felt bound to respect. It is affirmed that when they grew too numerous for the safety of the state, their numbers were thinned by a deliberate massacre of the surplus population.

The Legend of Lycurgus. — The laws and customs of the Spartans have excited more interest, perhaps, than any similar institutions of the ancient world. A mystery and halo were thrown about them by their being attributed to the creative genius of a single lawgiver, Lycurgus.

Lycurgus, according to tradition, lived about the ninth century B.C. He is represented as acquainting himself with the laws and institutions of different lands, by converse with their priests and sages. He is said to have studied with great zeal the laws of Minos, the legendary lawgiver of the Cretans. Like the great legislator Moses, he became learned in all the wisdom of the Egyptians.

After much opposition, a system of laws and regulations drawn up by Lycurgus was adopted by the Spartan people. Then, binding his countrymen by a solemn oath that they would carefully observe his laws during his absence, he set out on a pilgrimage to Delphi. In response to his inquiry, the oracle assured him that Sparta would endure and prosper as long as the people obeyed the laws he had given them. Lycurgus caused this answer to be carried to his countrymen; and then, that they might remain bound by the oath they had taken, he resolved never to return. He went into an unknown exile.

The Kings, the Senate, and the Popular Assembly. — The so-called Constitution of Lycurgus provided for two joint kings, a Senate of Elders, and a Popular Assembly.

The two kings corresponded in some respects to the two consuls in the later Roman republic. One served as a check upon the other. This double sovereignty worked admirably; for five centuries there were no attempts on the part of the Spartan kings to subvert the constitution. The power of the joint kings, it should be added, was rather nominal than real (save in time of war); so that while the Spartan government was monarchical in form, it was in reality an aristocracy, the Spartans corresponding very closely to the feudal lords of Mediæval Europe.

The Senate consisted of thirty elders. The powers of this body were at first almost unlimited. After a time, however, officers called ephors were elected by the Popular Assembly, and these gradually absorbed the powers and functions of the Senate, as well as the authority of the two associate kings.

The Popular Assembly was composed of all the citizens of Sparta over thirty years of age. By this body laws were made, and questions of peace and war decided. In striking contrast to what was the custom at Athens, all matters were decided without debate. The Spartans were fighters, not talkers; they hated discussion.

Regulations as to Lands and Money. — At the time of Lycurgus the lands of Laconia had become absorbed by the rich, leaving the masses in poverty and distress. It is certain that the lawgiver did much to remedy this ruinous state of affairs. Tradition says that all the lands were redistributed, an equal portion being assigned to each of the nine thousand Spartan citizens, and a smaller and less desirable portion to each of the thirty thousand Periœci, — but it is not probable that there was any such exact equalization of property.

The Spartans were forbidden to engage in trade ; all their time must be passed in the chase, or in gymnastic and martial exercise. Iron was made the sole money of the state. This, according to Plutarch, " was of great size and weight, and of small value, so that the equivalent for ten minæ (about $140) required a great room for its stowage, and a yoke of oxen to draw it." The object of this, he tells us, was to prevent its being used for the purchase of " foreign trumpery."

The Public Tables. — The most peculiar, perhaps, of the Lycurgean institutions were the public meals. In order to correct the extravagance with which the tables of the rich were often spread, Lycurgus ordered that all the Spartan citizens should eat at public and common tables. Excepting the ephors, none, not even the kings, were excused from sitting at the common mess. One of the kings, returning from a long expedition, presumed to dine privately with his wife, but received therefor a severe reproof.

A luxury-loving Athenian, once visiting Sparta and seeing the coarse fare of the citizens, is reported to have declared that now he understood the Spartan disregard of life in battle. "Any one," said he, "must naturally prefer death to life on such fare as this."

Education of the Youth. — Children were considered as belonging to the state. Every infant was brought before the Council of Elders ; and if it did not seem likely to become a robust and useful citizen, it was exposed in a mountain glen. At seven the education and training of the youth were committed to the charge of public officers, called boy-trainers. The aim of the entire course, as to the boys, was to make a nation of soldiers who should despise toil and danger and prefer death to military dishonor. Reading and writing were untaught, and the art of rhetoric was despised. Spartan brevity was a proverb, whence our word *laconic* (from Laconia), implying a concise and pithy mode of expression. Boys were taught to respond in the fewest words possible. At the public tables they were not permitted to speak until questioned : they sat "silent as statues." As Plutarch puts it, " Lycurgus was for having the money bulky, heavy, and of little value ; and the language, on the contrary, very pithy and short, and a great deal of sense compressed in a few words."

But before all things else the Spartan youth was taught to bear pain unflinchingly. Often he was scourged just for the purpose of accustoming his body to pain. Frequently, it is said, boys died under the lash, without betraying their suffering by look or moan.

Another custom tended to the same end as the foregoing usage. The boys were at times compelled to forage for their food. If detected, they were severely punished for having been so unskilful as not to get safely away with their booty. This custom, as well as the fortitude of the Spartan youth, is familiar to all through the story of the boy who, having stolen a young fox and concealed it beneath his tunic, allowed the animal to tear out his vitals, without betraying himself by the movement of a muscle.

The Cryptia, which has been represented as an organization of young Spartans who were allowed, as a means of rendering themselves ready and expert in war, to hunt and kill the Helots, seems in reality to have been a sort of police institution, designed to guard against uprisings of the serfs.

Estimate of the Spartan Institutions. — That the laws and regulations of the Spartan constitution were admirably adapted to the end in view, — the rearing of a nation of skilful and resolute warriors, — the long military supremacy of Sparta among the states of Greece abundantly attests. But when we consider the aim and object of the Spartan institutions, we must pronounce them low and unworthy. The true order of things was just reversed among the Lacedæmonians. Government exists for the individual: at Sparta the individual lived for the state. The body is intended to be the instrument of the mind: the Spartans reversed this, and attended to the education of the mind only so far as its development enhanced the effectiveness of the body as a weapon in warfare.

Spartan history teaches how easy it is for a nation, like an individual, to misdirect its energies — to subordinate the higher to the lower. It illustrates, too, the fact that only those nations that labor to develop that which is best and highest in man make helpful contributions to the progress of the world. Sparta, in significant contrast to Athens, bequeathed nothing to posterity.

The Messenian Wars. — The most important event in Spartan history between the age of Lycurgus and the commencement of the Persian War was the long contest with Messenia, known as the First and Second Messenian Wars (about 750–650 B.C.). Messenia was one of the districts of the Peloponnesus which, like Laconia, had been taken possession of by the Dorians at the time of the great invasion.

It is told that the Spartans, in the second war, falling into despair, sent to Delphi for advice. The oracle directed them to ask Athens for a commander. The Athenians did not wish to aid the Lacedæmonians, yet dared not oppose the oracle. So they sent Tyrtæus, a poet-schoolmaster, who they hoped and thought would prove of but little service to Sparta. Whatever truth there may be in this part of the story, it seems indisputable that during the

Second Messenian War, Tyrtæus, an Attic poet, reanimated the drooping spirits of the Spartans by the energy of his martial strains. Perhaps it would not be too much to say that Sparta owed her final victory to the inspiring songs of this martial poet.

The conquered Messenians were reduced to serfdom, and their condition made as degrading and bitter as that of the Helots of Laconia. Many, choosing exile, pushed out into the western seas in search of new homes. Some of the fugitives founded Rhegium, in Italy; others, settling in Sicily, gave name and importance to the still existing city of Messina.

Growth of the Power of Sparta. — After having secured possession of Messenia, Sparta conquered the southern part of Argolis. All the southern portion of the Peloponnesus was now subject to her commands.

On the north, Sparta extended her power over many of the villages, or townships, of Arcadia; but her advance in this direction having been checked by Tegea, one of the few important Arcadian cities, Sparta entered into an alliance with that city, which ever after remained her faithful friend and helper. This alliance was one of the main sources of Spartan preponderance in Greece during the next hundred years and more.

Sparta was now the most powerful state in the Peloponnesus. Her fame was spread even beyond the limits of Hellas. Crœsus, king of Lydia, sought an alliance with her in his unfortunate war with Persia, which just now was the rising power in Asia.

3. THE GROWTH OF ATHENS.

The Attic People. — The population of Attica in historic times was essentially Ionian in race, but there were in it strains of other Hellenic stocks, besides some non-Hellenic elements as well. This mixed origin of the population is believed to be one secret of the versatile yet well-balanced character which distinguished the Attic people above all other branches of the Hellenic family. It is not the absolutely pure, but the mixed races, like the English people, that have made the largest contributions to civilization.

The Site of Athens. — Four or five miles from the sea, a flat-topped rock, about one thousand feet in length and half as many in width, rises with abrupt cliffs, one hundred and fifty feet above the level of the plains of Attica. The security afforded by this eminence doubtless led to its selection as a stronghold by the early Attic settlers. Here a few buildings, perched upon the summit of the rock and surrounded by a palisade, constituted the beginning of the capital whose fame has spread over all the world.

The Kings of Athens. — During the Heroic Age Athens was ruled by kings, like all the other Grecian cities. The names of Theseus and Codrus are the most noted of the regal line.

THE ACROPOLIS AT ATHENS.   (From a Photograph.)

To Theseus tradition ascribed the work of uniting the different Attic villages, or cantons, twelve in number, into a single city, on the seat of the ancient Cecropia (see p. 92). This prehistoric union, however or by whomsoever effected, laid the basis of the greatness of Athens.

Respecting Codrus, the following legend is told: At one time the Dorians from the Peloponnesus invaded Attica. Codrus having learned that an oracle had assured them of success if they spared the life of the Athenian king, disguised himself, and, with a single companion, made an attack upon some Spartan soldiers, who instantly slew him. Discovering that the king of Athens had fallen by a Lacedæmonian sword, the Spartans despaired of taking the city, and withdrew from the country.

The Archons. — Codrus was the last hereditary king of Athens. His successor, elected by the nobles from the royal family, was simply ruler for life. There were twelve life-kings, and then (in 752 B.C.) the authority of the regal office was still further diminished by limiting the rule of the king first to ten years and later to one year. As the royal dignity was thus diminished, the old-time duties of the king were assigned to magistrates chosen by the nobles from among themselves. The outcome of these changes was that a little after the opening of the seventh century we find a board of nine persons, called Archons, of whom the king in a subordinate position was one, standing at the head of the Athenian state. The old Homeric monarchy had become an oligarchy.

Throughout these early times the common people had no part in the management of public affairs. Many of them were virtually serfs. If one became unable to pay his debts, both he and his wife and children might be seized by his creditor and sold as slaves. Thus because of their wretched economic condition, as well as because of their exclusion from the government, the commons were filled with bitterness against the nobles and were ready for Revolution.

The Rebellion of Cylon (probably 628 or 624 B.C.[1]). — Taking advantage of the unrest in the state, Cylon, a rich and ambitious noble, attempted to overthrow the government and make himself supreme. He seized the citadel of the Acropolis, where he was closely besieged by the Archons. Finally the Archon Megacles offered the insurgents their lives on condition of sur-

[1] Before the recent discovery of the Aristotelian treatise on the Athenian Constitution this conspiracy was by most historians placed after the legislation of Draco. In this issue of our History the text at this point as well as in the five paragraphs immediately following, which deal with the Solonian reforms, has been carefully revised in accordance with the demands of our new knowledge. For the text of the new-found work see Kenyon's *Aristotle on the Constitution of Athens.*

render.   They accepted the offer, but fearing to trust themselves among their enemies without some protection, fastened a string to a statue of Athena, and holding fast to this, descended from the citadel, into the streets of Athens.   As they came in front of the altars of the Furies, the line broke ; and Megacles, professing to believe that this mischance indicated that the goddess refused to shield them, caused them to be set upon and massacred.

The people were alarmed lest the anger of the gods had been incurred by this sacrilegious act.   They demanded and at last secured the banishment of the Alcmæonidæ, the family to which Megacles belonged.   Even the bones of the dead of the family were dug up, and cast beyond the frontiers of the state.   The people further insisted upon a publication of the laws, that they might be secured against the arbitrary and unjust decisions of the oligarchical magistrates, in whose hands was the entire administration of justice.

The Laws and Constitution of Draco (621 B.C.). — To meet these demands of the people, the nobles appointed one of their own number, Draco, to remodel the constitution and draw up a code of laws.

The most important constitutional change made by Draco related to the election of magistrates.   These had hitherto been chosen by the Council of the Areopagus (see p. 121).   This important function was now committed to the Ecclesia, or popular assembly, in which all persons had a place who were able to provide themselves with a full military equipment.

Besides making this reform in the constitution, Draco drew up a code of laws.   Tradition says that the legislator assigned to the least offence the penalty of death.   This alleged severity of the Draconian laws is what caused a later Athenian orator to say that they were written, " not in ink, but in blood."

The Reforms of Solon (594 B.C.). — There was one great defect in Draco's work.   He gave no relief to the poor who were the victims of the harsh law of debt.   Their condition grew continually worse, until some measures of relief became absolutely necessary.   Once more, as in the time of Draco, the Athenians placed their laws and constitution in the hands of a single man, to be remodelled as he might deem best. Solon, a man held in high esteem by all classes, was selected to discharge this responsible duty.

Solon turned his attention first to relieving the misery of the debtor class. He cancelled all debts of every kind, both public and private, and annulled the right of creditors to sell as slaves their debtors. No Athenian was ever after this sold for debt.

Changes in the Athenian Constitution: the Public Assembly. —Such was the most important of the economic reforms of Solon. His constitutional reforms were equally wise. The public assembly was at this time composed of all the members of the three highest of the four property classes into which the people were divided. The fourth and poorest class, the Thetes, were excluded. Solon opened the Ecclesia to them, giving them the right to vote, but not to hold office. Solon also made other changes in the constitution, whereby the magistrates became responsible to the people, who henceforth not only elected them, but judged them in case they did wrong.

A certain important council, one of whose duties it was to prepare measures to be laid before the public assembly, was reorganized by Solon. It was made to consist of four hundred members, and hence was called the Council of Four Hundred.

The Tribunal of the Areopagus.—Under the Solonian constitution the Areopagus, a venerable tribunal that from time out of memory had been held on the Areopagus, or Mars' Hill, near the Acropolis, remained the guardian of the laws. To this court was particularly committed the care of morals and religion. It was probably in the presence of this venerable tribunal that Paul stood when, six hundred years after Solon's time, he made his eloquent defence of Christianity.

The Tyrant Pisistratus (560–527 B.C.). —Solon had the misfortune of living to see his institutions used to set up a tyranny, by an ambitious kinsman, his nephew Pisistratus. This man courted popular favor, and called himself the "friend of the people." One day, having inflicted many wounds upon himself, he drove his

chariot hastily into the public square, and pretended that he had
been thus set upon by the nobles, because of his devotion to the
people's cause.   The people, moved with sympathy and indignation, voted him a guard of fifty men.   Under cover of raising this
company, Pisistratus gathered a much larger force, seized the
Acropolis, and made himself master of Athens.   Though twice
expelled from the city, he as often returned, and finally succeeded
in getting a permanent hold of the government.

The rule of the usurper was mild, and under him Athens enjoyed a period of great prosperity.   He adorned the city with
temples and other splendid buildings, and constructed great aqueducts.   Just beyond the city walls, he laid out the Lyceum, a sort
of public park, which became in after years the favorite resort of
the philosophers and poets of Athens.   He was a liberal patron
of literature ; and caused the Homeric poems to be collected and
edited.   He died 527 B.C., thirty-three years after his first seizure
of the citadel.   Solon himself said of him that he had no vice
save ambition.

Expulsion of the Tyrants from Athens (510 B.C.).—The two
sons of Pisistratus, Hippias and Hipparchus, succeeded to his
power.   At first they emulated the example of their father, and
Athens flourished under their parental rule.   But at length an
unfortunate event gave an entirely different tone to the government.   Hipparchus, having insulted a young noble, was assassinated.   Hippias escaped harm, but the event caused him to
become suspicious and severe.   His rule now became a tyranny
indeed, and was brought to an end in the following way.

After his last return to Athens, Pisistratus had sent the "accursed" Alcmæonidæ into a second exile.   During this period
of banishment an opportunity arose for them to efface the stain of
sacrilege which was still supposed to cling to them on account
of the old crime of Megacles.   The temple at Delphi having been
destroyed by fire, they contracted with the Amphictyons to rebuild
it.   They not only completed the work in the most honorable
manner throughout, but even went so far beyond the terms of their
contract as to use beautiful Parian marble for the front of the

temple, when only common stone was required by the specifications.

By this act the exiled family won to such a degree the favor of the priests of the sacred college, that they were able to influence the utterances of the oracle. The invariable answer now of the Pythia to Spartan inquirers at the shrine was, "Athens must be set free."

Moved at last by the repeated injunctions of the oracle, the Spartans resolved to drive Hippias from Athens. Their first attempt was unsuccessful; but in a second they were so fortunate as to capture the two children of the tyrant, who, to secure their release, agreed to leave the city (510 B.C.). He retired to Asia Minor, and spent the rest of his life, as we shall learn hereafter, seeking aid in different quarters to re-establish his tyranny in Athens. The Athenians passed a decree of perpetual exile against him and all his family.

The Reforms of Clisthenes (509 B.C.). — Straightway upon the expulsion of the Tyrant Hippias, there arose a great strife between the people, who of course wished to organize the government in accord with the constitution of Solon, and the nobles, who desired to re-establish the old aristocratical rule. Clisthenes, an aristocrat, espoused the cause of the popular party. Through his influence several important changes in the constitution, which rendered it still more democratical than under Solon, were now effected.

Athenian citizenship was conferred upon *all the free inhabitants of Attica.* This made such a radical change in the constitution in the interest of the masses, that Clisthenes rather than Solon is regarded by many as the real founder of the Athenian democracy.

Ostracism. — But of all the innovations or institutions of Clisthenes, that known as *ostracism* was the most characteristic. By means of this process any person who had excited the suspicions or displeasure of the people could, without trial, be banished from Athens for a period of ten years. Six thousand votes cast against any person in a meeting of the popular assembly was a decree of banishment. The name of the person whose banishment was sought was written on a piece of pottery or shell (in Greek *ostrakon*), hence the term *ostracism*.

The original design of this institution was to prevent the recurrence of such a usurpation as that of the Pisistratidæ. The power it gave the people was often abused, and many of the ablest statesmen of Athens were sent into exile through the influence of demagogues who for the moment had caught the popular ear.

No stigma or disgrace attached to the person ostracized. The vote came to be employed, as a rule, simply to settle disputes between rival leaders of political parties. Thus the vote merely expressed political preference.

The institution was short-lived. It was resorted to for the last time during the Peloponnesian War (417 B.C.). The people then, in a freak, ostracized a man whom all admitted to be the meanest man in Athens. This was regarded as such a degradation of the institution, as well as such an honor to the mean man, that never thereafter did the Athenians degrade a good man, or honor a bad one, by a resort to the measure.

Sparta opposes the Athenian Democracy. — The aristocratic party at Athens was naturally bitterly opposed to all these democratic innovations. The Spartans, also, viewed with disquiet and jealousy this rapid growth of the Athenian democracy, and tried to overthrow the new government and restore Hippias to power. But they did not succeed in their purpose, and Hippias went away to Persia to seek aid of King Darius. His solicitations, in connection with an affront which the Athenians just now offered the king himself by aiding his revolted subjects in Ionia, led directly up to the memorable struggle known as the Græco-Persian wars.

GREEK WARRIORS PREPARING FOR BATTLE.

CHAPTER XIII.

THE GRÆCO-PERSIAN WARS.

(500-479 B.C.)

Expeditions of Darius against Greece. — In narrating the history of the Persians, we told how Darius, after having subdued the revolt of his Ionian subjects in Asia Minor, turned his armaments against the European Greeks, to punish them for the part they had taken in the capture and burning of Sardis. It will be recalled how ill-fated was his first expedition, which was led by his son-in-law Mardonius (see p. 80).

Undismayed by this disaster, Darius issued orders for the raising and equipping of another and stronger armament. Meanwhile he sent heralds to the various Grecian states to demand earth and water, which elements among the Persians were symbols of submission. The weaker states gave the tokens required; but the Athenians and Spartans threw the envoys of the king into pits and wells, and bade them help themselves to earth and water. By the beginning of the year 490 B.C., another Persian army of 120,000 men had been mustered for the second attempt upon Greece. This armament was intrusted to the command of the experienced generals Datis and Artaphernes; but was under the guidance of the traitor Hippias. A fleet of six hundred ships bore the army from the coasts of Asia Minor over the Ægean towards the Grecian shores.

After receiving the submission of the most important of the Cyclades, and capturing and sacking the city of Eretria upon the island of Eubœa, the Persians landed at Marathon, barely two days' journey from Athens. Here is a sheltered bay, which is edged by a crescent-shaped plain, backed by the rugged ranges of Parnes and Pentelicus. Upon this level ground the Persian generals drew up their army, flushed and confident with their recent successes.

The Battle of Marathon (490 B.C.). — The Athenians were nerved by the very magnitude of the danger to almost superhuman energy. Slaves were transformed into soldiers by the promise of liberty. A fleet runner, Phidippides by name, was despatched to Sparta for aid. In just thirty-six hours he was in Sparta, which is one hundred and fifty miles from Athens. But it so happened that it lacked a few days of the full moon, during which interval the Spartans, owing to an old superstition, were averse to setting out upon a military expedition. They promised aid, but moved only in time to reach Athens when all was over. The Platæans, firm and grateful friends of the Athenians, on account of some former service, no sooner received the latter's appeal for help than they responded to a man.

The Athenians and their faithful allies, numbering about ten thousand in all, under the command of Miltiades, were drawn up in battle array just where the hills of Pentelicus sink down into the plain of Marathon. The vast host of the Persians filled the level ground in their front. The fate of Greece and the future of Europe were in the keeping of Miltiades and his trusty warriors. Without waiting for the attack of the Persians, the Greeks charged and swept like a tempest from the mountain over the plain, pushed the

Persians back towards the shore, and with great slaughter drove them to their ships.

Miltiades at once despatched a courier to Athens with intelligence of his victory. The messenger reached the city in a few hours, but so breathless from his swift run that, as the people thronged eagerly around him to hear the news he bore, he could merely gasp, " Victory is ours," and fell dead.

But the danger was not yet past. The Persian fleet, instead of returning to the coast of Asia, bore down upon Athens. Informed by watchers on the hills of the movements of the enemy, Miltiades immediately set out with his little army for the capital, which he reached just at evening, the battle at Marathon having been won in the forenoon of that same day. The next morning, when the Persian generals would have made an attack upon the city, they found themselves confronted by the same men who but yesterday had beaten them back from the plains of Marathon. Shrinking from another encounter with these citizen-soldiers of Athens, the Persians spread their sails, and bore away towards the Ionian shore.

Thus the cloud that had lowered so threateningly over Hellas was for a time dissipated. The most imposing honors were accorded to the heroes who had achieved the glorious victory, and their names and deeds were transmitted to posterity, in song and marble. And as the gods were believed to have interposed in behalf of Greece, suitable recognition of their favor was made in gifts and memorials. A considerable part of the brazen arms and shields gathered from the battle-field was melted into a colossal statue of Athena, which was placed upon the Acropolis, as the guardian of Athens.

Results of the Battle of Marathon. — The battle of Marathon is reckoned as one of the " decisive battles of the world." It marks an epoch, not only in the life of Greece, but in that of Europe. Hellenic civilization was spared to mature its fruit, not for itself alone, but for the world. The battle decided that no longer the despotism of the East, with its repression of all individual action, but the freedom of the West, with all its incentives to personal effort, should control the affairs and mould the ideas and institutions of the future. It broke the spell of the Persian name, and destroyed forever the prestige of the Persian arms. It gave the Hellenic peoples that position of authority and pre-eminence that had been so long enjoyed by the successive races of the East. It especially revealed the Athenians to themselves. The consciousness of resources and power became the inspiration of their future acts. They performed great deeds thereafter because they believed themselves able to perform them.

Miltiades falls into Disgrace. — The distinguished services Miltiades had rendered his country, made him the hero of the hour at Athens. Taking advantage of the public feeling in his favor, he persuaded the Athenians to put in his hands a fleet for an enterprise respecting the nature of which no one save himself was to know anything whatever. Of course it was generally supposed that he meditated an attack upon the Persians or their allies, and with full faith in the judgment as well as in the integrity of their favorite, the Athenians gave him the command he asked.

But Miltiades abused the confidence imposed in him. He led the expedition against the island of Paros, simply to avenge some private wrong. The undertaking was unsuccessful, and Miltiades, severely wounded, returned to Athens, where he was brought to trial for his conduct. His never-to-be-forgotten services at Marathon pleaded eloquently for him, and he escaped being sentenced to death, but was subjected to a heavy fine. This he was unable to pay, and in a short time he died of his wound. The unfortunate affair left an ineffaceable blot upon a fame otherwise the most resplendent in Grecian story.

Athens prepares for Persian Vengeance. — Many among the Athenians were inclined to believe that the battle of Marathon had freed Athens forever from the danger of a Persian invasion. But there was at least one among them who was clear-sighted enough to see that that battle was only the beginning of a great struggle. This was Themistocles, a sagacious, versatile, and ambitious statesman, who labored to persuade the Athenians to strengthen their navy, in order to be ready to meet the danger he foresaw.

Themistocles was opposed in this policy by Aristides, called the Just, a man of the most scrupulous integrity, who feared that Athens would make a serious mistake if she converted her land force into a naval armament. The contention grew so sharp between them that the ostracism was called into use to decide the matter. Six thousand votes were cast against Aristides, and he was sent into exile.

It is related that while the vote that ostracized him was being taken in the popular assembly, an illiterate peasant, who was a stranger to Aristides, asked him to write the name of Aristides upon his tablet. As he placed the name desired upon the shell, the statesman asked the man what wrong Aristides had ever done him. "None," responded the voter; "I don't even know him; but I am tired of hearing him called ' the Just.' "

After the banishment of Aristides, Themistocles was free to carry out his naval policy without any serious opposition, and soon Athens had the largest fleet of any Greek city, with a harbor at Piræus.

Xerxes' Preparations to invade Greece. — No sooner had the news of the disaster at Marathon been carried to Darius than he began to make gigantic preparations to avenge this second defeat and insult. It was in the midst of these plans for revenge that, as we have already learned, death cut short his reign, and his son Xerxes came to the throne (see p. 80).

Urged on by his nobles, as well as by exiled Greeks at his court, who sought to gratify ambition or enjoy revenge in the humiliation and ruin of their native land, Xerxes, though at first disinclined to enter into a contest with the Greeks, at length ordered the preparations begun by his father to be pushed forward with the utmost energy. For eight years all Asia resounded with the din of preparation. Levies were made upon all the provinces that acknowledged the authority of the Great King, from India to the

Hellespont. Vast contingents of vessels were furnished by the coast countries of the Mediterranean. Immense stores of provisions, the harvests of many years, were gathered into great storehouses along the intended line of march.

While all these preparations were going on in Asia itself, Phœnician and Egyptian architects were employed in spanning the Hellespont with a double bridge of boats, which was to unite the two continents as with a royal highway. At the same time, the isthmus at Mount Athos, in rounding which promontory the admirals of Mardonius had lost their fleet, was cut by a canal, traces of which may be seen at this day. Three years were consumed in these gigantic works. With them completed, or far advanced, Xerxes set out from his capital to join the countless hosts that from all quarters of the compass were gathering at Sardis, in Asia Minor.

Disunion of the Greeks: Congress at Corinth (481 B.C.). — Startling rumors of the gigantic preparations that the Persian king was making to crush them were constantly borne across the Ægean to the ears of the Greeks in Europe. Finally came intelligence that Xerxes was about to begin his march. Something must now be done to meet the impending danger. Mainly through the exertions of Themistocles, a council of the Greek cities was convened at Corinth in the fall of 481 B.C.

But on account of feuds, jealousies, and party spirit, only a small number of the states of Hellas could be brought to act in concert. Argos would not join the proposed confederation through hatred of Sparta; Thebes, through jealousy of Athens. The Cretans, to whom an embassy had been sent soliciting aid, refused all assistance. Gelon, the Tyrant of Syracuse, offered to send over a large armament, provided that he were given the chief command of the allied forces. His aid on such terms was refused.

Thus, through different causes, many of the Greek cities held aloof from the confederation, so that only about fifteen or sixteen states were brought to unite their resources against the Barbarians;

and even the strength of many of those cities that did enter into the alliance was divided by party spirit. The friends of aristocratical government were almost invariably friends of Persia, because a Persian victory in Greece proper meant what it had already meant in Ionia, — a suppression of the democracies as incompatible with the Persian form of government. Thus for the sake of a party victory, the aristocrats were ready to betray their country into the hands of the Barbarians. Furthermore, the Delphian oracle, aristocratical in its sympathies, was luke-warm and wavering, if not actually disloyal, and by its timid responses, disheartened the patriot party.

But under the inspiration of Themistocles the patriots in convention at Corinth determined upon desperate resistance to the Barbarians. It was at first decided to concentrate a strong force in the Vale of Tempe, and at that point to dispute the advance of the enemy; but this being found impracticable, it was resolved that the first stand against the invaders should be made at the pass of Thermopylæ.

The Spartans were given the chief command of both the land and the naval forces. The Athenians might fairly have insisted upon their right to the command of the allied fleet, but they patriotically waived their claim, for the sake of harmony.

The Hellespontine Bridges broken. — As the vast army of Xerxes was about to move from Sardis, intelligence came that the bridges across the Hellespont had been wrecked by a violent tempest. It is said that Xerxes, in great wrath, ordered the architects to be put to death, and the sea to be bound with fetters and scourged. The scourgers faithfully performed their duty, at the same time gratuitously cursing the traitorous and rebellious Hellespont with what Herodotus calls "non-Hellenic and blasphemous terms."

Other architects spanned the channel with two stronger and firmer bridges. Each roadway rested upon a row of from three to four hundred vessels, all securely anchored like modern pontoons. The bridges were each about one mile in length, and furnished with high parapets, that the horses and cattle might not be rendered uneasy at sight of the water.

Passage of the Hellespont. — With the first indications of the opening spring of 480 B.C., just ten years after the defeat at Marathon, the vast Persian army was astir and concentrating from all points upon the Hellespont. The passage of this strait, as pictured to us in the inimitable narration of Herodotus, is one of the most dramatic of all the spectacles afforded by history.

Before the passage commenced, the bridges were strewn with the sacred myrtle and perfumed with incense from golden censers, while the sea was placated with libations poured by the king himself. As the east reddened with the approach of day, prayers were offered, and the moment the rays of the sun touched the bridges the passage began. To avoid accidents and delays, the trains of baggage wagons and the beasts of burden crossed by one causeway, leaving the other free for the march of the army. The first of the host to cross was the sacred guard of the Great King, the Ten Thousand Immortals, all crowned with garlands as in festival procession. Preceding the king, the gorgeous Chariot of the Sun moved slowly, drawn by eight milk-white steeds. Herodotus affirms that for seven days and seven nights the bridges groaned beneath the living tide that Asia was pouring into Europe.[1]

Battle of Thermopylæ (480 B.C.). — Leading from Thessaly into Central Greece is a narrow pass, pressed on one side by the sea and on the other by rugged mountain ridges. At the foot of the cliffs break forth several hot springs, whence the name of the pass, Thermopylæ, or "Hot Gates."

At this point, in accordance with the decision of the Corinthian Congress, was offered the first resistance to the progress of the Persian army. Leonidas, king of Sparta, with three hundred Spartan soldiers and about six thousand allies from different states

---

[1] According to Herodotus, the land and naval forces of Xerxes amounted to 2,317,000 men, besides about 2,000,000 slaves and attendants. It is believed that these figures are a great exaggeration, and that the actual number of the Persian army could not have exceeded 900,000 men.

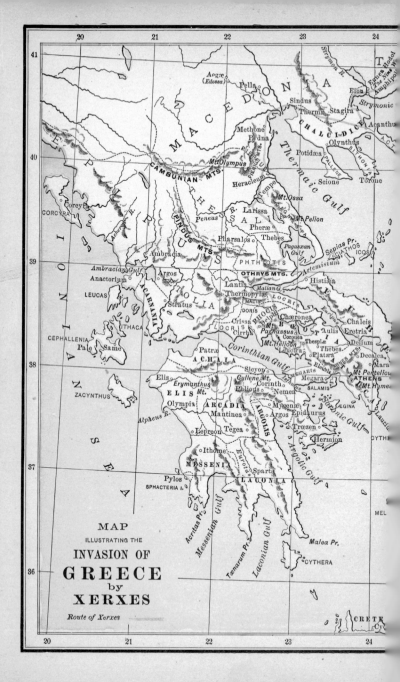

MAP

ILLUSTRATING THE

INVASION OF

GREECE

by

XERXES

Route of Xerxes

of Greece, held the pass. As the Greeks were about to celebrate
the Olympian games, which their religious scruples would not allow
them to postpone, they left this handful of men unsupported to hold
in check the army of Xerxes until the festival days should be past.

The Spartans could be driven from their advantageous position
only by an attack in front, as the Grecian fleet prevented Xerxes
from landing a force in their rear. Before assaulting them, Xerxes
summoned them to give up their arms. The answer of Leonidas
was, "Come and take them." For two days the Persians tried
to storm the pass. The Asiatics were driven to the attack by
their officers armed with whips. But every attempt to force the
way was repulsed ; even the Ten Thousand Immortals were hurled
back from the Spartan front like waves from a cliff.

But an act of treachery on the part of a native Greek rendered
unavailing all the bravery of the keepers of the pass. A by-way
leading over the mountains to the rear of the Spartans was
revealed to Xerxes. The startling intelligence was brought to
Leonidas that the Persians were descending the mountain-path
in his rear. He saw instantly that all was lost. The allies were
permitted to seek safety in flight while opportunity remained. But
for him and his Spartan companions there could be no thought of
retreat. Death in the pass, the defence of which had been
intrusted to them, was all that Spartan honor and Spartan law
now left them. The next day, surrounded by the Persian host,
they fought with desperate valor ; but, overwhelmed by mere
numbers, they were slain to the last man. With them also perished seven hundred Thespians who had chosen death with their
companions. Over the bodies of the Spartan soldiers a monument was afterwards erected with this inscription : "Stranger, tell
the Lacedæmonians that we lie here in obedience to their orders."

The Burning of Athens. — Athens now lay open to the invaders.
The Peloponnesians, thinking of their own safety simply, commenced throwing up defences across the isthmus of Corinth, working day and night under the impulse of an almost insane fear.
Athens was thus left outside to care for herself.

Counsels were divided. The Delphian oracle had obscurely declared, "When everything else in the land of Cecrops shall be taken, Zeus grants to Athena that the *wooden walls* alone shall remain unconquered, to defend you and your children." The oracle was believed to be, as was declared, "firm as adamant."

But there were various opinions as to what was meant by the "wooden walls." Some thought the Pythian priestess directed the Athenians to seek refuge in the forests on the mountains; but Themistocles (who it is thought may have himself prompted the oracle) contended that the ships were plainly indicated.

The last interpretation was acted upon. All the soldiers of Attica were crowded upon the vessels of the fleet at Salamis. The aged men, with the women and children, were carried out of the country to different places of safety. All the towns of Attica, with the capital, were thus abandoned to the conquerors.

A few days afterwards the Persians entered upon the deserted plain, which they rendered more desolate by ravaging the fields and burning the empty towns. Athens shared the common fate, and her splendid temples sank in flames. Sardis was avenged. The joy in distant Susa was unbounded.

The Naval Battle of Salamis (480 B.C.). — Just off the coast of Attica, separated from the mainland by a narrow passage of water, lies the island of Salamis. Here lay the Greek fleet, awaiting the Persian attack. To hasten on the attack before dissensions should divide the Greek forces, Themistocles resorted to the following stratagem. He sent a messenger to Xerxes representing that he himself was ready to espouse the Persian cause, and advised an immediate attack upon the Athenian fleet, which he represented as being in no condition to make any formidable resistance. Xerxes was deceived. He ordered an immediate attack. From a lofty throne upon the shore he himself overlooked the scene and watched the result. The Persian fleet was broken to pieces and two hundred of the ships destroyed.[1]

---

[1] The entire Persian fleet numbered about seven hundred and fifty vessels; the Grecian, about three hundred and eighty-five ships, mostly triremes.

The blow was decisive. Xerxes, fearing that treachery might burn or break the Hellespontine bridges, instantly despatched a hundred ships to protect them ; and then, leaving Mardonius with three hundred thousand men to retrieve the disaster of Salamis, and effect, as he promised to do, the conquest of the rest of Greece, the monarch set out on his ignominious retreat to Asia.[1]

The Battles of Platæa and Mycale (479 B.C.). — The next year the Persian fleet and army thus left behind in Europe were entirely destroyed, both on the same day — the army at Platæa, near Thebes, by the combined Greek forces under the Spartan Pausanias ; and the fleet, including the Asiatic land forces, at Mycale, on the Ionian coast.

The battles of Salamis, Platæa, and Mycale were the successive blows that shattered into fragments the most splendid armaments ever commanded by Asiatic despot.

Memorials and Trophies of the War. — The glorious issue of the war caused a general burst of joy and exultation throughout all Greece. Poets, artists, and orators, all vied with one another in commemorating the deeds of the heroes whose valor had warded off the impending danger.

Nor did the pious Grecians think that the marvellous deliverance had been effected without the intervention of the gods in their behalf. To the temple at Delphi was gratefully consecrated a tenth of the immense spoils in gold and silver from the field of Platæa ; and within the sanctuary of Athena, upon the Acropolis at Athens, were placed the broken cables of the Hellespontine bridges, at once a proud trophy of victory, and a signal illustration of the divine punishment that had befallen the audacious and impious attempt to lay a yoke upon the sacred waters of the Hellespont.

---

[1] On the very day of the battle of Salamis, Gelon of Syracuse gained a great victory over the Carthaginians at the battle of Himera, in the north of Sicily. So it was a memorable day for Hellas in the West as well as in the East.

CHAPTER XIV.

PERIOD OF ATHENIAN SUPREMACY.

(479–431 B.C.)

Rebuilding the Walls of Athens. — After the Persians had been expelled from Greece, the first care of the Athenians was the rebuilding of their homes. Their next task was the restoration of the city walls. The exalted hopes for the future which had been raised by the almost incredible achievements of the past few months, led the Athenians to draw a vast circuit of seven miles about the Acropolis as the line of the new ramparts.

The rival states of the Peloponnesus watched the proceedings of the Athenians with the most jealous interest. While they could not but admire Athens, they feared her. Sparta sent an embassy to dissuade the citizens from rebuilding the walls, hypocritically assigning as the cause of her interest in the matter her solicitude lest, in case of another Persian invasion, the city, if captured, might become a shelter and defence to the enemy. But the Athenians persisted in their purpose, and in a marvellously short time had raised the wall to such a height that they could defy interference.

Themistocles' Naval Policy. — Themistocles saw clearly that the supremacy of Athens among the Grecian states must be secured and maintained by her mastery of the sea. He had unbounded visions of the maritime power and glory that might come to her through her fleet, those " wooden walls " to which at this moment she owed her very existence ; and he succeeded in inspiring his countrymen with his own enthusiasm and sanguine hopes.

In the prosecution of his views, Themistocles persuaded the Athenians to enlarge the harbor of Piræus, the most spacious of the ports of Athens, and to surround the place with immense walls, far exceeding, both in compass and strength, those of the capital. He also led his countrymen to the resolution of adding each year twenty well-equipped triremes to their navy.

This policy, initiated by Themistocles, was, as we shall see, zealously pursued by the statesmen that after him successively assumed the lead in Athenian affairs.

His Ostracism. — Themistocles well deserved the honor of being called, as he was, the founder of the New Athens. But, although an able statesman, he was an unscrupulous man. He accepted bribes and sold his influence, thereby acquiring an enormous property. Finally he was ostracized (471 B.C.). After long wanderings, he became a resident at the court of the Persian king.

Tradition affirms that Artaxerxes, in accordance with Persian usage, provided for the courtier exile by assigning to three cities in Asia Minor the care of providing for his table : one furnished bread, a second meat, and a third wines. It is told that one day, as he sat down to his richly loaded board, he exclaimed, " How much we should have lost, my children, if we had not been ruined !"

The Confederacy of Delos (477 B.C.). — In order that they might be able to carry on the war more effectively against the Persians, the Ionian states of Asia Minor, the islands of the Ægean, and some of the states in Greece proper, shortly after the battle of Platæa, formed themselves into what is known as the Confederacy of Delos. Sparta, on account of her military reputation, had hitherto been accorded the place of pre-eminence and authority in all such alliances of the Hellenic cities. She had come, indeed, to regard herself as the natural guardian and leader of Greece. But at this time the unbearable arrogance of the Spartan general Pausanias, who presumed upon the great reputation he had gained at the battle of Platæa, led the states which had entered into the alliance to look to Athens to assume the position of leadership in the new confederacy.

The lofty character of Aristides, who was now the most prominent Athenian leader, and his great reputation for fairness and incorruptible integrity, also contributed to the same result. He was chosen the first president of the league (477 B.C.), and the sacred island of Delos was made the repository of the common funds. What proportion of the ships and money needed for carrying out the purposes of the union should be contributed by the different states, was left entirely to the decision of Aristides, such was the confidence all had in his equity ; and so long as he had control of the matter, none of the members of the alliance ever had cause of complaint.

Thus did Sparta lose, and Athens gain, the place of precedence among the Ionian states. The Dorian states of the Peloponnesus, in the main, still looked to Sparta as their leader and adviser. All Greece was thus divided into two great leagues, under the rival leadership of Sparta and Athens.

The Athenians convert the Delian League into an Empire. — The confederacy of Delos laid the basis of the imperial power of Athens. The Athenians misused their authority as leaders of the league, and gradually, during the interval between the formation of the union and the beginning of the Peloponnesian War, reduced their allies, or confederates, to the condition of tributaries and subjects.

Athens transformed the league into an empire in the following manner. The contributions assessed by Aristides upon the different members of the confederation consisted of ships and their crews for the larger states, and of money payments for the smaller ones. From the first, Athens attended to this assessment matter, and saw to it that each member of the league made its proper contribution. After a while, some of the cities preferring to make a money payment in lieu of ships, Athens accepted the commutation, and then building the ships herself, added them to her own navy. Thus the confederates disarmed themselves and armed their master.

Very soon the restraints which Athens imposed upon her allies became irksome, and they began to refuse, one after another, to pay the assessment in any form. Naxos, one of the Cyclades, was the first island to secede, as it were, from the league (466 B.C.). But Athens had no idea of admitting any such doctrine of state rights, and with her powerful navy forced the Naxians to remain within the union, and to pay an increased tribute.

What happened in the case of Naxos happened in the case of almost all the other members of the confederation. By the year 449 B.C. only three of the island members of the league still retained their independence.

Even before this date (probably about 457 B.C.) the Athenians had transferred the common treasury from Delos to Athens, and diverting the tribute from its original purpose, were beginning to spend it, not in the prosecution of war against the Barbarians, but in the execution of home enterprises, as though the treasure were their own revenue.

Thus what had been simply a voluntary confederation of sovereign and independent cities, was converted into what was practically an absolute monarchy, with the Attic democracy as the imperial master.

What made this servitude of the former allies of Athens all the more galling was the fact that they themselves had been compelled to forge the very chains which fettered them; for it was their money that had built and was maintaining the fleet by which they were kept in subjection and forced to do whatever might be the will of the Athenians.

The Leadership of Cimon; his Ostracism. — One of the ablest and most popular of the generals who commanded the forces of the Athenians during this same period when they were enslaving their confederates, was Cimon, the son of Miltiades. He was one of those whose spirits had been fired by the exciting events attendant upon the Persian invasion. He had acquired a certain reputation, at the time of the abandonment of Athens, by being the first to hang up his bridle in the sanctuary of the Acropolis, thus expressing his resolution to place all his confidence in the fleet, as Themistocles advised.

The popularity of Cimon at last declined, and he suffered ostra cism, as had Aristides and Themistocles before him. His loss of public favor came about in this manner. In the year 464 B.C., a terrible earthquake destroyed a large portion of Sparta. In the panic of the appalling disaster the Spartans were led to believe that the evil had befallen them as a punishment for their recent violation of the Temple of Poseidon, from which some Helots who had fled to the sanctuary for refuge had been torn. The Helots, on their part, were quick to interpret the event as an intervention of the gods in their behalf, and as an unmistakable signal for their uprising. Everywhere they flew to arms, and, being joined by some of the Periœci, furiously attacked their masters. The Spartans, after maintaining the bitter struggle for several years, finding themselves unable to reduce their former slaves to submission, were forced to ask aid of the other Grecian states.

The great Athenian statesman Pericles implored his countrymen not to lend themselves to the building up of the power of their rival. But the aristocratic Cimon, who had always entertained the most friendly feelings for the Spartans, exhorted the Athenians to put aside all sentiments of enmity or jealousy, and to extend succor to their kinsmen. "Let not Greece," said he, "be lamed, and thus Athens herself be deprived of her yokefellow." The assembly voted as he advised, and so the Athenian forces fought for some time side by side with the Lacedæmonians.

But the Spartans were distrustful of their Athenian allies, and fearing they might pass over to the side of the Helots, they dismissed them. The discourtesy of the act aroused the most bitter resentment at Athens. The party of Pericles took advantage of the exasperated feelings of the people to effect some important changes in the constitution in favor of the people, which made it almost purely democratical in character, and to secure the exercise of the ostracism against Cimon as the leader of the aristocratical party and the friend of Sparta (459 B.C.).

THE AGE OF PERICLES (459–431 B.C.).

General Features of the Age. — Under the inspiration of Pericles, the Athenian state now entered upon the most brilliant period of its history. The epoch embraces less than the lifetime of a single generation, yet its influence upon the civilization of the world can hardly be overrated. During this short period Athens gave birth to more great men — poets, artists, statesmen, and philosophers — than all the world besides has produced in any period of equal length.

Among all the great men of this age, Pericles stood pre-eminent. Such was the impression he left upon the period in which he lived, that it is called after him the Periclean Age. Yet Pericles' authority was simply that which talent and character justly confer. He ruled, as Plutarch says, by the art of persuasion.[1]

During the Periclean period the Athenian democracy was supreme. Every matter that concerned the empire was discussed and decided by the popular assembly. Never before had any people enjoyed such perfect political liberty as did the citizens of Athens at this time,

PERICLES.

and never before were any people, through so intimate a knowledge of public affairs, so well able to direct the policies of state. Every citizen, it is affirmed, was qualified to hold civil office.

Pericles fosters the Naval Power of Athens. — Cimon's policy had been to keep the Grecian cities united in order that they might offer effectual resistance to the Persian power. The aim of his rival Pericles was to maintain Athens as the leading state in Hellas, and to oppose the pretensions of Sparta. Accordingly he

---

[1] The only offices he held were those of strategus, superintendent of public works, and superintendent of the finances.

encouraged the Athenians to strengthen their naval armament and to perfect themselves in naval discipline, for with Themistocles he was convinced that the supremacy of Athens must depend chiefly upon her fleet.

As a part of his maritime policy, Pericles persuaded the Athenians to build what were known as the Long Walls, — great ramparts between four and five miles in length, — which united Athens to the ports of Piræus and Phalerum.   Later, as a double security,

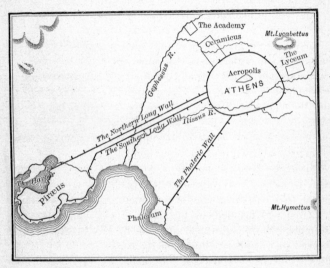

ATHENS AND THE LONG WALLS.

a third wall was built parallel to the one running to the former harbor.   By means of these walls Athens and her ports, with the intervening land, were converted into a vast fortified district, capable in time of war of holding the entire population of Attica. With her communication with the sea thus secured, and with a powerful navy at her command, Athens could bid defiance to her foes on sea and land.

Events leading up to the Thirty Years' Truce. — At the same time that Pericles was making the maritime supremacy of Athens more secure, he was endeavoring to build up for her a land empire in Central Greece. As her influence in this quarter increased, Sparta became more and more jealous, and strove to counteract it, chiefly by enhancing the power of Thebes.

The contest between the two rivals was long and bitter. It was ended by the well-known Peace of Pericles, or the Thirty Years' Truce (445 B.C.). By the terms of this treaty each of the rival cities was left at the head of the confederation it had formed, but neither was to interfere with the subjects or allies of the other, while those cities of Hellas which were not yet members of either league were to be left free to join either according to choice.

The real meaning of the Truce was that Athens gave up her ambition to establish a land empire, and was henceforth to be content with supremacy on the seas. It meant further that Greece was to remain a house divided against itself; that democratic Athens must share with aristocratic Sparta the hegemony, or leadership, of the Hellenic cities.

Pericles adorns Athens with Public Buildings. — Notwithstanding Pericles had failed to build up for Athens a land dominion, he had nevertheless succeeded in securing for her a place of proud pre-eminence in maritime Hellas. Athens having achieved such a position as she now held, it was the idea of Pericles that the Athenians should so adorn their city that it should be a fitting symbol of the power and glory of their empire. Nor was it difficult for him to persuade his art-loving countrymen to embellish their city with those masterpieces of genius that in their ruins still excite the admiration of the world.

Upon the commanding site of the Acropolis was erected the unrivalled Parthenon. Various other edifices, rich with sculptures, were also erected there and in different parts of Athens, until the whole city took on a surprisingly brilliant and magnificent appearance. The whole world looked up to the Attic city with the same surprised wonder with which a century before it had regarded the city of Babylon as adorned by the power and wealth of the great Nebuchadnezzar.

The Athenians secured the vast sums of money needed for the prosecution of their great architectural works, out of the treasury of the Delian confederacy. The allies naturally declaimed bitterly against this proceeding, complaining that Athens, with their money, was "gilding itself as a proud and vain woman decks herself out with jewels." But the answer of Pericles to them was, that the money was contributed to the end that the cities of the league should be protected from the Persians, and that so long as the Athenians kept the enemy at a distance they had a right to use the money as they pleased.

The Citizens are taken into the Pay of the State.— It was a fixed idea of Pericles that in a democracy there should be not only an equal distribution of political rights among all classes, but also an equalization of the means and opportunities of exercising these rights, as well as an equal participation by all in social and intellectual enjoyments.

In promoting his views Pericles carried to great length the system of payment for the most common public services. Thus, he introduced the custom of military pay; hitherto the Athenian soldier had served his country in the field as a matter of honor and duty. He also secured the payment of the citizen for serving as a juryman, as well as for his attendance upon the meetings of the popular assembly. Through his influence, also, salaries were attached to the various civil offices, the most of which had hitherto been unpaid positions.

These various measures enabled the poorer citizens to enjoy, without an inconvenient sacrifice, their franchise in the popular assembly, and to offer themselves for the different magistracies, which up to this time had been practically open only to men of means and leisure.

Furthermore, Pericles introduced or extended the practice of supplying all the citizens with free tickets to the theatre and other places of amusement, and of banqueting the people on festival days at the public expense.

Strength and Weakness of the Athenian Empire. — Under Pericles Athens had become the most powerful naval state in the world. In one of his last speeches, made at the outbreak of the Peloponnesian War, in which he recounts the resources of the Athenian empire, Pericles says to his fellow-citizens : " There is not now a king, there is not any nation in the universal world, able to withstand that navy which at this juncture you can launch out to sea."

But the most significant feature of this new imperial power was the combination of these vast material resources with the most imposing display of intellectual resources that the world had ever witnessed. Never before had there been such a union of the material and intellectual elements of civilization at the seat of empire. Literature and art had been carried to the utmost perfection possible to human genius. Art was represented by the inimitable creations of Phidias and Polygnotus. The drama was illustrated by the incomparable tragedies of Æschylus, Sophocles, and Euripides, and by the comedies of Aristophanes, while the writing of the world's annals had become an art in the graceful narrations of Herodotus.

But there were elements of weakness in the splendid imperial structure. The subject cities of the empire were the slaves of Athens. To her they paid tribute. To her courts they were dragged for trial. Naturally they regarded Athens as the destroyer of Hellenic liberties, and watched impatiently for the first favorable moment to revolt, and throw off the hateful yoke that she had imposed upon them. Hence the Athenian empire rested upon a foundation of sand.

Had Athens, instead of enslaving her confederates of the Delian league, only been able to find out some way of retaining them as allies in an equal union, — a great and perhaps impossible task in that age of the world, — as head of the federated Greek race, she might have secured for Hellas the sovereignty of the Mediterranean, and the history of Rome might have ended with the first century of the Republic.

Furthermore, in his system of payment for the most common public services, and of wholesale public gratuities, Pericles had introduced or encouraged practices that had the same demoralizing effects upon the Athenians that the free distribution of grain at Rome had upon the Roman populace. These pernicious customs cast discredit upon labor, destroyed frugality, and fostered idleness, thus sapping the virtues and strength of the Athenian democracy.

Illustrations of these weaknesses, as well as of the strength of the Athenian empire, will be afforded by the great struggle between Athens and Sparta known as the Peloponnesian War, the causes and chief incidents of which we shall next rehearse.

GREECE
in the
Fifth Century B.C.

Lacedæmonian Possessions & Allies

Athenian Possessions & Allies

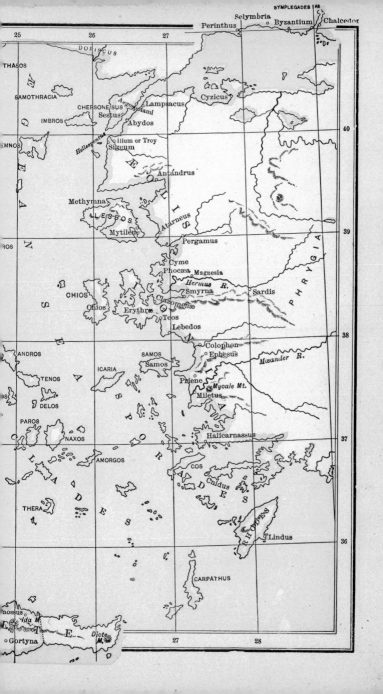

CHAPTER XV.

THE PELOPONNESIAN WAR: THE SPARTAN AND THE THEBAN SUPREMACY.

1. THE PELOPONNESIAN WAR (431–404 B.C.).

Causes of the War. — During the closing years of the life of Pericles, the growing jealousy between Athens and Sparta broke out in the long struggle known as the Peloponnesian War. Pericles had foreseen the coming storm: "I descry war," said he, "lowering from the Peloponnesus." His whole later policy looked toward the preparation of Athens for the "irrepressible conflict."

The immediate causes of the war were, first, the interference of Athens, on the side of the Corcyræns, in a quarrel between them and their mother city Corinth; and secondly, the blockade by the Athenians of Potidæa, on the Macedonian coast. This was a Corinthian colony, but it was a member of the Delian league, and was now being chastised by Athens for attempted secession. Corinth, as the ever-jealous naval rival of Athens, had endeavored to lend aid to her daughter, but had been worsted in an engagement with the Athenians.

With affairs in this shape, Corinth, seconded by other states that had causes of complaint against Athens, appealed to Sparta, as the head of the Dorian Alliance, for aid and justice. The Spartans, after listening to the deputies of both sides, decided that the Athenians had been guilty of injustice, and declared for war. The resolution of the Spartans was endorsed by the Peloponnesian confederation, and apparently approved by the Delphian oracle, which, in response to an inquiry of the Spartans as to what would be the issue of the proposed undertaking, assured them that "they would gain the victory, if they fought with all their might."

Comparison of the Resources of Sparta and of Athens. — The resources of Hellas were, at the outbreak of the war, very evenly divided between the two parties. With Sparta were all the states of the Peloponnesus, save Argos and Achaia, while beyond the Isthmus the Bœotian League, headed by Thebes, and other states were her allies. Together, these states could raise a land force of sixty thousand men, besides a considerable naval armament, Corinth being especially strong in ships.

Athens commanded all the resources of the subject cities — about three hundred in number, with twice as many smaller towns — of her great maritime empire. Her independent allies were Chios, Lesbos, Corcyra, and other states. Of course the chief strength of Athens lay in her splendid navy.

The Beginning: Attack upon Platæa by the Thebans. — The first act in the long and terrible drama was enacted at night, within the walls of Platæa. This city, though in Bœotia, was under the protection of Athens, and would have nothing to do with the Bœotian League.

Anxious to get possession of this place before the actual outbreak of the war which they saw to be inevitable, the Thebans planned its surprise and capture. Three hundred Thebans gained access to the unguarded city in the dead of night, and marching to the public square, summoned the Platæans to exchange the Athenian for a Bœotian alliance.

The Platæans were upon the point of acceding to all the demands made upon them, when, discovering the small number of the enemy, they attacked and overpowered them in the darkness, and took a hundred and eighty of them prisoners. These captives they afterwards murdered, in violation, as the Thebans always maintained, of a sacred promise that their lives should be spared. This wretched affair at Platæa precipitated the war (431 B.C.).

Invasion of Attica: Pestilence at Athens. — A Spartan army was soon overrunning Attica, while an Athenian fleet was ravaging the coasts of the Peloponnesus. Pericles persuaded the country people of Attica to abandon their villas and hamlets and gather within the defences of the city. He did not deem it prudent to risk a battle in the open fields. From the walls of Athens the people could see the flames of their burning villages and farmhouses, as the enemy ravaged the plains of Attica up to the very gates of the city. It required all the persuasion of Pericles to restrain them from issuing in a body from behind the ramparts and rushing to the defence of their homes.

The second year the Lacedæmonians again ravaged the fields about Athens, and drove the Athenians almost to frenzy with the sight of the flame and smoke of such property as had escaped the destruction of the previous year. To increase their misery, a pestilence broke out within the crowded city, and added its horrors to the already unbearable calamities of war. No pen could picture the despair and gloom that settled over the city. Athens lost, probably, one-fourth of her fighting men. Pericles, who had been the very soul and life of Athens through these dark days, fell a victim to the plague (429 B.C.). In dying, he said he considered his greatest praise to be that "he had never caused an Athenian to put on mourning."

After the death of Pericles the leadership of affairs at Athens fell into the hands of unprincipled demagogues, of whom Cleon was chief. The mob element got control of the popular assembly, so that hereafter we shall find many of its actions characterized neither by virtue nor wisdom.

Desperate and Cruel Character of the War. — On both sides the war was waged with the utmost vindictiveness and cruelty. As a rule, all the men captured by either side were killed.

In the year 428 B.C. the city of Mytilene, on the island of Lesbos, revolted from the Athenians. With the rebellion suppressed, the fate of the Mytileneans was in the hands of the Athenian assembly. Cleon proposed that all the men of the place, six thousand in number, should be slain, and the women and children sold as slaves. This infamous decree was passed, and a galley despatched bearing the sentence for execution to the Athenian general at Mytilene.

By the next morning, however, the Athenians had repented of their hasty and cruel resolution. A second meeting of the assembly was hurriedly called; the barbarous vote was repealed; and a swift trireme, bearing the reprieve, set out in anxious haste to overtake the former galley, which had twenty-four hours the start. The trireme reached the island just in time to prevent the execution of the barbarous edict.

The second resolution of the Athenians, though more discriminating than the first decree, was quite severe enough. Over one thousand of the nobles of Mytilene were killed, the city was destroyed, and the larger part of the lands of the island given to citizens of Athens.

Still more unrelenting and cruel were the Spartans. In the summer of the same year that the Athenians wreaked such vengeance upon the Mytileneans, the Spartans and their allies captured the city of Platæa, put to death all the men, sold the women as slaves, and turned the site of the city into pasture-land.

Events leading up to the Peace of Nicias (421 B.C.). — Soon after the affair at Mytilene and the destruction of Platæa, an enterprising general of the Athenians, named Demosthenes, seized and fortified a point of land (Pylos) on the coast of Messenia. The Spartans made every effort to dislodge the enemy. In the course of the siege, four hundred Spartans under Brasidas, having landed upon a little island (Sphacteria), were so unfortunate as to be cut off from the mainland by the sudden arrival of an Athenian fleet. About three hundred of them were at last captured and taken as prisoners to Athens.

But affairs now took a different turn; the Athenians were worsted (at the battle of Delium, 424 B.C.), and then much indecisive fighting followed. At last negotiations for peace were opened, which, after many embassies to and fro, resulted in what is known as the Peace of Nicias, from the prominent Athenian general who is supposed to have had most to do in bringing it about. The treaty arranged for a truce of fifty years. Each party was to give up to the other all prisoners and captured places.

Alcibiades and the Sicilian Expedition (415–413 B.C.). — The
Peace of Nicias was only a nominal one.   Some of the allies of
the two principal parties to the truce were dissatisfied with it, and
consequently its terms were not carried out in good faith or temper on either side.   So the war went on.   For about seven years,
however, Athens and Sparta refrained from invading each other's
territory ; but even during this period each was aiding its allies in
making war upon the dependents or confederates of the other.

Finally, hostilities flamed out in
open and avowed war, and all Hellas was again lit up with the fires of
the fratricidal strife.

The most prominent person on
the Athenian side during this latter
period of the struggle was Alcibiades,
a versatile and brilliant man, but a
reckless and unsafe counsellor.   He
was a pupil of Socrates, but he failed
to follow the counsels of his teacher.
His astonishing escapades only
seemed to attach the people more
closely to him, for he possessed all
those personal traits which make

ALCIBIADES.

men popular idols.   His influence over the democracy was
unlimited.   He was able to carry through the popular assembly
almost any measure that it pleased him to advocate.   The more
prudent of the Athenians were filled with apprehension for the
future of the state under such guidance.   The noted misanthrope
Timon gave expression to this feeling when, after Alcibiades had
secured the assent of the popular assembly to one of his impolitic
measures, he said to him : " Go on, my brave boy, and prosper ;
for your prosperity will bring on the ruin of all this crowd."
And it did, as we shall see.

The most prosperous enterprise of Alcibiades, in the Timonian
sense, was the inciting the Athenians to undertake an expedition

against the Dorian city of Syracuse, in Sicily. The scheme that Alcibiades was revolving in his mind was a most magnificent one. He proposed that the Athenians, after effecting the conquest of Sicily, should make that island the base of operations against both Africa and Italy. With the Italians and Carthaginians subdued, the armaments of the entire Hellenic world outside of the Peloponnesus, were to be turned against the Spartans, who with one blow should be forever crushed, and Athens be left the arbiter of the destinies of Hellas.

Alcibiades succeeded in persuading the Athenians to undertake at least the first part of the colossal enterprise. An immense fleet was carefully equipped and manned.[1] Anxiously did those remaining behind watch the squadron as it bore away from the port of Athens. Could the watchers have foreseen the fate of the splendid armament, their anxiety would have passed into despair. "Athens itself was sailing out of the Piræus, never again to return."

Scarcely had the expedition arrived at Sicily, before Alcibiades, who was one of the leading generals in command of the armament, was summoned back to Athens to answer a charge of impiety.[2] Fearing to trust himself in the hands of his enemies at Athens, he fled to Sparta, and there, by traitorous counsel, did all in his power to ruin the very expedition he had planned. He advised the Spartans to send at once their best general to the Syracusans. They sent Gylippus, an able commander, whose generalship contributed largely to the total and irretrievable defeat that the Athenians finally suffered. Their fleet and army were both virtually annihilated. Seven thousand prisoners were crowded into the

[1] It consisted of one hundred and thirty-four costly triremes, bearing thirty-six thousand soldiers and sailors. The commanders were Alcibiades, Nicias, and Lamachus. Later, Demosthenes was sent out with a reinforcement consisting of seventy-three triremes and five thousand soldiers.

[2] Just upon the eve of the departure of the expedition, the numerous statues of Hermes scattered throughout the city were grossly mutilated. Alcibiades was accused of having had a hand in the affair, and furthermore of having mimicked the sacred rites of the Eleusinian mysteries.

open stone quarries, where hundreds speedily died of exposure and starvation. Most of the wretched survivors were sold as slaves. The disaster was appalling and complete. The resources of Athens were wrecked.

The Decelean War: The Fall of Athens. — While the Athenians were before Syracuse, the Spartans, acting upon the advice of Alcibiades, had taken possession of and fortified a strong and commanding position known as Decelea, in Attica, only twelve miles from Athens. This was a thorn in the side of Athens. Secure in this stronghold, the Spartans could annoy and keep in terror almost all the Attic plain. The occupation by the Spartans of this strategic point had such a determining influence upon the remainder of the Peloponnesian War, that this latter portion of it is known as the Decelean War (413–404 B.C.).

Taking advantage of the terrible misfortunes of Athens, her subject-allies now revolted and fell away from her on every side. The Persians, ever ready to aid the Greeks in destroying one another, lent a willing ear to the solicitations of the traitor Alcibiades, and gave help to the Spartans.

The Athenians put forth almost superhuman efforts to retrieve their fortunes. Had they been united among themselves, perhaps their efforts might not have been in vain. But the oligarchical party, for the sake of ruining the democracy were willing to ruin the empire. While the army was absent from Athens, they overturned the government, and established a sort of aristocratical rule (411 B.C.) under which affairs were in the hands of a council of Four Hundred.

The Athenian troops, however, who were at Samos, would not recognize the new government. They voted themselves to be the true Athens, and forgetting and forgiving the past, recalled Alcibiades, and gave him command of the army, thereby well illustrating what the poet Aristophanes said respecting the disposition of the Athenians towards the spoiled favorite, — "They love, they hate, but cannot live without him."

Alcibiades detached the Persians from the side of the Spartans, and gained some splendid victories for Athens. But he could not undo the evil he had done. He had ruined Athens beyond redemption by any human power. Constantly the struggle grew more and more hopeless. Alcibiades was defeated, and fearing to face the Athenians, who had deposed him from his command, sought safety in flight.

Finally, at Ægospotami, on the Hellespont, the Athenian fleet was surprised and captured by the Spartans under Lysander (405 B.C.). The prisoners, three thousand in number, were massacred, and the usual rites of burial denied their bodies.

The battle of Ægospotami sealed the fate of Athens. "That night," writes the historian Xenophon, referring to the night upon which the news of the woful disaster reached Athens, "That night no man slept."

The towns on the Thracian and Macedonian coasts, and the islands of the Ægean belonging to the Athenian Empire, now fell into the hands of the Peloponnesians. Athens was besieged by sea and land, and soon forced to surrender. Some of the allies insisted upon the total destruction of the city, and the conversion of its site into pasture-land. The Spartans, however, with apparent magnanimity, declared that they would never consent thus " to put out one of the eyes of Greece."

The real motive, doubtless, of the Spartans in sparing the city was their fear lest, with Athens blotted out, Thebes or Corinth should become too powerful. So the city itself was spared, but the fortifications of Piræus and the Long Walls were levelled to the ground, the work of demolition being begun to the accompaniment of festive music (404 B.C.).

Sparta's power was now supreme. She had neither peer nor rival among all the Grecian states. Throughout the war she had maintained that her only purpose in warring against Athens was to regain liberty for the Grecian cities. We shall very soon see what sort of liberty it was that they enjoyed under her guardianship.

Results of the War. — " Never," says Thucydides, commenting upon the lamentable results of the Peloponnesian War, " Never had so many cities been made desolate by victories ; . . . never were there so many instances of banishment ; never so many scenes of slaughter either in battle or sedition."

Athens was but the wreck of her former self. She had lost two hundred ships and sixty thousand men, including the killed among her allies. Things were just the reverse now of what they were at the time of the Persian invasion. When, with all Athens in ruins, Themistocles at Salamis was taunted by the Spartans with being a man without a city, he replied grandly, "Athens is here in her ships." But now the real Athens was gone ; only the empty shell remained.

And all the rest of Hellas showed the marks of the cruel war. Spots where once had stood large towns were now pasture-land. But more lamentable than all else besides, was the effect of the war upon the intellectual and moral life of the Greek race. The Grecian world had sunk many degrees in morality ; while the vigor and productiveness of the intellectual and artistic life of Hellas, the centre and home of which had been Athens, were impaired beyond recovery. The achievements of the Greek intellect, especially in the fields of philosophic thought, in the century following the war were, it is true, wonderful ; but these triumphs merely show, we may believe, what the Hellenic mind would have done for art and general culture, had it been permitted, unchecked, and under the favoring and inspiring conditions of liberty and self-government, to disclose all that was latent in it.

2. THE SPARTAN AND THE THEBAN SUPREMACY.

Spartan Supremacy. — For just one generation following the Peloponnesian War (404–371 B.C.), Sparta held the leadership of the Grecian states. Aristocratical governments, with institutions similar to the Spartan, were established in the different cities of the old Athenian Empire. At Athens, the democratical constitution of Solon, under which the Athenians had attained their greatness, was abolished, and an oppressive oligarchy established in its stead. The Thirty Tyrants, however, who administered this government, were, after eight months' infamous rule, driven from the city, and the old democratic constitution, somewhat modified, was re-established (403 B.C.).

It was during this period that Socrates, the greatest moralist and teacher of antiquity that Europe had produced, was condemned to death, because his teachings were thought contrary to the religion of the Athenians. To this era also belongs the well-known expedition of the Ten Thousand Greeks.

Expedition of the Ten Thousand (401–400 B.C.). — Cyrus, satrap of the Persian province of Asia Minor, thinking that his brother Artaxerxes held the throne unjustly, planned to wrest it from him. For carrying out this purpose, he raised an army composed of a hundred thousand Barbarians and about eleven thousand Greek mercenaries.

With this force Cyrus set out from Sardis, in the spring of 401 B.C. He marched without opposition across Asia Minor and Mesopotamia to Babylonia, into the very heart of the Persian empire. Here, at Cunaxa, he was confronted by Artaxerxes with a force of more than half a million of men. The Barbarian allies of Cyrus were scattered at the first onset of the enemy; but the Greeks stood like a rampart of rock. Cyrus, however, was slain; and the other Greek generals, having been persuaded to enter into a council, were treacherously murdered by the Persians.

The Greeks, in a hurried night meeting, chose new generals to lead them back to their homes. One of these was Xenophon, the popular historian of the expedition. Now commenced one of the most memorable retreats in all history. After a most harassing march over the hot plains of the Tigris and the icy passes of Armenia, the survivors reached the Black Sea, the abode of sister Greek colonies.

Theban Supremacy (371–362 B.C.). — Throughout all the period of her supremacy, Sparta dealt selfishly and tyrannically with the other Grecian states. But at last the fiery resentment kindled by her oppressive measures inspired such a determined revolt against her as brought to an end her assumed supremacy over her sister cities. It was a city in Bœotia that led the uprising against Sparta. This was Thebes. The oligarchical government which the Lace-dæmonians had set up in that capital was overthrown by Pelopidas at the head of the so-called Sacred Band, a company of three hundred select men who were bound by oath to stand by each other to the last. Pelopidas was seconded in all his efforts by Epaminondas, one of the ablest generals the Grecian race ever produced. Under the masterly guidance and inspiration of these patriot leaders, Thebes very soon secured a predominating influence in the affairs of Greece.

It was Epaminondas who, when his enemies sought to disgrace and annoy him by electing him "public scavenger," made, in accepting the office, the memorable utterance, "If the office will not reflect honor upon me, I will reflect honor upon it."

At Leuctra (371 B.C.) the Thebans earned the renown of being the most invincible soldiers in the world by completely overthrowing, with a force of six thousand men, the Spartan army of twice that number. This is said to have been the first time that the Spartans were ever fairly defeated in open battle. Their forces had been annihilated, as at Thermopylæ, — but annihilation is not defeat.

From the victory of Leuctra dates the short but brilliant period of Theban supremacy. The year after that battle Epaminondas led an army into the Peloponnesus to aid the Arcadians, who had risen against Sparta. Laconia was ravaged, and for the first time Spartan women saw the smoke of fires kindled by an enemy.

To strengthen Arcadia's power of resistance to Sparta, Epaminondas perfected a league among the hitherto isolated towns and cantons of the district. As the mutual jealousies of the leading cities prevented him from making any one of them the capital of the confederation, he founded Megalopolis, or the Great City, and made it the head of the union. In the pursuit of the same policy, Epaminondas also restored the independence of Messenia.

But, moved by jealousy of the rapidly growing power of Thebes,

Athens now formed an alliance with her old rival Sparta against her. Three times more did Epaminondas lead an army into the Peloponnesus. During his third and last expedition he fought with the Spartans and Athenians the great battle of Mantinea, in Arcadia. On this memorable field, Epaminondas led the Thebans once more to victory; but he himself was slain, and with him fell the hopes and power of Thebes (362 B.C.).

All the states of Greece now lay exhausted, worn out by their endless domestic contentions and wars. There was scarcely sufficient strength left to strike one worthy blow against enslavement by the master destined soon to come from the North.

CHAPTER XVI.

PERIOD OF MACEDONIAN SUPREMACY: EMPIRE OF ALEXANDER.

(338–323 B.C.)

General Statement. — Macedonia lay to the north of Greece proper. The ruling class of the country was probably of Hellenic race ; at all events the Macedonian kings were allowed to take part in the Olympian games — a privilege accorded to none but pure Hellenes. Their efforts to spread Greek art and culture among their subjects, a race of rough but brave and martial men, unaccustomed to city life, had been so far successful that the country had, to a certain degree, become Hellenized.

So this period of Macedonian supremacy upon which we are entering belongs to the history of the political life of the Greek race, as well as the eras marked by Athenian, Spartan, or Theban leadership. It was Hellenic institutions, customs, and manners, Hellenic language and civilization, that the Macedonians, in the extended conquests which we are about to narrate, spread over the world.[1] It is this which makes the short-lived Macedonian empire so important in universal history.

Philip of Macedon. — Macedonia first rose to importance during the reign of Philip II. (359–336 B.C.), better known as Philip of Macedon. He was a man of pre-eminent ability, of wonderful

---

[1] Of course it was rather the outer forms than the real inner life and spirit of the old Greek civilization which were adopted by the non-Hellenic peoples of Egypt and Western Asia. Hence the resulting culture is given a special name, *Hellenism*, which, in Professor Jebbs' language, means, — "not '*being* Hellenes,' or Greeks, but — 'doing *like* Hellenes ' ; and as the adjective answering to *Hellas* is *Hellenic*, so the adjective answering to *Hellenism* is *Hellenistic*."

address in diplomacy, and possessed rare genius as an organizer and military chieftain. The art of war he had learned in youth as a hostage-pupil of Epaminondas of Thebes. He was the originator of the " Macedonian phalanx," a body as renowned in the military history of Macedonia as is the " legion " in that of Rome.

With his kingdom settled and consolidated at home, Philip's ambition led him to seek the leadership of the Grecian states. He sought to gain his purpose rather by artful diplomacy and intrigue than by open force. In the use of these weapons he might have been the teacher of the Athenian Themistocles.

The Second Sacred War (355–346 B.C.). — Philip quickly extended his power over a large part of Thrace and the Greek cities of Chalcidice. Meanwhile he was, in the following way, acquiring a commanding position in the affairs of the states of Greece proper.

The Phocians had put to secular use some of the lands which, at the end of the First Sacred War (see p. 108), had been consecrated to the Delphian Apollo. Taken to task and heavily fined for this act by the other members of the Delphian Amphictyony, the Phocians deliberately robbed the temple, and used the treasure in the maintenance of a large force of mercenary soldiers. The Amphictyons not being able to punish the Phocians for their impiety, were forced to ask help of Philip, who gladly rendered the assistance sought.

The Phocians were now quickly subdued, their cities were destroyed, and the inhabitants scattered in villages and forced to pay tribute to the Delphian Apollo. The place that the Phocians had held in the Delphian Amphictyony was given to Philip, upon whom was also bestowed the privilege of presiding at the Pythian games. The position he had now secured was just what Philip had coveted, in order that he might use it to make himself master of all Greece.

Battle of Chæronea (338 B.C.). — Demosthenes at Athens was one of the few who seemed to understand the real designs of Philip. His penetration, like that of Pericles, descried a cloud lowering over Greece — this time from the North. With all the energy of his wonderful eloquence, he strove to stir up the Athenians to resist the encroachments of the king of Macedon. He hurled against him his famous " Philippics," speeches so filled with fierce denunciation that they have given name to all writings characterized by bitter criticism or violent invective.

At length the Athenians and Thebans, aroused by the oratory of Demosthenes and by some fresh encroachments of the Macedonians, united their forces, and met Philip upon the memorable field of Chæronea in Bœotia. The Macedonian phalanx swept everything before it. The Theban band was annihilated. The power and authority of Philip were now extended and acknowledged throughout Greece (338 B.C.).

Plan to invade Asia. — While the Greek states were divided among themselves, they were united in an undying hatred of the Persians. They were at this time meditating an enterprise fraught with the greatest importance to the history of the world. This was a joint expedition against Persia. The march of the Ten Thousand Greeks through the very heart of the dominions of the Great King had encouraged this national undertaking, and illustrated the feasibility of the conquest of Asia. At a great council of the Grecian cities held at Corinth, Philip was chosen leader of this expedition. All Greece was astir with preparation. In the midst of all, Philip was assassinated during the festivities attending the marriage of his daughter, and his son Alexander succeeded to his place and power (336 B.C.).

Accession of Alexander the Great. — Alexander was only twenty years of age when he came to his father's throne. The spirit of the man is shown in the complaint of the boy when news of his father's victories came to him : " Friends," said he to his playmates, " my father will possess himself of everything and leave nothing for us to do."

For about two years Alexander was busy suppressing revolts against his power among the different cities of Hellas, and chastising hostile tribes on the northern frontiers of Macedonia. Thebes having risen against him, he razed the city to the ground, — sparing, however, the house of the poet Pindar, — and sold thirty thousand of the inhabitants into slavery. Thus was one of the most renowned of the cities of Greece blotted out of existence.

Alexander crosses the Hellespont (334 B.C.). — Alexander was now free to carry out his father's scheme in regard to the Asiatic expedition. In the spring of 334 B.C., he set out, at the head of an army numbering about thirty-five thousand men, for the con-

THE BATTLE OF ISSUS. (From a Mosaic found at Pompeii.)

quest of the Persian empire. Now commenced one of the most remarkable and swiftly executed campaigns recorded in history.

Crossing the Hellespont, Alexander routed the Persians at the important battle of the Granicus, by which victory all Asia Minor was laid open to the invader.

The Battle of Issus (333 B.C.). — At the northeast corner of the Mediterranean lies the plain of Issus. Here Alexander again defeated the Persian army, numbering six hundred thousand men.

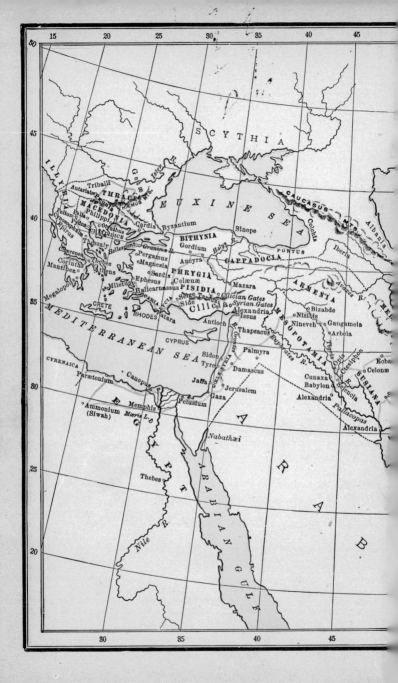

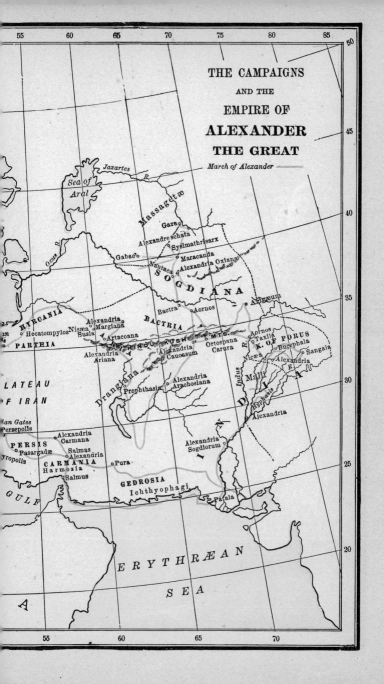

THE CAMPAIGNS

AND THE

EMPIRE OF

ALEXANDER

THE GREAT

March of Alexander ——————

Jaxartes

Sea of Aral

R.

Massagetæ

Gaza

Alexandre schata
Sysimathri sarx

Gabae

Nautaca
Maracanda
Alexandria Oxlana

SOGDIANA

Orus R.

HYRCANIA
Hecatompylos Nisæa
Alexandria
Margiana
Susia

Bactra
Aornos

Aorgæum

BACTRIA

PARTHIA
Artacoana
HINDOU KOUSH MTS.

Aornos
Taxila K. OF PORUS
Bucephala

Alexandria
Ariana
Alexandria
Caucasum
Ortospana
Carura
Nicæa
Alexandria
Sangala

Indus R.

I N D I A

PLATEAU
OF IRAN

Drangiana
Prophthasia
Alexandria
Arachosiana

Malli

an Gates
Persepolis

Hyphasis
Alexandria

PERSIS
Pasargadæ
yropolis

Alexandria
Carmana

Salmas
Alexandria

Alexandria
Sogdiorum

CARMANIA
Harmozia
Salmus

Pura

GEDROSIA
Ichthyophagi

Patala

GULF

E R Y T H R Æ A N

S E A

A

The family of Darius, including his mother, wife, and children, fell into the hands of Alexander; but the king himself escaped from the field, and hastened to his capital, Susa, to raise another army to oppose the march of the conqueror.

Siege of Tyre (332 B.C.). — Before penetrating to the heart of the empire, Alexander turned to the south, in order to effect the subjugation of Phœnicia, that he might command the Phœnician fleets and prevent their being used to sever his communication with Greece. The island-city of Tyre, after a memorable siege, was taken by means of a mole, or causeway, built with incredible labor through the sea to the city. Eight thousand of the inhabitants were slain, and thirty thousand sold into slavery — a terrible warning to those cities that should dare to close their gates against the Macedonian.

Alexander in Egypt. — With the cities of Phœnicia and the fleets of the Mediterranean subject to his control, Alexander easily effected the conquest of Egypt. The Egyptians, indeed, made no resistance to the Macedonians, but willingly exchanged masters.

While in the country, Alexander founded, at one of the mouths of the Nile, a city called, after himself, Alexandria. The city became the meeting-place of the East and West; and its importance through many centuries attests the far-sighted wisdom of its founder.

A less worthy enterprise of the conqueror was his expedition to the oasis of Siwah, located in the Libyan desert, where were a celebrated temple and oracle of Zeus Ammon. To gratify his own vanity, as well as to impress the superstitious barbarians, Alexander desired to be declared of celestial descent. The priests of the temple, in accordance with the wish of the king, gave out that the oracle pronounced Alexander to be the son of Zeus Ammon, and the destined ruler of the world.

The Battle of Arbela (331 B.C.). — From Egypt Alexander recommenced his march towards the Persian capital. He had received offers of peace from Darius, but to these he is said to have replied, " There cannot be two suns in the heavens." Pushing on, he crossed the Euphrates and the Tigris without opposition ; but upon the plain of Arbela, not far from ancient Nineveh, he found his further advance disputed by Darius with an immense army. Again the Macedonian phalanx "cut through the ranks of the Persians as a boat cuts through the waves." The fate of Darius has been already narrated in our story of the last of the Persian kings (see p. 82).

The battle of Arbela was one of the decisive combats of history. It marked the end of the long struggle between the East and the West, between Persia and Greece, and prepared the way for the spread of Hellenic civilization over all Western Asia.

Alexander at Babylon, Susa, and Persepolis. — From the field of Arbela Alexander marched south to Babylon, which opened its gates to him without opposition. Susa was next entered by the conqueror. Here he seized incredible quantities of gold and silver ($57,000,000, it is said), the treasure of the Great King.

From Susa Alexander's march was next directed to Persepolis, where he secured a treasure more than twice as great ($138,000,-000) as that found at Susa. Upon Persepolis Alexander wreaked vengeance, for all Greece had suffered at the hands of the Persians. Many of the inhabitants were massacred, and others sold into slavery ; while the palaces of the Persian kings were given to the flames.

Alexander, having thus overthrown the power of Darius, now began to regard himself, not only as his conqueror, but as his successor, and was thus looked upon by the Persians. He assumed the pomp and state of an Oriental monarch, and required the most obsequious homage from all who approached him. His Greek and Macedonian companions, unused to paying such servile adulation to their king, were much displeased at Alexander's conduct, and from this time on to his death, intrigues and conspiracies were being constantly formed among them against his power and life.

Conquest of Bactria. — Urged on by an uncontrollable desire to possess himself of the most remote countries of which any accounts had ever reached him, Alexander now led his army to the north, and, after subduing many tribes that dwelt about the Caspian Sea, boldly conducted his soldiers over the snowy passes of the Hindu Kush, and descended into the fair provinces of Bactria.

During the years 329–328 B.C. Alexander conquered not only Bactria but Sogdiana, a country lying north of the Oxus. Among his captives here was a beautiful Bactrian princess, Roxana by name, who became his bride.

Alexander's stay in Sogdiana was saddened by his murder of his dearest friend Clitus, who had saved his life at the Granicus. Both were flushed with wine when the quarrel arose; after the deed, Alexander was overwhelmed with remorse.

Conquests in India. — With the countries north of the Hindu Kush subdued and settled, Alexander recrossed the mountains, and led his army down upon the rich and crowded plains of India (327 B.C.). Here again he showed himself invincible, and received the submission of many of the native princes.

The most formidable resistance encountered by the Macedonians was offered by a strong and wealthy king named Porus. Captured at last and brought into the presence of Alexander, his proud answer to the conqueror's question as to how he thought he ought to be treated was, " Like a king." The impulsive Alexander gave him back his kingdom, to be held, however, subject to the Macedonian crown.

Alexander's desire was to extend his conquests to the Ganges, but his soldiers began to murmur because of the length and hardness of their campaigns, and he reluctantly gave up the undertaking. To secure the conquests already made, he founded, at different points in the valley of the Indus, Greek towns and colonies. One of these he named Alexandria, after himself; another Bucephala, in memory of his favorite steed; and still another Nicæa, for his victories. The modern museum at Lahore contains many relics of Greek art, dug up on the site of these Macedonian cities and camps.

Alexander's return route lay through the ancient Gedrosia, now Beluchistan, a region frightful with burning deserts, amidst which his soldiers endured almost incredible privations and sufferings. After a trying and calamitous march of over two months, Alexander, with the survivors of his army, reached Carmania. Here, to his unbounded joy, he was joined by Nearchus, the trusted admiral of his fleet, whom he had ordered to explore the sea between the Indus and the Euphrates.

To appropriately celebrate his conquests and discoveries, Alexander instituted a series of religious festivals, amidst which his soldiers forgot the dangers of their numberless battles and the hardships of their unparalleled marches, which had put to the test every power of human endurance. And well might these veterans glory in their achievements. In a few years they had conquered half the world, and changed the whole course of history.

Plans and Death of Alexander. — As the capital of his vast empire, which now stretched from the Ionian Sea to the Indus, Alexander chose the ancient Babylon, upon the Euphrates. His designs were to push his conquests as far to the west as he had extended them to the east. Arabia, Carthage, Italy, and Spain were to be added to his already vast domains. Indeed, the plans of Alexander embraced nothing less than the union and Hellenizing of the world. Not only were the peoples of Asia and Europe to be blended by means of colonies, but even the floras of the two continents were to be intermingled by the transplanting of fruits and trees from one continent to the other. Common laws and customs, a common language and a common religion, were to unite the world into one great family. Intermarriages were to blend the races. Alexander himself married a daughter of Darius III., and also one of Artaxerxes Ochus ; and to ten thousand of his soldiers, whom he encouraged to take Asiatic wives, he gave magnificent gifts.

In the midst of his vast projects, Alexander was seized by a fever, brought on by his insane excesses, and died at Babylon, 323 B.C., in the thirty-second year of his age. His soldiers could not let him die without seeing him. The watchers of the palace were obliged to open the doors to them, and the veterans of a hundred battle-fields filed sorrowfully past the couch of their dying commander. His body was carried to Alexandria, in Egypt, and there enclosed in a golden coffin, and a splendid mausoleum was raised over it. His ambition for celestial honors was gratified in his death; for in Egypt and elsewhere temples were dedicated to him, and divine worship was paid to his statues.

We cannot deny to Alexander, in addition to a remarkable genius for military affairs, a profound and comprehensive intellect. He had fine tastes, and liberally encouraged art, science, and literature. The artists of his times had in him a munificent patron; and to his preceptor Aristotle he sent large collections of natural-history objects, gathered in his extended expeditions. He had a kind and generous nature: he avenged the murder of his enemy Darius; and he repented in bitter tears over the body of his faithful Clitus. He exposed himself like the commonest soldier, sharing with his men the hardships of the march and the dangers of the battle-field.

But he was self-seeking, foolishly vain, and madly ambitious of military glory. He plunged into shameful excesses, and gave way to bursts of passion that transformed a usually mild and generous disposition into the fury of a madman. The contradictions of his life cannot, perhaps, be better expressed than in the words once applied to the gifted Themistocles: "He was greater in genius than in character."

Results of Alexander's Conquests. — The remarkable conquests of Alexander had far-reaching consequences. They ended the long struggle between Persia and Greece, and spread Hellenic civilization over Egypt and Western Asia. The distinction between Greek and Barbarian was obliterated, and the sympathies of men, hitherto so narrow and local, were widened, and thus an important preparation was made for the reception of the cosmopolitan creed of Christianity. The world was also given a universal language of culture, which was a further preparation for the spread of Christian teachings.

But the evil effects of the conquest were also positive and far-reaching. The sudden acquisition by the Greeks of the enormous wealth of the Persian empire, and contact with the vices and the effeminate luxury of the Oriental nations, had a most demoralizing effect upon Hellenic life. Greece became corrupt, and she in turn corrupted Rome. Thus the civilization of antiquity was undermined.

CHRONOLOGICAL SUMMARY OF GRECIAN HISTORY TO THE DEATH OF ALEXANDER THE GREAT.

Legendary Age . .	The Trojan War, legendary date	1194–1184
	The Dorians enter the Peloponnesus, about	1104
Early History of Sparta	Lycurgus gives laws to Sparta. . "	850
	The Messenian Wars . . . . . "	750–650
Early History of Athens. . .	Rule of the Archons . . . . "	1050–612
	Rebellion of Cylon . . . . . "	612
	Legislation of Solon . . . . . "	594
	Pisistratus rules	560–527
	Expulsion of the Pisistratidæ	510
Period of Græco-Persian War . .	First Expedition of Darius (led by Mardonius)	492
	Battle of Marathon	490
	Battle of Thermopylæ	480
	Battle of Salamis	480
	Battles of Platæa and Mycale	479
Period of Athenian Supremacy . .	Athens rebuilt	478
	Aristides chosen first president of the Confederacy of Delos	477
	Themistocles sent into exile	471
	Ostracism of Cimon	459
	Pericles at the head of affairs — Periclean Age	459–431
Events of the Peloponnesian War .	Beginning of the Peloponnesian War . .	431
	Pestilence at Athens	430
	Expedition against Syracuse	415
	Battle of Ægospotami	405
	Close of the War	404
Period of Spartan Supremacy . .	Rule of the Thirty Tyrants at Athens . .	404–403
	Expedition of the Ten Thousand	401–400
	Peace of Antalcidas	387
	Oligarchy established at Thebes	382
	Spartan power broken on the field of Leuctra	371

CHAPTER XVII.

STATES FORMED FROM THE EMPIRE OF ALEXANDER.

Division of the Empire of Alexander. — There was no one who could wield the sword that fell from the hand of Alexander. It is told that, when dying, being asked to whom the kingdom should belong, he replied, "To the strongest," and handed his signet ring to his general Perdiccas. But Perdiccas was not strong enough to master the difficulties of the situation.[1] Indeed, who is strong enough to rule the world?

Consequently the vast empire created by Alexander's unparalleled conquests was distracted by quarrels and wars, and before the close of the fourth century B.C., had become broken into many fragments. Besides minor states,[2] four well-defined and important monarchies arose out of the ruins. After the rearrangement of boundaries that followed the decisive battle of Ipsus (fought in Phrygia 301 B.C.), these principal states had the outlines shown by the accompanying map. Their rulers were Lysimachus, Seleucus Nicator, Ptolemy, and Cassander, who had each assumed the title of king. The great horn being broken, in its place came up four notable ones toward the four winds of heaven.[3]

[1] Perdiccas ruled as regent for Philip Arridæus (an illegitimate brother of Alexander), who was proclaimed titular king.

[2] Two of these lesser states, Rhodes and Pontus, deserve special notice : —

Rhodes. — Rhodes became the head of a maritime confederation of the cities and islands along the coasts of Asia Minor, and thus laid the basis of a remarkable commercial prosperity and naval power.

Pontus. — Pontus (Greek for *sea*), a state of Asia Minor, was so called from its position upon the Euxine. It was never thoroughly conquered by the Macedonians. It has a place in history mainly because of the lustre shed upon it by the transcendent ability of one of its kings, Mithridates the Great (120–63 B.C.), who for a long time made successful resistance to the Roman arms.

[3] Dan. viii. 8.

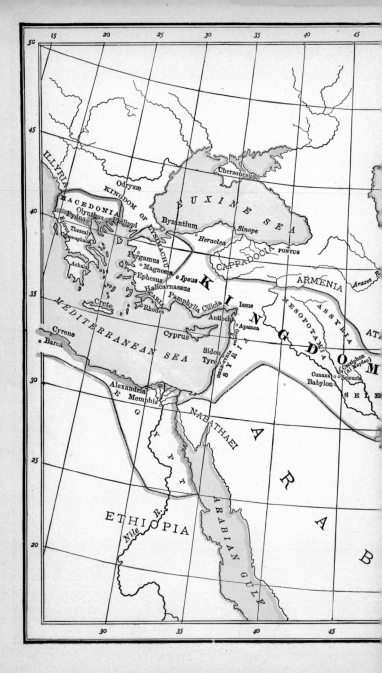

KINGDOMS
of the
SUCCESSORS of ALEXANDER
C. B. C. 300.

Dominions of Ptolemy

Jaxartes R.

Sea of
Aral

ASPI

Oxus R.

Maracanda

S O G D I A N A

NE   PARTHIA

B A C T R I A

HINDU KUSH MTS

OF S E L E U C

Indus R.

I   A

Drangiana

D

Hyphasis

rsepolis

PERSIS

N

CARMANIA

GEDROSIA

AN GULF

E R Y T H R E A N

A

S E A

Lysimachus held Thrace and the western part of Asia Minor; Seleucus Nicator, Syria and the countries eastward to the Indus; Ptolemy ruled Egypt; and Cassander governed Macedonia, and claimed authority over Greece.[1]

After barely mentioning the fate of the kingdom of Lysimachus, we will trace very briefly the fortunes of the other three monarchies until they were overthrown, one after the other, by the now rapidly rising power of Rome.

Thrace, or the Kingdom of Lysimachus. — The kingdom of Lysimachus soon disappeared. He was defeated by Seleucus in the year 281 B.C., and his dominions were divided. The lands in Asia Minor were joined to the Syrian kingdom, while Thrace was absorbed by Macedonia.

Syria, or the Kingdom of the Seleucidæ (312–63 B.C.). — This kingdom, during the two centuries and more of its existence, played an important part in the political history of the world. Under its first king it comprised nominally almost all the countries of Asia conquered by Alexander, thus stretching from the Hellespont to the Indus. Its rulers were called Seleucidæ, from the founder of the kingdom, Seleucus Nicator.

Seleucus Nicator (312–280 B.C.), besides being a ruler of unusual ability, was a most liberal patron of learning and art. He is declared to have been "the greatest founder of cities that ever lived." Throughout his dominions he founded a vast number, some of which endured for many centuries. Antioch, on the Orontes, in Northern Syria, became, after Seleucia on the Tigris, the capital of the kingdom, and obtained an influence and renown as a centre of population and trade which have given its name a sure place in history.

The successors of Seleucus Nicator led the kingdom through checkered fortunes. On different sides provinces fell away and became independent states.[2] Antiochus III. (223–187 B.C.), called

---

[1] Cassander never secured complete control of Greece, hence this country is not included in his domains as these appear upon the map.

[2] The most important of these were the following: —

1. **Pergamus.** — This was a state in western Asia Minor, which became

"the Great," raised the kingdom for a short time into great prominence; but attempting to make conquests in Europe, and further,

giving asylum to the Carthaginian general Hannibal, he incurred the fatal hostility of Rome. Quickly driven by the Roman legions across the Hel-

COIN OF ANTIOCHUS III. (THE GREAT).

lespont, he was hopelessly defeated at the battle of Magnesia (190 B.C.). After this, the Syrian kingdom was of very little importance in the world's affairs. At last, brought again into collision with Rome, the country was overrun by Pompey the Great, and became a part of the Roman Republic, 63 B.C.

Kingdom of the Ptolemies in Egypt (323–30 B.C.). — The Græco-Egyptian empire of the Ptolemies was by far the most important, in its influence upon the civilization of the world, of all the kingdoms that owed their origin to the conquests of Alexander. The founder of the house and dynasty was Ptolemy I., surnamed Soter (323–283 B.C.), one of Alexander's ablest generals. His de-

PTOLEMY SOTER.

scendants ruled in Egypt for nearly three centuries, a most important period in the intellectual life of the world. Under Ptolemy

independent upon the death of Seleucus Nicator (280 B.C.). Favored by the Romans, it gradually grew into a powerful kingdom, which at one time embraced a considerable part of Asia Minor. Its capital, also called Pergamus, became a most noted centre of Greek learning and civilization.

2. **Parthia.** — Parthia was a powerful Turanian state that grew up east of the Euphrates River (from about 255 B.C. to 226 A.D.). Its kings were at first formidable enemies of the rulers of Syria, and later of the Romans, whom they never allowed to make any considerable conquest beyond the Euphrates.

I., Alexandria became the great depot of exchange for the productions of the world. At the entrance of the harbor stood the Pharos, or light-house, — the first structure of its kind, — which Ptolemy built to guide the fleets of the world to his capital. This edifice was reckoned one of the Seven Wonders.

But it was not alone the exchange of material products that was comprehended in Ptolemy's scheme. His aim was to make his capital the intellectual centre of the world — the place where the arts, sciences, literatures, and even the religions, of the world should meet and mingle. He founded the famous Museum, a sort of college, which became the "University of the East," and established the renowned Alexandrian Library. Poets, artists, philosophers, and teachers in all departments of learning were encouraged to settle in Alexandria by the conferring of immunities and privileges, and by gifts and munificent patronage. His court embraced the learning and genius of the age.

Ptolemy II., Philadelphus (283–247 B.C.), followed closely in the footsteps of his father, carrying out, as far as possible, the plans and policies of the preceding reign. Under his successor, Ptolemy III., Euergetes (247–242 B.C.), the dominions of the Ptolemies touched their widest limits; while the capital Alexandria reached the culminating point in her fame as the centre of Hellenistic civilization.

Altogether the Ptolemies reigned in Egypt almost exactly three centuries (323–30 B.C.). Those rulers who held the throne for the last two hundred years were, with few exceptions, a succession of monsters, such as even Rome in her worst days could scarcely equal. The usage of intermarriage among the members of the royal family, — a usage in which the Ptolemies followed what was a custom of the ancient Pharaohs, — led to endless family quarrels, which resulted in fratricide, matricide, and all the dark deeds included in the calendar of royal crime. The story of the renowned Cleopatra, the last of the house of the Ptolemies, will be told in connection with Roman history, to which it properly belongs.

Macedonia and Greece. — From the time of the subjection of

Greece by Philip and Alexander to the absorption of Macedonia into the growing dominions of Rome, the Greek cities of the peninsula were very much under the control or influence of the Macedonian kings. But the Greeks were never made for royal subjects, and consequently they were in a state of chronic revolt against this foreign authority.

Thus, no sooner had they heard of the death of Alexander than several of the Grecian states rose against the Macedonian general Antipater, and carried on with him what is known as the Lamian War (323–321 B.C.). The struggle ended disastrously for the Greeks, and Demosthenes, who had been the soul of the movement, was forced to flee from Athens. He took refuge upon an island just off the coast of the Peloponnesus ; but being still hunted by Antipater, he put an end to his own life by means of poison.

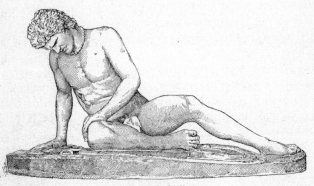

THE DYING GAUL.

The next matter of moment in the history of Macedonia, was an invasion of the Gauls (279 B.C.), kinsmen of the Celtic tribes that about a century before this time had sacked the city of Rome. These savage marauders inflicted terrible suffering upon both Macedonia and Greece. But they were at last expelled from Europe, and settling in Asia Minor, they there gave name to the province of Galatia. The celebrated Greek sculpture, The Dying Gaul, popularly but erroneously called The Dying Gladiator, is a most interesting memorial of this episode in Greek history.

Macedonia finally came in contact with a new enemy — the great military republic of the West. For lending aid to Carthage in the Second Punic War, she incurred the anger of Rome, and the result was that, after much intrigue and hard fighting, the country was brought into subjection to the Italian power. In the year 146 B.C. it was erected into a Roman province.

The political affairs of Greece proper during the period we are considering were chiefly comprehended in the fortunes of two confederacies, or leagues, one of which was called the Achæan, and the other the Ætolian League. United, these two confederacies might have maintained the political independence of Greece ; but that spirit of dissension which we have seen to be the bane of the Hellenic peoples caused them to become, in the hands of intriguing Rome, weapons first for crushing Macedonia, and then for grinding each other to pieces. Finally, in the year 146 B.C., the splendid city of Corinth was taken by the Roman army and laid in ashes. This was the last act in the long and varied drama of the political life of ancient Greece. Henceforth it constituted simply a portion of the Roman Empire.

Conclusion. — We have now traced the political fortunes of the Hellenic race through about seven centuries of authentic history. In succeeding chapters it will be our pleasanter task to trace the more brilliant and worthy fortunes of the artistic and intellectual life of Hellas, — to portray, though necessarily in scanty outline, the achievements of that wonderful genius which enabled her, "captured, to lead captive her captor."

End

CHAPTER XVIII.

GREEK ARCHITECTURE, SCULPTURE, AND PAINTING.

The Greek Sense of Beauty. — The Greeks were artists by nature. "Ugliness gave them pain like a blow." Everything they made was beautiful. Beauty they placed next to holiness; indeed, they almost or quite made beauty and right the same thing. They are said to have thought it strange that Socrates was good, seeing he was so unprepossessing in appearance.

PELASGIAN MASONRY.

1. ARCHITECTURE.

Pelasgian Architecture. — The term Pelasgian is applied to various structures of massive masonry found in different parts of Greece, Italy, and Asia Minor. The origin of these works was a mystery to the earliest Hellenes, who ascribed them to a race of giants called Cyclops; hence the name Cyclopean that also attaches to them.

These works exhibit three well-defined stages of development.

In the earliest and rudest structures the stones are gigantic in size and untouched by the chisel; in the next oldest the stones are worked into irregular polygonal blocks; while in the latest the blocks are cut into rectangular shapes and laid in regular courses. The walls of the old citadels or castles of several Grecian cities exhibit specimens of this primitive architecture (see p. 90).

Orders of Architecture. — There are three styles, or orders, of Grecian architecture — the Doric, the Ionic, and the Corinthian. They are distinguished from one another chiefly by differences in the proportions and ornamentation of the column.

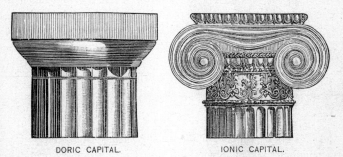

DORIC CAPITAL.   IONIC CAPITAL.

The Doric column is without a base, and has a simple and massive capital. At first the Doric temples of the Greeks were almost as massive as the Egyptian temples, but later they became more refined.

The Ionic column is characterized by the spiral volutes of the capital. This form was borrowed from the Assyrians, and was principally employed by the Greeks of Ionia, whence its name.

The Corinthian order is distinguished by its rich capital, formed of acanthus leaves. This type is made up of Egyptian, Assyrian, and Grecian elements. The addition of the acanthus leaves is said to have been suggested to the artist Callimachus by the pretty effect of a basket surrounded by the leaves of an acanthus plant, upon which it had accidentally fallen.

The entire structure was made to harmonize with its supporting columns. The general characteristics of the several orders are well portrayed by the terms we use when we speak of the "stern" Doric, the "graceful" Ionic, and the "ornate" Corinthian.

CORINTHIAN CAPITAL.

Temple of Diana at Ephesus. — The temple of Diana at Ephesus was regarded as one of the wonders of the world. The original structure was commenced about the beginning of the sixth century B.C., and, according to Pliny, was one hundred and twenty years in process of building. Crœsus gave liberally of his wealth to ornament the shrine.

In the year 356 B.C., on the same night, it is said, that Alexander was born, an ambitious youth, named Herostratus, fired the building, simply to immortalize his name. Alexander offered to rebuild the temple, provided that he be allowed to inscribe his name upon it. The Ephesians gracefully declined the proposal by replying that it was not right for one deity to erect a temple to another. Alexander was obliged to content himself with placing within the shrine his own portrait by Apelles — a piece of work which cost $30,000. The value of the gifts to the temple was beyond all calculation : kings and states vied with one another in splendid donations. Painters and sculptors were eager to have their masterpieces assigned a place within its walls, so that it became a great national gallery of paintings and statuary.

So inviolable was the sanctity of the temple that at all times, and especially in times of tumult and danger, property and treasures were carried to it as a safe repository.[1] But the riches of the

---

[1] The Grecian temples were, in a certain sense, banks of deposit. They contained special chambers or vaults for the safe-keeping of valuables. The

sanctuary proved too great a temptation to the Roman emperor Nero. He risked incurring the anger of the great Diana, and robbed the temple of many statues and a vast amount of gold. Later (in 262 A.D.), the barbarian Goths enriched themselves with the spoils of the shrine, and left it a ruin.

The Delphian Temple. — The first temple erected at Delphi over the spot whence issued the mysterious vapors (see p. 105) was a rude wooden structure. In the year 548 B.C., the temple then standing was destroyed by fire. All the cities and states of Hellas contributed to its rebuilding. Even the king of Egypt, Amasis, sent a munificent gift. More than half a million of dollars was collected; for the temple was to exceed in magnificence anything the world had yet seen. It will be recalled that the Athenian Alcmæonidæ were the contractors who undertook the rebuilding of the shrine (see p. 122).

The temple was crowded with the spoils of many battle-fields, with the rich gifts of kings, and with rare works of art. Like the temple at Ephesus, the Delphian shrine, after remaining for many years secure, through the awe and reverence which its oracle inspired, suffered frequent spoliation. The greed of conquerors overcame all religious scruples. The Phocians robbed the temple of a treasure equivalent, it is estimated, to more than $10,000,000 with us (see p. 160); and Nero plundered it of five hundred bronze images. But Constantine (emperor of Rome 306–337 A.D.,

heaps of gold and silver relics discovered by Di Cesnola at Sunium, in the island of Cyprus, were found in the secret subterranean vaults of a great temple. The priests often loaned out on interest the money deposited with them, the revenue from this source being added to that from the leased lands of the temple and from the tithes of war booty, to meet the expenses of the services of the shrine. Usually the temple property in Greece was managed solely by the priests; but the treasure of the Parthenon at Athens formed an exception to this rule. The treasure here belonged to the state, and was controlled and disposed of by the vote of the people. Even the personal property of the goddess, the gold drapery of the statue (see p. 185), which was worth about $600,000, could be used in case of great need, but it must be replaced in due time, with a fair interest.

and founder of Constantinople) was the Nebuchadnezzar who bore
off the sacred vessels and many statues as trophies to his new
capital then rising on the Hellespont.

The Athenian Acropolis and the Parthenon. — In the history
of art there is no other spot in the world possessed of such interest as the flat-topped rock, already described (see p. 118),
which constituted the Athenian Acropolis. We have seen that in
early times the eminence was used as a stronghold. But by the
fifth century B.C. the city had slipped down upon the plain, and
the summit of the rock was consecrated to the temples and the
worship of the deities, and came to be called "the city of the
gods." During the period of Athenian supremacy, especially in

ATHENIAN YOUTH IN PROCESSION.   (From the Frieze of the Parthenon.)

the Periclean Age, Hellenic genius and piety adorned this spot
with temples and statues that all the world has pronounced to be
faultless specimens of beauty and taste.

The most celebrated of the buildings upon the Acropolis was
the Parthenon, the "Residence of the virgin-goddess Athena."
This is considered the finest specimen of Greek architecture. It
was designed by the architect Ictinus, but the sculptures that
adorned it were the work of the celebrated Phidias.[1] It was built

[1] The subject of the wonderful frieze running round the temple was the procession which formed the most important feature of the Athenian festival

RESTORATION OF THE ACROPOLIS OF ATHENS.

in the Doric order, of marble from the neighboring Pentelicus. After standing for more than two thousand years, and having served successively as a Pagan temple, a Christian church, and a Mohammedan mosque, it finally was made to serve as a Turkish powder-magazine, in a war with the Venetians, in 1687. During the progress of this contest a bomb fired the magazine, and more than half of this masterpiece of ancient art was shivered into fragments. The front is nearly perfect, and is the most prominent feature of the Acropolis at the present time.

The Mausoleum at Halicarnassus. — This structure was another of the Seven Wonders of the World. It was a monumental tomb designed to preserve the memory of Mausolus, king of Caria, who died 353 B.C. Its erection was prompted by the love and grief of his wife Artemisia. The combined genius of the most noted artists of the age executed the wish of the queen. It is the traditions of this beautiful structure that have given the world a name for all magnificent monuments raised to perpetuate the memory of the dead.

Theatres. — The most noted of Greek theatres was the Theatre of Dionysus at Athens, which was the model of all the others. It was semi-circular in form, and was partly cut in the rock on the southeastern slope of the Acropolis, the Greeks in the construction of their theatres generally taking advantage of a hillside. There were about one hundred rows of seats, the lowest one, bordering the orchestra, consisting of sixty-seven marble arm-chairs. The structure would hold thirty thousand spectators.

2. SCULPTURE AND PAINTING.

Progress in Sculpture: Influence of the Gymnastic Art. — Wood was the material first employed by the Greek artists. About

known as the Great Panathenæa, which was celebrated every four years in honor of the patron-goddess of Athens. The larger part of the frieze is now in the British Museum, the Parthenon having been despoiled of its coronal of sculptures by Lord Elgin. Read Lord Byron's *The Curse of Minerva*. To the poet, Lord Elgin's act appeared worse than vandalism.

THE THEATRE OF DIONYSUS AT ATHENS. (Restored by G. Rehlender.)

the eighth century B.C. bronze and marble were generally substituted for the less durable material. With this change sculpture began to make rapid progress.

PITCHING THE DISCUS, OR QUOIT.
(Discobolus.)

But what exerted the most positive influence upon Greek sculpture was the gymnastic art. The exercises of the gymnasium and the contests of the sacred games afforded the artist unrivalled opportunities for the study of the human form. "The whole race," as Symonds says, "lived out its sculpture and its painting, rehearsed, as it were, the great works of Phidias and Polygnotus, in physical exercises, before it learned to express itself in marble or in color."

As the sacred buildings increased in number and costliness, the services of the artist were called into requisition for their adornment. At first the temple held only the statue of the god; but after a time it became, as we have already seen, a sort of national museum. The entablature, the pediments, and every niche of the interior of the shrine, as well as the surrounding grounds and groves, were peopled with statues and groups of figures, executed by the most renowned artists, and representing the national deities, the legendary heroes, victors at the public games, or incidents in the life of the state in which piety saw the special interposition of the god in whose honor the shrine had been reared.

Phidias. — Among all the great sculptors of antiquity, Phidias stands pre-eminent. He was an Athenian, and was born about 488 B.C. He delighted in the beautiful myths and legends of the

Heroic Age, and from these he drew subjects for his art. It was his genius that created the wonderful figures of the pediments and the frieze of the Parthenon.

The most celebrated of his colossal sculptures were the statue of Athena within the Parthenon, and that of Olympian Zeus in the temple at Olympia. The statue of Athena was of gigantic size, being about forty feet in height, and was constructed of ivory and gold, the hair, weapons, and drapery being of the latter material.

The statue of Olympian Zeus was also of ivory and gold. It was sixty feet high, and represented the god seated on his throne. The hair, beard, and drapery were of gold. The eyes were brilliant stones. Gems of great value decked the throne, and figures of exquisite design were sculptured on the golden robe. The colossal proportions of this wonderful work, as well as the lofty yet benign aspect of the countenance, harmonized well with the popular conception of the majesty and grace of the "father of gods and men." It was thought a great misfortune to die without having seen the Olympian Zeus.[1]

ATHENA PARTHENOS.

After a statue found at Athens in 1880, which is supposed to be a copy of the colossal statue of Athena by Phidias, described in the text.

[1] Phidias avowed that he took his idea from the representation which Homer gives in the first book of the *Iliad* in the passage thus translated by Pope : —

The statue was in existence for eight hundred years, being finally destroyed by fire in the fifth century A.D.

HEAD OF THE OLYMPIAN ZEUS BY
PHIDIAS.

Phidias also executed other works in both bronze and marble. He met an unworthy fate. Upon the famous shield at the feet of the statue of Athena in the Parthenon, among the figures in the representation of a battle between the Athenians and the Amazons, Phidias introduced a portrait of himself and also one of his patron Pericles. The enemies of the artist caused him to be prosecuted for this, which was considered an act of sacrilege. He died in prison (432 B.C.).

Polycletus. — At the same time that Phidias was executing his ideal representations of the gods, Polycletus the elder, whose home was at Argos, was producing his renowned bronze statues of athletes. Among his pieces was one representing a spear-bearer, which was so perfect as to be known as "the Rule."

Praxiteles. — This artist, after Polycletus, stands next to Phidias as one of the most eminent of Greek sculptors. His works were executed during the fourth century B.C. Among his chief pieces may be mentioned the "Cnidian Aphrodite." This stood in the Temple of Aphrodite at Cnidus, and was regarded by the ancients as the most perfect embodiment of the goddess of beauty. Pilgrimages were made from distant countries to Cnidus for the sake of looking upon the matchless statue.

Lysippus. — This artist is renowned for his works in bronze.

'He spake, and awful bends his sable brow,
   Shakes his ambrosial curls, and gives the nod,
   The stamp of fate, and sanction of the god.
   High heaven with reverence the dread signal took,
   And all Olympus to the centre shook."
                              BULFINCH'S *Age of Fable.*

He flourished about the middle of the fourth century B.C. His statues were in great demand. Many of these were of colossal size. Alexander gave the artist many orders for statues of himself, and also of the heroes that fell in his campaigns.

THE LAOCOÖN GROUP

The Rhodian Colossus and Schools of Art.—The most noted pupil of Lysippus was Chares, who gave to the world the celebrated Colossus at Rhodes (about 280 B.C.). This was another of the wonders of the world. Its height was about one hundred and seven feet, and a man could barely encircle with his arms the thumb of the statue.[1] After standing little more than half a century, it was overthrown by an earthquake. For nine hundred years the Colossus then lay, like a Homeric god, prone upon the ground. Finally, the Arabs, having overrun this part of the Orient (A.D. 672), appropriated the statue, and thriftily sold it to a Jewish merchant. It is said that it required a train of nine hundred camels to bear away the bronze.

This gigantic piece of statuary was not a solitary one at Rhodes; for that city, next after Athens, was the great art centre of the Grecian world. Its streets and gardens and public edifices were literally crowded with statues. The island became the favorite resort of artists, and the various schools there founded acquired a wide renown. Many of the most prized works of Grecian art in our modern museums were executed by members of these Rhodian schools. The "Laocoön Group," found at Rome in 1506, and now in the Museum of the Vatican, is generally thought to be the work of three Rhodian sculptors.

Greek Painting. — Although the Greek artists attained a high degree of excellence in painting, still they probably never brought the art to the perfection which they reached in sculpture. One reason for this was that paintings were never, like statues, objects of adoration ; hence less attention was directed to them.

With the exception of antique vases and a few patches of mural decoration, all specimens of Greek painting have perished. Consequently our knowledge of Greek painting is derived chiefly from the descriptions of renowned works, by the ancient writers, and their anecdotes of great painters.

Polygnotus. — Polygnotus (flourished 475–455 B.C.) has been called the Prometheus of painting, because he was the first to give fire and animation to the expression of the countenance. " In his hand," it is affirmed, " the human features became for the first

---

[1] The statue was not as large as the Statue of Liberty in New York harbor. The height of the latter is 151 feet.

time the mirror of the soul." Of a Polyxena[1] painted by this great master, it was said that "she carried in her eyelids the whole history of the Trojan War."

Zeuxis and Parrhasius. — These great artists lived and painted about 400 B.C. A favorite and familiar story preserves their names as companions, and commemorates their rival genius. Zeuxis, such is the story, painted a cluster of grapes which so closely imitated the real fruit that the birds pecked at them. His rival, for his piece, painted a curtain. Zeuxis asked Parrhasius to draw aside the veil and exhibit his picture. "I confess I am surpassed," generously admitted Zeuxis to his rival; "I deceived birds, but you have deceived the eyes of an experienced artist."

Apelles. — Apelles, who has been called the "Raphael of antiquity," was the court-painter of Alexander the Great. He was such a consummate master of the art of painting, and carried it to such a state of perfection, that the ancient writers spoke of it as the "art of Apelles."

That Apelles, like Zeuxis and Parrhasius, painted life-like pictures is shown by the following story. In a contest between him and some rival artists, horses were the objects represented. Perceiving that the judges were unfriendly to him, and partial, Apelles insisted that less prejudiced judges should pronounce upon the merit of the respective pieces, demanding, at the same time, that the paintings should be shown to some horses that were near. When brought before the pictures of his rival, the horses exhibited no concern; but upon being shown the painting of Apelles, they manifested by neighing and other intelligent signs their instant recognition of the companions the great master had created.

NOTE. — Recent excavations (1878–1886) on the site of ancient Pergamus, in Asia Minor, have brought to light a great Altar, dating seemingly from the second century B.C., whose sides were decorated with gigantic sculptures representing the Battle of the Giants against the Gods. The sculptures, which by some are placed next to those of the Parthenon, are now in the Berlin Museum.

[1] Polyxena was a daughter of the Trojan Priam, famous for her beauty and her sufferings.

CHAPTER XIX.

GREEK LITERATURE.

1. EPIC AND LYRIC POETRY.

The Greeks as Literary Artists. — It was that same exquisite sense of fitness and proportion and beauty which made the Greeks artists in marble that also made them artists in language. "Of all the beautiful things which they created," says Professor Jebb, "their own language was the most beautiful." This language they wrought into epics, lyrics, dramas, histories, and orations as incomparable in form and beauty as their temples and statues.

The Homeric Poems. — The earliest specimens of Greek poetry are the so-called "Homeric poems," consisting of the *Iliad* and the *Odyssey*. The subject of the *Iliad* (from Ilios, Troy) is the "Wrath of Achilles." The *Odyssey* tells of the long wanderings of the hero Odysseus (Ulysses) up and down over many seas while seeking his native Ithaca, after the downfall of Ilios. These poems exerted an incalculable influence upon the literary and religious life of the Hellenic race.

The *Iliad* must be pronounced the world's greatest epic. It has been translated into all languages and has been read with an ever fresh interest by generation after generation for nearly 3000 years. Alexander, it is told, slept with a copy beneath his pillow, — a copy prepared especially for him by his preceptor Aristotle, and called the "casket edition," from the jewelled box in which Alexander is said to have kept it. We preserve it quite as sacredly in all our courses of classical study. The poem has made warriors as well as poets. It incited the military ambition of Alexander, of Hannibal, and of Cæsar ; it inspired Virgil, Dante, and Milton. All epic writers have taken it as their model.

Date and Authorship of the Homeric Poems. — Until the rise of modern German criticism, the *Iliad* and the *Odyssey* were almost universally ascribed to a single bard named Homer, who was believed to have lived about the middle of the ninth or tenth century B.C., one or two centuries after the events commemorated in his poems. Though tradition represents many cities as contending for the honor of having been his birthplace, still he was generally regarded as a native of Smyrna, in Asia Minor. He travelled widely (so it was believed), lost his sight, and then, as a wandering minstrel, sang his immortal verses to admiring listeners in the different cities of Hellas.

HOMER.

But it is now the opinion of many scholars that the *Iliad* and the *Odyssey*, as they stand to-day, are not, either of them, the creation of a single poet. They are believed to be mosaics; that is, to be built up out of the fragments of an extensive ballad literature that grew up in an age preceding the Homeric. The "Wrath of Achilles," which forms the nucleus of the *Iliad* as we have it, may, with very great probability, be ascribed to Homer, whom we may believe to have been the most prominent of a brotherhood of bards who flourished about 850 or 750 B.C.

The Hesiodic Poems. — Hesiod, who lived a century or more after the age that gave birth to the Homeric poems, was the poet of nature and of real life, especially of peasant life, in the dim transition age of Hellas. The Homeric bards sing of the deeds of heroes, and of a far-away time when gods mingled with men.

Hesiod sings of common men, and of every-day, present duties. His greatest poem, a didactic epic, is entitled *Works and Days.* This is, in the main, a sort of farmers' calendar, in which the poet points out to the husbandman the lucky and unlucky days for doing certain kinds of work, eulogizes industry, and intersperses among all his practical lines homely maxims of morality and beautiful descriptive passages of the changing seasons.

Lyric Poetry: Pindar. — The Æolian island of Lesbos was the hearth and home of the earlier lyric poets. Among the earliest of the Lesbian singers was the poetess Sappho, whom the Greeks exalted to a place next to Homer. Plato calls her the Tenth Muse. Although her fame endures, her poetry, except some mere fragments, has perished.

Anacreon was a courtier at the time of the Greek tyrannies. He was a native of Ionia, but passed much of his time at the court of Polycrates of Samos. He seems to have enjoyed to the full the gay and easy life of a courtier, and sung so voluptuously of love and wine and festivity that the term "Anacreontic" has come to be used to characterize all poetry over-redolent of these themes.

But the greatest of the Greek lyric poets, and perhaps the greatest of all lyric poets of every age and race, was Pindar (about 522–443 B.C.). He was born at Thebes, but spent most of his time in the cities of Magna Græcia. Such was the reverence in which his memory was held that when Alexander, one hundred years after Pindar's time, levelled the city of Thebes to the ground on account of a revolt, the house of the poet was spared, and left standing amid the general ruin (see p. 161). The greater number of Pindar's poems were inspired by the scenes of the national festivals. They describe in lofty strains the splendors of the Olympian chariot-races, or the glory of the victors at the Isthmian, the Nemean, or the Pythian games.

Pindar insists strenuously upon virtue and self-culture. With deep meaning he says, "Become that which thou art;" that is, be that which you are made to be.

2. The Drama and Dramatists.

Origin of the Greek Drama. — The Greek drama, in both its branches of tragedy and comedy, grew out of the songs and dances instituted in honor of the god of wine — Dionysus (the same as the Roman Bacchus).

Tragedy (goat-song, possibly from the accompanying sacrifice of a goat) sprang from the graver songs, and comedy (village-song) from the lighter and more farcical ones. Gradually, recital and dialogue were added, there being at first but a single speaker, then two, and finally three, which last was the classical number.

Thespis (about 536 b.c.) is said to have introduced this idea of the dialogue; hence the term "Thespian" applied to the tragic drama.

Owing to its origin, the Greek drama always retained a religious character, and

BACCHIC PROCESSION.

further, presented two distinct features, the chorus (the songs and dances) and the dialogue. At first, the chorus was the all-important part; but later, the dialogue became the more prominent portion, the chorus, however, always remaining an essential feature of the performance. Finally, in the golden age of the Attic stage, the chorus dancers and singers were carefully trained, at great expense, and the dialogue became the masterpiece of some great poet, — and then the Greek drama, the most splendid creation of human genius, was complete.

The Three Great Tragic Poets. — There are three great names in Greek tragedy, — Æschylus, Sophocles, and Euripides. These dramatists all wrote during the splendid period which followed the victories of the Persian war, when the intellectual life of all Hellas, and especially that of Athens, was strung to the highest tension. This lent nervous power and intensity to almost all they wrote, particularly to the tragedies of Æschylus and Sophocles. Of the two hundred and more dramas produced by these poets, only thirty-two have escaped the accidents of time.

Æschylus (525–456 B.C.) knew how to touch the hearts of the generation that had won the victories of the Persian war; for he had fought with honor both at Marathon and at Salamis. But it was on a very different arena that he was destined to win his most enduring fame. Eleven times did he carry off the prize in tragic composition. The Athenians called him the "Father of Tragedy."

ÆSCHYLUS.

The central idea of his dramas is that "no mortal may dare raise his heart too high,'—that "Zeus tames excessive lifting up of heart.' *Prometheus Bound* is one of his chief works. Another of his great tragedies is *Agamemnon*, thought by some to be his masterpiece. The subject is the crime of Clytemnestra (see p. 96). It is a tragedy crowded with spirit-shaking terrors, and filled with more than human crimes and woes. Nowhere is portrayed with greater power the awful vengeance with which the implacable Nemesis is armed.

Sophocles (495–405 B.C.) while yet a youth gained the prize in a poetic contest with Æschylus. Plutarch says that Æschylus was so chagrined by his defeat that he left Athens and retired to Sicily. Sophocles now became the leader of tragedy at Athens. In almost every contest he carried away the first prize. He lived through nearly a century, a century, too, that comprised the most brilliant period of the life of Hellas. His dramas were perfect works of art. The leading idea of his pieces is the same as that which characterizes those of Æschylus; namely, that self-will and insolent pride arouse the righteous indignation of the gods, and that no mortal can contend successfully against the will of Zeus.

Euripides (485–406 B.C.) was a more popular drama- tist than either Æschylus or Sophocles. His fame passed far beyond the limits of Greece. Herodotus asserts that the verses of the poet were recited by the natives of the remote country of Ge- drosia ; and Plutarch says that the Sicilians were so fond of his lines that many of the Athenian prisoners, taken before Syracuse, bought their liberty by teaching their mas- ters his verses.

Comedy: Aristophanes.— Foremost among all writers of comedy must be placed Aristophanes (about 444– 380 B.C.). He introduces us to the every-day life of the least admirable classes of Athenian society. Four of his most noted works are the *Clouds*, the *Knights*, the *Birds*, and the *Wasps*.

SOPHOCLES.

In the comedy of the *Clouds*, Aristophanes especially ridicules the Sophists, a school of philosophers and teachers just then rising into prominence at Athens, of whom the satirist unfairly makes Socrates the representative.

The aim of the *Knights* was the punishment and ruin of Cleon, whom we already know as one of the most conceited and insolent of the demagogues of Athens.

The play of the *Birds* is "the everlasting allegory of foolish

sham and flimsy ambition." It was aimed particularly at the ambitious Sicilian schemes of Alcibiades; for at the time the play appeared, the Athenian army was before Syracuse, and elated by good news daily arriving, the Athenians were building the most gorgeous air-castles, and indulging in the most extravagant day-dreams of universal dominion.

In the *Wasps*, the poet satirizes the proceedings in the Athenian law-courts, by showing how the great citizen-juries, numbering sometimes

EURIPIDES.

five or six hundred, were befooled by the demagogues. But Aristophanes was something more than a master of mere mirth-provoking satire and ridicule: many of the choruses of his pieces are inexpressibly tender and beautiful.

3. History and Historians.

Poetry is the first form of literary expression among all peoples. So we must not be surprised to find that it was not until several centuries after the composition of the Homeric poems — that is, about the sixth century B.C. — that prose-writing appeared among the Greeks. Historical composition was then first cultivated. We can speak briefly of only three historians, — Herodotus, Thucydides and Xenophon, — whose names were cherished among the ancients, and whose writings are highly valued and carefully studied by ourselves.

HERODOTUS.

Herodotus. — Herodotus (about 484–402 B.C.), born at Halicarnassus, in Asia Minor, is called the " Father of History." He travelled over much of the then known world, visiting Italy, Egypt, and Babylonia, and as an eye-witness describes with a never-failing vivacity and freshness the wonders of the different lands he had seen. Herodotus lived in a story-telling age, and he is himself an inimitable story-teller. To him we are indebted for a large part of the tales of antiquity — stories of men and events which we never tire of repeating. He was over-credulous, and was often imposed upon by his guides in Egypt and at Babylon ; but he describes with great care and accuracy what he himself saw. It is sometimes very difficult, however, to determine just what he actually did see with his own eyes and experience in his own person ; for it seems certain that, following the custom of the story-tellers of his time, he often related as his own personal adventures the experiences of others, yet with no thought of deceiving. In this he might be likened to our modern writers of historical romances.

The central theme of his great History is the Persian wars, the struggle between Asia and Greece. Around this he groups the several stories of the nations of antiquity. In the pictures which the artist-historian draws, we see vividly contrasted, as in no other writings, the East and the West, Persia and Hellas.

Thucydides. — Thucydides (about 471–400 B.C.), though not so popular an historian as Herodotus, was a much more philosophical one. He was born near Athens. A pretty story is told of his youth, which must be repeated, though critics have pronounced it fabulous. The tale is that Thucydides, when only fifteen, was taken by his father to hear Herodotus recite his history at the Olympian games, and that the reading and the accompanying applause caused the boy to shed tears, and to resolve to become an historian.

THUCYDIDES.

Thucydides was engaged in military service during the first years of the Peloponnesian War ; but, on account of his being unfortunate, possibly through his own neglect, the Athenians deprived him of his command, and he went into an exile of twenty years. It is to this circumstance that we are indebted for his invaluable *History of the War between the Peloponnesians and the Athenians*.

Through the closest observation and study, he qualified himself to become the historian of what he from the first foresaw would prove a memorable war. " I lived," he says, " through its whole extent, in the very flower of my understanding and strength, and with a close application of my thoughts, to gain an exact insight into all its occurrences." He died before his task was completed. The work is considered a model of historical writing. Demosthenes read and re-read his writings to improve his own style ; and the greatest orators and historians of modern times have been equally diligent students of the work of the great Athenian.

Xenophon. — Xenophon (about 445–355 B.C.) was an Athenian, and is known both as a general and a writer. The works that render his name so familiar are his *Anabasis*, a simple yet thrilling narrative of the Expedition of the Ten Thousand Greeks ; and his *Memorabilia*, or Recollections of Socrates. This work by his devoted pupil is the most faithful portraiture that we possess of that philosopher.

4. ORATORY.

Influence of the Public Assembly. — The art of oratory among the Greeks was fostered and developed by the democratic character of their institutions. The public assemblies of the democratic cities were great debating clubs, open to all. The gift of eloquence secured for its possessor a sure pre-eminence. The law-courts, too, especially the great jury-courts of Athens, were schools of oratory ; for every citizen was obliged to be his own advocate and to defend his own case. Hence the attention bestowed upon public speaking, and the high degree of perfection attained by the Greeks in the difficult art of persuasion. Almost all the prominent Athenian statesmen were masters of oratory.

Themistocles and Pericles. — We have already become acquainted with Themistocles and Pericles as statesmen and leaders of Athenian affairs during the most stirring period of the history of Athens. They both were also great orators, and to that fact were largely indebted for their power and influence. Thucydides has preserved the oration delivered by Pericles in commemoration of those who fell in the first year of the Peloponnesian War. It is an incomparable picture of the beauty and glory of Athens at the zenith of her power, and has been pronounced one of the finest productions of antiquity. The language of the address, as we have it, is the historian's, but the sentiments are doubtless those of the great statesman. It was the habit of Thucydides to put speeches into the mouths of his characters.

DEMOSTHENES.

Demosthenes and Æschines. — It has been the fortune of Demosthenes (385-322 B.C.) to have his name become throughout the world the synonym of eloquence. The labors and struggles by which, according to tradition, he achieved excellence in his art are held up anew to each generation of youth as guides of the path to success. His first address before the public assembly was a complete failure, owing to defects of voice and manner. With indomitable will he set himself to the task of correcting these. He shut himself up in a cave, and gave himself to the diligent study of Thucydides. That he might not be tempted to spend his time in society, he rendered his appearance ridiculous by shaving one side of his head. To correct a stammering utterance, he spoke with pebbles in his mouth, and broke himself of an ungainly habit of shrugging his shoulders by speaking beneath a suspended sword. To accustom himself to the tumult and interruptions of a public assembly, he declaimed upon the noisiest seashore.

These are some of the many stories told of the world's greatest orator. There is doubtless this much truth in them at least — that Demosthenes attained success, in spite of great discouragements, by persevering and laborious effort. It is certain that he was a most diligent student of Thucydides, whose great history he is said to have known by heart. More than sixty of his orations have been preserved. "Of all human productions they present to us the models which approach the nearest to perfection."

The latter part of the life of Demosthenes is intertwined with that of another and rival Athenian orator, Æschines. For his services to the state, the Athenians proposed to award to Demosthenes a golden crown. Æschines opposed this. All Athens and strangers from far and near gathered to hear the rival orators; for every matter at Athens was decided by a great debate. Demosthenes made the grandest effort of his life. His address, known as the "Oration on the Crown," has been declared to be "the most polished and powerful effort of human oratory." Æschines was completely crushed, and was sent into exile, and became a teacher of oratory at Rhodes.

He is said to have once gathered his disciples about him and to have read to them the oration of Demosthenes that had proved so fatal to himself. Carried away by the torrent of its eloquence, his pupils, unable to restrain their enthusiasm, burst into applause. "Ah!" said Æschines, who seemed to find solace in the fact that his defeat had been at the hands of so worthy an antagonist, "you should have heard the wild beast himself!"

Respecting the orations of Demosthenes against Philip of Macedon, and the death of the eloquent patriot, we have already spoken
(see pp. 160, 174).

5. THE ALEXANDRIAN AGE.

The Alexandrian period of Greek literature embraces the time
between the break-up of Alexander's empire and the conquest
of Greece by Rome (300-146
B.C.). During this period Alexandria in Egypt was the centre of literary activity, hence the
term *Alexandrian*, applied to
the literature of the age. The
great Museum and Library of
the Ptolemies afforded in that
capital such facilities for students and authors as existed in
no other city in the world.

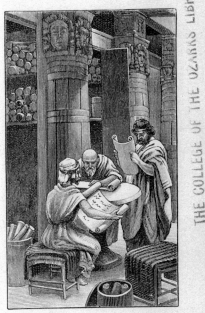

But the creative age of Greek
literature was over. With the
loss of political liberty, literature was cut off from its sources
of inspiration. Consequently
the Alexandrian literature
lacked freshness and originality. The writers of the period
were grammarians, commenta-
tors, and translators, — in a
word, book-worms.

IDEAL SCENE IN THE ALEXANDRIAN
LIBRARY.

One of the most important literary undertakings of the age was
the translation of the Old Testament into Greek. From the traditional number of translators (seventy) the version is known as
the *Septuagint* (Latin for seventy.) The work was probably begun by Ptolemy Philadelphus, and was completed under his successors.

Among the poets of the period one name, and only one, stands out clear and pre-eminent. This is that of Theocritus, a Sicilian idyllist, who wrote at Alexandria under Ptolemy Philadelphus. His idyls are beautiful pictures of Sicilian pastoral life.

Conclusion : Græco-Roman writers. — After the Roman conquest of Greece, the centre of Greek literary activity shifted from Alexandria to Rome. Hence Greek literature now passes into what is known as its Græco-Roman period (146 B.C.–527 A.D.).

The most noted historical writer of the first part of this period was Polybius (about 203–121 B.C.), who wrote a history of the Roman conquests from 264 to 146 B.C. His work, though the larger part of it has reached us in a very mutilated state, is of great worth ; for Polybius wrote of matters that had become history in his own day. He had lived to see the larger part of the world he knew absorbed by the ever-growing power of the Imperial City.

Plutarch (b. about 40 A.D.), " the prince of ancient biographers," will always live in literature as the author of the *Parallel Lives*, in which, with great wealth of illustrative anecdotes, he compares or contrasts Greek and Roman statesmen and soldiers.

CHAPTER XX.

GREEK PHILOSOPHY AND SCIENCE.

The Seven Sages; the Forerunners. — About the sixth century B.C. there lived and taught in different parts of Hellas many philosophers of real or reputed originality and wisdom. Among these were seven men, called the "Seven Sages," who held the place of pre-eminence.[1] To them belongs the distinction of having first aroused the Greek intellect to philosophical thought. The wise sayings — such as "Know thyself" and "Nothing in excess" — attributed to them, are beyond number.

The ethical maxims and practical proverbs ascribed to the sages, while, like the so-called proverbs of Solomon, they contain a vast amount of practical wisdom, still do not constitute philosophy proper, which is a systematic search for the reason and causes of things. They form simply the introduction or prelude to Greek philosophy.

The Ionic Philosophers. — The first Greek school of philosophy grew up in the cities of Ionia, in Asia Minor, where almost all forms of Hellenic culture seem to have had their beginning. The founder of the system was Thales of Miletus (about 640–550 B.C.), who was followed by Anaximander, Anaximenes, and Heraclitus.

One tenet held in common by all these philosophers was that matter and mind are inseparable; or, in other words, that all matter is animate. They never thought of the soul as something distinct and separable from matter as we do. Even the soul in

---

[1] As in the case of the Seven Wonders of the World, ancient writers were not always agreed as to what names should be accorded the honor of enrolment in the sacred number. Thales, Solon, Periander, Cleobulus, Chilo, Bias, and Pittacus are, however, usually reckoned as the Seven Wise Men.

Hades was conceived as having a body in every respect like that the soul possessed in the earthly life, only it was composed of a subtler substance. This conception of matter as being alive will help us to understand Greek mythology, which, it will be remembered, endowed trees, rivers, springs, clouds, the planets, all physical objects indeed, with intelligence and will.

Pythagoras. — Pythagoras (about 580–500 B.C.) was born on the island of Samos, whence his title of "Samian Sage." Probable tradition says that he spent many years of his early life in Egypt, where he became versed in all the mysteries of the Egyptians. He returned to Greece with a great reputation, and finally settled at Crotona, in Italy.

Like many another ancient philosopher, Pythagoras sought to increase the reverence of his disciples for himself by peculiarities of dress and manner. His uncut hair and beard flowed down upon his shoulders and over his breast. He never smiled. His dress was a white robe, with a golden crown. For the first years of their novitiate, his pupils were not allowed to look upon their master. They listened to his lectures from behind a curtain. *Ipse dixit,* "he himself said so," was the only argument they must employ in debate. It is to Pythagoras, according to legend, that we are indebted for the word *philosopher.* Being asked of what he was master, he replied that he was simply a "philosopher," that is, a "lover of wisdom."

Pythagoras held views of the solar system that anticipated by two thousand years those of Copernicus and his school. He taught, only to his most select pupils however, that the earth is a sphere; and that, like the other planets, it revolves about a central globe of fire. From him comes the pretty conceit of the "music of the spheres." He imagined that the heavenly spheres, by their swift, rolling motions, produced musical notes, which united in a celestial melody, too refined, however, for human ears.

He taught the doctrine of the transmigration of souls, an idea he had doubtless brought from Egypt. Because of this belief the

Pythagoreans were strict vegetarians, abstaining religiously from the use of all animal food.

Anaxagoras. — Anaxagoras (499–427 B.C.) was the first Greek philosopher who made *mind*, instead of necessity or chance, the arranging and harmonizing force of the universe. " Reason rules the world " was his first maxim.

Anaxagoras was the teacher in philosophy of Pericles, and it is certain that that statesman was greatly influenced by the liberal views of the philosopher ; for in his general conceptions of the universe, Anaxagoras was far in advance of his age. He ventured to believe that the moon was somewhat like the earth, and inhabited ; and taught that the sun was not a god, but a glowing rock, as large, probably, as the Peloponnesus.

But for his audacity, the philosopher suffered the fate of Galileo in a later age ; he was charged with impiety and exiled. Yet this did not disturb the serenity of his mind. In banishment he said, " It is not I who have lost the Athenians, but the Athenians who have lost me."

Empedocles and Democritus. — In the teachings of Empedocles (about 492–432 B.C.) and Democritus (about 460–370 B.C.) we meet with many speculations respecting the constitution of matter and the origin of things which are startlingly similar to some of the doctrines held by modern scientists. Empedocles, with the evolutionists of to-day, taught that the higher forms of life arise out of the lower ; Democritus conceived all things to be composed of invisible atoms, all alike in quality, but differing in form and combination.

The Sophists. — The Sophists, of whom the most noted were Protagoras, Gorgias, and Prodicus, were a class of philosophers or teachers who gave instruction in rhetoric and the art of disputation. They travelled about from city to city, and contrary to the usual custom of the Greek philosophers, took fees from their pupils. They were shallow but brilliant men, caring more for the dress in which the thought was arrayed than for the thought itself, more for victory than for truth ; and some of them inculcated a selfish morality. The better philosophers of the time despised them, and applied to them many harsh epithets, taunting them with selling wisdom, and accusing them of boasting that they could "make the worse appear the better reason."

Socrates. — Volumes would not contain what would be both instructive and interesting respecting the lives and works of the three great philosophers Socrates, Plato, and Aristotle. We can, however, accord to each only a few words. Of these three eminent thinkers, Socrates (469–399 B.C.), though surpassed in grasp

SOCRATES.

and power of intellect by both Plato and Aristotle, has the firmest hold upon the affections of the world.

Nature, while generous to the philosopher in the gifts of soul, was unkind to him in the matter of his person. His face was ugly as a satyr's, and he had an awkward, shambling walk, so that he invited the shafts of the comic poets of his time. He loved to gather a little circle about him in the Agora or in the streets, and then to draw out his listeners by a series of ingenious questions. His method was so peculiar to himself that it has received the designation of the "Socratic dialogue." He has very happily been called an *educator*, as opposed to an *instructor*. In the young men of his time Socrates found many devoted pupils. The youthful Alcibiades declared that " he was forced to stop his ears and flee away, that he might not sit down by the side of Socrates and grow old in listening."

Socrates was unfortunate in his domestic relations. Xanthippe, his wife, seems to have been of a practical turn of mind, and unable to sympathize with the abstracted ways of her husband.

This great philosopher believed that the proper study of mankind is man, his favorite maxim being " Know Thyself "; hence he is said to have brought philosophy from the heavens and introduced it to the homes of men.

Socrates held the Sophists in aversion, and in opposition to their selfish expediency taught the purest system of morals that the world had yet known, and which has been surpassed only by the precepts of the Great Teacher. He thought himself to be restrained from entering upon what was inexpedient or wrong by a tutelary spirit. He believed in the immortality of the soul and in a Supreme Ruler of the universe, but sometimes spoke slightingly of the temples and the popular deities. This led to his prosecution on the double charge of blasphemy and of corrupting the Athenian youth. The fact that Alcibiades had been his pupil was used to prove the demoralizing tendency of his teachings. He was condemned to drink the fatal hemlock. The night before his death he spent with his disciples, discoursing on the immortality of the soul.

Plato. — Plato (429–348 B.C.), "the broad-browed," was a philosopher of noble birth, before whom in youth a brilliant career in the world of Greek affairs opened ; but, coming under the influence of Socrates, he resolved to give up all his prospects in politics and devote himself to philosophy. Upon the condemnation and death of his master he went into voluntary exile. In many lands he gathered knowledge and met with varied experiences. He visited Sicily, where he was so unfortunate as to call upon himself the resentment of Dionysius, tyrant of Syracuse, through having worsted him in an argument, and also by an uncourtly plainness of speech. The king caused him to be sold into slavery

PLATO.

as a prisoner of war. Being ransomed by a friend, he found his way to his native Athens, and established a school of philosophy in the Academy, a public garden close to Athens. Here amid the disciples that thronged to his lectures, he passed the greater part of his long life, — he died 348 B.C., at the age of eighty-one years, — laboring incessantly upon the great works that bear his name.

Plato imitated in his writings the method of Socrates in conversation. The discourse is carried on by questions and answers, hence the term *Dialogues* that attaches to his works. He attributes to his master, Socrates, much of the philosophy that he teaches : yet his *Dialogues* are all deeply tinged with his own genius and thought. In the *Republic* Plato portrays his conception of an ideal state. He was opposed to the republic of Athens, and his system, in some of its main features, was singularly like the Feudal System of mediæval Europe.

The *Phædo* is a record of the last conversation of Socrates with his disciples — an immortal argument for the immortality of the soul.

Plato believed not only in a future life (post-existence), but also in pre-existence ; teaching that the ideas of reason, or our intuitions, are reminiscences of a past experience.[1] Plato's doctrines have exerted a profound influence upon all schools of thought and philosophies since his day. In some of his precepts he made a close approach to the teachings of Christianity. " We ought to become like God," he said, " as far as this is possible ; and to become like Him is to become holy and just and wise."

Aristotle. — As Socrates was surpassed by his pupil Plato, so in turn was Plato excelled in certain respects by his disciple Aristotle, " the master of those who know." In him the philosophical genius of the Hellenic intellect reached its culmination. He was born in the

---

[1] In the following lines from Wordsworth we catch a glimpse of Plato's doctrine of pre-existence : —

> " Our birth is but a sleep and a forgetting;
> The soul that rises with us, our life's star,
>   Hath had elsewhere its setting,
>   And cometh from afar:
>   Not in entire forgetfulness,
>   Nor yet in utter nakedness,
> But trailing clouds of glory, do we come
> From God, who is our home." — *Ode on Immortality.*

Macedonian city of Stagira (384 B.C.), and hence is frequently called the "Stagirite." As in the case of Socrates, his personal appearance gave no promise of the philosopher. His teacher, Plato, however, recognized the genius of his pupil, and called him the "Mind of the school."

ARISTOTLE.

After studying for twenty years in the school of Plato, Aristotle became the preceptor of Alexander the Great. When Philip invited him to become the tutor of his son, he gracefully complimented the philosopher by saying in his letter that he was grateful to the gods that the prince was born in the same age with him. Alexander became the liberal patron of his tutor, and aided him in his scientific studies by sending him large collections of plants and animals, gathered on his distant expeditions.

At Athens the great philosopher delivered his lectures while walking about beneath the trees and porticoes of the Lyceum; hence the term *peripatetic* (from the Greek *peripatein*, " to walk about") applied to his philosophy.

Among the productions of his fertile intellect are works on rhetoric, logic, poetry, morals and politics, physics and metaphysics. For centuries his works were studied and copied and commented upon by both European and Asiatic scholars, in the schools of Athens and Rome, of Alexandria and Constantinople. Until the time of Bacon in England, for nearly two thousand years, Aristotle ruled over the realm of mind with a despotic sway. All teachers and philosophers acknowledged him as their guide and master.

Zeno and the Stoics. — We are now approaching the period when the political life of Hellas was failing, and was being fast overshadowed by the greatness of Rome. But the intellectual life of the Greek race was by no means eclipsed by the calamity that ended its political existence. For centuries after that event the poets, scholars, and philosophers of this intellectual people led a brilliant career in the schools and universities of the Roman world.

From among all the philosophers of this long period, we can select for brief mention only a few. And first we shall speak of Zeno and Epicurus, who are noted as founders of schools of philosophy that exerted a vast influence upon both the thought and the conduct of many centuries.

Zeno, founder of the celebrated school of the Stoics, lived in the third century before our era (about 362–264). He taught at Athens in a public porch (in Greek, *stoa*), from which circumstance comes the name applied to his disciples.

The Stoical philosophy was the outgrowth, in part at least, of that of the Cynics, a sect of most rigid and austere morals. The typical representative of this sect is found in Diogenes, who lived, so the story goes, in a tub, and went about Athens by daylight with a lantern, in search, as he said, of a *man*. The Cynics were simply a race of pagan hermits.

The Stoics inculcated virtue for the sake of itself. They believed — and it would be very difficult to frame a better creed — that "man's chief business here is to do his duty." They schooled themselves to bear with perfect composure any lot that destiny might appoint. Any sign of emotion on account of calamity was considered unmanly and unphilosophical. Thus, when told of the sudden death of his son, the Stoic replied, "Well, I never imagined that I had given life to an immortal."

Stoicism became a favorite system of thought with certain classes of the Romans, and under its teachings and doctrines were nourished some of the purest and loftiest characters produced by the pagan world. It numbered among its representatives, in later times, the illustrious Roman emperor Marcus Aurelius, and the scarcely less renowned and equally virtuous slave Epictetus. In many of its teachings it anticipated Christian doctrines, and was, in the philosophical world, a very important preparation for Christianity.

Epicurus and the Epicureans. — Epicurus (342–270 B.C.), who was a contemporary of Zeno, taught, in opposition to the Stoics, that *pleasure* is the highest good.
He recommended virtue, indeed, but only as a means for the attainment of pleasure; whereas the Stoics made virtue an end in itself. In other words, Epicurus said, " Be virtuous, because virtue will bring you the greatest amount of happiness "; Zeno said, " Be virtuous, because you ought to be."

EPICURUS.

Epicurus had many followers in Greece, and his doctrines were eagerly embraced by many among the Romans during the corrupt period of the Roman empire. Many of these disciples carried the doctrines of their master to an excess that he himself would have been the first to condemn. Allowing full indulgence to every appetite and passion, their whole philosophy was expressed in the proverb, " Let us eat and drink, for to-morrow we die." No pure or exalted life could be nourished in the unwholesome atmosphere of such a philosophy. Epicureanism never produced a single great character.

The Skeptics; Pyrrho. — About the beginning of the third century B.C. skepticism became widespread in Greece. It seemed as though men were losing faith in everything. Many circumstances had worked together in bringing about this state of universal unbelief. A wider knowledge of the world had caused many to lose their faith in the myths and legends of the old mythologies.

The existence of so many opposing systems of philosophy caused men to doubt the truth of any of them. Many thoughtful minds were hopelessly asking, "What is truth?"

Pyrrho (about 360–270 B.C.) was the doubting Thomas of the Greeks. He questioned everything, and declared that the great problems of the universe could not be solved. He asserted that it was the duty of man, and the part of wisdom, to entertain no positive judgment on any matter, and thus to ensure serenity and peace of mind.

The disciples of Pyrrho went to absurd lengths in their skepticism, some of them even saying that they asserted nothing, not even that they asserted nothing. They doubted whether they doubted.

The Neo-Platonists. — Neo-Platonism was a blending of Greek philosophy and Oriental mysticism. It has been well called the "despair of reason," because it abandoned all hope of man's ever being able to attain the *highest* knowledge through reason alone, and looked for a Revelation. The centre of this last movement in Greek philosophical thought was Alexandria in Egypt, the meeting-place, in the closing centuries of the ancient world, of the East and the West.

Philo the Jew (b. about 30 B.C.), who labored to harmonize Hebrew doctrines with the teachings of Plato, was the forerunner of the Neo-Platonists. But the greatest of the school was Plotinus (A.D. 204–269), who spent the last years of his life at Rome, where he was a great favorite.

Conflict between Neo-Platonism and Christianity. — While the Neo-Platonists were laboring to restore, in modified form, the ancient Greek philosophy and worship, the teachers of Christianity were fast winning the world over to a new faith. The two systems came into deadly antagonism. Christianity triumphed. The gifted and beautiful Hypatia, almost the last representative of the old system of speculation and belief, was torn to pieces in the streets of Alexandria by a mob of fanatic Christian monks (A.D. 415). Finally the Roman emperor Justinian forbade the pagan philosophers to teach their doctrines (A.D. 529). This imperial edict closed forever the Greek schools, in which for more than a thousand years the world had received instruction upon the loftiest themes that can engage the human mind. The Greek philosophers, as living, personal teachers, had finished their work; but their systems of thought will never cease to attract and influence the best minds of the race.

SCIENCE AMONG THE GREEKS.

The contributions of the Greek observers to the physical sciences have laid us under no small obligation to them. Some of those whom we have classed as philosophers, were careful students of nature, and might be called scientists. The great philosopher Aristotle wrote some valuable works on anatomy and natural history. From his time onward the sciences were pursued with much zeal and success. Especially did the later Greeks do much good and lasting work in the mathematical sciences.

Mathematics: Euclid and Archimedes. — Alexandria, in Egypt, became the seat of the most celebrated school of mathematics of antiquity. Here, under Ptolemy Lagus, flourished Euclid, the great geometer, whose work forms the basis of the science of geometry as taught in our schools at the present time. Ptolemy himself was his pupil. The royal student, however, seems to have disliked the severe application required to master the problems of Euclid, and asked his teacher if there was not some easier way. Euclid replied, "There is no royal road to geometry."

In the third century B.C., Syracuse, in Sicily, was the home of Archimedes, the greatest mathematician that the Grecian world produced.

Astronomy. — Among ancient Greek astronomers, Aristarchus, Hipparchus, and Claudius Ptolemy are distinguished.

Aristarchus of Samos, who lived in the third century B.C., held that the earth revolves about the sun as a fixed centre, and rotates on its own axis. He was the Greek Copernicus. But his theory was rejected by his contemporaries and successors.

Hipparchus, who flourished about the middle of the second century B.C., was, through his careful observations, the real founder of scientific astronomy. He calculated eclipses, catalogued the stars, and wrote several astronomical works of a really scientific character.

Claudius Ptolemy lived in Egypt about the middle of the second century after Christ. His great reputation is due not so much to his superior genius as to the fortunate circumstance that a vast work compiled by him, preserved and transmitted to later times almost all the knowledge of the ancients on astronomical and geographical subjects. In this way it has happened that his name has become attached to various doctrines and views respecting the universe, though these probably were not originated by him. The phrase *Ptolemaic system*, however, links his name inseparably with that conception of the solar system set forth in his works, which continued to be the received theory from his time until Copernicus — fourteen centuries later.

Ptolemy combated the theory of Aristarchus in regard to the rotation and revolution of the earth ; yet he believed the earth to be a globe, and supported this view by exactly the same arguments that we to-day use to prove the doctrine.

CHAPTER XXI.

SOCIAL LIFE OF THE GREEKS.

Education. — Education at Sparta, where it was chiefly gymnastic, as we have seen (p. 115), was a state affair; but at Athens and throughout Greece generally, the youth were trained in private schools. These schools were of all grades, ranging from those kept by the most obscure teachers, who gathered their pupils in some recess of the street, to those established in the Athenian Academy and Lyceum by such philosophers as Plato and Aristotle.

A GREEK SCHOOL. (After a vase-painting.)

It was only the boys who received education. These Grecian boys, Professor Mahaffy imagines, were "the most attractive the world has ever seen." At all events, we may believe that they were trained more carefully and delicately than the youth among any other people before or since the days of Hellenic culture.

In the nursery, the boy was taught the beautiful myths and stories of the national mythology. At about seven he entered school, being led to and from the place of training by an old slave, who bore the name of *pedagogue,* which in Greek means a guide or leader of boys — not a teacher. His studies were grammar, music, and gymnastics, the aim of the course being to secure a symmetrical development of mind and body alike.

Grammar included reading, writing, and arithmetic ; music, which embraced a wide range of mental accomplishments, trained the boy to appreciate the masterpieces of the great poets, to contribute his part to the musical diversions of private entertainments, and to join in the sacred choruses and in the pæan of the battle-field. The exercises of the palestræ and the gymnasia trained him for the Olympic contests, or for those sterner hand-to-hand battle-struggles, in which so much depended upon personal strength and dexterity.

Upon reaching maturity, the youth was enrolled in the list of citizens. But his graduation from school was his " commencement " in a much more real sense than with the average modern graduate. Never was there a people besides the Greeks whose daily life was so emphatically a discipline in liberal culture. The schools of the philosophers, the debates of the popular assembly, the practice of the law-courts, the religious processions, the representations of an unrivalled stage, the Panhellenic games — all these were splendid and efficient educational agencies, which produced and maintained a standard of average intelligence and culture among the citizens of the Greek cities that probably has never been attained among any other people on the earth. Freeman, quoted approvingly by Mahaffy, says that " the average intelligence of the assembled Athenian citizens was higher than that of our [the English] House of Commons."

Social Position of Woman. — Woman's social position in ancient Greece may be defined in general as being about half-way between Oriental seclusion and Western freedom. Her main duties were to cook and spin, and to oversee the domestic slaves, of whom she herself was practically one. In the fashionable society of Ionian cities, she was seldom allowed to appear in public, or to meet, even in her own house, the male friends of her husband. In Sparta, however, and in Dorian states generally, she was accorded much greater freedom, and was a really important factor in society.

The low position generally assigned the wife in the home had a most disastrous effect upon Greek morals. She could exert no such elevating or refining influence as she casts over the modern home. The men were led to seek social and intellectual sympathy and companionship outside the family circle, among a class of women known as Hetairæ, who were esteemed chiefly for their brilliancy of intellect. As the most noted representative of this class stands Aspasia, the friend of Pericles. The influence of the Hetairæ was most harmful to social morality.

Theatrical Entertainments. — Among the ancient Greeks the theatre was a state establishment, "a part of the constitution." This arose from the religious origin and character of the drama (see p. 193), all matters pertaining to the popular worship being the care and concern of the state. Theatrical performances, being religious acts, were presented only during religious festivals, and were attended by all classes, rich and poor, men, women, and children. The women, however, except the Hetairæ, were, it would seem, permitted to witness tragedies only; the comic stage was too gross to allow of their presence. The spectators sat under the open sky; and the pieces followed one after the other in close succession from early morning till nightfall.

GREEK TRAGIC FIGURE.

There were companies of players who strolled about the country, just as the English actors of Shakespeare's time were wont to do. While the better class of actors were highly honored, ordinary players were held in very low esteem. The tragic actor increased his height and size by wearing thick-soled buskins, an enormous mask, and padded garments. The actor in comedy wore thin-soled slippers, or socks. The *sock* being thus a characteristic part of the make-up of the ancient comic actor, and the *buskin* that of the tragic actor, these foot coverings have come to be used as the symbols respectively of comedy and tragedy, as in the familiar lines of Dryden : —

> "Great Fletcher never treads in buskins here,
> Nor greater Jonson dares in socks appear."

The theatre exerted a great influence upon Greek life. It performed for ancient Greek society somewhat the same service as that rendered to modern society by the pulpit and the press. During the best days of Hellas the frequent rehearsal upon the stage of the chief incidents in the lives of the gods and the heroes served to deepen and strengthen the religious faith of the people ; and later, in the Macedonian period, the theatre was one of the chief agents in the diffusion of Greek literary culture over the world.

Banquets and Symposia. — Banquets and drinking-parties among the Greeks possessed some features which set them apart from similar entertainments among other peoples.

The banquet proper was partaken, in later times, by the guest in a reclining position, upon couches or divans, arranged about the table in the Oriental manner. After the usual courses, a libation was poured out and a hymn sung in honor of the gods, and then followed that characteristic part of the entertainment known as the *symposium*.

The symposium was "the intellectual side of the feast." It consisted of general conversation, riddles, and convivial songs rendered to the accompaniment of the lyre passed from hand to hand. Generally, professional singers and musicians, dancing-girls, jugglers, and jesters were called in to contribute to the merry-making. All the while the wine-bowl circulated freely, the rule being that a man might drink "as much as he could carry home without a guide,— unless he were far gone in years." Here also the Greeks applied their maxim, "Never too much."

The banqueters usually consumed the night in merry-making, sometimes being broken in upon from the street by other bands of revellers, who made themselves self-invited guests.

Occupation. — The enormous body of slaves in ancient Greece relieved the free population from most of those forms of labor classed as drudgery. The æsthetic Greek regarded as degrading any kind of manual labor that marred the symmetry or beauty of the body.

At Sparta, and in other states where oligarchical institutions prevailed, the citizens formed a sort of military class, strikingly similar to the military aristocracy of Feudal Europe. Their chief occupation was martial and gymnastic exercises and the administration of public affairs. The Spartans, it will be recalled, were forbidden by law to engage in trade. In other aristocratic states, as at Thebes, a man by engaging in trade disqualified himself for full citizenship.

In the democratic states, however, speaking generally, labor and trade were regarded with less contempt. A considerable portion of the citizens were traders, artisans, and farmers.

Life at Athens presented some peculiar features. All Attica being included in what we should term the corporate limits of the city, the roll of Athenian citizens included a large body of well-to-do farmers, whose residence was outside the city walls. The Attic plains, and the slopes of the half-encircling hills, were dotted with beautiful villas and inviting farmhouses.

And then Athens being the head of a great empire of subject cities, a large number of Athenian citizens were necessarily employed as salaried officials in the minor positions of the public service, and thus politics became a profession. In any event, the meetings of the popular assembly and the discussion of matters of state engrossed more or less of the time and attention of every citizen.

Again, the great Athenian jury-courts, which were busied with cases from all parts of the empire, gave constant employment to nearly one fourth of the citizens, the fee that the juryman received enabling him to live without other business. It is said that, in the early morning, when the jurymen were passing through the streets to the different courts, Athens appeared like a city wholly given up to the single business of law. Furthermore, the great public works, such as temples and commemorative monuments, which were in constant process of erection, afforded employment for a vast number of artists and skilled workmen of every class.

In the Agora, again, at any time of the day, a numerous class might have been found whose sole occupation, as in the case of Socrates, was to talk. The writer of the " Acts of the Apostles " was so impressed with this feature of life at Athens that he summarized the habits of the people by saying, "All the Athenians, and strangers which were there, spent their time in nothing else, but either to tell or to hear some new thing." (Chap. xvii. 21.)

Slavery. — There was a dark side to Greek life. Hellenic art, culture, refinement — "these good things were planted, like exquisite exotic flowers, upon the black, rank soil of slavery."

The proportion of slaves to the free population in many of the states was astonishingly large. In Corinth and Ægina there were ten slaves to every freeman. In Attica the proportion was four to one ; that is to say, out of a population of about 500,000, 400,000 were slaves.[1] Almost every freeman was a slave owner. It was accounted a real hardship to have to get along with less than half a dozen slaves.

This large class of slaves was formed in various ways. In the prehistoric period, the fortunes of war had brought the entire population of whole provinces into a servile condition, as in certain parts of the Peloponnesus. During later times, the ordinary captives of war still further augmented the ranks of these unfortunates. Their number was also largely added to by the slave

---

[1] The population of Attica in 317 B.C. is reckoned at about 527,000. That of Athens in its best days was probably not far from 150,000.

traffic carried on with the barbarian peoples of Asia Minor. Criminals and debtors, too, were often condemned to servitude ; while foundlings were usually brought up as slaves.

The relation of master and slave was regarded by the Greek as being, not only a legal, but a natural one. A free community, in his view, could not exist without slavery. It formed the natural basis of both the family and the state, — the relation of master and slave being regarded as "strictly analogous to the relation of soul and body." Even Aristotle and other Greek philosophers approved the maxim that "slaves are simply domestic animals possessed of intelligence." They were regarded as just as necessary in the economy of the family as cooking utensils.

In general, Greek slaves were not treated harshly — judging their treatment by the standard of humanity that prevailed in antiquity. Some held places of honor in the family, and enjoyed the confidence and even the friendship of their master. Yet at Sparta, where slavery assumed the form of serfdom, the lot of the slave was peculiarly hard and unendurable.

If slavery was ever justified by its fruits, it was in Greece. The brilliant civilization of the Greeks was its product, and could never have existed without it. As one truthfully says, " Without the slaves the Attic democracy would have been an impossibility, for they alone enabled the poor, as well as the rich, to take a part in public affairs." Relieving the citizen of all drudgery, the system created a class characterized by elegant leisure, refinement, and culture.

We find an almost exact historical parallel to all this in the feudal aristocracy of Mediæval Europe. Such a society has been well likened to a great pyramid, whose top may be gilded with light, while the base lies in dark shadows. The civilization of ancient Hellas was splendid and attractive, but it rested with a crushing weight upon all the lower orders of Greek society.

CHAPTER XXII.

THE ROMAN KINGDOM.

(Legendary Date, 753–509 B.C.)

Divisions of Italy. — The peninsula of Italy, like that of Greece, divides itself into three parts — Northern, Central, and Southern Italy. The first comprises the great basin of the Po, lying between the Alps and the Apennines. In ancient times this part of Italy included three districts — Liguria, Gallia Cisalpina, which means "Gaul on this (the Italian) side of the Alps," and Venetia.

The countries of Central Italy were Etruria, Latium, and Campania, facing the Western, or Tuscan Sea ; Umbria and Picenum, looking out over the Eastern, or Adriatic Sea ; and Samnium and the country of the Sabines, occupying the rough mountain districts of the Apennines.

Southern Italy comprised the countries of Apulia, Lucania, Calabria, and Bruttium. Calabria occupied the "heel," and Bruttium formed the "toe," of the peninsula. This part of Italy, as we have already learned, was called Magna Græcia, or "Great Greece," on account of the number and importance of the Greek cities that during the period of Hellenic supremacy were established in these regions.

The large island of Sicily, lying just off the mainland on the south, may be regarded simply as a detached fragment of Italy, so intimately has its history been interwoven with that of the peninsula. In ancient times it was the meeting-place and battle-ground of the Carthaginians, Greeks, and Romans.

Early Inhabitants of Italy. — There were, in early times, three chief races in Italy — the Italians, the Etruscans, and the Greeks. The Italians, a branch of the Aryan family, embraced many tribes (Latins, Umbrians, Sabines, Samnites, etc.), that occupied nearly all Central Italy. The Etruscans, a wealthy, cultured, and maritime people of uncertain race, dwelt in Etruria, now Tuscany. Before the rise of the Romans they were the leading race in the peninsula. Of the establishment of the Greek cities in Southern Italy, we have already learned in connection with Grecian History (p. 111).

Some five hundred years B.C., the Gauls, a Celtic race, came over the Alps, and settling in Northern Italy, became formidable enemies of the infant republic of Rome.

The Latins. — Most important of all the Italian peoples were the Latins, who dwelt in Latium, between the Tiber and the Liris. These people, like all the Italians, were near kindred of the Greeks, and brought with them into Italy those customs, manners, beliefs, and institutions which seem to have been the early common possession of the various Aryan-speaking peoples.

There are said to have been in all Latium thirty towns, and these formed an alliance known as the Latin League. The city which first assumed importance and leadership among the towns of this confederation was Alba Longa, the "Long White City," so called because its buildings stretched for a great distance along the summit of a whitish ridge.

The Beginnings of Rome. —The place of preëminence among the Latin towns was soon lost by Alba Longa, and gained by another city. This was Rome, the stronghold of the Ramnes, or Romans, located upon a low hill on the south bank of the Tiber, about fifteen miles from the sea.

The traditions of the Romans place the founding of their city in the year 753 B.C. The town was established, it would seem, as an outpost to guard the northern frontier of Latium against the Etruscans.

Recent excavations have revealed the foundations of the old

walls and two of the ancient gates. We thus learn that the city at first covered only the top of the Palatine Hill, one of a cluster of low eminences close to the Tiber, which, finally embraced within the limits of the growing city, became the famed " Seven Hills of Rome." From the shape of its enclosing walls, the original city was called *Roma Quadrata*, "Square Rome."

The Early Roman State : King, Senate, and Popular Assembly. — The early Roman state seems to have been formed by the union of three communities. These constituted three tribes, known as Ramnes (the Romans proper, who gave name to the mixed people), Tities, and Luceres. Each of these tribes was divided into ten wards, or districts (*curiæ*) ; each ward was made up of *gentes*, or clans, and each clan was composed of a number of families. The heads of these families were called *patres*, or " fathers," and all the members patricians, that is, " children of the fathers."

At the head of the nation stood the King, who was the father of the state. He was at once ruler of the people, commander of the army, judge and high priest of the nation, with absolute power as to life and death.

Next to the king stood the Senate, or " council of the old men," composed of the " fathers," or heads of the families. This council had no power to enact laws : the duty of its members was simply to advise with the king, who was free to follow or to disregard their suggestions.

The Popular Assembly (*comitia curiata*) comprised all the citizens of Rome, that is, all the members of the patrician families, old enough to bear arms. It was this body that enacted the laws of the state, determined upon peace or war, and also elected the king.

Classes of Society. — The two important classes of the population of Rome under the kingdom and the early republic, were the patricians and the plebeians. The former were the members of the three original tribes that made up the Roman people, and at first alone possessed political rights. They were proud, exclusive, and tenacious of their inherited privileges. The latter were made up chiefly of the inhabitants of subjected cities, and of refugees from various quarters that had sought an asylum at Rome. They were free to acquire property, and enjoyed personal freedom, but at first had no political rights whatever. The greater number were petty land-owners, who held and cultivated the soil about the city. A large part of the early history of Rome is simply the narration of the struggles of this class to secure social and political equality with the patricians.

Besides these two principal orders, there were two other classes — clients and slaves. The former were attached to the families of patricians, who became their patrons, or protectors. The condition of the client was somewhat like that of the serf in the feudal system of the Middle Ages. A large clientage was considered the crown and glory of a patrician house.

The slaves were, in the main, captives in war. Their number, small at first, gradually increased as the Romans extended their conquests, till they outnumbered all the other classes taken together, and more than once turned upon their masters in formidable revolts that threatened the very existence of the Roman state.

The Legendary Kings. — For nearly two and a half centuries after the founding of Rome (from 753 to 509 B.C., according to tradition), the government was a monarchy. To span this period, the legends of the Romans tell of the reigns of seven kings — Romulus, the founder of Rome ; Numa, the lawgiver ; Tullus Hostilius and Ancus Marcius, conquerors both ; Tarquinius Priscus, the great builder ; Servius Tullius, the reorganizer of the government and second founder of the state ; and Tarquinius Superbus, the haughty tyrant, whose oppressions led to the abolition by the people of the office of king.

The traditions of the doings of these monarchs and of what happened to them, blend hopelessly fact and fable. We cannot be quite sure even as to the names. Respecting Roman affairs, however, under the last three rulers (the Tarquins), who were of Etruscan origin, some important things are related, the substantial

truth of which we may rely upon with a fair degree of cer-
tainty; and these matters we shall notice in the following paragraphs.

Growth of Rome under the Tarquins. — The Tarquins extended
their authority over the whole of Latium. The position of supremacy thus given Rome was naturally attended by the rapid growth
in population and importance of the little Palatine city. The original walls soon became too strait for the increasing multitudes;
new ramparts were built — tradition says under the direction of

VIEW OF THE CAPITOLINE, WITH THE CLOACA MAXIMA.
(A Reconstruction.)

the king Servius Tullius — which, with a great circuit of seven
miles, swept around the entire cluster of the Seven Hills. A large
tract of marshy ground between the Palatine and Capitoline hills
was drained by means of the Cloaca Maxima, the "Great Sewer,"
which was so admirably constructed that it has been preserved to
the present day. It still discharges its waters through a great arch
into the Tiber. The land thus reclaimed became the Forum, the
assembling-place of the people. Upon the summit of the Capito-

line Hill, overlooking the Forum, was built the famous sanctuary called the Capitol, or the Capitoline temple, where beneath the same roof were the shrines of Jupiter, Juno, and Minerva, the three great national deities. Upon the level ground between the Aventine and the Palatine was laid out the Circus Maximus, the "Great Circus," where were celebrated the Roman games.

New Constitution of Servius Tullius. — The second king of the Etruscan house, Servius Tullius by name, effected a most important change in the constitution of the Roman state. He did here at Rome just what Solon at about this time did at Athens (see p. 120). He made property instead of birth the basis of the constitution. The entire population was divided into five classes, the first of which included all citizens, whether patricians or plebeians, who owned twenty *jugera* (about twelve acres) of land; the fifth and lowest embraced all that could show title to even two jugera. The army was made up of the members of the five classes; as it was thought right and proper that the public defence should be the care of those who, on account of their possessions, were most interested in the maintenance of order and in the protection of the boundaries of the state.

The assembling-place of the military classes thus organized was on a large plain just outside the city walls, called the Campus Martius, or "Field of Mars." The meeting of these military orders was called the *comitia centuriata,* or the "assembly of hundreds."[1] This body, which of course was made up of patricians and plebeians, gradually absorbed the powers of the earlier patrician assembly (*comitia curiata*).

The Expulsion of the Kings. — The legends make Tarquinius Superbus, or Tarquin the Proud, the last king of Rome. He is represented as a monstrous tyrant, whose arbitrary acts caused both patricians and plebeians to unite and drive him and all his house into exile. This event, according to tradition, occurred in

---

[1] This assembly was not organized by Servius Tullius, but it grew out of the military organization he created.

the year 509 B.C., only one year later than the expulsion of the
tyrants from Athens (see p. 122).

So bitterly did the people hate the tyranny they had abolished
that it is said they all, the nobles as well as the commons, bound
themselves by most solemn oaths never again to tolerate a king.
We shall hereafter see how well this vow was kept for nearly five
hundred years.

THE ROMAN RELIGION.

The Chief Roman Deities. — The basis of the Roman religious
system was the same as that of the Grecian : the germs of its
institutions were brought from the same early Aryan home. At
the head of the Pantheon stood Jupiter, identical in all essential
attributes with the Hellenic Zeus. He was the special protector
of the Roman people. To him, together with Juno and Minerva,
was consecrated, as we have already noticed, a magnificent temple
upon the summit of the Capitoline Hill, overlooking the Forum
and the city. Mars, the god of war, standing next in rank, was
the favorite deity and the fabled father of the Roman race, who
were fond of calling themselves the "children of Mars." They
proved themselves worthy offspring of the war-god. Martial games
and festivals were celebrated in his honor during the first month
of the Roman year, which bore, and still bears, in his honor, the
name of March. Janus was a double-faced deity, "the god of
the beginning and the end of everything." The month of January
was sacred to him, as were also all gates and doors. The gates of
his temple were always kept open in time of war and shut in time
of peace.

The fire upon the household hearth was regarded as the symbol
of the goddess Vesta. Her worship was a favorite one with the
Romans. The nation, too, as a single great family, had a common
national hearth in the Temple of Vesta, where the sacred fires
were kept burning from generation to generation by six virgins,
daughters of the Roman state. The Lares and Penates were
household gods. Their images were set in the entrance of the

dwelling. The Lares were the spirits of ancestors, which were thought to linger about the home as its guardians.

Oracles and Divination. — The Romans, like the Greeks, thought that the will of the gods was communicated to men by means of oracles, and by strange sights, unusual events, or singular coincidences. There were no true oracles at Rome. The Romans, therefore, often had recourse to those in Magna Græcia, even sending for advice, in great emergencies, to the Delphian shrine. From Etruria was introduced the art of the haruspices, or soothsayers, which consisted in discovering the divine mind by the appearance of victims slain for the sacrifices.

VESTAL VIRGIN.

The Sacred Colleges. — The four chief sacred colleges, or societies, were the Keepers of the Sibylline Books, the College of Augurs, the College of Pontiffs, and the College of the Heralds.

A curious legend is told of the Sibylline Books. An old woman came to Tarquinius Superbus and offered to sell him, for an extravagant price, nine volumes. As the king declined to pay the sum demanded, the woman departed, destroyed three of the books, and then, returning, offered the remainder at the very same sum that she had wanted for the complete number. The king still refused to purchase; so the sibyl went away and destroyed three more of the volumes, and bringing back the remaining three, asked the same price as before. Tarquin was by this time so curious respecting the contents of the mysterious books that he purchased the remaining volumes. It was found upon examination that they were filled with prophecies respecting the future of the Roman people. The books were placed in a stone chest, which was kept in a vault beneath the Capitoline temple; and special custodians were appointed to take charge of them and interpret them. The number of keepers, throughout the most important period of Roman history, was fifteen. The books were consulted only in times of extreme danger.

The duty of the members of the College of Augurs was to interpret the omens, or auspices, which were casual sights or appearances, by which means it was believed that Jupiter made known his will. Great skill was required in the "taking of the auspices," as it was called. No business of importance, public or private, was entered upon without first consulting the auspices, to ascertain whether they were favorable. The public assembly, for illustration, must not convene, to elect officers or to enact laws, unless the auspices had been taken and found propitious. Should a peal of thunder occur while the people were holding a meeting, that was considered an unfavorable omen, and the assembly must instantly disperse.

The College of Pontiffs was so called because one of the duties of its members was to keep in repair the bridges (*pontes*) over which the religious processions were accustomed to pass. This was the most important of all the religious institutions of the Romans; for to the pontiffs belonged the superintendence of all religious matters. In their keeping, too, was the calendar, and they could lengthen or shorten the year, which power they sometimes used to extend the office of a favorite or to cut short that of one who had incurred their displeasure. The head of the college was called Pontifex Maximus, or the Chief Bridge-builder, which title was assumed by the Roman emperors, and after them by the Christian bishops of Rome; and thus the name has come down to our own times.

The College of Heralds had the care of all public matters pertaining to foreign nations. If the Roman people had suffered any wrong from another state, it was the duty of the heralds to demand satisfaction. If this was denied, and war determined upon, then a herald proceeded to the frontier of the enemy's country and hurled over the boundary a spear dipped in blood. This was a declaration of war. The Romans were very careful in the observance of this ceremony.

Sacred Games. — The Romans had many religious games and festivals. Prominent among these were the so-called Circensian Games, or Games of the Circus, which were very similar to the sacred games of the Greeks (see p. 106). They consisted, in the main, of chariot-racing, wrestling, foot-racing, and various other athletic contests.

These festivals, as in the case of those of the Greeks, had their origin in the belief that the gods delighted in the exhibition of feats of skill, strength, or endurance ; that their anger might be appeased by such spectacles ; or that they might be persuaded by the promise of games to lend aid to mortals in great emergencies. At the opening of the year it was customary for the Roman magistrate, in behalf of the people, to promise to the gods games and festivals, provided good crops, protection from pestilence, and victory were granted the Romans during the year. So, too, a general in great straits in the field might, in the name of the state, vow plays to the gods, and the people were sacredly bound by his act to fulfil the promise. Plays given in fulfilment of vows thus made were called votive games.

Towards the close of the republic these games lost much of their religious character, and at last became degraded into mere brutal shows given by ambitious leaders for the purpose of winning popularity.

CHAPTER XXIII.

THE EARLY ROMAN REPUBLIC : CONQUEST OF ITALY.

(509–264 B.C.)

The First Consuls. — With the monarchy overthrown and the last king and his house banished from Rome, the people set to work to reorganize the government. In place of the king, there were elected (by the *comitia centuriata*, in which assembly the plebeians had a place) two patrician magistrates, called consuls,[1] who were chosen for one year, and were invested with all the powers, save some priestly functions, that had been held by the monarch during the regal period.

In public each consul was attended by twelve servants, called lictors, each of whom bore an axe bound in a bundle of rods (*fasces*), the symbols of the authority of the consul to flog and to put to death. Within the limits of the city, however, the axe must be removed from the *fasces*, by which was indicated that no Roman citizen could be put to death by the consuls without the consent of the public assembly.

Lucius Junius Brutus and Tarquinius Collatinus were the first consuls under the new constitution. But it is said that the very name of Tarquinius was so intolerable to the people that he was forced to resign the consulship, and that he and all his house were driven out of Rome.[2] Another consul, Publius Valerius, was chosen in his stead.

---

[1] That is, *colleagues.* Each consul had the power of obstructing the acts or vetoing the commands of the other. In times of great public danger the consuls were superseded by a special officer called a *dictator*, whose term of office was limited to six months, but whose power during this time was as unlimited as that of the kings had been.

[2] The truth is, he was related to the exiled royal family, and the people were distrustful of his loyalty to the republic.

First Secession of the Plebeians (494 B.C.). —Taking advantage of the disorders that followed the political revolution, the Latin towns which had been forced to acknowledge the supremacy of

LICTORS WITH FASCES.

(The symbolic fasces borne by these officers were probably of Etruscan origin. The Tarquins are said to have brought them to Rome along with other insignia of the kingly office.)

Rome rose in revolt, and the result was that almost all the conquests that had been made under the kings were lost. For a long time the little republic had to struggle hard for bare existence.

Troubles without brought troubles within. The poor plebeians, during this period of disorder and war, fell in debt to the wealthy class, — for the Roman soldier went to war at his own charge, equipping and feeding himself, — and payment was exacted with heartless severity. A debtor became the absolute property of his creditor, who might sell him as a slave to pay the debt, and in some cases even put him to death. All this was intolerable. The plebeians determined to secede from Rome and build a new city for themselves on a neighboring eminence, called afterwards the Sacred Hill. They marched away in a body from Rome to the chosen spot, and began making preparations for erecting new homes (494 B.C.).

The Covenant and the Tribunes. — The patricians saw clearly that such a division must prove ruinous to the state, and that the plebeians must be persuaded to give up their enterprise and come back to Rome. The consul Valerius was sent to treat with the insurgents. The plebeians were at first obstinate, but at last were persuaded to yield to the entreaties of the embassy to return, being won to this mind, so it is said, by one of the wise senators, Menenius, who made use of the well-known fable of the Body and the Members.

The following covenant was entered into, and bound by the most solemn oaths and vows before the gods : The debts of the poor plebeians were to be cancelled and those held in slavery set free ; and two magistrates (the number was soon increased to ten), called tribunes, whose duty it should be to watch over the plebeians, and protect them against the injustice, harshness, and partiality of the patrician magistrates, were to be chosen from the commons. The persons of these officers were made sacred. Any one interrupting a tribune in the discharge of his duties, or doing him any violence, was declared an outlaw, whom any one might kill. That the tribunes might be always easily found, they were not allowed to go more than one mile beyond the city walls. Their houses were to be open night as well as day, that any plebeian unjustly dealt with might flee thither for protection and refuge.

We cannot overestimate the importance of the change effected in the Roman constitution by the creation of this office of the tribunate. Under the protection and leadership of the tribunes, who were themselves protected by oaths of inviolable sanctity, the plebeians carried on a struggle for a share in the offices and dignities of the state which never ceased until the Roman government, as yet only republican in name, became in fact a real democracy, in which patrician and plebeian shared equally in all emoluments and privileges.

Coriolanus. — The tradition of Coriolanus illustrates in what manner the tribunes cared for the rights of the common people and protected them from the oppression of the nobles. During a severe famine at Rome, Gelon, the King of Syracuse, sent large quantities of grain to the capital for distribution among the suffering poor. A certain patrician, Coriolanus by name, made a proposal that none of the grain should be given to the plebeians save on condition that they give up their tribunes. These officials straightway summoned him before the plebeian assembly,[1] on the charge of having broken the solemn covenant of the Sacred Mount, and so bitter was the feeling against him that he was obliged to flee from Rome.

He now allied himself with the Volscians, enemies of Rome, and even led their armies against his native city. An embassy from the Senate was sent to him, to sue for peace. But the spirit of Coriolanus was bitter and revengeful, and he would listen to none of their proposals. Nothing availed to move him until his mother, at the head of a train of Roman matrons, came to his tent, and with tears pleaded with him to spare the city. Her entreaties and the " soft prayers " of his own wife and children

---

[1] The Assembly of Tribes (*comitia tributa*), an assembly which came into existence about this time. It was made up wholly of plebeians, and was presided over by the tribunes. Later, there came into existence another tribal assembly, which was composed of patricians and plebeians, and presided over by consuls or prætors. Some authorities are inclined to regard these two assemblies as one and the same body ; but others, among whom is Mommsen, with probably better reason, look upon them as two distinct organizations.

prevailed, and with the words "Mother, thou hast saved Rome, but lost thy son," he led away the Volscian army.

Cincinnatus made Dictator. — The enemies of Rome, taking advantage of the dissensions of the nobles and commons, pressed upon the frontiers of the republic on all sides. In 458 B.C., the Æquians, while one of the consuls was away fighting the Sabines, defeated the forces of the other, and shut them up in a narrow valley, whence escape seemed impossible. There was great terror in Rome when news of the situation of the army was brought to the city.

The Senate immediately appointed Cincinnatus, a noble patrician, dictator. The ambassadors that carried to him the message from the Senate found him upon his little farm near the Tiber, at work behind the plough. Accepting the office at once, he hastily gathered an army, marched to the relief of the consul, captured the entire army of the Æquians, and sent them beneath the yoke.[1] Cincinnatus then led his army back to Rome in triumph, laid down his office, and sought again the retirement of his farm.

The Decemvirs and the Tables of Laws. — Written laws are always a great safeguard against oppression. Until what shall constitute a crime and what shall be its penalty are clearly written down and well known and understood by all, judges may render unfair decisions, or inflict unjust punishment, and yet run little risk — unless they go altogether too far — of being called to an account; for no one but themselves knows what the law or the penalty really is. Hence in all struggles of the people against the tyranny of the ruling class, the demand for written laws is one of the first measures taken by the people for the protection of their persons and property. Thus we have seen the people of Athens, early in their struggle with the nobles, demanding and obtaining a code of written laws (see p. 119). The same thing now took place at Rome. The plebeians demanded that a code

---

[1] This was formed of two spears thrust firmly into the ground and crossed a few feet from the earth by a third. Prisoners of war were forced to pass beneath this yoke as a symbol of submission.

of laws be drawn up, in accordance with which the consuls, who exercised judicial powers, should render their decisions. The patricians offered a stubborn resistance to their wishes, but finally were forced to yield to the popular clamor.

A commission was sent to the Greek cities of Southern Italy and to Athens to study the Grecian laws and customs. Upon the return of this embassy, a commission of ten magistrates, who were known as decemvirs, was appointed to frame a code of laws (451 B.C.). These officers, while engaged in this work, were also to administer the entire government, and so were invested with the supreme power of the state. The patricians gave up their consuls and the plebeians their tribunes. At the end of the first year, the task of the board was quite far from being finished, so a new decemvirate was elected to complete the work. Appius Claudius was the only member of the old board that was returned to the new.

The code was soon finished, and the laws were written on twelve tablets of brass, which were fastened to the Rostra, or orator's platform in the Forum, where they might be seen and read by all. These "Laws of the Twelve Tables" were to Roman jurisprudence what the good laws of Solon (see p. 120) were to the Athenian constitution. They formed the basis of all new legislation for many centuries, and constituted a part of the education of the Roman youth — every school-boy being required to learn them by heart.

Misrule and Overthrow of the Decemvirs. — The first decemvirs used the great power lodged in their hands with justice and prudence; but the second board, under the leadership of Appius Claudius, instituted a most infamous and tyrannical rule. The result was a second secession of the plebeians to the Sacred Hill. This procedure, which once before had proved so effectual in securing justice to the oppressed, had a similar issue now. The situation was so critical that the decemvirs were forced to resign. The consulate and the tribunate were restored. Eight of the decemvirs were forced to go into exile ; Appius Claudius and one other, having been imprisoned, committed suicide.

Consular, or Military Tribunes. — The overthrow of the decemvirate was followed by a long struggle between the nobles and the commons, which was an effort on the part of the latter to gain admission to the consulship ; for up to this time only a patrician could hold that office. The contention resulted in a compromise. It was agreed that, in place of the two consuls, the people *might* elect from either order magistrates, who should be known as " military tribunes with consular powers." These officers, whose numbers varied, differed from consuls more in name than in functions or authority. In fact, the plebeians had gained the office, but not the name (444 B.C.).

The Censors. — No sooner had the plebeians virtually secured admission to the consulship, than the jealous and exclusive patricians commenced scheming to rob them of the fruit of the victory they had gained. They effected this by taking from the consulate some of its most distinctive duties and powers, and conferring them upon two new patrician officers called censors. The functions of these magistrates were many and important. They took the census, and thus assigned to every man his position in the different classes of the citizens ; and they could, for immorality or any improper conduct, not only degrade a man from his rank, but deprive him of his vote. It was their duty to watch the public morals and in case of necessity to administer wholesome advice. Thus we are told of their reproving the young Romans for wearing tunics with long sleeves — an Oriental and effeminate custom — and for neglecting to marry upon arriving at a proper age. From the name of these Roman officers comes our word *censorious*, meaning fault-finding.

The first censors were elected probably in the year 444 B.C. ; about one hundred years afterwards, in 351 B.C., the plebeians secured the right of holding this office also.

Siege and Capture of Veii. — We must now turn to notice the fortunes of Rome in war. Almost from the founding of the city, we find its warlike citizens carrying on a fierce contest with their powerful Etruscan neighbors on the north. Veii was one of the largest and richest of the cities of Etruria. Around this the war gathered. The Romans, like the Grecians at Troy, attacked its walls for ten years. The length of the siege, and the necessity of maintaining a force permanently in the field, led to the establishment of a paid standing army; for hitherto the soldier had not only equipped himself, but had served without pay. Thus was laid the basis of that military power which was destined to effect the conquest of the world, and then, in the hands of ambitious and favorite generals, to overthrow the republic itself.

ROMAN SOLDIER.

The capture of Veii by the dictator Camillus (396 B.C.) was followed by that of many other Etruscan towns. Rome was enriched by their spoils, and became the centre of a large and lucrative trade. The frontiers of the republic were pushed out even beyond the utmost limits of the kingdom before its overthrow. All that was lost by the revolution had been now regained, and much besides had been won. At this moment there broke upon the city a storm from the north, which all but cut short the story we are narrating.

Sack of Rome by the Gauls (390 B.C.). — We have already mentioned how, in very remote times, the tribes of Gaul crossed the Alps and established themselves in Northern Italy (see p. 223). While the Romans were conquering the towns of Etruria, these barbarian hordes were moving southward, and overrunning and devastating the countries of Central Italy.

News was brought to Rome that they were advancing upon that city. A Roman army met them on the banks of the river Allia, eleven miles from the capital. The Romans were driven in great panic from the field. It would be impossible to picture the consternation and despair that reigned at Rome when the fugitives brought to the city intelligence of the terrible disaster. It was never forgotten, and the day of the battle of Allia was ever after a black day in the Roman calendar. The sacred vessels of the temples were buried; the eternal fires of Vesta were hurriedly

GAULS IN SIGHT OF ROME.

borne by their virgin keepers to a place of safety in Etruria; and a large part of the population fled in dismay across the Tiber. No attempt was made to defend any portion of the city save the citadel. This stronghold was kept by a little garrison, under the command of the hero Marius Manlius. A tradition tells how, when the barbarians, under cover of the darkness of night, had climbed the steep rock and had almost effected an entrance to the citadel, the defenders were awakened by the cackling of some geese, which the piety of the famishing soldiers had spared, because these birds were sacred to Juno.

News was now brought the Gauls that the Venetians were over-running their possessions in Northern Italy. This led them to open negotiations with the Romans. For one thousand pounds of gold, according to the historian Livy, the Gauls agreed to retire from the city. As the story runs, while the gold was being weighed out in the Forum, the Romans complained that the weights were false, when Brennus, the Gallic leader, threw his sword also into the scales, exclaiming, " *Væ victis!* " "Woe to the vanquished." Just at this moment, so the tale continues, Camillus, a brave patrician general, appeared upon the scene with a Roman army that had been gathered from the fugitives ; and, as he scattered the barbarians with heavy blows, he exclaimed, " Rome is ransomed with steel and not with gold." According to one account Brennus himself was taken prisoner ; but another tradition says that he escaped, carrying with him not only the ransom, but a vast booty besides.

The Rebuilding of Rome. — When the fugitives returned to Rome after the withdrawal of the Gauls, they found the city a heap of ruins. Some of the poorer classes, shrinking from the labor of rebuilding their old homes, proposed to abandon the site and make Veii their new capital. But love for the old spot at last prevailed over all the persuasions of indolence, and the people, with admirable courage, set themselves to the task of rebuilding their homes. It was a repetition of the scene at Athens after the retreat of the Persians (see p. 136). The city was speedily restored, and was soon enjoying her old position of supremacy among the surrounding states. There were some things, however, which even Roman resolution and perseverance could not restore. These were the ancient records and documents, through whose irreparable loss the early history of Rome is involved in great obscurity and uncertainty.

Treason and Death of Manlius. — The ravages of the Gauls left the poor plebeians in a most pitiable condition. In order to rebuild their dwellings and restock their farms, they were obliged to borrow money of the rich patricians, and consequently soon began again to experience the insult and oppression that were ever incident to the condition of the debtor class at Rome.

The patrician Manlius, the hero of the brave defence of the Capitol, now came forward as the champion of the plebeians. He sold the larger part of his estates, and devoted the proceeds to the relief of the debtor class. It seems evident that in thus undertaking the cause of the commons he had personal aims and ambitions. The patricians determined to crush him. He was finally brought to trial before the popular assembly, on the charge of conspiring to restore the office of king. From the Forum, where the people were gathered, the Capitol, which Manlius had so bravely defended against the barbarians, was in full sight. Pointing to the temples he had saved, he appealed to the gods and to the gratitude of the Roman people. The people responded to the appeal in a way altogether natural. They refused to condemn him. But brought to trial a second time, and now in a grove whence the citadel could not be seen, he was sentenced to death, and was thrown from the Tarpeian Rock.[1] This event occurred 384 B.C.

Plebeians admitted to the Consulship. — For nearly half a century after the death of Manlius the most important events in the history of Rome centre about the struggle of the plebeians for admission to those offices of the government whence the jealousy of the patricians still excluded them. The Licinian laws, so called from one of their proposers, the tribune C. Licinius, besides relieving the poor of usurious interest, and effecting a more just division of the public lands, also provided that consuls should be chosen yearly, as at first (see p. 238), and that one of the consuls should

---

[1] The Tarpeian Rock was the name given to the cliff which the Capitoline Hill formed on the side towards the Tiber (or towards the Palatine, according to some). It received its name from Tarpeia, daughter of one of the legendary keepers of the citadel. State criminals were frequently executed by being thrown from this rock.

be a plebeian. This last provision opened to any one of the plebeian class the highest office in the state. The nobles, when they saw that it would be impossible to resist the popular demand, had recourse to the old device. They effected a compromise, whereby the judicial powers of the consuls were taken from them and conferred upon a new magistrate, who bore the name of prætor. Only patricians, of course, were to be eligible to this new office. They then permitted the Licinian laws to pass (367 B.C.).

During the latter half of the fourth century B.C. (between the years 356–300) the plebeians gained admittance to the dictatorship, the censorship, the prætorship, and to the College of Augurs and the College of Pontiffs. They had been admitted to the College of Priests having charge of the Sibylline books, at the time of the passing of the Licinian laws. With plebeians in all these positions, the rights of the lower order were fairly secured against oppressive and partisan decisions on the part of the magistrates, and against party fraud in the taking of the auspices and in the regulation of the calendar. There was now political equality between the nobility and the commonalty.

Wars for the Mastery of Italy.

The First Samnite War (343–341 B.C.). — The union of the two orders in the state allowed the Romans now to employ their undivided strength in subjugating the different states of the peninsula. The most formidable competitors of the Romans for supremacy in Italy were the Samnites, rough and warlike mountaineers who held the Apennines to the east of Latium. They were worthy rivals of the "children of Mars." The successive struggles between these martial races are known as the First, Second, and Third Samnite wars. They extended over a period of half a century, and in their course involved almost all the states of Italy.

Of the first of this series of wars we know very little, although Livy wrote a long, but unfortunately very unreliable, narration of it. In the midst of the struggle, Rome was confronted by a dangerous revolt of her Latin allies, and, leaving the war unfinished, turned her forces upon the insurgents.

Revolt of the Latin Cities (340–338 B.C.). — The strife between the Romans and their Latin allies was simply the old contest within the walls of the capital between the patricians and the plebeians transferred to a larger arena. As the nobles had oppressed the commons, so now both these orders united in the oppression of the Latins — the plebeians in their bettered circumstances forgetting the lessons of adversity. The Latin allies demanded a share in the government, and that the lands acquired by conquest should be distributed among them as well as among Roman citizens. The Romans refused. All Latium rose in revolt against the injustice and tyranny of the oppressor.

After about three years' hard fighting, the rebellion was subdued. The Latin League was now broken up. Some of the towns retained their independence (Tibur, Præneste, and Cora); some received full Roman citizenship (Aricia, Lanuvium, and Nomentum); while others received only the private rights of Roman citizens, the right of suffrage being withheld.

Second and Third Samnite Wars (326–290 B.C.). — In a few years after the close of the Latin contest, the Romans were at war again with their old rivals, the Samnites. Notwithstanding the latter were thoroughly defeated in this second contest, still it was not long before they were again in arms and engaged in their third struggle with Rome. This time they had formed a powerful coalition which embraced the Etruscans, the Umbrians, the Gauls, and other nations.

Roman courage rose with the danger. The united armies of the league met with a most disastrous defeat (at Sentinum, 295 B.C.), and the power of the coalition was broken. One after another the states that had joined the alliance were chastised, and the Samnites were forced to acknowledge the supremacy of Rome. A few years later, almost all of the Greek cities of Southern Italy, save Tarentum, also came under the growing power of the imperial city.

War with Pyrrhus (282–272 B.C.). — Tarentum was one of the most noted of the Hellenic cities of Magna Græcia. It was a sea-port on the Calabrian coast, and had grown opulent through the extended trade of its merchants. The capture of some Roman vessels, and an insult offered to an envoy of the republic by the Tarentines, led to a declaration of war against them by the Roman Senate. The Tarentines turned to Greece for aid. Pyrrhus, king of Epirus, a cousin of Alexander the Great, who had an ambition to build up such an empire in the West as his renowned kinsman had established in the East, responded to their entreaties, and crossed over into Italy with a small army of Greek mercenaries and twenty war-elephants. He organized and drilled the effeminate Taren-tines, and soon felt prepared to face the Romans.

The hostile armies met at Heraclea (280 B.C.). It is said that when Pyrrhus, who had underestimated his foe, observed the skill which the Romans evinced in forming their line of battle, he ex-claimed, in admiration, " In war, at least, these men are not bar-barians." The battle was won for Pyrrhus by his war-elephants, the sight of which, being new to the Romans, caused them to flee from the field in dismay. But Pyrrhus had lost thousands of his bravest troops. Victories gained by such losses in a country where he could not recruit his army, he saw clearly, meant final defeat. As he looked over the battle-field, he is said to have turned to his companions and remarked, " Another such victory, and I must return to Epirus alone." He noticed also, and not without appre-ciating its significance, that the wounds of the Roman soldiers killed in the action were all in front. " Had I such soldiers," said he, " I should soon be master of the world."

The prudence of the victorious Pyrrhus led him to send to the Romans an embassy with proposals of peace. When the Senate hesitated, its resolution was fixed by the eloquence of the aged Appius : " Rome," exclaimed he, " shall never treat with a victori-ous foe." The ambassadors were obliged to return to Pyrrhus unsuccessful in their mission.

Pyrrhus, according to the Roman story-tellers, who most lavishly embellished this chapter of their history, was not more successful in attempts at bribery than in the arts of negotiation. Upon his attempting by large offers of gold to win Fabricius, who had been intrusted by the Senate with an important embassy, the sturdy old Roman replied, "Poverty, with an honest name, is more to be desired than wealth."

After a second victory, as disastrous as his first, Pyrrhus crossed over into Sicily, to aid the Grecians there in their struggle with the Carthaginians. At first he was everywhere successful; but finally fortune turned against him, and he was glad to escape from the island. Recrossing the straits into Italy, he once more engaged the Romans, but at the battle of Beneventum suffered a disastrous and final defeat at the hands of the consul Curius Dentatus (274 B.C.). Leaving a sufficient force to garrison Tarentum, the baffled and disappointed king set sail for Epirus. He had scarcely embarked before Tarentum surrendered to the Romans (272 B.C.). This ended the struggles for the mastery of Italy. Rome was now mistress of all the peninsula south of the Arnus and the Rubicon. It was now her care to consolidate these possessions, and to fasten her hold upon them, by means of a perfect network of colonies [1] and military roads.

[1] "Colonies were not all of the same character. They must be distinguished into two classes — the colonies of Roman citizens and the Latin colonies. The colonies of Roman citizens consisted usually of three hundred men of approved military experience, who went forth with their families to occupy conquered cities of no great magnitude, but which were important as military positions, being usually on the sea-coast. These three hundred families formed a sort of patrician caste, while the old inhabitants sank into the condition formerly occupied by the plebeians at Rome. The heads of these families retained all their rights as Roman citizens, and might repair to Rome to vote in the popular assemblies." — Liddell's *History of Rome*.

The Latin colonies numbered about thirty at the time of the Second Punic War. A few of these were colonies that had been founded by the old Latin Confederacy; but the most were towns that had been established by Rome subsequent to the dissolution of the League (see p. 244). The term Latin was applied to these later colonies of purely Roman origin, for the reason that they enjoyed the same rights as the Latin towns that had retained their independence. Thus the inhabitants of a Latin colony possessed some of the most valuable of the private rights of Roman citizens, but they had no political rights at the capital.

CHAPTER XXIV.

THE FIRST PUNIC WAR.

(264–241 B.C.)

Carthage and the Carthaginian Empire. — Foremost among the cities founded by the Phœnicians upon the different shores of the Mediterranean was Carthage, upon the northern coast of Africa. The city is thought to have had its beginnings in a small trading-post, established late in the ninth century B.C., about one hundred years before the founding of Rome. Carthage was simply another Tyre. She was mistress and queen of the Western Mediterranean. At the period we have now reached, she held sway, through peaceful colonization or by force of arms, over all the northern coast of Africa from the Greater Syrtis to the Pillars of Hercules, and possessed the larger part of Sicily, as well as Sardinia, Cõrsica, the Balearic Isles, Southern Spain, and scores of little islands scattered here and there in the neighboring seas. With all its shores dotted with her colonies and fortresses, and swept in every direction by the Carthaginian war-galleys, the Western Mediterranean had become a " Phœnician lake," in which, as the Carthaginians boasted, no one dared wash his hands without their permission.

Carthaginian Government and Religion. — The government of Carthage, like that of Rome, was republican in form. Corresponding to the Roman consuls, two magistrates, called Suffetes, stood at the head of the state. The Senate was composed of the heads of the leading families ; its duties and powers were very like those of the Roman Senate. So well-balanced was the constitution, and so prudent was its administration, that six hundred years of Carthaginian history exhibited not a single revolution.

The religion of the Carthaginians was the old Canaanitish worship of Baal, or the Sun. To Moloch, — another name for the fire-god, — " who rejoiced in human victims and in parents' tears," they offered human sacrifices.

Rome and Carthage compared. — These two great republics, which for more than five centuries had been slowly extending their limits and maturing their powers upon the opposite shores of the Mediterranean, were now about to begin one of the most memorable struggles of all antiquity — a duel that was to last, with every vicissitude of fortune, for over one hundred years.

As was the case in the contest between Athens and Sparta, so now the two rival cities, with their allies and dependencies, were very nearly matched in strength and resources. The Romans, it is true, were almost destitute of a navy; while the Carthaginians had the largest and most splendidly equipped fleet that ever patrolled the waters of the Mediterranean. But although the Carthaginians were superior to the Romans in naval warfare, they were greatly their inferiors in land encounters. The Carthaginian territory, moreover, was widely scattered, embracing extended coasts and isolated islands; while the Roman possessions were compact, and confined to a single and easily defended peninsula. Again, the Carthaginian armies were formed chiefly of mercenaries, while those of Rome were recruited very largely from the ranks of the Roman people. And then the subject states of Carthage were mostly of another race, language, and religion from their Phœnician conquerors, and were ready, upon the first disaster to the ruling city, to drop away from their allegiance; while the Latin allies and Italian dependencies of Rome were close kindred to her in race and religion, and so, through natural impulse, for the most part remained loyal to her during even the darkest periods of her struggle with her rival.

The Beginning of the War. — Lying between Italy and the coast of Africa is the large island of Sicily. It is in easy sight of the former, and its southernmost point is only ninety miles from the latter. At the commencement of the First Punic War, the Carthaginians held possession of all the island save a strip of the eastern coast, which was under the sway of the Greek city of Syracuse. The Greeks and Carthaginians had carried on an almost uninterrupted struggle through two centuries for the control of the island. The Romans had not yet set foot upon it. But it was destined to become the scene of the most terrible encounters between the armaments of the two rivals. Pyrrhus had foreseen it all. As he withdrew from the island, he said, "What a fine battle-field we are leaving for the Romans and Carthaginians."

In the year 264 B.C., on a flimsy pretext of giving protection to some friends, the Romans crossed over to the island. That act committed them to a career of foreign conquest destined to continue till their arms had made the circuit of the Mediterranean.

The Syracusans and Carthaginians, old enemies and rivals though they had been, joined their forces against the insolent new-comers. The allies were completely defeated in the first battle, and the Roman army obtained a sure foothold upon the island.

In the following year both consuls were placed at the head of formidable armies for the conquest of Sicily. A large portion of the island was quickly overrun, and many of the cities threw off their allegiance to Syracuse and Carthage, and became allies of Rome. Hiero, king of Syracuse, seeing that he was upon the losing side, deserted the cause of the Carthaginians, and formed an alliance with the Romans, and ever after remained their firm friend.

The Romans gain their First Naval Victory (260 B.C.). — Their experience during the past campaigns had shown the Romans that if they were to cope successfully with the Carthaginians, they must be able to meet them upon the sea as well as upon the land. So they determined to build a fleet. A Carthaginian galley that had been wrecked upon the shores of Italy, served as a pattern. It is affirmed that, within the almost incredibly short space of sixty days, a growing forest was converted into a fleet of one hundred and twenty war galleys.

The consul C. Duillius was entrusted with the command of the fleet. He met the Carthaginian squadron near the city and promontory of Mylæ, on the northern coast of Sicily. Now, distrusting their ability to match the skill of their enemy in naval tactics, the Romans had provided each of their vessels with a drawbridge. As soon as a Carthaginian ship came near enough to a Roman vessel, this gangway was allowed to fall upon the approaching galley ; and the Roman soldiers, rushing along the bridge, were soon engaged in a hand-to-hand conflict with their enemies, in which species of encounter the former were unequalled. The result was a complete victory for the Romans.

The joy at Rome was unbounded. It inspired in the more sanguine splendid visions of maritime command and glory. The Mediterranean should speedily become a Roman lake, in which no vessel might float without the consent of Rome.

The Romans carry the War into Africa. — The results of the naval engagement at Mylæ encouraged the Romans to push the war with redoubled energy. They resolved to carry it into Africa. An immense Carthaginian fleet that disputed the passage of the Roman squadron was almost annihilated, and the Romans disembarked near Carthage. Regulus, one of the consuls who led the army of invasion, sent word to Rome that he had sealed up the gates of Carthage with terror. Finally, however, Regulus suffered a crushing defeat, and was made prisoner. A fleet which was sent to bear away the remnants of the shattered army was wrecked in a terrific storm off the coast of Sicily, and the shores of the island were strewn with the wreckage of between two and three hundred ships and with the bodies of one hundred thousand men.

Undismayed at the terrible disaster that had overtaken the transport fleet, the Romans set to work to build another, and made a second descent upon the African coast. The expedition, however, accomplished nothing of importance ; and the fleet on its return voyage was almost destroyed, just off the coast of Italy, by a tremendous storm.

Regulus and the Carthaginian Embassy. — For a few years the Romans refrained from tempting again the hostile powers of the sea, and Sicily became once more the battle-ground of the contending rivals. At last, having lost a great battle (battle of Panormus, 251 B.C.), the Carthaginians became dispirited, and sent an embassy to Rome, to negotiate for peace, or, if that could not be reached, to effect an exchange of prisoners. Among the commissioners was Regulus, who since his capture, five years before, had been held a prisoner in Africa. Before setting out from Carthage he had promised to return if the embassy were unsuccessful. For the sake of his own release, the Carthaginians supposed he would counsel peace, or at least urge an exchange of prisoners. But it is related, that upon arrival at Rome, he counselled war instead of peace, at the same time revealing to the Senate the enfeebled condition of Carthage. As to the exchange of prisoners, he said, " Let those who have surrendered when they ought to have died, die in the land which has witnessed their disgrace."

The Roman Senate, following his counsel, rejected all the proposals of the embassy; and Regulus, in spite of the tears and entreaties of his wife and friends, turned away from Rome, and set out for Carthage to bear such fate as he well knew the Carthaginians, in their disappointment and anger, would be sure to visit upon him.

The tradition goes on to tell how, upon his arrival at Carthage, he was confined in a cask driven full of spikes, and then left to die of starvation and pain. This part of the tale has been discredited, and the finest touches of the other portions are supposed to have been added by the story-tellers.

Loss of Two More Roman Fleets. — After the failure of the Carthaginian embassy, the war went on for several years by land and sea with varying vicissitudes. At last, on the coast of Sicily, one of the consuls, Claudius, met with an overwhelming defeat. Almost a hundred vessels of his fleet were lost. The disaster caused the greatest alarm at Rome. Superstition increased the fears of the people. It was reported that just before the battle, when the auspices were being taken, and the sacred chickens would not eat, Claudius had given orders to have them thrown

into the sea, irreverently remarking, " At any rate, they shall drink."
Imagination was free to depict what further evils the offended
gods might inflict upon the Roman state.

The gloomiest forebodings might have found justification in
subsequent events. The other consul just now met with a great
disaster. He was proceeding along the southern coast of Sicily
with a squadron of eight hundred merchantmen and over one
hundred war galleys, the former loaded with grain for the Roman
army on the island. A severe storm arising, the squadron was
beaten to pieces upon the rocks. Not a single ship escaped.
The coast for miles was strewn with broken planks, and with
bodies, and heaped with vast windrows of grain cast up by the
waves.

Close of the First Punic War. — The war had now lasted for
fifteen years. Four Roman fleets had been destroyed, three of
which had been sunk or broken to pieces by storms. Of the
fourteen hundred vessels which had been lost, seven hundred were
war galleys, — all large and costly quinqueremes, that is, vessels
with five banks of oars. Only one hundred of these had fallen
into the hands of the enemy ; the remainder were a sacrifice to
the malign and hostile power of the waves. Such successive
blows from an invisible hand were enough to blanch the faces
even of the sturdy Romans. Neptune manifestly denied to the
" Children of Mars " the realm of the sea.

It was impossible for the six years following the last disaster to
infuse any spirit into the struggle. In 247 B.C., Hamilcar Barcas,
the father of the great Hannibal, assumed the command of the
Carthaginian forces, and for several years conducted the war with
great ability on the island of Sicily, even making Rome tremble
for the safety of her Italian possessions.

Once more the Romans determined to commit their cause to
the element that had been so unfriendly to them. A fleet of two
hundred vessels was built and equipped, but entirely by private
subscription ; for the Senate feared that public sentiment would
not sustain them in levying a tax for fitting up another costly

armament as an offering to the insatiable Neptune. This people's squadron, as we may call it, was intrusted to the command of the consul Catulus. He met the Carthaginian fleet under the command of the Admiral Hanno, near the Ægatian islands, and inflicted upon it a crushing defeat.

The Carthaginians now sued for peace. A treaty was at length arranged, the terms of which required that Carthage should give up all claims to the island of Sicily, surrender all her prisoners, and pay an indemnity of 3200 talents (about $4,000,000), one-third of which was to be paid down, and the balance in ten yearly payments. Thus ended (241 B.C.), after a continuance of twenty-four years, the first great struggle between Carthage and Rome.

CHAPTER XXV.

THE SECOND PUNIC WAR.

(218–201 B.C.)

ROME BETWEEN THE FIRST AND THE SECOND PUNIC WAR.

The First Roman Province. — For the twenty-three years that followed the close of the first struggle between Rome and Carthage, the two rivals strained every power and taxed every resource in preparation for a renewal of the contest.

The Romans settled the affairs of Sicily, organizing all of it, save the lands belonging to Syracuse, as a province of the republic. This was the first territory beyond the limits of Italy that Rome had conquered, and the Sicilian the first of Roman provinces. But as the imperial city extended her conquests, her provincial possessions increased in number and size until they formed at last a perfect cordon about the Mediterranean. Each province was governed by a magistrate sent out from the capital, and paid an annual tribute, or tax, to Rome.

Rome acquires Sardinia and Corsica. — The first acquisition by the Romans of lands beyond the peninsula seems to have created in them an insatiable ambition for foreign conquests. They soon found a pretext for seizing the island of Sardinia, the most ancient and, after Sicily, the most prized of the possessions of the Carthaginians. The island, in connection with Corsica, which was also seized, was formed into a Roman province. With her hands upon these islands, the authority of Rome in the Western, or Tuscan Sea, was supreme.

The Illyrian Corsairs are punished. — At about the same time, the Romans also extended their influence over the seas that wash the eastern shores of Italy. For a long time the Adriatic and Ionian

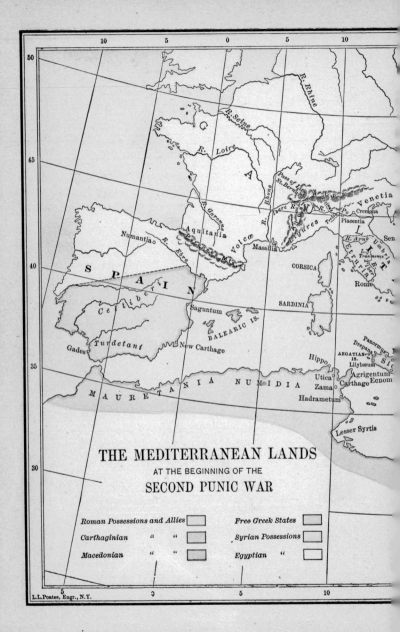

THE MEDITERRANEAN LANDS

AT THE BEGINNING OF THE

SECOND PUNIC WAR

Roman Possessions and Allies ☐   Free Greek States ☐

Carthaginian " " ☐   Syrian Possessions ☐

Macedonian " " ☐   Egyptian " ☐

L.L.Poates, Engr., N.Y.

THRACE

Olbia

Bosprus

Chersonesus

Paphlagonia

Byzantium

Heraclea

Nicæa

Galatia

KINGDOM OF THE SELEUCIDÆ

Epidamnos

Apollonia

Pydna

Macedonia

Strymon

R. Axios

Thessaly

Cynoscephalæ

LEMNOS

Pergamus

Magnesia

Ephesus

R. Mæander

Cilicia

Tarsus

Antioch

CORCYRA

Ætolia

Elis

Athens

CHIOS

LESBOS

SAMOS

Caria

Lycia

Syria

Corinth

Megalopolis

Sparta

RHODES

CYPRUS

Salamis

CRETE

Paphus

Cyrene

Alexandria

Barca

CYRENAICA

Greater
Syrtis

Altars of
Philainoi

EGYPT

R. Nile

or

Danube

YRIA

Epiros

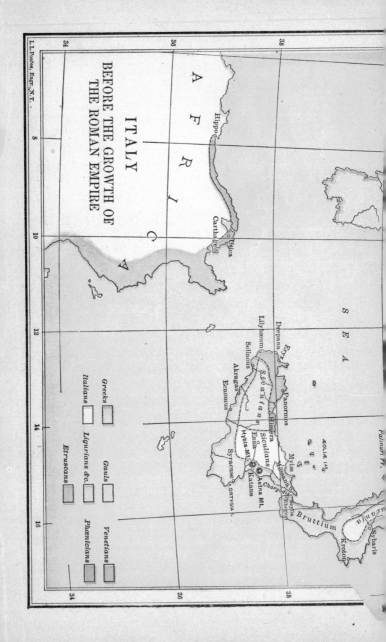

L.L.Poates, Engr., N.Y.

ITALY
BEFORE THE GROWTH OF
THE ROMAN EMPIRE

A F R I C A

Hippo
Utica
Carthage

S E A

Palmuri Pr.

Greeks
Italians

Gauls
Ligurians &c.

Venetians
Phoenicians

Etruscans

Lilybaeum
Drepana
Eryx
Panormus
Selinus
Himera
Mylae
Messana
AEOLIAE I^s.
Akragas
Sicani
Siculians
Hybla Mt.
Enna
Scylla
Charybdis
Rhegion
Enomus
Syracuse
Aetna Mt.
Katane
ORTYGIA I.
Bruttium
Sybaris
Kroton

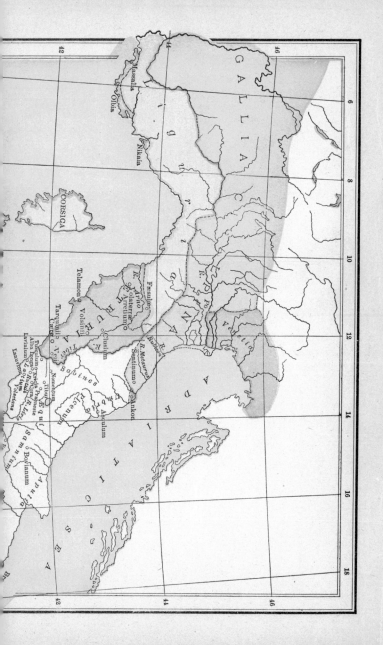

waters had been infested with Illyrian pirates, who issued from the roadsteads of the northeastern coasts of the former sea. The Roman fleet chased these corsairs from the Adriatic, and captured several of their strongholds. Rome now assumed a sort of protectorate over the Greek cities of the Adriatic coasts. This was her first step towards final supremacy in Macedonia and Greece.

War with the Gauls. — In the north, during this same period, Roman authority was extended from the Apennines and the Rubicon to the foot of the Alps. Alarmed at the advance of the Romans, who were pushing northward their great military road, called the Flaminian Way, and also settling with discharged soldiers and needy citizens the tracts of frontier land wrested some time before from the Gauls, the Boii, a tribe of that race, stirred up all the Gallic peoples already in Italy, besides their kinsmen who were yet beyond the mountains, for an assault upon Rome. Intelligence of this movement among the northern tribes threw all Italy into a fever of excitement. At Rome the terror was great ; for not yet had died out of memory what the city had once suffered at the hands of the ancestors of these same barbarians that were now again gathering their hordes for sack and pillage. An ancient prediction, found in the Sibylline books, declared that a portion of Roman territory must needs be occupied by Gauls. Hoping sufficiently to fulfil the prophecy and satisfy Fate, the Roman Senate caused two Gauls to be buried alive in one of the public squares of the capital.

Meanwhile the barbarians had advanced into Etruria, ravaging the country as they moved southward. After gathering a large amount of booty, they were carrying this back to a place of safety, when they were surrounded by the Roman armies at Telamon, and almost annihilated (225 B.C.). The Romans, taking advantage of this victory, pushed on into the plains of the Po, captured the city which is now known as Milan, and extended their authority to the foot-hills of the Alps.

CARTHAGE BETWEEN THE FIRST AND THE SECOND PUNIC WAR.

The Truceless War. — Scarcely had peace been concluded with Rome at the end of the First Punic War, before Carthage was plunged into a still deadlier struggle, which for a time threatened her very existence. The mercenary troops, upon their return from Sicily, revolted, on account of not receiving their pay. Their appeal to the native tribes of Africa was answered by a general uprising throughout the dependencies of Carthage. The extent of the revolt shows how hateful and hated was the rule of the great capital over her subject states.

The war was unspeakably bitter and cruel. It is known in history as " The Truceless War." At one time Carthage was the only city remaining in the hands of the government. But the genius of the great Carthaginian general Hamilcar Barcas at last triumphed, and the authority of Carthage was everywhere restored.

The Carthaginians in Spain. — After the disastrous termination of the First Punic War, the Carthaginians determined to repair their losses by new conquests in Spain. Hamilcar Barcas was sent over into that country, and for nine years he devoted his commanding genius to organizing the different Iberian tribes into a compact state, and to developing the rich gold and silver mines of the southern part of the peninsula. He fell in battle 228 B.C.

Hamilcar Barcas was the greatest general that up to this time the Carthaginian race had produced. As a rule, genius is not heritable ; but in the Barcine family the rule was broken, and the rare genius of Hamilcar reappeared in his sons, whom he himself, it is said, was fond of calling the "lion's brood." Hannibal, the oldest, was only nineteen at the time of his father's death, and being thus too young to assume command, Hasdrubal,[1] the son-in-law of Hamilcar, was chosen to succeed him. He carried out the unfinished plans of Hamilcar, extended and consolidated the Cartha-

---

[1] Not to be confounded with Hannibal's own brother Hasdrubal. See p. 264.

ginian power in Spain, and upon the eastern coast founded New Carthage as the centre and capital of the newly acquired territory. The native tribes were conciliated rather than conquered. The Barcine family knew how to rule as well as how to fight.

Hannibal's Vow. — Upon the death of Hasdrubal, which occurred 221 B.C., Hannibal, now twenty-six years of age, was by the unanimous voice of the army called to be their leader. When a child of nine years he had been led by his father to the altar ; and there, with his hands upon the sacrifice, the little boy had sworn eternal hatred to the Roman race. He was driven on to his gigantic undertakings and to his hard fate, not only by the restless fires of his warlike genius, but, as he himself declared, by the sacred obligations of a vow that could not be broken.

Hannibal attacks Saguntum. — In two years Hannibal extended the Carthaginian power to the Ebro. Saguntum, a native city upon the east coast of Spain, alone remained unsubdued. The Romans, who were jealously watching affairs in the peninsula, had entered into an alliance with this city, and taken it, with some Greek cities in that quarter of the Mediterranean, under their protection. Hannibal, although he well knew that an attack upon this place would precipitate hostilities with Rome, laid siege to it in the spring of 219 B.C. He was eager for the renewal of the old contest. The Roman Senate sent messengers to him forbidding his making war upon a city which was a friend and ally of the Roman people ; but Hannibal, disregarding their remonstrances, continued the siege, and, after an investment of eight months, gained possession of the town.

The Romans now sent commissioners to Carthage to demand of the Senate that they should give up Hannibal to them, and by so doing repudiate the act of their general. The Carthaginians hesitated. Then Quintus Fabius, chief of the embassy, gathering up his toga, said : " I carry here peace and war ; choose, men of Carthage, which ye will have." " Give us whichever ye will," was the reply. " War, then," said Fabius, dropping his toga. The " die was now cast ; and the arena was cleared for the foremost

man of his race and his time, perhaps the mightiest military genius
of any race and of any time."

THE SECOND PUNIC WAR.

Hannibal's Passage of the Alps. — The Carthaginian empire
was now stirred with preparations for the impending struggle.

HANNIBAL.

Hannibal was the life and soul of every movement. His bold
plan was to cross the Pyrenees and the Alps and descend upon
Rome from the north.

With his preparations completed, Hannibal left New Carthage early in the spring of 218 B.C., with an army numbering about one hundred thousand men, and including thirty-seven war elephants. Crossing the Pyrenees and the Rhone, he reached the foot-hills of the Alps. Nature and man joined to oppose the passage. The season was already far advanced — it was October — and snow was falling upon the higher portions of the trail. Day after day the army toiled painfully up the dangerous path. In places the narrow way had to be cut wider for the monstrous bodies of the elephants. Often avalanches of stone were hurled upon the trains by the hostile bands that held possession of the heights above. At last the summit was gained, and the shivering army looked down into the warm haze of the Italian plains. The sight alone was enough to rouse the drooping spirits of the soldiers; but Hannibal stirred them to enthusiasm by addressing them with these words: "Ye are standing upon the Acropolis of Italy; yonder lies Rome." The army began its descent, and at length, after toils and losses equalled only by those of the ascent, its thinned battalions issued from the defiles of the mountains upon the plains of the Po. Of the fifty thousand men and more with which Hannibal had begun the passage, barely half that number had survived the march, and these "looked more like phantoms than men."

Battles of the Ticinus, the Trebia, and Lake Trasimenus. — The Romans had not the remotest idea of Hannibal's plans. With war determined upon, the Senate had sent one of the consuls, L. Sempronius Longus, with an army into Africa by the way of Sicily; while the other, Publius Cornelius Scipio, they had directed to lead another army into Spain.

While the Senate were watching the movements of these expeditions, they were startled with the intelligence that Hannibal, instead of being in Spain, had crossed the Pyrenees and was among the Gauls upon the Rhone. Sempronius was hastily recalled from his attempt upon Africa, to the defence of Italy. Scipio, on his way to Spain, had touched at Massilia, and there learned of the movements of Hannibal. He turned back, hurried into Northern Italy, and took command of the levies there. The cavalry of the two armies met upon the banks of the Ticinus, a tributary of the Po. The Romans were driven from the field by the fierce onset of the Numidian horsemen. Scipio now awaited the arrival of the other consular army, which was hurrying up through Italy by forced marches.

In the battle of the Trebia the united armies of the two consuls were almost annihilated. The Gauls, who had been waiting to see to which side fortune would incline, now flocked to the standard of Hannibal, and hailed him as their deliverer.

The spring following the victory at the Trebia, Hannibal led his army, now recruited by many Gauls, across the Apennines, and moved southward. At Lake Trasimenus he entrapped the Romans under Flaminius in a mountain defile, where, bewildered by a fog that filled the valley, the greater part of the army was slaughtered, and the consul himself was slain.

The way to Rome was now open. Believing that Hannibal would march directly upon the capital, the Senate caused the bridges that spanned the Tiber to be destroyed, and appointed Fabius Maximus dictator.

In one respect only had events disappointed Hannibal's expectations. He had thought that all the states of Italy were, like the Gauls, ready to revolt from Rome at the first opportunity that might offer itself. But not a single city had thus far proved unfaithful to her.

Fabius "the Delayer." — The fate of Rome was now in the hands of Fabius. Should he risk a battle and lose it, the destiny of the capital would be sealed. He determined to adopt a more prudent policy — to follow and annoy the Carthaginian army, but to refuse all proffers of battle. Thus time might be gained for raising a new army and perfecting measures for the public defence. In every possible way Hannibal endeavored to draw his enemy into an engagement. He ravaged the fields far and wide and fired the homesteads of the Italians, in order to force Fabius to fight in their defence. The soldiers of the dictator began to murmur. They called him *Cunctator*, or " the Delayer." They even accused him of treachery to the cause of Rome. But nothing moved him from the steady pursuit of the policy which he clearly saw was the only prudent one to follow.

The Battle of Cannæ. — The time gained by Fabius enabled the Romans to raise and discipline an army that might hope successfully to combat the Carthaginian forces. Early in the summer of the year 216 B.C. these new levies, numbering 80,000 men, confronted the army of Hannibal, amounting to not more than half that number, at Cannæ, in Apulia. It was the largest army the Romans had ever gathered on any battle-field. But it had been collected only to meet the most overwhelming defeat that ever befell the forces of the republic. Through the skilful manœuvres of Hannibal, the Romans were completely surrounded, and huddled together in a helpless mass upon the field, and then for eight hours were cut down by the Numidian cavalry. From fifty to seventy thousand were slain ; a few thousand were taken prisoners ; only the merest handful escaped, including one of the consuls. The slaughter was so great that, according to Livy, when Mago, a brother of Hannibal, carried the news of the victory to Carthage, he, in confirmation of the intelligence, poured down in the porch of the Senate-house, nearly a peck of gold rings taken from the fingers of Roman knights.

Events after the Battle of Cannæ. — The awful news flew to Rome. Consternation and despair seized the people. The city would have been emptied of its population had not the Senate ordered the gates to be closed. Never did that body display greater calmness, wisdom, prudence, and resolution. By word and act they bade the people never to despair of the republic. Little by little the panic was allayed. Measures were concerted for the defence of the capital, as it was expected that Hannibal would immediately march upon Rome. Swift horsemen were sent out along the Appian Way to gather information of the conqueror's movements, and to learn, as Livy expresses it, " if the immortal gods, out of pity to the empire, had left any remnant of the Roman name."

The leader of the Numidian cavalry, Maharbal, urged Hannibal to follow up his victory closely. "Let me advance with the cavalry," said he, "and in five days thou shalt dine in the capital." But Hannibal refused to adopt the counsel of his impetuous general. Maharbal turned away, and, with mingled reproach and impatience, exclaimed, "Alas! thou knowest how to gain a victory, but not how to use one." The great commander, while he knew he was invincible in the open field, did not think it prudent to fight the Romans behind their walls.

Hannibal now sent an embassy to Rome to offer terms of peace. The Senate, true to the Appian policy never to treat with a victorious enemy (see p. 245), would not even permit the ambassadors to enter the gates. Not less disappointed was Hannibal in the temper of the Roman allies. For the most part they adhered to the cause of Rome with unshaken loyalty through all these trying times. Some tribes in the South of Italy, however, among which were the Lucanians, the Apulians, and the Bruttians, went over to the Carthaginians. Hannibal marched into Campania and quartered his army for the winter in the luxurious city of Capua, which had opened its gates to him. Here he rested and sent urgent messages to Carthage for re-inforcements, while Rome exhausted every resource in raising and equipping new levies, to take the place of the legions lost at Cannæ. For several years there was an ominous lull in the war, while both parties were gathering strength for a renewal of the struggle.

The Fall of Syracuse and of Capua. — In the year 216 B.C., Hiero, King of Syracuse, who loved to call himself the friend and ally of the Roman people, died, and the government fell into the hands of a party unfriendly to the republic. An alliance was formed with Carthage, and a large part of Sicily was carried over to the side of the enemies of Rome. The distinguished Roman general, Marcus Claudius Marcellus, called "the Sword of Rome," was intrusted with the task of reconquering the island. After reducing many towns, he at last laid siege to Syracuse.

This noted capital was then one of the largest and richest cities of the Grecian world. For three years it held out against the Roman forces. It is said that Archimedes (see p. 213), the great mathematician, rendered valuable aid to the besieged with curious and powerful engines contrived by his genius. But the city fell at last, and was given over to sack and pillage. Rome was adorned with the rare works of Grecian art—paintings and sculptures—which for centuries

MARCELLUS, "The Sword of Rome."

had been accumulating in this the oldest and most renowned of the colonies of ancient Hellas. Syracuse never recovered from the blow inflicted upon her at this time by the relentless Romans.

Capua must next be punished for opening her gates and extending her hospitalities to the enemies of Rome. A line of circumvallation was drawn about the devoted city, and two Roman armies held it in close siege. Hannibal, ever faithful to his allies and friends, hastened to the relief of the Capuans. Unable to break the enemy's lines, he marched directly upon Rome, as if to make an attack upon that city, hoping thus to draw off the legions about Capua to the defence of the capital. The "dread Hannibal" himself rode alongside the walls of the hated city, and, tradition says, even hurled a defiant spear over the defences. The Romans certainly were trembling with fear; yet Livy tells how they manifested their confidence in their affairs by selling at public auction the land upon which Hannibal was encamped. He in turn, in the same manner, disposed of the shops fronting the Forum. The story is that there were eager purchasers in both cases.

Failing to draw the legions from Capua as he had hoped, Hannibal now retired from before Rome, and, retreating into the southern part of Italy, abandoned Capua to its fate. It soon fell, and paid the penalty that Rome never failed to inflict upon an unfaithful ally. The chief men in the city were put to death, and a large part of the inhabitants sold as slaves. Capua had aspired to the first place among the cities of Italy : scarcely more than the name of the ambitious capital now remained.

Hasdrubal attempts to carry Aid to his Brother. — During all the years Hannibal was waging war in Italy, his brother Hasdrubal was carrying on a desperate struggle with the Roman armies in Spain. At length he determined to leave the conduct of the war in that country to others, and go to the relief of his brother, who was sadly in need of aid. Like Pyrrhus, Hannibal had been brought to realize that even constant victories won at the cost of soldiers that could not be replaced, meant final defeat.

Hasdrubal followed the same route that had been taken by his brother Hannibal, and in the year 207 B.C. descended from the Alps upon the plains of Northern Italy. Thence he advanced southward, while Hannibal moved northward from Bruttium to meet him. Rome made a last great effort to prevent the junction of the armies of the two brothers. At the river Metaurus, Hasdrubal's march was withstood by a large Roman army. Here his forces were cut to pieces, and he himself was slain (207 B.C.). His head was severed from his body and sent to Hannibal. Upon recognizing the features of his brother, Hannibal exclaimed sadly, " Carthage, I see thy fate."

War in Africa: Battle of Zama. — The defeat and death of Hasdrubal gave a different aspect to the war. Hannibal now drew back into the rocky peninsula of Bruttium, the southernmost point of Italy. There he faced the Romans like a lion at bay. No one dared attack him. It was resolved to carry the war into Africa, in hopes that the Carthaginians would be forced to call their great commander out of Italy to the defence of Carthage. Publius Cornelius Scipio,[1] who after the departure of Hasdrubal from Spain had quickly brought the peninsula under the power of Rome, led the army of invasion. He had not been long in Africa before the Carthaginian Senate sent for Hannibal to conduct the war. At Zama, not far from Carthage, the hostile armies came face to face. Fortune had deserted Hannibal ; he was fighting

[1] Son of the consul mentioned on page 259.

against fate. He here met his first and final defeat. His army, in which were many of the veterans that had served through all the Italian campaigns, was almost annihilated (202 B.C.). Scipio was accorded a splendid triumph at Rome, and given the surname Africanus in honor of his achievements.[1]

PUBLIUS CORNELIUS SCIPIO (Africanus).

The Close of the War. — Carthage was now completely exhausted, and sued for peace. Even Hannibal himself could no longer counsel war. The terms of the treaty were much severer than those imposed upon the city at the end of the First Punic War. She was required to give up all claims to Spain and the islands of the Mediterranean; to surrender her war elephants, and all her ships of war save ten galleys; to pay an indemnity of five thousand talents at once, and two hundred and fifty talents annu-

[1] Some time after the close of the Second Punic War, the Romans, persuading themselves that Hannibal was preparing Carthage for another war, demanded his surrender of the Carthaginians. He fled to Syria, and thence to Asia Minor, where, to avoid falling into the hands of his implacable foes, he committed suicide by means of poison (183 B.C.).

ally for fifty years ; and not to engage in any war without the consent of Rome.   Five hundred of the costly Phœnician war galleys were towed out of the harbor of Carthage and burned in the sight of the citizens.

Such was the end of the Second Punic, or Hannibalic War, as called by the Romans, the most desperate struggle ever maintained by rival powers for empire.

CHAPTER XXVI.

THE THIRD PUNIC WAR.

(149–146 B.C.)

EVENTS BETWEEN THE SECOND AND THE THIRD PUNIC WAR.

THE terms imposed upon Carthage at the end of the Second Punic War left Rome mistress of the Western Mediterranean. During the fifty eventful years that elapsed between the close of that struggle and the breaking-out of the last Punic war, her authority became supreme also in the Eastern seas. In a preceding chapter (see p. 170), while narrating the fortunes of the most important states into which the great empire of Alexander was broken at his death, we followed them until one after another they fell beneath the arms of Rome, and were successively absorbed into her growing kingdom. We shall therefore speak of them here only in the briefest manner, simply indicating the connection of their several histories with the series of events which mark the advance of Rome to universal empire.

The Battle of Cynoscephalæ (197 B.C.). — During the Hannibalic War, Philip V. (III.) of Macedonia had aided the Carthaginians, or at least had entered into an alliance with them. He was now troubling the Greek cities which were under the protection of Rome. For these things the Roman Senate determined to punish him. An army under Flamininus was sent into Greece, and on the plains of Cynoscephalæ, in Thessaly, the Roman legion demonstrated its superiority over the un-

PHILIP V., of Macedonia.

wieldy Macedonian phalanx by subjecting Philip to a most disastrous defeat (197 B.C.). The king was forced to give up all his conquests, and Rome extended her protectorate over Greece.

The Battle of Magnesia (190 B.C.). — Antiochus the Great of Syria had at this time not only overrun all Asia Minor, but had crossed the Hellespont into Europe, and was intent upon the conquest of Thrace and Greece. Rome, that could not entertain the idea of a rival empire upon the southern shores of the Mediterranean, could much less tolerate the establishment in the East of such a colossal kingdom as the ambition of Antiochus proposed to itself. Just as soon as intelligence was carried to Italy that the Syrian king was leading his army into Greece, the legions of the republic were set in motion. Some reverses caused Antiochus to retreat in haste across the Hellespont into Asia, whither he was followed by the Romans, led by Scipio, a brother of Africanus.

At Magnesia, Antiochus was overthrown, and a large part of Asia Minor fell into the hands of the Romans. Not yet prepared to maintain provinces so distant from the Tiber, the Senate conferred the new territory, with the exception of Lycia and Caria, which were given to the Rhodians, upon their friend and ally Eumenes, King of Pergamus (see p. 171). This "Kingdom of Asia," as it was called, was really nothing more than a dependency of Rome, and its nominal ruler only a puppet-king in the hands of the Roman Senate.

Scipio enjoyed a magnificent triumph at Rome, and, in accordance with a custom that had now become popular with successful generals, erected a memorial of his deeds in his name by assuming the title of Asiaticus.

The Battle of Pydna (168 B.C.). — In a few years Macedonia,

under the leadership of Perseus, son of Philip V., was again in arms and offering defiance to Rome ; but in the year 168 B.C. the Roman consul Æmilius Paulus crushed the Macedonian power forever upon the memorable field of Pydna. This was one of the decisive battles fought by the Romans in their struggle for the dominion of the

PERSEUS, of Macedonia. world. The last great power in the East was here broken. The Roman Senate was henceforth recognized by the whole civilized world as the source and fountain of supreme political wisdom and power. We shall have yet to record many campaigns of the Roman legions; but these were efforts to suppress revolt among dependent or semi-vassal states, or were struggles with barbarian tribes that skirted the Roman dominions.

The Destruction of Corinth (146 B.C.). — Barely twenty years had passed after the destruction of the Macedonian monarchy before the cities and states that formed the Achæan League (see p. 175) were goaded to revolt by the injustice of their Roman protectors. In the year 146 B.C. the consul Mummius signalized the suppression of the rebellion by the complete destruction of the brilliant city of Corinth, the "eye of Hellas," as in expressive figure it has been called. This fair capital, the most beautiful and renowned of all the cities of Greece after the fall of Athens, was sacked, and razed to the ground. Much of the booty was sold on the spot at public auction. Numerous works of art, — rare paintings and sculptures, — with which the city was crowded, were carried off to Italy. "Never before or after," says Long, "was such a display of the wonders of Grecian art carried in triumphal procession through the streets of Rome."

The Third Punic War.

"Carthage must be destroyed." — The same year that Rome destroyed Corinth (146 B.C.), she also blotted her great rival Carthage from the face of the earth. It will be recalled that one of the conditions imposed upon the last-named city at the close of the Second Punic War was that she should, under no circumstances, engage in any war without the permission of the Roman Senate. Taking advantage of the helpless condition of Carthage, Masinissa, King of Numidia, began to make depredations upon her territories. She appealed to Rome for protection. The envoys sent to Africa by the Senate to settle the dispute, unfairly adjudged every case in favor of the robber Masinissa. In this way Carthage was deprived of her lands and towns.

Chief of one of the embassies sent out was Marcus Cato the Censor. When he saw the prosperity of Carthage, — her immense trade, which crowded her harbor with ships, and the country for miles back of the city a beautiful landscape of gardens and villas, — he was amazed at the growing power and wealth of the city, and returned home convinced that the safety of Rome demanded the destruction of her rival. Never afterwards did he address the Romans, no matter upon what subject, but he always ended with the words, "Carthage must be destroyed" (*delenda est Carthago*).

Roman Perfidy. — A pretext for the accomplishment of the hateful work was not long wanting. In 150 B.C. the Carthaginians, when Masinissa made another attack upon their territory, instead of calling upon Rome, from which source the past had convinced them they could hope for neither aid nor justice, gathered an army, and resolved to defend themselves. Their forces, however, were defeated by the Numidians, and sent beneath the yoke.

In entering upon this war without the consent of Rome, Carthage had broken the conditions of the last treaty. The Carthaginian Senate, in great anxiety, now sent an embassy to Italy to offer any reparation the Romans might demand. They were told that if they would give three hundred hostages, members of the noblest Carthaginian families, the independence of their city should be respected. They eagerly complied with this demand. But no sooner were these in the hands of the Romans than the consular armies, numbering eighty thousand men, secured against attack by the hostages so perfidiously drawn from the Carthaginians, crossed from Sicily into Africa, and disembarked at Utica, only ten miles from Carthage.

The Carthaginians were now commanded to give up all their arms; still hoping to win their enemy to clemency, they complied with this demand also. Then the consuls made known the final decree of the Roman Senate — "That Carthage must be destroyed, but that the inhabitants might build a new city, provided it were located ten miles from the coast."

When this resolution of the Senate was announced to the Carthaginians, and they realized the baseness and perfidy of their enemy, a cry of indignation and despair burst from the betrayed city.

The Carthaginians prepare to defend their City. — It was resolved to resist to the bitter end the execution of the cruel decree. The gates of the city were closed. Men, women, and children set to work and labored day and night manufacturing arms. The entire city was converted into one great workshop. The utensils of the home and the sacred vessels of the temples, statues, and vases were melted down for weapons. Material was torn from the buildings of the city for the construction of military engines. The women cut off their hair and braided it into strings for the catapults. By such labor, and through such means, the city was soon put in a state to withstand a siege.

When the Romans advanced to take possession of the place, they were astonished to find the people they had just treacherously disarmed, with weapons in their hands, manning the walls of their capital, and ready to bid them defiance.

The Destruction of Carthage. — It is impossible for us here to give the circumstances of the siege of Carthage. For four years the city held out against the Roman army. At length the consul Scipio Æmilianus succeeded in taking it by storm. When resistance ceased, only 50,000 men, women, and children, out of a population of 700,000, remained to be made prisoners. The city was fired, and for seventeen days the space within the walls was a sea of flames. Every trace of building which the fire could not destroy was levelled, a plough was driven over the site, and a dreadful curse invoked upon any one who should dare attempt to rebuild the city.

Such was the hard fate of Carthage. It is said that Scipio, as he gazed upon the smouldering ruins, seemed to read in them the fate of Rome, and, bursting into tears, sadly repeated the lines of Homer :

> "The day shall come in which our sacred Troy,
>   And Priam, and the people over whom
>   Spear-bearing Priam rules, shall perish all."

The Carthaginian territory in Africa was made into a Roman province, with Utica as the leading city; and Roman civilization was spread rapidly, by means of traders and settlers, throughout the regions that lie between the ranges of the Atlas and the sea.

War in Spain.

Siege of Numantia. — It is fitting that the same chapter which narrates the destruction of Corinth in Greece, and the blotting-out of Carthage in Africa, should tell the story of the destruction of Numantia in Spain.

The expulsion of the Carthaginians from the Spanish peninsula really gave Rome the control of only a small part of that country. The war-like native tribes — the Celtiberians and Lusitanians — of the North and the West were ready stubbornly to dispute with the new-comers the possession of the soil.

The war gathered about Numantia, the siege of which was brought to a close by Scipio Æmilianus, the conqueror of Carthage. Before the surrender of the place, almost all the inhabitants had met death, either in defence of the walls, or by deliberate suicide. The miserable remnant which the ravages of battle, famine, pestilence, and despair had left alive were sold into slavery, and the city was levelled to the ground (133 B.C.).

The capture of Numantia was considered quite as great an achievement as the taking of Carthage. Scipio celebrated another triumph at Rome, and to his surname Africanus, which he had received for his achievements in Africa, added that of Numantinus. Spain became a favorite resort of Roman merchants, and many colonies were established in different parts of the country. As a result of this great influx of Italians, the laws, manners, customs, language, and religion of the conquerors were introduced everywhere, and the peninsula became rapidly Romanized.

CHAPTER XXVII.

THE LAST CENTURY OF THE ROMAN REPUBLIC.

(133–31 B.C.)

WE have now traced the growth of the power of republican Rome, as through two centuries and more of conquest she has extended her authority, first throughout Italy, and then over almost all the countries that border upon the Mediterranean. It must be our less pleasant task now to follow the declining fortunes of the republic through the last century of its existence. We shall here learn that wars waged for spoils and dominion are in the end more ruinous, if possible, to the conqueror than to the conquered.

The Servile War in Sicily (134–132 B.C.). — With the opening of this period we find a terrible struggle going on in Sicily between masters and slaves — or what is known as " The First Servile War." The condition of affairs in that island was the legitimate result of the Roman system of slavery. The captives taken in war were usually sold into servitude. The great number of prisoners furnished by the numerous conquests of the Romans caused slaves to become a drug in the slave-markets of the Roman world. They were so cheap that masters found it more profitable to wear their slaves out by a few years of unmercifully hard labor, and then to buy others, than to preserve their lives for a longer period by more humane treatment. In case of sickness, they were left to die without attention, as the expense of nursing exceeded the cost of new purchases. Some Sicilian estates were worked by as many as 20,000 slaves. That each owner might know his own, the poor creatures were branded like cattle. What makes all this the more revolting is the fact that many of these slaves were in every way the peers of their owners, and often were their superiors. The fortunes of war alone had made one servant and the other master.

The wretched condition of these slaves and the cruelty of their masters at last drove them to revolt. The insurrection spread throughout the island, until 200,000 slaves were in arms, and in possession of many of the strongholds of the country. They defeated four Roman armies sent against them, and for three years defied the power of Rome. Finally, however, in the year 132 B.C., the revolt was crushed, and peace was restored to the distracted island.[1]

The Public Lands. — In Italy itself affairs were in a scarcely less wretched condition than in Sicily. When the different states of the peninsula were subjugated, large portions of the conquered territory had become public land (*ager publicus*); for upon the subjugation of a state Rome never left to the conquered people more than two-thirds of their lands, and often not so much as this. The land appropriated was disposed of at public sale, leased at low rentals, allotted to discharged soldiers, or allowed to lie unused.[2]

Now, it had happened that, in various ways, the greater part of the public lands had fallen into the hands of the wealthy. They alone had the capital necessary to stock and work them to advantage ; hence the possessions of the small proprietors were gradually absorbed by the large landholders. These great proprietors, also, disregarding a law which forbade any person to hold more than five hundred jugera of land, held many times that amount. Almost all the lands of Italy, about the beginning of the first century B.C., are said to have been held by not more than two thousand

---

[1] In the year 102 B.C. another insurrection of the slaves broke out in the island, which it required three years to quell. This last revolt is known as "The Second Servile War."

[2] These land matters may be made plain by a reference to the public lands of the United States. The troubles in Ireland between the land-owners and their tenants will also serve to illustrate the agrarian disturbances in ancient Rome.

persons; for the large proprietors, besides the lands they had secured by purchase from the government, or had wrested from the smaller farmers, claimed enormous tracts to which they had only a squatter's title. So long had they been left in undisturbed possession of these government lands that they had come to look upon them as absolutely their own. In many cases, feeling secure through great lapse of time, — the lands having been handed down through many generations, — the owners had expended large sums in their improvement, and now resisted as very unjust every effort to dispossess them of their hereditary estates. Money-lenders, too, had, in many instances, made loans upon these lands, and they naturally sided with the owners in their opposition to all efforts to disturb the titles.

These wealthy " possessors " employed slave rather than free labor, as they found it more profitable; and so the poorer Romans, left without employment, crowded into the cities, especially congregating at Rome, where they lived in vicious indolence. The proprietors also found it to their interest to raise stock rather than to cultivate the soil. All Italy became a great sheep-pasture.

Thus, largely through the workings of the public land system, the Roman people had become divided into two great classes, which are variously designated as the Rich and the Poor, the Possessors and the Non-Possessors, the Optimates (the " Best "), and the Populares (the " People "). We hear nothing more of patricians and plebeians. As one expresses it, " Rome had become a commonwealth of millionaires and beggars."

For many years before and after the period at which we have now arrived, a bitter struggle was carried on between these two classes; just such a contest as we have seen waged between the nobility and the commonalty in the earlier history of Rome. The most instructive portion of the story of the Roman republic is found in the records of this later struggle. The misery of the great masses naturally led to constant agitation at the capital. Popular leaders introduced bill after bill into the Senate, and brought measure after measure before the assemblies of the people, all aiming at the redistribution of the public lands and the correction of existing abuses.

The Reforms of the Gracchi. — The most noted champions of the cause of the poorer classes against the rich and powerful were Tiberius and Caius Gracchus. These reformers are reckoned among the most popular orators that Rome ever produced. They eloquently voiced the wrongs of the people. Said Tiberius, " You are called ' lords of the earth ' without possessing a single clod to call your own." The people made him tribune ; and in that position he secured the passage of a law for the redistribution of the public lands, which gave some relief. It took away from Possessors without sons all the land they held over five hundred jugera ; Possessors with one son might hold seven hundred and fifty jugera, and those with two sons one thousand.

As the end of his term of office drew near, Tiberius stood again for the tribunate. The nobles combined to defeat him. Foreseeing that he would not be re-elected, Tiberius resolved to use force upon the day of voting. His partisans were overpowered, and he and three hundred of his followers were killed in the Forum, and their bodies thrown into the Tiber (133 B.C.). This was the first time that the Roman Forum had witnessed such a scene of violence and crime.

Caius Gracchus, the younger brother of Tiberius, now assumed the position made vacant by the death of Tiberius. It is related that Caius had a dream in which the spirit of his brother seemed to address him thus : " Caius, why do you linger ? There is no escape : one life for both of us, and one death in defence of the people, is our fate." The dream came true. Caius was chosen tribune in 123 B.C. He secured the passage of grain-laws which provided that grain should be sold to the poor from public granaries, at half its value or less. This was a very unwise and pernicious measure. It was not long before grain was distributed free to all applicants ; and a considerable portion of the population of the capital were living in vicious indolence and feeding at the public crib.

Caius proposed other measures in the interest of the people, which were bitterly opposed by the Optimates; and the two orders at last came into collision. Caius sought death by a friendly sword (121 B.C.), and three thousand of his adherents were massacred. The consul offered for the head of Caius its weight in gold. "This is the first instance in Roman history of head-money being offered and paid, but it was not the last" (Long).

The people ever regarded the Gracchi as martyrs to their cause, and their memory was preserved by statues in the public square. To Cornelia, their mother, a monument was erected, simply bearing the inscription, "The Mother of the Gracchi."

The War with Jugurtha (111–106 B.C.). — After the death of the Gracchi there seemed no one left to resist the heartless oppressions and to denounce the scandalous extravagances of the aristocratic party. Many of the laws of the Gracchi respecting the public lands were annulled. Italy fell again into the hands of a few over-rich land-owners. The provinces were plundered by the Roman governors, who squandered their ill-gotten wealth at the capital. The votes of senators and the decisions of judges, the offices at Rome and the places in the provinces — everything pertaining to the government had its price, and was bought and sold like merchandise. Affairs in Africa at this time illustrate how Roman virtue and integrity had declined since Fabricius indignantly refused the gold of Pyrrhus.

Jugurtha, king of Numidia, had seized all that country, having put to death the rightful rulers of different provinces of the region, who had been confirmed in their possessions by the Romans at the close of the Punic wars. Commissioners sent from Rome to look into the matter were bribed by Jugurtha. Even the consul Bestia, who had been sent into Africa with an army to punish the insolent usurper, sold himself to the robber. An investigation was ordered; but many prominent officials at Rome were implicated in the offences, and the matter was hushed up with money. The venality of the Romans disgusted even Jugurtha, who exclaimed, "O venal city, thou wouldst sell thyself if thou couldst find a purchaser!"

In the year 106 B.C. the war against Jugurtha was brought to a close by Caius Marius, a man who had risen to the consulship from the lowest ranks of the people. Under him fought a young nobleman named Sulla, of whom we shall hear much hereafter. Marius celebrated a grand triumph at Rome. Jugurtha, after having graced the triumphal procession, was thrown into the Mamertine dungeon, beneath the Capitoline, where he died of starvation.

Invasion of the Cimbri and Teutones. — The war was not yet ended in Africa before terrible tidings came to Rome from the north. Two mighty nations of "horrible barbarians," three hundred thousand strong in fighting-men, coming whence no one could tell, had invaded, and were now desolating, the Roman provinces of Gaul, and might any moment cross the Alps and pour down into Italy.

The mysterious invaders proved to be two Germanic tribes, the Teutones and Cimbri, the vanguard of that great German migration which was destined to change the face and history of Europe. These intruders were seeking new homes. They carried with them, in rude wagons, all their property, their wives, and their children. The Celtic tribes of Gaul were no match for the newcomers, and fled before them as they advanced. Several Roman armies beyond the Alps were cut to pieces. The terror at Rome was only equalled by that occasioned by the invasion of the Gauls two centuries before. The Gauls were terrible enough ; but now the conquerors of the Gauls were coming.

Marius, the conqueror of Jugurtha, was looked to by all as the only man who could save the state in this crisis. Accompanied by Sulla as one of his most skilful lieutenants, Marius hastened into Northern Italy. The barbarians had divided into two bands. The Cimbri were to cross the Eastern Alps, and join in the valley of the Po the Teutones, who were to force the defiles of the Western, or Maritime Alps. Marius determined to prevent the union of the barbarians, and to crush each band separately.

Anticipating the march of the Teutones, he hurried over the Alps into Gaul, and falling upon them at a favorable moment (at

Aquæ Sextiæ, not far from Marseilles, 102 B.C.), almost annihilated the entire host. Two hundred thousand barbarians are said to have been slain. Marius now recrossed the Alps, and, after visiting Rome, hastened to meet the Cimbri, who were entering the northeastern corner of Italy. He was not a day too soon. Already the barbarians had defeated the Roman army under the nobleman Catulus, and were ravaging the rich plains of the Po. The Cimbri, unconscious of the fate of the Teutones, sent an embassy to Marius, to demand that they and their kinsmen should be given lands in Italy. Marius sent back in reply, " The Teutones have got all the land they need on the other side of the Alps." The devoted Cimbri were soon to have all they needed on this side.

A terrible battle almost immediately followed at Vercellæ (101 B.C.). The barbarians were drawn up in an enormous hollow square, the men forming the outer ranks being fastened together with chains, to prevent the lines being broken. This proved their ruin. More than 100,000 were killed and 60,000 taken prisoners to be sold as slaves in the Roman markets. Marius was hailed as the " Saviour of his Country."

" The forlorn-hope of the German migration had performed its duty; the homeless people of the Cimbri and their comrades were no more " (Mommsen). Their kinsmen yet behind the Danube and the Rhine were destined to exact a terrible revenge for their slaughter.

The Social, or Marsic War (91–89 B.C.). — Scarcely was the danger of the barbarian invasion past, before Rome was threatened by another and greater evil arising within her own borders. At this time all the free inhabitants of Italy were embraced in three classes, — *Roman citizens, Latins,* and *Italian allies.* The Roman citizens included the inhabitants of the capital and of the various Roman colonies planted in different parts of the peninsula (see p. 246, note), besides the people of a number of towns called *municipia;* the Latins were the inhabitants of the Latin colonies (see p. 246, note) ; the Italian allies (*socii*) included the various subjugated races of Italy.

The Social, or Marsic War (as it is often called on account of the prominent part taken in the insurrection by the warlike Marsians) was a struggle that arose from the demands of the Italian allies for the privileges of Roman citizenship, from which they were wholly excluded. Their demands were stubbornly resisted by both the aristocratic and the popular party at Rome. Some, however, recognized the justice of these claims of the Italians. The tribune Livius Drusus championed their cause, but he was killed by an assassin. The Italians now flew to arms. They determined upon the establishment of a rival state. A town called Corfinium, among the Apennines, was chosen as the capital of the new republic, and its name changed to Italica. Thus, in a single day, almost all Italy south of the Rubicon was lost to Rome. The Etrurians, the Umbrians, the Campanians, the Latins, and some of the Greek cities were the only states that remained faithful.

COIN OF THE ITALIAN
CONFEDERACY.
(The Sabellian Bull goring the
Roman Wolf.)

The greatness of the danger aroused all the old Roman courage and patriotism. Aristocrats and democrats hushed their quarrels, and fought bravely side by side for the endangered life of the republic. The war lasted three years. Finally Rome prudently extended the right of suffrage to the Latins, Etruscans, and Umbrians, who had so far remained true to her, but now began to show signs of wavering in their loyalty. Shortly afterwards she offered the same to all Italians who should lay down their arms within sixty days. This tardy concession to the just demands of the Italians virtually ended the war. It had been extremely disastrous to the republic. Hundreds of thousands of lives had been lost, many towns had been depopulated, and vast tracts of the country made desolate by those ravages that never fail to characterize civil contentions.

In after-years, under the empire, the rights of Roman citizenship, which the most of the Italians had now so hardly won, were extended to all the free inhabitants of the various provinces, beyond the confines of Italy (see p. 327).

The Civil War of Marius and Sulla. — The Social War was not yet ended when a formidable enemy appeared in the East. Mithridates the Great, king of Pontus (see p. 170, note), taking advantage of the distracted condition of the republic, had encroached upon the Roman provinces in Asia Minor, and had caused a general massacre of the Italian traders and residents in that country. The number of victims of this wholesale slaughter has been variously estimated at from 80,000 to 150,000. The Roman Senate instantly declared war.

A contest straightway arose between Marius and Sulla for the command of the forces. The sword settled the dispute. Sulla, at the head of the legions he commanded, marched upon Rome, entered the gates, and " for the first time in the annals of the city a Roman army encamped within the walls." The party of Marius was defeated, and he and ten of his companions were proscribed. Marius escaped and fled to Africa; Sulla embarked with the legions to meet Mithridates in the East (87 B.C.).

MARIUS.

The Wanderings of Marius: His Return to Italy. — Leaving Sulla to carry on the Mithridatic War, we must first follow the fortunes of the outlawed Marius. The ship in which he embarked for Africa was driven back upon the Italian coast at Circeii, and he was captured. A Cimbrian slave was sent to despatch him in prison. The cell where Marius lay was dark, and the eyes of the old soldier " seemed to flash fire." As the slave advanced, Marius shouted, " Man, do you dare to kill Caius Marius?" The frightened slave dropped his sword, and fled from the chamber, half dead with fear.

A better feeling now took possession of the captors of Marius, and they resolved that the blood of the "Saviour of Italy" should not be upon their hands. They put him aboard a vessel, which bore him and his friends to an island just off the coast of Africa. When he attempted to set foot upon the mainland near Carthage, Sextius, the Roman governor of the province, sent a messenger to forbid him to land. The legend says that the old general, almost choking with indignation, only answered, "Go, tell your master, that you have seen Marius a fugitive sitting amidst the ruins of Carthage."

A successful move of his friends at Rome brought Marius back to the capital. He now took a terrible revenge upon his enemies. The consul Octavius was assassinated, and his head set up in front of the Rostrum. Never before had such a thing been seen at Rome — a consul's head exposed to the public gaze. The senators, equestrians, and leaders of the Optimate party fled from the capital. For five days and nights a merciless slaughter was kept up. The life of every man in the capital was in the hands of the revengeful Marius. If he refused to return the greeting of any citizen, that sealed his fate : he was instantly despatched by the soldiers who awaited the dictator's nod. The bodies of the victims lay unburied in the streets. Sulla's house was torn down, and he himself declared a public enemy.

Rumors were now spread that Sulla, having overthrown Mithridates, was about to set out on his return with his victorious legions. He would surely exact speedy and terrible vengeance. Marius, old and enfeebled by the hardships of many campaigns, seemed to shrink from again facing his hated rival. He plunged into dissipation to drown his remorse and gloomy forebodings, and died in his seventy-first year (86 B.C.).

Sulla and the Mithridatic War. — When Sulla left Italy with his legions for the East, he knew very well that his enemies would have their own way in Italy during his absence ; but he also knew that, if successful in his campaign against Mithridates, he could easily regain Italy, and wrest the government from the hands of the Marian party.

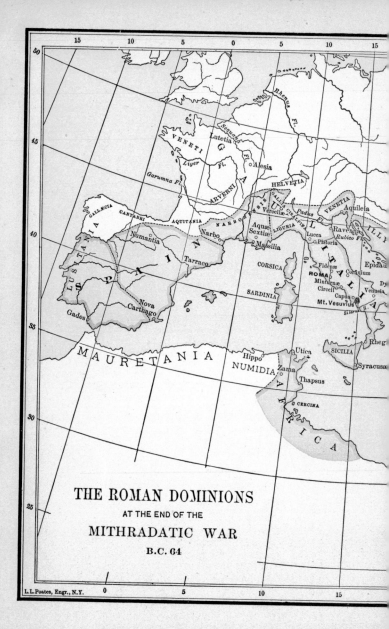

THE ROMAN DOMINIONS

AT THE END OF THE

MITHRADATIC WAR

B.C. 64

L.L.Poates, Engr., N.Y.

We can here take space to give simply the results of Sulla's campaigns in the East. After driving the army of Mithridates out of Greece, Sulla crossed the Hellespont, and forced the king to sue for peace. He gave up his conquered territory, surrendered his war ships, and paid a large indemnity to cover the expenses of the war.

SULLA.

With the Mithridatic War ended, Sulla wrote to the Senate, saying that he was now coming to take vengeance upon the Marian party,— his own and the republic's foes.

The terror and consternation produced at Rome by this letter were increased by the accidental burning of the Capitol. The Sibylline books, which held the secrets of the fate of Rome, were consumed. Such an event, it was believed, could only foreshadow the most direful calamities to the state.

The Proscriptions of Sulla. — The returning army from the East landed in Italy. With his veteran legions at his back, Sulla marched into Rome with all the powers of a dictator. The leaders of the Marian party were proscribed, rewards were offered for their heads, and their property was confiscated. Sulla was implored to make out a list of those he designed to put to death, that those he intended to spare might be relieved of the terrible suspense in which all were now held. He made out a list of eighty, which was attached to the Rostrum. The people murmured at the length of the roll. In a few days it was extended to over three hundred, and grew rapidly, until it included the names of thousands of the best citizens of Italy. Hundreds were murdered, not for any offence, but because some favorites of Sulla coveted their estates. A wealthy noble coming into the Forum, and reading his own name in the list of the proscribed, exclaimed, " Alas ! my villa has proved my ruin." The infamous Catiline, by having the name of a brother placed upon the fatal roll, secured his property. Julius Cæsar, at this time a mere boy of eighteen, was proscribed on account of his relationship to Marius; but, upon the intercession of friends, Sulla spared him : as he did so, however, he said warningly, and, as the event proved, prophetically, "There is in that boy many a Marius."

Senators, knights, and wealthy land-owners fell by hundreds and by thousands; but the poor Italians who had sided with the Marian party were simply slaughtered by tens of thousands. Nor did the provinces escape. In Sicily, Spain, and Africa the enemies of the dictator were hunted and exterminated like noxious animals. It is estimated that the civil war of Marius and Sulla cost the republic over one hundred and fifty thousand lives.

When Sulla had sated his revenge, he celebrated a splendid triumph at Rome, and the Senate enacted a law declaring all that he had done legal and right, caused to be erected in the Forum a gilded equestrian statue of the dictator, which bore the legend, "To Lucius Cornelius Sulla, the Commander Beloved by Fortune," and made him dictator for life. Sulla used his position and influence in recasting the constitution in the interest of the aristocratic party. After enjoying the unlimited power of an Asiatic despot for three years, he suddenly resigned the dictatorship, and retired to his villa at Puteoli, where he gave himself up to the grossest dissipations. He died the year following his abdication (78 B.C.).

CHAPTER XXVIII.

THE LAST CENTURY OF THE ROMAN REPUBLIC (*concluded*).

(133–31 B.C.)

Pompey the Great in Spain. — The fires of the Civil War, though quenched in Italy, were still smouldering in Spain. Sertorius, an adherent of Marius, had there stirred up the martial tribes of Lusitania, and incited a general revolt against the power of the aristocratic government at Rome. Cnæus Pompey, a rising young leader of the oligarchy, upon whom the title of Great had already been conferred as a reward for crushing the Marian party in Sicily and Africa, was sent into Spain to perform a similar service there.

For several years the war was carried on with varying fortunes. At times the power of Rome in the peninsula seemed on the verge of utter extinction. Finally, the brave Sertorius was assassinated, and then the whole of Spain was quickly regained. Pompey boasted of having forced the gates of more than eight hundred cities in Spain and Southern Gaul. Throughout all the conquered regions he established military colonies, and reorganized the local governments, putting in power those who would be, not only friends and allies of the Roman state, but also his own personal adherents. How he used these men as instruments of his ambition, we shall learn a little later.

Spartacus : War of the Gladiators. — While Pompey was subduing the Marian faction in Spain, a new danger broke out in the midst of Italy. Gladiatorial combats had become, at this time, the favorite sport of the amphitheatre. At Capua was a sort of training-school, from which skilled fighters were hired out for public or private entertainments. In this seminary was a Thracian slave, known by the name of Spartacus, who incited his companions to revolt.   The insurgents fled to the crater of Vesuvius, and made that their stronghold.   There they were joined by gladiators from other schools, and by slaves and discontented men from every quarter.   Some slight successes enabled them to arm themselves with the weapons of their enemies.   Their number at length increased to one hundred thousand men.   For three years they defied the power of Rome, and even gained control of the larger part of Southern Italy.   Four Roman armies sent against them were cut to pieces.   But at length Spartacus himself was slain, and the insurgents were crushed.

The rebellion was punished with Roman severity.   The slaves that had taken part in the revolt were hunted through the mountains and forests, and exterminated like dangerous beasts.   The Appian Way was lined with six thousand crosses, bearing aloft as many bodies — a terrible warning of the fate awaiting slaves that should dare to strike for freedom.

The Abuses of Verres. — Terrible as was the state of society in Italy, still worse was the condition of affairs outside the peninsula. At first the rule of the Roman governors in the provinces, though severe, was honest and prudent.   But during the period of profligacy and corruption upon which we have now entered, the administration of these foreign possessions was shamefully dishonest and incredibly cruel and rapacious.   The prosecution of Verres, the proprætor of Sicily, exposed the scandalous rule of the oligarchy, into whose hands the government had fallen.   For three years Verres plundered and ravaged that island with impunity.   He sold all the offices, and all his decisions as judge.   He demanded of the farmers the greater part of their crops, which he sold, to swell his already enormous fortune.   Agriculture was thus ruined, and the farms were abandoned.   Verres had a taste for art, and when on his tours through the island confiscated gems, vases, statues, paintings, and other things that struck his fancy, whether in temples or private dwellings.   He even caused a Roman trader, for a slight offence, to be crucified, " the cross being set on the beach within sight of Italy, that he might address to his native shores the ineffectual cry ' I am a Roman citizen.' "

Verres could not be called to account while in office ; and it was doubtful whether, after the end of his term, he could be convicted, so corrupt and venal had become the members of the Senate, before whom all such offenders must be tried. Indeed, Verres himself openly boasted that he intended two thirds of his gains for his judges and lawyers, while the remaining one third would satisfy himself.

At length, after Sicily had come to look as though it had been ravaged by barbarian conquerors, the infamous robber was impeached. The prosecutor was Marcus Tullius Cicero, the brilliant orator, who was at this time just rising into prominence at Rome. The storm of indignation raised by the developments of the trial caused Verres to flee into exile to Massilia, whither he took with him much of his ill-gotten wealth.

War with the Mediterranean Pirates (66 B.C.). — The Roman republic was now threatened by a new danger from the sea. The Mediterranean was swarming with pirates. Roman conquests in Africa, Spain, and especially in Greece and Asia Minor, had caused thousands of adventurous spirits from those maritime countries to flee to their ships, and seek a livelihood by preying upon the commerce of the seas. The cruelty and extortions of the Roman governors had also driven large numbers to the same course of life. These corsairs had banded themselves into a sort of government, and held possession of numerous strongholds — four hundred, it is said — in Cilicia, Crete, and other countries. With a full thousand swift ships they scoured the waters of the Mediterranean, so that no merchantman could spread her sails in safety. They formed a floating empire, which Michelet calls " a wandering Carthage, which no one knew where to seize, and which floated from Spain to Asia."

These buccaneers, the Vikings of the South, made descents upon the coast everywhere, plundered villas and temples, attacked and captured cities, and sold the inhabitants as slaves in the various slave-markets of the Roman world. They carried off merchants and magistrates from the Appian Way itself, and held them for ransom. At last the grain-ships of Sicily and Africa were intercepted, and Rome was threatened with the alternative of starvation or the paying of an enormous ransom.

The Romans now bestirred themselves. Pompey was invested with dictatorial power for three years over the Mediterranean and all its coasts for fifty miles inland. An armament of five hundred ships and one hundred thousand men was intrusted to his command. The great general acted with his characteristic energy. Within forty days he had swept the pirates from the Western Mediterranean, and in forty-nine more hunted them from all the waters east of Italy, captured their strongholds in Cilicia, and settled the twenty thousand prisoners that fell into his hands in various colonies in Asia Minor and Greece. Pompey's vigorous and successful conduct of this campaign against the pirates gained him great honor and reputation.

Pompey and the Mithridatic War. — In the very year that Pompey suppressed the pirates (66 B.C.), he was called to undertake a more difficult task. Mithridates the Great, led on by his ambition and encouraged by the discontent created throughout the Eastern provinces by Roman rapacity and misrule, was again in arms against Rome. He had stirred almost all Asia Minor to revolt. The management of the war was eventually intrusted to Pompey, whose success in the war of the pirates had aroused unbounded enthusiasm for him.

In a great battle in Lesser Armenia, Pompey almost annihilated the army of Mithridates. The king fled from the field, and, after seeking in vain for a refuge in Asia Minor, sought an asylum beyond the Caucasus Mountains, whose bleak barriers interposed their friendly shield between him and his pursuers. Desisting from the pursuit, Pompey turned south and conquered Syria, Phœnicia, and Cœle-Syria, which countries he erected into a Roman province. Still pushing southward, the conqueror entered Palestine, and after a short siege captured Jerusalem (63 B.C.).

While Pompey was thus engaged, Mithridates was straining every energy to raise an army among the Scythian tribes with which to carry out a most daring project.
He proposed to cross Europe and fall upon Italy from the north. A revolt on the part of his son Pharnaces ruined all his plans and hopes; and the disappointed monarch, to avoid falling into the hands of the Romans, took his own life (63 B.C.). His death removed one of the most formidable enemies that Rome had ever encountered. Hamilcar, Hannibal, and Mithridates were the three great names

MITHRIDATES VI.
(The Great.)

that the Romans always pronounced with respect and dread.

Pompey's Triumph. —After regulating the affairs of the different states and provinces in the East, Pompey set out on his return to Rome, where he enjoyed such a triumph as never before had been seen since Rome had become a city. The spoils of all the East were borne in the procession; 322 princes walked as captives before the triumphal chariot of the conqueror; legends upon the banners proclaimed that he had conquered 21 kings, captured 1000 strongholds, 900 towns, and 800 ships, and subjugated more than 12,000,000 people; and that he had put into the treasury more than $25,000,000, besides doubling the regular revenues of the state. He boasted that three times he had triumphed, and each time for the conquest of a continent — first for Africa, then for Europe, and now for Asia, which completed the conquest of the world.

The Conspiracy of Catiline. — While the legions were absent from Italy with Pompey in the East, a most daring conspiracy against the government was formed at Rome. Catiline, a ruined spendthrift, had gathered a large company of profligate young nobles, weighed down with debt and desperate like himself, and had deliberately planned to murder the consuls and the chief men of the state, and to plunder and burn the capital. The offices of the new government were to be divided among the conspirators. They depended upon receiving aid from Africa and Spain, and proposed to invite to their standard the gladiators in the various schools of Italy, as well as slaves and criminals. The proscriptions of Sulla were to be renewed, and all debts were to be cancelled.

Fortunately, all the plans of the conspirators were revealed to the consul Cicero, the great orator. The Senate immediately clothed the consuls with dictatorial power with the usual formula, that they should take care that the republic received no harm. The gladiators were secured; the city walls were manned; and at every point the capital and state were armed against the "invisible foe." Then in the Senate-chamber, with Catiline himself present, Cicero exposed the whole conspiracy in a famous philippic, known as "The First Oration against Catiline." The senators shrank from the conspirator, and left the seats about him empty. After a feeble effort to reply to Cicero, overwhelmed by a sense of his guilt, and the cries of "traitor" and "parricide" from the senators, Catiline fled from the chamber, and hurried out of the city to the camp of his followers, in Etruria. In a desperate battle fought near Pistoria (62 B.C.), he was slain with many of his followers. His head was borne as a trophy to Rome. Cicero was hailed as the "Saviour of his Country."

Cæsar, Crassus, and Pompey. — Although the conspiracy of Catiline had failed, it was very easy to foresee that the downfall of the Roman republic was near at hand. Indeed, from this time on only the name remains. The basis of the institutions of the republic — the old Roman virtue, integrity, patriotism, and faith in the gods — was gone, having been swept away by the tide of luxury, selfishness, and immorality produced by the long series of foreign conquests and robberies in which the Roman people had been engaged. The days of liberty at Rome were over. From this time forward the government was really in the hands of ambitious and popular leaders, or of corrupt combinations and "rings." Events gather about a few great names, and the annals of the republic become biographical rather than historical.

There were now in the state three men — Cæsar, Crassus, and Pompey — who were destined to shape affairs. Caius Julius Cæsar was born in the year 100 B.C. Although descended from an old patrician family, still his sympathies, and an early marriage to the daughter of Cinna, one of the adherents of Marius, led him early to identify himself with the Marian, or democratic party. In every way Cæsar courted public favor. He lavished enormous sums upon public games and tables. His debts are said to have amounted to 25,000,000 sesterces ($1,250,000). His popularity was unbounded. A successful campaign in Spain had already made known to himself, as well as to others, his genius as a commander.

Crassus belonged to the senatorial, or aristocratic party. He owed his influence to his enormous wealth, being one of the richest men in the Roman world. His property was estimated at 7100 talents (about $7,500,000).

With Pompey and his achievements we are already familiar. His influence throughout the Roman world was great; for, in settling and reorganizing the many countries he subdued, he had always taken care to reconstruct them in his own interest, as well as in that of the republic. The offices, as we have seen, were filled with his friends and adherents (see p. 285). This patronage had secured for him incalculable authority in the provinces. His veteran legionaries, too, were naturally devoted to the general who had led them so often to victory.

The First Triumvirate. — What is known as the First Triumvirate rested on the genius of Cæsar, the wealth of Crassus, and the achievements of Pompey. It was a coalition or private arrangement entered into by these three men for the purpose of securing to themselves the control of public affairs. Each pledged himself to work for the interests of the others. Cæsar was the manager of the "ring," and through the aid of his colleagues secured the consulship (59 B.C.).

Cæsar's Conquests in Gaul and Britain. — At the end of his consulship, the administration of the provinces of Cisalpine and Transalpine Gaul was assigned to Cæsar. Already he was revolving in his mind plans for seizing supreme power. Beyond the Alps the Gallic and Germanic tribes were in restless movement. He saw there a grand field for military exploits, which should gain for him such glory and prestige as, in other fields, had been won and were now enjoyed by Pompey. With this achieved, and with a veteran army devoted to his interests, he might hope easily to attain that position at the head of affairs towards which his ambition was urging him.

In the spring of 58 B.C. alarming intelligence from beyond the Alps caused Cæsar to hasten from Rome into Transalpine Gaul. Now began a series of eight brilliant campaigns directed against the various tribes of Gaul, Germany, and Britain. In his *Commentaries* Cæsar himself has left us a faithful and graphic account of all the memorable marches, battles, and sieges that filled the years between 58 and 50 B.C.

The year 55 B.C. marked two great achievements. Early in the spring of this year Cæsar constructed a bridge across the Rhine, and led his legions against the Germans in their native woods and swamps. In the autumn of the same year he crossed, by means of hastily constructed ships, the channel that separates the mainland from Britain, and after maintaining a foothold upon that island for two weeks withdrew his legions into Gaul for the winter. The following season he made another invasion of Britain ; but, after some encounters with the fierce barbarians, recrossed to the mainland without having established any permanent garrisons in the island. Almost one hundred years passed away before the natives of Britain were again molested by the Romans (see p. 311).

In the year 52 B.C., while Cæsar was absent in Italy, a general revolt occurred among the Gallic tribes. It was a last desperate struggle for the recovery of their lost independence. Vercingetorix, chief of the Arverni, was the leader of the insurrection. For a time it seemed as though the Romans would be driven from the country. But Cæsar's despatch and military genius saved the province to the republic.

In his campaigns in Gaul, Cæsar had subjugated three hundred tribes, captured eight hundred cities, and slain a million of barbarians — one third of the entire population of the country. Another third he had taken prisoners. Great enthusiasm was aroused at Rome by these victories. " Let the Alps now sink," exclaimed Cicero : " the gods raised them to shelter Italy from the barbarians : they are now no longer needed."

Results of the Gallic Wars. — The most important result of the Gallic wars of Cæsar was the Romanizing of Gaul. The country was opened to Roman traders and settlers, who carried with them the language, customs, and arts of Italy.

Another result of the conquest was the checking of the migratory movements of the German tribes, which gave Græco-Roman civilization time to become thoroughly rooted, not only in Gaul, but also in Spain and other lands.

Rivalry between Cæsar and Pompey: Cæsar crosses the Rubicon. — While Cæsar was in the midst of his Transalpine wars, Crassus was leading an army against the Parthians, hoping to rival there the brilliant conquests of Cæsar in Gaul. But his army was almost annihilated by the Parthian cavalry, and he himself was slain (54 B.C.). His captors, so it is said, poured molten gold down his throat, that he might be sated with the metal which he had so coveted during life. In the death of Crassus, Cæsar lost his stanchest friend, one who had never failed him, and whose wealth had been freely used for his advancement.

The world now belonged to Cæsar and Pompey. That the insatiable ambition of these two rivals should sooner or later bring them into collision was inevitable. Their alliance in the triumvirate was simply one of selfish convenience, not of friendship. While Cæsar was carrying on his campaigns in Gaul, Pompey was at Rome watching jealously the growing reputation of his great rival. He strove, by a princely liberality, to win the affections of the common people.   On the Field of Mars he erected an immense theatre with seats for forty thousand spectators.   He gave magnificent games, and set public tables ; and when the interest of the people in the sports of the Circus flagged, he entertained them with gladiatorial combats.   In a similar manner Cæsar strengthened himself with the people for the struggle which he plainly foresaw.   He sought in every way to ingratiate himself with the Gauls ; increased the pay of his soldiers ; conferred the privileges of Roman citizenship upon the inhabitants of different cities in his province ; and sent to Rome enormous sums of gold to be expended in the erection of temples, theatres, and other public structures, and in the celebration of games and shows that should rival in magnificence those given by Pompey.

The terrible condition of affairs at the capital favored the ambition of Pompey.   So selfish and corrupt were the members of the Senate, so dead to all virtue and to every sentiment of patriotism were the people, that even such patriots as Cato and Cicero saw no hope for the maintenance of the republic.   The former favored the appointment of Pompey as sole consul for one year, which was about the same thing as making him dictator.   "It is better," said Cato, "to choose a master than to wait for the tyrant whom anarchy will impose upon us."   The "tyrant" in his and everybody's mind was Cæsar.

Pompey now broke with Cæsar, and attached himself again to the old aristocratic party, which he had deserted for the alliance and promises of the triumvirate.   The death at this time of his wife Julia, the daughter of Cæsar, severed the bonds of relationship at the same moment that those of ostensible friendship were broken.

The Senate, hostile to Cæsar, now issued a decree that he should resign his office, and disband his Gallic legions by a stated day.   The crisis had now come.   Cæsar ordered his legions to hasten from Gaul into Italy.   Without waiting for their arrival, at the head of a small body of veterans that he had with him at Ravenna, he crossed the Rubicon, a little stream that marked the boundary of his province. This was a declaration of war. As he plunged into the river, he exclaimed, "The die is cast."

The Civil War of Cæsar and Pompey (49–48 B.C.). — The bold movement of Cæsar produced great consternation at Rome. Realizing the danger of delay, Cæsar, without waiting for the Gallic legions to join him, marched southward. One city after another threw open its gates to him ; legion after legion went over to his standard. Pompey and the Senate hastened from Rome to Brundisium, and thence, with about twenty-five thousand men, fled across the Adriatic into Greece. Within sixty days Cæsar made himself undisputed master of all Italy.

Pompey and Cæsar now controlled the Roman world. It was large, but not large enough for both these ambitious men. As to which was likely to become sole master, it were difficult for one watching events at that time to foresee. Cæsar held Italy, Illyricum, and Gaul, with the resources of his own genius and the idolatrous attachment of his soldiers ; Pompey controlled Spain, Africa, Sicily, Sardinia, Greece, and the provinces of Asia, with the prestige of his great name and the indefinite resources of the East.

Cæsar's first care was to pacify Italy. His moderation and prudence won all classes to his side. Many had looked to see the terrible scenes of the days of Marius and Sulla re-enacted. Cæsar, however, soon gave assurance that life and property should be held sacred. He needed money ; but, to avoid laying a tax upon the people, he asked for the treasure kept beneath the Capitol. Legend declared that this gold was the actual ransom-money which Brennus had demanded of the Romans, and which Camillus had saved by his timely appearance (see p. 241). It was esteemed sacred, and was never to be used save in case of another Gallic invasion. When Cæsar attempted to get possession of the treasure, the tribune Metellus prevented him ; but Cæsar impatiently brushed him aside, saying, "The fear of a Gallic invasion is over : I have subdued the Gauls."

With order restored in Italy, Cæsar's next movement was to gain control of the wheat-fields of Sicily, Sardinia, and Africa. A single

legion brought over Sardinia without resistance to the side of
Cæsar. Cato, the lieutenant of Pompey, fled from before Curio
out of Sicily. In Africa, however, the lieutenant of Cæsar sustained a severe defeat, and the Pompeians held their ground there
until the close of the war. Cæsar, meanwhile, had subjugated
Spain. In forty days the entire peninsula was brought under his
authority. Massilia had ventured to close her gates against the
conqueror ; but a brief siege forced the city to capitulate. Cæsar
was now free to turn his forces against Pompey in the East.

The Battle of Pharsalus (48 B.C.). — From Brundisium Cæsar
embarked his legions for Epirus. The armies of the rivals met
upon the plains of Pharsalia, in Thessaly. The adherents of Pompey were so confident of an easy victory that they were already
disputing about the offices at Rome, and were renting the most
eligible houses fronting the public squares of the capital. The
battle was at length joined. It proved Pompey's Waterloo. His
army was cut to pieces. He himself fled from the field, and escaped to Egypt. Just as he was landing there, he was assassinated.

The head of the great general was severed from his body ; and
when Cæsar, who was pressing after Pompey in hot pursuit, landed
in Egypt, the bloody trophy was brought to him. He turned from
the sight with generous tears. It was no longer the head of his
rival, but of his old associate and son-in-law. He ordered the assassins to be executed, and directed that fitting obsequies should
be performed over the body.

Close of the Civil War. — Cæsar was detained at Alexandria nine
months in settling a dispute respecting the throne of Egypt. After
a severe contest he overthrew the reigning Ptolemy, and secured
the kingdom to the celebrated Cleopatra and a younger brother.
Intelligence was now brought from Asia Minor that Pharnaces, son
of Mithridates the Great, was inciting a revolt among the peoples
of that region. Cæsar met the Pontic king at Zela, defeated him,
and in five days put an end to the war. His laconic message to
the Senate, announcing his victory, is famous. It ran thus : *Veni,
vidi, vici,* — " I came, I saw, I conquered."

Cæsar now hurried back to Italy, and thence proceeded to Africa, which the friends of the old republic had made their last chief rallying-place. At the great battle of Thapsus (46 B.C.) they were crushed. Fifty thousand lay dead upon the field. Cato, who had been the very life and soul of the army, refusing to out-live the republic, took his own life.

Cæsar's Triumph. — Cæsar was now virtually lord of the Roman world. Although he refrained from assuming the title of king, no Eastern monarch was ever possessed of more absolute power, or surrounded by more abject flatterers and sycophants. He was invested with all the offices and dignities of the state. The Senate made him perpetual dictator, and conferred upon him the powers of censor, consul, and tribune, with the titles of Pontifex Maximus and Imperator (whence Emperor). "He was to sit in a golden chair in the Senate-house, his image was to be borne in the procession of the gods, and the seventh month of the year was changed in his honor from Quintilis to Julius [whence our July]."

His triumph celebrating his many victories far eclipsed in mag-nificence anything that Rome had before witnessed. In the procession were led captive princes from all parts of the world. Beneath his standards marched soldiers gathered out of almost every country beneath the heavens. Seventy-five million dollars of treasure were displayed. Splendid games and tables attested the liberality of the conqueror. Sixty thousand couches were set for the multitudes. The shows of the theatre and the combats of the arena followed one another in an endless round. "Above the combats of the amphitheatre floated for the first time the awning of silk, the immense velarium of a thousand colors, woven from the rarest and richest products of the East, to protect the people from the sun" (Gibbon).

Cæsar as a Statesman. — Cæsar was great as a general, yet greater, if possible, as a statesman. The measures which he in-stituted evince profound political sagacity and surprising breadth of view. He sought to reverse the jealous and narrow policy of Rome in the past, and to this end rebuilt both Carthage and Corinth, and founded numerous colonies in all the different provinces, in which he settled about one hundred thousand of the poorer citizens of the capital. Upon some of the provincials he conferred full Roman citizenship, and upon others Latin rights (see p. 246, note), and thus strove to blend the varied peoples and races within the boundaries of the empire in a real nationality, with community of interests and sympathies. He reformed the calendar so as to bring the festivals once more in their proper seasons, and provided against further confusion by making the year consist of 365 days, with an added day for every fourth or leap year.

Besides these achievements, Cæsar projected many vast undertakings, which the abrupt termination of his life prevented his carrying into execution. Among these was his projected conquest of the Parthians and the Germans. He proposed, in revenge for the defeat and death of his friend Crassus, to break to pieces the Parthian empire; then, sweeping with an army around above the Euxine, to destroy the dreaded hordes of Scythia; and then, falling upon the German tribes in the rear, to crush their power forever, and thus relieve the Roman empire of their constant threat. He was about to set out on the expedition against the Parthians, when he was struck down by assassins.

The Death of Cæsar. — Cæsar had his bitter personal enemies, who never ceased to plot his downfall. There were, too, sincere lovers of the old republic, who longed to see restored the liberty which the conqueror had overthrown. The impression began to prevail that Cæsar was aiming to make himself king. A crown was several times offered him in public by Mark Antony; but, seeing the manifest displeasure of the people, he each time pushed it aside. Yet there is no doubt that secretly he desired it. It was reported that he proposed to rebuild the walls of Troy, whence the Roman race had sprung, and make that ancient capital the seat of the new Roman empire. Others professed to believe that the arts and charms of the Egyptian Cleopatra, who had borne him a son at Rome, would entice him to make Alexandria the centre of the proposed kingdom. So many, out of love for Rome and the old republic, were led to enter into a conspiracy against the life of Cæsar with those who sought to rid themselves of the dictator for other and personal reasons.

The Ides (the 15th day) of March, 44 B.C., upon which day the Senate convened, witnessed the assassination. Seventy or eighty conspirators, headed by Cassius and Brutus, both of whom had received special favors from the hands of Cæsar, were concerned in the plot. The soothsayers must have had some knowledge of the plans of the conspirators, for they had warned Cæsar to "beware of the Ides of March." On his way to the Senate-meeting that day, a paper warning him of his danger was thrust into his hand; but, not suspecting its urgent nature, he did not open it. As he entered the assembly chamber he observed the astrologer Spurinna, and remarked carelessly to him, referring to his prediction, "The Ides of March have come." "Yes," replied Spurinna, "but not gone."

No sooner had Cæsar taken his seat than the conspirators crowded about him as if to present a petition. Upon a signal from one of their number their daggers were drawn. For a moment Cæsar defended himself; but seeing Brutus, upon whom he had lavished gifts and favors, among the conspirators, he exclaimed reproachfully, *Et tu, Brute!* — "Thou, too, Brutus!" drew his mantle over his face, and received unresistingly their further thrusts. Pierced with twenty-three wounds, he sank dead at the foot of Pompey's statue.

Funeral Oration by Mark Antony. — The conspirators, or "liberators," as they called themselves, had thought that the Senate would confirm, and the people applaud, their act. But both people and senators, struck with consternation, were silent. Men's faces grew pale as they recalled the proscriptions of Sulla, and saw in the assassination of Cæsar the first act in a similar reign of terror. As the conspirators issued from the assembly hall, and entered the Forum, holding aloft their bloody daggers, instead of the expected acclamations they were met by an ominous silence. The liberators hastened for safety to the Temple of Jupiter Capitolinus. Upon the day set for the funeral ceremonies, Mark Antony, the trusted friend and secretary of Cæsar, mounted the rostrum in the Forum to deliver the usual funeral oration. He recounted the great deeds of Cæsar, the glory he had conferred upon the Roman name, and dwelt upon his liberality and his

CICERO.

munificent bequests to the people. When he had wrought the feelings of the multitude to the highest tension, he raised the robe of Cæsar, and showed the rents made by the daggers of the assassins. Cæsar had always been beloved by the people and idolized by his soldiers. They were now driven almost to frenzy with grief and indignation. Seizing weapons and torches, they rushed through the streets, vowing vengeance upon the conspirators. The liberators, however, escaped from the fury of the mob, and fled from Rome, Brutus and Cassius seeking refuge in Greece.

The Second Triumvirate. — Antony had gained possession of the will and papers of Cæsar, and now, under color of carrying out the testament of the dictator, according to a decree of the Senate, entered upon a course of high-handed usurpation. He was aided in his designs by Lepidus, one of Cæsar's old lieutenants. Very soon he was exercising all the powers of a real dictator. "The tyrant is dead," said Cicero, "but the tyranny still lives." This was a bitter commentary upon the words of Brutus, who, as he drew his dagger from the body of Cæsar, turned to Cicero, and exclaimed, "Rejoice, O Father of your Country, for Rome is free." Rome could not be free, the republic could not be reestablished because the old love for virtue and liberty had died

out from among the people — had been overwhelmed by the rising
tide of vice, corruption, sensuality, and irreligion that had set in
upon the capital.

To what length Antony would have gone in his career of usurpation it is difficult to say, had he not been opposed at this point by
Caius Octavius,
the grand-neph-
ew of Julius
Cæsar, and the
one whom he
had named in
his will as his
heir and adopt-
ed as his son.
The Senate de-
claring in favor
of Octavius,
civil war imme-
diately broke
out between
him and Anto-
ny and Lepi-
dus. After
several indeci-
sive battles be-
tween the for-
ces of the rival
competitors,

JULIUS CÆSAR. (From a Bust in the Museum of the Louvre.)

Octavius proposed to Antony and Lepidus a reconciliation. The
three met on a small island in the Rhenus, a little stream in Northern Italy, and there formed a league known as the Second Triumvirate (43 B.C.).

The plans of the triumvirs were infamous. They first divided
the world among themselves: Octavius was to have the government of the West; Antony, that of the East; while to Lepidus

fell the control of Africa. A general proscription, such as had marked the coming to power of Sulla (see p. 283), was then resolved upon. It was agreed that each should give up to the assassin such friends of his as had incurred the ill will of either of the other triumvirs. Under this arrangement Octavius gave up his friend Cicero, — who had incurred the hatred of Antony by opposing his schemes, — and allowed his name to be put at the head of the list of the proscribed.

The friends of the orator urged him to flee the country. "Let me die," said he, "in my fatherland, which I have so often saved!" His attendants were hurrying him, half unwilling, towards the coast, when his pursuers came up and despatched him in the litter in which he was being carried. His head was taken to Rome, and set up in front of the rostrum, "from which he had so often addressed the people with his eloquent appeals for liberty." It is told that Fulvia, the wife of Antony, ran her gold bodkin through the tongue, in revenge for the bitter philippics it had uttered against her husband. The right hand of the victim — the hand that had penned the eloquent orations — was nailed to the rostrum.

Cicero was but one victim among many hundreds. All the dreadful scenes of the days of Sulla were re-enacted. Three hundred senators and two thousand knights were murdered. The estates of the wealthy were confiscated, and conferred by the triumvirs upon their friends and favorites.

Last Struggle of the Republic at Philippi (42 B.C.). — The friends of the old republic, and the enemies of the triumvirs, were meanwhile rallying in the East. Brutus and Cassius were the animating spirits. The Asiatic provinces were plundered to raise money for the soldiers of the liberators. Octavius and Antony, as soon as they had disposed of their enemies in Italy, crossed the Adriatic into Greece, to disperse the forces of the republicans there. The liberators, advancing to meet them, passed over the Hellespont into Thrace.

Tradition tells how one night a spectre appeared to Brutus and seemed to say, "I am thy evil genius; we will meet again at Phil ippi." At Philippi, in Thrace, the hostile armies met (42 B.C.). In two successive engagements the new levies of the liberators were cut to pieces, and both Brutus and Cassius, believing the cause of the republic forever lost, committed suicide. It was, indeed, the last effort of the republic. The history of the events that lie between the action at Philippi and the establishment of the empire is simply a record of the struggles among the triumvirs for the possession of the prize of supreme power. After various redistributions of provinces, Lepidus was at length expelled from the triumvirate, and then again the Roman world, as in the times of Cæsar and Pompey, was in the hands of two masters — Antony in the East, and Octavius in the West.

Antony and Cleopatra. — After the battle of Philippi, Antony went into Asia for the purpose of settling the affairs of the provinces and vassal states there. He summoned Cleopatra, the fair queen of Egypt, to meet him at Tarsus, in Cilicia, there to give account to him for the aid she had rendered the liberators. She obeyed the summons, relying upon the power of her charms to appease the anger of the triumvir. She ascended the Cydnus in a gilded barge, with oars of silver, and sails of purple silk. Beneath awnings wrought of the richest manufactures of the East, the beautiful queen, attired to personate Venus, reclined amidst lovely attendants dressed to represent cupids and nereids. Antony was completely fascinated, as had been the great Cæsar before him, by the dazzling beauty of the " Serpent of the Nile." Enslaved by her enchantments, and charmed by her brilliant wit, in the pleasure of her company he forgot all else — ambition and honor and country.

Once, indeed, Antony did rouse himself and break away from his enslavement to lead the Roman legions across the Euphrates against the Parthians. But the storms of approaching winter, and the incessant attacks of the Parthian cavalry, at length forced him to make a hurried and disastrous retreat. He hastened back to Egypt, and sought to forget his shame and disappointment amidst the revels of the Egyptian court.

The Battle of Actium (31 B.C.). — Affairs could not long continue in their present course. Antony had put away his faithful wife Octavia for the beautiful Cleopatra. It was whispered at Rome, and not without truth, that he proposed to make Alexandria the capital of the Roman world, and announce Cæsarion, son of Julius Cæsar and Cleopatra, as heir of the empire. All Rome was stirred. It was evident that a conflict was at hand in which the question for decision would be whether the West should rule the East, or the East rule the West. All eyes were instinctively turned to Octavius as the defender of Italy, and the supporter of the sovereignty of the Eternal City. Both parties made the most gigantic preparations. Octavius met the combined fleets of Antony and Cleopatra just off the promontory of Actium, on the Grecian coast. While the issue of the battle that there took place was yet undecided, Cleopatra turned her galley in flight. The Egyptian ships, to the number of fifty, followed her example. Antony, as soon as he perceived the withdrawal of Cleopatra, forgot all else, and followed in her track with a swift galley. Overtaking the fleeing queen, the infatuated man was received aboard her vessel, and became her partner in the disgraceful flight.

The abandoned fleet and army surrendered to Octavius. The conqueror was now sole master of the civilized world. From this decisive battle (31 B.C.) are usually dated the end of the republic and the beginning of the empire. Some, however, make the establishment of the empire date from the year 27 B.C., as it was not until then that Octavius was formally invested with imperial powers.

Deaths of Antony and Cleopatra. — Octavius pursued Antony to Egypt, where the latter, deserted by his army, and informed by a messenger from the false queen that she was dead, committed suicide. Cleopatra then sought to enslave Octavius with her charms ; but, failing in this, and becoming convinced that he proposed to take her to Rome that she might there grace his triumph, she took her own life, being in the thirty-eighth year of her age. Tradition says that she effected her purpose by applying an asp to her arm. But it is really unknown in what way she killed herself.

CHAPTER XXIX.

THE ROMAN EMPIRE.

(From 31 B.C. to A.D. 180.)

Reign of Augustus Cæsar (31 B.C. to A.D. 14). — The hundred years of strife which ended with the battle of Actium left the Roman republic, exhausted and helpless, in the hands of one wise enough and strong enough to remould its crumbling fragments in such a manner that the state, which seemed ready to fall to pieces, might prolong its existence for another five hundred years. It was a great work thus to create anew, as it were, out of anarchy and chaos, a political fabric that should exhibit such elements of perpetuity and strength. "The establishment of the Roman empire," says Merivale, "was, after all, the greatest political work that any human being ever wrought. The achievements of Alexander, of Cæsar, of Charlemagne, of Napoleon, are not to be compared with it for a moment."

The government which Octavius established was a monarchy in fact, but a republic in form. Mindful of the fate of Julius Cæsar, who fell because he gave the lovers of the republic reason to think that he coveted the title of king, Octavius carefully veiled his really absolute sovereignty under the forms of the old republican state. The Senate still existed ; but so completely subjected were its members to the influence of the conqueror that the only function it really exercised was the conferring of honors and titles and abject flatteries upon its master. All the republican officials remained ; but Octavius absorbed and exercised their chief powers and functions. He had the powers of consul, tribune, censor, and Pontifex Maximus. All the republican magistrates — the consuls, the tribunes, the prætors — were elected as usual ; but they were simply the nominees and creatures of the emperor. They were the effigies and figure-heads to delude the people into believing that the republic still existed. Never did a people seem more content with the shadow after the loss of the substance.

The Senate, acting under the inspiration of Octavius, withheld from him the title of king, which ever since the expulsion of the Tarquins, five centuries before this time, had been intolerable to the people ; but they conferred upon him the titles of Imperator and Augustus, the latter having been hitherto sacred to the gods. The sixth month of the Roman year was called Augustus (whence our August) in his honor, an act in imitation of that by which the preceding month had been given the name of Julius in honor of Julius Cæsar.

The domains over which Augustus held sway were imperial in magnitude. They stretched from the Atlantic to the Euphrates, and upon the north were hemmed by the forests of Germany and the bleak steppes of Scythia, and were bordered on the south by

AUGUSTUS.

the sands of the African desert and the dreary wastes of Arabia, which seemed the boundaries set by nature to dominion in those directions. Within these limits were crowded more than 100,000,-000 people, embracing every conceivable condition and variety in race and culture, from the rough barbarians of Gaul to the refined voluptuary of the East.

Octavius was the first to moderate the ambition of the Romans, and to counsel them not to attempt to conquer any more of the world, but rather to devote their energies to the work of consolidating the domains already acquired. He saw the dangers that would attend any further extension of the boundaries of the state.

The reign of Augustus lasted forty-four years, from 31 B.C. to A.D. 14. It embraced the most splendid period of the annals of Rome. Under the patronage of the emperor, and that of his favorite minister Mæcenas, poets and writers flourished and made this the "golden age" of Latin literature. During this reign Virgil composed his immortal epic of the *Æneid*, and Horace his famous odes ; while Livy wrote his inimitable history, and Ovid his *Metamorphoses*. Many who lamented the fall of the republic sought solace in the pursuit of letters ; and in this they were encouraged by Augustus, as it gave occupation to many restless spirits that would otherwise have been engaged in political intrigues against his government.

Augustus was also a munificent patron of architecture and art. He adorned the capital with many splendid structures. Said he proudly, " I found Rome a city of brick ; I left it a city of marble." The population of the city at this time was probably about one million.

Although the government of Augustus was disturbed by some troubles upon the frontiers, still never before, perhaps, did the world enjoy so long a period of general rest from the preparation and turmoil of war. Three times during this auspicious reign the gates of the Temple of Janus at Rome, which were open in time of war and closed in time of peace, were shut. Only twice before during the entire history of the city had they been closed, so constantly had the Roman people been engaged in war. It was in the midst of this happy reign, when profound peace prevailed throughout the civilized world, that Christ was born in Bethlehem of Judea. The event was unheralded at Rome ; yet it was filled with profound significance, not only for the Roman empire, but for the world.

The latter years of the life of Augustus were clouded both by domestic bereavement and national disaster. His beloved nephew Marcellus, and his two grandsons Caius and Lucius, whom he purposed making his heirs, were all removed by death ; and then, far away in the German forest, his general Varus, who had attempted to rule the freedom-loving Teutons as he had governed the abject Asiatics of the Eastern provinces, was surprised by the barbarians, led by their brave chief Hermann, — Arminius, as called by the Romans, — and his army destroyed almost to a man (A.D. 9). Twenty thousand of the legionaries lay dead and unburied in the tangled woods and morasses of Germany.

The victory of Arminius over the Roman legions was an event of the greatest significance in the history of European civilization. Germany was almost overrun by the Roman army. The Teutonic tribes were on the point of being completely subjugated and Romanized, as had been the Celts of Gaul before them. Had this occurred, the entire history of Europe would have been changed ; for the Germanic element is the one that has given shape and color to the important events of the last fifteen hundred years. Those barbarians, too, were our ancestors. Had Rome succeeded in exterminating or enslaving them, Britain, as Creasy says, would never have received the name of England, and the great English nation would never have had an existence.

In the year A.D. 14, Augustus died, having reached the seventy-sixth year of his age. It was believed that his soul ascended visibly amidst the flames of the funeral pyre. By decree of the Senate divine worship was accorded to him, and temples were erected in his honor.

One of the most important of the acts of Augustus, in its influence upon following events, was the formation of the Prætorian Guard, which was designed for a sort of body-guard to the emperor. In the succeeding reign this body of soldiers, about ten thousand in number, was given a permanent camp alongside the city walls. It soon became a formidable power in the state, and made and unmade emperors at will.

Reign of Tiberius (A.D. 14–37). — Tiberius succeeded to an unlimited sovereignty. The Senate conferred upon him all the titles that had been worn by Augustus. One of the first acts of Tiberius gave the last blow to the ancient republican institutions. He took away from the popular assembly the privilege of electing the consuls and prætors, and bestowed the same upon the Senate, which, however, as a rule elected candidates presented by the emperor. As the Senate was the creation of the emperor, through virtue of his power to name new members, he was now of course the source and fountain of all patronage. During the first years of nis reign, Tiberius used his practically unrestrained authority with moderation and justice, but soon yielding to the promptings of a naturally cruel, suspicious, and jealous nature, he entered upon a course of the most high-handed tyranny. He enforced oppressively an old law, known as the *law of majestas*, which made it a capital offence for any one to speak a careless word, or even to entertain an unfriendly thought, respecting the emperor. " It was dangerous to speak, and equally dangerous to keep silent," says Leighton, " for silence even might be construed into discontent." Rewards were offered to informers, and hence sprang up a class of persons called " delators," who acted as spies upon society. Often false charges were made, to gratify personal enmity ; and many, especially of the wealthy class, were accused and put to death that their property might be confiscated.

Tiberius appointed, as his chief minister and as commander of the prætorians, one Sejanus, a man of the lowest and most corrupt life. This officer actually persuaded Tiberius to retire to the little island of Capreæ, in the Bay of Naples, and leave to him the management of affairs at Rome. The emperor built several villas in different parts of the beautiful islet, and, having gathered a band of congenial companions, passed in this pleasant retreat the later years of his reign. Both Tacitus the historian and Suetonius the biographer tell many stories of the scandalous profligacy of the emperor's life on the island; but these tales, it should be added, are discredited by some.

Meanwhile, Sejanus was ruling at Rome very much according to his own will. No man's life was safe. He even grew so bold as to plan the assassination of the emperor himself. His designs, however, became known to Tiberius; and the infamous and disloyal minister was arrested and put to death.

After the execution of his minister, Tiberius ruled more despotically than ever before. Multitudes sought refuge from his tyranny in suicide. Death at last relieved the world of the monster. His end was probably hastened by his attendants, who are believed to have smothered him in his bed, as he lay dying.

It was in the midst of the reign of Tiberius that, in a remote province of the Roman empire, the Saviour was crucified. Animated by an unparalleled missionary spirit, His followers traversed the length and breadth of the empire, preaching everywhere the "glad tidings." Men's loss of faith in the gods of the old mythologies, the softening and liberalizing influence of Greek culture, the unification of the whole civilized world under a single government, the widespread suffering and the inexpressible weariness of the oppressed and servile classes, — all these things had prepared the soil for the seed of the new doctrines. In less than three centuries the Pagan empire had become Christian not only in name, but also very largely in fact. This conversion of Rome is one of the most important events in all history. A new element is here introduced into civilization, an element which we shall find giving color and character to very much of the story of the eighteen centuries that we have yet to study.

Reign of Caligula (A.D. 37–41). — Caius Cæsar, better known as Caligula, was only twenty-five years of age when the death of Tiberius called him to the throne. His career was very similar to that of Tiberius. After a few months spent in arduous application to the affairs of the empire, during which time his many acts of kindness and piety won for him the affections of all classes, the mind of the young emperor became unsettled, and he began to indulge in all sorts of insanities. The cruel sports of the amphitheatre possessed for him a strange fascination. When animals failed, he ordered spectators to be seized indiscriminately, and thrown to the beasts. He entered the lists himself, and fought as a gladiator upon the arena. In a sanguinary mood, he wished that "the people of Rome had but one neck." As an insult to his nobles, he gave out that he proposed to make his favorite horse, Incitatus, consul. He declared himself divine, and removing the heads of Jupiter's statues, put on his own.

After four years the insane career of Caligula was brought to a close by some of the officers of the prætorian guard, whom he had wantonly insulted.

Reign of Claudius (A.D. 41–54). — The reign of Claudius, Caligula's successor, was signalized by the conquest of Britain. Nearly a century had now passed since the invasion of the island by Julius Cæsar, who, as has been seen (see p. 292), simply made a reconnoissance of the island and then withdrew. Claudius conquered all the southern portion of the island, and founded many towns, which in time became important centres of Roman trade and culture. The leader of the Britons was Caractacus. He was taken captive and carried to Rome. Gazing in astonishment upon the magnificence of the imperial city, he exclaimed, "How can a people possessed of such splendor at home envy Caractacus his humble cottage in Britain?"

Claudius distinguished his reign by the execution of many important works. At the mouth of the Tiber he constructed a magnificent harbor, called the Portus Romanus. The Claudian Aqueduct, which he completed, was a stupendous work, bringing water to the city from a distance of forty-five miles.

The delight of the people in gladiatorial shows had at this time become almost an insane frenzy. Claudius determined to give an entertainment that should render insignificant all similar efforts. Upon a large lake, whose sloping bank afforded seats for the vast multitudes of spectators, he exhibited a naval battle, in which two opposing fleets, bearing nineteen thousand gladiators, fought as though in real battle, till the water was filled with thousands of bodies, and covered with the fragments of the broken ships.

Throughout his life Claudius was ruled by intriguing favorites and unworthy wives. For his fourth wife Claudius married the "wicked Agrippina," who secured his death by means of a dish of poisoned mushrooms, in order to make place for the succession of her son Nero.

Reign of Nero (A.D. 54–68). — Nero was fortunate in having for his preceptor the great philosopher and moralist Seneca ; but never was teacher more unfortunate in his pupil. For five years Nero ruled with moderation and equity. He then broke away from the guidance of his tutor Seneca, and entered upon a career filled with crimes of almost incredible enormity. The dagger and poison — the latter a means of murder the use of which at Rome had become a "fine art," and was in the hands of those who made it a regular profession — were employed almost unceasingly, to remove persons that had incurred his hatred, or who possessed wealth that he coveted.

It was in the tenth year of his reign that the so-called Great Fire laid more than half of Rome in ashes. It was rumored that Nero had ordered the conflagration to be lighted, and that from the roof of his palace he had enjoyed the spectacle, and amused himself by singing a poem which he had written, entitled the "Sack of Troy."

Nero did everything in his power to discredit the rumor. To turn attention from himself, he accused the Christians of having conspired to destroy the city, in order to help out their prophecies. The doctrine which was taught by some of the new sect respecting the second coming of Christ, and the destruction of the world by fire, lent color to the charge. The persecution that followed was one of the most cruel recorded in the history of the Church

Many victims were covered with pitch and burned at night, to serve as torches in the imperial gardens. Tradition preserves the names of the Apostles Peter and Paul as victims of this Neronian persecution.

As to Rome, the conflagration was a blessing in disguise. The city rose from its ashes as quickly as Athens from her ruins at the close of the Persian wars. The new buildings were made fire-proof; and the narrow, crooked streets reappeared as broad and beautiful avenues. A considerable portion of the burnt region was appropriated by Nero for the buildings and grounds of an immense palace, called the "Golden House." It covered so much space that the people "maliciously hinted" that Nero had fired the old city, in order to make room for it.

The emperor secured money for his enormous expenditures by new extortions, murders, and confiscations. No one of wealth knew but that his turn might come next. A conspiracy was formed among the nobles to relieve the state of the monster. The plot was discovered, and again "the city was filled with funerals." Lucan the poet, and Seneca, the old preceptor of Nero, both fell victims to the tyrant's rage.

Nero now made a tour through the East, and there plunged deeper and deeper into every shame, sensuality, and crime. The tyranny and the disgrace were no longer endurable. Almost at the same moment the legions in several of the provinces revolted. The Senate decreed that Nero was a public enemy, and condemned him to a disgraceful death by scourging, to avoid which he instructed a slave how to give him a fatal thrust. His last words were, "What a loss my death will be to art!"

Nero was the sixth and last of the Julian line. The family of the Great Cæsar was now extinct; but the name remained, and was adopted by all the succeeding emperors.

Galba, Otho, and Vitellius (A.D. 68–69). — These three names are usually grouped together, as their reigns were all short and uneventful. The succession, upon the death of Nero and the extinction in him of the Julian line, was in dispute, and the legions

in different quarters supported the claims of their favorite leaders.
One after another the three aspirants named were killed in bloody
struggles for the imperial purple. The last, Vitellius, was hurled
from the throne by the soldiers of Flavius Vespasian, the old and
beloved commander of the legions in Palestine, which were at this
time engaged in a war with the Jews.

Reign of Vespasian (A.D. 69–79). — The accession of Flavius
Vespasian marks the beginning of a period, embracing three reigns,
known as the *Flavian Age* (A.D. 69–96). Vespasian's reign was
signalized both by important military achievements abroad and by
stupendous public works undertaken at Rome.

After one of the most harassing sieges recorded in history,
Jerusalem was taken by Titus, son of Vespasian. The Temple

COIN OF VESPASIAN.

was destroyed,
and more than
a million of
Jews that were
crowded in the
city are believed
to have perished.
Great multitudes
suffered death by
crucifixion. The
miserable remnants of the nation were scattered everywhere over
the world. Josephus, the great historian, accompanied the conqueror to Rome. In imitation of Nebuchadnezzar, Titus robbed
the Temple of its sacred utensils, and bore them away as trophies.
Upon the triumphal arch at Rome that bears his name may be
seen at the present day the sculptured representation of the
golden candlestick, which was one of the memorials of the
war.

In the opposite corner of the empire a dangerous revolt of the
Gauls was suppressed, and in the island of Britain the Roman
commander Agricola subdued or crowded back the native tribes
until he had extended the frontiers of the empire into what is now

Scotland. Then, as a protection against the incursions of the Caledonians, the ancestors of the Scottish Highlanders, he constructed a line of fortresses from the Frith of Forth to the Frith of Clyde.

Vespasian rebuilt the Capitoline temple, which had been burned during the struggle between his soldiers and the adherents of Vitellius; he constructed a new forum which bore his own name; and also began the erection of the celebrated Flavian amphitheatre, which was completed by his successor. After a most prosperous reign of ten years, Vespasian died A.D. 79, the first emperor after Augustus that did not meet with a violent death.

TRIUMPHAL PROCESSION FROM THE ARCH OF TITUS:
Showing the Seven-branched Candlestick and other Trophies from the Temple at Jerusalem.

At the last moment he requested his attendants to raise him upon his feet that he might "die standing," as befitted a Roman emperor.

Reign of Titus (A.D. 79–81). — In a short reign of two years

Titus won the title, the "Delight of Mankind." He was un-wearied in acts of benevolence and in bestowal of favors. Having let a day slip by without some act of kindness performed, he is said to have exclaimed reproachfully, "I have lost a day."

Titus completed and dedicated the great Flavian amphitheatre begun by his father, Vespasian. This vast structure, which accommodated more than eighty thousand spectators, is better known as the Colosseum — a name given it either because of its gigantic proportions, or on account of a colossal statue of Nero which happened to stand near it.

A STREET IN POMPEII.

The reign of Titus, though so short, was signalized by two great disasters. The first was a conflagration at Rome, which was almost as calamitous as the Great Fire in the reign of Nero. The second was the destruction, by an eruption of Vesuvius, of the Campanian cities of Pompeii and Herculaneum. The cities were buried beneath showers of cinders, ashes, and streams of volcanic mud. Pliny the elder, the great naturalist, venturing too near the mountain to investigate the phenomenon, lost his life.[1]

Domitian — Last of the Twelve Cæsars (A.D. 81–96). — Domitian, the brother of Titus, was the last of the line of emperors known as " the Twelve Cæsars." The title, however, was assumed by, and is applied to, all succeeding emperors ; the sole reason that the first twelve princes are grouped together is because the Roman biographer Suetonius completed the lives of that number only.

Domitian's reign was an exact contrast to that of his brother Titus. It was one succession of extravagances, tyrannies, confiscations, and murders. Under this emperor took place what is known in Church history as "the second persecution of the Christians." This class, as well as the Jews, were the special objects of Domitian's hatred, because they refused to worship the statues of himself which he had set up (see p. 322).

The last of the Twelve Cæsars perished in his own palace, and by the hands of members of his own household. The Senate ordered his infamous name to be erased from the public monuments, and to be blotted from the records of the Roman state.

The Five Good Emperors: Reign of Nerva (A.D. 96–98). — The five emperors — Nerva, Trajan, Hadrian, and the two Antonines — that succeeded Domitian were elected by the Senate, which during this period assumed something of its former weight and influence in the affairs of the empire. The wise and beneficent administration of the government by these rulers secured for them the enviable distinction of being called "the five good emperors." Nerva died after a short reign of sixteen months,

---

[1] In the year 1713, sixteen centuries after the destruction of the cities, the ruins were discovered by some persons engaged in digging a well, and since then extensive excavations have been made, which have uncovered a large part of Pompeii, and revealed to us the streets, homes, theatres, baths, shops, temples, and various monuments of the ancient city — all of which presents to us a very vivid picture of Roman life during the imperial period, eighteen hundred years ago.

and the sceptre passed into the stronger hands of the able commander Trajan, whom Nerva had previously made his associate in the government.

Reign of Trajan (A.D. 98–117). — Trajan was a native of Spain, and a soldier by profession and talent. His ambition to achieve military renown led him to undertake distant and important conquests. It was the policy of Augustus — a policy adopted by most of his successors — to make the Danube in Europe and the Euphrates in Asia the limits of the Roman empire in those respective quarters. But Trajan determined to push the frontiers of his dominions beyond both these rivers, scorning to permit Nature by these barriers to mark out the confines of Roman sovereignty.

TRAJAN.

He crossed the Danube by means of a bridge, the foundations of which may still be seen, and subjugated the bold and warlike Dacian tribes lying behind that stream — tribes that had often threatened the peace of the empire. After celebrating his victories in a magnificent triumph at Rome, Trajan turned to the East, led his legions across the Euphrates, reduced Armenia, and wrested from the Parthians most of the territory which anciently formed

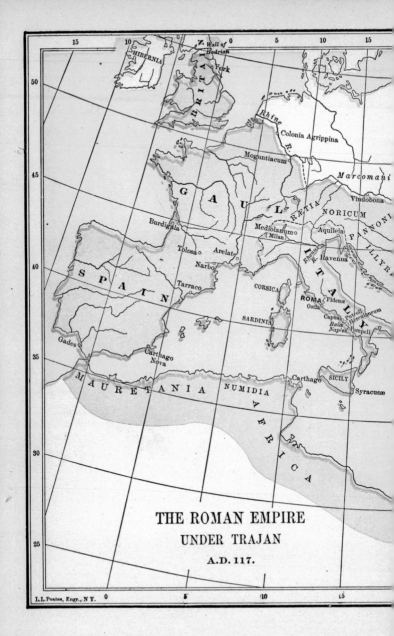

THE ROMAN EMPIRE

UNDER TRAJAN

A.D. 117.

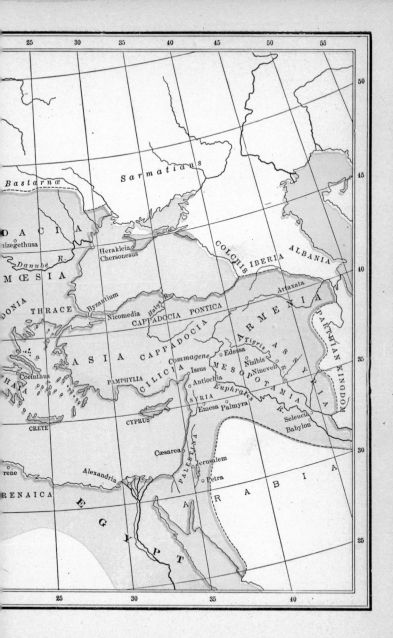

Bastarnæ

Sarmatians

DOACIA

izegethusa

Heraklein
Chersonesus

COLCHIS IBERIA ALBANIA

Danube R.

MŒSIA

DONIA THRACE Byzantium Artaxata

Nicomedia Halys R. ARMENIA

CAPPADOCIA PONTICA

ASIA CAPPADOCIA Tigris R. Edessa A PARTHIAN KINGDOM

Commagene Nisibis S

HAIA Corinthus PAMPHYLIA CILICIA Issus Nineveh S

Antiochia MESOPOTAMIA Y

SYRIA Euphrates R. R

CRETE CYPRUS Emesa Palmyra Seleucia I

Babylon A

Cæsarea Cæsarea

Jerusalem

rene Alexandria PALESTINA Petra A R A B I A

RENAICA E G Y P T

the heart of the Assyrian monarchy. To Trajan belongs the distinction of extending the boundaries of the empire to the most distant points to which Roman ambition and prowess were ever able to push them.

But Trajan was something besides a soldier. He had a taste for literature : Juvenal, Plutarch, and the younger Pliny wrote under his patronage ; and, moreover, as is true of almost all great conquerors, he had a perfect passion for building. Among the great works with which he embellished the capital was the Trajan Forum. Here he erected the celebrated marble shaft known as Trajan's column. It is one hundred and forty-seven

BESIEGING A DACIAN CITY. (From Trajan's Column.)

feet high, and is wound from base to summit by a spiral band of sculptures, containing more than twenty-five thousand human figures. The column is nearly as perfect to-day as when reared eighteen centuries ago. It was intended to commemorate the Dacian conquests of Trajan ; and its pictured sides are the best, and almost the only, record we now possess of those wars.

Respecting the rapid spread of Christianity at this time, the character of the early professors of the new faith, and the light in which they were viewed by the rulers of the Roman world, we have very important evidence in a certain letter written by Pliny the Younger to the emperor in regard to the Christians of Pontus,

in Asia Minor, of which remote province Pliny was governor.
Pliny speaks of the new creed as a "contagious superstition, that
had seized not cities only, but the lesser towns also, and the open
country." Yet he could find no fault in the converts to the new
doctrines. Notwithstanding this, however, because the Christians
steadily refused to sacrifice to the Roman gods, he ordered many
to be put to death for their "inflexible obstinacy."

Trajan died A.D. 117, after a reign of nineteen years, one of the
most prosperous and fortunate that had yet befallen the lot of the
Roman people.

Reign of Hadrian (A.D. 117–138). — Hadrian, a kinsman of
Trajan, succeeded him in the imperial office. He possessed great
ability, and displayed admirable moderation and prudence in the
administration of the government. He gave up the territory conquered by Trajan in the East, and made the Euphrates once more
the boundary of the empire in that quarter. He also broke down
the bridge that Trajan had built over the Danube, and made that
stream the real frontier line, notwithstanding the Roman garrisons
were still maintained in Dacia. Hadrian saw plainly that Rome
could not safely extend any more widely the frontiers of the
empire. Indeed, so active and threatening were the enemies of
the empire in the East, and so daring and numerous had now
become its barbarian assailants of the North, that there was reason for the greatest anxiety lest they should break through even
the old and strong lines of the Danube and the Euphrates, and
pour their devastating hordes over the provinces.

More than fifteen years of his reign were spent by Hadrian in
making tours of inspection through all the different provinces of
the empire. He visited Britain, and secured the Roman possessions there against the Picts and Scots by erecting a continuous
wall across the island. Next he journeyed through Gaul and
Spain, and then visited in different tours all the remaining countries bordering upon the Mediterranean. He ascended the Nile,
and, traveller-like, carved his name upon the vocal Memnon.
The cities which he visited he decorated with temples, theatres,
and other monuments.

In the year 131, the Jews in Palestine, who had in a measure recovered from the blow Titus had given their nation, broke out in desperate revolt, because of the planting of a Roman colony upon the almost desolate site of Jerusalem, and the placing of the statue of Jupiter in the Holy Temple. More than half a million of Jews perished in the useless struggle, and the survivors were driven into exile — the last dispersion of the race.

The latter years of his reign Hadrian passed at Rome. It was here that this princely builder erected his most splendid structures. Among these was the Mole, or Mausoleum, of Hadrian, an immense structure surmounted by a gilded dome, erected on the banks of the Tiber, and designed as a tomb for himself.

The Antonines (A.D. 138–180). — Aurelius Antoninus, surnamed Pius, the adopted son of Hadrian, and his successor, gave the Roman empire an administration singularly pure and parental. Of him it has been said that "he was the first, and, saving his colleague and successor Aurelius, the only one of the emperors who devoted himself to the task of government with a single view to the happiness of his people." Throughout his long reign of twenty-three years, the empire was in a state of profound peace. The attention of the historian is attracted by no striking events, which, as many have not failed to observe, illustrates admirably the oft-repeated maxim, "Happy is that people whose annals are brief."

Antoninus, early in his reign, united with himself in the government his adopted son Marcus Aurelius, and upon the death of the former (A.D. 161) the latter succeeded quietly to his place and work. His studious habits won for him the title of "Philosopher." He belonged to the school of the Stoics, and was a most thoughtful writer. His *Meditations* breathe the tenderest sentiments of devotion and benevolence, and make the nearest approach to the spirit of Christianity of all the writings of Pagan antiquity. He established an Institution, or Home, for orphan girls; and, finding the poorer classes throughout Italy burdened by their taxes and greatly in arrears in paying them, he caused all the tax-claims to be heaped in the Forum and burned.

The tastes and sympathies of Aurelius would have led him to choose a life passed in retirement and study at the capital; but hostile movements of the Parthians, and especially invasions of the barbarians along the Rhenish and Danubian frontiers, called him from his books, and forced him to spend most of the latter years of his reign in the camp. The Parthians, who had violated their treaty with Rome, were chastised by the lieutenants of the emperor, and Mesopotamia again fell under Roman authority.

This war drew after it a series of terrible calamities. The returning soldiers brought with them the Asiatic plague, which swept off vast numbers, especially in Italy, where entire cities and districts were depopulated. In the general distress and panic, the superstitious people were led to believe that it was the new sect of Christians that had called down upon the nation the anger of the gods. Aurelius permitted a fearful persecution to be instituted against them, during which the famous Christian fathers and bishops, Justin Martyr and Polycarp, suffered death.

It should be noted that the persecution of the Christians under the Pagan emperors, sprung from political rather than religious motives, and that this is why we find the names of the best emperors, as well as those of the worst, in the list of persecutors. It was believed that the welfare of the state was bound up with the careful performance of the rites of the national worship; and hence, while the Roman rulers were usually very tolerant, allowing all forms of worship among their subjects, still they required that men of every faith should at least recognize the Roman gods, and burn incense before their statues. This the Christians steadily refused to do. Their neglect of the service of the temple, it was believed, angered the gods, and endangered the safety of the state, bringing upon it drought, pestilence, and every disaster. This was the main reason of their persecution by the Pagan emperors.

But pestilence and persecution were both forgotten amidst the imperative calls for immediate help that now came from the North. The barbarians were pushing in the Roman outposts, and pouring impetuously over the frontiers. To the panic of the plague was added this new terror. Aurelius placed himself at the head of his legions, and hurried beyond the Alps. For many years, amidst the snows of winter and the heats of summer, he strove to beat back the assailants of the empire.

The efforts of the devoted Aurelius checked the inroads of the barbarians; but he could not subdue them, so weakened was the empire by the ravages of the pestilence, and so exhausted was the treasury from the heavy and constant drains upon it. At last his weak body gave way beneath the hardships of his numerous campaigns, and he died in his camp at Vindobona (now Vienna), in the nineteenth year of his reign (A.D. 180).

The united voice of the Senate and people pronounced him a god, and divine worship was accorded to his statue. Never was Monarchy so justified of her children as in the lives and works of the Antonines. As Merivale, in dwelling upon their virtues, very justly remarks, " the blameless career of these illustrious princes has furnished the best excuse for Cæsarism in all after-ages."

ROMAN EMPERORS FROM AUGUSTUS TO MARCUS AURELIUS.

(From 31 B.C. to A.D. 180.)

Augustus reigns	31 B.C. to A.D. 14	Titus	A.D. 79–81
Tiberius	A.D. 14–37	Domitian	81–96
Caligula	37–41	Nerva	96–98
Claudius	41–54	Trajan	98–117
Nero	54–68	Hadrian	117–138
Galba	68–69	Antoninus Pius	138–161
Otho	69	Marcus Aurelius	161–180
Vitellius	69	Verus associated with Au-	
Vespasian	69–79	relius	161–169

The first eleven, in connection with Julius Cæsar, are called the Twelve Cæsars. The last five (excluding Verus) are known as the Five Good Emperors.

CHAPTER XXX.

DECLINE AND FALL OF THE ROMAN EMPIRE IN THE WEST; BEGINNING OF THE GREAT GERMAN MIGRATION.

(A.D. 180–476.)

Reign of Commodus (A.D. 180–192). — Under the wise and able administration of "the five good emperors" — Nerva, Trajan, Hadrian, and the two Antonines — the Roman empire reached its culmination in power and prosperity; and now, under the enfeebling influences of vice and corruption within, and the heavy blows of the barbarians without, it begins to decline rapidly to its fall.

COMMODUS (as Hercules).

Commodus, son of Marcus Aurelius, and the last of the Antonines, was a most unworthy successor of his illustrious father. For three years, however, surrounded by the able generals and wise counsellors that the prudent administration of the preceding emperors had drawn to the head of affairs, Commodus ruled with fairness and lenity, when an unsuccessful conspiracy against his life seemed suddenly to kindle all the slumbering passions of a Nero. He secured the favor of the rabble with the shows of the amphitheatre, and purchased the support of the prætorians with bribes and flatteries. Thus he was enabled for ten years to retain the throne, while perpetrating all manner of cruelties, and staining the imperial purple with the most detestable debaucheries and crimes.

Commodus had a passion for gladiatorial combats, and attired in a lion's skin, and armed with the club of Hercules, he valiantly set upon and slew antagonists arrayed to represent mythological monsters, and armed with great sponges for rocks. The Senate, so obsequiously servile had that body become, conferred upon him the title of the Roman Hercules, and also voted him the additional surnames of Pius and Felix, and even proposed to change the name of Rome and call it Colonia Commodiana.

The empire was finally relieved of the insane tyrant by some members of the royal household, who anticipated his designs against themselves by putting him to death.

"The Barrack Emperors." — For nearly a century after the death of Commodus (from A.D. 192 to 284), the emperors were elected by the army, and hence the rulers for this period have been called "the Barrack Emperors." The character of the period is revealed by the fact that of the twenty-five emperors who mounted the throne during this time all except four came to their deaths by violence. "Civil war, pestilence, bankruptcy, were all brooding over the empire. The soldiers had forgotten how to fight, the rulers how to govern." On every side the barbarians were breaking into the empire to rob, to murder, and to burn.

The Public Sale of the Empire (A.D. 193). — The beginning of these troublous times was marked by a shameful proceeding on the part of the prætorians. Upon the death of Commodus, Pertinax, a distinguished senator, was placed on the throne; but his efforts to enforce discipline among the prætorians aroused their anger, and he was slain by them after a short reign of only three months. These soldiers then gave out notice that they would sell the empire to the highest bidder. It was, accordingly, set up for sale at the prætorian camp, and struck off to Didius Julianus, a wealthy senator, who promised $1000 to each of the 12,000 soldiers at this time composing the guard. So the price of the empire was about $12,000,000.

But these turbulent and insolent soldiers at the capital of the empire were not to have things entirely their own way. As soon as the news of the disgraceful transaction reached the legions on the frontiers, they rose as a single man in indignant revolt. Each of the three armies that held the Euphrates, the Rhine, and the Danube, proclaimed its favorite commander emperor. The leader of the Danubian troops was Septimius Severus, a man of great energy and force of character. He knew that there were other competitors for the throne, and that the prize would be his who first seized it. Instantly he set his veterans in motion and was soon at Rome. The prætorians were no match for the trained legionaries of the frontiers, and did not even attempt to defend their emperor, who was taken prisoner and put to death after a reign of sixty-five days.

Reign of Septimius Severus (A.D. 193–211). — One of the first acts of Severus was to organize a new body-guard of 50,000 legionaries, to take the place of the unworthy prætorians, whom, as a punishment for the insult they had offered to the Roman state, he disbanded, and banished from the capital, and forbade to approach within a hundred miles of its walls. He next crushed his two rival competitors, and was then undisputed master of the empire. He put to death forty senators for having favored his late rivals, and completely destroyed the power of their body. Committing to the prefect of the new prætorian guard the management of affairs at the capital, Severus passed the greater part of his long and prosperous reign upon the frontiers. At one time he was chastising the Parthians beyond the Euphrates, and at another, pushing back the Caledonian tribes from the Hadrian wall in the opposite corner of his dominions. Finally, in Britain, in his camp at York, death overtook him.

Reign of Caracalla (A.D. 211–217). — Severus conferred the empire upon his two sons, Caracalla and Geta. Caracalla murdered his brother, and then ordered Papinian, the celebrated jurist, to make a public argument in vindication of the fratricide. When that great lawyer refused, saying that " it was easier to commit such a crime than to justify it," he put him to death. Thousands fell victims to his senseless rage. Driven by remorse and fear, he fled from the capital, and wandered about the most distant provinces. At Alexandria, on account of some uncomplimentary remarks by the citizens upon his appearance, he ordered a general massacre. Finally, after a reign of six years, the monster was slain in a remote corner of Syria.

Caracalla's sole political act of real importance was the bestowal of citizenship upon all the free inhabitants of the empire ; and this he did, not to give them a just privilege, but that he might collect from them certain special taxes which only Roman citizens had to pay. Before the reign of Caracalla it was only particular classes of subjects, or the in-

CARACALLA.

habitants of some particular city or province, that, as a mark of special favor, had, from time to time, been admitted to the rights of citizenship (see p. 280). By this wholesale act of Caracalla, the entire population of the empire was made Roman, at least in name and nominal privilege. " The city had become the world, or, viewed from the other side, the world had become the city " (Merivale).

Reign of Alexander Severus (A.D. 222–235). — Severus restored the virtues of the Age of the Antonines. His administration was pure and energetic ; but he strove in vain to resist the corrupt and downward tendencies of the times. He was assassinated, after a reign of fourteen years, by his seditious soldiers, who were angered by his efforts to reduce them to discipline. They invested with the imperial purple an obscure officer named Maximin, a Thracian peasant, whose sole recommendation for this dignity was his gigantic stature and his great strength of limbs. Rome had now sunk to the lowest possible degradation. We may pass rapidly over the next fifty years of the empire.

The Thirty Tyrants (A.D. 251–268). — Maximin was followed swiftly by Gordian, Philip, and Decius, and then came what is

TRIUMPH OF SAPOR OVER VALERIAN.

called the "Age of the Thirty Tyrants." The imperial sceptre being held by weak emperors, there sprang up in every part of the empire, competitors for the throne — several rivals frequently appearing in the field at the same time. The barbarians pressed upon all the frontiers, and thrust themselves into all the provinces. The empire seemed on the point of falling to pieces.[1] But a fortunate succession of five good emperors — Claudius, Aurelian,

[1] It was during this period that the Emperor Valerian (A.D. 253–260), in a battle with the Persians before Edessa, in Mesopotamia, was defeated and taken prisoner by Sapor, the Persian king. A large rock tablet (see cut above), still to be seen near the Persian town of Shiraz, is believed to commemorate the triumph of Sapor over the unfortunate emperor.

Tacitus, Probus, and Carus (A.D. 268–284) — restored for a time the ancient boundaries, and again forced together into some sort of union the fragments of the shattered state.

The Fall of Palmyra. — The most noted of the usurpers of authority in the provinces during the period of anarchy of which we have spoken, was Odenatus, Prince of Palmyra, a city occupying an oasis in the midst of the Syrian Desert, midway between the Mediterranean and the Euphrates. In gratitude for the aid he had rendered the Romans against the Parthians, the Senate had bestowed upon him titles and honors. When the empire began to show signs of weakness and approaching dissolution, Odenatus conceived the ambitious project of erecting upon its ruins in the East a great Palmyrian kingdom. Upon his death, his wife, Zenobia, succeeded to his authority and to his ambitions. This famous princess claimed descent from Cleopatra, and it is certain that in the charms of personal beauty she was the rival of the Egyptian queen. Boldly assuming the title of " Queen of the East," she bade defiance to the emperor of Rome. Aurelian marched against her, defeated her armies, and carried her a captive to Italy (273 A.D.). After having been led in golden chains in the triumphal procession of Aurelian, the queen was given a beautiful villa in the vicinity of Tibur, where, surrounded by her children, she passed the remainder of her checkered life.

The ruins of Palmyra are among the most interesting remains of Græco-Roman civilization in the East.

Reign of Diocletian (A.D. 284–305). — The reign of Diocletian marks an important era in Roman history. Up to this time the imperial government had been more or less carefully concealed under the forms and names of the old republic. The government now became an unveiled and absolute monarchy. Diocletian's reforms, though radical, were salutary, and infused such fresh vitality into the frame of the dying state as to give it a new lease of life for another term of nearly two hundred years.

He determined to divide the numerous and increasing cares of the distracted empire, so that it might be ruled from two centres—

one in the East and the other in the West.   In pursuance of this
plan, he chose as a colleague a companion soldier, Maximian,
upon whom he conferred the title of Augustus.   After a few years,

DIOCLETIAN.

finding the cares of the co-sovereignty
still too heavy, each sovereign associated with himself an assistant, who
took the title of Cæsar, and was considered the son and heir of the emperor.   There were thus two Augusti
and two Cæsars.   Milan, in Italy, became the capital and residence of
Maximian ; while Nicomedia, in Asia
Minor, became the seat of the court
of Diocletian.   The Augusti took
charge of the countries near their respective capitals, while the younger
and more active Cæsars were assigned
the government of the more distant
and turbulent provinces.   The vigor-
ous administration of the government in every quarter of the
empire was thus secured.   The authority of each of the rulers was
supreme within the territory allotted him ; but all acknowledged
Diocletian as " the father and head of the state."

The most serious drawback to the system of government thus
instituted was the heavy expense incident to the maintenance of
four courts with their trains of officers and dependants.   The taxes
became unendurable, husbandry ceased, and large masses of the
population were reduced almost to starvation.

While the changes made in the government have rendered the
name of Diocletian famous in the political history of the Roman
state, the cruel persecutions which he ordered against the Christians have made his name in an equal degree infamous in ecclesiastical annals ; for it was during this reign that the tenth — the
last and severest — of the persecutions of the Church took place.
By an imperial decree the churches of the Christians were ordered

to be torn down, and they themselves were outlawed. For ten years the fugitives were hunted in forest and cave. The victims were burned, were cast to the wild beasts in the amphitheatre — were put to death by every torture and in every mode that ingenious cruelty could devise. But nothing could shake the constancy of their faith. They courted the death that secured them, as they firmly believed, immediate entrance upon an existence of unending happiness. The exhibition of devotion and constancy shown by the martyrs won multitudes to the persecuted faith.

It was during this and the various other persecutions that vexed the Church in the second and third centuries that the Christians sought refuge in the Catacombs, those vast subterranean galleries and chambers under the city of Rome. Here the Christians hopefully buried their dead, and on the walls of the chambers sketched

CHRIST AS THE GOOD SHEPHERD.
(From the Catacombs.)

rude symbols of their confident faith. It was in the darkness of these subterranean abodes that Christian art had its beginnings.

After a prosperous reign of twenty years, becoming weary of the cares of state, Diocletian abdicated the throne, and forced or induced his colleague Maximian also to lay down his authority on the same day. Galerius and Constantius were, by this act, advanced to the purple and made Augusti; and two new associates were appointed as Cæsars. Diocletian, having enjoyed the extreme satisfaction of seeing the imperial authority quietly and successfully transmitted by his system, without the dictation of the insolent prætorians or the interference of the turbulent legionaries, now retired to his country-seat at Salona, on the eastern shore of the Adriatic, and there devoted himself to rural pursuits. It is related that, when Maximian wrote him urging him to endeavor, with him, to regain the power they had laid aside, he replied : " Were you but to come to Salona and see the vegetables which I raise in my garden with my own hands, you would no longer talk to me of empire."

Reign of Constantine the Great (A.D. 306–337) ; **the Empire becomes Christian.** — Galerius and Constantius had reigned together only one year, when the latter died at York, in Britain ; and his soldiers, disregarding the rule of succession as determined by the system of Diocletian, proclaimed his son Constantine emperor.   Six competitors for the throne arose in different quarters. For eighteen years Constantine fought to gain supremacy.   At the end of that time every rival was crushed, and he was the sole ruler of the Roman world.

Constantine was the first Christian emperor.   He was converted to the new religion — such is the story — by seeing in the heavens, during one of his campaigns against his rivals, a luminous cross with this inscription : "With this sign you will conquer." He made the cross the royal standard ; and the Roman legions now for the first time marched beneath the emblem of Christianity.

By a decree issued from Milan A.D. 313, Christianity was made in effect the state religion ; but all other forms of worship were tolerated.   With the view of harmonizing the different sects that had sprung up among the Christians, and to settle the controversy between the Arians and the Athanasians respecting the nature of Christ, — the former denied his equality with God the Father, — Constantine called the first Œcumenical, or General Council of the Church, at Nicæa, a town of Asia Minor, A.D. 325.   Arianism was denounced, and a formula of Christian faith adopted, which is known as the Nicene Creed.

After the recognition of Christianity, the most important act of Constantine was the selection of Byzantium, on the Bosporus, as the new capital of the empire.   One reason which led the emperor to choose this site in preference to Rome was the ungracious conduct towards him of the inhabitants of the latter city, because he had abandoned the worship of the old national deities.

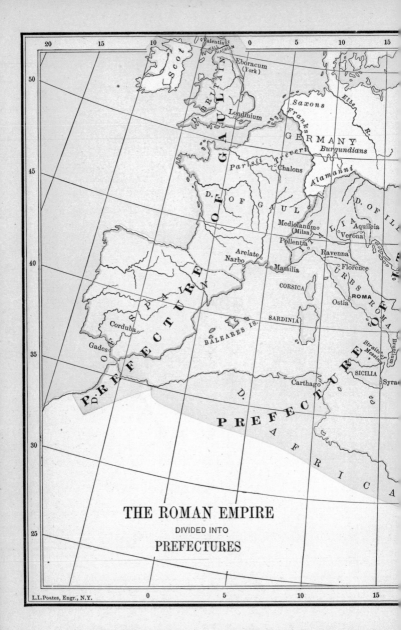

THE ROMAN EMPIRE

DIVIDED INTO

PREFECTURES

L.L.Poates, Engr., N.Y.

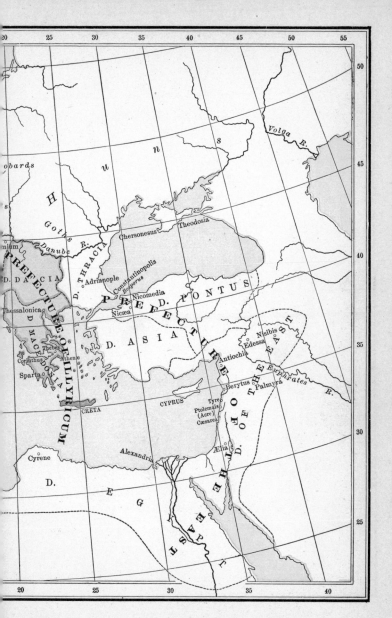

But there were political reasons for such a change. Through the Eastern conquests of Rome, the centre of the population, wealth, and culture of the empire had shifted eastward. The West — Gaul, Britain, Spain — was rude and barbarous; the East — Egypt, Syria, Asia Minor — was the abode of ancient civilizations from which Rome was proud to trace her origin. Constantine was not the first to entertain the idea of seeking in the East a new centre for the Roman world. The Italians were inflamed against the first Cæsar by the report that he intended to restore Ilium, the cradle of the Roman race, and make that the capital of the empire.

Constantine organized at Byzantium a new Senate, while that at Rome sank to the obscure position of the council of a provincial municipality. Multitudes eagerly thronged to the new capital, and almost in a night the little colony grew into an imperial city. In honor of the emperor its name was changed to Constantinople, the "City of Constantine." Hereafter the eyes of the world were directed towards the Bosporus instead of the Tiber.

To aid in the administration of the government, Constantine laid out the empire into four great divisions, called prefectures (see map), which were subdivided into thirteen dioceses, and these again into one hundred and sixteen provinces.

The character of Constantine has been greatly eulogized by Christian writers, while pagan historians very naturally painted it in dark colors. It is probable that he embraced Christianity, not entirely from conviction, but partly from political motives. As the historian Hodgkin puts it, " He was half convinced of the truth of Christianity, and wholly convinced of the policy of embracing it." In any event, Constantine's religion was a strange mixture of the old and the new faith : on his medals the Christian cross is held by the pagan deity, Victory. In his domestic relations he was tyrannical and cruel. He died in the thirty-first year of his reign, leaving his kingdom to his three sons, Constans, Constantius, and Constantine.

Reign of Julian the Apostate (A.D. 361–363). — The parcelling out of the empire by Constantine among his sons led to strife and wars, which, at the end of sixteen years, left Constantius master of the whole. He reigned as sole emperor for about eight years, engaged in ceaseless warfare with German tribes in the West and with the Persians[1] in the East. Constantius was followed by his cousin Julian, who was killed while in pursuit of the troops of Sapor, king of the Persians (A.D. 363).

Julian is called the Apostate because he abandoned Christianity and labored to restore the pagan faith. In his persecution of the Christians, however, he could not resort to the old means — "the sword, the fire, the lions;" for, under the softening influences of the very faith he sought to extirpate, the Roman world had already learned a gentleness and humanity that rendered impossible the renewal of the Neronian and Diocletian persecutions. Julian's weapons were sophistry and ridicule, in the use of which he was a master. To degrade the Christians, and place them at a disadvantage in controversy, he excluded them from the schools of logic and rhetoric.

Furthermore, to cast discredit upon the predictions of the Scriptures, Julian determined to rebuild the Temple at Jerusalem, which the Christians contended could not be restored because of the prophecies against it. He actually began excavations, but his workmen were driven in great panic from the spot by terrific explosions and bursts of flame. The Christians regarded the occurrence as miraculous; and Julian himself, it is certain, was so dismayed by it that he desisted from the undertaking.[2]

It was in vain that the apostate emperor labored to uproot the

---

[1] The great Parthian empire, which had been such a formidable antagonist of Rome, was, after an existence of five centuries, overthrown (A.D. 226) by a revolt of the Persians, and the New Persian, or Sassanian monarchy established. This empire lasted till the country was overrun by the Saracens in the seventh century A.D.

[2] The explosions which so terrified the workmen of Julian are supposed to have been caused by accumulations of gases — similar to those that so frequently occasion accidents in mines — in the subterranean chambers of the Temple foundations.

new faith; for the purity of its teachings, the universal and eternal character of its moral precepts, had given it a name to live. Equally in vain were his efforts to restore the worship of the old Grecian and Roman divinities. Polytheism was a transitional form of religious belief which the world had now outgrown : Great Pan was dead.

The disabilities under which Julian had placed the Christians were removed by his successor Jovian (A.D. 363–4), and the Christian worship was re-established.

GERMANS CROSSING THE RHINE. (After Alphonse de Neuville.)

Valentinian and Valens.—Upon the death of Jovian, Valentinian, the commander of the imperial guard, was elected emperor by a council of the generals of the army and the ministers of the court. He appointed his brother Valens as his associate in office, and assigned to him the Eastern provinces, while reserving for himself the Western. He set up his own court at Milan, while his brother established his residence at Constantinople.

The Movements of the Barbarians.—The reigns of Valentinian and Valens were signalized by threatening movements of the barbarian tribes, that now, almost at the same moment, began to press with redoubled energy against all the barriers of the empire. The Alemanni (Germans) crossed the Rhine — sometimes swarming over the river on the winter's ice — and, before pursuit could be made, escaped with their booty into the depths of the German forests. The Saxons, pirates of the northern seas, who issued from the mouth of the Elbe, ravaged the coasts of Gaul and Britain, even pushing their light skiffs far up the rivers and creeks of those countries, and carrying spoils from the inland cities. In Britain, the Picts broke through the Wall of Antoninus, and wrested almost the entire island from the hands of the Romans. In Africa, the Moorish and other tribes, issuing from the ravines of the Atlas Mountains and swarming from the deserts of the south, threatened to obliterate the last trace of Roman civilization occupying the narrow belt of fertile territory skirting the sea.

The barbarian tide of invasion seemed thus on the point of overwhelming the empire in the West ; but for twelve years Valentinian defended with signal ability and energy, not only his own territories, but aided with arms and counsel his weaker brother Valens in the defence of his. Upon the death of Valentinian, his son Gratian succeeded to his authority (A.D. 375).

The Goths cross the Danube. — The year following the death of Valentinian, an event of the greatest importance occurred in the East. The Visigoths (Western Goths) dwelling north of the Lower Danube, who had often in hostile bands crossed that river to war against the Roman emperors, now appeared as suppliants in vast multitudes upon its banks. They said that a terrible race, whom they were powerless to withstand, had invaded their territories, and spared neither their homes nor their lives. They begged permission of the Romans to cross the river and settle in Thrace, and promised, should this request be granted, ever to remain the grateful and firm allies of the Roman state.

Valens consented to grant their petition on condition that they should surrender their arms, give up their children as hostages, and all be baptized in the Christian faith. Their terror and despair led them to assent to these conditions. So the entire nation, numbering one million souls, — counting men, women, and children, — were allowed to cross the river. Several days and nights were consumed in the transport of the vast multitudes. The writers of the times liken the passage to that of the Hellespont by the hosts of Xerxes.

The enemy that had so terrified the Goths were the Huns, a monstrous race of fierce nomadic horsemen, that two centuries and more before the Christian era were roving the deserts north of the Great Wall of China (see p. 13). Migrating from that region, they moved slowly to the west, across the great plains of Central Asia, and, after wandering several centuries, appeared in Europe. They belonged to a different race (the Turanian) from all the other European tribes with which we have been so far concerned. Their features were hideous, their noses being flattened, and their cheeks gashed, to render their appearance more frightful, as well as to prevent the growth of a beard. Even the barbarous Goths called them " barbarians."

Scarcely had the fugitive Visigoths been received within the limits of the empire before a large company of their kinsmen, the Ostrogoths (Eastern Goths), also driven from their homes by the same terrible Huns, crowded to the banks of the Danube, and pleaded that they might be allowed, as their countrymen had been, to place the river between themselves and their dreaded enemies. But Valens, becoming alarmed at the presence of so many barbarians within his dominions, refused their request; whereupon they, dreading the fierce and implacable foe behind more than the wrath of the Roman emperor in front, crossed the river with arms in their hands. At this moment the Visigoths, rising in revolt, joined their kinsmen that were just now forcing the passage of the Danube, and began to ravage the Danubian provinces. Valens despatched swift messengers to Gratian in the West, asking for assistance against the foe he had so imprudently admitted within the limits of the empire.

Theodosius the Great (A.D. 379–395). — Gratian was hurrying to the help of his colleague Valens, when news of his defeat and death at the hands of the barbarians was brought to him, and he at once appointed as his associate Theodosius, known afterwards as the Great, and entrusted him with the government of the Eastern provinces. Theodosius, by wise and vigorous measures, quickly reduced the Goths to submission. Vast multitudes of the Visigoths were settled upon the waste lands of Thrace, while the Ostrogoths were scattered in various colonies in different regions of Asia Minor. The Goths became allies of the Emperor of the East, and more than 40,000 of these warlike barbarians, who were destined to be the subverters of the empire, were enlisted in the imperial legions.

While Theodosius was thus composing the East, the West, through the jealous rivalries of different competitors for the control of the government, had fallen into great disorder. Theodosius twice interposed to right affairs, and then took the government into his own hands. For four months he ruled as sole monarch of the empire.

Final Division of the Empire (A.D. 395). — The Roman world was now united for the last time under a single master. Just before his death, Theodosius divided the empire between his two sons, Arcadius and Honorius, assigning the former, who was only eighteen years of age, the government of the East, and giving the latter, a mere child of eleven, the sovereignty of the West. This was the final partition of the Roman empire — the issue of that growing tendency, which we have observed in its immoderately extended dominions, to break apart. The separate histories of the East and the West now begin.

The Eastern Empire. — The story of the fortunes of the Empire in the East need not detain us long at this point of our history. This monarchy lasted over a thousand years — from the accession to power of Arcadius, A.D. 395, to the capture of Constantinople by the Turks, A.D. 1453. It will thus be seen that the greater part of its history belongs to the mediæval period. Up to the time of the overthrow of the Empire in the West, the sovereigns of the East were engaged almost incessantly in suppressing uprisings of their Gothic allies or mercenaries, or in re-pelling invasions of the Huns and the Vandals. Frequently during this period, in order to save their own territories, the Eastern emperors, by dishonorable inducements, persuaded the barbarians to direct their ravaging expeditions against the provinces of the West.

LAST DAYS OF THE EMPIRE IN THE WEST.

First Invasion of Italy by Alaric. — Only a few years had elapsed after the death of the great Theodosius, before the barbarians were trooping in vast hordes through all the regions of the West. First, from Thrace and Mœsia came the Visigoths, led by the great Alaric. They poured through the Pass of Thermopylæ, and devastated almost the entire peninsula of Greece ; but, being driven from that country by Stilicho, the renowned Vandal general of Honorius, they crossed the Julian Alps, and spread terror throughout all Italy. Stilicho followed the barbarians cautiously, and, attacking them at a favorable moment, inflicted a terrible and double defeat upon them at Pollentia and Verona (A.D. 402–403). The captured camp was found filled with the spoils of Thebes, Corinth, and Sparta. Gathering the remnants of his shattered army, Alaric forced his way with difficulty through the defiles of the Alps, and escaped.

Last Triumph at Rome (A.D. 404). — A terrible danger had been averted. All Italy burst forth in expressions of gratitude and joy. The days of the Cimbri and Teutones were recalled, and the name of Stilicho was pronounced with that of Marius. A magnificent triumph at Rome celebrated the victory and the deliverance. It was the last triumph that Rome ever saw. Three hundred times — such is asserted to be the number — the Imperial City had witnessed the triumphal procession of her victorious generals, celebrating conquests in all quarters of the world.

Last Gladiatorial Combat of the Amphitheatre. — The same year that marks the last military triumph at Rome also signalizes the last gladiatorial combat in the Roman amphitheatre. It is to

Christianity that the credit of the suppression of the inhuman exhibitions of the amphitheatre is entirely, or almost entirely, due. The pagan philosophers usually regarded them with indifference, often with favor. Thus Pliny commends a friend for giving a gladiatorial entertainment at the funeral of his wife. And when the pagan moralists did condemn the spectacles, it was rather for other reasons than that they regarded them as inhuman and absolutely contrary to the rules of ethics. They were defended on the ground that they fostered a martial spirit among the people and inured the soldier to the sights of the battle-field. Hence gladiatorial games were actually exhibited to the legions before they set out on their campaigns. Indeed, all classes appear to have viewed the matter in much the same light, and with exactly the same absence of moral disapprobation, that we ourselves regard the slaughter of animals for food.

But the Christian fathers denounced the combats as absolutely immoral, and labored in every possible way to create a public opinion against them. The members of their own body who attended the spectacles were excommunicated. At length, in A.D. 325, the first imperial edict against them was issued by Constantine. This decree appears to have been very little regarded; nevertheless, from this time forward the exhibitions were under something of a ban, until their final abolition was brought about by an incident of the games that closed the triumph of Honorius. In the midst of the exhibition a Christian monk, named Telemachus, descending into the arena, rushed between the combatants, but was instantly killed by a shower of missiles thrown by the people, who were angered by this interruption of their sports. But the people soon repented of their act; and Honorius himself, who was present, was moved by the scene. Christianity had awakened the conscience and touched the heart of Rome. The martyrdom of the monk led to an imperial edict "which abolished forever the human sacrifices of the amphitheatre."

Invasion of Italy by Various German Tribes. — While Italy was celebrating her triumph over the Goths, another and more formidable invasion was preparing in the North. The tribes beyond the Rhine — the Vandals, the Suevi, the Burgundians, and other peoples — driven onward by some unknown cause, poured in impetuous streams from the forests and morasses of Germany, and bursting the barriers of the Alps, overspread the devoted plains of Italy. The alarm caused by them among the Italians was even greater than that inspired by the Gothic invasion ; for Alaric was a Christian, while Radagaisus, the leader of the new hordes, was a superstitious savage, who paid worship to gods that required the bloody sacrifice of captive enemies.

By such efforts as Rome put forth in the younger and more vigorous days of the republic, when Hannibal was at her gates, an army was now equipped and placed under the command of Stilicho. Meanwhile the barbarians had advanced as far as Florence, and were now besieging that place. Stilicho here surrounded the vast host — variously estimated from 200,000 to 400,000 men — and starved them into a surrender. Their chief, Radagaisus, was put to death, and great multitudes of the barbarians that the sword and famine had spared were sold as slaves (A.D. 406).

The Ransom of Rome (A.D. 409). — Shortly after the victory of Stilicho over the German barbarians, he came under the suspicion of the weak and jealous Honorius, and was executed. Thus fell the great general whose sword and counsel had twice saved Rome from the barbarians, and who might again have averted similar dangers that were now at hand. Listening to the rash counsels of his unworthy advisers, Honorius provoked to revolt the 30,000 Gothic mercenaries in the Roman legions by a massacre of their wives and children, who were held as hostages in the different cities of Italy. The Goths beyond the Alps joined with their kinsmen to avenge the perfidious act. Alaric again crossed the mountains, and pillaging the cities in his way, led his hosts to the very gates of Rome. Not since the time of the dread Hannibal (see p. 263) — more than six hundred years before — had Rome been insulted by the presence of a foreign foe beneath her walls.

The barbarians laying siege to the city, famine soon forced the Romans to sue for terms of surrender. The ambassadors of the Senate, when they came before Alaric, began, in lofty language, to warn him not to render the Romans desperate by hard or dishonorable terms : their fury when driven to despair, they represented, was terrible, and their number enormous. "The thicker the grass, the easier to mow it," was Alaric's derisive reply. The barbarian chieftain at length named the ransom that he would accept, and spare the city. Small as it comparatively was, the Romans were able to raise it only by the most extraordinary measures. The images of the gods were stripped of their ornaments of gold and precious stones, and even the statues themselves were melted down.

Sack of Rome by Alaric (A.D. 410). — Upon retiring from Rome, Alaric established his camp in Etruria. Here he was joined by great numbers of fugitive slaves, and by fresh accessions of barbarians from beyond the Alps. The Gallic king now demanded for his followers lands of Honorius, but the emperor treated all the proposals of the barbarian with foolish insolence. Rome paid the penalty. Alaric turned upon the devoted city, determined upon its sack and plunder. The barbarians broke into the capital by night, "and the inhabitants were awakened by the tremendous sound of the Gothic trumpet." Precisely eight hundred years had passed since its sack by the Gauls. During that time the Imperial City had carried its victorious standards over three continents, and had gathered within the temples of its gods and the palaces of its nobles the plunder of the world. Now it was given over for a spoil to the fierce tribes from beyond the Danube.

Alaric commanded his soldiers to respect the lives of the people, and to leave untouched the treasures of the Christian temples ; but the wealth of the citizens he encouraged them to make their own. For six days and nights the rough barbarians trooped through the streets of the city on their mission of pillage. Their wagons were heaped with the costly furniture, the rich plate, and the silken garments stripped from the palaces of the wealthy patricians and the temples of the gods. Amidst the license of the sack, the barbarian instincts of the robbers broke loose from all restraint, and the city was everywhere wet with blood, while the nights were lighted with burning buildings.

Effects of the Disaster upon Paganism. — The overwhelming disaster that had befallen the Imperial City produced a profound impression upon both Pagans and Christians throughout the Roman world. The former asserted that these unutterable calamities had fallen upon the Roman state because of the abandonment by the people of the worship of the gods of their forefathers, under whose protection and favor Rome had become the mistress of the world. The Christians, on the other hand, saw in the fall of the Eternal City the fulfilment of the prophecies against the Babylon of the Apocalypse. The latter interpretation of the appalling calamity gained credit amidst the panic and despair of the times. The temples of the once popular deities were deserted by their worshippers, who had lost faith in gods that could neither save themselves nor protect their shrines from spoliation. "Henceforth," says Merivale, "the power of paganism was entirely broken, and the indications which occasionally meet us of its continued existence are rare and trifling. Christianity stepped into its deserted inheritance. The Christians occupied the temples, transforming them into churches."

The Death of Alaric. — After withdrawing his warriors from Rome, Alaric led them southward. As they moved slowly on, they piled still higher the wagons of their long trains with the rich spoils of the cities and villas of Campania and other districts of Southern Italy. In the villas of the Roman nobles the rough barbarians spread rare banquets from the stores of their well-filled cellars, and drank from jewelled cups the famed Falernian wine.

Alaric led his soldiers to the extreme southern point of Italy, intending to cross the Straits of Messina into Sicily, and, after subduing that island, to carry his conquests into the provinces of Africa. His designs were frustrated by his death, which occurred A.D. 410. With religious care his followers secured the body of their hero against violation by his enemies. The little river Busentinus, in Northern Bruttium, was turned from its course with great labor, and in the bed of the stream was constructed a tomb, in which was placed the body of the king, with his jewels and trophies. The river was then restored to its old channel, and, that the exact spot might never be known, the prisoners who had been forced to do the work were all put to death.

The Barbarians Seize the Western Provinces. — We must now turn our eyes from Rome and Italy to observe the movement of events in the provinces. In his efforts to defend Italy, Stilicho had withdrawn the last legion from Britain, and had drained the camps and fortresses of Gaul. The Wall of Antoninus was left unmanned ; the passages of the Rhine were left unguarded ; and the agitated multitudes of barbarians beyond these defences were free to pour their innumerable hosts into all the fair provinces of the empire. Hordes of Suevi, Alani, Vandals, and Burgundians overspread all the plains and valleys of Gaul. The Vandals pushed on into the south of Spain, and there occupied a large tract of country, which, in its present name of Andalusia, preserves the memory of its barbarian settlers. From these regions they crossed the Straits of Gibraltar, overran the Roman provinces of Northern Africa, captured Carthage (A.D. 439), and made that city the seat of the dread empire of the Vandals. The Goths, with Italy pillaged, recrossed the Alps, and establishing their camps in the south of Gaul and the north of Spain, set up in those regions what is known as the Kingdom of the Visigoths.

In Britain, upon the withdrawal of the Roman legions, the Picts breaking over the Wall of Antoninus, descended upon and pillaged the cities of the South. The half-Romanized and effeminate provincials — no match for their hardy kinsmen who had never bowed their necks to the yoke of Rome — were driven to despair by the ravages of their relentless enemies, and, in their helplessness, invited to their aid the Angles and Saxons from the shores of the North Sea. These people came in their rude boats, drove back the invaders, and, being pleased with the soil and climate of the island, took possession of the country for themselves, and became the ancestors of the English people.

Invasion of the Huns: Battle of Chalons. — The barbarians that were thus overrunning and parcelling out the inheritance of the dying empire were now, in turn, pressed upon and terrified by a foe more hideous and dreadful in their eyes than were they in the sight of the peoples among whom they had thrust themselves. These were the non-Aryan Huns, of whom we have already caught a glimpse as they drove the panic-stricken Goths across the Danube. At this time their leader was Attila, whom the affrighted inhabitants of Europe called the "Scourge of God." It was declared that the grass never grew again where once the hoof of Attila's horse had trod.

Attila defeated the armies of the Eastern emperor, and exacted tribute from the court of Constantinople. Finally he turned westward, and, at the head of a host numbering, it is asserted, 700,000 warriors, crossed the Rhine into Gaul, purposing first to ravage that province, and then to traverse Italy with fire and sword, in order to destroy the last vestige of the Roman power.

The Romans and their Gothic conquerors laid aside their animosities, and made common cause against the common enemy. The Visigoths were rallied by their king, Theodoric; the Italians, the Franks, the Burgundians, flocked to the standard of the Roman general Aëtius. Attila drew up his mighty hosts upon the plain of Châlons, in the north of Gaul, and there awaited the onset of the Romans and their allies. The conflict was long and terrible. Theodoric was slain; but at last fortune turned against the barbarians. The loss of the Huns is variously estimated at from 100,000 to 300,000 warriors. Attila succeeded in escaping from the field, and retreated with his shattered hosts across the Rhine (A.D. 451).

This great victory is placed among the significant events of history; for it decided that the Christian Germanic races, and not the pagan Scythic Huns, should inherit the dominions of the expiring Roman Empire, and control the destinies of Europe.

The Death of Attila. — The year after his defeat at Châlons, Attila again crossed the Alps, and burned or plundered all the important cities of Northern Italy. The Veneti fled for safety to the morasses at the head of the Adriatic (A.D. 452). Upon the islets where they built their rude dwellings, there grew up in time the city of Venice, the "eldest daughter of the Roman Empire," the "Carthage of the Middle Ages."

The conqueror threatened Rome; but Leo the Great, bishop of the capital, went with an embassy to the camp of Attila, and pleaded for the city. He recalled to the mind of Attila the fact that death had overtaken the impious Alaric soon after he had given the Imperial City to be sacked, and warned him not to call down upon himself the like judgment of heaven. To these admonitions of the Christian bishop was added the persuasion of a golden bribe from the Emperor Valentinian; and Attila was induced to spare Southern Italy, and to lead his warriors back beyond the Alps. Shortly after he had crossed the Danube, he died suddenly in his camp. His followers gradually withdrew from Europe into the wilds of their native Scythia, or were absorbed by the peoples they had conquered.

Sack of Rome by the Vandals (A.D. 455). — Rome had been saved a visitation from the spoiler of the North, but a new destruction was about to burst upon it by way of the sea from the South. Africa sent out another enemy whose greed for plunder proved more fatal to Rome than the eternal hate of Hannibal. The kings of the Vandal Empire in Northern Africa had acquired as perfect a supremacy in the Western Mediterranean as Carthage ever enjoyed in the days of her commercial pride. Vandal corsairs swept the seas and harassed the coasts of Sicily and Italy, and even plundered the maritime towns of the Eastern provinces. In the year 455 a Vandal fleet, led by the dread Genseric, sailed up the Tiber.

Panic seized the people; for the name of Vandal was pronounced with terror throughout the world. Again the great Leo, who had once before saved his flock from the fury of an Attila, went forth to intercede in the name of Christ for the Imperial City. Genseric granted to the pious bishop the lives of the citizens, but said that the plunder of the capital belonged to his warriors. For fourteen days and nights the city was given over to the ruthless barbarians. The ships of the Vandals, which almost hid with their number the waters of the Tiber, were piled, as had been the wagons of the Goths before them, with the rich and weighty spoils of the capital. Palaces were stripped of their ornaments and furniture, and the walls of the temples denuded of their statues and of the trophies of a hundred Roman victories. From the Capitoline sanctuary were borne off the golden candlestick and other sacred articles that Titus had stolen from the Temple at Jerusalem.

The greed of the barbarians was sated at last, and they were ready to withdraw. The Vandal fleet sailed for Carthage,[1] bearing, besides the plunder of the city, more than 30,000 of the inhabitants as slaves. Carthage, through her own barbarian conquerors, was at last avenged upon her hated rival. The mournful presentiment of Scipio had fallen true (see p. 271). The cruel fate of Carthage might have been read again in the pillaged city that the Vandals left behind them.

Fall of the Roman Empire in the West (A.D. 476). — Only the shadow of the Empire in the West now remained. All the provinces — Illyricum, Gaul, Britain, Spain, and Africa — were in the hands of the Goths, the Vandals, the Franks, the Burgundians, the Angles and Saxons, and various other intruding tribes. Italy, as well as Rome herself, had become again and again the spoil of the insatiable barbarians. The story of the twenty years following the sack of the capital by Genseric affords only a repetition of the events we have been narrating. During these years several pup-

---

[1] The fleet was overtaken by a storm and suffered some damage, but the most precious of the relics it bore escaped harm. "The golden candlestick reached the African capital, was recovered a century later, and lodged in Constantinople by Justinian, and by him replaced, from superstitious motives, in Jerusalem. From that time its history is lost." — *Merivale.*

pet emperors were set up by the different leaders of the invading tribes. A final seditious movement placed upon the shadow-throne a child of six years, named Romulus Augustus. Chiefly because of the imperial farce he was forced to play, this child-emperor became known as Augustulus, "the little Augustus." He had reigned only a year, when Odoacer, the leader of a tribe of German mercenaries, dethroned him, and abolishing the title of emperor, took upon himself the government of Italy.

The Roman Senate now sent an embassy to Constantinople, with the royal vestments and the insignia of the imperial office, to represent to the Emperor Zeno that the West was willing to give up its claims to an emperor of its own, and to request that the German chief, with the title of "Patrician," might rule Italy as his viceroy. This was granted; and Italy now became in effect a province of the Empire in the East (A.D. 476). The Roman Empire in the West had come to an end, after an existence from the founding of Rome of 1229 years.

THE APPIAN WAY. (From a photograph).

ROMAN EMPERORS FROM COMMODUS TO ROMULUS AUGUSTUS.

(A.D. 180–476.)

	A.D.			A.D.
Commodus	180–192	{ Diocletian	. . . . .	284–305
Pertinax	193	{ Maximian	. . . . .	286–305
Didius Julianus	193	{ Constantius I.	. . .	305–306
Septimius Severus	193–211	{ Galerius	. . . .	305–311
{ Caracalla	211–217	Constantine the Great	.	306–337
{ Geta	211–212	Reigns as sole ruler	.	323–337
Macrinus	217–218	Constantine II.	. . .	337–340
Elagabalus	218–222	Constans I.	. . . .	337–350
Alexander Severus	222–235	Constantius II.	. . .	337–361
Maximin	235–238	Reigns as sole ruler	.	350–361
Gordian III	238–244	Julian the Apostate	.	361–363
Philip	244–249	Jovian	. . . . .	363–364
Decius	249–251	{ Valentinian I.	.	364–375
Period of the Thirty Tyrants	251–268	{ Valens (in the East)	.	364–378
Claudius	268–270	Gratian	. . . .	375–383
Aurelian	270–275	Maximus	. . . .	383–388
Tacitus	275–276	Valentinian II.	. .	375–392
Probus	276–282	Eugenius	. . . .	392–394
Carus	282–283	Theodosius the Great	.	379–395
{ Carinus	283–284	Reigns as sole emperor	.	394–395
{ Numerian	283–284			

FINAL PARTITION OF THE ROMAN EMPIRE.

(A.D. 395.)

EMPERORS IN THE EAST.		EMPERORS IN THE WEST.	
(From A.D. 395 to Fall of Rome.)			A.D.
	A.D.	Honorius	395–423
Arcadius	395–408	Valentinian III. . . .	425–455
Theodosius II. . . .	408–450	Maximus	455
Marcian	450–457	Avitus	455–456
Leo I.	457–474	Count Ricimer creates and	
Zeno	474–491	deposes emperors . .	456–472
		Romulus Augustus . . .	475–476

CHAPTER XXXI.

ARCHITECTURE, LITERATURE, LAW, AND SOCIAL LIFE AMONG THE ROMANS.

1. ARCHITECTURE.

Greek Origin of Roman Architecture: the Arch. — The architecture of the Romans was, in the main, an imitation of Greek models. But the Romans were not mere servile imitators. They not only modified the architectural forms they borrowed, but they gave their structures a distinct character by the prominent use of the arch, which the Greek and Oriental builders seldom employed, though they were acquainted with its properties. By means of it the Roman builders vaulted the roofs of the largest buildings, carried stupendous aqueducts across the deepest valleys, and spanned the broadest streams with bridges that have resisted all the assaults of time and flood to the present day.

Sacred Edifices. — The temples of the Romans were in general so like those of the Greeks that we need not here take time and space to enter into a particular description of them. Mention, however, should be made of their circular vaulted temples, as this was a style of building almost exclusively Italian. The best representative of this style of sacred edifices is the Pantheon at Rome, which has come down to our own times in a state of wonderful preservation. This structure is about 140 feet in diameter. The immense stone dome which vaults the building, is one of the boldest pieces of masonry executed by the master-builders of the world.

Circuses, Theatres, and Amphitheatres. — The circuses of the Romans were what we should call race-courses. There were several at Rome, the most celebrated being the Circus Maximus,

THE ROMAN FORUM IN 1885.

which was first laid out in the time of the Tarquins, and afterwards enlarged as the population of the capital increased, until it was capable of holding two or three hundred thousand spectators.

The Romans borrowed the plan of their theatres from the Greeks; their amphitheatres, however, were original with them. The Flavian Amphitheatre, known as the Colosseum, has already come under our notice (see p. 316). The edifice was 574 feet in its greatest diameter, and was capable of seating eighty-seven thousand spectators. The ruins of this immense structure stand to-day as "the embodiment of the power and splendor of the Roman Empire."

Aqueducts. — The aqueducts of ancient Rome were among the most important of the utilitarian works of the Romans. The water-system of the capital was commenced by Appius Claudius (about 313 B.C.), who secured the building of an aqueduct which led water into the city from the Sabine hills. During the republic four aqueducts in all were completed; under the emperors the number was increased to fourteen.[1] The longest of these was about fifty-five miles in length. The aqueducts usually ran beneath the surface, but when a depression was to be crossed, they were lifted on arches, which sometimes were over one hundred feet high. These lofty arches running in long broken lines over the plains beyond the walls of Rome, are the most striking feature of the Campagna at the present time.

Thermæ, or Baths. — The greatest demand upon the streams of water poured into Rome by the aqueducts was made by the Thermæ, or baths. Among the ancient Romans, bathing, regarded at first simply as a troublesome necessity, became in time a luxurious art. Under the republic, bathing-houses were erected in considerable numbers. But it was during the imperial period that those magnificent structures to which the name of Thermæ properly attaches, were erected. These edifices were among the most elaborate and expensive of the imperial works. They contained chambers for cold, hot, tepid, sudatory, and swimming baths;

---

[1] Several of these are still in use.

dressing-rooms and gymnasia ; museums and libraries ; covered colonnades for lounging and conversation, extensive grounds filled with statues and traversed by pleasant walks ; and every other adjunct that could add to the sense of luxury and relaxation. Being intended to exhibit the liberality of their builders, they were thrown open to the public free of charge.

Memorial Architecture. — Among the memorial structures of the Romans, their triumphal arches are especially characteristic.

ARCH OF CONSTANTINE.

These were modelled after the city gates, being constructed with single and with triple archways. Two of the most noted monuments of this character, and the most interesting because of their historic connections, are the Arch of Titus (see p. 315) and the Arch of Constantine, both of which are still standing. The Arch of Constantine was intended to commemorate the victory of that emperor over his rival Maxentius, which event established Christianity as the imperial and favored religion of the empire.

2. LITERATURE, PHILOSOPHY, AND LAW.

Relation of Roman to Greek Literature : the Poets of the Republican Era. — Latin literature was almost wholly imitative or borrowed, being a reproduction of Greek models ; still it performed a most important service for civilization : it was the medium for the dissemination throughout the world of the rich literary treasures of Greece.

It was the dramatic productions of the Greeks which were first studied and copied at Rome. Livius Andronicus, Nævius, Ennius, Plautus, and Terence, all of whom wrote under the republic, are the most noted of the Roman dramatists. Most of their plays were simply adaptations or translations of Greek masterpieces.

Lucilius (born 148 B.C.) was one of the greatest of Roman satirists. The later satirists of the corrupt imperial era were his imitators. Besides Lucilius, there appeared during the later republican era only two other poets of distinguished merit, Lucretius and Catullus. Lucretius (95–51 B.C.) was an evolutionist, and in his great poem, *On the Nature of Things*, we find anticipated many of the conclusions of modern scientists.

Poets of the Augustan Age. — We have in another place (see p. 307) spoken of the effects of the fall of the republic upon the development of Latin literature. Many, who if the republican institutions had continued would have been absorbed in the affairs of state, were led, by the change of government, to seek solace for their disappointed hopes, and employment for their enforced leisure, in the graceful labors of elegant composition. Four names have cast an unfading lustre over the period covered by the reign of Augustus, — Virgil, Horace, Ovid, and Livy. So distinguished have these writers rendered the age in which they lived, that any period in a people's literature marked by unusual literary taste and refinement is called, in allusion to the Roman era, an *Augustan Age*. Of the three poets, Virgil, Horace, and Ovid, a word

has already been said; of Livy we shall find place to say something a little later, under the head of the Roman historians.

Satire and Satirists. — Satire thrives best in the reeking soil
and tainted atmosphere of an age of selfishness, immorality, and
vice. Such an age was that which followed the Augustan era
at Rome. The throne was held by such imperial monsters as
Caligula, Nero, and Domitian. The profligacy of fashionable life
at the capital and the various watering-places of the empire, and
the degradation of the court gave venom and point to the shafts
of those who were goaded by the spectacle into attacking the
immoralities and vices which were silently yet rapidly sapping the
foundations of both society and state. Hence arose a succession
of writers whose mastery of sharp and stinging satire has caused
their productions to become the models of all subsequent attempts
in the same species of literature. Two names stand out in special
prominence — Persius and Juvenal, who lived and wrote during
the last half of the first and the beginning of the second century
of our era.

Oratory among the Romans. — " Public oratory," as has been
truly said, " is the child of political freedom, and cannot exist
without it." We have seen this illustrated in the history of republican Athens. Equally well is the same truth exemplified by the
records of the Roman state. All the great orators of Rome arose
under the republic.

Roman oratory was senatorial, popular, or judicial. These
different styles of eloquence were represented by the grave and
dignified debates of the Senate, the impassioned and often noisy
and inelegant harangues of the Forum, and the learned pleadings
or ingenious appeals of the courts. Among the orators of ancient
Rome, Hortensius (114–50 B.C.), an eloquent advocate, and
Cicero (106–43 B.C.) are easily first.

Historians. — Ancient Rome produced four writers of history
whose works have won for them a permanent fame — Cæsar, Sallust, Livy, and Tacitus. Of Cæsar and his *Commentaries on the
Gallic War*, we have learned in a previous chapter. His *Com-*

mentaries will always be mentioned with the *Anabasis* of Xenophon, as a model of the narrative style of writing. Sallust (86–34
B.C.) was the contemporary and friend of Cæsar. The two works
upon which his fame rests are the *Conspiracy of Catiline* and the
Jugurthine War.

Livy (59 B.C. — A.D. 17) was one of the brightest ornaments of
the Augustan age. Herodotus among the ancient, and Macaulay
among the modern, writers of historical narrative, are the names
with which his is most frequently compared. His greatest work
is his *Annals*, a history of Rome from the earliest times to the
year 9 B.C. Unfortunately, all save thirty-five of the books[1] — the
work filled one hundred and forty-two volumes — perished during
the disturbed period that followed the overthrow of the empire.
Many have been the laments over "the lost books of Livy." As
a chronicle of actual events, Livy's history, particularly in its
earlier parts, is very unreliable ; however, it is invaluable as an account of what the Romans themselves believed respecting the
origin of their race, the founding of their city, and the deeds
and virtues of their forefathers.

The most highly prized work of Tacitus is his *Germania*, a
treatise on the manners and customs of the Germans. Tacitus
dwells with delight upon the simple life of the uncivilized Germans, and sets their virtues in strong contrast with the immoralities of the refined and cultured Romans.

Ethics, Science, and Philosophy. — Under this head may be
grouped the names of Seneca, Pliny the Elder, Marcus Aurelius,
and Epictetus. Seneca (about A.D. 1–65), moralist and philosopher, has already come to our notice as the tutor of Nero (see
p. 312). He was a disbeliever in the popular religion of his
countrymen, and entertained conceptions of God and his moral

---

[1] It should be borne in mind that a book in the ancient sense was simply
a roll of manuscript or parchment, and contained nothing like the amount
of matter held by an ordinary modern volume. Thus Cæsar's *Gallic Wars*,
which makes a single volume of moderate size with us, made eight Roman
books.

government not very different from the doctrines of Socrates. Pliny the Elder (A.D. 23–79) is almost the only Roman who won renown as a naturalist. The only work of his that has been spared to us is his *Natural History*, a sort of " Roman Encyclopædia," embracing thirty-seven books.

SENECA.

(From the double bust of Seneca and Socrates in the Berlin Museum.)

Marcus Aurelius the emperor and Epictetus the slave hold prominent places among the ethical teachers of Rome. Of the emperor as a philosopher we have already spoken (see p. 321).

Epictetus (b. about 60 A.D.) was for many years a slave at the capital; but, securing in some way his freedom, he became a teacher of philosophy. Epictetus and Aurelius were the last eminent representatives and expositors of the philosophy of Zeno. Christianity, giving a larger place to the affections than did Stoicism, was already fast winning the hearts of men.

Writers of the Early Latin Church. — The Christian authors of the first three centuries, like the writers of the New Testament, employed the Greek, that being the language of learning and culture. As the Latin tongue, however, came into more general use throughout the extended provinces of the Roman empire, the Christian authors naturally began to use the same in the composition of their works. Hence, almost all the writings of the Fathers of the Church, produced during the last two centuries of the empire, were composed in Latin. Among the many names that adorn the Church literature of this period may be mentioned Saint Jerome and Saint Augustine, — the former celebrated for his translation of the Scriptures into Latin,[1] and the latter for his "City of God." This was truly a wonderful work. It was written just when Rome was becoming the spoil of the barbarians, and was designed to answer the charge of the pagans that Christianity, turning the hearts of the people away from the worship of the ancient gods, was the cause of the calamities that were befalling the Roman state.

Roman Law and Law Literature. — Although the Latin writers in all the departments of literary effort which we have so far reviewed did much valuable work, yet the Roman intellect in all these directions was under Greek guidance. Its work was largely imitative. But in another department it was different. We mean, of course, the field of legal and political science. Here the Romans ceased to be pupils, and became teachers. Nations, like men, have their mission. Rome's mission was to give laws to the world.

In the year 527 A.D. Justinian became emperor of the Roman empire in the East. He almost immediately appointed a commission, headed by the great lawyer Tribonian, to collect and arrange in a systematic manner the immense mass of Roman laws, and the writings of the jurists. The undertaking was like that of the Decemvirs in connection with the Twelve Tables (see p. 236), only far greater. The result of the work of the commission was what is known as the *Corpus Juris Civilis*, or "Body of the Civil Law." This consisted of three parts: the *Code*, the *Pandects* and the *Institutes*.[2] The Code was a revised and compressed collection of all the laws, instructions to judicial officers, and opinions on legal subjects, promulgated by the different emperors since

[1] The *Vulgate*, which is the version still used in the Roman Catholic Church.
[2] A later work called the *Novels* comprised the laws of Justinian subsequent to the completion of the *Code*.

the time of Hadrian ; the Pandects (all-containing) were a digest or abridgment of the writings, opinions, and decisions of the most eminent of the old Roman jurists and lawyers. The Institutes were a condensed edition of the Pandects, and were intended to form an elementary text-book for the use of students in the great law-schools of the empire.

The Body of the Roman Law thus preserved and transmitted was the great contribution of the Latin intellect to civilization. It has exerted a profound influence upon all the law-systems of Europe. Thus does the once little Palatine city of the Tiber still rule the world. The religion of Judea, the arts of Greece, and the laws of Rome are three very real and potent elements in modern civilization.

3. SOCIAL LIFE.

Education. — Roman children were subject in an extraordinary manner to their father (*paterfamilias*). They were regarded as his property, and their life and liberty were in general at his abso-lute disposal. This power he exercised by usually drowning at birth the deformed or sickly child. Even the married son re-mained legally subject to his father, who could banish him, sell him as a slave, or even put him to death. It should be said, how-ever, that the right of putting to death was seldom exercised, and that in the time of the empire the law put some limitations upon it.

The education of the Roman boy differed from that of the Greek youth in being more practical. The Laws of the Twelve Tables were committed to memory ; and rhetoric and oratory were given special attention, as a mastery of the art of public speaking was an almost indispensable acquirement for the Roman citizen who aspired to take a prominent part in the affairs of state.

After the conquest of Magna Græcia and of Greece, the Romans were brought into closer relations than had hitherto existed with Greek culture. The Roman youth were taught the language of Athens, often to the neglect, it appears, of their native tongue. Young men belonging to families of means, not unusually went to

Greece, just as the graduates of our schools go to Europe, to finish their education. Many of the most prominent statesmen of Rome, as for instance Cicero and Julius Cæsar, received the advantages of this higher training in the schools of Greece.

Somewhere between the age of fourteen and eighteen the boy exchanged his purple-hemmed toga, or gown, for one of white wool, which was in all places and at all times the significant badge of Roman citizenship.

Social Position of Woman. — Until after her marriage, the daughter of the family was kept in almost Oriental seclusion. Marriage gave her a certain freedom. She might now be present at the races of the circus and the various shows of the theatre and the arena, a privilege rarely accorded to her before marriage. In the early virtuous period of the Roman state, divorce was unusual, but in later and more degenerate times, it became very common. The husband had the right to divorce his wife for the slightest cause, or for no cause at all. In this disregard of the sanctity of the family relation, may doubtless be found one cause of the degeneracy and failure of the Roman stock.

Public Amusements. — The entertainments of the theatre, the games of the circus, and the combats of the amphitheatre were the three principal public amusements of the Romans. These entertainments in general increased in popularity as liberty declined, the great festive gatherings at the various places of amusement taking the place of the political assemblies of the republic. The public exhibitions under the empire were, in a certain sense, the compensation which the emperors offered the people for their surrender of the right of participation in public affairs, — and the people were content to accept the exchange.

Tragedy was never held in high esteem at Rome : the people saw too much real tragedy in the exhibitions of the amphitheatre to care much for the make-believe tragedies of the stage. The entertainments of the theatres usually took the form of comedies, farces, and pantomimes. The last were particularly popular, both because the vast size of the theatres made it quite impossible for the actor to make his voice heard throughout the structure, and for the reason that the language of signs was the only language that could be readily understood by an audience made up of so many different nationalities as composed a Roman assemblage.

More important and more popular than the entertainments of the theatre were the various games, especially the chariot races, of the circus. But surpassing in their terrible fascination all other public amusements were the animal-baitings and the gladiatorial combats of the arena.

'The beasts required for the baitings were secured in different parts of the world, and transported to Rome and the other cities of the empire at an enormous expense. The wildernesses of Northern Europe furnished bears and wolves; Africa contributed lions, crocodiles, and leopards; Asia elephants and tigers. These creatures were pitted against one another in every conceivable way. Often a promiscuous multitude would be turned loose in the arena at once. But even the terrific scene that then ensued, became at last too tame to stir the blood of the Roman populace. Hence a new species of show was introduced, and grew rapidly into favor with the spectators of the amphitheatre. This was the gladiatorial combat.

The Gladiatorial Combats. — Gladiatorial games seem to have had their origin in Etruria, whence they were brought to Rome. It was a custom among the early Etruscans to slay prisoners upon the warrior's grave, it being thought that the spirit of the dead delighted in the blood of such victims. In time the condemned prisoners were allowed to fight and kill one another, this being deemed more humane than their cold-blooded slaughter. Thus it happened that sentiments of humanity gave rise to an institution which, afterwards perverted, became the most inhuman of any that ever existed among a civilized people.

The first gladiatorial spectacle at Rome was presented by two sons at the funeral of their father, in the year 264 B.C. This exhibition was arranged in one of the forums, as there were at that time no amphitheatres in existence. From this time the public taste for this species of entertainment grew rapidly, and by the beginning of the imperial period had mounted into a perfect passion.   It was now no longer the manes of the dead, but the spirits of the living, that they were intended to appease.   At first the combatants were slaves, captives, or condemned criminals ; but at last knights, senators, and even women descended into the arena. Training-schools were established at Rome, Capua, Ravenna, and other cities.   Free citizens often sold themselves to the keepers of these seminaries ; and to them flocked desperate men of all classes, and ruined spendthrifts of the noblest patrician houses. Slaves and criminals were encouraged to become proficient in this art by the promise of freedom if they survived the combats

GLADIATORS. (After an old Mosaic.)

beyond a certain number of years.

Sometimes the gladiators fought in pairs ; again great companies engaged at once in the deadly fray.   They fought in chariots, on horse-back, on foot — in all the ways that soldiers were accustomed to fight in actual battle.   The contestants were armed with lances,

swords, daggers, tridents, and every manner of weapon.   Some were provided with nets and lassos, with which they entangled their adversaries, and then slew them.

The life of a wounded gladiator was in the hands of the audience.   If in response to his appeal for mercy, which was made by outstretching the forefinger, the spectators reached out their hands with thumbs extended, that indicated that his prayer had been heard and that the sword was to be sheathed ; but if they extended their hands with thumbs turned in, that was the signal for the victor to complete his work upon his wounded foe.   Sometimes the dying were aroused and forced on to the fight by burning with a hot iron.   The dead bodies were dragged from the arena with hooks, like the carcasses of animals, and the pools of blood soaked up with dry sand.

These shows increased to such an extent that they entirely over-shadowed the entertainments of the circus and the theatre. Ambitious officials and commanders arranged such spectacles in order to curry favor with the masses; magistrates were expected to give them in connection with the public festivals; the heads of aspiring families exhibited them "in order to acquire social position"; wealthy citizens prepared them as an indispensable feature of a fashionable banquet; the children caught the spirit of their elders and imitated them in their plays. The demand for gladiators was met by the training-schools; the managers of these hired out bands of trained men, that travelled through the country like opera troupes among us, and gave exhibitions in private houses or in the provincial amphitheatres.

The rivalries between ambitious leaders during the later years of the republic tended greatly to increase the number of gladiatorial shows, as liberality in arranging these spectacles was a sure passport to popular favor. It was reserved for the emperors, however, to exhibit them on a truly imperial scale. Titus, upon the dedication of the Flavian Amphitheatre, provided games, mostly gladiatorial combats, that lasted one hundred days. Trajan celebrated his victories with shows that continued still longer, in the progress of which 10,000 gladiators fought upon the arena, and more than that number of wild beasts were slain. (For the suppression of the gladiatorial games, see p. 339.)

State Distribution of Corn. — The free distribution of corn at Rome has been characterized as the "leading fact of Roman life." It will be recalled that this pernicious practice had its beginnings in the legislation of Caius Gracchus (see p. 276). Just before the establishment of the empire, over 300,000 Roman citizens were recipients of this state bounty. In the time of the Antonines the number is asserted to have been even larger. The corn for this enormous distribution was derived in large part from a grain tribute exacted of the African and other corn-producing provinces. The evils that resulted from this misdirected state charity can hardly be overstated. Idleness and all its accompanying vices were fostered to such a degree that we probably shall not be wrong in enumerating the practice as one of the most prominent causes of the demoralization of society at Rome under the emperors.

Slavery. — A still more demoralizing element in Roman life than that of the state largesses of corn, was the institution of slavery. The number of slaves in the Roman state under the later republic and the earlier empire was probably as great or even greater than the number of freemen. The love of ostentation led to the multiplication of offices in the households of the wealthy, and the employment of a special slave for every different kind of work. Thus there was the slave called the *sandalio*, whose sole duty it was to care for his master's sandals; and another, called the *nomenclator*, whose exclusive business it was to accompany his master when he went upon the street, and give him the names of such persons as he ought to recognize. The price of slaves varied from a few dollars to ten or twenty thousand dollars, — these last figures being of course exceptional. Greek slaves were the most valuable, as their lively intelligence rendered them serviceable in positions calling for special talent.

The slave class was recruited chiefly, as in Greece, by war, and by the practice of kidnapping. Some of the outlying provinces in Asia and Africa were almost depopulated by the slave hunters. Delinquent tax payers were often sold as slaves, and frequently poor persons sold themselves into servitude.

Slaves were treated better under the empire than under the later republic (see p. 273), a change to be attributed doubtless to the softening influence of the Stoical philosophy and of Christianity. The feeling entertained towards this unfortunate class in the later republican period is illustrated by Varro's classification of slaves as "vocal agricultural implements," and again by Cato the Elder's recommendation that old and worn-out slaves be sold, as a matter of economy. Sick and hopelessly infirm slaves were taken to an island in the Tiber and left there to die of starvation and exposure. In many cases, as a measure of precaution, the slaves were forced to work in chains, and to sleep in subterranean prisons. Their bitter hatred towards their masters, engendered by harsh treatment, is witnessed by the well-known proverb, "As many enemies as slaves," and by the servile revolts and wars of the republican period. But from the first century of the empire there is observable a growing sentiment of humanity towards the bondsman. Imperial edicts take away from the master the right to kill his slave, or to sell him to the trader in gladiators, or even to treat him with any undue severity. This marks the beginning of a slow reform which in the course of ten or twelve centuries resulted in the complete abolition of slavery in Christian Europe.

SARCOPHAGUS OF CORNELIUS SCIPIO BARBATUS (Consul 298 B.C.).

PART II.

MEDIÆVAL AND MODERN HISTORY.

INTRODUCTION.

Divisions of the Subject. — As we have already noted, the fourteen centuries since the fall of the Roman empire in the West (A.D. 476) are usually divided into two periods, — the *Middle Ages*, or the period lying between the fall of Rome and the discovery of America by Columbus in 1492, and the *Modern Age*, which extends from the latter event to the present time. The Middle Ages, again, naturally subdivide into two periods, — the *Dark Ages*, and the *Age of Revival;* while the Modern Age also falls into two divisions, — the *Era of the Protestant Reformation*, and the *Era of the Political Revolution.*

Chief Characteristics of the Four Periods. — The so-called *Dark Ages* embrace the years intervening between the fall of Rome and the opening of the eleventh century. The period was one of *origins*, — of the beginnings of peoples and languages and institutions. During this time arose the Papacy and Feudalism, the two great institutions of the Mediæval Ages.

The *Age of Revival* begins with the opening of the eleventh century, and ends with the discovery of America by Columbus in 1492. During all this time civilization was making slow but sure advances. The last century of the period, especially, was marked by a great revival of classical learning (known as the *Renaissance*, or New Birth), by improvements, inventions, and discoveries, which greatly stirred men's minds, and awakened them as from a sleep. The Crusades, or Holy Wars, were the most remarkable undertakings of the age.

The *Era of the Reformation* embraces the sixteenth century and the first half of the seventeenth. The period is characterized by the great religious movement known as the Reformation, and the tremendous struggle between Catholicism and Protestantism. Almost all the wars of the period were religious wars. The last great combat was the Thirty Years' War in Germany, which was closed by the celebrated Peace of Westphalia, in 1648. After this date the disputes and wars between parties and nations were political rather than religious in character.

The *Era of the Political Revolution* extends from the Peace of Westphalia to the present time. This age is especially marked by the great conflict between despotic and liberal principles of government, resulting in the triumph of democratic ideas. The central event of the period is the French Revolution.

Having now made a general survey of the ground we are to traverse, we must return to our starting-point, — the fall of Rome.

Relation of the Fall of Rome to World-History. — The calamity which in the fifth century befell the Roman empire in the West is sometimes represented as having destroyed the treasures of the Old World. It was not so. All that was really valuable in the accumulations of antiquity escaped harm, and became sooner or later the possession of the succeeding ages. The catastrophe simply prepared the way for the shifting of the scene of civilization from the south to the north of Europe, simply transferred at once political power, and gradually social and intellectual preëminence, from one branch of the Aryan family to another, — from the Græco-Italic to the Teutonic.

The event was not an unrelieved calamity, because, fortunately, the floods that seemed to be sweeping so much away were not the mountain torrent, which covers fruitful fields with worthless drift, but the overflowing Nile with its rich deposits. Over all the regions covered by the barbarian inundation a new stratum of population was deposited, a new soil formed that was capable of nourishing a better civilization than any the world had yet seen.

The Three Elements of Civilization. — We must now notice what survived the catastrophe of the fifth century, what it was that Rome transmitted to the new rulers of the world, the Teutonic race. This renders necessary an analysis of the elements of civilization.

Modern civilization is the result of the blending of three historic elements, — the *Classical*, the *Hebrew*, and the *Teutonic.*

By the classical element in civilization is meant that whole body of arts, sciences, literatures, laws, manners, ideas, and social arrangements, — everything, in a word, save Christianity, that Greece and Rome gave to mediæval and modern Europe. Taken together, these things constituted a valuable gift to the new northern race that was henceforth to represent civilization.

By the Hebrew element in history is meant Christianity. This has been the most potent factor in modern civilization. It has so colored the whole life, and so moulded all the institutions of the European people that their history is very largely a story of the fortunes and influences of this religion, which, first going forth from Judea, was given to the younger world by the missionaries of Rome.

By the Teutonic element in history is meant of course the Germanic race. The Teutons were poor in those things in which the Romans were rich. They had neither arts, nor sciences, nor philosophies, nor literatures. But they had something better than all these; they had personal worth. Three prominent traits of theirs we must especially notice; namely, their capacity for civilization, their love of personal freedom, and their reverence for womanhood.

The Teutons fortunately belonged to a progressive family of peoples. As Kingsley puts it, they came of a royal race. They were Aryans. It was their boundless capacity for growth, for culture, for civilization, which saved the countries of the West from the sterility and barbarism reserved for those of the East that were destined to be taken possession of by the Turanian Turks.

The Teutons loved personal freedom. They never called any man master, but followed their chosen leader as companions and equals. They could not even bear to have the houses of their villages set close together. And again we see the same independent spirit expressed in their assemblies of freemen, in which meetings, all matters of public interest were debated and decided. In this trait of the Teutonic disposition lay the germ of representative government and of Protestant, or Teutonic Christianity.

A feeling of respect for woman characterized all the northern, or Teutonic peoples. Tacitus says of the Germans that they deemed something sacred to reside in woman's nature. This sentiment guarded the purity and sanctity of the home. In their high estimation of the sacredness of the family relation, the barbarians stood in marked contrast with the later Romans. Our own sacred word *home*, as well as all that it represents, comes from our Teutonic ancestors.

Celts, Slavonians, and Other Peoples. — Having noticed the Romans and Teutons, the two most prominent peoples that present themselves to us at the time of the downfall of Rome, if we now name the Celts, the Slavonians, the Persians, the Arabians, and the Turanian tribes of Asia, we shall have under view the chief actors in the drama of mediæval and modern history.

At the commencement of the mediæval era the Celts were in front of the Teutons, clinging to the western edge of the European continent, and engaged in a bitter contest with these latter peoples, which, in the antagonism of England and Ireland, was destined to extend itself to our own day.

The Slavonians were in the rear of the Teutonic tribes, pressing them on even as the Celts in front were struggling to resist their advance. These peoples, progressing but little beyond the pastoral state before the Modern Age, will play only an obscure part in the events of the mediæval era, but in the course of the modern period will assume a most commanding position among the European nations.

The Persians were in their old seat beyond the Euphrates,

maintaining there what is called the New Persian Empire, the kings of which, until the rise of the Saracens in the seventh century, were the most formidable rivals of the emperors of Constantinople.

The Arabians were hidden in their deserts; but in the seventh century we shall see them, animated by a wonderful religious fanaticism, issue from their peninsula and begin a contest with the Christian nations of the East and the West which, in its varying phases, was destined to fill a large part of the mediæval period.

The Tartar tribes were buried in Central Asia. They will appear late in the eleventh century, proselytes for the most part of Mohammedanism; and, as the religious ardor of the Semitic Arabians grows cool, we shall see the Crescent upheld by these zealous converts of another race, and finally, in the fifteenth century, placed by the Turks upon the dome of St. Sophia in Constantinople.

As the Middle Ages draw to a close, the remote nations of Eastern Asia will gradually come within our circle of vision; and, as the Modern Age dawns, we shall catch a glimpse of new continents and strange races of men beyond the Atlantic.

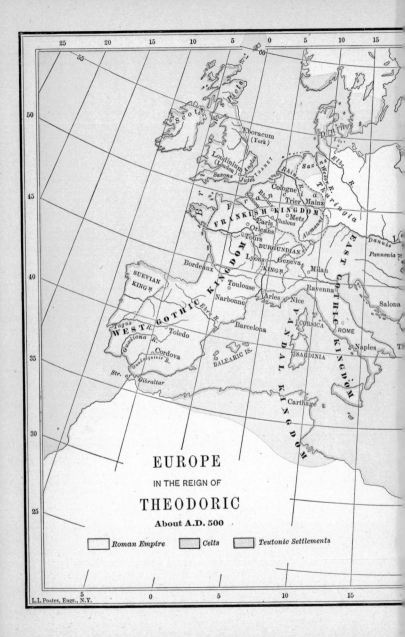

EUROPE

IN THE REIGN OF

THEODORIC

About A.D. 500

| | Roman Empire | | Celts | | Teutonic Settlements |

L.L. Poates, Engr., N.Y.

FIRST PERIOD. — THE DARK AGES.

(FROM THE FALL OF ROME, A.D. 476, TO THE ELEVENTH CENTURY.)

CHAPTER XXXII.

THE TEUTONIC KINGDOMS.

Introductory. — In connection with the history of the break-up of the Roman empire in the West, we have already given some account of the migrations and settlements of the German tribes. In the present chapter we shall relate briefly the political fortunes, for the two centuries following the fall of Rome, of the principal kingdoms set up by the German chieftains in the different provinces of the old empire.

Kingdom of the Ostrogoths (A.D. 493–554). — Odoacer will be recalled as the barbarian chief who dethroned the last of the Western Roman emperors (see p. 348). His feeble government in Italy lasted only seventeen years, when it was brought to a close by the invasion of the Ostrogoths (Eastern Goths) under Theodoric, the greatest of their chiefs, who set up in Italy a new dominion, known as the Kingdom of the Ostrogoths.

The reign of Theodoric covered thirty-three years — years of such quiet and prosperity as Italy had not known since the happy era of the Antonines. The king made good his promise that his reign should be such that " the only regret of the people should be that the Goths had not come at an earlier period."

The kingdom established by the rare abilities of Theodoric

lasted only twenty-seven years after his death, which occurred A.D.
527. Justinian, emperor of the East, taking advantage of that
event, sent his generals, first Belisarius and afterwards Narses, to
deliver Italy from the rule of the barbarians. The last of the
Ostrogothic kings fell in battle, and Italy, with her fields ravaged
and her cities in ruins, was reunited to the empire (A.D. 554).

Kingdom of the Visigoths (A.D. 415–711). — The Visigoths
(Western Goths) were already in possession of Spain and Southern
Gaul at the time of the fall of Rome. Being driven south of the
Pyrenees by Clovis, king of the Franks, they held possession of
Spain until the beginning of the eighth century, when the Saracens
crossed the Straits of Gibraltar, destroyed the kingdom of Rod-
erick, the last of the Gothic kings, and established throughout
the country the authority of the Koran (A.D. 711). The Visigothic empire when thus overturned had lasted nearly three
hundred years. During this time the conquerors had mingled
with the old Romanized inhabitants of Spain, so that in the veins
of the Spaniard of to-day is blended the blood of Iberian, Celt,
Roman, and Teuton, together with that of the last comers, the Moors.

Kingdom of the Burgundians (A.D. 443–534). — The Burgundians, who were near kinsmen of the Goths, built up a kingdom
in Southeastern Gaul. A portion of this ancient domain still
retains, from these German settlers, the name of "Burgundy."
The Burgundians soon came in collision with the Franks on the
north, and were reduced by the Frankish kings to a state of
dependence.

Kingdom of the Vandals (A.D. 429–533). — We have already
spoken of the establishment in North Africa of the kingdom of
the Vandals, and told how, under the lead of their king Genseric,
they bore in triumph down the Tiber the heavy spoils of Rome.
(see p. 346).

Being Arian Christians, the Vandals persecuted with furious
zeal the orthodox party, the followers of Athanasius. Moved by
the entreaties of the African Catholics, the Emperor Justinian sent
his general Belisarius to drive the barbarians from Africa, and to

restore that province to the bosom of the true Catholic Church.
The expedition was successful, and Carthage and the fruitful fields
of Africa were restored to the em-
pire, after having suffered the insolence of the barbarian conquerors
for the space of one hundred years.
The Vandals remaining in the
country were gradually absorbed
by the old Roman population, and
after a few generations no certain
trace of the barbarian invaders
could be detected in the physical appearance, the language, or
the customs of the inhabitants of
the African coast. The Vandal
nation had disappeared; the name
alone remained.

**The Franks under the Mero-
vingians** (A.D. 486–752). — The
Franks, who were destined to give
a new name to Gaul and form the
nucleus of the French nation,
made their first settlement west
of the Rhine about two hundred
years before the fall of Rome.
The name was the common designation of a number of Teutonic
tribes that had formed a confederation while dwelling beyond the
Rhine. The Salian Franks were
the leading tribe of the league,
and it was from the members of
their most powerful family, who

CLOVIS AND THE VASE OF SOISSONS.[1]

(After Alphonse de Neuville.)

[1] The story of the Vase of Soissons illustrates at once the customs of the
Franks and the power and personal character of their leader Clovis. Upon

traced their descent from Merovæus, a legendary sea-king of the Franks, that leaders were chosen by the free vote of all the warriors.

After the downfall of Rome, Clovis, then chief of the Franks, conceived the ambition of erecting a kingdom upon the ruins of the Roman power. He attacked Syagrius, the Roman governor of Gaul, and at Soissons gained a decisive victory over his forces (A.D. 486). Thus was destroyed forever in Gaul that Roman authority established among its barbarous tribes more than five centuries before by the conquests of Julius Cæsar.

During his reign, Clovis extended his authority over the greater part of Gaul, reducing to the condition of tributaries the various Teutonic tribes that had taken possession of different portions of the country. About a century and a half of discord followed his energetic rule, by the end of which time the princes of the house of Merovæus had become so feeble and inefficient that they were contemptuously called "do-nothings," and an ambitious officer of the crown, who bore the title of Mayor of the Palace, pushed aside his imbecile master, and gave to the Frankish monarchy a new royal line,— the Carolingian (see p. 404).

Kingdom of the Lombards (A.D. 568–774).— The circumstances attending the establishment of the Lombards in Italy were very like those marking the settlement of the Ostrogoths. The Lombards (Langobardi), so called either from their long beards, or their long battle-axes, came from the region of the Upper Danube. In just such a march as the Ostrogoths had made nearly a century before, the Lombard nation crossed the Alps and descended upon the plains of Italy. After many years

---

the division at Soissons of some spoils, Clovis asked his followers to set aside a rule whereby they divided the booty by lot, and to let him have a certain beautiful vase. One of his followers objected, and broke the vase to pieces with his battle-axe. Clovis concealed his anger at the time, but some time afterwards, when reviewing his troops, he approached the man who had offended him, and chiding him for not keeping his arms bright, cleft his head with a battle-axe, at the same time exclaiming, "Thus didst thou to the vase of Soissons."

of desperate fighting, they wrested from the empire [1] all the peninsula save some of the great cities, and set up in the country a monarchy which lasted almost exactly two centuries.

The rule of the Lombard princes was brought to an end by Charlemagne, the greatest of the Frankish rulers (see p. 405); but the blood of the invaders had by this time become intermingled with that of the former subjects of the Roman empire, so that throughout all that part of the peninsula which is still called Lombardy after them, the people at the present day reveal, in the light hair and fair features which distinguish them from the inhabitants of Southern Italy, their partly German origin.

The Anglo-Saxons in Britain. — We have already seen how in the time of Rome's distress the Angles and Saxons secured a foothold in Britain (see p. 344). The advance of the invaders here was stubbornly resisted by the half-Romanized Celts of the island. At the end of a century and a half of fighting, the German tribes had gained possession of only the eastern half of what is now England. On the conquered soil they set up eight or nine, or perhaps more, petty kingdoms. For the space of two hundred years there was an almost perpetual strife among these states for supremacy. Finally Egbert, king of the West Saxons, brought all the other states into a subject or tributary condition, and became the first king of the English, and the founder of the long line of Saxon monarchs (A.D. 827).

Teutonic Tribes outside the Empire. — We have now spoken of the most important of the Teutonic tribes that forced themselves within the limits of the Roman empire in the West, and that there, upon the ruins of the civilization they had overthrown, laid or helped to lay the foundations of the modern nations of Italy, Spain, France, and England. Beyond the boundaries of the old empire were still other tribes and clans of this same mighty

---

[1] Italy, it will be borne in mind, had but recently been delivered from the hands of the Ostrogoths by the lieutenants of the Eastern emperor (see p. 372).

family of nations, — tribes and clans that were destined to play great parts in European history.

On the east, beyond the Rhine, were the ancestors of the modern Germans. Notwithstanding the immense hosts that the forests and morasses of Germany had poured into the Roman provinces, the Father-land, in the sixth century of our era, seemed still as crowded as before the great migration began. These tribes were yet savages in manners and for the most part pagans in religion.

In the northwest of Europe were the Scandinavians, the ancestors of the modern Danes, Swedes, and Norwegians. They were as yet untouched either by the civilization or the religion of Rome. We shall scarcely get a glimpse of them before the ninth century, when they will appear as the Northmen, the dreaded corsairs of the northern seas.

CHAPTER XXXIII.

THE CONVERSION OF THE BARBARIANS.

Introductory. — The most important event in the history of the tribes that took possession of the Roman empire in the West was their conversion to Christianity. Many of the barbarians were converted before or soon after their entrance into the empire ; to this circumstance the Roman provinces owed their immunity from the excessive cruelties which pagan barbarians seldom fail to inflict upon a subjected enemy. Alaric left untouched the treasures of the churches of the Roman Christians, because his own faith was also Christian (see p. 342). For like reason the Vandal king Genseric yielded to the prayers of Pope Leo the Great, and promised to leave to the inhabitants of the Imperial City their lives (see p. 346). The more tolerable fate of Italy, Spain, and Gaul, as compared with the hard fate of Britain, is owing, in part at least, to the fact that the tribes which overran those countries had become, in the main, converts to Christianity before they crossed the boundaries of the empire, while the Saxons, when they entered Britain, were still untamed pagans.

Conversion of the Goths, Vandals, and Other Tribes. — The first converts to Christianity among the barbarians beyond the limits of the empire were won from among the Goths. Foremost of the apostles that arose among them was Ulfilas, who translated the Scriptures into the Gothic language, omitting from his version, however, "the Book of Kings," as he feared that the stirring recital of wars and battles in that portion of the Word might kindle into too fierce a flame the martial ardor of his new converts.

When the Visigoths, distressed by the Huns, besought the Eastern Emperor Valens for permission to cross the Danube, one of the conditions imposed upon them was that they should all be baptized in the Christian faith (see p. 336). This seems to have crowned the work that had been going on among them for some time, and thereafter they were called Christians.

What happened to the Goths happened also to most of the barbarian tribes that participated in the overthrow of the Roman empire in the West. By the time of the fall of Rome, the Goths, the Vandals, the Suevi, the Burgundians, had all become proselytes to Christianity. The greater part of them, however, professed the Arian creed, which had been condemned by the great council of the church held at Nicæa during the reign of Constantine the Great (see p. 332). Hence they were regarded as heretics by the Roman Church, and all had to be reconverted to the orthodox creed, which was gradually effected.

The remaining Teutonic tribes of whose conversion we shall speak, — the Franks, the Anglo-Saxons, the Scandinavians, and the chief tribes of Germany, — embraced at the outset the Catholic faith.

Conversion of the Franks. — The Franks, when they entered the empire, like the Angles and Saxons when they landed in Britain, were still pagans. Christianity gained way very slowly among them until a supposed interposition by the Christian God in their behalf led the king and nation to adopt the new religion in place of their old faith. The circumstances were these. In the year 496 of our era, the Alemanni crossed the Rhine and fell upon the Franks. A desperate battle ensued. In the midst of it, Clovis, falling upon his knees, called upon the God of the Christians, and solemnly vowed that if He would give victory to his arms, he would become his faithful follower. The battle turned in favor of the Franks, and Clovis, faithful to his vow, was baptized, and with him several thousand of his warriors. This incident illustrates how the very superstitions of the barbarians, their belief in omens and divine interpositions, contributed to their conversion.

Augustine's Mission to the Angles and Saxons in Britain. — In the year 596 Pope Gregory I. sent the monk Augustine with a band of forty companions to teach the Christian faith in Britain. Gregory had become interested in the inhabitants of that remote region in the following way. One day, some years before his elevation to the papal chair, he was passing through the slave-market at Rome, and noticed there some English captives, whose fair features awakened his curiosity respecting them. Inquiring of what nation they were, he was told that they were called Angles. "Right," said he, "for they have an angelic face, and it becomes such to become co-heirs with the angels in heaven." A little while afterwards he was elected Pope, and still mindful of the incident of the slave-market, he sent to the Angles the embassy to which we have alluded.

The monks were favorably received by the English, who listened attentively to the story the strangers had come to tell them, and being persuaded that the tidings were true, they burned the temples of Woden and Thor, and were in large numbers baptized in the Christian faith.

The Celtic Church. — It here becomes necessary for us to say a word respecting the Celtic Church. Christianity, it must be borne in mind, held its place among the Celts whom the Saxons crowded slowly westward. Now, during the very period that England was being wrested from the Celtic warriors, the Celtic missionaries were effecting the spiritual conquest of Ireland. Among these messengers of the Cross, was a zealous priest named Patricius, better known as Saint Patrick, the patron saint of the Irish.

Never did any race receive the Gospel with more ardent enthusiasm. The Irish Church sent out its devoted missionaries into the Pictish Highlands, into the forests of Germany, and among the wilds of Alps and Apennines. "For a time it seemed," says the historian Green, "that the course of the world's history was to be changed; as if the older Celtic race that Roman and German had driven before them had turned to the moral conquest of their conquerors; as if Celtic, and not Latin, Christianity was to mould the destinies of the churches of the West."

Among the numerous religious houses founded by the Celtic

missionaries was the famous monastery established about A.D. 564 by the Irish monk Saint Columba, on the little isle of Iona, just off the Pictish coast. Iona became a most renowned centre of Christian learning and missionary zeal, and for almost two centuries was the point from which radiated light through the darkness of the surrounding heathenism. Fitly has it been called the Nursery of Saints and the Oracle of the West.

Rivalry between the Roman and the Celtic Church. — Now, from the very moment that Augustine touched the shores of Britain and summoned the Welsh clergy to acknowledge the discipline of the Roman Church, there had been a growing jealousy between the Latin and the Celtic Church, which by this time had risen into the bitterest rivalry and strife. So long had the Celtic Church been cut off from all relations with Rome, that it had come to differ somewhat from it in the matter of certain ceremonies and observances, such as the time of keeping Easter and the form of the tonsure. Furthermore, it was inclined to look upon St. John rather than upon St. Peter as the apostle of pre-eminence.

The Council of Whitby (A.D. 664). — With a view to settling the quarrel Oswy, king of Northumbria, called a synod composed of representatives of both parties, at the monastery of Whitby. The chief question of debate, which was argued before the king by the ablest advocates of both Churches, was the proper time for the observance of Easter. Finally Wilfred, the speaker for the Roman party, happening to quote the words of Christ to Peter, "To thee will I give the keys of the kingdom of heaven," the king asked the Celtic monks if these words were really spoken by Christ to that apostle, and upon their admitting that they were, Oswy said, "He being the door-keeper, . . . I will in all things obey his decrees, lest when I come to the gates of the kingdom of heaven, there should be none to open them."[1]

The decision of the prudent Oswy gave the British Isles to Rome; for not only was all England quickly won to the Roman side, but the Celtic churches and monasteries of Wales and Ire-

[1] Bede's *Eccl. Hist.* III. 25.

land and Scotland soon came to conform to the Roman standard and custom. "By the assistance of our Lord," says the pious Latin chronicler, "the monks were brought to the canonical observation of Easter, and the right mode of the tonsure."

The Roman Victory Fortunate for England. — There is no doubt but that it was very fortunate for England that the controversy turned as it did. For one of the most important of the consequences of the conversion of Britain was the re-establishment of that connection of the island with Roman civilization which had been severed by the calamities of the fifth century. As Green says, — he is speaking of the embassy of St. Augustine, — "The march of the monks as they chanted their solemn litany was in one sense a return of the Roman legions who withdrew at the trumpet call of Alaric. . . . Practically Augustine's landing renewed that union with the western world which the landing of Hengest had destroyed. The new England was admitted into the older Commonwealth of nations. The civilization, art, letters, which had fled before the sword of the English conquerors returned with the Christian faith."

Now all this advantage would have been lost had Iona instead of Rome won at Whitby. England would have been isolated from the world, and would have had no part or lot in that rich common life which was destined to the European peoples as co-heirs of the heritage bequeathed to them by the dying empire.

A second valuable result of the Roman victory was the hastening of the political unity of England through its ecclesiastical unity. The Celtic Church, in marked contrast with the Latin, was utterly devoid of capacity for organization. It could have done nothing in the way of developing among the several Anglo-Saxon states the sentiment of nationality. On the other hand, the Roman Church, through the exercise of a central authority, through national synods and general legislation, overcame the isolation of the different kingdoms, and helped powerfully to draw them together into a common political life.

The Conversion of Germany. — The conversion of the tribes of

Germany was effected by Celtic, Anglo-Saxon, and Frankish missionaries, — and the sword of Charlemagne (see p. 406). The great apostle of Germany was the Saxon Winfred, or Winifred, better known as St. Boniface. During a long and intensely active life he founded schools and monasteries, organized churches, preached and baptized ; and at last died a martyr's death (A.D. 753).

The christianizing of the tribes of Germany relieved the Teutonic states of Western Europe from the constant peril of massacre by their heathen kinsmen, and erected a strong barrier in Central Europe against the advance of the waves of Turanian paganism and Mohammedanism which for centuries beat so threateningly against the eastern frontiers of Germany.[1]

Christianity in the North. — The progress of Christianity in the North was slow ; but gradually, during the ninth, tenth, and eleventh centuries, the missionaries of the Church won over all the Scandinavian peoples. One important effect of their conversion was the checking of their piratical expeditions, which previously had vexed almost every shore to the south.

By the opening of the fourteenth century all Europe was claimed by Christianity, save a limited district in Southern Spain held by the Moors, and another in the Baltic regions possessed by the still pagan Finns and Lapps.

Monasticism. — It was during this very conflict with the barbarians that the Church developed the remarkable institution known as Monasticism, which denotes a life of seclusion from the world, with the object of promoting the interests of the soul. The central idea of the system is, that the body is a weight upon the spirit, and that to " mortify the flesh " is a prime duty.

The monastic system embraced two prominent classes of ascetics :

[1] The conversion of Russia dates from about the close of the tenth century. Its evangelization was effected by the missionaries of Constantinople, that is, of the Greek, or Eastern Church. Of the Turanian tribes, only the Hungarians, or Magyars, embraced Christianity. All the other Turanian peoples that appeared on the eastern edge of Europe during the Middle Ages, came as pagan or Moslem enemies.

1. Hermits, or anchorites, persons who, retiring from the world, lived solitary lives in desolate places; 2. Cenobites, or monks, who formed communities and lived under a common roof.

St. Antony, an Egyptian ascetic, who by his example and influence gave a tremendous impulse to the strange enthusiasm, is called the "father of the hermits." The persecutions that arose under the Roman emperors, driving thousands into the deserts, contributed vastly to the movement. The cities of Egypt became almost emptied of their Christian population.

About the close of the fourth century the cenobite system was introduced into Europe, and in an astonishingly short space of time spread throughout all the western countries where Christianity had gained a foothold. Monasteries arose on every side, in the wilds of the desert and in the midst of the crowded city. The number that fled to these retreats was vastly augmented by the disorder and terror attending the invasion of the barbarians and the overthrow of the empire in the West.

With the view of introducing some sort of system and uniformity among the numerous communities, fraternities or associations were early organized and spread rapidly. The three essential vows required of their members were poverty, chastity, and obedience. The most celebrated of these fraternities was the Order of the Benedictines, so called from its founder St. Benedict (A.D. 480–543). This order became immensely popular. At one time it embraced about 40,000 abbeys.

Advantages of the Monastic System. — The early establishment of the monastic system in the Church resulted in great advantages to the new world that was shaping itself out of the ruins of the old.

The monks became missionaries, and it was largely to their zeal and devotion that the Church owed her speedy and signal victory over the barbarians; they also became teachers, and under the shelter of the monasteries established schools which were the nurseries of learning during the Middle Ages; they became copyists, and with great care and industry gathered and multiplied ancient manuscripts, and thus preserved and transmitted to the modern world much classical learning and literature that would otherwise have been lost; they became agriculturists, especially the Benedictines, and by skilful labor converted the wilderness about their retreats into fair gardens, thus redeeming from barrenness some of the most desolate districts of Europe; they became further the almoners of the pious and the wealthy, and distributed alms to the poor and needy. Everywhere the monasteries opened their hospitable doors to the weary, the sick, and the discouraged. In a word, these retreats were the inns, the asylums, and the hospitals, as well as the schools of learning and the nurseries of religion, of mediæval Europe. Nor should we fail to mention how the asceticism of the monks checked those flagrant social evils that had sapped the strength of the Roman race, and which uncounteracted would have contaminated and weakened the purer peoples of the North; nor how, through its requirements of self-control and self-sacrifice, it gave prominence to the inner life of the spirit.

Conclusion. — With a single word or two respecting the general consequences of the conversion to Christianity of the Teutonic tribes, we will close the present chapter.

The adoption of a common faith by the European peoples drew them together into a sort of religious brotherhood, and rendered it possible for the continent to employ its undivided strength, during the succeeding centuries, in staying the threatening progress toward the West of the colossal Mohammedan power of the East. The Christian Church set in the midst of the seething, martial nations and races of Europe an influence that fostered the gentler virtues, and a power that was always to be found on the side of order, and usually of mercy. It taught the brotherhood of man, the essential equality in the sight of God of the high and the low, and thus pleaded powerfully and at last effectually for the freedom of the slave and the serf. It prepared the way for the introduction among the barbarians of the arts, the literature, and the culture of Rome, and contributed powerfully to hasten the fusion into a single people of the Latins and Teutons, of which important matter we shall treat in the following chapter.

CHAPTER XXXIV.

FUSION OF THE LATIN AND TEUTONIC PEOPLES.

Introductory. — Having seen how the Hebrew element, that is, the ideas, beliefs, and sentiments of Christianity, became the common possession of the Latins and Teutons, it yet remains to notice how these two races, upon the soil of the old empire, intermingled their blood, their language, their laws, their usages and customs, to form new peoples, new tongues, and new institutions.

The Romance Nations. — In some districts the barbarian invaders and the Roman provincials were kept apart for a long time by the bitter antagonism of race, and a sense of injury on the one hand and a feeling of disdainful superiority on the other. But for the most part the Teutonic intruders and the Latin-speaking inhabitants of Italy, Spain, and Gaul very soon began freely to mingle their blood by family alliances. It is quite impossible to say what proportion the Teutons bore to the Romans. Of course the proportion varied in the different countries. In none of the countries named, however, was it large enough to absorb the Latinized population; on the contrary, the barbarians were themselves absorbed, yet not without changing very essentially the body into which they were incorporated. By the close of the ninth century the two elements had become quite intimately blended, and a century or two later Roman and Teuton have alike disappeared, and we are introduced to Italians, Spaniards, and Frenchmen. These we call Romance nations, because at base they are Roman.[1]

---

[1] Britain did not become a Romance nation on account of the nature of the barbarian conquest of that island. The Romanized provincials, as has been seen, were there almost destroyed by the fierce Teutonic invaders.

The Formation of the Romance Languages. — During the five centuries of their subjection to Rome, the natives of Spain and Gaul forgot their barbarous dialects and came to speak a corrupt Latin. Now in exactly the same way that the dialects of the Celtic tribes of Gaul and of the Celtiberians of Spain had given way to the more refined speech of the Romans, did the rude languages of the Teutons yield to the more cultured speech of the Roman provincials. In the course of two or three centuries after their entrance into the empire, Goths, Lombards, Burgundians, and Franks had, in a large measure, dropped their own tongue, and were speaking that of the people they had subjected. But of course this provincial Latin underwent a great change upon the lips of the mixed descendants of the Romans and Teutons. Owing to the absence of a common popular literature, the changes that took place in one country did not exactly correspond to those going on in another. Hence, in the course of time, we find different dialects springing up, and by about the ninth century the Latin has virtually disappeared as a spoken language, and its place been usurped by what will be known as the Italian, Spanish, and French languages, all more or less resembling the ancient Latin, and all called Romance tongues, because children of the old Roman speech.

Personal Character of the Teutonic Legislation. — The legislation of the barbarians was generally personal instead of territorial, as with us ; that is, instead of all the inhabitants of a given country being subject to the same laws, there were different ones for the different classes of society. The Latins, for instance, were subject in private law only to the old Roman code, while the Teutons lived under the rules and regulations which they had brought with them from beyond the Rhine.

Even among themselves the Teutons knew nothing of the modern legal maxim that all should stand equal before the law. The penalty inflicted upon the evil-doer depended, not upon the nature of his crime, but upon his rank, or that of the party injured. Thus slaves and serfs could be beaten and put to death for minor offences, while a freeman might atone for any crime, even for murder, by the payment of a fine, the amount of the penalty being determined by the rank of the victim. Among the Saxons the life of a king's thane was worth 1200 shillings, while that of a common free man was valued only one-sixth as high.

Ordeals. — The modes by which guilt or innocence was ascertained show in how rude a state was the administration of justice among the barbarians. One very common method of proof was by what were called ordeals, in which the question was submitted to the judgment of God. Of these the chief were the *ordeal by fire*, the *ordeal by water*, and the *ordeal by battle*.

The *ordeal by fire* consisted in taking in the hand a red-hot iron, or in walking blindfolded with bare feet over a row of hot ploughshares laid lengthwise at irregular distances. If the person escaped without serious harm, he was held to be innocent. Another way of performing the fire ordeal was by running through the flame of two fires built close together, or by walking over live brands; hence the phrase "to haul over the coals."

The *ordeal by water* was of two kinds, by hot water and cold. In the hot-water ordeal the accused person thrust his arm into boiling water, and if no hurt was visible upon the arm three days after the operation, the person was considered guiltless. When we speak of one's being "in hot water," we use an expression which had its origin in this ordeal.

In the cold-water trial the suspected person was thrown into a stream or pond : if he floated, he was held guilty ; if he sank, innocent. The water, it was believed, would reject the guilty, but receive the innocent into its bosom. The practice common in Europe until a very recent date of trying supposed witches by weighing them, or by throwing them into a pond of water to see whether they would sink or float, grew out of this superstition.

The *trial by combat*, or *wager of battle*, was a solemn judicial duel. It was resorted to in the belief that God would give victory to the right. Naturally it was a favorite mode of trial among a people who found their chief delight in fighting. Even religious disputes were sometimes settled in this way. The modern duel may probably be regarded as a relic of this form of trial.

The ordeal was frequently performed by deputy, that is, one person for hire or for the sake of friendship would undertake it for another; hence the expression " to go through fire and water to serve one." Especially was such substitution common in the judicial duel, as women and ecclesiastics were generally forbidden to appear personally in the lists. The champions, as the deputies were called, became in time a regular class in society, like the gladiators in ancient Rome. Religious houses and chartered towns hired champions at a regular salary to defend all the cases to which they might become a party.

The Revival of the Roman Law. — Now the barbarian law-system, if such it can be called, the character of which we have simply suggested by the preceding illustrations, gradually displaced the Roman law in all those countries where the two systems at first existed alongside each other, save in Italy and Southern France, where the provincials greatly outnumbered the invaders. But the admirable jurisprudence of Rome was bound to assert its superiority. About the close of the eleventh century, there was a great revival in the study of the Roman law as embodied in the *Corpus Juris Civilis* of Justinian (see p. 358), and in the course of a century or two this became either the groundwork or a strong modifying element in the jurisprudence of almost all the peoples of Europe.

What took place may be illustrated by reference to the fate of the Teutonic languages in Gaul, Italy, and Spain. As the barbarian tongues, after maintaining a place in those countries for two or three centuries, at length gave place to the superior Latin, which became the basis of the new Romance languages, so now in the domain of law the barbarian maxims and customs, though holding their place more persistently, likewise finally give way, almost everywhere and in a greater or less degree, to the more excellent law-system of the empire. Rome must fulfil her destiny and give laws to the nations.

CHAPTER XXXV.

THE ROMAN EMPIRE IN THE EAST.

The Reign of Justinian (A.D. 527–565).—During the fifty years immediately following the fall of Rome, the Eastern emperors struggled hard and doubtfully to withstand the waves of the barbarian inundation which constantly threatened to overwhelm Constantinople with the same awful calamities that had befallen the imperial city of the West. Had the new Rome — the destined refuge for a thousand years of Græco-Roman learning and culture — also gone down at this time before the storm, the loss to the cause of civilization would have been incalculable.

Fortunately, in the year 527, there ascended the Eastern throne a prince of unusual ability, to whom fortune gave a general of such rare genius that his name has been allotted a place in the short list of the great commanders of the world. Justinian was the name of the prince, and Belisarius that of the soldier. The sovereign has given name to the period, which is called after him the " Era of Justinian."

It will be recalled that it was during this reign that Africa was recovered from the Vandals and Italy from the Goths (see p. 372). These conquests brought once more within the boundaries of the empire some of the fairest lands of the West.

But that which has given Justinian's reign a greater distinction than any conferred upon it by brilliant military achievements, is the collection and publication, under the imperial direction, of the *Corpus Juris Civilis*, or " Body of the Roman Law." This work is the most precious legacy of Rome to the modern world. In causing its publication, Justinian earned the title of " The Lawgiver of Civilization " (see p. 358).

In the midst of this brilliant reign an awful pestilence, bred probably in Egypt, fell upon the empire, and did not cease its ravages until about fifty years afterwards. This plague was the most terrible scourge of which history has any knowledge, save perhaps the so-called Black Death, which afflicted Europe in the fourteenth century. The number of victims of the plague has been estimated at 100,000,000.

The Reign of Heraclius (A.D. 610–641). — For half a century after the death of Justinian, the annals of the Byzantine empire are unimportant. Then we reach the reign of Heraclius, a prince about whose worthy name gather matters of significance in world-history.

About this time Chosroes II., king of Persia, wrested from the empire the fortified cities that guarded the Euphratean frontier, and overran all Syria, Egypt, and Asia Minor. What was known as the True Cross was torn from the church at Jerusalem and carried off in triumph to Persia. In order to compel Chosroes to recall his armies, which were distressing the provinces of the empire, Heraclius, pursuing the same plan as that by which the Romans in the Second Punic War forced the Carthaginians to call Hannibal out of Italy (see p. 264), with a small company of picked men marched boldly into the heart of Persia, and in revenge for the insults heaped by the infidels upon the Christian churches, overturned the altars of the fire-worshippers and quenched their sacred flames.

The struggle between the two rival empires was at last decided by a terrible combat known as the Battle of Nineveh (A.D. 627), which was fought around the ruins of the old Assyrian capital. The Persian army was almost annihilated. In a few days grief or violence ended the life of Chosroes. With him passed away the glory of the Second Persian Empire. The new Persian king negotiated a treaty of peace with Heraclius. The articles of this treaty left the boundaries of the two empires unchanged.

The Empire becomes Greek. — The two combatants in the fierce struggle which we have been watching, were too much absorbed in their contentions to notice the approach of a storm from the deserts of Arabia, — a storm destined to overwhelm both alike in its destructive course. Within a few years from the date of the Battle of Nineveh, the Saracens entered upon their surprising career of conquest, which in a short time completely changed the face of the entire East, and set the Crescent, the emblem of a new faith, alike above the fire-altars of Persia and the churches of the Empire. Heraclius himself lived to see — so cruel are the vicissitudes of fortune — the very provinces which he had wrested from the hands of the fire-worshippers, in the hands of the more insolent followers of the False Prophet, and the Crescent planted within sight of the walls of Constantinople.

The conquests of the Saracens cut off from the empire those provinces that had the smallest Greek element and thus rendered the population subject to the emperor more homogeneous, more thoroughly Greek. The Roman element disappeared, and the court of Constantinople became Greek in tone, spirit, and manners. Hence, instead of longer applying to the empire the designation *Roman*, we shall from this on call it the *Greek*, or Byzantine empire.

We shall trace no further as a separate story the fortunes of the Eastern emperors. In the eighth century the so-called Iconoclastic controversy [1] will draw our attention to them; and then again in the twelfth and thirteenth centuries the Crusades will once more bring their affairs into prominence, and we shall see a line of Latin princes seated for a time (from 1204 to 1261) upon the throne of Constantine. [2] Finally, in the year 1453, we shall witness the capture of Constantinople by the Turks, [3] which disaster closes the long and checkered history of the Græco-Roman empire in the East.

[1] See p. 417. [2] See p. 446. [3] See p. 462.

CHAPTER XXXVI.

MOHAMMED AND THE SARACENS.

Introductory Statement. — The Arabs, or Saracens, who are now about to play their surprising part in history, are, after the Hebrews, the most important people of the Semitic race. Secure in their inaccessible deserts, the Arabs have never as a people bowed their necks to a foreign conqueror, although portions of the Arabian peninsula have been repeatedly subjugated by different races.

AN ARAB RIDER.

Religious Condition of Arabia before Mohammed. — Before the reforms of Mohammed, the Arabs were idolaters. Their holy city was Mecca. Here was the ancient and most revered shrine of the Caaba, where was preserved a sacred black stone believed to have been given by an angel to Abraham.

But though the native tribes of the peninsula were idolaters, still there were many followers of other faiths; for Arabia at this time was a land of religious freedom. The altar of the fire-worshipper rose alongside the Jewish synagogue and the Christian church.

The Jews especially were to be found everywhere in great numbers, having been driven from Palestine by the Roman persecutions. It was from the Jews and Christians, doubtless, that Mohammed learned many of the doctrines that he taught.

Mohammed. — Mohammed, the great prophet of the Arabs, was born in the holy city of Mecca, about the year 570 of our era. He sprang from the distinguished tribe of the Koreishites, the custodians of the sacred shrine of the Caaba. Like Moses, he spent many years of his life as a shepherd.

THE CAABA AT MECCA.

Mohammed possessed a deeply religious nature, and it was his wont often to retire to a cave a few miles from Mecca, and there spend long vigils in prayer. He declared that here he had visions, in which the angel Gabriel appeared to him, and made to him revelations which he was commanded to make known to his fellow-men. The sum of the new faith which he was to teach was this: "There is but one God, and Mohammed is his Prophet."

Mohammed communicated the nature of his visions to his wife, and she became his first convert. At the end of three years his disciples numbered forty persons.

The Hegira (622). — The teachings of Mohammed at last

aroused the anger of a powerful party among the Koreishites, who feared that they, as the guardians of the national idols of the Caaba, would be compromised in the eyes of the other tribes by allowing such heresy to be openly taught by one of their number, and accordingly plots were formed against his life. Barely escaping assassination, he fled to the city of Medina.

This Hegira, or Flight, as the word signifies, occurred in the year 622, and was considered by the Moslems as such an important event in the history of their religion that they adopted it as the beginning of a new era, and from it still continue to reckon their dates.

The Faith extended by the Sword. — His cause being warmly espoused by the inhabitants of Medina, Mohammed threw aside the character of an exhorter, and assumed that of a warrior. He declared it to be the will of God that the new faith should be spread by the sword. Accordingly, the year following the Hegira, he began to attack and plunder caravans. The flames of a sacred war were soon kindled. The reckless enthusiasm of his wild converts was intensified by the assurance of the Apostle that death met in fighting those who resisted the true faith ensured the martyr immediate entrance upon the joys of Paradise. Within ten years from the time of the assumption of the sword by Mohammed, Mecca had been conquered, and the new creed established among all the tribes of Arabia.

Mohammed died in the year 632. No character in all history has been the subject of more conflicting speculations than the Arabian Prophet. By some he has been called a self-deluded enthusiast, while others have denounced him as the boldest of impostors. We shall, perhaps, reconcile these discordant views, if we bear in mind that the same person may, in different periods of a long career, be both.

The Koran and the Doctrines of Islam. — Before going on to trace the conquests of the successors of Mohammed, we must form some acquaintance with the religion of the great Prophet.

The doctrines of Mohammedanism, or Islam, which means

" submission," are contained in the Koran, the sacred book of the Moslems. They declare that God has revealed himself through four holy men : to Moses he gave the Pentateuch ; to David, the Psalms ; to Jesus, the Gospels ; and to Mohammed, the last and greatest of all the prophets, he gave the Koran.

" There is no God save Allah," is the fundamental doctrine of Islamism, and to this is added the equally binding declaration that " Mohammed is the Prophet of Allah." The faithful Moslem must also believe in the sacredness and infallibility of the Koran. He is also required to believe in the resurrection and the day of judgment, and an after-state of happiness and of misery. Also he must believe in the absoluteness of the decrees of God, — that he foreordains whatsoever comes to pass, and that nothing man can do can change his appointments.

The Koran, while requiring assent to the foregoing creed, inculcates the practice of four virtues. The first is prayer ; five times each day must the believer turn his face towards Mecca and engage in devotion. The second requirement is almsgiving. The third is keeping the Fast of Ramadan, which lasts a whole month. The fourth duty is making a pilgrimage to Mecca.

Abubekr, First Successor of Mohammed (632–634). — Upon the death of Mohammed a dispute at once arose as to his successor ; for the Prophet left no children, nor had he designated upon whom his mantle should fall. Abubekr, the Apostle's father-in-law, was at last chosen to the position, with the title of Caliph, or Vicar, of the Prophet, although many thought that the place belonged to Ali, the Prophet's cousin and son-in-law, and one of his first and most faithful companions. This question of succession was destined at a later period to divide the Mohammedan world into two sects, animated by the most bitter and lasting hostility towards each other.[1]

During the first part of his caliphate, Abubekr was engaged in

[1] The Mohammedans of Persia, who are known as Shiites, are the leaders of the party of Ali ; while the Turks, known as Sunnites, are the chief adherents of the opposite party.

suppressing revolts in different parts of the peninsula. These
commotions quieted, he was free to carry out the last injunction
of the Prophet to his followers, which enjoined them to spread his
doctrines by the sword, till all men had confessed the creed of
Islam, or consented to pay tribute to the Faithful.

The Conquest of Syria. — The country which Abubekr resolved
first to reduce was Syria. A call addressed to all the Faithful
throughout Arabia was responded to with the greatest alacrity and
enthusiasm. From every quarter the warriors flocked to Medina,
until the desert about the city was literally covered with their black
tents, and crowded with men and horses and camels. After
invoking the blessing of God upon the hosts, Abubekr sent them
forward upon their holy mission.

Heraclius made a brave effort to defend the holy places against
the fanatical warriors of the desert, but all in vain. His armies
were cut to pieces. Seeing there was no hope of saving Jerusalem,
he removed from that city to Constantinople the True Cross, which
he had rescued from the Persians (see p. 390). " Farewell, Syria,"
were his words, as he turned from the consecrated land which he
saw must be given up to the followers of the False Prophet.

The Conquest of Persia (632–641). — While one Saracen army
was overrunning Syria, another was busy with the subjugation of
Persia. Enervated as this country was through luxury, and weakened by her long wars with the Eastern emperors, she could offer
but feeble resistance to the terrible energy of the Saracens.

Soon after the conquest of Persia, the Arabs crossed the mountains that wall Persia on the north, and spread their faith among
the Turanian tribes of Central Asia. Among the most formidable
of the clans that adopted the new religion were the Turks. Their
conversion was an event of the greatest significance, for it was
their swords that were destined to uphold and to spread the creed
of Mohammed when the fiery zeal of his own countrymen should
abate, and their arms lose the dreaded power which religious fanaticism had for a moment imparted to them.

The Conquest of Egypt (638). — The reduction of Persia was not yet fully accomplished, when the Caliph Omar, the successor of Abubekr, commissioned Amrou, the chief whose valor had won many of the cities of Palestine, to carry the standard of the Prophet into the Valley of the Nile. Alexandria, after holding out against the arms of the Saracens for more than a year, was at length abandoned to the enemy. Amrou, in communicating the intelligence of the important event to Omar, wrote him also about the great Alexandrian Library, and asked him what he should do with the books. Omar is said to have replied : " If these books agree with the Koran, they are useless ; if they disagree, they are pernicious : in either case they ought to be destroyed." Accordingly the books were distributed among the four thousand baths of the capital, and served to feed their fires for six months.

The Conquest of Northern Africa (643–689). — The lieutenants of the Caliphs were obliged to do much and fierce fighting before they obtained possession of the oft-disputed shores of North Africa. They had to contend not only with the Græco-Roman Christians of the coast, but to battle also with the idolatrous Moors of the interior. Furthermore, all Europe had begun to feel alarm at the threatening advance of the Saracens ; so now Roman soldiers from Constantinople, and Gothic warriors from Italy and Spain hastened across the Mediterranean to aid in the protection of Carthage, and to help arrest the alarming progress of these wild fanatics of the desert.

But all was of no avail. Destiny had allotted to the followers of the Apostle the land of Hannibal and Augustine. Carthage was taken and razed to the ground, and the entire coast from the Nile to the Atlantic was forced to acknowledge the authority of the Caliphs. By this conquest all the countries of Northern Africa, whose history for a thousand years had been intertwined with that of the opposite shores of Europe, and which at one time seemed destined to share in the career of freedom and progress opening to the peoples of that continent, were drawn back into the fatalism, the despotism, and the stagnation of the East. From being an extension of Europe, they became once more an extension of Asia.

Attacks upon Constantinople. — Only fifty years had now passed since the death of Mohammed; but during this short time his standard had been carried by the lieutenants of his successors through Asia to the Hellespont on the one side, and across Africa to the Straits of Gibraltar on the other. From each of these two points, so remote from each other, the fanatic warriors of the desert were casting longing glances across those narrow passages of water which alone separated them from the single continent that their swift coursers had not yet traversed, or whence the spoil of the unbelievers had not yet been borne to the feet of the Vicar of the Prophet of God. We may expect to see the Saracens at one or both of these points attempt the invasion of Europe.

The first attempt was made in the East (in 668), where the Arabs endeavored to gain control of the Bosporus, by wresting Constantinople from the hands of the Eastern emperors. But the capital was saved through the use, by the besieged, of a certain bituminous compound, called Greek Fire. In 716, the city was again besieged by a powerful Moslem army; but its heroic defence by the Emperor Leo III. saved the capital for several centuries longer to the Christian world.

The Conquest of Spain (711). — While the Moslems were thus being repulsed from Europe at its eastern extremity, the gates of the continent were opened to them by treachery at the western, and they gained a foothold in Spain. At the great battle of Xeres (711), Roderic, the last of the Visigothic kings, was hopelessly defeated, and all the peninsula, save some mountainous regions in the northwest, quickly submitted to the invaders. Thus some of the fairest provinces of Europe were lost to Christendom for a period of nearly eight hundred years.

No sooner had the subjugation of the country been effected than multitudes of colonists from Arabia, Syria, and North Africa crowded into the peninsula, until in a short time the provinces of Seville, Cordova, Toledo, and Granada became Arabic in dress, manners, language, and religion.

Invasion of France: Battle of Tours (732). — Four or five years after the conquest of Spain, the Saracens crossed the Pyrenees, and established themselves upon the plains of Gaul. This advance of the Moslem hosts beyond the northern wall of Spain was viewed with the greatest alarm by all Christendom. It looked as though the followers of Mohammed would soon possess all the continent. As Draper pictures it, the Crescent, lying in a vast semi-circle upon the northern shore of Africa and the curving coast of Asia, with one horn touching the Bosporus and the other the Straits of Gibraltar, seemed about to round to the full and overspread all Europe.

In the year 732, exactly one hundred years after the death of the great Prophet, the Franks, under their renowned chieftain, Charles, and their allies met the Moslems upon the plains of Tours in the centre of Gaul, and committed to the issue of a single battle the fate of Christendom and the future course of history. The desperate valor displayed by the warriors of both armies was worthy of the prize at stake. Abderrahman, the Mohammedan leader, fell in the thick of the fight, and night saw the complete discomfiture of the Moslem hordes. The loss that the sturdy blows of the Germans had inflicted upon them was enormous, the accounts of that age swelling the number killed to the impossible figures of 375,000. The disaster at all events was too overwhelming to permit the Saracens ever to recover from the blow, and they soon retreated behind the Pyrenees.

The young civilization of Europe was thus delivered from an appalling danger, such as had not threatened it since the fearful days of Attila and the Huns. The heroic Duke Charles who had led the warriors of Christendom to the glorious victory was given the surname *Martel*, the "Hammer," in commemoration of the mighty blows of his huge battle-axe.

Changes in the Caliphate. — During the century of conquests we have traced, there were many changes in the caliphate. Abubekr was followed by Omar (634–644), Othman (644–655), and Ali (655–661), all of whom fell by the hands of assassins, for from the very first dissensions were rife among the followers of

the Prophet.   Ali was the last of the four so-called "Orthodox Caliphs," all of whom were relatives or companions of the
Prophet.

Moawiyah, a usurper, was now recognized as Caliph (661).
He succeeded in making the office hereditary, instead of elective,
as it hitherto had been, and thus established what is known as the
dynasty of the Ommiades,[1] the rulers of which family for nearly
a century issued their commands from the city of Damascus.

The house of the Ommiades was overthrown by the adherents
of the house of Ali, who established a new dynasty (750), known
as that of the Abbassides, so called from Abbas, an uncle of
Mohammed.   The new family, soon after coming to power, established the seat of the royal residence on the lower Tigris, and
upon the banks of that river founded the renowned city of Bagdad, which was destined to remain the abode of the Abbasside
Caliphs for a period of five hundred years, — until the subver-
sion of the house by the Tartars of the North.

The golden age of the caliphate of Bagdad covers the latter
part of the eighth and the ninth century of our era, and was illustrated by the reign of the renowned Haroun-al-Raschid (786–
809), the hero of the Arabian Nights.   During this period science,
philosophy, and literature were most assiduously cultivated by
the Arabian scholars, and the court of the Caliphs presented in
culture and luxury a striking contrast to the rude and barbarous
courts of the kings and princes of Western Christendom.

The Dismemberment of the Caliphate. — "At the close of the
first century of the Hegira," writes Gibbon, "the Caliphs were
the most potent and absolute monarchs of the globe.   The word
that went forth from the palace at Damascus was obeyed on the
Indus, on the Jaxartes, and on the Tagus."   Scarcely less potent
was the word that at first went forth from Bagdad.   But in a short
time the extended empire of the Abbassides, through the quarrels
of sectaries and the ambitions of rival aspirants for the honors of
the caliphate, was broken in fragments, and from three capitals —

---

[1] So called from Ommaya, an ancestor of Moawiyah.

Bagdad upon the Tigris, Cairo upon the Nile, and Cordova upon the Guadalquivir — were issued the commands of three rival Caliphs, each of whom was regarded by his adherents as the sole rightful spiritual and civil successor of the Apostle. All, however, held the great Arabian Prophet in the same reverence, all maintained with equal zeal the sacred character of the Koran, and all prayed with their faces turned toward the holy city of Mecca.

Spread of the Religion and Language of the Arabs. — Just as the Romans Romanized the peoples they conquered, so did the Saracens Saracenize the populations of the countries subjected to their authority. Over a large part of Spain, over North Africa, Egypt, Syria, Babylonia, Persia, Northern India, and portions of Central Asia, were spread — to the more or less perfect exclusion of native customs, speech, and worship — the manners, the language, and the religion of the Arabian conquerors.[1]

In Arabia no religion was tolerated save the faith of the Koran. But in all the countries beyond the limits of the peninsula, freedom of worship was allowed (save to *idolaters*, who were to be "rooted out") ; unbelievers, however, must purchase this liberty by the payment of a moderate tribute. Yet notwithstanding this toleration, the Christian and Zoroastrian religions gradually died out almost everywhere throughout the domains of the Caliphs.[2]

The Defects of Islam. — Civilization certainly owes a large debt to the Saracens. They preserved and transmitted much that was valuable in the science of the Greeks and the Persians (see p. 472). They improved trigonometry and algebra, and from India they

[1] Beyond the eastern edge of Mesopotamia, the Arabs failed to impress their language upon the subjected peoples, or in any way, save in the matter of creed, to leave upon them any important permanent trace of their conquests.

[2] The number of Guebers, or fire-worshippers, in Persia at the present time is estimated at from 50,000 to 100,000. About the same number may be counted in India, the descendants of the Guebers who fled from Persia at the time of the Arabian invasion. They are there called Parsees, from the land whence they came.

borrowed the decimal system of notation and introduced it into the West.

Many of the doctrines of Islam, however, are most unfavorable to human liberty, progress, and improvement. It teaches fatalism, and thus discourages effort and enterprise. It allows polygamy and puts no restraint upon divorce, and thus destroys the sanctity of the family life. It permits slavery and fosters despotism. It inspires a blind and bigoted hatred of race and creed, and thus puts far out of sight the salutary truth of the brotherhood of man. Because of these and other scarcely less prominent defects in its teachings, Islam has proved a blight and curse to almost every race embracing its sterile doctrines.

Mohammedism is vastly superior, however, either to fetichism or idolatry, and consequently, upon peoples very low in the scale of civilization, it has an elevating influence. Thus, upon the negro tribes of Central Africa, where it is to-day spreading rapidly, it is acknowledged to have a civilizing effect.

CHAPTER XXXVII.

CHARLEMAGNE AND THE RESTORATION OF THE EMPIRE IN THE WEST.

General Remarks. — In the foregoing chapter we traced the rise and decline of the power of the Saracens. We saw the Semitic East roused for a moment to a life of tremendous energy by the miracle of religious enthusiasm, and then beheld it sinking rapidly again into inaction and weakness, disappointing all its early promises. Manifestly the " Law " is not to go forth from Mecca. The Semitic race is not to lead the civilization of the world.

But returning again to the West, we discover among the Teutonic barbarians indications of such youthful energy and life, that we are at once persuaded that to them has been given the future. The Franks, who, with the aid of their confederates, withstood the advance of the Saracens upon the field of Tours, and saved Europe from subjection to the Koran, are the people that first attract our attention. It is among them that a man appears who makes the first grand attempt to restore the laws, the order, the institutions of the ancient Romans. Charlemagne, their king, is the imposing figure that moves amidst all the events of the times ; indeed, is the one who makes the events, and renders the period in which he lived an epoch in universal history. The story of this era affords the key to very much of the subsequent history of Europe.

How Duke Pepin became King of the Franks. — Charles Martel, whose tremendous blows at Tours earned for him his significant surname (see p. 399), although the real head of the Frankish nation, was nominally only an officer of the Merovingian court. He died without ever having borne the title of king, notwithstanding he had exercised all the authority of that office.

But Charles's son Pepin, called *le Bref* (the Short), on account of his diminutive stature, aspired to the regal title and honors. He resolved to depose his titular master, and to make himself king. Not deeming it wise, however, to do this without the sanction of the Pope, he sent an embassy to represent to him the state of affairs, and to solicit his advice. Mindful of recent favors that he had received at the hands of Pepin, the Pope gave his approval to the proposed scheme by replying that it seemed altogether reasonable that the one who was king in power should be king also in name. This was sufficient. Chilperic — such was the name of the Merovingian king — was straightway deposed, and placed in a monastery; while Pepin, whose own deeds together with those of his illustrious father had done so much for the Frankish nation and for Christendom, was anointed and crowned king of the Franks (752), and thus became the first of the Carolingian line, the name of his illustrious son Charlemagne giving name to the house.

Beginning of the Temporal Power of the Popes. — In the year 754 Pope Stephen II., who was troubled by the Lombards (see p. 374), besought Pepin's aid. Quick to return the favor which the head of the Church had rendered him in the establishment of his power as king, Pepin straightway crossed the Alps with a large army, expelled the Lombards from their recent conquests, and made a donation to the Pope of these captured cities and provinces (755).

This famous gift may be regarded as having laid the basis of the temporal power of the Popes; for though Pepin probably did not intend to convey to the Papal See the absolute sovereignty of the transferred lands, after a time the Popes claimed this, and finally came to exercise within the limits of the donated territory all the rights and powers of independent temporal rulers. So here we have the beginning of the celebrated *Papal States*, and of the story of the Popes as temporal princes.

Accession of Charlemagne. — Pepin died in the year 768, and his kingdom passed into the hands of his two sons, Carlo-

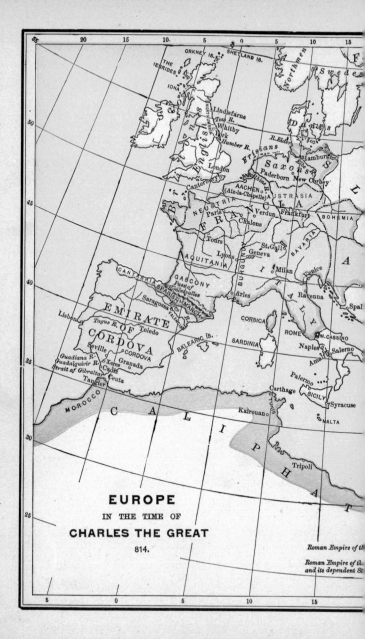

EUROPE

IN THE TIME OF

CHARLES THE GREAT

814.

Roman Empire of th[e]

Roman Empire of th[e]
and its dependent St[ates]

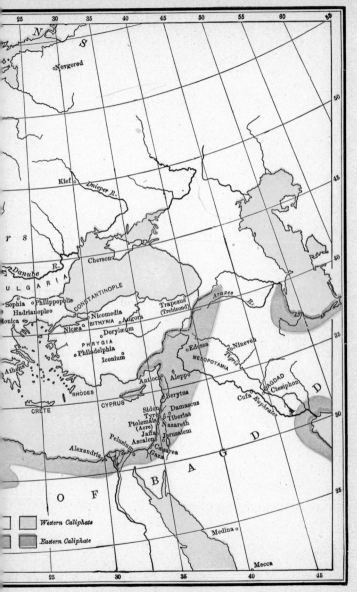

Western Caliphate

Eastern Caliphate

man and Charles; but within three years the death of Carloman and the free votes of the Franks conferred the entire kingdom upon Charles, better known as Charlemagne, or "Charles the Great."

His Campaigns. — Charlemagne's long reign of nearly half a century — he ruled forty-six years — was filled with military expeditions and conquests, by which he so extended the boundaries of his dominions, that at his death they embraced the larger part of Western Europe. He made fifty-two military campaigns, the chief of which were against the Lombards, the Saracens, and the Saxons. Of these we will speak briefly.

CHARLEMAGNE.
(Head of a bronze equestrian statuette.)

Among Charlemagne's first undertakings was a campaign against the Lombards, whose king, Desiderius, was troubling the Pope. Charlemagne wrested from Desiderius all his possessions, shut up the unfortunate king in a monastery, and placed on his own head the iron crown of the Lombards. While in Italy he visited Rome, and, in return for the favor of the Pope, confirmed the donation of his father, Pepin (774).

In the ninth year of his reign Charlemagne gathered his warriors for a crusade against the Saracens in Spain. He crossed the Pyrenees, and succeeded in wresting from the Moslems all the northeastern corner of the peninsula. As he was leading his victorious bands back across the Pyrenees, the rear of his army under the lead of the renowned paladin Roland, while hemmed in by the walls of the Pass of Roncesvalles, was set upon by the wild mountaineers (the Gascons and Basques), and cut to pieces before Charlemagne could give relief. Of the details of this event no authentic account has been preserved; but long afterwards it formed the favorite theme of the tales and songs of the Trouveurs of Northern France.

But by far the greater number of the campaigns of Charlemagne were directed against the pagan Saxons, who almost alone of the German tribes still retained their ancient idolatry. Thirty years and more of his reign were occupied in these wars across the Rhine. Reduced to submission again and again, as often did the Saxons rise in desperate revolt. The heroic Witikind was the "second Arminius" (see p. 308) who encouraged his countrymen to resist to the last the intruders upon their soil. Finally, Charlemagne, angered beyond measure by the obstinacy of the barbarians, caused 4500 prisoners in his hands to be massacred in revenge for the contumacy of the nation. The Saxons at length yielded, and accepted Charlemagne as their sovereign, and Christianity as their religion.

Restoration of the Empire in the West (800). — An event of seemingly little real moment, yet, in its influence upon succeeding affairs, of the very greatest importance, now claims our attention. Pope Leo III. having called upon Charlemagne for aid against a hostile faction at Rome, the king soon appeared in person at the capital, and punished summarily the disturbers of the peace of the Church. The gratitude of Leo led him at this time to make a most signal return for the many services of the Frankish king. To understand his act a word of explanation is needed.

For a considerable time a variety of circumstances had been fostering a growing feeling of enmity between the Italians and the emperors at Constantinople. Disputes had arisen between the churches of the East and those of the West, and the Byzantine rulers had endeavored to compel the Italian churches to introduce certain changes and reforms in their worship, which had aroused the most determined opposition of the Roman bishops, who denounced the Eastern emperors as schismatics and heretics. Furthermore, while persecuting the orthodox churches of the West, these unworthy emperors had allowed the Christian lands of the East to fall a prey to the Arabian infidels.

Just at this time, moreover, by the crime of the Empress Irene, who had deposed her son Constantine VI., and put out his eyes, that she might have his place, the Byzantine throne was vacant, in the estimation of the Italians, who contended that the crown of the Cæsars could not be worn by a woman. Confessedly it was time that the Pope should exercise the power reposing in him as Head of the Church, and take away from the heretical and effeminate Greeks the Imperial crown, and bestow it upon some strong, orthodox, and worthy prince in the West.

Now, among all the Teutonic chiefs of Western Christendom, there was none who could dispute the claims to the honor with the king of the Franks, the representative of a most illustrious house, and the strongest champion of the young Christianity of the West against her pagan foes. Accordingly, as Charlemagne was participating in the festivities of Christmas Day in the Cathedral of St. Peter at Rome, the Pope approached the kneeling king, — who declared afterwards that he was wholly ignorant of the designs of his friend, — and placing a crown of gold upon his head, proclaimed him emperor of the Romans, and the rightful and consecrated successor of Cæsar Augustus and Constantine (800).

The intention of Pope Leo was, by a sort of reversal of the act of Constantine, to bring back from the East the seat of the Imperial court ; but what he really accomplished was a restoration of the line of emperors in the West, which 324 years before had been ended by Odoacer, when he dethroned Romulus Augustus and sent the royal vestments to Constantinople (see p. 348). We say this was what he actually effected ; for the Greeks of the East, disregarding wholly what the Roman people and the Pope had done, maintained their line of emperors just as though nothing had occurred in Italy. So now from this time on for centuries there were two emperors, one in the East, and another in the West, each claiming to be the rightful successor of Cæsar Augustus.[1]

[1] From this time on it will be proper for us to use the terms *Western* Empire and *Eastern* Empire. These names should not, however, be employed before this time, for the two parts of the old Roman Empire were simply administrative divisions of a single empire ; we may though, properly

Charlemagne's Death; his Work. — Charlemagne enjoyed the Imperial dignity only fourteen years, dying in 814. Within the cathedral at Aachen, in a tomb which he himself had built, the dead monarch, so tradition relates, was placed upon a throne, with his royal robes around him, his good sword by his side, and the Bible open on his lap. It seemed as though men could not believe that his reign was over; and it was not.

By the almost universal verdict of students of the mediæval period, Charles the Great has been pronounced the most imposing personage that appears between the fall of Rome and the fifteenth century. His greatness has erected an enduring monument for itself in his name, the one by which he is best known — Charlemagne.

Charlemagne must not be regarded as a warrior merely. His most noteworthy work was that which he effected as a reformer and statesman. He founded schools, reformed the laws, collected libraries, and extended to the Church a patronage worthy of a Constantine. In a word, he laid "the foundation of all that is noble and beautiful and useful in the history of the Middle Ages."

Division of the Empire; Treaty of Verdun (843). — Like the kingdom of Alexander, the mighty empire of Charlemagne fell to pieces soon after his death. "His sceptre was the bow of Ulysses which could not be drawn by any weaker hand." After a troublous period of dissension and war, the empire was divided, by the important Treaty of Verdun, among Charlemagne's three grandchildren, — Charles, Lewis, and Lothar. To Charles was given France; to Lewis, Germany; and to Lothar, Italy and the valley of the Rhone, together with a narrow strip of land extending from Switzerland to the mouth of the Rhine. With these possessions of Lothar went also the Imperial title.

enough, speak of the Roman empire *in* the West, and the Roman empire *in* the East, or of the Western and Eastern emperors. See Bryce's *Holy Roman Empire*. The Eastern Empire was destroyed by the Turks in 1453; the line of Western Teutonic emperors was maintained until the present century, when it was ended by the act of Napoleon in the dismemberment of Germany (1806).

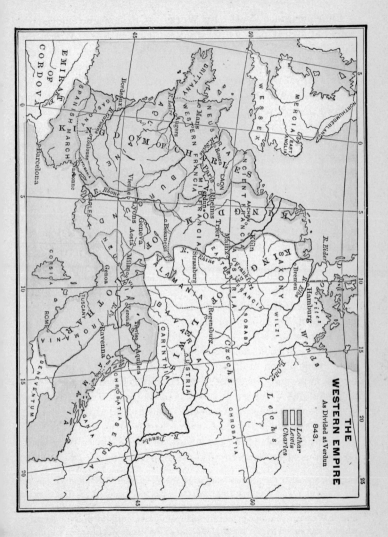

THE
WESTERN EMPIRE
As Divided at Verdun.
843.

Lothar
Lewis
Charles

This treaty is celebrated, not only because it was the first great treaty among the European states, but also on account of its marking the divergence from one another, and in some sense the origin, of three of the great nations of modern Europe, — of France, Germany, and Italy.

Conclusion.— After this dismemberment of the dominions of Charlemagne, the annals of the different branches of the Carolingian family become intricate, wearisome, and uninstructive. A fate as dark and woeful as that which, according to Grecian story, overhung the royal house of Thebes, seemed to brood over the house of Charlemagne. In all its different lines a strange and adverse destiny awaited the lineage of the great king. The tenth century witnessed the extinction of the family.

CHAPTER XXXVIII.

THE NORTHMEN.

The People. — Northmen, Norsemen, Scandinavians, are different names applied in a general way to the early inhabitants of
Denmark, Norway, and Sweden.   These people formed the northern branch of the Teutonic family.   We cannot be certain when
they took possession of the northern peninsulas, but it is probable
that they had entered those countries long before Cæsar invaded
Gaul.

The Northmen as Pirates and Colonizers. — For the first eight
centuries of our era the Norsemen are hidden from our view in
their remote northern home ; but with the opening of the ninth
century their black piratical crafts are to be seen creeping along
all the coasts of Germany, Gaul, and the British Isles, and even
venturing far up their inlets and creeks.   Every summer these
dreaded sea-rovers made swift descents upon the exposed shores
of these countries, plundering, burning, murdering ; then upon
the approach of the stormy season, they returned to winter in the
sheltered fiords of the Scandinavian peninsula.   After a time the
bold corsairs began to winter in the lands they had harried during
the summer ; and soon all the shores of the countries visited were
dotted with their stations or settlements.

These marauding expeditions and colonizing enterprises of the
Northmen did not cease until the eleventh century was far advanced.   The consequences of this wonderful outpouring of the
Scandinavian peoples were so important and lasting that the movement has well been compared to the great migration of their German kinsmen in the fifth and sixth centuries.   Europe is a second
time inundated by the Teutonic barbarians.

The most noteworthy characteristic of these Northmen was the readiness with which they laid aside their own manners, habits, ideas, and institutions, and adopted those of the country in which they established themselves. " In Russia they became Russians ; in France, Frenchmen ; in England, Englishmen."

Colonization of Iceland and Greenland. — Iceland was settled by the Northmen in the ninth century,[1] and about a century later Greenland was discovered and colonized. In 1874 the Icelanders celebrated the thousandth anniversary of the settlement of their island, an event very like our Centennial of 1876.

America was reached by the Northmen as early as the beginning of the eleventh century : the Vineland of their traditions was possibly some part of the New England coast. It is believed that these first visitors to the continent made settlements in this new land ; but no certain remains of these exist.

The Norsemen in Russia. — While the Norwegians were sailing boldly out into the Atlantic and taking possession of the isles and coasts of the western seas, the Swedes were pushing their crafts across the Baltic and troubling the Slavonian tribes that dwelt upon the eastern shore of that sea. Either by right of conquest or through the invitation of the contentious Slavonian clans, the renowned Scandinavian chieftain Ruric acquired, in the year 862, kingly dignity, and became the founder of the first royal line of Russia, the successive kings of which family gradually consolidated the monarchy which was destined to become one of the foremost powers of Europe.

The Danish Conquest of England. — The Danes began to make descents upon the English coast about the beginning of the ninth

---

[1] Iceland became the literary centre of the Scandinavian world. There grew up here a class of scalds, or bards, who, before the introduction of writing, preserved and transmitted orally the sagas, or legends, of the Northern races. About the twelfth century these poems and legends were gathered into collections known as the Elder, or poetic, Edda, and the Younger, or prose, Edda. These are among the most interesting and important of the literary memorials that we possess of the early Teutonic peoples. They reflect faithfully the beliefs, manners, and customs of the Norsemen, and the wild, adventurous spirit of their Sea-Kings.

century. These sea-rovers spread the greatest terror through the
island; for they were not content with plunder, but being pagans,
they took special delight in burning the churches and monasteries
of the now Christian Anglo-Saxons, or English, as we shall hereafter call them. After a time the Danes began to make permanent settlements in the land. The wretched English were subjected
to exactly the same treatment that they had inflicted upon the
Celts. Much need had they to pray the petition of the Litany of
those days, — " From the fury of the Northmen, Good Lord, deliver us." Just when it began to look as though they would be
entirely annihilated or driven from the island by the barbarous
intruders, the illustrious Alfred (871–901) came to the throne of
Wessex.

For six years the youthful king fought heroically at the head of
his brave thanes; but each succeeding year the possessions of the
English grew smaller, and finally Alfred and his few remaining followers were driven to take refuge in the woods and morasses.
After a time, however, the affairs of the English began to brighten.
The Danes were overpowered, and though allowed to hold the
northeastern half of the land, still they were forced nominally to
acknowledge the authority of the English king.

For a full century following the death of Alfred, his successors
were engaged in a constant struggle to hold in subjection the
Danes already settled in the land, or to protect their domains from
the plundering inroads of fresh bands of pirates from the northern
peninsulas. In the end, the Danes got the mastery, and Canute,
king of Denmark, became king of England (1016). For eighteen
years he reigned in a wise and parental way.

Altogether the Danes ruled in England about a quarter of a century (from 1016 to 1042), and then the old English line was
restored in the person of Edward the Confessor.

The great benefit which resulted to England from the Danish
conquest, was the infusion of fresh blood into the veins of the
English people, who through contact with the half-Romanized
Celts, and especially through the enervating influence of a mo-

nastic church, had lost much of that bold, masculine vigor which characterized their hardy ancestors.

Settlement of the Northmen in Gaul. — The Northmen began to make piratical descents upon the coasts of Gaul before the end of the reign of Charlemagne. Tradition tells how the great king, catching sight one day of some ships of the Northmen, burst into tears as he reflected on the sufferings that he foresaw the new foe would entail upon his country.

The record of the raids of the Northmen in Gaul, and of their final settlement in the north of the country, is simply a repetition of the tale of the Danish forays and settlement in England. At last, in the year 918, Charles the Simple did exactly what Alfred the Great had done across the Channel only a very short time before. He granted the adventurous Rollo, the leader of the Northmen that had settled at Rouen, a considerable section of country in the north-west of Gaul, upon condition of homage and conversion.

In a short time the barbarians had adopted the language, the manners, and the religion of the French, and had caught much of their vivacity and impulsiveness of spirit, without, however, any loss of their own native virtues. This transformation in their manners and life we may conceive as being recorded in their transformed name — *Northmen* becoming softened into *Norman*. As has been said, they were simply changed from heathen Vikings, delighting in the wild life of sea-rover and pirate, into Christian knights, eager for pilgrimages and crusades.

CHAPTER XXXIX.

RISE OF THE PAPAL POWER.

Introduction. — In an early chapter of our book we told how Christianity as a system of beliefs and precepts took possession of the different nations and tribes of Europe. We purpose in the present chapter to tell how the Christian Church grew into a great spiritual monarchy, with the bishop of Rome as its head.

It must be borne in mind that the bishops of Rome put forth a double claim, namely, that they were the supreme head of the Church, and also the rightful, divinely appointed suzerain of all temporal princes, the "earthly king of kings." Their claim to supremacy in all spiritual matters was very generally acknowledged throughout at least the West as early as the sixth century, and continued to be respected by almost every one until the great Reformation of the sixteenth century, when the nations of Northern Europe revolted, denied the spiritual authority of the Pope, and separated themselves from the ancient ecclesiastical empire.

The papal claim to supremacy in temporal affairs was never fully and willingly allowed by the secular rulers of Europe; yet during a considerable part of the Middle Ages, particularly throughout the thirteenth century, the Pope was very generally acknowledged by kings and princes as their superior and suzerain in temporal as well as in spiritual matters.

Early Organization of the Church. — The Christian Church very early in its history became an organized body, with a regular gradation of officers, such as presbyters, bishops, metropolitans or archbishops, and patriarchs. There were at first four regular patriarchates, that is, districts superintended by patriarchs. These centred in the great cities of Rome, Constantinople,

Alexandria, and Antioch. Jerusalem was also made an honorary patriarchate.

Primacy of the Bishop of Rome. — It is maintained by some that the patriarchs at first had equal and coördinate powers ; that is, that no one of the patriarchs had preëminence or authority over the others. But others assert that the bishop of Rome from the very first was regarded as above the others in dignity and authority, and as the divinely appointed head of the visible Church on earth.

However this may be, the pontiffs of Rome began very early to *claim* supremacy over all other bishops and patriarchs. This claim of the Roman pontiffs was based on several alleged grounds, the chief of which was that the Church at Rome had been founded by St. Peter himself, the first bishop of that capital, to whom Christ had given the keys of the kingdom of heaven, and had further invested with superlative authority as a teacher and interpreter of the Word by the commission, " Feed my Sheep ; . . . feed my Lambs," thus giving into his charge the entire flock of the Church. This authority and preëminence conferred by the great Head of the Church upon Peter was held to be transmitted to his successor in the holy office.

Advantage to the Roman Bishops of the Misfortunes of the Empire. — The claims of the Roman bishops were greatly favored from the very first by the spell in which the world was held by the name and prestige of imperial Rome. Thence it had been accustomed to receive its commands in all temporal matters ; how very natural, then, that thither it should turn for command and guidance in spiritual affairs. The Roman bishops in thus occupying the geographical and political centre of the world enjoyed a great advantage over all other bishops and patriarchs.

Nor was this advantage lost when misfortune befell the imperial city. Thus the removal by Constantine the Great of the seat of government to the Bosporus (see p. 332), instead of diminishing the power and dignity of the Roman bishops, tended powerfully to promote their claims and authority. In the phrase of Dante, it "gave the Shepherd room." It left the pontiff the foremost personage of Rome.

Again, when the barbarians came, there came another occasion for the Roman bishops to increase their influence, and to raise themselves to a position of absolute supremacy throughout the West. Rome's extremity was their opportunity. Thus it will be recalled how, mainly through the intercession of Leo the Great, the fierce Attila was persuaded to turn back and leave Rome unpillaged ; and how, through the intercession of the same pious bishop, the savage Genseric was prevailed upon to spare the lives of the inhabitants of the city at the time of its sack by the Vandals (see pp. 346, 347). So when the emperors, the natural defenders of the capital, were unable to protect it, the unarmed pastor was able, through the awe and reverence inspired by his holy office, to render services that could not but result in bringing increased honor and dignity to the Roman See.

But if the misfortunes of Rome tended to the enhancement of the reputation and influence of the Roman bishops, much more did the final downfall of the capital tend to the same end. Upon the surrender of the sovereignty of the West into the hands of the emperor of the East, the bishops of Rome became the most important persons in Western Europe, and being so far removed from the court at Constantinople, gradually assumed almost imperial powers. They became the arbiters between the barbarian chiefs and the Italians, and to them were referred for decision the disputes arising between cities, states, and kings. It is easy to understand how directly and powerfully these things tended to strengthen the authority and increase the influence of the Roman See.

The Missions of Rome. — Again, the early missionary zeal of the church at Rome made her the mother of many churches, all of whom looked up to her with affectionate and grateful loyalty. Thus the Angles and Saxons, won to the faith by the missionaries of Rome, conceived a deep veneration for the Holy See and became her most devoted children. To Rome it was that they made their most frequent pilgrimages, and thither they sent their offering of " St. Peter's penny." And when the Saxons became missionaries to their pagan kinsmen of the continent, they transplanted into the heart of Germany these same feelings of filial attachment and love. Thus was Rome exalted in the eyes of the children of the churches of the West, until Gregory II. (715–731), writing the Eastern emperor, could say that to these peoples the very statue of the founder of the Roman church seemed "a god on earth."

The Iconoclasts. — The dispute about the worship of images, known in church history as the Iconoclastic controversy, which broke out in the eighth century between the Greek churches of the East and the Latin churches of the West, drew after it far-reaching consequences as respects the growing power of the Roman pontiffs.

Even long before the seventh century, the churches both in the East and in the West had become crowded with images or pictures of the apostles, saints, and martyrs, which to the ignorant classes at least were objects of adoration and worship. A strong party opposed to the use of images[1] at last arose in the East. These reformers were given the name of Iconoclasts (image-breakers).

Leo the Isaurian, who came to the throne of Constantinople in 717, was a most zealous Iconoclast. The Greek churches of the East having been cleared of images, the emperor resolved to clear also the Latin churches of the West of these symbols. To this end he issued a decree that they should not be used.

The bishop of Rome not only opposed the execution of the edict, but by the ban of excommunication cut off the emperor and all the iconoclastic churches of the East from communion with the true Catholic Church. Though images were permanently restored in the Eastern churches in 842, still by this time other causes of alienation had arisen, and the breach between the two sections of Christendom could not now be closed. The final outcome was the permanent separation, about the middle of the eleventh century, of the churches of the East from those of the West. The

---

[1] The so-called images of the Greek Church were not statues, but mosaics, or paintings. The Eastern Church has at no period sanctioned the use of sculptures in worship.

former became known as the Greek, Byzantine, or Eastern Church; the latter as the Latin, Roman, or Catholic Church.

The East was thus lost to the Roman See. But the loss was more than made good by fresh accessions of power in the West. In this quarrel with the Eastern emperors the Roman bishops cast about for an alliance with some powerful Western prince. We have already told the story of the friendship of the Carolingian kings and the Roman pontiffs, and of the favors they exchanged (see ch. xxxvii). Never did friends render themselves more serviceable to each other. The Popes made the descendants of Charles Martel kings and emperors; the grateful Frankish princes defended the Popes against all their enemies, imperial and barbarian, and dowering them with cities and provinces, laid the basis of their temporal sovereignty, which continued for more than a thousand years (until 1870).

Ecclesiastical Jurisdiction: Appeals to Rome. — Charlemagne had recognized the principle, held from early times by the Church, that ecclesiastics should be amenable only to the ecclesiastical tribunals, by freeing the whole body of the clergy from the jurisdiction of the temporal courts, in criminal as well as civil cases. Gradually the bishops acquired the right to try all cases relating to marriage, trusts, perjury, simony, or concerning widows, orphans, or crusaders, on the ground that such cases had to do with religion. Even the right to try all criminal cases was claimed on the ground that all crime is sin, and hence can properly be dealt with only by the Church. Persons convicted by the ecclesiastical tribunals were subjected to penance, imprisoned in the monasteries, or handed over to the civil authorities for punishment.

Thus by the end of the twelfth century the Church had absorbed, not only the whole criminal administration of the clergy, but in part that of the laity also.[1] Now the particular feature of this enormous extension of the jurisdiction of the Church tribunals which at present it especially concerns us to notice, is the establishment of the principle that all cases might be appealed or cited

[1] Hallam, *Middle Ages*, ch. vii.

from the courts of the bishops and archbishops of the different European countries to the Papal See, which thus became the court of last resort in all cases affecting ecclesiastics or concerning religion. The Pope thus came to be regarded as the fountain of justice, and, in theory at least, the supreme judge of Christendom, while emperors and kings and all civil magistrates bore the sword simply as his ministers to carry into effect his sentences and decrees.

The Papacy and the Empire. — We must now speak of the relation of the Popes to the Emperors. About the middle of the tenth century Otto the Great of Germany, like a second Charlemagne, restored once more the fallen Imperial power, which now became known as the Holy Roman Empire, the heads of which from this on were the German kings (see p. 502). Here now were two world-powers, the Empire and the Papacy, whose claims and ambitions were practically antagonistic and irreconcilable.

There were three different theories of the divinely constituted relation of the "World-King" and the "World-Priest." The first was that Pope and Emperor were each independently commissioned by God, the first to rule the spirits of men, the second to rule their bodies. Each reigning thus by original divine right, neither is set above the other, but both are to coöperate and to help each other. The special duty of the temporal power is to maintain order in the world and to be the protector of the Church.

The second theory, the one held by the Imperial party, was that the Emperor was superior to the Pope. Arguments from Scripture and from the transactions of history were not wanting to support this view of the relation of the two world-powers. Thus Christ's payment of tribute money was cited as proof that he regarded the temporal power as superior to the spiritual; and again, his submission to the jurisdiction of the Roman tribunal was held to be a recognition on his part of the supremacy of the civil authority. Further, the gifts of Pepin and Charlemagne to the Roman See made the Popes, it was maintained, the vassals of the Emperors.

The third theory, the one held by the Papal party, maintained that the ordained relation of the two powers was the subordination of the temporal to the spiritual authority. This view was maintained by such texts of Scripture as these : " But he that is spiritual judgeth all things, yet he himself is judged of no man ; "[1] "See, I have this day set thee over the nations and over the kingdoms, to root out and to pull down, and to destroy and to throw down, to build and to plant."[2] The conception was further illustrated by such comparisons as the following. As God has set in the heavens two lights, the sun and the moon, so has he established on earth two powers, the spiritual and the temporal ; but as the moon is inferior to the sun and receives its light from it, so is the Emperor inferior to the Pope and receives all power from him. Again, the two authorities were likened to the soul and body ; as the former rules over the latter, so is it ordered that the spiritual power shall rule over and subject the temporal.

The first theory was the impracticable dream of lofty souls who forgot that men are human. Christendom was virtually divided into two hostile camps, the members of which were respectively supporters of the Imperial and the Papal theory. The most interesting and instructive chapters of mediæval history after the tenth century are those that record the struggles between Pope and Emperor, springing from their efforts to reduce to practice these irreconcilable theories.[3]

[1] 1 Cor. ii. 15.   [2] Jer. i. 10.

[3] For a most admirable presentation of this whole subject, consult Bryce's *The Holy Roman Empire*.

CHAPTER XL.

FEUDALISM AND CHIVALRY.

1. FEUDALISM.

Feudalism defined. — Feudalism is the name given to a special form of society and government, based upon a peculiar military tenure of land which prevailed in Europe during the latter half of the Middle Ages, attaining, however, its most perfect development in the eleventh, twelfth, and thirteenth centuries.

A feudal estate, which might embrace a few acres or an entire province, was called a *fief*, or *feud*, whence the term Feudalism. The person granting a fief was called the *suzerain*, *liege*, or *lord ;* the one receiving it, his *vassal*, *liegeman*, or *retainer*.

The Ideal System. — The few definitions given above will render intelligible the following explanation of the theory of the Feudal System.

In theory, all the soil of the country was held by the king as a fief from God (in practice, the king's title was his good sword), granted on conditions of fealty to right and justice. Should the king be unjust or wicked, he forfeited the kingdom, and it might be taken from him and given to another. According to Papal theorists it was the Pópe who, as God's vicar on earth, had the right to pronounce judgment against a king, depose him, and put another in his place.

In the same way that the king received his fief from God, so he might grant it out in parcels to his chief men, they, in return for it, promising, in general, to be faithful to him as their lord, and tô serve and aid him. Should these men, now vassals, be in any way untrue to their engagement, they forfeited their fiefs, and these might be resumed by their suzerain and bestowed upon others.

In like manner these immediate vassals of the king or suzerain might parcel out their domains in smaller tracts to others, on the same conditions as those upon which they had themselves received theirs ; and so on down through any number of stages.

We have thus far dealt only with the soil of a country. We must next notice what disposition was made of the people under this system.

The king in receiving his fief was intrusted with sovereignty over all persons living upon it : he became their commander, their law-maker, and their judge — in a word, their absolute and irresponsible ruler.   Then, when he parcelled out his fief among his great men, he invested them, within the limits of the fiefs granted, with all his own sovereign rights.   Each vassal became a virtual sovereign in his own domain.   And when these great vassals divided their fiefs and granted them to others, they in turn invested their vassals with those powers of sovereignty with which they themselves had been clothed.   Thus every holder of a fief became " monarch of all he surveyed."

To illustrate the workings of the system, we will suppose the king or suzerain to be in need of an army.   He calls upon his own immediate vassals for aid ; these in turn call upon their vassals ; and so the order runs down through the various ranks of retainers. The retainers in the lowest rank rally around their respective lords, who, with their bands, gather about their lords, and so on up through the rising tiers of the system, until the immediate vassals of the suzerain, or chief lord, present themselves before him with their graduated trains of followers.   The array constitutes a feudal army, — a splendidly organized body in theory, but in fact an extremely poor instrument for warfare.

Such was the ideal feudal state. It is needless to say that the ideal was never perfectly realized. The system simply made more or less distant approaches to it in the several European countries.

Roman and Teutonic Elements in the System. — Like many another institution that grew up on the conquered soil of the empire, Feudalism was of a composite character; that is, it contained both Roman and Teutonic elements. The spirit of the institution was barbarian, but the form was classical. We might illustrate the idea we are trying to convey, by referring to the mediæval papal church. It, while Hebrew in spirit, was Roman in form. It had shaped itself upon the model of the empire, and was thoroughly imperial in its organization. Thus was it with Feudalism. Beneath the Roman garb it assumed, beat a German life.

The Ceremony of Homage. — A fief was conferred by a very solemn and peculiar ceremony called homage. The person about to become a vassal, kneeling with uncovered head, placed his hands in those of his future lord, and solemnly vowed to be henceforth his man (Latin *homo*, whence " homage "), and to serve him faithfully even with his life. This part of the ceremony, sealed with a kiss, was what properly constituted the ceremony of homage. It was accompanied by an oath of fealty, and the whole was concluded by the act of investiture, whereby the lord put his vassal in actual possession of the land, or by placing in his hand a clod of earth or a twig, symbolized the delivery to him of the estate for which he had just now done homage and sworn fealty.

The Relations of Lord and Vassal. — In general terms the duty of the vassal was service; that of the lord, protection. The most honorable service required of the vassal, and the one most willingly rendered in a martial age, was military aid. The liegeman must always be ready to follow his lord upon his military expeditions; he must defend his lord in battle; if he should be unhorsed, must give him his own animal; and, if he should be made a prisoner, must offer himself as a hostage for his release.

Among other incidents attaching to a fief were *escheat, for-*

feiture, and *aids*. By Escheat was meant the falling back of the fief into the hands of the lord through failure of heirs. If the fief lapsed through disloyalty or other misdemeanor on the part of the vassal, this was known as Forfeiture. Aids were sums of money which the lord had a right to demand, in order to defray the expense of knighting his eldest son, of marrying his eldest daughter, or for ransoming his own person in case of captivity.

The chief return that the lord was bound to make to the vassal as a compensation for these various services, was counsel and protection — by no means a small return in an age of turmoil and insecurity.

Development of the Feudal System. — After the death of Charlemagne and the partition of his great empire among his feeble successors, it seemed as though the world was again falling back into chaos. The bonds of society seemed entirely broken. The strong oppressed the weak ; the nobles became highway-robbers and marauders.

It was this distracted state of things that, during the ninth and tenth centuries, caused the rapid development of the Feudal System. It was the only form of social organization, the only form of government that it was practicable to maintain in that rude, transitional age. All classes of society, therefore, hastened to enter the system, in order to secure the protection which it alone could afford. Kings, princes, and wealthy persons who had large landed possessions which they had never parcelled out as fiefs, were now led to do so, that their estates might be held by tenants bound to protect them by all the sacred obligations of homage and fealty. Again, the smaller proprietors who held their estates by allodial tenure voluntarily surrendered them into the hands of some neighboring lord, and then received them again from him as fiefs, that they might claim protection as vassals. They deemed this better than being robbed of their property altogether. Thus it came that almost all the allodial lands of France, Germany, Italy, and Northern Spain were, during the ninth, tenth, and eleventh centuries, converted into feudal estates, or fiefs.

Moreover, for like reasons and in like manner, churches, monasteries, and cities became members of the Feudal System. They granted out their vast possessions as fiefs, and thus became suzerains and lords. Bishops and abbots became the heads of great bands of retainers, and led military expeditions, like temporal chiefs. On the other hand, these same monasteries and towns, as a means of security and protection, did homage to some powerful lord, and thus came in vassalage to him.

In this way were Church and State, all classes of society from the wealthiest suzerain to the humblest tenant, bound together by feudal ties. Everything was impressed with the stamp of Feudalism.

Classes of Feudal Society. — Besides the nobility, or the landed class, there were under the Feudal System three other classes, namely, *freemen, serfs* or *villeins,* and *slaves.* These lower classes made up the great bulk of the population of a feudal state. The freemen were the inhabitants of chartered towns, and in some countries the yeomanry, or small farmers, who did not hold their lands by a regular feudal tenure. The serfs, or villeins, were the laborers who cultivated the ground. The peculiarity of their condition was that they were not allowed to move from the estate where they lived, and when the land was sold they passed with it just like any fixture. The slaves constituted a still lower class made up of captives in war or of persons condemned to bondage as a penalty for crime. These chattel slaves, however, almost disappeared before the thirteenth century, being converted into the lowest order of serfs, which was a step toward freedom.

Castles of the Nobles. — The lawless and violent character of the times during which Feudalism prevailed is well shown by the nature of the residences of the nobles. These were strong stone fortresses, usually perched upon some rocky eminence, and defended by moats and towers. France, Germany, Italy, Northern Spain, England, and Scotland, in which countries the Feudal System became most thoroughly developed, fairly bristled with these fortified residences of the nobility. One of the most striking and picturesque features of the scenery of many districts of Europe at the present time is the ivy-mantled towers and walls of these feudal castles, now falling into ruins.

Causes of the Decay of Feudalism. — Chief among the various causes which undermined and at length overthrew Feudalism, were the hostility to the system of the kings and the common people, the Crusades, the revolt of the cities, and the introduction of fire-arms in the art of war.

FEUDAL CASTLE AT ROUEN.

The Feudal System was hated and opposed by both the royal power and the people. Kings opposed it and sought to break it down, because it left them only the semblance of power. The people always hated it for the reason that under it they were re-garded as of less value than the game in the lord's hunting-park.

The Crusades, or Holy Wars, that agitated all Europe during the twelfth and thirteenth centuries did much to weaken the power of the nobles; for in order to raise money for their expeditions, they frequently sold or mortgaged their estates, and in this way power and influence passed into the hands of the kings or of the wealthy merchants of the cities. Many of the great nobles also perished in battle with the Infidels, and their lands escheated to their suzerain, whose domains were thus augmented.

The growth of the towns also tended to the same end. As they increased in wealth and influence, they became able to resist the exactions and tyranny of the lord in whose fief they happened to be, and eventually were able to secede, as it were, from his authority, and to make of themselves little republics (see p. 464).

Again, the use of gunpowder in war hastened the downfall of Feudalism, by rendering the yeoman foot-soldier equal to the armor-clad knight. "It made all men of the same height," as Carlyle puts it.

But it is to be noted that, though Feudalism as a system of government virtually disappeared during the latter part of the mediæval age, it still continued to exist as a social organization. The nobles lost their power and authority as rulers and magistrates, as petty sovereigns, but retained generally their titles, privileges, and social distinctions.

Defects of the Feudal System. — Feudalism was perhaps the best form of social organization that it was possible to maintain in Europe during the mediæval period ; yet it had many and serious defects, which rendered it very far from being a perfect social or political system. Among its chief faults may be pointed out the two following. First, it rendered impossible the formation of strong national governments. Every country was divided and subdivided into a vast number of practically independent principalities. Thus, in the tenth century France was partitioned among nearly two hundred overlords, all exercising equal and coördinate powers of sovereignty. The enormous estates of these great lords were again divided into about 70,000 smaller fiefs.

In theory, as we have seen, the holders of these petty estates were bound to serve and obey their overlords, and these great nobles were in turn the sworn vassals of the French king. But many of these lords were richer and stronger than the king himself, and if they chose to cast off their allegiance to him, he found it impossible to reduce them to obedience.

A second evil of the institution was its exclusiveness. It was, in theory, only the person of noble birth that could become the holder of a fief. The feudal lords constituted a proud and oppressive aristocracy. It was only as the lower classes in the different countries gradually wrested from the feudal nobility their special and unfair privileges, that a better form of society arose, and civilization began to make more rapid progress.

Good Results of the System. — The most noteworthy of the good results springing from the Feudal System was the development among its privileged members of that individualism, that love of personal independence, which we have seen to be a marked trait of the Teutonic character (see p. 369). Turbulent, violent, and refractory as was the feudal aristocracy of Europe, it performed the grand service of keeping alive during the later mediæval period the spirit of liberty. It prevented Royalty from becoming as despotic as it would otherwise have become. Thus in England, for instance, the feudal lords held such tyrannical rulers as King John in check, until such time as the yeomen and the burghers were bold enough and strong enough alone to resist their despotically inclined sovereigns. In France, where, unfortunately, the power of the feudal nobles was broken too soon, — before the common people, the Third Estate, were prepared to take up the struggle for liberty, — the result was the growth of that autocratic, despotic Royalty which led the French people to the Revolution and the Reign of Terror.

Another of the good effects of Feudalism was the impulse it gave to certain forms of polite literature. Just as learning and philosophy were fostered by the seclusion of the cloister, so were poetry and romance fostered by the open and joyous hospitalities of the baronial hall. The castle door was always open to the wandering singer and story-teller, and it was amidst the scenes of festivity within that the ballads and romances of mediæval minstrelsy and literature had their birth.

Still another service which Feudalism rendered to civilization was the development within the baronial castle of those ideas and sentiments — among others, a nice sense of honor and an exalted consideration for the female sex — which found their noblest expression in Chivalry, of which institution and its good effects upon the social life of Europe we shall now proceed to speak.

2. CHIVALRY.

Chivalry defined: Origin of the Institution. — Chivalry has been aptly defined as the "Flower of Feudalism." It was a military institution, or order, the members of which, called *knights*, were pledged to the protection of the church, and to the defence of the weak and the oppressed. Although the germs of the system may be found in society before the age of Charlemagne, still Chivalry did not assume its distinctive character until the eleventh century, and died out during the fifteenth.

Chivalry seems to have had France for its cradle. That

A KNIGHT IN FULL ARMOR.
(After Alphonse de Neuville.)

country at least was its true home. There it was that it exhibited its most complete and romantic development. Yet its influence was felt everywhere and in everything. It colored all the events and enterprises of the latter half of the Middle Ages. The literature of the period is instinct with its spirit. The Crusades, or Holy Wars, the greatest undertakings of the mediæval ages, were predominantly enterprises of the Christian chivalry of Europe.

Training of the Knight. — When Chivalry had once become established, all the sons of the nobility, save such as were to enter the holy orders of the Church, were set apart and disciplined for its service. The sons of the poorer nobles were usually placed in the

family of some superior lord of renown and wealth, whose castle became a sort of school, where they were trained in the duties and exercises of knighthood.

This education began at the early age of seven, the youth bearing the name of page or varlet until he attained the age of fourteen, when he acquired the title of squire or esquire. At the age of twenty-

CONFERRING KNIGHTHOOD ON THE FIELD OF BATTLE.

one the squire became a knight, being then introduced to the order of knighthood by a peculiar and impressive service. After a long fast and vigil, the candidate listened to a lengthy sermon on his duties as a knight. Then kneeling, as in the feudal ceremony of homage, before the lord conducting the services, he vowed to defend religion and the ladies, to succor the distressed, and ever to be faithful to his companion knights. His arms were now presented to him, and his sword girded on, when the lord, striking him with the flat of his sword on the shoulders or the neck, said, " In the name of God, of St. Michael, and of St. George, I dub thee knight : be brave, bold, and loyal."

Sometimes knighthood was conferred with less ceremony upon the battle-field, as the reward of signal bravery or address.

The Tournament. — The tournament was the favorite amusement of the age of Chivalry. It was a mimic battle between two companies of noble knights, armed usually with pointless swords or

A TOURNAMENT.

blunted lances. In the universal esteem in which the participants were held, it reminds us of the Sacred Games of the Greeks ; while in the fierce and sanguinary character it sometimes assumed, especially before it was brought fully under the spirit of Chivalry, it recalls the gladiatorial combats of the Roman amphitheatre.

Decline of Chivalry. — The fifteenth century was the evening of Chivalry. The decline of the system resulted from the operation of the same causes that effected the overthrow of Feudalism. The changes in the mode of warfare which helped to do away with the feudal baron and his mail-clad retainers, likewise tended to destroy knight-errantry. And then as civilization advanced, new feelings and sentiments began to claim the attention, and to work upon the imagination of men. Governments, too, became more regular, and the increased order and security of society rendered less needful the services of the gallant knight in behalf of distressed maidens.

Influence of Chivalry. — The system of Chivalry had many vices, chief among which were its exclusive, aristocratic tendencies. An indignant writer declares that " it is not probable that the knights supposed they could be guilty of injustice to the lower classes." These were regarded with indifference or contempt, and considered as destitute of any claims upon those of noble birth as were beasts of burden or the game of the chase. It is always the young and beautiful lady of *gentle* birth whose wrongs the valiant knight is risking his life to avenge, always the smiles of the "queen of love and beauty" for which he is splintering his lance in the fierce tournament. The fostering of this aristocratic spirit was one of the most serious faults of Chivalry.

But to speak of the beneficial, refining influences of Chivalry, we should say that it undoubtedly contributed powerfully to lift that sentiment of respect for the gentler sex that characterized all the Northern nations, into that reverence for womanhood which forms one of the distinguishing characteristics of the present age.

Again, Chivalry did much towards producing that type of manhood among us which we rightly think to surpass any ever formed under the influences of antiquity. Just as Christianity gave to the world an ideal manhood which it was to strive to realize, so did Chivalry hold up an ideal to which men were to conform their lives. Men, indeed, have never perfectly realized either the ideal of Christianity or that of Chivalry; but the influence which these two ideals have had in shaping and giving character to the lives of men cannot be overestimated. Together, through the enthusiasm and effort awakened for their realization, they produced a new type of manhood, which we indicate by the phrase "a knightly and Christian character."

LANDING IN ENGLAND OF WILLIAM OF NORMANDY. (From the Bayeux Tapestry.)

CHAPTER XLI.

THE NORMAN CONQUEST OF ENGLAND.

Introductory. — The history of the Normans — the name, it will be recalled, of the transformed Scandinavians who settled in Northern Gaul (see p. 413) — is simply a continuation of the story of the Northmen. The most important of the enterprises of the Normans, and one followed by consequences of the greatest magnitude not only to the conquered people, but indirectly to the world, was their conquest of England.[1]

Events leading up to the Conquest. — In the year 1066 Edward the Confessor died, in whose person, it will be recalled, the old English line was restored after the Danish usurpation (see p. 412). Immediately the Witan, that is, the assembly of the chief men

---

[1] Not long before the Normans conquered England, they succeeded in gaining a foothold in the south of Italy, where they established a sort of republic, which ultimately included the island of Sicily. The fourth president of the commonwealth was the celebrated Robert Guiscard (d. 1085), who spread the renown of the Norman name throughout the Mediterranean lands. This Norman state, converted finally into a kingdom, lasted until late in the twelfth century (1194).

of the nation, in accordance with the dying wish of the king, chose Harold, Earl of the West Saxons, son of the famous Godwin, and the best and strongest man in all England, to be his successor.

When the news of the action of the Witan and of Harold's acceptance of the English crown was carried across the channel to William, Duke of Normandy, he was really or feignedly transported with rage. He declared that Edward, who was his cousin, had during his lifetime promised the throne to him, and that Harold had assented to this, and by solemn oath engaged to sustain him. He now demanded of Harold that he surrender to him the usurped throne, threatening the immediate invasion of the island in case he refused. King Harold answered the demand by expelling from the country the Normans who had followed Edward into the kingdom, and by collecting fleets and armies for the defence of his dominions.

While Harold was watching the southern coasts against the Normans, a Danish host appeared in the north, led by Tostig, the traitor brother of the English king, and Harold Hardrada, king of Norway. The English army in that quarter, attempting to withstand the invaders, was cut to pieces; and the important city of York fell into the hands of the Northmen. As soon as news of this disaster was borne to King Harold in the south, he instantly marched northward with his army, and at Stamford Bridge met the invaders, and there gained a decisive victory over them.

The Battle of Hastings (1066). — The festivities that followed the victory of Stamford Bridge were not yet ended, when a messenger from the south brought to Harold intelligence of the landing of the Normans. Hurrying southward with his army, Harold came face to face with the forces of William at Senlac, a short distance from the port of Hastings.

The battle soon opened — the battle that was to determine the fate of England. It was begun by a horseman riding out from the Norman lines and advancing alone toward the English army, tossing up his sword and skilfully catching it as it fell, and singing all the while the stirring battle-song of Charlemagne and Roland (see p. 405). The English watched with astonishment this exhibition of "careless dexterity," and if they did not contrast the vivacity and nimbleness of the Norman foe with their own heavy and clumsy manners, others at least have not failed to do so for them.

The battle once joined, the conflict was long and terrific. The day finally went against the English. Harold fell, pierced through the eye by an arrow; and William was master of the field (1066).

The conqueror now marched upon London, and at Westminster Abbey, on Christmas Day, 1066, was crowned and anointed king of England.

BATTLE OF HASTINGS. (From the Bayeux Tapestry.)

The Distribution of the Land. — Almost the first act of William after he had established his power in England was to fulfil his promise to the nobles who had aided him in his enterprise, by distributing among them the unredeemed[1] estates of the English who had fought at Hastings in defence of their king and country. Large as was the number of these confiscated estates, there would have been a lack of land to satisfy all, had not subsequent uprisings against the authority of William afforded him an opportunity

---

[1] "When the lands of all those who had fought for Harold were confiscated, those who were willing to acknowledge William were allowed to redeem theirs, either paying money at once, or giving hostages for the payment." — Stubbs, *Const. Hist.* I. 258.

to confiscate almost all the soil of England as forfeited by trea-son.

Profiting by the lesson taught by the wretched condition of France, which country was kept in a state of constant turmoil by a host of feudal chiefs and lords many of whom were almost or quite as powerful as the king himself, William took care that in the distribution no feudatory should receive an entire shire, save in two or three exceptional cases. To the great lord to whom he must needs give a large fief, he granted, not a continuous tract of land, but several estates, or manors, scattered in different parts of the country, in order that there might be no dangerous concentration of property or power in the hands of the vassal. He also re-quired of all the sub-vassals of the realm, in addition to their oath of allegiance to their own lord, an oath of fealty to the crown. This was a most important modification of feudal custom. On the Continent, the sub-tenant swore allegiance to his own lord simply, and was in duty bound to aid him in all his wars, even in one against the sovereign. But the oath of allegiance to himself exacted by William of all holders of fiefs, just reversed this, and made it the first duty of the sub-vassal, even in the case of a war between his lord and the king, to follow and obey the king. Furthermore, William denied to his feudatories the right of coin-ing money or making laws; and by other wise restrictions upon their power, he saved England from those endless contentions and petty wars that were distracting almost every other country of Europe.

The Norman Successors of the Conqueror. — For nearly three-quarters of a century after the death of William the Conqueror, England was ruled by Norman kings.[1] The latter part of this period was a troublous time. The succession to the crown com-ing into dispute, civil war broke out. The result of the contention

[1] William II., known as Rufus "the Red" (1087–1100); Henry I., sur-named Beauclerc, "the good scholar" (1100–1135); and Stephen of Blois (1135–1154). William and Henry were sons, and Stephen a grandson, of the conqueror.

was a decline in the royal power, and the ascendency of the Norman barons, who for a time made England the scene of the same feudal anarchy that prevailed at this time upon the Continent. Finally, in 1154, the Norman dynasty gave place to that of the Plantagenets. Under Henry II., the first king of the new house, and an energetic and strong ruler, the barons were again brought into proper subjection to the crown, and many castles which had been built without royal permission during the preceding anarchical period, and some of which at least were little better than robbers' dens, were destroyed.

Advantages to England of the Norman Conquest. — The most important and noteworthy result of the Norman Conquest of England, was the establishment in the island of a strong centralized government. England now for the first time became a real kingdom.

A second result of the Conquest was the founding of a new feudal aristocracy. The Saxon thane was displaced by the Norman baron.

A third result was the bringing of England into more intimate relations with the nations of continental Europe, by which means her advance in art, science, and general culture was greatly promoted.

CRUSADERS ON THE MARCH.

CHAPTER XLII.

THE CRUSADES.

(1096–1272.)

I. INTRODUCTORY: CAUSES OF THE CRUSADES.

General Statement. — The Crusades were great military expeditions undertaken by the Christian nations of Europe for the purpose of rescuing from the hands of the Mohammedans the holy places of Palestine. They were eight in number, the first four being sometimes called the Principal Crusades, and the remaining four the Minor Crusades. Besides these there were a Children's Crusade, and several other expeditions, which, being insignificant in numbers or results, are not usually enumerated.

Causes of the Crusades. — Among the early Christians it was thought a pious and meritorious act to undertake a journey to some sacred place. Especially was it thought that a pilgrimage to the land that had been trod by the feet of the Saviour of the world, to the Holy City that had witnessed his martyrdom, was a peculiarly pious undertaking, and one which secured for the pilgrim the special favor and blessing of Heaven.

The Saracen caliphs, for the four centuries and more that they held possession of Palestine, pursued usually an enlightened policy towards the pilgrims, even encouraging pilgrimages as a source of revenue. But in the eleventh century the Seljukian Turks, a prominent Tartar tribe, zealous proselytes of Islam, wrested from the caliphs almost all their Asiatic possessions. The Christians were not long in realizing that power had fallen into new hands. Pilgrims were insulted and persecuted in every way. The churches in Jerusalem were, in some cases, destroyed or turned into stables.

Now, if it were a meritorious thing to make a pilgrimage to the Holy Sepulchre, much more would it be a pious act to rescue the sacred spot from the profanation of infidels. This was the conviction that changed the pilgrim into a warrior, — this the sentiment that for two centuries and more stirred the Christian world to its profoundest depths, and cast the population of Europe in wave after wave upon Asia.

Although this religious feeling was the principal cause of the Crusades, still there was another concurring cause which must not be overlooked. This was the restless, adventurous spirit of the Teutonic peoples of Europe, who had not as yet outgrown their barbarian instincts. The feudal knights and lords, just now animated by the rising spirit of chivalry, were very ready to enlist in an undertaking so consonant with their martial feelings and their new vows of knighthood.

Preaching of Peter the Hermit. — One inciting cause of the First Crusade was the preaching of Peter the Hermit, a native of Picardy, in France. Having been commissioned by Pope Urban II. to preach a crusade, the Hermit traversed the lands of France, addressing everywhere, in the church, in the street, and in the open field, the crowds that flocked about him, moving all hearts with sympathy or firing them with indignation, as he recited the sufferings of their brethren at the hands of the infidels, or pictured the profanation of the holy places, polluted by the presence and insults of the unbelievers.

The Councils of Placentia and Clermont. — While Peter the Hermit had been arousing the warriors of the West, the Turks had been making constant advances in the East, and were now threatening Constantinople itself. The Greek emperor (Alexius Comnenus) sent urgent letters to the Pope, asking for aid against the infidels, representing that, unless assistance was extended immediately, the capital with all its holy relics must soon fall into the hands of the barbarians.

Urban called a great council of the Church at Placentia, in Italy, to consider the appeal (1095), but nothing was effected. Later in the same year a new council was convened at Clermont, in France, Urban purposely fixing the place of meeting among the warm-tempered and martial Franks. The Pope himself was one of the chief speakers. He was naturally eloquent, so that the man, the cause, and the occasion all conspired to achieve one of the greatest triumphs of human oratory. He pictured the humiliation and misery of the provinces of Asia ; the profanation of the places made sacred by the presence and footsteps of the Son of God ; and then he detailed the conquests of the Turks, until now, with all Asia Minor in their possession, they were threatening Europe from the shores of the Hellespont. "When Jesus Christ summons you to his defence," exclaimed the eloquent pontiff, " let no base affection detain you in your homes ; whoever will abandon his house, or his father, or his mother, or his wife, or his children, or his inheritance, for the sake of my name, shall be recompensed a hundred-fold, and possess life eternal."

Here the enthusiasm of the vast assembly burst through every restraint. With one voice they cried, *Dieu le volt ! Dieu le volt !* "It is the will of God ! It is the will of God ! " Thousands immediately affixed the cross to their garments,[1] as a pledge of

[1] Hence the name *Crusade* given to the Holy Wars, from old French *crois*, cross.

their sacred engagement to go forth to the rescue of the Holy Sepulchre. The fifteenth day of August of the following year was set for the departure of the expedition.

2. The First Crusade (1096–1099).

Mustering of the Crusaders. — All Western Europe now rang with the cry, " He who will not take up his cross and follow me, is not worthy of me." The contagion of enthusiasm seized all classes ; for while the religious feelings of the age had been specially appealed to, all the various sentiments of ambition, chivalry, love of license, had also been skilfully enlisted on the side of the undertaking. The council of Clermont had declared Europe to be in a state of peace, and pronounced anathemas against any one who should invade the possessions of a prince engaged in the holy war. By further edicts of the assembly, the debtor was released from meeting his obligations while a soldier of the Cross, and during this period the interest on his debt was to cease ; and the criminal, as soon as he assumed the badge of the crusader, was by that act instantly absolved from all his sins of whatever nature.

Under such inducements princes and nobles, bishops and priests, monks and anchorites, saints and sinners, rich and poor, hastened to enroll themselves beneath the consecrated banner. " Europe," says Michaud, " appeared to be a land of exile, which every one was eager to quit."

The Vanguard. — Before the regular armies of the crusaders were ready to move, those who had gathered about Peter the Hermit, becoming impatient of delay, urged him to place himself at their head and lead them at once to the Holy Land. Dividing command of the mixed multitudes with a poor knight, called Walter the Penniless, and followed by a throng of about 80,000 persons, among whom were many women and children, the Hermit set out for Constantinople by the overland route through Germany and Hungary. Thousands of the crusaders fell in battle with the natives of the countries through which they marched, and thousands more perished miserably of hunger and exposure. Those that crossed the Bosporus were surprised by the Turks, and almost all were slaughtered. Thus perished the forlorn hope of the First Crusade.

March of the Main Body. — Meanwhile there were gathering in the West disciplined armies composed of men worthy to be champions of the holy cause they had espoused. Godfrey of Bouillon, Duke of Lorraine, and Tancred, " the mirror of knighthood," were among the most noted of the leaders of the different divisions of the army. The expedition numbered about 300,000 men, of whom many were full-mailed knights.

The crusaders traversed Europe by different routes and reassembled at Constantinople. Crossing the Bosporus, they first captured Nicæa, the Turkish capital, in Bithynia, and then set out across Asia Minor for Syria. The line of their dreary march between Nicæa and Antioch was whitened with the bones of nearly one-half their number. Arriving at Antioch, the survivors captured that place, and then, after some delays, pushed on towards Jerusalem.

When at length the Holy City burst upon their view, a perfect delirium of joy seized the crusaders. They embraced one another with tears of joy, and even embraced and kissed the ground on which they stood. As they passed on, they took off their shoes, and marched with uncovered head and bare feet, singing the words of the prophet : " Jerusalem, lift up thine eyes, and behold the liberator who comes to break thy chains."

The first assault made by the Christians upon the walls of the city was repulsed ; but the second was successful, and the city was in the hands of the crusaders (1099). A terrible slaughter of the infidels now took place. For seven days the carnage went on, at the end of which time scarcely any of the Moslem faith were left alive. The Christians took possession of the houses and property of the infidels, each soldier having a right to that which he had first seized and placed his mark upon.

Founding of the Latin Kingdom of Jerusalem. — No sooner

was Jerusalem in the hands of the crusaders than they set themselves to the task of organizing a government for the city and country they had conquered. The government which they established was a sort of feudal league, known as the Latin Kingdom of Jerusalem. At its head was placed Godfrey of Bouillon, the most valiant and devoted of the crusader knights. The prince refused the title and vestments of royalty, declaring that he would never wear a crown of gold in the city where his Lord and Master had worn a crown of thorns. The only title he would accept was that of " Defender of the Holy Sepulchre."

Many of the crusaders, considering their vows fulfilled, now set out on their return to their homes, some making their way back by sea and some by land. Godfrey, Tancred, and a few hundred other knights, were all that stayed behind to maintain the conquests that had been made, and to act as guardians of the holy places.

3. The Second Crusade (1147–1149).

Origin of the Religious Orders of Knighthood. — In the interval between the First and the Second Crusade, the two famed religious military orders, known as the Hospitallers and the Templars,[1] were formed. A little later, during the Third Crusade, still another fraternity, known as the Teutonic Knights was established. The objects of all the orders were the care of the sick and wounded crusaders, the entertainment of Christian pilgrims, the guarding of the holy places, and ceaseless battling for the Cross. These fraternities soon acquired a military fame that was spread throughout the Christian world. They were joined by many of the most illustrious knights of the West, and through the gifts of

[1] The Hospitallers, or Knights of St. John, took their name from the fact that the organization was first formed among the monks of the Hospital of St. John, at Jerusalem; while the Templars, or Knights of the Temple, were so called on account of one of the buildings of the brotherhood occupying the site of Solomon's Temple.

the pious acquired great wealth, and became possessed of numerous estates and castles in Europe as well as in Asia.

Preaching of St. Bernard; Failure of the Crusade. — In the year 1146, the city of Edessa, the bulwark of the Latin Kingdom of Jerusalem on the side towards Mesopotamia, was taken by the Turks, and the entire population was slaughtered, or sold into slavery. This disaster threw the entire West into a state of the greatest alarm, lest the little Christian state, established at such cost of tears and suffering, should be completely overwhelmed, and all the holy places should again fall into the hands of the infidels.

The scenes that marked the opening of the First Crusade were now repeated in all the countries of the West. St. Bernard, an eloquent monk, was the second Peter the Hermit, who went everywhere, arousing the warriors of the Cross to the defence of the birthplace of their religion. The contagion of the holy enthusiasm seized not only barons, knights, and the common people, which classes alone participated in the First Crusade, but kings and emperors were now infected with the sacred frenzy. Conrad III., emperor of Germany, was persuaded to leave the affairs of his distracted empire in the hands of God, and consecrate himself to the defence of the sepulchre of Christ. Louis VII., king of France, was led to undertake the crusade through remorse for an act of great cruelty that he had perpetrated upon some of his revolted subjects.[1]

The strength of both the French and the German division of the expedition was wasted in Asia Minor, and the crusade accomplished nothing.

4. The Third Crusade (1189–1192).

The Three Leaders. — The Third Crusade was caused by the capture of Jerusalem (1187) by Saladin, the sultan of Egypt.

---

[1] The act which troubled the king's conscience was the burning of thirteen hundred people in a church, whither they had fled for refuge.

Three of the great sovereigns of Europe, Frederick Barbarossa of Germany, Philip Augustus of France, and Richard I. of England, assumed the Cross, and set out, each at the head of a large army, for the recovery of the Holy City.

The English king, Richard, afterwards given the title of *Cœur de Lion*, the "Lion-hearted," in memory of his heroic exploits in Palestine, was the central figure among the Christian knights of this crusade. He raised money for the enterprise by the persecution and robbery of the Jews; by the imposition of an unusual tax upon all classes; and by the sale of offices, dignities, and the royal lands. When some one expostulated with him on the means employed to raise money, he declared that "he would sell the city of London, if he could find a purchaser."

Death of Frederick Barbarossa: Siege of Acre. — The German army, attempting the overland route, was consumed in Asia Minor by the hardships of the march and the swords of the Turks. The Emperor Frederick, according to the most probable accounts, was drowned while crossing a swollen stream, and the most of the survivors of his army, disheartened by the loss of their leader, returned to Germany.

The English and French kings finally mustered their forces beneath the walls of Acre, which city the Christians were then besieging. It is estimated that 600,000 men were engaged in the investment of the place. After one of the longest and most costly sieges they ever carried on in Asia, the crusaders at last forced the place to capitulate, in spite of all the efforts of Saladin to render the garrison relief.

Richard and Saladin. — The knightly adventures and chivalrous exploits which mark the career of Richard in the Holy Land read like a romance. Nor was the chief of the Mohammedans, the renowned Saladin, lacking in any of those knightly virtues with which the writers of the time invested the character of the English hero. At one time, when Richard was sick with a fever, Saladin, knowing that he was poorly supplied with delicacies, sent him a gift of the choicest fruits of the land. And on another occasion, Richard's horse having been killed in battle, the sultan caused a fine Arabian steed to be led to the Christian camp as a present for his rival.

For two years did Richard the Lion-hearted vainly contend in almost daily combat with his generous antagonist for the posses-sion of the tomb of Christ. He finally concluded a truce of three years and eight months with Saladin, which provided that the Christians during that period should have free access to the holy places, and remain in undisturbed possession of the coast from Jaffa to Tyre.

5. THE FOURTH CRUSADE (1202–1204).

Capture of Constantinople by the Latins. — None of the Cru-sades after the Third effected much in the Holy Land ; either their force was spent before reaching it, or they were diverted from their purpose by different objects and ambitions.

The crusaders of the Fourth expedition captured Constantino-ple instead of Jerusalem. The circumstances were these : A usur-per had seized upon the Byzantine throne. The rightful claimant, Alexius, besought the aid of the Frankish warriors to regain the sceptre. The Christian knights listened favorably to his appeals. The Venetians, in consideration of a share of the conquests that might be made, also joined their forces to those of the crusaders. Constantinople was taken by storm, and Alexius was invested with the Imperial authority.

Scarcely was Alexius seated upon the throne, before the turbu-lent Greeks engaged in a revolt which resulted in his death. The crusaders now resolved to take possession of the capital, and set a Latin prince on the throne of Constantine. The determina-tion was carried out. Constantinople was taken a second time by storm, and sacked, and Baldwin, Count of Flanders, was crowned Emperor of the East.

The Latin empire thus established lasted only a little over half a century (1204–1261). The Greeks, at the end of this period, succeeded in regaining the throne, which they then held until the capture of Constantinople by the Turks in 1453.

6. CLOSE OF THE CRUSADES : THEIR RESULTS.

The Children's Crusade (1212). — During the interval between the Fourth and the Fifth Crusade, the epidemical fanaticism that had so long agitated Europe seized upon the children, resulting in what is known as the Children's Crusade.

The preacher of this crusade was a child about twelve years of age, a French peasant lad, named Stephen, who became persuaded that Jesus Christ had commanded him to lead a crusade of children to the rescue of the Holy Sepulchre. The children became wild with excitement, and flocked in vast crowds to the places appointed for rendezvous. Nothing could restrain them or thwart their purpose. "Even bolts and bars," says an old chronicler, "could not hold them."

The movement excited the most diverse views. Some declared that it was inspired by the Holy Spirit, and quoted such Scriptural texts as these to justify the enthusiasm : "A child shall lead them ; " " Out of the mouth of babes and sucklings thou hast ordained praise." Others, however, were quite as confident that the whole thing was the work of the Devil.

The great majority of those who collected at the rallying places were boys under twelve years of age, but there were also many girls. The German children, 50,000 in number, crossed the Alps, and marched down the Italian shores, looking for a miraculous pathway through the Mediterranean. From Brundusium 2000 or 3000 of the little crusaders sailed away into oblivion. Not a word ever came back from them.

The French children — about 30,000 in number — set out from the place of rendezvous for Marseilles. Those that sailed from that port were betrayed, and sold as slaves in Alexandria and other Mohammedan slave markets.

This remarkable spectacle of the children's crusade affords the most striking exhibition possible of the ignorance, superstition, and fanaticism that characterized the period. Yet we cannot but reverence the holy enthusiasm of an age that could make such sacrifices of innocence and helplessness in obedience to what was believed to be the will of God.

The children's expedition marked at once the culmination and the decline of the crusading movement. The fanatic zeal that inspired the first crusaders was already dying out. "These children," said the Pope, referring to the young crusaders, "reproach us with having fallen asleep, whilst they were flying to the assistance of the Holy Land."

The Minor Crusades: End of the Kingdom of Jerusalem.— The last four expeditions — the Fifth, Sixth, Seventh, and Eighth — undertaken by the Christians of Europe against the infidels of the East, may be conveniently grouped as the Minor Crusades. They were marked by a less fervid and holy enthusiasm than that which characterized the first movements, and exhibit among those taking part in them the greatest variety of objects and ambitions.[1] The flame of the Crusades had burned itself out, and the fate of the little Christian kingdom in Asia, isolated from Europe, and surrounded on all sides by bitter enemies, became each day more and more apparent. Finally the last of the places

---

[1] The *Fifth Crusade* (1216–1220) was led by the kings of Hungary and Cyprus. Its strength was wasted in Egypt, and it resulted in nothing. The *Sixth Crusade* (1227–1229), headed by Frederick II. of Germany, succeeded in securing from the Saracens the restoration of Jerusalem, together with several other cities of Palestine. The *Seventh Crusade* (1249–1254) was under the lead of Louis IX. of France, surnamed the Saint. The *Eighth Crusade* (1270–1272) was incited by the fresh misfortunes that, towards the close of the thirteenth century, befell the Christian kingdom in Palestine. The two principal leaders of the expedition were Louis IX. of France, and Prince Edward of England, afterwards Edward I. Louis directed his forces against the Moors about Tunis, in North Africa. Here the king died of the plague. Nothing was effected by this division of the expedition. The division led by the English prince, was, however, more fortunate. Edward succeeded in capturing Nazareth, and in compelling the sultan of Egypt to agree to a treaty favorable to the Christians (1272).

(Acre) held by the Christians fell before the attacks of the Mamelukes of Egypt, and with this event the Latin Kingdom of Jerusalem came to an end (1291). The second great combat between Mohammedanism and Christianity was over, and "silence reigned along the shore that had so long resounded with the world's debate."

Results of the Crusades. — The Crusades kept all Europe in a tumult for two centuries, and directly and indirectly cost Christendom several millions of lives (from 2,000,000 to 6,000,000 according to different estimates), besides incalculable expenditures in treasure and suffering. They were, moreover, attended by all the disorder, license, and crime with which war is always accompanied.

On the other hand, the Holy Wars were productive indirectly of so much and lasting good that they form a most important factor in the history of the progress of civilization. To show this to be so, we will speak briefly of their influence upon the Church, and upon the political, the social, the intellectual, and the material progress and development of the European nations.

The Crusades contributed to increase the wealth of the Church and the power of the Papacy. Thus the prominent part which the Popes took in the enterprises naturally fostered their authority and influence, by placing in their hands, as it were, the armies and resources of Christendom, and accustoming the people to look to them as guides and leaders. As to the wealth of the churches and monasteries, this was augmented enormously by the sale to them, often for a mere fraction of their actual value, of the estates of those preparing for the expeditions, or by the out and out gift of the lands of such in return for prayers and pious benedictions. Again, thousands of the crusaders, returning broken in spirits and in health, sought an asylum in cloistral retreats, and endowed the establishments that they entered with all their worldly goods. Besides all this, the stream of the ordinary gifts of piety was swollen by the extraordinary fervor of religious enthusiasm which characterized the period into enormous proportions. In all these ways, the power of the Papacy and the wealth of the Church were vastly augmented.[1]

As to the political effects of the Crusades, they helped to break down the power of the feudal aristocracy, and to give prominence to the kings and the people. Many of the nobles who set out on the expeditions never returned, and their estates, through failure of heirs, escheated to the Crown; while many more wasted their fortunes in meeting the expenses of their undertaking. At the same time, the cities also gained many political advantages at the expense of the crusading barons and princes. Ready money in the twelfth and thirteenth centuries was largely in the hands of the burgher class, and in return for the contributions and loans they made to their overlords, or suzerains, they received charters conferring special and valuable privileges. And under this head of the political effects of the Crusades, it should be noticed that, in checking the advance of the Turks, they postponed the fall of Constantinople for three centuries or more. This gave the young Christian civilization of Germany time to acquire sufficient strength to roll back the returning tide of Mohammedan invasion when it broke upon Europe in the fifteenth century.

The effects of the Crusades upon the social life of the Western nations were marked and important. Giving opportunity for romantic adventure, they were one of the principal fostering influences of Chivalry; while by bringing the rude peoples of the West in contact with the culture of the East, they exerted upon them a general refining influence.

The influence of the Crusades upon the intellectual development of Europe can hardly be overestimated. Above all, they liberalized the minds of the crusaders. Furthermore, the knowledge of the science and learning of the East gained by the crusaders

[1] It should be said in regard to this increase in the riches of the Church and the authority of the Popes, that while Catholics count this as one of the good results of the Holy Wars, Protestants consider it as one of the evils of the movements, urging that it led to papal tyranny and to the corruption of monastic morals.

through their expeditions, greatly stimulated the Latin intellect, and helped to awaken in Western Europe that mental activity which resulted finally in the great intellectual outburst known as the Revival of Learning (see p. 471).

Among the effects of the Holy Wars upon the material development of Europe must be mentioned the spur they gave to commercial enterprise, especially to the trade and commerce of the Italian cities. During this period, Venice, Pisa, and Genoa acquired great wealth and reputation through the fostering of their trade by the needs of the crusaders, and the opening up of the East. The Mediterranean was whitened with the sails of their transport ships, which were constantly plying between the various ports of Europe and the towns of the Syrian coast. Moreover, various arts, manufactures, and inventions before unknown in Europe, were introduced from Asia. This enrichment of the civilization of the West with the "spoils of the East" we may allow to be emblemized by the famous bronze horses that the crusaders carried off from Constantinople, and set up before St. Mark's Cathedral in Venice.

Lastly, the incentive given to geographical discovery led various travellers, such as the celebrated Italian, Marco Polo, and the scarcely less noted Englishman, Sir John Mandeville, to explore the most remote countries of Asia. Even that spirit of maritime enterprise and adventure which rendered illustrious the fifteenth century, inspiring the voyages of Columbus, Vasco da Gama, and Magellan, may be traced back to that lively interest in geographical matters awakened by the expeditions of the crusaders.

CHAPTER XLIII.

SUPREMACY OF THE PAPACY: DECLINE OF ITS TEMPORAL POWER.

Introductory. — In a previous chapter we traced the gradual rise of the spiritual and temporal power of the Papacy, and stated the several theories respecting its relation to secular rulers. In the present chapter, we purpose to follow its increasing power to the culmination of its authority in the thirteenth century, and then to speak of some of the circumstances that caused, or that marked, the decline of its temporal power.

Pope Gregory VII. (Hildebrand) and his Reforms. — One of the greatest promoters of the papal fortunes was Pope Gregory VII., perhaps better known as Hildebrand, the most noteworthy character after Charlemagne that the Middle Ages produced. In the year 1049 he was called from the cloisters of a French monastery to Rome, there to become the maker and adviser of Popes, and finally to be himself elevated to the pontifical throne, which he held from 1073 to 1080. Being a man of great force of character and magnificent breadth of view, he did much towards establishing the universal spiritual and temporal sovereignty of the Holy See.

In carrying out his purpose of exalting the Papal See above all prelates and princes, Gregory, as soon as he became Pope, set about two important reforms, — the enforcement of celibacy among the secular clergy, and the suppression of simony. By the first measure he aimed to effect not only a much-needed moral reform, but, by separating the clergy from all the attachments of home and neighborhood and country, to render them more devoted to the interests of the Church.

The second reform, the correction of simony, had for its ulti-mate object the freeing of the lands and offices of the Church from the control of temporal lords and princes, and the bringing of them more completely into the hands of the Roman bishop.

The evil of simony [1] had grown up in the Church in the follow-ing way : As the feudal system took possession of European soci-ety, the Church, like individuals and cities, assumed feudal relations. Thus, as we have already seen, abbots and bishops, as the heads of monasteries and churches, for the sake of protection, became the vassals of powerful barons or princes. When once a prelate had rendered homage for his estates, or temporalities, as they were called, these became thenceforth a permanent fief of the overlord, and upon the death of the holder could be re-bestowed by the lord upon whomsoever he chose. These Church estates and positions that thus came within the gift of the temporal princes were often given to unworthy court favorites, or sold to the highest bidder. So long as a considerable portion of the clergy sustained this vas-sal relation to the feudal lords, the Papal See could not hope to exercise any great authority over them.

To remedy the evil, Gregory issued a decree that no ecclesias-tic should do homage to a temporal lord, but that he should receive the ring and staff, the symbols of investiture, from the hands of the Pope alone. Any one who should dare disobey the decree was threatened with the anathemas of the Church.

Such was the bold measure by which Gregory proposed to wrest out of the hands of the feudal lords and princes the vast patron-age and immense revenues resulting from the relation they had gradually come to sustain to a large portion of the lands and riches of the Church. To realize the magnitude of the proposed revolu-tion, we must bear in mind that the Church at this time was in possession of probably one-half of the lands of Europe.

Excommunications and Interdicts. — The principal instru-

---

[1] By simony is meant the purchase of an office in the Church, the name of the offence coming from Simon Magus, who offered Peter money for the power to confer the Holy Spirit. See Acts viii, 9–24.

ments relied upon by Gregory for the carrying out of his reforms were Excommunication and Interdict.

The first was directed against individuals. The person excommunicated was cut off from all relations with his fellow-men. If a king, his subjects were released from their oath of allegiance. Any one providing the accursed with food or shelter incurred the wrath of the Church. The Interdict was directed against a city, province, or kingdom. Throughout the region under this ban, the churches were closed; no bell could be rung, no marriage celebrated, no burial ceremony performed. The rites of baptism and extreme unction alone could be administered. These spiritual punishments rarely failed during the eleventh and twelfth centuries in bringing the most contumacious offender to a speedy and abject confession. This will appear in the following paragraph.

Gregory VII. and Henry IV. of Germany. — The decree of Gregory respecting the relation of the clergy to the feudal lords created a perfect storm of opposition, not only among the temporal princes and sovereigns of Europe, but also among the clergy themselves. The dispute thus begun distracted Europe for centuries.

Gregory experienced in Germany the most formidable opposition to his reforms. The Emperor Henry IV. refused to recognize his decree, and even called a council of the clergy of Germany and deposed him. Gregory in turn gathered a council at Rome, and deposed and excommunicated the emperor. This encouraged a revolt on the part of some of Henry's discontented subjects. He was shunned as a man accursed by heaven. His authority seemed to have slipped entirely out of his hands, and his kingdom was on the point of going to pieces. In this wretched state of his affairs there was but one thing for him to do, — to go to Gregory, and humbly sue for pardon and re-instatement in the favor of the Church.

Henry sought the Pontiff at Canossa among the Apennines. But Gregory refused to admit the penitent to his presence. It was winter, and for three successive days the king, clothed in sackcloth, stood with bare feet in the snow of the court-yard of the palace, waiting for permission to kneel at the feet of the Pontiff and to receive forgiveness. On the fourth day the penitent king was admitted to the presence of Gregory, who re-instated him in favor — to the extent of removing the sentence of excommunication (1077).

Henry afterwards avenged his humiliation. He raised an army, invaded Italy, and drove Gregory into exile at Salerno, where he died. His last words were, " I have loved justice and hated iniquity, and therefore I die in exile " (1085).

But the quarrel did not end here. It was taken up by the successors of Gregory, and Henry was again excommunicated. After maintaining a long struggle with the power of the Church, and with his own sons, who were incited to rebel against him, he at last died of a broken heart (1106).

The Popes and the Hohenstaufen Emperors. — In the twelfth century began the long and fierce contention — lasting more than a hundred years — between the Papal See and the emperors of the proud House of Hohenstaufen (see p. 504). It was simply the continuation and culmination of the struggle begun long before to decide which should be supreme, the " world-priest" or the " world-king." The outcome was the final triumph of the Roman bishops and the utter ruin of the Hohenstaufen.

The Papacy at its Height. — The authority of the Popes was at its height during the thirteenth century. The beginning of this period of papal splendor is marked by the accession to the pontifical throne of Innocent III. (1198–1216), the greatest of the Popes after Gregory VII., Under him was very nearly made good the papal claim that all earthly sovereigns were merely vassals of the Roman Pontiff. Almost all the kings and princes of Europe swore fealty to him as their overlord. " Rome was once more the mistress of the world."

Pope Innocent III. and Philip Augustus of France. — One of Innocent's most signal triumphs in his contest with the kings of Europe was gained over Philip Augustus (1180–1223) of France.

That king having put away his wife, Innocent commanded him to take her back, and forced him to submission by means of an interdict. "This submission of such a prince," says Hallam, "not feebly superstitious like his predecessor Robert, nor vexed with seditions, like the Emperor Henry IV., but brave, firm, and victorious, is perhaps the proudest trophy in the scutcheon of Rome."

Pope Innocent III. and King John of England. — Innocent's quarrel with King John (1199–1216) of England will afford another illustration of the power of the Popes. The See of Canterbury falling vacant, John ordered the monks who had the right of election to give the place to a favorite of his. They obeyed; but the Pope immediately declared the election void, and caused the vacancy to be filled with one of his own friends, Stephen Langton. John declared that the Pope's archbishop should never enter England as primate, and proceeded to confiscate the estates of the See. Innocent III. now laid all England under an interdict, excommunicated John, and incited the French king, Philip Augustus, to undertake a crusade against the contumacious rebel.

The outcome of the matter was that John, like the German Emperor before him, was compelled to yield to the power of the Church. He gave back the lands he had confiscated, acknowledged Langton to be the rightful primate of England, and even went so far as to give England to the Pope as a perpetual fief. In token of his vassalage he agreed to pay to the Papal See the annual sum of 1000 marks. This tribute money was actually paid, though with very great irregularity, until the seventeenth year of the reign of Edward I. (1289).

The Mendicants, or Begging Friars. — The authority of the immediate successors of Innocent III. was powerfully supported by the monastic orders of the Dominicans and Franciscans, established early in the thirteenth century. They were named after their respective founders, St. Dominic (1170–1221) and St. Francis (1182–1226). The principles on which these fraternities were established were very different from those which had shaped all previous monastic institutions. Until now the monk had sought cloistral solitude in order to escape from the world, and through penance and prayer and contemplation to work out his own salvation. In the new orders, the monk was to give himself wholly to the work of securing the salvation of others.

Again, the orders were also as *orders* to renounce all earthly possessions, and, "espousing Poverty as a bride," to rely entirely for support upon the alms of the pious. Hitherto, while the individual members of a monastic order must affect extreme poverty, the house or fraternity might possess any amount of communal wealth.

The new fraternities grew and spread with marvellous rapidity, and in less than a generation they quite overshadowed all of the old monastic orders of the Church. The Popes conferred many and special privileges upon them, and they in turn became the staunchest friends and supporters of the Roman See. They were to the Papacy of the thirteenth century what the later order of the Jesuits was to the Roman Church of the seventeenth (see p. 528).

Removal of the Papal Seat to Avignon (1309). — Having now noticed some of the most prominent circumstances and incidents that marked the gradual advance of the bishops of Rome to almost universal political and ecclesiastical sovereignty, we shall next direct attention to some of the chief events that marked the decline of their temporal power, and prepared the way for the rejection, at a later date, by a large part of Christendom, of their spiritual authority.

One of the severest blows given both the temporal and the spiritual authority of the Popes was the removal, in 1309, through the influence of the French king, Philip the Fair, of the papal chair from Rome to Avignon, in Provence, near the frontier of France. Here it remained for a space of about seventy years, an era known in Church history as the Babylonian Captivity. While it was established here, all the Popes were French, and of course all their policies were shaped and controlled by the French kings. "In that city," says Stillé, " the Papacy ceased, in the eyes of a very large part of Christendom, to possess that sacred cosmopolitan character which no doubt had had much to do with the veneration and respect with which the Catholic authority had been regarded."

The Great Schism (1378). — The discontent awakened among the Italians by the situation of the papal court at length led to an open rupture between them and the French party. In 1378 the opposing factions each elected a Pope, and thus there were two heads of the Church, one at Avignon and the other at Rome.

The spectacle of two rival Popes, each claiming to be the rightful successor of St. Peter and the sole infallible head of the Church, very naturally led men to question the claims and infallibility of both. It gave the reverence which the world had so generally held for the Roman See a rude shock, and one from which it never recovered.

The Church Councils of Pisa and Constance. — Finally, in 1409, a general council of the Church assembled at Pisa, for the purpose of composing the shameful quarrel. This council deposed both Popes, and elected Alexander V. as the supreme head of the Church. But matters instead of being mended hereby were only made worse ; for neither of the deposed pontiffs would lay down his authority in obedience to the demands of the council, and consequently there were now three Popes instead of two.

In 1414 another council was called, at Constance, for the settlement of the growing dispute. Two of the claimants were deposed, and one resigned. A new Pope was then elected, — Pope Martin V. In his person the Catholic world was again united under a single spiritual head. The schism was outwardly healed, but the wound had been too deep not to leave permanent marks upon the Church.

The Revolt of the Temporal Princes. — Taking advantage of the declining authority of the Papal See, the temporal rulers in France, Germany, and England successively revolted, and freed themselves from the authority of the Papacy as touching political or governmental affairs. But it must be borne in mind that the princes or governments that at this time repudiated the temporal authority of the Papal See, did not think of challenging the claims of the Popes to recognition as the supreme head of the *Church*, and the rightful arbiters in all *spiritual* matters. At the very time that they were striving to emancipate themselves from papal control in temporal matters, they were lending the Church all their strength to punish heresy and schism. Thus the Albigenses[1] in Southern France, the Lollards[2] in England, and the Hussites[3] in Bohemia, were extirpated or punished by the civil authorities, acting either in accordance with the then universal idea of how heresy should be dealt with, or in obedience to the commands of the Roman See.

[1] See p. 493. [2] See p. 491. [3] See p. 506.

CHAPTER XLIV.

CONQUESTS OF THE TURANIAN TRIBES.

The Huns and the Hungarians. — The Huns, of whom we have already told, were the first Turanians that during historic times pushed their way in among the peoples of Europe (see p. 345).

The next Turanian invaders of Europe that we need here notice were the Magyars, or Hungarians, another branch of the Hunnic race, who in the ninth century of our era succeeded in thrusting themselves far into the continent, and establishing there the important Kingdom of Hungary. These people, in marked contrast to almost every other tribe of Turanian origin, adopted the manners, customs, and religion of the peoples about them — became, in a word, thoroughly Europeanized, and for a long time were the main defence of Christian Europe against the Turkish tribes of the same race that followed closely in their footsteps.

The Seljukian Turks. — The Seljukian Turks, so called from the name of one of their chiefs, are the next Tartar people that thrust themselves prominently upon our notice. It was the capture of the holy places in Palestine by this intolerant race, and their threatening advance towards the Bosporus, that alarmed the Christian nations of Europe, and led to the First Crusade.

The blows dealt the empire of the Seljuks by the crusaders, and disputes respecting the succession, caused the once formidable sovereignty to crumble to pieces, only, however, to be replaced by others of equally rapid growth, destined to as quick a decay.

The Mongols, or Moguls. — While the power of the Seljukian Turks was declining in Western Asia, the Mongols, or Moguls, a fierce and utterly untamed Tartar tribe that first issued from the easternmost part of Chinese Tartary, were building up a new dynasty among the various tribes of the central portion of the continent. In the year 1156 was born their greatest chieftain, Temujin, afterwards named Genghis Khan, or "Universal Sovereign," the most terrible scourge that ever afflicted the human race. At the head of vast armies, made up of numerous Turanian hordes, he traversed with sword and torch a great part of Asia. It is estimated that his enormous empire was built up at the cost of fifty thousand cities and towns and five millions of lives, — a greater waste, probably, than resulted from all the Crusades.

The successors of Genghis Khan still farther enlarged and strengthened the monarchy, so that it came to embrace, besides the best part of Asia, a considerable portion of Europe as well. At length the immoderately extended empire fell into disorder, and became broken into many petty states. It was restored by Tamerlane, or Timour the Lame (born about 1336), a descendant of Genghis Khan. With his wild Mongolian hordes he traversed anew almost all the countries that had been desolated by the sanguinary marches of his predecessors. The route of the barbarians was everywhere marked by ruined fields and burned villages.

Asia has never recovered from the terrible devastation of the Mongol conquerors. Many districts, swarming with life, were entirely swept of their population by these destroyers of the race, and have remained to this day desolate as the tomb.

The immense empire of Tamerlane crumbled to pieces after his death. One of its fragments had a remarkable history. This was the dynasty established in India, which became known as the Kingdom of the Great Moguls. This Mongol state lasted upwards of 300 years, — until destroyed by the English in the present century. The magnificence of the court of the Great Moguls at Delhi and Agra is one of the most splendid traditions of the East.

The Ottoman Empire.

Founding of the Empire. — The latest, most permanent, and most important of the Tartar sovereignties was established by the Ottoman Turks, who were an offshoot of the Seljukians. Gradually

this martial race seized province after province of the Asiatic possessions of the Byzantine emperors. Through the quarrels that
were constantly distracting Constantinople, they at last gained
a foothold in Europe (1353). During the reign of Amurath I.
(1360–1389), a large part of the country known as Turkey in
Europe fell into their hands.

Conquests of Bajazet (1389–1403). — Amurath was followed by
his son Bajazet who, by the rapid advance of his arms, spread the
greatest alarm throughout Western Europe. The warriors of Hungary, Germany, and France united their armies to arrest his progress; but their combined forces, numbering 100,000 men, were
cut to pieces by the sabres of the Turks on the fatal field of Nicop-
olis, in Bulgaria (1396). Bajazet now vowed that he would
stable his horse in the Cathedral of St. Peter at Rome, and there
seemed no power in Christendom to prevent the sacrilege.

Before proceeding to fulfil his threat, however, Bajazet turned
back to capture Constantinople, which he believed in the present
despondent state of its inhabitants would make little or no resistance. Now it happened that just at this time Tamerlane was leading the Mongols on their career of conquest. He directed them
against the Turks in Asia Minor, and Bajazet was forced to raise
the siege of Constantinople, and hasten across the Bosporus, to
check the advance in his dominions of these new enemies. The
Turks and Mongols met upon the plains of Angora, where the
former suffered a disastrous defeat (1402). The battle of Angora
checked for a time the conquests of the Ottomans, and saved
Constantinople to the Christian world for another period of fifty
years.

The Capture of Constantinople (1453). — The Ottomans gradually recovered from the blow they had received at Angora. In
the year 1421 they made another attempt upon Constantinople,
but were unsuccessful. Finally, in the year 1453, Mohammed II.,
the Great, sultan of the Ottomans, laid siege to the capital, with
an army of over 200,000 men. After a short investment, the
place was taken by storm. The Cross, which since the time of

Constantine the Great had surmounted the dome of St. Sophia, was replaced by the Crescent, which remains to this day.

Check to the Ottoman Arms. — The consternation which the fall of Byzantium created throughout Christendom was like the dismay which filled the world upon the downfall of Rome in the fifth century. All Europe now lay open to the Moslem barbarians, and there seemed nothing to prevent their marching to the Atlantic. But the warriors of Hungary made a valiant stand against the invaders, and succeeded in checking their advance upon the continent, while the Knights of St. John (see p. 443), now established in the island of Rhodes, held them in restraint in the Mediterranean. Mohammed II. did succeed in planting the Crescent upon the shores of Italy — capturing and holding for a year the city of Otranto, in Calabria ; but by the time of the death of that energetic prince, the conquering energy of the Ottomans seems to have nearly spent itself, and the limits of their empire were not afterwards materially enlarged.

The Turks have ever remained quite insensible to the influences of European civilization, and their government has been a perfect blight and curse to the countries subjected to their rule. They have always been looked upon as intruders in Europe, and their presence there has led to several of the most sanguinary wars of modern times. Gradually they are being pushed out from their European possessions, and the time is probably not very far distant when they will be driven back across the Bosporus, as their Moorish brethren were expelled long ago from the opposite corner of the continent by the Christian chivalry of Spain.

CHAPTER XLV.

GROWTH OF THE TOWNS: THE ITALIAN CITY-REPUBLICS.

Relation of the Cities to the Feudal Lords. — When Feudalism took possession of Europe, the cities became a part of the system. Each town formed a part of the fief in which it happened to be situated, and was subject to all the incidents of feudal ownership. It owed allegiance to its lord, must pay to him feudal tribute, and aid him in his war enterprises. As the cities, through their manufactures and trade, were the most wealthy members of the Feudal System, the lords naturally looked to them for money when in need. Their exactions at last became unendurable, and a long struggle broke out between them and the burghers, which resulted in what is known as the enfranchisement of the towns.

It was in the eleventh century that this revolt of the cities against the feudal lords became general. During the course of this and the succeeding century, the greater number of the towns of the countries of Western Europe either bought, or wrested by force of arms, charters from their lords or suzerains. The cities thus chartered did not become independent of the feudal lords, but they acquired the right of managing, with more or less supervision, their own affairs, and were secured against arbitrary and oppressive taxation. This was a great gain ; and as, under the protection of their charters, they increased in wealth and population, very many of them grew at last strong enough to cast off all actual dependence upon lord or suzerain, and became in effect independent states — little commonwealths. Especially was this true in the case of the Italian cities, and in a less marked degree in that of the German towns.

Rise of the Italian City-Republics. — The Italian cities were the first to rise to power and importance. Several things conspired to secure their early and rapid development, but the main cause of their prosperity was their trade with the East, and the enormous impulse given to this commerce by the Crusades.

With wealth came power, and all the chief Italian cities became

A MEDIÆVAL SIEGE, SHOWING BALLISTAE, ETC. (After Alphonse de Neuville.)

distinct, self-governing states, with just a nominal dependence upon the pope or the emperor. Towards the close of the thirteenth century, Northern and Central Italy was divided among about two hundred contentious little city-republics. Italy had become another Greece.

The Establishment of Tyrannies. — Just what happened among the contending republics of Greece took place in the case of the quarrelling city-commonwealths of Italy. Their republican constitutions were overthrown, and the supreme power fell into the hands of an ambitious aristocracy, or was seized by some bold usurper, who often succeeded in making the government hereditary in his family. Before the close of the fourteenth century almost all the republics of the peninsula had become converted into exclusive oligarchies or hereditary principalities.

We shall now relate some circumstances, for the most part of a commercial character, which concern some of the most renowned of the Italian city-states.

Venice. — Venice, the most celebrated of the Italian republics, had its beginnings in the fifth century, in the rude huts of some

refugees who fled out into the marshes of the Adriatic to escape the fury of the Huns of Attila (see p. 346). Conquests and negotiations gradually extended the possessions of the island-city until she came to control the coasts and waters of the East-

PALACE OF THE DOGES.   (From a photograph.)

ern Mediterranean in much the same way that Carthage had mastery of the Western Mediterranean at the time of the First Punic War. Even before the Crusades her trade with the East was very extensive, and by those expeditions was expanded into enormous proportions.

Venice was at the height of her power during the thirteenth, fourteenth, and fifteenth centuries. Her supremacy on the sea was celebrated each year by the brilliant ceremony of "Wedding the Adriatic," by the dropping of a ring into the sea.

The decline of Venice dates from the fifteenth century. The conquests of the Turks during that century deprived her of much of the territory she held east of the Adriatic, and finally the voyage of Vasco da Gama round the Cape of Good Hope (1497–8), showing a new path to India, gave a death-blow to her commerce. From this time forward, the trade of Europe with the East was to be conducted from the Atlantic ports of the continent instead of from those in the Mediterranean.

Genoa. — Genoa, on the western coast of Italy, was the most formidable commercial rival of Venice. The period of her greatest prosperity dates from the recapture of Constantinople from the Latins by the Greeks in 1261 ; for the Genoese had assisted the Greek princes in the recovery of their throne, and as a reward were shown commercial favors by the Greek emperors.

The jealousy with which the Venetians regarded the prosperity of the Genoese led to oft-renewed war between the two rival republics. For nearly two centuries their hostile fleets contended, as did the navies of Rome and Carthage during the First Punic War, for the supremacy of the sea.

The merchants of Genoa, like those of Venice, reaped a rich harvest during the Crusades. Their prosperity was brought to an end by the irruption of the Mongols and Turks, and the capture of Constantinople by the latter in 1453. The Genoese traders were now driven from the Black Sea, and their traffic with Eastern Asia was completely broken up ; for the Venetians had control of the ports of Egypt and Syria and the southern routes to India and the countries beyond — that is, the routes by way of the Euphrates and the Red Sea.

Florence. — Florence, although shut out, by her inland location upon the Arno, from engaging in those naval enterprises that conferred wealth and importance upon the coast cities of Venice and Genoa, became, notwithstanding, through the skill, industry, enterprise, and genius of her citizens, the great manufacturing, financial, literary, and art centre of the Middle Ages. The list of her illustrious citizens, of her poets, statesmen, historians, architects, sculptors, and painters, is more extended than that of any other city of mediæval times ; and indeed, as respects the number of her great men, Florence is perhaps unrivalled by any city, excepting Athens, of the ancient or the modern world.[1]

The Hanseatic League. — From speaking of the Italian city-republics, we must now turn to say a word respecting the free cities of Germany, in which country, next after Italy, the mediæval municipalities had their most perfect development, and acquired their greatest power and influence.

ROBBER KNIGHTS.

When, in the eleventh and twelfth centuries, the towns of Northern Europe began to extend their commercial connections, the greatest drawback to their trade was the general insecurity and disorder that everywhere prevailed. The trader who entrusted his goods designed for the Italian market to the overland routes was in danger of losing them at the hands of the robber nobles, who

[1] In her long roll of fame we find the names of Dante, Petrarch, Boccaccio, Macchiavelli, Michael Angelo, Leonardo da Vinci, Galileo, Amerigo Vespucci, and the Medici.

watched all the lines of travel, and either robbed the merchant outright, or levied an iniquitous toll upon his goods. The plebeian tradesmen, in the eyes of these patrician barons, had no rights which they felt bound to respect. Nor was the way to Italy by the Baltic and the North Sea beset with less peril. Piratical crafts scoured those waters, and made booty of any luckless merchant-man they might overpower, or lure to wreck upon the dangerous shores.

This state of things led some of the German cities, about the middle of the fourteenth century, to form, for the protection of their merchants, an alliance called the Hanseatic League. The confederation eventually embraced eighty-five of the principal towns of North Germany. In order to facilitate the trading operations of its members, the League established in different parts of the world trading-posts and warehouses. The four most noted centres of the trade of the confederation were the cities of Bruges, London, Bergen, and Novgorod. The League thus became a vast monopoly, which endeavored to control, in the interests of its own members, the entire commerce of Northern Europe.

Among other causes of the dismemberment of the association may be mentioned the maritime discoveries of the fifteenth century, which disarranged all the old routes of trade in the north of Europe as well as in the south ; the increased security which the formation of strong governments gave to the merchant class upon sea and land ; and the heavy expense incident to membership in the association, resulting from its ambitious projects. All these things combined resulted in the decline of the power and usefulness of the League, and finally led to its formal dissolution about the middle of the seventeenth century.

Influence of the Mediæval Cities. — The chartered towns and free cities of the mediæval era exerted a vast influence upon the commercial, social, artistic, and political development of Europe.

They were the centres of the industrial and commercial life of the Middle Ages, and laid the foundations of that vast system of international exchange and traffic which forms a characteristic feature of modern European civilization.

Their influence upon the social and artistic life of Europe cannot be overestimated. It was within the walls of the cities that the civilization uprooted by the Teutonic invaders first revived. With their growing wealth came not only power, but those other usual accompaniments of wealth, — culture and refinement. The Italian cities were the cradle and home of mediæval art, science, and literature.

Again, these cities were the birthplace of political liberty, of representative government. It was the burghers, the inhabitants of the cities, that in England, in France, and in Germany finally grew into the Third Estate, or Commons, the controlling political class in all these countries. In a word, municipal freedom was the germ of national liberty.

CHAPTER XLVI.

THE REVIVAL OF LEARNING.

By the Revival of Learning, in the most general sense, is meant the intellectual awakening of Europe after the languor and depression of the first mediæval centuries. In a narrower sense, however, the phrase is used to designate that wonderful renewal of interest in the old Greek and Latin authors which sprung up in Italy about the beginning of the fourteenth century. We shall use the expression in its most comprehensive sense, thus making the restoration of classical letters simply a part of the great Revival of Learning.

Scholasticism and the Schoolmen. — One of Charlemagne's most fruitful labors was the establishment of schools, in connection with the cathedrals and monasteries, throughout his dominions. Within these schools there grew up in the course of time a form of philosophy called, from the place of its origin, Scholasticism, while its expounders were known as Schoolmen. This philosophy was a fusion of Christianity and Aristotelian logic. It might be defined as being, in its later stages, an effort to reconcile revelation and reason, faith and philosophy. Viewed in this light, it was not altogether unlike that theological philosophy of the present day whose aim is to harmonize the Bible with the facts of modern science.

The greatest of the Schoolmen appeared in the thirteenth century. Among them were Albertus Magnus, Roger Bacon, Thomas Aquinas, and Duns Scotus. The most eminent of these was Thomas Aquinas (died 1274), who was called the "Angel of the Schools." He was the strongest champion of mediæval orthodoxy. His remarkable work, entitled the *Summa Theologica*, outlines and defends the whole scheme of Roman Catholic theology.

The Schoolmen often busied themselves with the most unprofitable questions in metaphysics and theology, yet their discussions were not without good results. These debates sharpened the wits of men, created activity of thought and deftness in argument. The schools of the times became real mental gymnasia, in which the young awakening mind of Europe received its first training and gained its earliest strength.

The Universities. — Closely related to the subject of Scholasticism is the history of the universities, which, springing up in the thirteenth century, became a powerful agency in the Revival of Learning. They were for the most part expansions of the old cathedral and abbey schools, their transformation being effected largely through the reputation of the Schoolmen, who drew such multitudes to their lectures that it became necessary to reorganize the schools on a broader basis. Popes and kings granted them charters which conferred special privileges upon their faculties and students, as, for instance, exemption from taxation and from the jurisdiction of the ordinary courts. The celebrated University of Paris was the first founded, and that of Bologna was probably next in order.

The usual course of study in the universities was divided into what was known as the *trivium* and the *quadrivium*. The trivium embraced Grammar, Logic, and Rhetoric ; the quadrivium, Arithmetic, Geometry, Astronomy, and Music. These constituted the seven liberal arts. Greek, Hebrew, and the physical sciences received but little attention. Medicine had not yet freed itself from the influence of magic and astrology, and alchemy had not yet given birth to chemistry. The Ptolemaic theory of the universe still held sway. However, in all these matters the European mind was making progress, was blindly groping its way towards the light.

Influence of the Saracens. — The progress of the Christian scholars of Europe in the physical sciences was greatly accelerated by the Saracens, who, during the Dark Ages, were almost the sole repositories of the scientific knowledge of the world. A part of this they gathered for themselves, for the Arabian scholars were original investigators, but a larger share of it they borrowed from the Greeks. While the Western nations were too ignorant to know the value of the treasures of antiquity, the Saracens preserved them by translating into Arabic the scientific works of Aristotle and other Greek authors; and then, when Europe was prepared to appreciate these accumulations of the past, gave them back to her. This learning came into Europe in part through the channel of the Crusades, but more largely, and at an earlier date, through the Arabian schools in Spain. Two of the greatest scholars of the thirteenth century, or perhaps of all the mediæval ages, Roger Bacon and Albertus Magnus, owed very much of their scientific knowledge to the Arabians.

Effects of the Crusades. — Having in a previous chapter dwelt on the effects of the Crusades upon the intellectual development of the European peoples (see p. 449) there is no need that we here do more than refer to the matter, in order that we may fix in mind the place of the Holy Wars among the agencies that conspired to bring about the Revival of Learning. The stimulating, quickening, liberalizing tendency of these chivalric enterprises was one of the most potent forces concerned in the mental movement we are tracing.

Rise of Modern Languages and Literatures. — Between the tenth and the fourteenth century the native tongues of Europe began to form literatures of their own. We have already spoken of the formation and gradual growth of these languages (see p. 386). As soon as their forms became somewhat settled, then literature was possible, and all these speeches bud and blossom into song and romance. This formation of modern European languages and birth of native literatures, was one of the greatest gains in the interest of general intelligence; for the Schoolmen used the Latin language, and their discussions and writings consequently influenced only a limited class; while the native literatures addressed themselves to the masses, and thus stirred the universal mind and heart of Europe.

The Revival of Classical Learning. — About the beginning of the fourteenth century there sprung up in Italy a great enthusiasm for Greek and Latin literature and art. This is what is generally known as the Italian Renaissance, or the New Birth.

The Renaissance divides itself as follows: 1. The revival of classical learning; 2. The revival of classical art. It is with the first only, the intellectual and literary phase of the movement, that we are now concerned. This feature of the movement is called *Humanism*, and the promoters of it are known as *Humanists*.[1] The

DANTE.[2]

real originator of the humanistic movement was Petrarch[2] (1304–1374). His love for the old Greek and Latin writers was a passion amounting to a worship. He often wrote love-letters to his favorite authors. In one to Homer he laments the lack of taste among his countrymen, and declares that there are not more than ten persons in all Italy who could appreciate the Iliad. Next to Petrarch stands Boccaccio (1313–1375), as the second of the Humanists.

Just as the antiquarians of to-day search the mounds of Assyria for relics of the ancient civilizations of the East, so did the Humanists ransack the libraries of the monasteries and cathedrals, and all the out-of-the-way places of Europe, for old manuscripts of the classic writers. The precious documents were found covered with mould in damp cellars, or loaded with dust in the attics of monasteries. This late search for these remains of classical authors saved to the world hundreds of valuable manuscripts which, a little

---

[1] That is, students of the *humanities*, or polite literature.

[2] The great Florentine poet, Dante (1265–1321), was the forerunner of Humanism, but was not, properly speaking, a Humanist. His Divine Comedy is the " Epic of Mediævalism."

longer neglected, would have been forever lost. Libraries were founded in which the new treasures might be stored, and copies of the manuscripts were made and distributed among all who could appreciate them. It was at this time that the celebrated Vatican Library was established by Pope Nicholas V. (1447–1455), one of the most generous promoters of the humanistic movement.

This reviving interest in the literature of ancient Greece was vastly augmented by the disasters just now befalling the Greek empire (see p. 462). From every part of the crumbling state scholars fled before the approach of the barbarians, and sought shelter in the West, especially in Italy, bringing with them many valuable manuscripts of the old Greek masters, who were almost unknown in Western Europe, and always an enthusiasm for Greek learning. There was now a repetition of what took place at Rome upon the conquest of Greece in the days of the Republic. Italy was conquered a second time by the genius of Greece.

Before the close of the fifteenth century, the enthusiasm for classical authors had infected the countries beyond the Alps. The New Learning, as it was called, found a place in the colleges and universities of Germany, France, and England. Greek was added to Latin as one of the requirements in a liberal education, and from that day to this has maintained a prominent place in all our higher institutions of learning. In Northern Europe, however, the humanistic movement became blended with other tendencies. In Italy it had been an exclusive passion, a single devotion to classical literature; but here in the North there was added to this enthusiasm for Græco-Roman letters an equal and indeed supremer interest in what we have called the Hebrew element in civilization (see p. 368). Petrarch hung over the pages of Homer; Luther pores over the pages of the Bible. The Renaissance, in a word, becomes the Reformation; the Humanist becomes the Reformer.

Evil and Good Results of the Classical Revival. — There were some serious evils inherent in the classical revival. In Italy, especially, where the humanistic spirit took most complete possession of society, it was "disastrous to both faith and morals." The study of the old pagan writers produced the result predicted by the monks, — caused a revival of paganism. To be learned in Greek was to excite suspicion of heresy. With the New Learning came also those vices and immoralities that characterized the decline of classical civilization. Italy was corrupted by the new influences that flowed in upon her, just as Rome was corrupted by Grecian luxury and vice in the days of the failing republic.

On the other hand, the benefits of the movement to European civilization were varied and positive. The classical revival gave to Europe, not only faultless literary models, but large stores of valuable knowledge. As Woolsey says, "The old civilization contained treasures of permanent value which the world could not spare, which the world will never be able or willing to spare. These were taken up into the stream of life, and proved true aids to the progress of a culture which is gathering in one the beauty and truth of all the ages." And to the same effect are the words of Symonds, who closes his appreciative review of the Italian Revival of Letters as follows : "Such is the Lampadephoria, or torch-race, of the nations. Greece stretches out her hand to Italy ; Italy consigns the sacred fire to Northern Europe ; the people of the North pass on the flame to America, to India, and the Australasian Isles."

JOHN GUTENBERG.

Printing. — One of the most helpful agencies concerned in the Revival of Learning, was the invention of printing from movable blocks, or type, — the most important discovery, in the estimation of Hallam, recorded in the annals of mankind. For this improvement the world is probably indebted to John Gutenberg of Mentz (1438).[1]

The new art would have been much restricted in its usefulness had it not been for the bringing to perfection about this time of

[1] Dutch writers maintain that the honor of the invention belongs to Costar of Haarlem.

the art of making paper from linen rags. This article took the place of the costly parchment, and rendered it possible to place books within the reach of all classes.

The first book printed from movable types was a Latin copy of the Bible, issued at Mentz, in Germany, between the years 1450 and 1455. The art spread rapidly, and before the close of the fifteenth century presses were busy in every country of Europe, multiplying books with a rapidity undreamed of by the patient copyists of the cloister.

It is needless to dwell upon the tremendous impulse which the new art gave, not only to the humanistic movement, but to the general intellectual progress of the European nations. Without it, the Revival of Learning must have languished, and the Reformation could hardly have become a fact in history. Its instrument, the *press*, is fitly chosen as the symbol of the new era of intelligence and freedom which it ushered in.

CHAPTER XLVII.

GROWTH OF THE NATIONS. — FORMATION OF NATIONAL GOVERNMENTS AND LITERATURES.

Introductory. — The most important movement that marked the latter part of the Middle Ages was the grouping, in several of the countries of Europe, of the petty feudal states and half-independent cities and towns into great nations with strong centralized governments. This movement was accompanied by, or rather consisted in, the decline of Feudalism as a governmental system, the loss by the cities of their freedom, and the growth of the power of the kings.

Many things contributed to this consolidation of peoples and governments, different circumstances favoring the movement in the several countries. In some countries, however, events were opposed to the centralizing tendency, and in these the Modern Age was reached without nationality having been found. But in England, in France, and in Spain circumstances all seemed to tend towards unity, and by the close of the fifteenth century there were established in these countries strong despotic monarchies. Yet even among those peoples where national governments did not appear, some progress was made towards unity through the formation of national languages and literatures, and the development of common feelings, sentiments, and aspirations, so that these peoples were manifestly only awaiting the opportunities of a happier period for the maturing of their national life.

This rise of Monarchy and decline of Feudalism, this substitution of strong centralized governments in place of the feeble, irregular, and conflicting authorities of the feudal nobles, was a very great gain to the cause of law and good order. It paved the way for modern progress and civilization.

1. ENGLAND.

General Statement. — In preceding chapters we have told of the origin of the English people, and traced their growth under Saxon, Danish, and Norman rulers (see pp. 375, 411, 433). We shall, in the present section, tell very briefly the story of their progress under the Plantagenet kings, thus carrying on our narrative to the accession of the Tudors in 1485, from which event dates the beginning of the modern history of England.

The era of the Plantagenets,[1] which covers three hundred and thirty-one years, was a most eventful one in English history. The chief political matters that we shall notice were the wresting of Magna Charta from King John, the formation of the House of Commons, the Conquest of Wales, the Wars with Scotland, the Hundred Years' War with France, and the Wars of the Roses.

Magna Charta (1215). — *Magna Charta*, the "Great Charter," held sacred as the basis of English liberties, was an instrument which the English barons and clergy forced King John to grant, in which the ancient rights and privileges of the people were clearly defined and guaranteed.

King John (1199–1216), the third of the Plantagenet line, was as tyrannical as he was unscrupulous and wicked. His course led to an open revolt of the barons, who were resolved upon the recovery of their ancient liberties. The tyrant was forced to bow

---

[1] The name Plantagenet came from the peculiar badge, a sprig of broom-plant (*plante de genêt*), adopted by one of the early members of the House. Following is a table of the sovereigns of the family : —

		HOUSE OF LANCASTER.	
Henry II.	1154–1189		
Richard I.	1189–1199	Henry IV.	1399–1413
John	1199–1216	Henry V.	1413–1422
Henry III.	1216–1272	Henry VI.	1422–1461
Edward I.	1272–1307	HOUSE OF YORK.	
Edward II.	1307–1327	Edward IV.	1461–1483
Edward III.	1327–1377	Edward V.	1483
Richard II.	1377–1399	Richard III.	1483–1485

to the storm he had raised. He met his barons at Runnymede, a meadow on the Thames, and there affixed his seal to the instrument that had been prepared to receive it.

Among the important articles of the paper were the following : No freeman should be deprived of life, liberty, or property, "save by legal judgment of his peers." No taxes (save several feudal aids specified) should be imposed "save by the Common Council of the realm."[1]

Besides these articles, which form the foundation of the English Constitution, there were others abolishing numerous abuses and confirming various time-honored rights and privileges of the towns and of different classes of freemen.

The Great Charter was often disregarded and broken by despotic sovereigns; but the people always clung to it as the warrant and basis of their liberties, and again and again forced tyrannical kings to renew and confirm its provisions, and swear solemnly to observe all its articles.

Considering the far-reaching consequences that resulted from the granting of *Magna Charta*, — the securing of constitutional liberty as an inheritance for the English-speaking race in all parts of the world, — it must always be considered the most important concession that a freedom-loving people ever wrung from a tyrannical sovereign.

Beginning of the House of Commons (1265). — The reign of Henry III. (1216–1272), John's son and successor, witnessed the second important step taken in English constitutional freedom. This was the formation of the House of Commons, Parliament having up to this time consisted of a single House, made up of nobles and bishops. It was again the royal misbehavior that led to this great change in the form of the English national assembly.

---

[1] This article respecting taxation was suffered to fall into abeyance in the reign of John's successor, Henry III., and it was not until about one hundred years after the granting of *Magna Charta* that the great principle that the people should be taxed only through their representatives in Parliament, became fully established.

Henry had violated his oath to rule according to the Great Charter, and had become even more tyrannical than his father. The indignant barons rose in revolt, and Henry and his son being worsted in a great engagement, known as the battle of Lewes (1264), were made prisoners.

Simon de Montfort, a Frenchman, whom Henry had given a prominent position in the government, now assumed control of affairs. He issued, in the king's name, writs of summons to the nobles and bishops to meet in Parliament; and at the same time sent similar writs to the sheriffs of the different shires, directing them " to return two knights for the body of their county, with two citizens or burghers for every city and borough contained in it." This was the first time that plain untitled citizens or burghers had been called to take their place with the knights, lords, and bishops in the great council of the nation, to join in deliberations on the affairs of the realm.[1] The Commons were naturally at first a weak and timorous body, quite overawed by the great lords, but were destined eventually to grow into the controlling branch of the British Parliament.

Conquest of Wales.— For more than a thousand years the Celtic tribes of Wales maintained among their mountain fastnesses an ever-renewed struggle with the successive invaders and conquerors of England — with Roman, Saxon, and Norman. They never submitted their necks to the Roman yoke, but they were forced to acknowledge the overlordship of some of the Saxon and Norman kings. They were restless vassals, however, and were constantly withholding tribute and refusing homage.

When Edward I. came to the English throne in 1272, Llewellyn, the overlord of the Welsh chiefs, with the title of Prince of Wales, refused to render homage to the new king. War followed. Llewellyn was slain, and the independence of his race forever

---

[1] At first the Commons could only take part in questions relating to taxation, but gradually they acquired the right to share in all matters that might come before Parliament.

extinguished (1282). The title of the Welsh chieftain has ever since been borne by the eldest son of the English sovereign.

Wars with Scotland (1296–1328). — In 1285 the ancient Celtic line of Scottish chiefs became extinct. Thirteen claimants for the vacant throne immediately arose. Chief among these were Robert Bruce and John Balliol, distinguished noblemen of Norman descent, attached to the Scottish court. King Edward I. of England, who claimed suzerain rights over the Scottish realm, was asked to act as arbitrator, and decide to whom the crown should be given. He decided the question of the succession in favor of Balliol, who now took the crown of Scotland as the acknowledged vassal of the English sovereign.

Edward's unjust demands on the Scottish king led him to cast off his feudal allegiance. In the war that followed, the Scots were defeated, and Scotland now fell back as a fief forfeited by treason, into the hands of Edward (1296). As a sign that the Scottish kingdom had come to an end, Edward carried off to London the royal regalia, and with this a large stone, known as the Stone of Scone, upon which the Scottish kings, from time out of memory, had been accustomed to be crowned. Legend declared that the relic was the very stone on which Jacob had slept at Bethel. The block was taken to Westminster Abbey, and there made to support the seat of a stately throne-chair, which to this day is used in the coronation ceremonies of the English sovereigns. It is said that the stone once bore this legend : —

> " Should fate not fail, where'er this stone be found,
> The Scot shall monarch of that realm be crowned,"

which prophecy was fulfilled when James VI. of Scotland became James I. of England.[1]

---

[1] "Whether the prophecy was actually inscribed on the stone may be doubted, though this seems to be implied, and on the lower side is still visible a groove which may have contained it ; but the fact that it was circulated and believed as early as the fourteenth century, is certain." — Dean Stanley's *Memorials of Westminster Abbey.*

The two countries were not long united. The Scotch people loved too well their ancient liberties to submit quietly to this extinguishment of their national independence. Under the inspiration and lead of the famous Sir William Wallace, an outlaw knight, all the Lowlands were soon in determined revolt. It was chiefly from the peasantry that the patriot hero drew his followers. Wallace gained some successes, but at length was betrayed into Edward's hands. He was condemned to death as a traitor, and his head, garlanded with a crown of laurel, was exposed on London Bridge (1305). The romantic life of Wallace, his patriotic service, his heroic exploits, and his tragic death, at once lifted him to the place that he has ever since held, as the national hero of Scotland.

The struggle in which Wallace had fallen, was soon renewed by the almost equally renowned hero Robert Bruce (grandson of the Robert Bruce mentioned on p. 482), who was the representative of the nobles, as Wallace had been of the common people. With Edward II. Bruce fought the great *Battle of Bannockburn,* near Stirling. Edward's army was almost annihilated (1314). It was the most appalling disaster that had befallen the arms of the English people since the memorable defeat of Harold at Hastings.

The independence of Scotland really dates from the great victory of Bannockburn, but the English were too proud to acknowledge it until fourteen years more of war. Finally, in the year 1328, the young king Edward III. gave up all claim to the Scottish crown, and Scotland with the hero Bruce as its king, took its place as an independent power among the nations of Europe.

The independence gained by the Scotch at Bannockburn was maintained for nearly three centuries, — until 1603, — when the crowns of England and Scotland were peacefully united in the person of James Stuart VI. of Scotland. During the greater part of these three hundred years the two countries were very quarrelsome neighbors.

The Hundred Years' War (1336–1453).

Causes of the War. — The long and wasteful war between England and France, known in history as the Hundred Years' War, was a most eventful one, and its effects upon both England and France so important and lasting as to entitle it to a prominent place in the records of the closing events of the Middle Ages. Freeman likens the contest to the Peloponnesian War in ancient Greece.

The war with Scotland was one of the things that led up to this war. All through that struggle, France, as the jealous rival of England, was ever giving aid and encouragement to the Scotch rebels. Then the English lands in France, for which the English king did homage to the French king as overlord, were a source of constant dispute between the two countries. Furthermore, upon the death of Charles IV., the last of the Capetian line, Edward III. laid claim, through his mother, to the French crown, in much the same way that William of Normandy centuries before had laid claim to the crown of England.

The Battle of Crécy (1346). — The first great combat of the long war was the memorable battle of Crécy. Edward had invaded France with an army of 30,000 men, made up largely of English bowmen, and had penetrated far into the country, ravaging as he went, when he finally halted, and faced the pursuing French army near the village of Crécy, where he inflicted upon it a most terrible defeat; 1200 knights, the flower of French chivalry, and 30,000 foot-soldiers lay dead upon the field.

The great battle of Crécy is memorable for several reasons, but chiefly because Feudalism and Chivalry there received their death-blow. The yeomanry of England there showed themselves superior to the chivalry of France. "The churl had struck down the noble; the bondsman proved more than a match, in sheer hard fighting, for the knight. From the day of Crécy, Feudalism tottered slowly but surely to its grave." The battles of the world were hereafter, with few exceptions, to be fought and won, not by mail-clad knights with battle-axe and lance, but by common foot-soldiers with bow and gun.

The Capture of Calais. — From the field of Crécy Edward led his army to the siege of Calais. At the end of a year's investment, the city fell into the hands of the English. The capture of this sea-port was a very important event for the English, as it gave them control of the commerce of the Channel, and afforded them a convenient landing-place for their expeditions of invasion into France.

The Battle of Poitiers (1356). — The terrible scourge of the "Black Death," [1] which desolated all Europe about the middle of the fourteenth century, caused the contending nations for a time to forget their quarrel. But no sooner had a purer atmosphere breathed upon the continent than the old struggle was renewed with fresh eagerness.

Edward III. planned a double invasion of France. He

CHARGE OF FRENCH KNIGHTS AND FLIGHT OF ENGLISH ARROWS.

himself led an army through the already wasted provinces of the North, while the Black Prince with another army ravaged the fields of the South. As the Prince's army, numbering about 8000 men, loaded with booty, was making its way back to the coast, it found its path, near Poitiers, obstructed by a French army of

---

[1] The Black Death was so called on account of the black spots which covered the body of the person attacked. It was a contagious fever, which, like the pestilence in the reign of Justinian, entered Europe from the East, and made terrible ravages during the years 1347–49. In Germany over 1,000,000 persons fell victims to the plague, while in England, according to some authori-

50,000. A battle ensued which proved for the French a second Crécy. The arrows of the English bowmen drove them in fatal panic from the field, which was strewn with 11,000 of their dead.

Battle of Agincourt (1415). — For half a century after the Peace [1] that followed the battle of Poitiers there was a lull in the war. But while Henry V. (1413–1422) was reigning in England, France was unfortunate in having an insane king, Charles VI.; and Henry, taking advantage of the disorder into which the French kingdom naturally fell under these circumstances, invaded the country with a powerful army, defeated the French in the great battle of Agincourt (1415), and five years later concluded the Treaty of Troyes, in which, so discouraged had the French become, a large party agreed that the crown of France should be given to him upon the death of Charles.

Joan of Arc. — But patriotism was not yet wholly extinct among the French people. There were many who regarded the concessions of the Treaty of Troyes as not only weak and shameful, but as unjust to the Dauphin Charles, who was thereby disinherited, and they accordingly refused to be bound by its provisions. Consequently, when the poor insane king died, the terms of the treaty were not carried out, and the war dragged on. The party that stood by their native prince, afterwards crowned as Charles VII., were at last reduced to most desperate straits. A great part of the northern section of the country was in the hands of the English, who were holding in close siege the important city of Orleans.

But the darkness was the deep gloom that precedes the dawn. A strange deliverer now appears, — the famous Joan of Arc, Maid of Orleans. This young peasant girl, with imagination all

ties, one-half of the population was swept away. The pestilence was also especially severe in Florence, in Italy. Under the terror and excitement of the dreadful visitation, religious penitents, thinking to turn away the wrath of heaven by unusual penances, went about in procession, lacerating themselves with whips (hence they were called *flagellants*). This religious frenzy had its most remarkable manifestation in Germany.

[1] The Treaty of Bretigny (1360).

aflame from brooding over her country's wrongs and sufferings, seemed to see visions and hear voices, which bade her undertake the work of delivering France. She was obedient unto the heavenly vision.

The warm, impulsive French nation, ever quick in responding to appeals to the imagination, was aroused exactly as it was stirred by the voice of the preachers of the Crusades. Religious enthusiasm now accomplished what patriotism alone could not do.

Received by her countrymen as a messenger from heaven, the maiden kindled throughout the land a flame of enthusiasm that nothing could resist. Inspiring the dispirited French soldiers with new courage, she forced the English to raise the siege of Orleans (from which exploit she became known as the Maid of Orleans), and speedily brought about the coronation of Prince Charles at Reims (1429). Shortly afterward she fell into the hands of the English, and was condemned and burned as a heretic and witch.

But the spirit of the Maid had already taken possession of the French nation. From this on, the war, though long continued, went steadily against the English. Little by little they were pushed back and off from the soil they had conquered, until, by the middle of the fifteenth century, they were driven quite out of the country, retaining no foothold in the land save Calais (see p. 553).

Thus ended the Hundred Years' War, in 1453, the very year which saw Constantinople fall before the Turks.

Effects upon England of the War. — The most lasting and important effects upon England of the war were the enhancement of the power of the Lower House of Parliament, and the awakening of a national spirit and feeling. The maintaining of the long and costly quarrel called for such heavy expenditures of men and money that the English kings were made more dependent than hitherto upon the representatives of the people, who were careful to make their grants of supplies conditional upon the correction of abuses or the confirming of their privileges. Thus the war served to make the Commons a power in the English government.

Again, as the war was participated in by all classes alike, the great victories of Crécy, Poitiers, and Agincourt roused a national pride, which led to a closer union between the different elements of society. Normans and English were fused by the ardor of a common patriotic enthusiasm into a single people. The real *national* life of England dates from this time. (For the effects of the war on France, see p. 494.)

The Wars of the Roses (1455-1485).

General Statement. — The Wars of the Roses is the name given to a long, shameful, and selfish contest between the adherents of the Houses of York and Lancaster, rival branches of the royal family of England. The strife, which was for place and power, was so named because the Yorkists adopted as their badge a white rose and the Lancastrians a red one.

The battle of Bosworth Field (1485) marks the close of the war. In this fight King Richard III., the last of the House of York, was overthrown and slain by Henry Tudor, the Earl of Richmond, who was crowned on the field with the diadem which had fallen from the head of Richard, and saluted as King Henry VII., the first of the Tudors.

The Effects of the War. — The most important result of the Wars of the Roses was the ruin of the baronage of England. One-half of the nobility was slain. Those that survived were ruined, their estates having been wasted or confiscated during the progress of the struggle. Not a single great house retained its old-time wealth and influence.

The second result of the struggle sprung from the first. This was the great peril into which English liberty was cast by the ruin of the nobility. It will be recalled that it was the barons who forced the Great Charter from King John (see p. 479), and who kept him and his successors from reigning like absolute monarchs. Now that once proud and powerful baronage were ruined, and their confiscated estates had gone to increase the influence and patronage of the king. He being no longer in wholesome fear of Parliament, for the Commons were as yet weak and timid, did pretty much as he pleased, and became insufferably oppressive and tyrannical; raising taxes, for instance, without the consent of Parliament, and imprisoning and executing persons without due process of law. For the hundred years following the Wars of the Roses the government of England was rather an absolute than a limited monarchy. Not until the final Revolution of the seventeenth century (see Chap. LV.) did the people, by overturning the throne of the Stuarts, fully recover their lost liberties.

Growth of the English Language and Literature.

The Language. — From the Norman Conquest to the middle of the fourteenth century there were in use in England three languages: Norman French was the speech of the conquerors and the medium of polite literature; Old English was the tongue of the common people; while Latin was the language of the laws and records, of the church services, and of the works of the learned.

Modern English is the Old English worn and improved by use, and enriched by a large infusion of Norman-French words, with less important additions from the Latin and other languages. It took the place of the Norman-French in the courts of law about the middle of the fourteenth century. At this time the language was broken up into many dialects, and the expression "King's English" is supposed to have referred to the standard form employed in state documents and in use at court.

Effect of the Norman Conquest on English Literature. — The blow that struck down King Harold and his brave thanes on the field of Hastings silenced for the space of about a century the voice of English literature. The tongue of the conquerors became the speech of the court, the nobility, and the clergy; while the language of the despised English was, like themselves, crowded out of every place of honor. But when, after a few generations, the down-trodden race began to re-assert itself, English literature emerged from its obscurity, and with an utterance somewhat changed — yet it is unmistakably the same voice — resumes its interrupted lesson and its broken song.

Chaucer (1328?–1400). — Holding a position high above all other writers of early English is Geoffrey Chaucer. He is the first in time, and, after Shakespeare, perhaps the first in genius, among the great poets of the English-speaking race. He is

WYCLIFFE.

reverently called the "Father of English Poetry."

Chaucer stands between two ages, the mediæval and the modern. He felt not only the influences of the age of Feudalism which was passing away, but also those of the new age of learning and freedom which was dawning. It is because he reflects his surroundings so faithfully in his writings, that these are so valuable as interpreters of the period in which he lived. Chaucer's greatest work is his *Canterbury Tales*, wherein the poet represents himself as one of a company of story-telling pilgrims who have set out from London on a journey to the tomb of Thomas Becket, at Canterbury.

Wycliffe and the Reformation (1324–1384). — Foremost among the reformers and religious writers of the period under review was

Wycliffe, "The Morning Star of the Reformation." He gave the English people the first translation of the entire Bible in their native tongue. There was no press at that time to multiply editions of the book, but by means of manuscript copies it was widely circulated and read. Its influence was very great, and from its appearance may be dated the beginning of the Reformation in England.

The followers of Wycliffe became known as "Lollards" (babblers), a term applied to them in derision. They grew to be very numerous, and threatened by their excesses and imprudent zeal the peace of the state. They were finally suppressed by force.

2. FRANCE.

Beginning of the French Kingdom. — The kingdom of France begins properly with the accession of the first of the Capetian rulers, late in the tenth century. The Merovingian and Carolingian kings were simply German princes reigning in Gaul. The Capetians held the throne for more than three centuries, when they were followed by the Valois kings. The last of the main line of the Valois family gave way to the first of the Valois-Orleans sovereigns in 1498, which date may be allowed to mark the beginning of modern French history.

We shall now direct attention to the most important transactions of the period covered by the Capetian and Valois dynasties. Our aim will be to give prominence to those matters which concern the gradual consolidation of the French monarchy.

France under the Capetians [1] (987–1328).

The first Capetian king differed from his vassal counts and dukes simply in having a more dignified title; his power was scarcely

[1] Table of the Capetian Kings (direct line): —

Hugh Capet	987– 996	Louis VIII.(Lion-hearted)	1223–1226
Robert II. (the Sage) . .	996–1031	Louis IX. (the Saint) . .	1226–1270
Henry I.	1031–1060	Philip III. (the Hardy) .	1270–1285
Philip I.	1060–1108	Philip IV. (the Fair) . .	1285–1314
Louis VI. (the Fat) . .	1108–1137	Louis X. (the Stubborn) .	1314–1316
Louis VII. (the Young) .	1137–1180	Philip V. (the Tall) . .	1316–1322
Philip II. (Augustus) . .	1180–1223	Charles IV.(the Handsome)	1322–1328

greater than that of many of the lords who paid him homage as their suzerain. The fourth king of the line (Philip I.) confessed that he had grown gray while trying to capture a castle which stood within sight of Paris ; and evidently he had abandoned all hope of getting possession of it, for he charged his son, to whom he one day pointed it out, to watch it well. How various events and circumstances — conquests, treaties, politic marriage alliances, and unjust encroachments — conspired to build up the power of the kings will appear as we go on.

The most noteworthy events of the Capetian period were the acquisition by the French crown of the English possessions in France, the Holy Wars for the recovery of Jerusalem, the crusade against the Albigenses, and the creation of the States-General. Of these several matters we will now speak in order.

The English Possessions in France. — The issue of the battle of Hastings, in 1066, made William of Normandy king of England. He ruled that country by right of conquest. But we must bear in mind that he still held his possessions in France as a fief from the French king, whose vassal he was. This was the beginning of the possessions on the continent of the English kings. Then, when Henry, Count of Anjou, came to the English throne as the first of the Plantagenets, these territories were greatly increased by the French possessions of that prince. The larger part of Henry's dominions, indeed, was in France, almost the whole of the western coast of the country being in his hands ; but for all of this he, of course, paid homage to the French king.

As was inevitable, a feeling of intense jealousy sprang up between the two sovereigns. The French king was ever watching for some pretext upon which he might deprive his rival of his possessions in France. The opportunity came when King John, in 1199, succeeded Richard the Lion-hearted upon the English throne. That odious tyrant was accused, and doubtless justly, of having murdered his nephew Arthur. Philip Augustus, who then held the French throne, as John's feudal superior, ordered him to clear himself of the charge before his French peers. John refus-

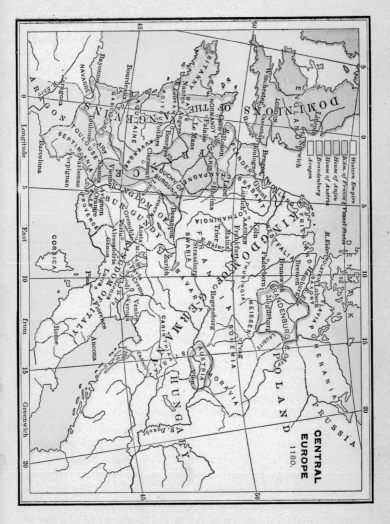

CENTRAL
EUROPE
1180.

Western Empire
Adm. of France & Vassal States
House of Anjou
House of Austria
House of Brandenburg

DOMINIONS

OF

ENGLAND

London
Canterbury
Winchester
Norwich
Lincoln
Baldwins

BRITANNY
NORMANDY
Rouen
Falaise
Nantes
Angers
Le Mans
Tours
Chartres
Orleans
Brabant
Ghent
Bruges
Holland
Cologne
Liège
Aachen
Lothringia
Westfalia
Trier
Mainz
Frankfurt
Paderborn
Thuringia
Meissen
Brunswick
Magdeburg
Bremen
Hamburg
R.Elder
Holstein
Lübeck
Schleswig
Pomerania

DENMARK
Odense

DUCHY OF
BURGUNDY
Laon
Rheims
Sens

PARIS
Bourges
Clermont
Poitiers

POITOU
AQUITAINE
GASCOGNE
GUIENNE

ANGOULEME
Limoges

KINGDOM OF FRANCE

Bayonne
Bordeaux
Toulouse
Narbonne
Perpignan
Nismes
Avignon
Arles
Provence
Vienne
Lyons
Geneva
Grenoble
Besançon
Aosta
Turin
Alessandria
Genoa
Lucca
Pisa
Florence
Ancona
Rome

NAVARRE
Saragossa
ARAGON
Barcelona
R.Ebro
SEPTIMANIA

KINGDOM OF BURGUNDY

KINGDOM OF ITALY

PROVENCE
SAVOY
Piacenza
Parma
Modena
Venice
Milan
Pavia

CORSICA

SWABIA
Strassburg
Zürich
BAVARIA
Regensburg
FRANCONIA
F.R.Rhine
CARINTHIA
CARNIOLA
AUSTRIA
STYRIA
MORAVIA
BOHEMIA
Prag
LAUSITZ
BRANDENBURG
R.Oder

KINGDOM OF GERMANY

FRIESLAND

HUNGARY
R.Danube

POLAND

PRUSSIA

Longitude 0 East 5 10 from 15 Greenwich 20

45 50

ing to do so, Philip declared forfeited all the lands he held as fiefs of the French Crown,[1] and thereupon proceeded to seize Normandy and other possessions of John in the North of France, leaving him scarcely anything save the Duchy of Aquitaine in the South. The annexation of these large possessions to the crown of France brought a vast accession of power and patronage to the king, who was now easily the superior of any of his great vassals.

The French and the Crusades. — The age of the Capetians was the age of the Crusades. These romantic expeditions, while stirring all Christendom, appealed especially to the ardent, imaginative genius of the Gallic race. Three Capetian kings, Louis VII., Philip Augustus, and Louis IX., themselves headed several of the wild expeditions.

It is the influence of the Crusades on the French monarchy that we alone need to notice in this place. They tended very materially to weaken the power and influence of the feudal nobility, and in a corresponding degree to strengthen the authority of the crown and add to its dignity. The way in which they brought about this transfer of power from the aristocracy to the king has been explained in the chapter on the Crusades (see p. 450).

Crusade against the Albigenses (1207–1229). — During this age of religious enthusiasm holy wars were directed as well against heretics as infidels. In the South of France was a sect of Christians called Albigenses,[2] who had departed so far from the faith of the Church, and had embraced such dangerous social heresies, that Pope Innocent III. felt constrained to call upon the French king and his nobles to lead a crusade against them. The outcome was the almost total extirpation of the heretical sect, and the acquisition by the French crown of large and rich territories that were

---

[1] This was the second condemnation of John. A year before this time (in 1202), John having refused to answer a charge of tyranny preferred by the nobles of Poitou, Philip had declared his fief to be forfeited. It was in the turmoil which followed this sentence, that Arthur was taken prisoner by John and afterwards murdered.

[2] From *Albi*, the name of a city and district in which their tenets prevailed.

formerly the possessions of the Counts of Toulouse, the patrons of the heretics.

Creation of the States-General (1302). — The event of the greatest significance in the Capetian age was the admission, in the reign of Philip the Fair, of the commons to the feudal assembly, or council, of the king. This transaction is in French history what the first summoning of the House of Commons is in English (see p. 480).

A dispute having arisen between Philip and the Pope respecting the control of the offices and revenues of the French Church, in order to rally to his support all classes throughout his kingdom, Philip called an assembly, to which he invited representatives of the burghers, or inhabitants of the cities (1302). The royal council had hitherto been made up of two estates only, — the nobles and the clergy ; now is added what comes to be known as the *Tiers État*, or Third Estate, and henceforth the assembly is known as the *States-General.* Eventually, before the power of this Third Estate, we shall see the Church, the nobility, and the monarchy all go down, through revolution ; just as in England we shall see clergy, nobles, and king gradually yield to the rising power of the English Commons.

France under the House of Valois[1] (1328–1498).

Effects upon France of the Hundred Years' War. — The chief interest of that period of French history upon which we here enter attaches to that long struggle between England and France known as the Hundred Years' War. Having already, in connection with English affairs (see p. 484), touched upon the causes and incidents of this war, we shall here simply speak of

---

[1] Names of the sovereigns of the main line of the House of Valois : —

Philip VI.	1328–1350	Charles VII. (the Victori-	
John (the Good)	1350–1364	ous)	1422–1461
Charles V. (the Wise)	1364–1380	Louis XI.	1461–1483
Charles VI. (the Well-		Charles VIII. (the Affa-	
Beloved)	1380–1422	ble)	1483–1498

the effects of the struggle on the French people and kingdom. Among these results must be noticed the almost complete prostration, by the successive shocks of Crécy, Poitiers, and Agincourt, of the French feudal aristocracy, which was already tottering to its fall through the undermining influences of the Crusades; the growth of the power of the king, a consequence, largely, of the ruin of the nobility; and, lastly, the awakening of a feeling of nationality, and the drawing together of the hitherto isolated sections of the country by the attraction of a common and patriotic enthusiasm.

Speaking in a very general manner, we may say that by the close of the war Feudalism in France was over, and that France had become, partly in spite of the war but more largely by reason of it, not only a great monarchy, but a great nation.

Louis XI. and Charles the Bold of Burgundy. — The foundations of the French monarchy were greatly enlarged and strengthened by the unscrupulous measures of Louis XI. (1461–1483), who was a perfect Ulysses in cunning and deceit. His maxim was, " He who knows how to deceive, knows how to reign." The great feudal lords that still retained power and influence, he brought to destruction one after another, and united their fiefs to the royal domains. Of all the vassal nobles ruined by the craft and cunning of Louis, the most famous and powerful was Charles the Bold, Duke of Burgundy, with whom the French king was almost constantly warring, and against whom he was forever intriguing. Upon the death of the duke, Louis, without clear right, seized a great part of his dominions, which were almost large and rich enough to sustain the dignity of a king. By inheritance and treaty, Louis also gained large accessions of territory in the South of France, which gave his kingdom a wide frontage upon the Mediterranean, and made the Pyrenees its southern defence.

Invasion of Italy by Charles VIII. — Charles VIII., the son of Louis XI., was the last of the direct line of the Valois. Through the favor of a long series of circumstances, the persistent policy of his predecessors, and his own politic marriage,[1] he found himself at the head of a state that had been gradually transformed from a feudal league into a true monarchy. The strength of this kingdom he determined to employ in some enterprise beyond the limits of France. With a standing army, created by Charles VII. during the latter years of the war with England,[2] at his command, he invaded Italy, intent on the conquest of Naples, — to which he laid claim on the strength of some old bequest, — proposing, with that state subdued, to lead a crusade to the East against the Turks. He reached Naples in triumph, but was soon forced, with heavy losses, to retreat into France.

This enterprise of Charles is noteworthy not only because it marks the commencement of a long series of brilliant yet disastrous campaigns carried on by the French in Italy, but also on account of Charles' army having been made up largely of paid troops instead of feudal retainers, which fact assures us that the Feudal System in France, as a governmental organization, had come to an end.

Beginnings of French Literature.

The Troubadours. — The contact of the old Latin speech in Gaul with that of the Teutonic invaders gave rise there to two very distinct dialects. These were the *Langue d'Oc*, or Provençal, the tongue of the South of France and of the adjoining regions of Spain and Italy ; and the *Langue d'Oil*, or French proper, the language of the North.[3]

---

[1] He married Anne of Brittany, and thus brought that large province, which had hitherto constituted an almost independent state, under the authority of the French crown.

[2] The paid force of infantry and cavalry created by Charles VII. in 1448, was the first standing army in Europe, and the beginning of that vast military system which now burdens the great nations of that continent with the support of several millions of soldiers constantly under arms.

[3] The terms *Langue d'Oc* and *Langue d'Oil* arose from the use of different words for *yes*, which in the tongue of the South was *oc*, and in that of the North *oil*.

About the beginning of the twelfth century, by which time the Provençal tongue had become settled and somewhat polished, literature in France first began to find a voice in the songs of the Troubadours, the poets of the South. It is instructive to note that it was the home of the Albigensian heresy, the land that had felt the influence of every Mediterranean civilization, that was also the home of the Troubadour literature. The Counts of Toulouse, the protectors of the heretics, were also the patrons of the poets. The same fierce persecution that uprooted the heretical faith of the Albigenses, also stilled the song of the Troubadours (see p. 493).

The verses of the Troubadours were sung in every land, and to the stimulating influence of their musical harmonies the early poetry of almost every people of Europe is largely indebted.

The Trouveurs. — These were the poets of Northern France, who composed in the *Langue d' Oil*, or Old French tongue. They flourished during the twelfth and thirteenth centuries. While the compositions of the Troubadours were almost exclusively lyrical songs, those of the Trouveurs were epic, or narrative poems, called *romances.* They gather about three great names, — King Arthur, Alexander the Great, and Charlemagne. It will be noted that the poet story-tellers thus drew their material from the heroic legends of all the different races that blended to form the French nation, namely, the Celtic, the Græco-Roman, and the Teutonic.

The influence of these French romances upon the springing literatures of Europe was most inspiring and helpful. Nor has their influence yet ceased. Thus in English literature, not only did Chaucer and Spenser and all the early island-poets draw inspiration from these fountains of continental song, but the later Tennyson, in his *Idylls of the King,* has illustrated the power over the imagination yet possessed by the Arthurian poems of the old Trouveurs.

Froissart's Chronicles. — The first really noted prose writer in French literature was Froissart (1337–1410), whose entertaining credulity and artlessness, and skill as a story-teller, have won for him the title of the French Herodotus. Born, as he was, only a little after the opening of the Hundred Years' War, and knowing personally many of the actors in that struggle, it was fitting that he should become, as he did, the annalist of those stirring times.

3. SPAIN.

The Beginnings of Spain. — When, in the eighth century, the Saracens swept like a wave over Spain, the mountains of Asturia, in the northwest corner of the peninsula, afforded a refuge for the most resolute of the Christian chiefs who refused to submit their necks to the Moslem yoke. These brave and hardy warriors not only successfully defended the hilly districts that formed their retreat, but gradually pushed back the invaders, and regained control of a portion of the fields and cities that had been lost. This work of reconquest was greatly furthered by Charlemagne, who, it will be recalled, drove the Saracens out of all the northeastern portion of the country as far south as the Ebro, and made the subjugated district a province of his great empire, under the name of the Spanish March.

By the opening of the eleventh century several little Christian states, among which we must notice the names of Castile and Aragon, because of the prominent part they were to play in later history, had been established upon the ground thus recovered or always maintained. Castile was at first simply "a line of castles" against the Moors, whence its name.

Union of Castile and Aragon (1479). — For several centuries the princes of the little states to which we have referred kept up an incessant warfare with their Mohammedan neighbors ; owing however to dissensions among themselves, they were unable to combine in any effective way for the reconquest of their ancient possessions. But the marriage, in 1469, of Ferdinand, prince of Aragon, to Isabella, princess of Castile, paved the way for the union a little later of these two leading states. Thus the quarrels of these rival principalities were composed, and they were now free to employ their united strength in effecting what the Christian princes amidst all their contentions had never lost sight of, — the expulsion of the Moors from the peninsula.

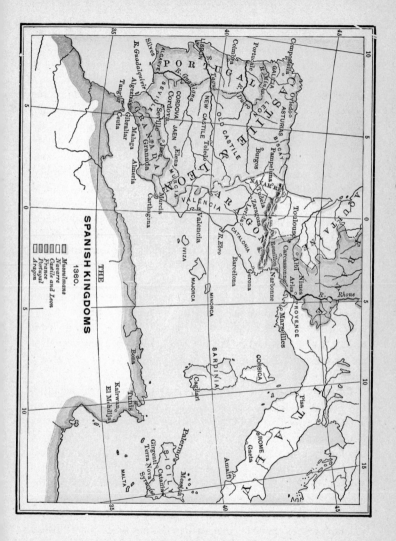

THE
SPANISH KINGDOMS
1360.

Mussulmans
Navarre
Castile and Leon
France
Portugal
Aragon

The Conquest of Granada (1492). — At the time when the basis of the Spanish monarchy was laid by the union of Castile and Aragon, the Mohammedan possessions had been reduced, by the constant pressure of the Christian chiefs through eight centuries, to a very limited dominion in the south of Spain. Here the Moors had established a strong, well-compacted state, known as the Kingdom of Granada.

As soon as Ferdinand and Isabella had settled the affairs of their dominions, they began to make preparation for the conquest of Granada, eager to signalize their reign by the reduction

THE ALHAMBRA. PALACE OF THE MOORISH KINGS AT GRANADA.
(From a photograph.)

of this last stronghold of the Moorish power in the peninsula. The Moors made a desperate defence of their little state. The struggle lasted for ten years. City after city fell into the hands of the Christian knights, and finally the capital, Granada, pressed by an army of seventy thousand, was forced to surrender, and the Cross replaced the Crescent on its walls and towers (1492). The Moors, or Moriscoes, as they were called, were allowed to remain in the country and to retain their Mohammedan worship, though under many annoying restrictions. What is known as their *expulsion* occurred at a later date (see p. 538).

The fall of Granada holds an important place among the many significant events that mark the latter half of the fifteenth century. It ended, after an existence of eight hundred years, the Mohammedan kingdom in the Spanish peninsula, and thus formed an offset to the progress of the Moslem power in Eastern Europe and the loss to the Christian world of Constantinople. It advanced Spain to the first rank among the nations of Europe, and gave her arms a prestige that secured for her position, influence, and deference long after the decline of her power had commenced.

The Inquisition. — Ferdinand greatly enhanced his power by the active and tyrannical use of the Inquisition, a court that had been established by the Church for the purpose of detecting and punishing heresy. The chief victims of the tribunal were the Moors and Jews, but it was also directed against the enemies of the sovereign among the nobility and the clergy. The Holy Office, as the tribunal was styled, thus became the instrument of the most incredible cruelty. Thousands were burned at the stake, and tens of thousands more condemned to endure penalties scarcely less terrible. Queen Isabella, in giving her consent to the establishment of the tribunal in her dominions, was doubtless actuated by the purest religious zeal, and sincerely believed that in suppressing heresy she was discharging a simple duty, and rendering God good service. " In the love of Christ and his Maid-Mother," she says, " I have caused great misery. I have depopulated towns and districts, provinces and kingdoms."

Death of Ferdinand and of Isabella. — Queen Isabella died in 1504, and Ferdinand followed her in the year 1516, upon which latter event the crown of Spain descended upon the head of his grandson, Charles, of whom we shall hear much as Emperor Charles V. With his reign the modern history of Spain begins.

Beginnings of the Spanish Language and Literature.

The Language. — After the union of Castile and Aragon it was the language of the former that became the speech of the Spanish court. During the reign of Ferdinand and Isabella it gradually gained the ascendancy over the numerous dialects of the country, and became the national speech, just as in France the Langue d'Oil finally crowded out all other dialects. By the conquests and colonizations of the sixteenth century this Castilian speech was destined to become only less widely spread than the English tongue.

The Poem of the Cid. — Castilian, or Spanish literature, begins in the twelfth century with the romance-poem of the *Cid* (that is, *Chief*, the title of the hero of the poem), one of the great literary productions of the mediæval period. This grand national poem was the outgrowth of the sentiments inspired by the long struggle between the Spanish Christians and the Mohammedan Moors.

SARCOPHAGUS OF FERDINAND AND ISABELLA, AT GRANADA.
(From a photograph.)

4. GERMANY.

Beginnings of the Kingdom of Germany. — The history of Germany as a separate kingdom begins with the break-up of the empire of Charlemagne (see p. 408). Germany at that time comprised several groups of tribes, — the Saxons, the Suabians, the Thuringians, the Bavarians, and the Franks. Closely allied in race, speech, manners, and social arrangements, all these peoples seemed ready to be welded into a close and firm nation ; but, unfortunately, the circumstances tending to keep the several states or communities apart were stronger than those operating to draw them together, so that for a thousand years after Charlemagne we find them constituting hardly anything more than a very loose confederation, the members of which were constantly struggling among themselves for supremacy, or were engaged in private wars with the neighboring nations.[1]

That which more than all else operated to prevent Germany from becoming a powerful, closely-knit nation, was the adoption by the German rulers of an unfortunate policy respecting a world-empire. This matter will be explained in the following paragraphs.

Renewal of the Roman Empire by Otto the Great (962). — When the dominions of Charlemagne were divided among his three grandsons (see p. 408), the Imperial title was given to Lothair, to whom fell Italy and the Rhine-land. The title, however, meant scarcely anything, carrying with it little or no real authority. Thus matters ran on for more than a century, the empty honor of the title sometimes being enjoyed by the kings of Italy, and again by those of Germany.

But with the accession of the second of the Saxon line, Otto I., who was crowned king at Aachen in 936, there appeared among the princes of Europe a second Charlemagne. He was easily first among them all. Besides being king of Germany, he became, through interference on request in the affairs of Italy, king of that country also. Furthermore, he wrested large tracts of land from the Slavonians, and forced the Danes, Poles, and Hungarians to acknowledge his suzerainty. Thus favored by fortune, he natur-

---

[1] During the mediæval period, Germany was under the following lines of kings and emperors: —

Carolingians	843– 911	The Interregnum	1254–1273
Conrad of Franconia	911– 918	Emperors of different	
Saxon Emperors	919–1024	Houses	1273–1438
Franconian Emperors	1024–1125	Emperors of the House of	
Lothair of Saxony	1125–1137	Austria	1438–
Hohenstaufen Emperors	1138–1254		

ally conceived the idea of restoring once more the Roman empire, even as it had been revived by Charles the Great (see p. 406).

So in 962, just a little more than a century and a half after the coronation at Rome of Charlemagne as emperor, Otto, at the same place and by the same papal authority, was crowned Emperor of the Romans. For a generation no one had borne the title. From this time on it was the rule that the German king who was crowned at Aachen had a right to be crowned king of Italy at Milan, and emperor at Rome (Freeman). Thus three crowns, and in time still more, came to be heaped upon a single head.

Consequences to Germany of the Revival of the Empire. — The scheme of Otto respecting a world-empire was a grand one, but, as had been demonstrated by the failure of the attempt of Charlemagne, was an utterly impracticable idea. It was simply a dream, and never became anything more than a ghostly shadow. Yet the pursuit of this phantom by the German kings resulted in the most woeful consequences to Germany. Trying to grasp too much, these rulers seized nothing at all. Attempting to be emperors of the world, they failed to become even kings of Germany. While engaged in their schemes of foreign conquest, their home affairs were neglected, and their vassals succeeded in increasing their power and making it hereditary. Thus while the kings of England, France, and Spain were gradually consolidating their dominions, and building up strong centralized monarchies on the ruins of Feudalism, the sovereigns of Germany, neglecting the affairs of their own kingdom, were allowing it to become split up into a vast number of virtually independent states, the ambitions and jealousies of whose rulers were to postpone the unification of Germany for four or five hundred years — until our own day.

Had the emperors inflicted loss and disaster upon Germany alone through their pursuit of this phantom, the case would not be so lamentable ; but Italy was made the camping field of the Imperial armies, and the whole peninsula kept distracted with the bitter quarrels of Guelphs and Ghibellines (see p. 504), and thus the nationalization of the Italian people was also delayed for centuries.

Germany received just one positive compensation for all this loss accruing from the ambition of her kings. This was the gift of Italian civilization, which came into the country through the connections of the emperors with the peninsula.

Germany under the Hohenstaufen Emperors (1138–1254).— The Hohenstaufen, or Suabian dynasty was a most notable line of emperors. The matter of chief importance in German history under the Hohenstaufen is the long and bitter conflict, begun generations before, that was waged between them and the Popes (see p. 455). Germany and Italy were divided into two great parties, known as Welfs and Waiblings, or, as designated in Italy, Guelphs and Ghibellines, the former adhering to the Pope, the latter to the Emperor. The issue of a century's contention was the complete ruin of the House of Hohenstaufen.

The most noted ruler of the line was Frederick I. (1152–1190), better known as *Frederick Barbarossa*, from his red beard. He gave Germany a good and strong government, and gained a sure place in the affections of the German people, who came to regard him as the representative of the sentiment of German nationality. When news of his death was brought back from the East, — it will be recalled that he took part in the Third Crusade, and lost his life in Asia Minor (see p. 445), — they refused to believe that he was dead, and, as time passed, a tradition arose which told how he slept in a cavern beneath one of his castles on a mountain-top, and how, when the ravens should cease to circle about the hill, he would appear, to make the German people a nation united and strong.

Frederick Barbarossa was followed by his son Henry VI. (1190–1197), who, by marriage, had acquired a claim to the kingdom of Sicily.[1] Almost all his time and resources were spent in reducing

[1] The Hohenstaufen held the kingdom until 1265, when the Pope gave it as a fief to Charles I. of Anjou (brother of Louis IX. of France), who beheaded the rightful heir, the ill-starred boy Conradin, the last of the Hohenstaufen race (1268). Charles' oppressive rule led to a revolt of his island subjects, and to the great massacre known as the Sicilian Vespers (1282). All of the hated race of Frenchmen were either killed or driven out of the island.

that remote realm to a state of proper subjection to his authority. By thus leading the emperors to neglect their German subjects and interests, this southern kingdom proved a fatal dower to the Suabian house.

By the close of the Hohenstaufen period, Germany was divided into two hundred and seventy-six virtually independent states, the princes and nobles having taken advantage of the prolonged absences of the emperors, or their troubles with the Popes, to free themselves almost completely from the control of the crown. There was really no longer either a German kingdom or a Roman empire.

Cathedral-building. — The age of the Hohenstaufen was the age of the Crusades, which is to say that it was the age of religious faith. The most striking expression of the spirit of the period, if we except the Holy Wars, is to be found in the sacred architecture of the time. The style of architecture first employed was the Romanesque, characterized by the rounded arch and the dome ; but towards the close of the twelfth century this was superseded by the Gothic, distinguished by the pointed arch, the tower or the slender spire, and rich ornamentation.

The enthusiasm for church-building was universal throughout Europe ; yet nowhere did it find nobler or more sustained expression than in Germany. Among the most noted of the German cathedrals are the one at Strasburg, begun in the eleventh century, and that at Cologne, commenced in 1248, but not wholly finished until our own day (in 1880).

Rise of the Swiss Republic. — The most noteworthy matters in German history during the fourteenth and fifteenth centuries, are the struggles between the Swiss and the dukes of Austria ; the religious movement of the Hussites ; and the growing power of the House of Austria.

From early in the eleventh century, the country now known as Switzerland was a part of the Holy Roman Empire ; but its liberty-loving people never acknowledged any man as their master, save the German emperor, to whom they yielded a merely nominal obedience. The dukes of Austria, princes of the empire, laid claim to a certain authority over them, and tried to make themselves masters in Switzerland. This led to a memorable struggle between the dukes and the brave mountaineers. To the early part of the contest belongs the legend of William Tell, which historical criticism now pronounces a myth, with nothing but the revolt as the nucleus of fact.

In 1315, at the noted battle of Morgarten Pass, the Austrians suffered a severe defeat at the hands of the Swiss patriots. Later in the same century, the Austrians sustained another defeat on the memorable field of Sempach (1386). It was here, tradition says, that Arnold of Winkelried broke the ranks of the Austrians, by collecting in his arms as many of their lances as he could, and, as they pierced his breast, bearing them with him to the ground, exclaiming, " Comrades, I will open a road for you."

Shortly after the battle of Sempach, the Eidgenossen, or Confederates, as the Swiss were at this time called, gained another victory over the Austrians at Näfels (1388), which placed on a firm basis the growing power of the League.

The Hussites. — About the beginning of the fifteenth century, the doctrines of the English reformer, Wycliffe (see p. 490) began to spread in Bohemia. The chief of the new sect was John Huss, a professor of the University of Prague. The doctrines of the reformer were condemned by the great Council of Constance, and Huss himself, having been delivered over into the hands of the civil authorities for punishment, was burned at the stake (1415). The following year Jerome of Prague, another reformer, was likewise burned.

Shortly after the burning of Huss a crusade was proclaimed against his followers, who had risen in arms. Then began a cruel, desolating war of fifteen years, the outcome of which was the almost total extermination of the radical party among the Hussites. With the more moderate of the reformers, however, a treaty was made which secured them freedom of worship.

The Imperial Crown becomes Hereditary in the House of Austria (1438). — In the year 1438, Albert, Duke of Austria,

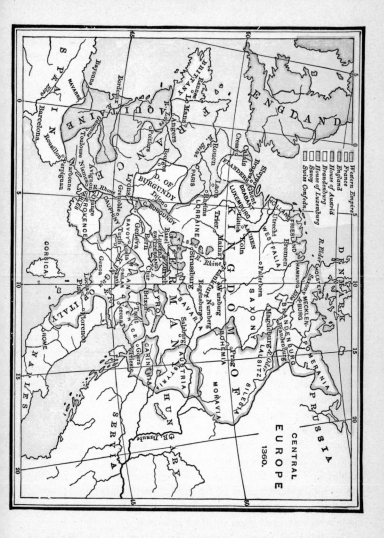

CENTRAL
EUROPE
1360.

Western Empire
France
England
House of Austria
Brandenburg
House of Luxemburg
Savoy
Swiss Confed'n.

was raised by the Electors[1] to the Imperial throne. His accession marks an epoch in German history, for from this time until the dissolution of the empire by Napoleon in 1806, the Imperial crown was regarded as hereditary in the Hapsburg[2] family, the Electors, although never failing to go through the formality of an election, almost always choosing one of the members of that house as king.

GERMAN FOOT-SOLDIER.
(15th Century.)

From the beginning of the practically uninterrupted succession upon the Imperial throne of the princes of the House of Austria, up to the close of the Middle Ages, the power and importance of the family steadily increased, until it seemed that Austria would overshadow all the other German states, and subject them to her sway ; would, in a word, become Germany, just as Francia in Gaul had become France. But this, as we shall learn, never came about.

The greatest of the Hapsburg line during the mediæval period was Maximilian I. (1493–1519). His reign is in every way a noteworthy one in German history, marking, as it does, a strong tendency to centralization, and the material enhancement of the Imperial authority.

[1] When, in the beginning of the tenth century, the German Carolingian line became extinct, the great nobles of the kingdom assumed the right of choosing the successor of the last of the house, and Germany thus became an elective feudal monarchy. In the course of time a few of the leading nobles usurped the right of choosing the king, and these princes became known as Electors. There were, at the end of the Hohenstaufen period, seven princes who enjoyed this important privilege, four of whom were secular princes and three spiritual.

[2] The House of Austria is often so called from the Castle of Hapsburg in Switzerland, the cradle of the family.

Beginning of German Literature.

Song of the Nibelungen. — It was under the patronage of the Hohenstaufen that Germany produced the first pieces of a national literature. The "Song of the Nibelungen" is the great German mediæval epic. It was reduced to writing about 1200, being a recast, by some Homeric genius, perhaps, of ancient German and Scandinavian legends and lays dating from the sixth and seventh centuries. The hero of the story is Siegfried, the Achilles of Teutonic legend and song.

The Minnesingers. — Under the same emperors, during the twelfth and thirteenth centuries, the Minnesingers, or lyric poets, flourished. They were the "Troubadours of Germany." For the most part, refined and tender and chivalrous and pure, the songs of these poets tended to soften the manners and lift the hearts of the German people.

5. RUSSIA.

Beginnings of Russia. — We have seen how, about the middle of the ninth century, the Swedish adventurer Ruric laid, among the Slavonian tribes dwelling eastward from the Baltic, the foundation of what was destined to become one of the leading powers of Europe (see p. 411). The state came to be known as Russia, probably from the word *Ruotsi* (corsairs?), the name given by the Finns to the foreigners.

The Tartar Conquest. — In the thirteenth century an overwhelming calamity befell Russia. This was the overrunning and conquest of the country by the Tartar hordes (see p. 461). The barbarian conquerors inflicted the most horrible atrocities upon the unfortunate land, and for more than two hundred years held the Russian princes in a degrading bondage, forcing them to pay homage and tribute. This misfortune delayed for centuries the nationalization of the Slavonian peoples.

Russia freed from the Mongols. — It was not until the reign of Ivan the Great (1462-1505) that Russia, — now frequently called

Muscovy from the fact that it had been reorganized with Moscow as a centre, — after a terrible struggle, succeeded in freeing itself from the hateful Tartar domination, and began to assume the character of a well-consolidated monarchy.

Thus, by the end of the Middle Ages, Russia had become a really great power; but she was as yet too much hemmed in by hostile states to be able to make her influence felt in the affairs of Europe. Between her and the Caspian and Euxine were the Tartars; shutting her out from the Baltic were the Swedes and other peoples; and between her and Germany were the Lithuanians and Poles.

6. Italy.

No National Government. — In marked contrast to all those countries of which we have thus far spoken, unless we except Germany, Italy came to the close of the Middle Ages without a national or regular government. This is to be attributed in large part to that unfortunate rivalry between Pope and Emperor which resulted in dividing Italy into the two hostile camps of Guelph and Ghibelline. And yet the mediæval period did not pass without attempts on the part of patriot spirits to effect some sort of political union among the different cities and states of the peninsula. The most noteworthy of these movements, and one which gave assurance that the spark of patriotism which was in time to flame into an inextinguishable passion for national unity was kindling in the Italian heart, was that headed by the hero Rienzi, in the fourteenth century.

Rienzi, Tribune of Rome (1347). — During the greater part of the fourteenth century the seat of the Papal See was at Avignon, beyond the Alps (see p. 457). Throughout this period of the "Babylonish captivity," Rome, deprived of her natural guardians, was in a state of the greatest confusion. The nobles terrorized the country about the capital, and kept the streets of the city itself in constant turmoil with their bitter feuds.

In the midst of these disorders there appeared from among the lowest ranks of the people a deliverer in the person of one Nicola di Rienzi. Possessed of considerable talent and great eloquence, Rienzi easily incited the people to a revolt against the rule, or rather misrule, of the nobles, and succeeded in having himself, with the title of Tribune, placed at the head of a new government for Rome.

Encouraged by the success that had thus far attended his schemes, Rienzi now began to concert measures for the union of all the principalities and commonwealths of Italy in a great republic, with Rome as its capital. He sent ambassadors throughout Italy to plead, at the courts of the princes and in the council-chamber of the municipalities, the cause of Italian unity and freedom. The splendid dream of Rienzi was shared by other Italian patriots besides himself, among whom was the poet Petrarch, who was the friend and encourager of the "plebeian hero."

But the moment for Italy's unification had not yet come. Not only were there hindrances to the national movement in the ambitions and passions of rival parties and classes, but there were still greater impediments in the character of the plebeian patriot himself. Rienzi proved to be an unworthy leader. His sudden elevation and surprising success completely turned his head, and he soon began to exhibit the most incredible vanity and weakness. The people withdrew from him their support, and he was finally assassinated.

Thus vanished the dream of Rienzi and Petrarch, of the hero and the poet. Centuries of division, of shameful subjection to foreign princes, — French, Spanish, and Austrian, — of wars and suffering, were yet before the Italian people ere Rome should become the centre of a free, orderly, and united Italy.

The Renaissance. — Though the Middle Ages closed in Italy without the rise there of a national government, still before the end of the period much had been done to awaken those common ideas and sentiments upon which political unity can alone safely repose. Literature and art here performed the part that war did in other countries in arousing a national spirit. The Renaissance (see p.

474) did much toward creating among the Italians a common pride in race and country ; and thus this great literary and artistic enthusiasm was the first step in a course of national development which was to lead the Italian people to a common political life.

Upon the literary phase of the Italian Renaissance we have said something in the chapter on the Revival of Learning (see p. 474) ; we shall here say just a word respecting the artistic side of the movement.

The most splendid period of the art revival covered the latter part of the fifteenth century and the first half of the sixteenth. The characteristic art of the Renaissance in Italy was painting, although the æsthetic genius of the Italians also expressed itself both in architecture and sculpture.[1] The mediæval artists devoted themselves to painting instead of sculpture, for the reason that it best expresses the ideas and sentiments of Christianity. The art that would be the handmaid of the Church needed to be able to represent faith and hope, ecstasy and suffering, — none of which things can well be expressed by sculpture, which is essentially the art of repose.

Savonarola (1452–1498). — A word must here be said respecting the Florentine monk and reformer Girolamo Savonarola, who stands as the most noteworthy personage in Italy during the closing years of the mediæval period.

Savonarola was at once Roman censor and Hebrew prophet. Such a preacher of righteousness the world had not seen since the days of Elijah. His powerful preaching alarmed the conscience of the Florentines. At his suggestion the women brought their

---

[1] The four supreme masters of the Italian Renaissance were Leonardo da Vinci (1452–1519), Michael Angelo (1475–1564), Raphael (1483–1520), and Titian (1477–1576). All were great painters. Perhaps the one of greatest, at least of most varied, genius, was Michael Angelo, who was at once architect, painter, and sculptor. His grandest architectural triumph was the majestic dome of St. Peter's, — which work, however, he did not live to see completed.

finery and ornaments, and others their beautiful works of art, and piling them in great heaps in the streets of Florence, burned them as "vanities." Savonarola even persuaded the people of Florence to set up a sort of theocratic government, of which Christ was the acknowledged head. But at length the activity of his enemies brought about the reformer's downfall, and he was condemned to death, executed, and his body burned. Savonarola may be regarded as the last great mediæval forerunner of the reformers of the sixteenth century.

7. THE NORTHERN COUNTRIES.

The Union of Calmar. — The great Scandinavian Exodus of the ninth and tenth centuries drained the Northern lands of some of the best elements of their population. For this reason these countries did not play as prominent a part in mediæval history as they would otherwise have done. The constant quarrels between their sovereigns and the nobility were also another cause of internal weakness.

In the year 1397, by what is known as the Union of Calmar, the three kingdoms of Norway, Denmark, and Sweden were united under Margaret of Denmark, " the Semiramis of the North." The treaty provided that each country should make its own laws. But the treaty was violated, and though the friends of the measure had hoped much from it, it brought only jealousies, feuds, and wars.

The Swedes arose again and again in revolt, and finally, under the lead of a nobleman named Gustavus Vasa, made good their independence (1523). During the seventeenth century, under the descendants and successors of the Liberator, Sweden was destined to play an important part in the affairs of the continent.

Norway became virtually a province of Denmark, and the Norwegian nobles were driven into exile or killed. The country remained attached to the Danish Crown until the present century.

SECTION II.— MODERN HISTORY.

INTRODUCTION.

As an introduction to the history of the Modern Age, we shall give a brief account of the voyages and geographical discoveries of Columbus, Vasco da Gama, and Magellan, and of the beginning of European conquests and settlements in the New World, inasmuch as these great events lie at the opening of the era and form the prelude of its story.

Discovery of the New World by Columbus (1492). — Christopher Columbus was one of those Genoese navigators who, when Genoa's Asiatic lines of trade were broken by the irruption of the Turks (see p. 467), conceived the idea of reaching India by an ocean route. While others were endeavoring to reach that country by sailing around the southern point of Africa, he proposed the bolder plan of reaching this eastern land by sailing directly westward. The sphericity of the earth was a doctrine held by many at that day; but the theory was not in harmony with the religious ideas of the time, and so it was not prudent for one to publish too openly one's belief in the notion.

COLUMBUS.
(After the Yanez Portrait in the Madrid Library.)

In his endeavors to secure a patron for his enterprise, Columbus met at first with repeated repulse and disappointment. At last, however, he gained the ear of Queen Isabella of Spain; a little fleet was fitted out for the explorer, — and the New World was found.

Columbus never received a fitting reward for the great service he had rendered mankind. Even the continent to which he had shown the way, instead of being called after him as a perpetual memorial, was named from a Florentine navigator, Amerigo Vespucci, whose chief claim to this distinction was his having published the first account of the new lands.

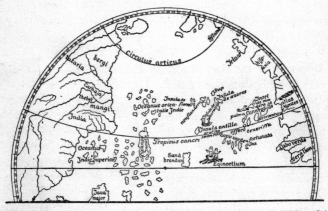

THE OCEAN AND ISLANDS BETWEEN WESTERN EUROPE AND EASTERN ASIA.
From the Globe of Martin Behaim, 1492. (Cathaja = China; Cipango = Japan.)

The Voyage of Vasco da Gama (1497–1498). — The favorable position of Portugal upon the Atlantic seaboard naturally led her sovereigns to conceive the idea of competing with the Italian cities for the trade of the East Indies, by opening up an ocean route to those lands. During all the latter part of the fifteenth century Portuguese sailors were year after year penetrating a little farther into the mysterious tropical seas, and exploring new reaches of the western coast of Africa.

In 1487 the most southern point of the continent was reached, and was named the Cape of Good Hope, as the possibility of reaching India by sea now seemed assured. A decade later Vasco da Gama, a Portuguese admiral, doubled the Cape, crossed the Indian Sea, and landed on the coast of Malabar (1498).

The discovery of a water-path to India effected, as we have already noticed (see p. 467), most important changes in the traffic of the world. It made the ports of Portugal and of other countries on the Atlantic seaboard the depots of the Eastern trade. "The front of Europe was suddenly changed." The Italian merchants were ruined. The great warehouses of Egypt and Syria were left empty. The traffic of the Mediterranean dwindled to insignificant proportions. Portugal established trading-posts and colonies in the East, and built up there a great empire, — like that which England is maintaining in the same region at the present day.

The Voyage around the Globe (1519–1522). — Upon the return of Columbus from his successful expedition, Pope Alexander VI., with a view to adjusting the conflicting claims of Spain and Portugal, divided the world by a meridian line drawn about midway through the Atlantic, and gave to the Spanish sovereigns all unclaimed pagan lands that their subjects might find west of this line, and to the Portuguese kings all new pagan lands discovered by Portuguese navigators east of the designated meridian.

The determination on the part of the king of Spain to acquire title under the papal grant to the valuable Spice Islands of the Pacific by reaching them through sailing westward, led him to organize an expedition of discovery in the western seas. The little fleet was entrusted to the command of Magellan, a Portuguese admiral.

Magellan directed his fleet in a southwesterly course across the Atlantic, hoping to find towards the south a break in the land discovered by Columbus. Near the most southern point of Patagonia he found the narrow strait that now bears his name, through which he pushed his vessel into the sea beyond. From the calm, unruffled face of the new ocean, so different from the stormy Atlantic, he gave to it the name *Pacific*.

After a most adventurous voyage upon the hitherto untraversed waters of the new sea, the expedition reached the Spice Islands, and eventually arrived home, after an absence of over three years. For the first time men had gone around the globe that they had so long lived upon. The achievement of course settled forever the question as to the shape of the earth. It pushed aside all the old narrow geographical ideas, and broadened immensely the physical horizon of the world.

Conquest of Mexico (1519–1521). — Soon after the discovery of the New World, Spanish settlements were established upon the islands in front of the Gulf of Mexico. Among the colonists here were constantly spread reports of a great and rich Indian monarchy upon the mainland to the west. These stories inflamed the imagination of the more adventurous among the settlers, and an expedition was organized and placed under the command of Hernando Cortez, for the conquest and "conversion" of the heathen nation. The expedition was successful, and soon the Spaniards were masters of the greater part of Mexico.

The state that the conquerors destroyed was hardly an "empire," as termed by the Spanish writers, but rather a confederacy, somewhat like the Iroquois confederacy in the North. It embraced three tribes, of which the Aztecs were leaders. At the head of the league was a war-chief, who bore the name of Montezuma.

The Mexican Indians had taken some steps in civilization. They employed a system of picture-writing, and had cities and temples. But they were cannibals, and offered human sacrifices to their gods. They had no knowledge of the horse or of the ox, and were of course ignorant of the use of fire-arms.

The Conquest of Peru (1532–1536). — Shortly after the conquest of the Indians of Mexico, the subjugation of the Indians of Peru was also effected. The civilization of the Peruvians was superior to that of the Mexicans. Not only were the great cities of the Peruvian empire filled with splendid temples and palaces, but throughout the country were magnificent works of public utility, such as roads, bridges, and aqueducts. The government of the Incas, the royal, or ruling race, was a mild, parental autocracy. •

Glowing reports of the enormous wealth of the Incas, — the commonest articles in whose palaces, it was asserted, were of solid gold, reached the Spaniards by way of the Isthmus of Darien, and it was not long before an expedition was organized for the conquest of the country. The leader of the band was Francisco Pizarro, an iron-hearted, perfidious, and illiterate adventurer.

Through treachery, Pizarro made a prisoner of the Inca Atahualpa. The captive offered, as a ransom for his release, to fill the room in which he was confined "as high as he could reach" with vessels of gold. Pizarro accepted the offer, and the palaces and temples throughout the empire were stripped of their golden vessels, and the apartment was filled with the precious relics. The value of the treasure is estimated at over $17,000,000. When this vast wealth was once under the control of the Spaniards, they seized it all, and then treacherously put the Inca to death (1533). With the death of Atahualpa the power of the Inca dynasty passed away forever.

Spanish Colonization in the New World. — Not until more than one hundred years after the discovery of the Western Hemisphere by Columbus, was there established a single permanent English settlement within the limits of what is now the United States, the portion of the New World destined to be taken possession of by the peoples of Northern Europe, and to become the home of civil and religious freedom.

But into those parts of the new lands opened up by Spanish exploration and conquest there began to pour at once a tremendous stream of Spanish adventurers and colonists, in search of fortune and fame. It was a sort of Spanish migration. The movement might be compared to the rush of population from the Eastern States to California, after the announcement of the discovery there of gold, in 1848–9. Upon the West India Islands, in Mexico, in Central America, all along the Pacific slope of the Andes, and everywhere upon the lofty and pleasant table-lands that had formed the heart of the empire of the Incas, there sprang up rapidly great cities as the centres of mining and agricultural industries, of commerce and of trade. Thus did a Greater Spain grow up in the New World. It was, in a large measure, the treasures derived from these new possessions that enabled the sovereigns of Spain to play the imposing part they did in the affairs of Europe during the century following the discovery of America.[1]

[1] After having robbed the Indians of their wealth in gold and silver, the slow accumulation of centuries, the Spaniards further enriched themselves by the enforced labor of the unfortunate natives. Unused to such toil as was exacted of them under the lash of worse than Egyptian task-masters, the Indians wasted away by millions in the mines of Mexico and Peru, and upon the sugar plantations of the West Indies. More than half of the native population of Peru is thought to have been consumed in the Peruvian mines. To save the Indians, negroes were introduced as a substitute for native laborers. This was the beginning of the African slave-trade in the New World. The traffic was especially encouraged by a benevolent priest named Las Casas (1474–1566), known as the "Apostle of the Indians." Thus the gigantic evil of African slavery in the Western Hemisphere, like the gladiatorial shows of the Romans, was brought into existence, or, rather, in its beginning was fostered, by a philanthropic desire and effort to mitigate human suffering.

(FROM THE DISCOVERY OF AMERICA TO THE PEACE OF WESTPHALIA, IN 1648.)

CHAPTER XLVIII.

THE BEGINNING OF THE REFORMATION UNDER LUTHER.

General Statement. — We have already indicated (see pp. 366–7), the two periods of modern history; namely, the *Era of the Protestant Reformation* and the *Era of the Political Revolution.* We need here simply to remind the reader that the first period, extending from the opening of the sixteenth century to the Peace of Westphalia in 1648, is characterized by the revolt of the nations of Northern Europe against the spiritual jurisdiction of Rome, and the great combat between Protestantism and Catholicism; and that the second period, running from the Peace of Westphalia to our own day, is distinguished by the contest between the people and their rulers, or, in other words, by the conflict between liberal and despotic principles of government.

We shall now proceed to speak of the causes and general features of the Reformation, and in succeeding chapters shall follow its fortunes in the various countries of Europe.

Extent of Rome's Spiritual Authority at the Opening of the Sixteenth Century. — In a preceding chapter on the Papacy it was shown how perfect at one time was the obedience of the West, not only to the spiritual, but to the temporal, authority of the Pope. It was also shown how the papal claim of the right to dictate in temporal or governmental affairs was practically rejected

by the princes and sovereigns of Europe as early as the fourteenth
century (see p. 458). But previous to the opening of the sixteenth
century there had been comparatively few — though there had
been some, like the Albigenses in the South of France, the Wick-
liffites in England, and the Hussites in Bohemia — who denied the
supreme and infallible authority of the bishops of Rome in all
matters touching religion. Speaking in a very general manner,
it would be correct to say that at the close of the fifteenth century
all the nations of Western Europe professed the faith of the Latin,
or Roman Catholic Church, and yielded spiritual obedience to
the Papal See.

Causes of the Reformation. — We must now seek the causes
which led one-half of the nations of Europe to secede, as it were,
from the Roman Catholic Church. The causes were many.
Among others may be mentioned the great mental awakening
which marked the close of the mediæval and the opening of the
modern age ; for the intellectual revival, though often spoken of,
in so far as it concerned the Northern nations, as an effect of the
religious revival, was in reality at once cause and effect. It
hastened the Reformation, and was itself hastened by it. And in
connection with the Revival of Learning must be mentioned the
invention of printing as a powerful agency in the promotion of the
religious movement. The press scattered broadcast over Europe,
not only the Bible, but the writings of the men who had begun to
doubt the scriptural authority for many of the doctrines and ceremonies of the Church, — such as devotion to the Virgin Mary, the
invoking of saints, the use of images, confession to a priest, and the
nature of the elements in the Eucharist. These writings of course
stirred up debate, and led to questioning and criticism.

A second cause was the existence of most serious scandals and
abuses in the Church. During the fifteenth century, the morality
of the Church was probably lower than at any other period in its
history. The absolute necessity of its thorough reform in both
" head and members " was recognized by all earnest and spiritual-
minded men. The only difference of opinion among such was

as to the manner in which the work of purification should be effected.

A third cause may be found in the claims of the Popes to the right to interfere in the internal, governmental affairs of a nation; for, although these claims had been rejected by the sovereigns of Europe, they were nevertheless still maintained by the Roman bishops, and this caused the temporal princes to regard with great jealousy the papal power.

But foremost among the proximate causes, and the actual *occasion* of the revolution, was the controversy which arose about the doctrine of indulgences. These were remissions of punishment granted to persons who preferred to pay a sum of money rather than perform the penances imposed upon them by the Church. It is, and always has been, the theory of the Catholic Church, that the indulgence remits merely temporal penalties, — that is, penalties imposed by ecclesiastical authority, and the pains of Purgatory, — and that it can take effect only upon certain conditions, among which is that of sincere repentance. Indulgences were frequently granted by various pontiffs, as a means of raising funds for pious enterprises. A considerable portion of the money for building the Cathedral of St. Peter at Rome was raised in this manner.

Tetzel and the Preaching of Indulgences. — Leo X., upon his election to the papal dignity, in 1513, found the coffers of the Church almost empty; and, being in pressing need of money to carry on his various undertakings, among which was work upon St. Peter's, he had recourse to the then common expedient of a grant of indulgences. He delegated the power of dispensing these in Germany to the archbishop of Magdeburg, who employed a Dominican friar by the name of Tetzel as his deputy in Saxony.

The archbishop was unfortunate in the selection of his agent. Tetzel carried out his commission in such a way as to give rise to great scandal. The language that he, or at least his subordinates, used, in exhorting the people to comply with the conditions of gaining the indulgences, one of which was a donation of money, was unseemly and exaggerated. The result was that erroneous views as to the effect of indulgences began to spread among the ignorant and credulous, some being so far misled as to think that if they only contributed this money to the building of St. Peter's at Rome they would be exempt from all penalty for sins, paying little heed to the other conditions, such as sorrow for sin, and purpose of amendment. Hence, many were led to declaim against the procedure of the zealous friar. These protests were the near mutterings of a storm that had long been gathering, and that was soon to shake all Europe from the Baltic to the Mediterranean.

Martin Luther. — Foremost among those who opposed and denounced Tetzel was Martin Luther (1483–1546), an Augustine

monk, and a teacher of theology in the university of Wittenberg. He was of humble parentage, his father being a poor miner. The boy possessed a good voice, and frequently, while a student, earned his bread by singing from door to door. The natural bent of his mind, and, if we may believe a somewhat doubtful legend, the death of a friend struck down at his side by lightning, led him to resolve to enter a monastery and devote himself to the service of the Church.

MARTIN LUTHER.

Before Tetzel appeared in Germany, Luther had already earned a wide reputation for learning and piety.

The Ninety-five Theses. — The form which Church penances had taken in the hands of Tetzel and his associates, together with other circumstances, awakened in Luther's mind doubts and questionings as to many of the doctrines of the Church. Especially was there gradually maturing within him a conviction that the entire system of ecclesiastical penances and indulgences was unscriptural and wrong. His last lingering doubt respecting this matter appears to have been removed while, during an official visit to Rome in 1510, he was penitentially ascending on his knees the sacred stairs (*scala santa*) of the Lateran, when he seemed to hear an inner voice declaring, " The just shall live by faith."

At length Luther drew up ninety-five theses, or articles, wherein he fearlessly stated his views respecting indulgences. These theses, written in Latin, he nailed to the door of the church at Wittenberg, and invited all scholars to examine and criticise them, and to point out if in any respect they were opposed to the teachings of the Word of God, or of the early Fathers of the Church (1517). By means of the press the theses were scattered with incredible rapidity throughout every country in Europe.

Burning of the Papal Bull (1520).—All the continent was now plunged into a perfect tumult of controversy. Luther, growing bolder, was soon attacking the entire system and body of teachings of the Roman Catholic Church. At first the Pope, Leo X., was inclined to regard the whole matter as " a mere squabble of monks," but at length he felt constrained to issue a bull against the audacious reformer (1520). His writings were condemned as heretical, and all persons were forbidden to read them ; and he himself, if he did not recant his errors within sixty days, was to be seized and sent to Rome to be dealt with as an heretic. Luther in reply publicly burned the papal bull at one of the gates of Wittenberg.

The Diet of Worms (1521).— Leo now invoked the aid of the recently elected Emperor Charles the Fifth in extirpating the spreading heresy. The emperor complied by summoning Luther before the Diet of Worms, an assembly of the princes, nobles, and clergy of Germany, convened at Worms to deliberate upon the affairs of Germany, and especially upon matters touching the great religious controversy.

Called upon in the Imperial assembly to recant his errors, Luther steadily refused to do so, unless his teachings could be shown to be inconsistent with the Bible. Although some wished to deliver the reformer to the flames, the safe-conduct of the emperor under which he had come to the Diet protected him. So Luther was allowed to depart in safety, but was followed by a decree of the assembly which pronounced him a heretic and an outlaw.

But Luther had powerful friends among the princes of Germany, one of whom was his own prince, Frederick the Wise, Elector of Saxony. Solicitous for the safety of the reformer, the prince caused him to be seized on his way from the Diet by a company of masked horsemen, who carried him to the castle of the Wartburg, where he was kept about a year, his retreat being known only to a few friends. During this period of forced retirement from the world, Luther was hard at work upon his celebrated translation of the Bible.

The Peasants' War (1524–1525). — Before quite a year had passed, Luther was called from the Wartburg by the troubles caused by a new sect that had appeared, known as the Anabaptists, whose excesses were casting great discredit upon the whole reform movement. Luther's sudden appearance at Wittenberg gave a temporary check to the agitation.

But in the course of two or three years the trouble broke out afresh, and in a more complex and aggravated form. The peasants of Suabia and Franconia, stung to madness by the oppressions of their feudal lords, stirred by the religious excitement that filled the air, and influenced by the incendiary preaching of their prophets Carlstadt and Münzer, rose in revolt against the nobles and priests. Castles and monasteries were sacked and burned, and horrible outrages were committed. The rebellion was at length crushed, but not until one hundred thousand lives had been sacrificed, a large part of South Germany ravaged, and great reproach cast upon the reformers, whose teachings were held by their enemies to be the whole cause of the ferment.

The Reformers are called Protestants. — Notwithstanding all the efforts that were made to suppress the doctrines of Luther, they gained ground rapidly, and in the year 1529 another assembly, known as the Second Diet of Spires, was called to consider the matter. This body issued an edict forbidding all persons doing anything to promote the spread of the new doctrines, until a general council of the Church should have investigated them and pronounced authoritatively upon them. Seven of the German princes, and a large number of the cities of the empire, issued a formal *protest* against the action of the Diet. Because of this protest, the reformers from this time began to be known as *Protestants*.

Causes that checked the Progress of the Reformation. — Even before the death of Luther,[1] which occurred in the year 1546, the Reformation had gained a strong foothold in most of the countries of Western Christendom, save in Spain and Italy, and even in these parts the new doctrines had made some progress. It seemed as if the revolt from Rome was destined to become universal, and the old ecclesiastical empire to be completely broken up.

But several causes now conspired to check the hitherto triumphant advance of Protestantism, and to confine the movement to the Northern nations. Chief among these were the *divisions among the Protestants*; the *Catholic counter-reform*, the *increased activity of the Inquisition*, and the *rise of the Order of the Jesuits*.

Divisions among the Protestants. — Early in their contest with Rome, the Protestants became divided into numerous hostile sects. In Switzerland arose the Zwinglians (followers of Ulrich Zwingle, 1484–1531), who differed from the Lutherans in their views regarding the Eucharist, and on some other points of doctrine. The Calvinists were followers of John Calvin (1509–1564), a Frenchman by birth, who, forced to flee from France

---

[1] After the death of Luther, the leadership of the Reformation in Germany fell to Philip Melanchthon (1497–1560), one of Luther's friends and fellow-workers. Melanchthon's disposition was exactly the opposite of Luther's. He often reproved Luther for his indiscretion and vehemence, and was constantly laboring to effect, through mutual concessions, a reconciliation between the Roman Catholics and the Protestants.

on account of persecution, found a refuge at Geneva, of which city he became a sort of Protestant pope.[1]

JOHN CALVIN.

The great Protestant communions quickly broke up into a large number of denominations, or churches, each holding to some minor point of doctrine, or adhering to some form of worship disregarded by the others, yet all agreeing in the central doctrine of the Reformation, "Justification by faith."

Now the contentions between these different sects were sharp and bitter. The liberal-minded reformer had occasion to lament the same state of things as that which troubled the apostle Paul in the early days of Christianity. One said, I am of Luther; another said, I am of Calvin; and another said, I am of Zwingle. Even Luther himself denounced Zwingle as a heretic; and the Calvinists would have no dealings with the Lutherans.

The influence of these sectarian divisions upon the progress of the Reformation was most disastrous. They afforded the Catholics a strong and effective argument against the entire movement as tending to uncertainty and discord.

The Catholic Counter-Reform. — While the Protestants were thus breaking up into numerous rival sects, the Catholics were removing the causes of dissension within the old Church by a

---

[1] Calvin was, next after Luther, the greatest of the reformers. The doctrines of Calvin came to prevail very widely, and have exerted a most remarkable influence upon the general course of history. "The Huguenots of France, the Covenanters of Scotland, the Puritans of England, the Pilgrim Fathers of New England, were all the offspring of Calvinism."

thorough reform in its head and members, and by a clear and authoritative restatement of the doctrines of the Catholic faith. This was accomplished very largely by the labors of the celebrated Council of Trent (1545–1563). The correction of the abuses that had so much to do in causing the great schism, smoothed the way for the return to the ancient Church of thousands who had become alarmed at the dangers into which society seemed to drift when once it cast loose from anchorage in the safe harbor of tradition and authority.

The Inquisition. — The Roman Catholic Church having purified itself and defined clearly its articles of faith, demanded of all a more implicit obedience than hitherto. The Inquisition, or Holy Office (see p. 500), now assumed new vigor and activity, and heresy was sternly dealt with. The tribunal was assisted in the execution of its sentences by the secular authorities in all the Romance countries, but outside of these it was not generally recognized by the temporal princes, though it did succeed in establishing itself for a time in the Netherlands and in some parts of Germany. Death, usually by burning, and loss of property were the penalty of obstinate heresy. Without doubt the Holy Office did much to check the advance of the Reformation in Southern Europe, aiding especially in holding Italy and Spain compactly obedient to the ancient Church.

At this point, in connection with the persecutions of the Inquisition, we should not fail to recall that in the sixteenth century a refusal to conform to the established worship was regarded by all, by Protestants as well as by Catholics, as a species of treason against society, and was dealt with accordingly. Thus we find Calvin at Geneva consenting to the burning of Servetus (1553), because he published views that the Calvinists thought heretical; and in England we see the Anglican Protestants waging the most cruel, bitter, and persistent persecutions, not only against the Catholics, but also against all Protestants that refused to conform to the Established Church.

The Jesuits. — The Order of Jesuits, or Society of Jesus, was

another most powerful agent concerned in the re-establishment
of the threatened authority of the Papal See. The founder of
the institution was St. Ignatius Loyola (1491–1556), a native of

Spain. Loyola's object was to
form a society, the devotion and
energy of whose numbers should
counteract the zeal and activity
of the reformers.

As the well-disciplined, watchful, and uncompromising foes of
the Protestant reformers, now divided into many and often hostile
sects, the Jesuits did very much
to bring about a reaction, to retrieve the failing fortunes of the

LOYOLA. (From a medal.)

papal power in Europe, and to extend the authority and doctrines
of the Roman Catholic Church in all other parts of the world.
Most distinguished of the missionaries of the order to pagan lands
was Francis Xavier (1506–1552), known as the Apostle of the
Indies. His labors in India, Japan, and other lands of the East
were attended with astonishing results.

Outcome of the Revolt. — As in following chapters we are to
trace the fortunes of the Reformation in the leading European
countries, we shall here say only a word as to the issue of the
great contest.

The outcome of the revolt, very broadly stated, was the separation from the Roman Catholic Church of the Northern, or Teutonic nations ; that is to say, of Northern Germany, of portions
of Switzerland and of the Netherlands, of Denmark, Norway,
Sweden, England, and Scotland. The Romance nations, namely,
Italy, France and Spain, together with Celtic Ireland, adhered to
the old Church.

What this separation from Rome meant in the political realm is
well stated by Seebohm : " It was the claiming by the civil power
in each nation of those rights which the Pope had hitherto claimed

within it as head of the great ecclesiastical empire. The clergy and monks had hitherto been regarded more or less as foreigners — that is, as subjects of the Pope's ecclesiastical empire. Where there was a revolt from Rome the allegiance of these persons to the Pope was annulled, and the civil power claimed as full a sovereignty over them as it had over its lay subjects. Matters relating to marriage and wills still for the most part remained under ecclesiastical jurisdiction, but then, as the ecclesiastical courts themselves became national courts and ceased to be Roman or papal, all these matters came under the control of the civil power."

In a spiritual or religious point of view, this severance by the Northern nations of the bonds that formerly united them to the ecclesiastical empire of Rome, meant a transfer of their allegiance from the *Church* to the *Bible*. The decrees of Popes and the decisions of Councils were no longer to be regarded as having divine and binding force; the Scriptures alone were to be held as possessing divine and infallible authority, and, theoretically, this rule and standard of faith and practice each one was to interpret for himself.

Thus one-half of Western Christendom was lost to the Roman Church. Yet notwithstanding this loss, notwithstanding the earlier loss of the Eastern part of Christendom (see p. 417), and notwithstanding the fact that its temporal power has been entirely taken from it, the Papacy still remains, as Macaulay says, "not a mere antique, but full of life and youthful vigor." The Pope is to-day the supreme Head of a Church that, in the words of the brilliant writer just quoted, "was great and respected before Saxon had set foot on Britain, before the Frank had passed the Rhine, when Grecian eloquence still flourished in Antioch, when idols were still worshipped in the temple of Mecca. And she may still exist in undiminished vigor when some traveller from New Zealand shall, in the midst of a vast solitude, take his stand on a broken arch of London Bridge to sketch the ruins of St. Paul's."

CHAPTER XLIX.

THE ASCENDENCY OF SPAIN.

1. REIGN OF THE EMPEROR CHARLES V. (1519–1556).

Charles' Dominions. — Charles I. of Spain, better known to fame as Emperor Charles V., was the son of Philip the Handsome, Archduke of Austria, and Joanna, daughter of Ferdinand and Isabella of Spain. He was "the converging point and heir of four great royal lines, which had become united by a series of happy matrimonial alliances." These were the houses of Austria, Burgundy, Castile, and Aragon. Before Charles had completed his nineteenth year, there were heaped upon his head, through the removal of his ancestors by death, the crowns of the four dynasties.

But vast as were the *hereditary* possessions of the young prince, there was straightway added to these (in 1519), by the vote of the Electors of Germany, the sovereignty of the Holy Roman Empire. After this election he was known as *Emperor Charles V.*, whereas hitherto he had borne the title of *Don Carlos I.* of Spain.

Charles and the Reformation. — It is Charles' relations to the Lutheran movement which constitute the significant feature of his life and work. Here his policies and acts concerned universal history. It would hardly be asserting too much to say that Charles, at the moment he ascended the Imperial throne, held in his hands the fortunes of the Reformation, so far as regards the countries of Southern Europe. Whether these were to be saved to Rome or not, seemed at this time to depend largely upon the attitude which Charles should assume towards the reform movement. Fortunately for the Catholic Church, the young emperor placed himself at the head of the Catholic party, and during his

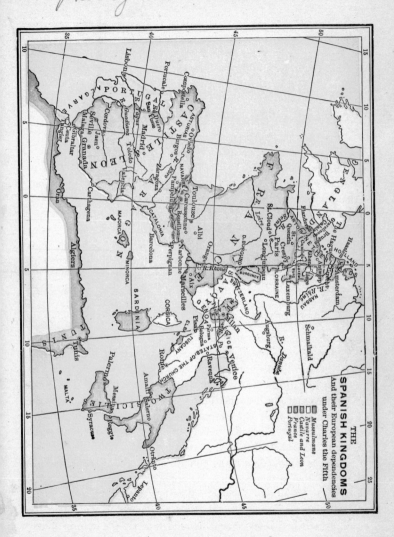

THE SPANISH KINGDOMS
And their European dependencies
under Charles the Fifth

Mussulmans
Navarre
Castile and Leon
France
Portugal

reign employed the strength and resources of his empire in repressing the heresy of the reformers.

His Two Chief Enemies. — Had Charles been free from the outset to devote all his energies to the work of suppressing the Lutheran heresy, it is difficult to see what could have saved the reform doctrines within his dominions from total extirpation. But fortunately for the cause of the reformers, Charles' attention, during all the first part of his reign, was drawn away from the serious consideration of Church questions, by the attacks upon his dominions of two of the most powerful monarchs of the times, — Francis I. (1515–1547) of France, and Solyman the Magnificent (1520–1566), Sultan of Turkey. Whenever Charles was inclined to proceed to severe measures against the Protestant princes of Germany, the threatening movements of one or both of these enemies, at times acting in concert and alliance, forced him to postpone his proposed crusade against heretics for a campaign against foreign foes.

Rivalry and Wars between Charles and Francis[1] (1521–1544). — Francis I. was the rival of Charles in the contest for Imperial honors. When the Electors conferred the title of emperor upon the Spanish monarch, Francis was sorely disappointed, and during all the remainder of his reign kept up a jealous and almost incessant warfare with Charles, whose enormous possessions now nearly surrounded the French kingdom. Italy was the field of much of the fighting, as the securing of dominion in that peninsula was the chief aim of each of the rivals.

The so-called *First War* between Francis and the emperor was full of misfortunes for Francis. His army was driven out of Northern Italy by the Imperial forces; his most skilful and trusted commander, the Constable of Bourbon, turned traitor and went

---

[1] Table of Wars: —

First War (ended by Peace of Madrid) 1521–1526	Third War (ended by Truce of Nice) . . . 1536–1538
Second War (ended by Ladies' Peace) . . . 1527–1529	Fourth War (ended by Peace of Crespy) . . 1542–1544

over to Charles, and another of his most valiant nobles, the celebrated Chevalier Bayard, the knight *sans peur*, *sans reproche*,
"without fear and without reproach," was killed ; while, to crown
all, Francis himself, after suffering a crushing defeat at Pavia, in
Italy, was wounded and taken prisoner. In his letter to his
mother informing her of the disaster, he is said to have laconically
written, " All is lost save honor." He was liberated by the Peace
of Madrid (1526).

The most memorable incident of the *Second War* between the
king and the emperor, was the sack of Rome by an Imperial army,
made up chiefly of Lutherans. Rome had not witnessed such
scenes since the terrible days of the Goth and Vandal.

In the *Third War* Francis shocked all Christendom by forming
an alliance with the Turkish Sultan, who ravaged with his fleets
the Italian coasts, and sold his plunder and captives in the port of
Marseilles. Thus was a Christian city shamefully opened to the
Moslems as a refuge and a slave-market.

The *Fourth War*, which was the last between the rivals, left
their respective possessions substantially the same as at the beginning of the strife, in 1521.

Disastrous Effects of the Wars. — The results of these royal
contentions had been extremely calamitous. For a quarter of a
century they had kept nearly all Europe in a perfect turmoil, and
by preventing alliances of the Christian states, had been the occasion of the severe losses which Christendom during this period
suffered at the hands of the Turks. Hungary had been ravaged
with fire and sword ; Rhodes had been captured from the Knights
of St. John ; and all the Mediterranean shores pillaged, and thousands of Christian captives chained to the oars of Turkish galleys.[1]

---

[1] The worst feature of this advance of the Sultan's authority in the Mediterranean was the growth, under his protection, of the power of the Algerian
pirates. One of the chief strongholds of the pirates on the African coast was
Tunis, which was held by the famous Barbarossa. In the interval between
his second and third wars with Francis, Charles, with a large army and fleet,
made an assault upon this place, defeated the corsair, and set free 20,000

Persecution of the French Protestants by Francis. — The cessation of the wars between Francis and Charles left each free to give his attention to his heretical subjects. And both had work enough on hand ; for while the king and the emperor had been fighting each other, the doctrines of the reformers had been spreading rapidly in all directions and among all classes.

The severest blow dealt by Francis against the heretics of his kingdom fell upon the Vaudois, or Waldenses,[1] the inhabitants of a number of hamlets in Piedmont and Provence. Thousands were put to death by the sword, thousands more were burned at the stake, and the land was reduced to a wilderness. Only a miserable remnant, who found an asylum among the mountains, were left to hand down their faith to later times.

Charles' Wars with the Protestant German Princes. — Charles, on his part, turned his attention to the reformers in Germany. Inspired by religious motives and convictions, and apprehensive, further, of the effect upon his authority in Germany of the growth there of a confederacy of the Protestant princes, known as the League of Schmalkald, Charles resolved to suppress the reform movement by force. He was at first successful, but in the end, the war proved the most disastrous and humiliating to him of any in which he had engaged. Successive defeats of his armies forced him to give up his undertaking to make all his German subjects think alike in matters of religion.

The Religious Peace of Augsburg (1555). — In the celebrated Diet of Augsburg, convened in 1555 to compose the distracted affairs of the German states, it was arranged and agreed that every prince should be allowed to choose between the Catholic religion

Christian captives. For this brilliant and knightly achievement, the emperor received great applause throughout Europe. Just after his third war with Francis, the emperor made an unsuccessful and most disastrous assault upon Algiers, another stronghold of the corsairs.

[1] So called from the founder of the sect, Peter Waldo, or Pierre de Vaux, who lived about the beginning of the thirteenth century.

and the Augsburg Confession,[1] and should have the right to make his religion the worship of his people. This, it will be noted, was simply toleration as concerns princes or governments. The people individually had no freedom of choice; every subject must follow his prince, and think and believe as he thought and believed. Of course, this was no real toleration.

Even to the article of toleration as stated above, the Diet made one important exception. The Catholics insisted that *ecclesiastical* princes, *i.e.*, bishops and abbots who were heads of states, on becoming Protestants, should lose their offices and revenues; and this provision, under the name of the *Ecclesiastical Reservation*, was finally made a part of the treaty. This was a most fortunate article for the Catholics. It is said that but for it all Germany would have turned Protestant.

Abdication and Death of Charles. — While the Diet of Augsburg was arranging the Religious Peace, the Emperor Charles was enacting the part of a second Diocletian (see p. 331). There had long been forming in his mind the purpose of spending his last days in monastic seclusion. The disappointing issue of his contest with the Protestant princes of Germany, the weight of advancing years, together with menacing troubles which began " to thicken like dark clouds about the evening of his reign," now led the emperor to carry this resolution into effect. Accordingly he abdicated in favor of his son Philip the crown of the Netherlands (1555), and that of Spain and its colonies (1556), and then retired to the monastery of San Yuste, situated in a secluded region in the western part of Spain (1556).

In his retreat at Yuste, Charles passed the remaining short term of his life in participating with the monks in the exercises of relig-

[1] The " Augsburg Confession " was the formula of belief of the adherents of Luther. It was drawn up by the scholar Melanchthon, and laid before the Imperial Diet assembled at Augsburg by Charles V. in 1530. It formed the basis of the Lutheran Church. The Peace of Augsburg, it is to be specially noted, made no provision for the Calvinists — that is, the confessors of the *Genevan* creed.

ion, and in watching the current of events without; for Charles never lost interest in the affairs of the empire over which he had ruled, and Philip constantly had the benefit of his father's wisdom and experience.

There is a tradition which tells how Charles, after vainly endeavoring to make some clocks that he had about him at Yuste run together, made the following reflection: "How foolish I have been to think I could make all men believe alike about religion, when here I cannot make even two clocks keep the same time."

This story is probably mythical. Charles seems never to have doubted either the practicability or the policy of securing uniformity of belief by force. While in retirement at Yuste, he expressed the deepest regret that he did not burn Luther at Worms. He was constantly urging Philip to use greater severity in dealing with his heretical subjects, and could scarcely restrain himself from leaving his retreat, in order to engage personally in the work of extirpating the pestilent doctrines, which he heard were spreading in Spain.

2. SPAIN UNDER PHILIP II. (1556–1598).

Philip's Domains. — With the abdication of Charles V. the Imperial crown passed out of the Spanish line of the House of Hapsburg.[1] Yet the dominions of Philip were scarcely less extensive than those over which his father had ruled. All the hereditary possessions of the Spanish crown were of course his. Then just before his father's abdication gave him these domains, he had become king-consort of England by marriage with Mary Tudor. And about the middle of his reign he conquered Portugal and added to his empire that kingdom and its rich dependencies in Africa and the East Indies, — an acquisition which more than made good to the Spanish crown the loss of the Imperial dignity. After this accession of territory, Philip's sovereignty was acknowledged by more than 100,000,000 persons — probably as large a

[1] The Imperial crown went to Charles' brother, Ferdinand, of Austria.

number as was embraced within the limits of the Roman empire at the time of its greatest extension.

But notwithstanding that Philip's dominions were so extensive, his resources enormous, and many of the outward circumstances of his reign striking and brilliant, there were throughout the period causes at work which were rapidly undermining the greatness of Spain and preparing her fall. By wasteful wars and extravagant buildings Philip managed to dissipate the royal treasures; and by his tyrannical course in respect of his Moorish, Jewish, and Protestant subjects, he ruined the industries of the most flourishing of the provinces of Spain, and drove the Netherlands into a desperate revolt, which ended in the separation of the most valuable of those provinces from the Spanish crown.

As the most important matters of Philip's reign — namely, his war against the revolted Netherlands, and his attempt upon England with his "Invincible Armada" — belong more properly to the respective histories of England and the Netherlands, and will be treated of in connection with the affairs of those countries (see pp. 558, 564), we shall give here only a very little space to the history of the period.

Philip's War with France. — Philip took up his father's quarrel with France. He was aided by the English, who were persuaded to this step by their queen, Mary Tudor, now the wife of the Spanish sovereign. Fortune favored Philip. The French were defeated in two great battles, and were forced to agree to the terms of a treaty (Peace of Cateau-Cambrésis, 1559) so advantageous to Spain as to give Philip great distinction in the eyes of all Europe.

Philip's Crusade against the Moors. — It will be recalled that after the conquest of Granada the Moors were still allowed the exercise of their religion (see p. 499). Philip conceived it to be his duty to impose upon them conditions that should thoroughly obliterate all traces of their ancient faith and manners. So he issued a decree that the Moors should no longer use their native tongue; and that they should give their children Christian names, and send them to Christian schools. A determined revolt followed. Philip repressed the uprising with terrible severity (1571). The fairest provinces of Spain were almost depopulated, and large districts relapsed into primeval wilderness.

Defeat of the Turkish Fleet at Lepanto (1571). — Philip rendered an eminent service to civilization in helping to stay the progress of the Turks in the Mediterranean. They had captured the important island of Cyprus, and had assaulted the Hospitallers at Malta,[1] which island had been saved from falling into the hands of the infidels only by the splendid conduct of the knights. All Christendom was becoming alarmed. Pope Pius V. called upon the princes of Europe to rally to the defence of the Church. An alliance was formed, embracing the Pope, the Venetians, and Philip II. An immense fleet was equipped, and put under the command of Don John of Austria, Philip's half-brother, a young general whose consummate ability had been recently displayed in the crusade against the Moors.

The Christian fleet met the Turkish squadron in the Gulf of Lepanto, on the western coast of Greece. The battle was unequalled by anything the Mediterranean had seen since the naval encounters of the Romans and Carthaginians in the First Punic War. More than 600 ships and 200,000 men mingled in the struggle. The Ottoman fleet was almost totally destroyed. Thousands of Christian captives, who were found chained to the oars of the Turkish galleys, were liberated. All Christendom rejoiced as when Jerusalem was captured by the first crusaders.

The battle of Lepanto holds an important place in history, because it marks the turning-point of the long struggle between the Mohammedans and the Christians, which had now been going on for nearly one thousand years. The Ottoman Turks, though they afterwards made progress in some quarters, never recovered the

[1] After the knights had been driven from the island of Rhodes by the Turks (see p. 532), Charles gave the survivors of the Order the island of Malta (1530).

prestige they lost in that disaster, and their authority and power thenceforward steadily declined.[1]

The Death of Philip: Later Events. — In the year 1588 Philip made his memorable attempt with the so-called "Invincible Armada" upon England, at this time the stronghold of Protestantism. As we shall see a little later, he failed utterly in the undertaking (see p. 558). Ten years after this he died in the palace of the Escurial. With his death closed that splendid era of Spanish history which began with the discovery of the New World by Columbus. From this time forward the nation steadily declined in power, reputation, and influence.

Thus, under Philip III. (1598–1621), a severe loss, and one from which they never recovered, was inflicted upon the manufactures and various other industries of Spain, by the expulsion of the Moors, or Moriscoes. More than half a million of the most intelligent, skilful, and industrious inhabitants of the Peninsula were driven into exile. And then in 1609, the Protestant Netherlands, whose revolt against the tyranny of Philip II. has been mentioned, virtually achieved their independence (see p. 570). In the secession of these provinces the Spanish crown lost her most valuable possessions, and she now sank rapidly to the position of a third or fourth rate power.[2]

---

[1] After the battle of Lepanto the next most critical moment in the history of the Turkish conquests was in 1683. In that year the Turks besieged Vienna, and had all but secured the prize, when the city was relieved by the distinguished Polish general Sobieski.

[2] The loss of the Netherlands was followed in 1639 by the loss of Portugal. During the latter part of the seventeenth century Spain was involved in disastrous wars with France, and suffered a decline of 8,000,000 in her population. After the revolt of her American colonies, in the early part of the present century, and her cession to the United States of Florida (in 1819), Spain was almost shorn — she still held Cuba and a few other patches of territory scattered about the world — of those rich and magnificent colonial possessions which had been her pride in the time of her ascendency.

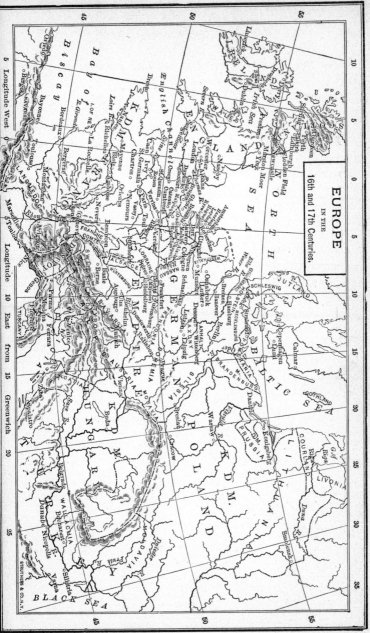

EUROPE
IN THE
16th and 17th Centuries.

STRUTHERS & CO. N.Y.

CHAPTER L.

THE TUDORS AND THE ENGLISH REFORMATION.

(1485–1603.)

1. INTRODUCTORY.

The Tudor Period. — The Tudor period[1] in English history covers the sixteenth century, and overlaps a little the preceding and the following century. It was an eventful and stirring time for the English people. It witnessed among them great progress in art, science, and trade, and a literary outburst such as the world had not seen since the best days of Athens. But the great event of the period was the Reformation. It was under the Tudors that England was severed from the spiritual empire of Rome, and Protestantism firmly established in the island. To tell how these great results were effected will be our chief aim in the present chapter.

The English Reformation first a Revolt and then a Reform. — The Reformation in England was, more distinctly than elsewhere, a double movement. First, England was separated violently from the ecclesiastical empire of Rome. The authority of the Pope was cast off, but without any essential change being made in creed or mode of worship. This was accomplished under Henry VIII.

Secondly, the English Church, thus rendered independent of Rome, gradually changed its creed and ritual. This was effected chiefly under Edward VI. So the movement was first a *revolt* and then a *reform*.

The Revival of Learning in England. — The soil in England

[1] The Tudor sovereigns were Henry VII. (1485–1509); Henry VIII. (1509–1547); Edward VI. (1547–1553); Mary (1553–1558); and Elizabeth (1558–1603).

was, in a considerable measure, prepared for the seed of the Reformation by the labors of the Humanists (see p. 474). Three men stand preëminent as lovers and promoters of the New Learning. Their names are Colet, Erasmus, and More.

Colet was leader and master of the little band. His generous enthusiasm was kindled at Florence, in Italy. It was an important event in the history of the Reformation when Colet crossed the Alps to learn Greek at the feet of the Greek exiles; for on his return to England he brought back with him not only an increased love for classical learning, but a fervent zeal for religious

ERASMUS.

reform, inspired, it would seem, by the stirring eloquence of Savonarola (see p. 511).

Erasmus was probably superior in classical scholarship to any student of his times. "He bought Greek books first, and clothes afterwards." His Greek testament, published in 1516, was one of the most powerful agents concerned in bringing about the Reformation. Indeed, his relation to the reform movement is well indicated by the charge made against him by the enemies of the Reformation, who declared that "Erasmus laid the egg, and Luther hatched it."

Thomas More was drawn, or rather forced, into political life, and of him and his writings we shall have occasion to speak hereafter, in connection with the reign of Henry VIII. (see p. 549).

The Lollards. — Another special preparation for the entrance into England of the Reformation was the presence among the lower classes there of a considerable body of Lollards (see p. 491). Persecution had driven the sect into obscurity, but had not been able to extirpate the heresy. In holding the Scriptures as the sole rule of faith, and in the maintenance of other doctrines denounced by the Roman Catholic Church, the Lollards occupied a position similar to that held by the German reformers, and consequently, when the teachings of Luther were disseminated in England, they received them gladly.

2. THE REIGN OF HENRY VII. (1485-1509).

The Union of the Roses. — Henry VII. and his queen united the long-disputed titles of the two Roses [1] (see p. 488) ; but the bitter feelings engendered by the contentions of the rival families still existed. Particularly was there much smothered discontent among the Yorkists, which manifested itself in two attempts to place impostors upon the throne, both of which, however, were unsuccessful.

Benevolences. — Avarice and a love of despotic rule were Henry's chief faults. Much of his attention was given to heaping up a vast fortune. One device adopted by the king for wringing money from his wealthy subjects was what was euphoniously termed *Benevolences*. Magna Charta forbade the king to impose taxes without the consent of Parliament. But Henry did not like to convene Parliament, as he wished to rule like the kings of the Continent, guided simply by his own free will. Furthermore, his title not being above question, it was his policy to relieve the poorer classes of the burden of tax-paying, in order to secure their good-will and support. So Benevolences were made to take the place of regular taxes. These were nothing more nor less than gifts extorted from the well-to-do, generally by moral pressure. One of Henry's favorite ministers, named Morton, was particularly successful in his appeals for gifts of this kind. To those who lived splendidly he would say that it was very evident they were quite able to make a generous donation to their sovereign ; while to others who lived in a narrow and pinched way he would represent that their economical mode of life must have made them

---

[1] Henry represented the claims of the House of Lancaster, and soon after his coronation he married the Princess Elizabeth, a daughter of Edward IV., and the representative of the claims of the House of York.

wealthy. This famous dilemma received the name of " Morton's Fork."

Maritime Discoveries. — It was during this reign that great geographical discoveries enlarged the boundaries of the world. In 1492 Columbus announced to Europe the existence of land to the west. In 1497 Vasco da Gama sailed around the cape of Good Hope and found a water-road to the East Indies.

The same year of this last enterprise, Henry fitted out a fleet under the command of John Cabot, a Venetian sailor doing business in England, and his son Sebastian, for exploration in the western seas. The Cabots first touched at Newfoundland (or Cape Breton Island), and then the following year Sebastian explored the coast they had run against, from that point to what is now Virginia or the Carolinas. They were the first Europeans, if we except the Northmen, to look upon the American continent, for Columbus at this time had seen only the islands in front of the Gulf of Mexico. These explorations of the Cabots were of great importance for the reason that they gave England a title to the best portion of the North American coast.

Foreign Matrimonial Alliances. — The marriages of Henry's children must be noted by us here, because of the great influence these alliances had upon the after-course of English history. A common fear of France caused Ferdinand and Isabella of Spain and Henry to form a protective alliance. To secure the permanency of the union it was deemed necessary to cement it by a marriage bond. The Spanish Infanta was accordingly betrothed to Arthur, Prince of Wales. Unfortunately, the prince died soon after the celebration of the nuptials. The Spanish sovereigns, still anxious to retain the advantages of an English alliance, now urged that the young widow be espoused to Arthur's brother Henry, and the English king, desirous on his side to preserve the friendship of Spain, assented to the betrothal. A rule of the Church, however, which forbade a man to marry his brother's widow, stood in the way of this arrangement; but the queen-mother Isabella managed to secure a decree from the Pope granting permission in this case, and so the young widow was betrothed to Prince Henry, afterward Henry VIII. This alliance of the royal families of England and Spain led to many important consequences, as we shall learn.

To relieve England of danger on her northern frontier, Henry steadily pursued the policy of a marriage alliance with Scotland. His wishes were realized when his eldest daughter Margaret became the wife of James IV., king of that realm. This was a most fortunate marriage, and finally led to the happy union of the two countries under a single crown (see p. 601).

Henry VII. died in 1509, leaving his throne to his son Henry, an energetic and headstrong youth of eighteen years.

3. England severed from the Papacy by Henry VIII.
(1509–1547).

Cardinal Wolsey. — We must here, at the opening of Henry VIII.'s reign,[1] introduce his greatest minister, Thomas Wolsey (1471–1530). This man was one of the most remarkable characters of his generation. Henry VIII. elevated him to the office of Archbishop of York, and made him lord chancellor of the realm. The Pope, courting the minister's influence, made him a cardinal, and afterwards papal legate in England. He was now at the head of affairs in both State and Church. His revenues from his many offices were enormous, and enabled him to assume a style of living astonishingly magnificent. His household numbered five hundred persons; and a truly royal train, made up of

---

[1] In 1512, joining what was known as the Holy League, — a union against the French king, of which the Pope was the head, — Henry made his first campaign in France. While Henry was across the Channel, James IV. of Scotland thought to give aid to the French king by invading England. The Scottish army was met by the English force at Flodden, beneath the Cheviot Hills, and completely overwhelmed (1513). King James was killed, and the flower of the Scottish nobility were left dead upon the field. It was the most terrible disaster that had ever befallen the Scottish nation. Scott's poem entitled *Marmion, a Tale of Flodden Field*, commemorates the battle.

bishops and nobles, attended him with great pomp and parade wherever he went.

Henry as Defender of the Faith. — It was early in the reign of Henry VIII. that Martin Luther tacked upon the door of the Wittenberg church his epoch-making theses. England was stirred with the rest of Western Christendom. Henry wrote a Latin treatise replying to the articles of the audacious monk. The Pope, Leo X., rewarded Henry's Catholic zeal by conferring upon him the title of "Defender of the Faith" (1521). This title was retained by Henry after the secession of the Church of England from the Papal See, and is borne by his successors at this day, though they are "defenders" of quite a different faith from that in the defence of which Henry first earned the title.

HENRY VIII. OF ENGLAND.

Henry seeks to be divorced from Catherine. — We have now to relate some circumstances which changed Henry from a zealous supporter of the Papacy into its bitterest enemy.

Henry's marriage with Catherine of Aragon had been prompted by policy and not by love. Of the five children born of the union, all had died save a sickly daughter named Mary. In these successive afflictions which left him without a son to succeed him, Henry saw, or feigned to see, a certain sign of Heaven's displeasure because he had taken to wife the widow of his brother.

And now a new circumstance arose, — if it had not existed for some time previous to this. Henry conceived a violent passion for Anne Boleyn, a beautiful and vivacious maid of honor in the queen's household. This new affection so quickened the king's conscience, that he soon became fully convinced that it was his duty to put Catherine aside.[1]

Accordingly, Henry asked the Pope, Clement VII., to grant him a divorce. The request placed Clement in a very embarrassing position ; for if he refused to grant it, he would offend Henry ; and if he granted it, he would offend Charles V., who was Catherine's relative. So Clement in his bewilderment was led to temporize, to make promises to Henry and then evade them. At last, after a year's delay, he appointed Cardinal Wolsey and an Italian cardinal named Campeggio as commissioners to hold a sort of court in England to determine the validity of Henry's marriage to Catherine. A year or more dragged along without anything being accomplished, and then Clement, influenced by the Emperor Charles, ordered Henry and Catherine both to appear before him at Rome. (Respecting appeals to Rome, see p. 418).

The Fall of Wolsey. — Henry's patience was now completely exhausted. Becoming persuaded that Wolsey was not exerting himself as he might to secure the divorce, he banished him from the court. The hatred of Anne Boleyn and of others pursued the fallen minister. He was deposed from all his offices save the archbishopric, and eventually was arrested on the charge of high treason. While on his way to London the unhappy minister, broken in spirits and health, was prostrated by a fatal fever. As he lay dying, he uttered these words, which have lived so long after him : "Had I served my God as diligently as I have served my king, He would not have given me over in my gray hairs" (1530).

Thomas Cromwell. — A man of great power and mark now

---

[1] Political considerations, without doubt, had much if not most to do in bringing Henry to this state of mind. He was ready to divorce Catherine and openly break with Spain, because the Emperor Charles V., to whom he had offered the hand of the Princess Mary, had married the Infanta of Portugal, and thus cast aside the English alliance. On this point consult Seebohm, *The Era of the Protestant Revolution*, pp. 178–180.

rises to our notice. Upon the disgrace of Wolsey, a faithful attendant of his named Thomas Cromwell straightway assumed in Henry's regard the place from which the Cardinal had fallen. He was just the opposite of Wolsey in caring nothing for pomp and parade. For the space of ten years this wonderful man shaped the policy of Henry's government. What he proposed to himself was the establishment of a royal despotism upon the ruin of every other power in the State. The executioner's axe was constantly wet with the blood of those who stood in his way, or who in any manner incurred his displeasure.

It was to the bold suggestions of this man that Henry now listened, when all other means of gratifying his passion had been tried in vain. Cromwell's advice to the king was to waste no more time in negotiating with the Pope, but at once to renounce the jurisdiction of the Roman pontiff, proclaim himself Supreme Head of the Church in England, and then get a decree of divorce from his own courts.

The Breach with Rome. — The advice of Cromwell was acted upon, and by a series of steps England was swiftly and forever carried out from under the authority of the Roman See. Henry first virtually cut the Gordian knot by a secret marriage with Anne Boleyn, notwithstanding a papal decree threatening him with excommunication should he dare to do so. Parliament, which was entirely subservient to Henry's wishes, now passed a law known as the Statute of Appeals, which made it a crime for any Englishman to carry a case out of the kingdom to the courts at Rome. Cranmer, a Cambridge doctor who had served Henry by writing a book in favor of the divorce, was, in accordance with the new programme, made archbishop of Canterbury. He at once formed a court, tried the case, and of course declared the king's marriage with Catherine null and void from the very first, and his union with Anne legal and right.

The Act of Supremacy (1534). — The decisive step had now been taken: the Rubicon had been crossed. The Pope issued a decree excommunicating Henry and relieving his subjects from their allegiance. Henry on his part called Parliament, and a celebrated bill known as the Act of Supremacy was passed (1534). This statute made Henry the Supreme Head of the Church in England, vesting in him absolute control over all its offices, and turning into his hands the revenues which had hitherto flowed into the coffers of the Roman See. A denial of the title given the king by the statute was made high treason. This statute established the independence of the Anglican Church.

Henry as Supreme Head of the Church. — Henry now set up in England a little Popedom of his own. He drew up a sort of creed which everybody must believe, or at least pretend to believe. The doctrines of purgatory, of indulgences, of masses for the dead, of pilgrimages, of the adoration of images and relics, were condemned; but the doctrines of transubstantiation and of confession to a priest were retained. Every head of a family and every teacher was commanded to teach his children or pupils the Lord's Prayer, the Ten Commandments, and the new Creed.

Thus was the English Church cared for by its self-appointed shepherd. What it should be called under Henry it would be hard to say. It was not Protestant; and it was just as far from being Catholic.

The Suppression of the Monasteries. — The suppression of the monasteries was one of Henry's most high-handed measures. Several things led him to resolve on the extinction of these religious houses. For one thing, he coveted their wealth, which at this time included probably one-fifth of the lands of the realm. Then the monastic orders were openly or secretly opposed to Henry's claims of supremacy in religious matters; and this naturally caused him to regard them with jealousy and disfavor. Hence their ruin was planned.

In order to make the act appear as reasonable as possible, it was planned to make the charge of immorality the ostensible ground of their suppression. Accordingly two royal commissioners were appointed to inspect the monasteries, and make a report upon what they might see and learn. If we may believe the report, the smaller houses were conducted in a most shameful manner. The larger houses, however, were fairly free from faults. Many of them served as schools, hospitals, and inns, and all distributed alms to the poor who knocked at their gates. But the undoubted usefulness and irreproachable character of the larger foundations did not avail to avert the indiscriminate ruin of all. A bill was passed which at once dissolved between three and four hundred of the smaller monasteries, and gave all their property to the king (1536).

The unscrupulous act stirred up a rebellion in the north of England, known as the "Pilgrimage of Grace." This was suppressed with great severity, and soon afterwards the larger monasteries were also dissolved, their possessors generally surrendering the property voluntarily into the hands of the king, lest a worse thing than the loss of their houses and lands should come upon them.[1] Pensions were granted to the dispossessed monks, which relieved in part the suffering caused by the proceeding.

A portion of the confiscated wealth of the houses was used in founding schools and colleges, and a part for the establishment of bishoprics; but by far the greater portion was distributed among the adherents and favorites of the king. The leading houses of the English aristocracy of to-day, may, according to Hallam, trace the title of their estates back to these confiscated lands of the religious houses. Thus a new nobility was raised up whose interests led them to oppose any return to Rome; for in such an event their estates were liable of course to be restored to the monasteries.

Persecution of Catholics and Protestants. — Our disapproval of Henry's unscrupulous conduct in compassing the ruin of the religious houses flames into hot indignation when we come to speak of his atrocious crimes against the lives and consciences of

[1] Altogether there were 90 colleges, 110 hospitals, 2374 chantries and chapels, and 645 monasteries broken up. Such Roman Catholic church property as was spared at this time, was confiscated during the reign of Edward VI., and a portion of it used to establish schools and hospitals.

his subjects. The royal reformer persecuted alike Catholics and Protestants. Thus, on one occasion, three Catholics who denied that the king was the rightful Head of the Church, and three Protestants who disputed the doctrine of the real presence in the sacrament (a dogma which Henry had retained in his creed), were dragged on the same sled to the place of execution.

The most illustrious of the king's victims were the learned Sir Thomas More and the aged Bishop Fisher, both of whom were brought to the block because their consciences would not allow them to acknowledge that the king was rightfully the Supreme Head of the Church of England.

Henry's Wives. — Henry's troubles with his wives form a curious and shameful page in the history of England's kings. Anne Boleyn retained the affections of her royal husband only a short time. She was charged with unfaithfulness and beheaded, leaving a daughter who became the famous Queen Elizabeth. The day after the execution of Anne the king married Jane Seymour, who died the following year. She left a son by the name of Edward. The fourth marriage of the king was to Anne of Cleves, who enjoyed her queenly honors only a few months. The king becoming enamoured of a young lady named Catherine Howard, Anne was divorced on the charge of a previous betrothal, and a new alliance formed. But Catherine was proved guilty of misconduct and her head fell upon the block. The sixth and last wife of this amatory monarch was Catherine Parr. She was a discreet woman, and managed to outlive her husband.

His Death and the Succession. — Henry died in 1547. His many marriages and divorces had so complicated the question of the succession, that Parliament, to avoid disputes after Henry's death, had given him power, with some restrictions, to settle the matter by will. This he did, directing that the crown should descend to his son Edward and his heirs; in case Edward died childless, it was to go to Mary and her heirs, and then to Elizabeth and her heirs.

Literature under Henry VIII.: More's Utopia. — The most

prominent literary figure of this period is Sir Thomas More.   The
work upon which his fame as a writer mainly rests is his *Utopia*, or
" Nowhere," a political romance like Plato's *Republic* or Sir Philip
Sidney's *Arcadia*.   It pictures an imaginary kingdom away on an
island beneath the equinoctial in the New World, then just discovered, where the laws, manners, and customs of the people were
represented as being ideally perfect.   In this wise way More suggested improvements in social, political, and religious matters :
for it was the wretchedness, the ignorance, the social tyranny, the
religious intolerance, the despotic government of the times which
inspired the *Utopia*.   More did not expect, however, that Henry
would follow all his suggestions, for he closes his account of the
Utopians with this admission : " I confess that many things in the
commonwealth of Utopia I rather *wish* than *hope* to see adopted
in our own."   And, indeed, More himself, before his death, materially changed his views regarding religious persecution.   Although in his book he had expressed his decided disapproval of
persecution for conscience' sake, yet he afterwards, driven into
reaction by the terrible excesses of the Peasants' War in Germany,
and by other popular tumults which seemed to be the outgrowth
of the Protestant movement, favored persecution, and advised
that unity of faith be preserved by the use of force.

4. Changes in the Creed and Ritual under Edward VI.
(1547–1553).

Changes in the Creed. — In accordance with the provisions of
Henry's will, his only son Edward, by Jane Seymour, succeeded
him.   As Edward was but a child of nine years, the government was entrusted to a board of regents made up of both Protestants and Catholics.   But the Protestants usurped authority in
the body, and conducted the government in the interests of their
party.   The young king was carefully taught the doctrines of the
reformers, and changes were made in the creed and service of the
English Church which carried it still farther away from the Roman
Catholic Church.   By a royal decree all pictures, images, and

crosses were cleared from the churches; the use of tapers, holy water, and incense were forbidden; the worship of the Virgin and the invocation of saints was prohibited; belief in purgatory was denounced as a superstition, and prayers for the dead were interdicted; the real or bodily presence of Christ in the bread and wine of the sacrament was denied; the prohibition against the marriage of the clergy was annulled (a measure which pleased the clergy and reconciled them to the other sweeping innovations); and the services of the Church, which had hitherto been conducted in Latin, were ordered to be said in the language of the people.

In order that the provision last mentioned might be effectually carried out, the English Book of Common Prayer was prepared by Archbishop Cranmer, and the first copy issued in 1549. This book, which was in the main simply a translation of the old Latin service-books, with the subsequent change of a word here and a passage there to keep it in accord with the growing new doctrines, is the same that is used in the Anglican Church at the present time.

In 1552 were published the well-known Forty-two Articles of Religion, which formed a compendious creed of the reformed faith. These Articles, reduced finally to thirty-nine, form the present standard of faith and doctrine in the Church of England.

Persecutions to secure Uniformity. — These sweeping changes in the old creed and in the services of the Church would have worked little hardship or wrong had only everybody, as in More's happy republic, been left free to follow what religion he would. But unfortunately it was only away in " Nowhere " that men were allowed perfect freedom of conscience and worship. By royal edict all preachers and teachers were forced to sign the Forty-two Articles; and severe enactments, known as "Acts for the Uniformity of Service," punished with severe penalties any departure from the forms of the new prayer-book. The Princess Mary, who remained a firm and conscientious adherent of the old faith, was not allowed to have the Roman Catholic service in her own private chapel. Even the powerful intercession of the Emperor Charles V.

availed nothing. What was considered idolatry in high places could not be tolerated.

Many persons during the reign were imprisoned for refusing to conform to the new worship ; while two at least were given to the flames as " heretics and contemners of the Book of Common Prayer." Probably a large majority of the English people were still at this time good Catholics at heart.

5. Reaction under Mary (1553-1558).

Reconciliation with Rome. — Upon the death of Edward, an

MARY TUDOR.

attempt was made, in the interest of the Protestant party, to place upon the throne Lady Jane Grey,[1] a grandniece of Henry VIII.; but the people, knowing that Mary was the rightful heir to the throne, rallied about her, and she was proclaimed queen amidst great demonstrations of loyalty. Soon after her accession, she was married to Prince Philip of Spain.

Mary was an earnest Catholic, and her zeal effected the full reëstablishment of the Catholic worship throughout the realm. Parliament voted that the nation should return to its obedience to the Papal See ; and then the members of both houses fell

[1] The leaders of this movement were executed, and Lady Jane Grey was also eventually brought to the block.

upon their knees to receive at the hands of the legate of the Pope absolution from the sin of heresy and schism. The sincerity of their repentance was attested by their repeal of all the acts of Henry and of Edward by which the new worship had been set up in the land. The joy at Rome was unbounded.

But not quite everything done by the reformers was undone. Parliament refused to restore the confiscated Church lands, which was very natural, as much of this property was now in the hands of the lords and commoners (see p. 548). Mary, however, in her zeal for the ancient faith, restored a great part of the property still in the possession of the crown, and refounded many of the ruined monasteries and abbeys.

Persecution of the Protestants. — With the reëstablishment of the Roman worship, the Protestants in their turn became the victims of persecution. The three most eminent martyrs of what is known as the Marian persecutions were Latimer, Ridley, and Cranmer. Altogether, between two and three hundred persons suffered death, during this reign, on account of their religion.

For the part she took in the persecutions that marked her reign, Mary should be judged not by the standard of our time, but by that of her own. Punishment of heresy was then regarded, by both Catholics and Protestants alike, as a duty which could be neglected by those in authority only at the peril of Heaven's displeasure. Believing this, those of that age could consistently do nothing less than labor to exterminate heresy with axe, sword, and fagot.

The Loss of Calais. — The marriage of Philip and Mary had been earnestly wished for by the Emperor Charles V., in order that Philip, in those wars with France which he well knew must be a part of the bequest which he should make to his son, might have the powerful aid of England. This was Philip's chief reason in seeking the alliance ; and in due time he called upon Mary for assistance against the French king. The result of England's participation in the war was her mortifying loss of Calais (see p. 487), which the French, by an unexpected attack, snatched out of the hands of its garrison (1558). The unfortunate queen did not live out the year that marked this calamity, which she most deeply deplored.

6. Final Establishment of Protestantism under Elizabeth (1558–1603).

The Queen. — Elizabeth was the daughter of Henry VIII. and Anne Boleyn. She seems to have inherited the characteristics of both parents ; hence the inconsistencies of her disposition.

QUEEN ELIZABETH.

When the death of Mary called Elizabeth to the throne, she was twenty-five years of age. Like her father, she favored the reformed faith rather from policy than conviction. It was to the Protestants alone that she could look for support ; her title to the crown was denied by every true Catholic in the realm, for she was the child of that marriage which the Pope had forbidden under pain of the anathemas of the Church.

Elizabeth possessed a strong will, indomitable courage, admirable judgment, and great political tact. It was these qualities which rendered her reign the strongest and most illustrious in the record of England's sovereigns, and raised the nation from a position of insignificance to a foremost place among the states of Europe.

Along with her good and queenly qualities and acccomplishments, Elizabeth had many unamiable traits and unwomanly ways. She was capricious, treacherous, unscrupulous, ungrateful, and cruel. She seemed almost wholly devoid of a moral or religious sense. Deception and falsehood were her usual weapons in diplomacy. "In the profusion and recklessness of her lies," declares Green, "Elizabeth stood without a peer in Christendom."

Her Ministers. — One secret of the strength and popularity of Elizabeth's government was the admirable judgment she exercised in her choice of advisers. Around her Council-board she gathered the wisest and strongest men to be found in the realm. The most eminent of the queen's ministers was Sir William Cecil (Lord Burleigh), a man of great sagacity and ceaseless industry, to whose able counsel and prudent management is largely due the success of Elizabeth's reign. He stood at the head of the Queen's Council for forty years. His son Robert, Sir Nicholas Bacon, and Sir Francis Walsingham were also prominent among the queen's advisers.

Reëstablishment of the Reformed Church. — As Mary undid the work in religion of Henry and Edward, so now her work is undone by Elizabeth. The religious houses that had been reestablished by Mary were again dissolved, and Parliament, by two new Acts of Supremacy and Uniformity, relaid the foundations of the Anglican Church.

The Act of Supremacy required all the clergy, and every person holding office under the crown, to take an oath declaring the queen to be the supreme governor of the realm in all spiritual as well as temporal things, and renouncing the authority or jurisdiction of any foreign prince or prelate. For refusing to take this oath, many Catholics during Elizabeth's reign suffered death, and many more endured within the Tower the worse horrors of the rack.

The Act of Uniformity forbade any clergyman to use any but the Anglican liturgy, and required every person to attend the Established Church on Sunday and other holy days. For every absence a fine of one shilling was imposed. The persecutions which arose under this law caused many Catholics to seek freedom of worship in other countries.

The Protestant Non-Conformists. — The Catholics were not the only persons among Elizabeth's subjects who were opposed to the Anglican worship. There were Protestant non-conformists — the Puritans and the Separatists — who troubled her almost as much as the Romanists.

The Puritans were so named because they desired a *purer* form of worship than the Anglican. To these earnest reformers the Church Elizabeth had established seemed but half-reformed. Many rites and ceremonies, such as wearing the surplice and making the cross in baptism, had been retained ; and these things, in their eyes, appeared mere Popish superstitions. What they wanted was a more sweeping change, a form of worship more like that of the Calvinistic churches of Geneva, in which city very many of them had lived as exiles during the Marian persecution. They, however, did not at once withdraw from the Established Church, but remaining within its pale, labored to reform it, and to shape its doctrines and discipline to their notions.

The Separatists were still more zealous reformers than the Puritans : in their hatred of everything that bore any resemblance to the Roman worship, they flung away the surplice and the Prayer-book, severed all connection with the Established Church, and refused to have anything to do with it. Under the Act of Conformity they were persecuted with great severity, so that multitudes were led to seek an asylum upon the continent. It was from among these exiles gathered in Holland that a little later came the passengers of the Mayflower, — the Pilgrim Fathers, who laid the foundations of civil liberty in the New World.

Mary Stuart, Queen of Scots. — A large part of the history of Elizabeth's reign is intertwined with the story of her cousin, Mary Stuart, Queen of Scots. Mary Stuart was the daughter of James V. of Scotland, and to her *in right of birth* — according to all Catholics who denied the validity of Henry's marriage with Anne Boleyn — belonged the English crown next after Mary Tudor. Upon the death, in 1560, of her husband Francis II. of France, Mary gave up life at the French court, and returned to her native land. She was now in her nineteenth year. The subtle charm of her beauty seems to have bewitched all who came into her presence — save the more zealous of the Protestants, who could never forget that their young sovereign was a Catholic. The stern old reformer, John Knox, made her life miserable. He was a veritable Elijah, in whose eyes Mary appeared a modern Jezebel. He called her a "Moabite," and the "Harlot of Babylon," till she wept from sheer vexation. She dared not punish the impudent preacher, for she knew too well the strength of the Protestant feeling among her subjects.

Other things now conspired with Mary's hated religion to alienate entirely the love of her people. Her second husband, Henry Stuart, Lord Darnley, was murdered. The queen was suspected of having some guilty knowledge of the affair. She was imprisoned and forced to abdicate in favor of her infant son James.

Escaping from prison, Mary fled into England (1568). Here she threw herself upon the generosity of her cousin Elizabeth, and entreated aid in recovering her throne. But the part which she was generally believed to have had in the murder of her husband, her disturbing claims to the English throne, and the fact that she was a Catholic, all conspired to determine her fate. She was placed in confinement, and for nineteen years she remained a prisoner. During all this time Mary was the centre of innumerable plots and conspiracies on the part of the Catholics, which aimed at setting her upon the English throne. The Pope aided these conspirators by a bull excommunicating Elizabeth, denying her right to the crown she wore, and releasing her subjects from their allegiance.

Events just now occurring on the continent tended to inflame the Protestants of England with a deadly hatred against Mary and her Catholic friends and abettors. In 1572 the Huguenots of France were slaughtered on St. Bartholomew's Day. In 1584 the Prince of Orange fell at the hands of a hired assassin. That there were daggers waiting to take the life of Elizabeth was well known. It was evident that so long as Mary lived the queen's life was in constant danger. In the feverish state of the public mind, it was natural that the air should be filled with rumors of plots of every kind. Finally, a carefully laid conspiracy to assassinate Elizabeth and place Mary on the throne, was unearthed. Mary was tried for complicity in the plot, was declared guilty, and, after some hesitation, feigned or otherwise, on the part of Elizabeth, was ordered to the block (1587).

The Invincible Armada. — The execution of Mary Stuart led immediately to the memorable attempt against England by the Spanish Armada. Before her death the Queen of Scots had bequeathed to Philip II. of Spain her claims to the English crown. To enforce these rights, to avenge the death of Mary, to punish Elizabeth for rendering aid to his rebellious subjects in the Netherlands, and to deal a fatal blow to the Reformation in Europe by crushing the Protestants of England, Philip resolved upon making a tremendous effort for the conquest of the heretical and troublesome island. Vast preparations were made for carrying out the project. Great fleets were gathered in the harbors of Spain, and a large army was assembled in the Netherlands to coöperate with the naval armament. The Pope, Sixtus V., blessed the enterprise, which was thus rendered a sort of crusade.

These threatening preparations produced a perfect fever of excitement in England ; for we must bear in mind that the Spanish king was at this time the most powerful potentate in Europe, commanding the resources of a large part of two worlds. Never did Roman citizens rise more splendidly to avert some terrible peril threatening the republic than the English people now arose as a single man to defend their island-realm against the revengeful and ambitious project of Spain. The imminent danger served to unite all classes, the gentry and the yeomanry, Protestants and Catholics. The latter might intrigue to set a Mary Stuart on the English throne, but they were not ready to betray their land into the hands of the hated Spaniards.

July 19, 1588, the Invincible Armada, as it was boastfully called, was first descried by the watchmen on the English cliffs. It swept up the channel in the form of a great crescent, seven miles in

SPANISH AND ENGLISH WAR-VESSELS OF THE SIXTEENTH CENTURY.

width from tip to tip of horn. The English fleet, commanded by Drake, Howard, and Lord Henry Seymour, disputed its advance. The light build and quick movements of the English ships gave them a great advantage over the clumsy, unwieldy Spanish galleons. The result was the complete defeat of the immense Armada, and the destruction of many of the ships. The remaining galleons sought to escape by sailing northward around the British Isles; but a terrible tempest arising, many of the fleeing ships were dashed to pieces on the Scottish or the Irish shores. Barely one-third of the ships of the Armada ever reëntered the harbors whence they sailed. When intelligence of the woeful disaster was carried to Philip, he simply said, " God's will be done ; I sent my fleet to fight with the English, not with the elements."

The destruction of the Invincible Armada was not only a terrible blow to Spanish pride, but an equally heavy blow to Spanish supremacy among the states of Europe. From this time on, Spain's prestige and power rapidly declined.

As to England, she had been delivered from a great peril ; and as to the cause of Protestantism, it was now safe.

Maritime and Colonial Enterprises. — The crippling of the naval power of Spain left England mistress of the seas. The little island-realm now entered upon the most splendid period of her history. The old Norse blood of her people, stirred by recent events, seemed to burn with a feverish impatience for maritime adventure and glory. Many a story of the daring exploits of English sea-rovers during the reign of Elizabeth seems like a repetition of some tale of the old Vikings.[1]

Especially deserving of mention among the enterprises of these stirring and romantic times are the undertakings of Sir Walter Raleigh (1552–1618). Several expeditions were sent out by him for the purpose of making explorations and forming settlements in the New World. One of these, which explored the central coasts of North America, returned with such glowing accounts of the beauty and richness of the land visited, that, in honor of the Virgin Queen, it was named " Virginia."

Sir Walter Raleigh sent two colonies to the new land, but they both failed to form permanent settlements. It is said that the

---

[1] Among all these sea-rovers, half explorer, half pirate, Sir Francis Drake (1545–1595) was preëminent. Before the Armada days he had sailed around the globe (1577–1579), and for the achievement had been knighted by Queen Elizabeth. The whole life of this sixteenth century Viking was spent in fighting the fleets of his sovereign's enemy, Philip II., in capturing Spanish treasure-vessels on the high sea, and in pillaging the warehouses and settlements on every Spanish shore in the Old and the New World.

returning colonists first acquainted the English with the Indian custom of smoking tobacco, and that Sir Walter Raleigh made the practice popular. This may be true ; yet prior to this, Europeans had acquired a knowledge of the plant and some of its uses through Spanish explorers and settlers. At this same time also, the potato, likewise a native product of the New World, was introduced into the British Isles.

The Queen's Death. — The closing days of Elizabeth's reign were, to her personally, dark and gloomy. She seemed to be burdened with a secret grief,[1] as well as by the growing infirmities of age. She died March 24, 1603, in the seventieth year of her age, and the forty-fifth of her reign. With her ended the Tudor line of English sovereigns.

Literature of the Elizabethan Era.

Influences favorable to Literature. — The years covered by the reign of Elizabeth constitute the most momentous period in history. It was the age when Europe was most deeply stirred by the Reformation. It was, too, a period of marvellous physical and intellectual expansion and growth. The discoveries of Columbus and Copernicus had created, as Froude affirms, "not in any metaphor, but in plain and literal speech, a new heaven and a new earth." The New Learning had, at the same time, discovered the old world — had revealed an unsuspected treasure in the philosophies and literatures of the past.

No people of Europe felt more deeply the stir and movement of the times, nor helped more to create this same stir and movement, than the English nation. There seemed to be nothing too great or arduous for them to undertake. They made good their resistance to the Roman See ; they humbled the pride of the

[1] In 1601 she sent to the block her chief favorite, the Earl of Essex, who had been found guilty of treason. She wished to spare him, and probably would have done so, had a token which he sent her from his prison reached her. Read the story as told in all the histories of England.

strongest monarch in Christendom; they sailed round the globe, and penetrated all its seas.

An age of such activity and achievement almost of necessity gives birth to a strong and vigorous literature. And thus is explained, in part at least, how the English people during this period should have developed a literature of such originality and richness and strength as to make it the prized inheritance of all the world.

The Writers. — To make special mention of all the great writers who adorned the Elizabethan era would carry us quite beyond the limits of our book. Having said something of the influences under which they wrote, we will simply add that this age was the age of Shakespeare and Spenser and Bacon.[1]

---

[1] William Shakespeare (1564–1616); Edmund Spenser (1552?–1599); Francis Bacon (1561–1626). Shakespeare and Bacon, it will be noticed, outlived Elizabeth. Two other names hold a less prominent place, — that of Sir Philip Sidney (1554–1586), the courtly knight, who wrote the *Arcadia*, a sort of pastoral romance, and *A Defence of Poesy*, a work intended to counteract the Puritanical spirit then rising; and that of Richard Hooker (1553–1600), who in his *Ecclesiastical Polity* defends the Anglican Church.

REDUCED FAC-SIMILE OF THE SIGNATURE OF QUEEN ELIZABETH.

CHAPTER LI.

THE REVOLT OF THE NETHERLANDS: RISE OF THE DUTCH REPUBLIC.

(1572–1609.)

The Country. — The term Netherlands (low-lands) was formerly applied to all that low, marshy district in the northwest of Europe, sunk much of it below the level of the sea, now occupied by the kingdoms of Holland and Belgium. The entire strip of land is simply the delta accumulations of the Rhine and other rivers emptying into the North Sea. Originally it was often overflowed by its streams and inundated by the ocean. But this unpromising morass, protected at last by heavy dykes against the invasions of the ocean and the overflow of its streams, was destined to become the site of cities which at one period were the richest and most potent of Europe, and the seat of one of the foremost commonwealths of modern times.

No country in Europe made greater progress in civilization during the mediæval era than the Netherlands. At the opening of the sixteenth century they contained a crowded and busy population of 3,000,000 souls. The ancient marshes had been transformed into carefully kept gardens and orchards. The walled cities alone numbered between two and three hundred.

The Low Countries under Charles V. (1515–1555). — The Netherlands were part of those possessions over which Charles V. ruled by hereditary right. Though Charles could not prevent the growth of Protestantism in Germany, he resolved to root out the heresy from his hereditary possessions of the Netherlands. By an Imperial edict he condemned to death all persons presuming to read the Scriptures, or even to discuss religious topics. The Inquisition was introduced, and thousands perished at the stake and upon the scaffold, or were strangled, or buried alive. But when Charles retired to the monastery at Yuste (see p. 534), the reformed doctrines were, notwithstanding all his efforts, far more widely spread and deeply rooted in the Netherlands than when he entered upon their extirpation by fire and sword.

Accession of Philip II. — In 1555, in the presence of an august and princely assembly at Brussels, and amidst the most imposing and dramatic ceremonies, Charles V. abdicated the crown whose weight he could no longer bear, and placed the same upon the head of his son Philip (see p. 534), who was a most zealous Catholic. Philip remained in the Netherlands after his coronation four years, employing much of his time in devising means to root out the heresy of Protestantism. In 1559 he set sail for Spain, never to return.

Long live the Beggars. — Upon his departure from the Netherlands Philip entrusted their government to his half-sister, Margaret, Duchess of Parma, as Regent. Under the administration of Margaret (1559–1567) the persecution of the Protestants went on with renewed bitterness. Philip declared that "he would rather lose a hundred thousand lives, were they all his own, than allow the smallest deviation from the standards of the Roman Catholic Church." Thousands fled the country, many of the fugitives finding a home in England. At last the nobles leagued together for the purpose of resisting the Inquisition. They demanded of the Regent a redress of grievances. When the petition was presented to the Duchess, she displayed great agitation, whereupon one of her councillors exclaimed, "Madam, are you afraid of a pack of beggars?"

The expression was carried to the nobles, who were assembled at a banquet. Immediately one of their number suspended a beggar's wallet from his neck, and filling a wooden bowl with wine, proposed the toast, "Long live the Beggars." The name was tumultuously adopted, and became the party designation of the patriot Netherlanders during their long struggle with the Spanish power.

The Iconoclasts (1566). — Affairs now rapidly verged towards violence and open revolt. The only reply of the government to the petition of the nobles was a decree termed the *Moderation,* which substituted hanging for burning in the case of condemned heretics. The pent-up indignation of the people at length burst forth in an uncontrollable fury. They gathered in great mobs, and arming themselves with whatever implements they could first seize, proceeded to demolish every image they could find in the churches throughout the country. The rage of the insurgents was turned in this direction, because in their eyes these churches represented the hated Inquisition under which they were suffering. Scarcely a church in all the Netherlands escaped. The monasteries, too, were sacked, their libraries burned, and the inmates driven from their cloisters. In the province of Flanders alone there were four hundred sacred buildings visited by the mob, and sacked. The tempest destroyed innumerable art treasures, which have been as sincerely mourned by the lovers of the beautiful as the burned rolls of the Alexandrian Library have been lamented by the lovers of learning.

These image-breaking riots threw Philip into a perfect transport of rage. He tore his beard, and exclaimed, " It shall cost them dear ! I swear it by the soul of my father ! "

The Duke of Alva and William of Orange. — The year following the outbreak of the Iconoclasts, Philip sent to the Netherlands a veteran Spanish army, headed by the Duke of Alva. The duke was one of the ablest generals of the age ; and the intelligence of his coming threw the provinces into a state of the greatest agitation and alarm. Those who could do so hastened to get out of the country. William the Silent, Prince of Orange, fled to Germany, where he began to gather an army of volunteers for the struggle which he now saw to be inevitable. Egmont and Horn, noblemen of high rank and great distinction, were seized, cast into prison, and afterwards beheaded (1568).

The eyes of all Netherlanders were now turned to the Prince of Orange as their only deliverer. Towards the close of the year 1568, he marched from Germany against Alva, at the head of an

army of 30,000 men, which he had raised and equipped principally at his own expense. The war was now fully joined. The
struggle lasted for more than a generation, — for thirty-seven years.

WILLIAM OF ORANGE (the Silent).

The Spanish armies were
commanded successively by
the most experienced and
distinguished generals of Europe, — the Duke of Alva,
Don John of Austria (the
conqueror of the Moors and
the hero of the great naval
fight of Lepanto), and the
Duke of Parma ; but the
Prince of Orange coped ably
with them all, and in the
masterly service which he
rendered his country, thus
terribly assaulted, earned
the title of "the Founder of Dutch Liberties."

Isolation of the Provinces. — The Netherlanders sustained the
unequal contest almost single-handed ; for, though they found
much sympathy among the Protestants of Germany, France, and
England, they never received material assistance from any of these
countries, excepting England, and it was not until late in the struggle that aid came from this source. Elizabeth did, indeed, at first
furnish the patriots with secret aid, and opened the ports of England to the "Beggars of the Sea" ; but after a time the fear of
involving herself in a war with Philip led her to withhold for a long
period all contributions and favors. As regards the German states,
they were too much divided among themselves to render efficient
aid ; and just at the moment when the growing Protestant sentiment in France encouraged the Netherlanders to look for help
from the Huguenot party there, the massacre of St. Bartholomew
extinguished forever all hope of succor from that quarter (see
p. 576). So the little revolted provinces were left to carry on un-

aided, as best they might, a contest with the most powerful monarch of Christendom.

The details of this memorable struggle we must, of course, leave unnoticed, and hurry on to the issue of the matter. In so doing we shall pass unnoticed many memorable sieges and battles.[1]

Pacification of Ghent (1576). — The year 1576 was marked by a revolt of the Spanish soldiers, on account of their not receiving their pay, the costly war having drained Philip's treasury. The mutinous army marched through the land, pillaging city after city, and paying themselves with the spoils. The beautiful city of Antwerp was ruined. The horrible massacre of its inhabitants, and the fiendish atrocities committed by the frenzied soldiers, caused the awful outbreak to be called the " Spanish Fury."

The terrible state of affairs led to an alliance between Holland and Zealand and the other fifteen provinces of the Netherlands, known in history as the Pacification of Ghent (1576). The resistance to the Spanish crown had thus far been carried on without concerted action among the several states, the Prince of Orange having hitherto found it impossible to bring the different provinces to agree to any plan of general defence. But the awful experiences of the Spanish Fury taught the necessity of union, and led all the seventeen provinces solemnly to agree to unite in driving the Spaniards from the Netherlands, and in securing full liberty for all in matters of faith and worship. William of Orange, with the title of Stadtholder, was placed at the head of the union. It was mainly the strong Catholic sentiment in the Southern provinces that had prevented such a union and pacification long before.

The Union of Utrecht (1579). — With the Spanish forces under the lead first of Don John of Austria, the hero-victor of Lepanto, and afterwards of Prince Alexander of Parma, a commander of most distinguished ability, the war now went on with increased vigor, fortune, with many vacillations, inclining to the side of the Spaniards. Disaffection arose among the Netherland-

---

[1] Read in Motley's *Rise of the Dutch Republic* the siege and sack of Harlem and the relief of Leyden.

ers, the outcome of which was the separation of the provinces. The Prince of Orange, seeing the impossibility of uniting all the states, devoted his efforts to effecting a confederation of the Northern ones. His endeavors were fortunately crowned with success, and the seven Protestant states of the North,[1] the chief of which were Holland and Zealand, by the treaty of Utrecht (1579), were united in a permanent confederation, known as the Seven United Provinces of the Netherlands. In this league was laid the foundation of the Dutch Republic.

Fortunate would it have been for the Netherlands, could all of the states at this time have been brought to act in concert. Under the leadership of the Prince of Orange, the seventeen provinces might have been consolidated into a powerful nation, that might now be reckoned among the great powers of Europe.

The " Ban " and the " Apology." — William of Orange was, of course, the animating spirit of the confederacy formed by the treaty of Utrecht. In the eyes of Philip and his viceroys he appeared the sole obstacle in the way of the pacification of the provinces and their return to civil and ecclesiastical obedience. In vain had Philip sent against him the ablest and most distinguished commanders of the age ; in vain had he endeavored to detach him from the cause of his country by magnificent bribes of titles, offices, and fortune.

Philip now resolved to employ assassination for the removal of the invincible general and the incorruptible patriot. He published a ban against the prince, declaring him an outlaw, and offering to any one who should kill him the pardon of all his sins, a title of nobility, and 25,000 gold crowns.

The prince responded to the infamous edict in a remarkable paper, entitled " The Apology of the Prince of Orange," — the

---

[1] The ten Catholic provinces of the South, although they continued their contest with Philip a little longer, ultimately submitted to Spanish tyranny. A portion of these provinces were absorbed by France, while the remainder, after varied fortunes amidst the revolutions and dynastic changes of the European states, finally became the present kingdom of Belgium.

most terrible arraignment of tyranny that was ever penned. The "Apology" was scattered throughout Europe, and everywhere produced a profound impression. The friends of the prince, while admiring his boldness, were filled with alarm for his safety. Their apprehensions, as the issue shows, were not unfounded.

Assassination of the Prince of Orange. — "The ban soon bore fruit." Upon the 10th day of July, 1584, five previous unsuccessful attempts having been made upon his life, the Prince of Orange was fatally shot by an assassin. The heirs of the murderer received substantially the reward which had been offered in the ban, being enriched with the estates of the prince, and honored by elevation to the ranks of the Spanish nobility.

The character of William the Silent is one of the most admirable portrayed in all history.[1] His steadfast and unselfish devotion to the cause of his country deservedly won for him the love of all classes. His people fondly called him " Father William."

Prince Maurice: Sir Philip Sidney. — Severe as was the blow sustained by the Dutch patriots in the death of the Prince of Orange, they did not lose heart, but continued the struggle with the most admirable courage and steadfastness. Prince Maurice, a youth of seventeen years, the second son of William, was chosen Stadtholder in his place, and proved himself a worthy son of the great chief and patriot. The war now proceeded with unabated fury. The Southern provinces were, for the most part, in the hands of the Spaniards, while the revolutionists held control, in the main, of the Northern states.

Substantial aid from the English now came to the struggling Hollanders. Queen Elizabeth, alarmed by the murder of the Prince of Orange, — for she well knew that hired agents of the king of Spain watched likewise for her life, — openly espoused

---

[1] He was not, however, without faults. The most serious of these was his habit of dissimulation. Some charge to this the separation of the Northern and Southern provinces after the Pacification of Ghent. The Southern provinces would not trust the " double-dealer." For references to various writers on this point, consult Young's *History of the Netherlands*, p. 320.

the cause of the Dutch. Among the English knights who led the British forces sent into the Netherlands was the gallant Sir Philip Sidney, the "Flower of Chivalry." At the siege of Zutphen (1586), he received a mortal wound. A little incident that occurred as he rode from the field, suffering from his terrible hurt, is always told as a memorial of the gentle knight. A cup of water having been brought him, he was about to lift it to his lips, when his hand was arrested by the longing glance of a wounded soldier who chanced at that moment to be carried past. "Give it to him," said the fainting knight; "his necessity is greater than mine."

Progress of the War: Treaty of 1609. — The circle of war grew more and more extended. France as well as England became involved, both fighting against Philip, who was now laying claims to the crowns of both these countries. The struggle was maintained on land and on sea, in the Old World and in the New. The English fleet, under the noted Sir Francis Drake (see p. 560, n.), ravaged the Spanish settlements in Florida and the West Indies, and intercepted the treasure-ships of Philip returning from the mines of Mexico and Peru ; the Dutch fleet wrested from Spain many of her possessions in the East Indies and among the islands of the South Pacific.

Europe at last grew weary of the seemingly interminable struggle, and the Spanish commanders becoming convinced that it was impossible to reduce the Dutch rebels to obedience by force of arms, negotiations were entered into, and by the celebrated treaty of 1609, comparative peace was secured to Christendom.

The treaty of 1609 was in reality an acknowledgment by Spain of the independence of the United Provinces of the Netherlands, although the Spanish king was so unwilling to admit the fact of his being unable to reduce the rebel states to submission, that the treaty was termed simply "a truce for twelve years." Spain did not formally acknowledge their independence until forty years afterwards, in the Peace of Westphalia, at the end of the Thirty Years' War (1648) (see p. 586).

Development of the Provinces during the War. — One of the most remarkable features of the war for Dutch independence was the vast expansion of the trade and commerce of the revolted provinces, and their astonishing growth in population, wealth, and resources, while carrying on the bitter and protracted struggle. When the contest ended, notwithstanding the waste of war, the number of inhabitants crowded on that little patch of sea-bottom and morass constituting the Dutch Republic, was equal to the entire population of England; that is to say, to three or four millions. But the home-land was only a small part of the dominions of the commonwealth. Through the enterprise and audacity of its bold sailors, it had made extensive acquisitions in the East Indies and other parts of the world, largely at the expense of the Spanish and the Portuguese colonial possessions. The commerce of the little republic had so expanded that more than one hundred thousand of its citizens found a home upon the sea. No idlers or beggars were allowed a place in the industrious commonwealth. And hand in hand with industry went intelligence. Throughout the United Provinces it was rare to meet with a person who could not both read and write.

CHAPTER LII.

THE HUGUENOT WARS IN FRANCE.

(1562–1629.)

Beginning of the Reformation in France. — Before Luther posted his ninety-five theses at Wittenberg, there appeared in the University of Paris and elsewhere in France men who, from their study of the Scriptures, had come to entertain opinions very like those of the German reformer. The land which had been the home of the Albigenses was again filled with heretics. The movement thus begun received a fresh impulse from the uprising in Germany under Luther.

The Reformation in France, as elsewhere, brought dissension, persecution, and war. We have already seen how Francis I., the second of the Valois-Orleans dynasty,[1] waged an exterminating crusade against his heretical Waldensian subjects (see p. 533). His son and successor, Henry II., also conceived it to be his duty to uproot heresy ; and it was his persecution of his Protestant subjects that sowed the seeds of those long and woful civil and religious wars which he left as a terrible legacy to his three feeble sons, Francis, Charles, and Henry, who followed him in succession upon the throne. At the time these wars began, which was about the middle of the sixteenth century, the confessors of the reformed creed, who later were known as *Huguenots*,[2] numbered probably 400,000. The new doctrines found adherents especially among

---

[1] The *Valois-Orleans* sovereigns, whose reigns cover the greater part of the period treated in the present chapter, were Louis XII. (1498–1515), Francis I. (1515–1547), Henry II. (1547–1559), Francis II. (1559–1560), Charles IX. (1560–1574), Henry III. (1574–1589). The successor of Henry III. — Henry IV. — was the first of the Bourbons.

[2] This word is probably a corruption of the German *Eidgenossen*, meaning "oath-comrades" or "confederates."

the nobility and the higher classes, and had taken particularly deep root in the South, — the region of the old Albigensian heresy.

The Catholic and the Huguenot Leaders. — The leaders of the Catholic party were the notorious Catherine de Medici, and the powerful chiefs of the family of the Guises. Catherine, the queen-mother of the last three Valois-Orleans sovereigns, was an intriguing, treacherous Italian. Nominally she was a Catholic ; but only nominally, for it seems certain that she was almost destitute of religious convictions of any kind. What she sought was power, and this she was ready to secure by any means. When it suited her purpose, she favored the Huguenots ; and when it suited her purpose better, she incited the Catholics to make war upon them. Perhaps no other woman ever made so much trouble in the world. She made France wretched through the three successive reigns of her sons, and brought her house to a shameful and miserable end.

At the head of the family of the Guises stood Francis, Duke of Guise, a famous commander, who had gained great credit and popularity among his countrymen by many military exploits, especially by his capture of Calais from the English in the recent Spanish wars (see p. 553). By his side stood a younger brother Charles, Cardinal of Lorraine. Both of these men were ardent Catholics. Mary Stuart, the queen of the young king Francis II., was their niece, and through her they ruled the boy-king. The Pope and the king of Spain were friends and allies of the Guises.

The chiefs of the Huguenots were the Bourbon princes, Anthony, king of Navarre, and Louis, Prince of Condé, who, next after the brothers of Francis II., were heirs to the French throne ; and Gaspard de Coligny, Admiral of France. Anthony was not a man of deep convictions. He at first sided with the Protestants, probably because it was only through forming an alliance with them that he could carry on his opposition to the Guises. He afterwards went over to the side of the Catholics. A man of very different character was Admiral Coligny. Early in life he had embraced the doctrines of the reformers, and he remained to the last

the trusted and consistent, though ill-starred, champion of the
Protestants.

The Conspiracy of Amboise (1560). — The foregoing notice of
parties and their chiefs will render intelligible the events which we
now have to narrate. The harsh measures adopted against the
reformers by Francis II., who of course was entirely under the
influence of the Guises, led the chiefs of the persecuted party to
lay a plan for wresting the government from the hands of these
"new Mayors of the Palace." The Guises were to be arrested
and imprisoned, and the charge of the young king given to the
Prince of Condé. The plot was revealed to the Guises, and was
avenged by the execution of more than a thousand of the Huguenots.

The Massacre of Vassy (1562). — After the short reign of
Francis II. (1559–1560), his brother Charles came to the throne
as Charles IX. He was only ten years of age, so the queen-mother
assumed the government in his name. Pursuing her favorite
maxim to rule by setting one party as a counterpoise to the other,
she gave the Bourbon princes a place in the government, and also
by a royal edict gave the Huguenots a limited toleration, and forbade their further persecution.

These concessions in favor of the Huguenots angered the Catholic chiefs, particularly the Guises; and it was the violation by the
adherents of the Duke of Guise of the edict of toleration that
finally caused the growing animosities of the two parties to break
out in civil war. While passing through the country with a body
of armed attendants, at a small place called Vassy, the Duke came
upon a company of Huguenots assembled in a barn for worship.
His retainers first insulted and then attacked them, killing about
forty of the company and wounding many more.

Under the lead of Admiral Coligny and the Prince of Condé,
the Huguenots now rose throughout France. Philip II. of Spain
sent an army to aid the Catholics, while Elizabeth of England extended help to the Huguenots.

The Treaty of St. Germain (1570). — Throughout the series of lamentable civil wars [1] upon which France now entered, both parties displayed a ferocity of disposition more befitting pagans than Christians. But it should be borne in mind that many on both sides were actuated by political ambition, rather than by religious conviction, knowing little and caring less about the distinctions in the creeds for which they were ostensibly fighting.

Sieges, battles, and truces followed one another in rapid and confusing succession. Conspiracies, treacheries, and assassinations help to fill up the dreary record of the period. The Treaty of St. Germain (in 1570) brought a short but, as it proved, delusive peace. The terms of the treaty were very favorable to the Huguenots. They received four towns, — among which was La Rochelle, the stronghold of the Huguenot faith, — which they might garrison and hold as places of safety and pledges of good faith.

To cement the treaty, Catherine de Medici now proposed that the Princess Marguerite, the sister of Charles IX., should be given in marriage to Henry of Bourbon, the new young king of Navarre. The announcement of the proposed alliance caused great rejoicing

---

[1] What are usually designated as the *First*, *Second*, and *Third Wars* were really one. The table below exhibits the wars of the entire period of which we are treating. Some make the Religious Wars proper end with the Edict of Nantes (1598); others with the fall of La Rochelle (1628).

First War (ended by Peace of Amboise)	1562–1563.
Second War (ended by Peace of Longjumeau)	1567–1568.
Third War (ended by Peace of St. Germain)	1568–1570.
Massacre of St. Bartholomew's Day, Aug. 24	1572.
Fourth War (ended by Peace of La Rochelle)	1572–1573.
Fifth War (ended by Peace of Chastenoy)	1574–1576.
Sixth War (ended by Peace of Bergerac)	1577.
Seventh War (ended by Treaty of Fleix)	1579–1580.
Eighth War (War of the Three Henries)	1585–1589.
Henry of Bourbon, King of Navarre, secures the throne	1589.
Edict of Nantes	1598.
Siege and fall of La Rochelle	1627–1628.

By the fall of La Rochelle the political power of the Huguenots was completely prostrated.

among Catholics and Protestants alike, and the chiefs of both parties crowded to Paris to attend the wedding, which took place on the 18th of August, 1572.

The Massacre of St. Bartholomew's Day (Aug. 24, 1572).— Before the festivities which followed the nuptial ceremonies were over, the world was shocked by one of the most awful crimes of which history has to tell, — the massacre of the Huguenots in Paris on St. Bartholomew's Day.

The circumstances which led to this fearful tragedy were as follows : Among the Protestant nobles who came up to Paris to attend the wedding was the Admiral Coligny. Upon coming in contact with Charles IX., the Admiral secured almost immediately an entire ascendency over his mind. This influence Coligny used to draw the king away from the queen-mother and the Guises. Fearing the loss of her influence over her son, Catherine resolved upon the death of the Admiral. The attempt miscarried, Coligny receiving only a slight wound from the assassin's ball.

The Huguenots at once rallied about their wounded chief with loud threats of revenge. Catherine, driven on by insane fear and hatred, now determined upon the death of all the Huguenots in Paris as the only measure of safety. By the 23d of August, the plans for the massacre were all arranged. On the evening of that day, Catherine went to her son, and represented to him that the Huguenots had formed a plot for the assassination of the royal family and the leaders of the Catholic party, and that the utter ruin of their house and cause could be averted only by the immediate destruction of the Protestants within the city walls. The order for the massacre was then laid before him for his signature. The king at first refused to sign the decree, but, overcome at last by the representations of his mother, he exclaimed, " I agree to the scheme, provided not one Huguenot be left alive in France to reproach me with the deed."

A little past the hour of midnight on St. Bartholomew's Day (Aug. 24, 1572), at a preconcerted signal, — the tolling of a bell, — the massacre began. Coligny was one of the first victims,

After his assassins had done their work, they tossed the body out of the window of the chamber in which it lay, into the street, in order that the Duke of Guise, who stood below, might satisfy himself that his enemy was really dead. For three days and nights the massacre went on within the city. King Charles himself is said to have joined in the work, and from one of the windows of the palace of the Louvre to have fired upon the Huguenots as they fled past. The number of victims in Paris is variously estimated at from 3,000 to 10,000.

With the capital cleared of Huguenots, orders were issued to the principal cities of France to purge themselves in like manner of heretics. In many places the instincts of humanity prevailed over fear of the royal resentment, and the decree was disobeyed. But in other places the orders were carried out, and frightful massacres took place. The entire number of victims throughout the country was probably between 20,000 and 30,000.

The massacre of St. Bartholomew's Day raised a cry of execration in almost every part of the civilized world, among Catholics and Protestants alike. Philip II., however, is said to have received the news with unfeigned joy; while Pope Gregory XIII. caused a *Te Deum*, in commemoration of the event, to be sung in the church of St. Mark, in Rome. Respecting this it should in justice be said that Catholic writers maintain that the Pope acted under a misconception of the facts, it having been represented to him that the massacre resulted from a thwarted plot of the Huguenots against the royal family of France and the Catholic Church.

Reign of Henry III. (1574–1589). — The massacre of St. Bartholomew's Day, instead of exterminating heresy in France, only served to rouse the Huguenots to a more determined defence of their faith. Throughout the last two years of the reign of Charles IX., and the fifteen succeeding years of the reign of his brother Henry III., the country was in a state of turmoil and war. At length the king, who, jealous of the growing power and popularity of the Duke of Guise, had caused him to be assassinated, was himself struck down by the avenging dagger of a Dominican monk. With him ended the House of Valois-Orleans.

Henry of Bourbon, king of Navarre, who for many years had been the most prominent leader of the Huguenots, now came to the throne as the first of the Bourbon kings.

Accession of Henry IV. (1589). — Notwithstanding that the doctrines of the reformers had made rapid progress in France under the sons of Henry II., still the majority of the nation at the time of the death of Henry III. were Roman Catholics in faith and worship. Under these circumstances, we shall hardly expect to find the entire nation quietly acquiescing in the accession to the French throne of a Protestant prince, and he the leader and champion of the hated Huguenots. Nor did Henry secure without a struggle the crown that was his by right. The Catholics declared for Cardinal Bourbon, an uncle of the king of Navarre, and France was thus kept in the whirl of civil war. Elizabeth of England aided the Protestants, and Philip II. of Spain assisted the Catholics.

Henry turns Catholic (1593). — After the war had gone on for about four years, — during which time was fought the noted battle of Ivry, in which Henry led his soldiers to victory by telling them to follow the white plume on his hat, — the quarrel was closed, for the time being, by Henry's abjuration of the Huguenot faith, and his adoption of that of the Roman Catholic Church (1593).

Mingled motives led Henry to do this. He was personally liked even by the Catholic chiefs, and he was well aware that it was only his Huguenot faith that prevented their being his hearty supporters. Hence duty and policy seemed to him to concur in urging him to remove the sole obstacle in the way of their ready loyalty, and thus bring peace and quiet to distracted France.

The Edict of Nantes (1598). — As soon as Henry had become the crowned and acknowledged king of France, he gave himself to the work of composing the affairs of his kingdom. The most noteworthy of the measures he adopted to this end was the publication of the celebrated Edict of Nantes (April 15, 1598). This decree granted the Huguenots practical freedom of worship, opened to them all offices and employments, and gave them as places of refuge and defence a large number of fortified towns, among which was the important city of La Rochelle.

The temporary hushing of the long-continued quarrels of the Catholics and Protestants by the adoption of the principle of religious toleration, paved the way for a revival of the trade and industries of the country, which had been almost destroyed by the anarchy and waste of the civil wars. France now entered upon such a period of prosperity as she had not known for many years.

Louis XIII. and his Minister, Cardinal Richelieu. — Henry IV. was assassinated by a fanatic named Ravaillac, who regarded him as an enemy of the Roman Catholic Church. As his son Louis, who succeeded him as Louis XIII. (1610–1643), was a child of nine years, during his minority the government was administered by his mother, Mary de Medici. Upon attaining his majority, Louis took the government into his own hands. He chose, as his chief minister, Cardinal Richelieu, one of the most remarkable characters of the seventeenth century. From the time that Louis admitted the young prelate to his cabinet (in

CARDINAL RICHELIEU.

1622), the ecclesiastic became the virtual sovereign of France, and for the space of twenty years swayed the destinies not only of that country, but, it might almost be said, those of Europe as well.

Richelieu's policy was twofold : first, to render the authority of the French king absolute in France ; secondly, to make the power of France supreme in Europe.

To attain the first end, Richelieu sought to crush the political power of the Huguenots, and to trample out the last vestige of independence among the old feudal aristocracy; to secure the second, he labored to break down the power of both branches of the House of Hapsburg, — that is, of Austria and Spain.

For nearly the life-time of a generation Richelieu, by intrigue, diplomacy, and war, pursued with unrelenting purpose these objects of his ambition. His own words best indicate how he proposed to use his double authority as cardinal and prime minister to effect his purpose : " I shall trample all opposition under foot," said he, " and then cover all errors with my scarlet robe."

In the following paragraph we shall speak very briefly of the cardinal's dealings with the Huguenots, which feature alone of his policy especially concerns us at present.

Political Power of the Huguenots crushed. — In the prosecution of his plans, Cardinal Richelieu's first step was to break down the political power of the Huguenot chiefs, who, dissatisfied with their position in the government, and irritated by religious grievances, were revolving in mind the founding in France of a Protestant commonwealth like that which the Prince of Orange and his adherents had set up in the Netherlands. The capital of the new Republic was to be La Rochelle, on the southwestern coast of France. In 1627, an alliance having been formed between England and the French Protestant nobles, an English fleet and army were sent across the Channel to aid the Huguenot enterprise.

Richelieu now resolved to ruin forever the power of these Protestant nobles who were constantly challenging the royal authority and threatening the dismemberment of France. Accordingly he led in person an army to the siege of La Rochelle, which, after a gallant resistance of more than a year, was compelled to open its gates to the cardinal (1628). That the place might never again be made the centre of resistance to the royal power, Louis ordered that " the fortifications be razed to the ground, in such wise that the plough may plough through the soil as through tilled land."

The Huguenots maintained the struggle a few months longer in the south of France, but were finally everywhere reduced to submission. The result of the war was the complete destruction of the political power of the French Protestants. A treaty of peace, called the Edict of Grace, negotiated the year after the fall of La Rochelle, left them, however, freedom of worship, according to the provisions of the Edict of Nantes (see p. 578).

The Edict of Grace properly marks the close of the religious wars which had desolated France for two generations (from 1562 to 1629). It is estimated that this series of wars and massacres cost France a million lives, and that between three and four hundred hamlets and towns were destroyed by the contending parties.

Richelieu and the Thirty Years' War. — When Cardinal Richelieu came to the head of affairs in France, there was going on in Germany the Thirty Years' War (1618–1648), of which we shall tell in the following chapter. This was very much such a struggle between the Catholic and Protestant German princes as we have seen waged between the two religious parties in France.

Although Richelieu had just crushed French Protestantism, he now gives aid to the Protestant princes of Germany, because their success meant the division of Germany and the humiliation of Austria. Richelieu did not live to see the end either of the Thirty Years' War or of that which he had begun with Spain; but this foreign policy of the great minister, carried out by others, finally resulted, as we shall learn hereafter, in the humiliation of both branches of the House of Hapsburg, and the lifting of France to the first place among the powers of Europe.

CHAPTER LIII.

THE THIRTY YEARS' WAR.

(1618–1648.)

Nature and Causes of the War. — The long and calamitous Thirty Years' War was the last great combat between Protestantism and Catholicism in Europe. It started as a struggle between the Protestant and Catholic princes of Germany, but gradually involved almost all the states of the continent, degenerating at last into a shameful and heartless struggle for power and territory.

The real cause of the war was the enmity existing between the German Protestants and Catholics. Each party by its encroachments gave the other occasion for complaint. The Protestants at length formed for their mutual protection a league called the Evangelical Union (1608). In opposition to the Union, the Catholics formed a confederation known as the Holy League (1609). All Germany was thus prepared to burst into the flames of a religious war.

The Bohemian Period of the War (1618–1623). — The flames that were to desolate Germany for a generation were first kindled in Bohemia, where were still smouldering embers of the Hussite wars, which two centuries before had desolated that land (see p. 506). A church which the Protestants maintained they had a right to build was torn down by the Catholics, and another was closed. The Protestants rose in revolt against their Catholic king, Ferdinand, elected a new Protestant king,[1] and drove out the Jesuits. The Thirty Years' War had begun (1618). Almost an exact century had passed since Luther posted his theses on the door of the court church at Wittenberg. It is estimated that at this time more than nine-tenths of the population of the empire were Protestants.

---

[1] Frederick V. of the Palatinate, son-in-law of James I. of England.

The war had scarcely opened when, the Imperial office falling vacant, the Bohemian king, Ferdinand, was elected emperor. With the power and influence he now wielded, it was not a difficult matter for him to quell the Protestant insurrection in his royal dominions. The leaders of the revolt were executed, and the reformed faith in Bohemia was almost uprooted.

The Danish Period (1625–1629). — The situation of affairs at this moment in Germany filled all the Protestant rulers of the North with the greatest alarm. Christian IV., king of Denmark, supported by England and Holland, threw himself into the struggle as the champion of German Protestantism. He now becomes the central figure on the side of the reformers. On the side of the Catholics are two noted commanders, — Tilly, the leader of the forces of the Holy League, and Wallenstein, the commander of the Imperial army. What is known as the Danish period of the war now begins (1625).

The war, in the main, proved disastrous to the Protestant allies, and Christian IV. was constrained to conclude a treaty of peace with the emperor (Peace of Lübeck, 1629), and retire from the struggle.

By what is known as the Edict of Restitution (1629), the Emperor Ferdinand now restored to the Catholics all the ecclesiastical lands and offices in North Germany of which possession had been taken by the Protestants in violation of the terms of the Peace of Augsburg. This decree gave back to the Catholic Church two archbishoprics, twelve bishoprics, besides many monasteries and other ecclesiastical property.

The Swedish Period (1630–1635) : **Gustavus Adolphus, Wallenstein, and Tilly**. — At this moment of seeming triumph, Ferdinand was constrained by rising discontent and jealousies to dismiss from his service his most efficient general, Wallenstein, who had made almost all classes, save his soldiers, his bitter enemies. In his retirement, Wallenstein maintained a court of fabulous magnificence. Wherever he went he was followed by an imperial train of attendants and equipages. He was reserved and silent, but his eye was upon everything going on in Germany, and indeed in Europe. He was watching for a favorable moment for revenge, and the retrieving of his fortunes.

The opportunity which Wallenstein, inspired by faith in his star, was so confidently awaiting was not long delayed. Only a few months before his dismissal from the Imperial service, Gustavus Adolphus, king of Sweden, with a veteran and enthusiastic army of 16,000 Swedes, had appeared in Northern Germany as the champion of the dispirited and leaderless Protestants. The Protestant princes, however, through fear of the emperor, as well as from lack of confidence in the disinterestedness of the motives of Gustavus, were shamefully backward in rallying to the support of their deliverer. But through an alliance formed just now with France, the Swedish king received a large annual subsidy from that country, which, with the help he was receiving from England, made him a formidable antagonist.

The wavering, jealous, and unworthy conduct of the Protestant princes now led to a most terrible disaster. At this moment Tilly was besieging the city of Magdeburg, which had dared to resist the Edict of Restitution (see p. 583). Gustavus was prevented from giving relief to the place by the hindrances thrown in his way by the Electors of Brandenburg and Saxony, both of whom should have given him every assistance. In a short time the city was obliged to surrender, and was given up to sack and pillage. Everything was burned, save two churches and a few hovels. 30,000 of the inhabitants perished miserably.

The cruel fate of Magdeburg excited the alarm of the Protestant princes. The Elector of Saxony now at once united his forces with those of the Swedish king. Tilly was defeated with great loss in the celebrated battle of Leipsic (1631), and Gustavus, emboldened by his success, pushed southward into the very heart of Germany. Attempting to dispute his march, Tilly's army was again defeated, and he himself received a fatal wound. In the death of Tilly, Ferdinand lost his most trustworthy general (1632).

The Imperial cause appeared desperate. There was but one man in Germany who could turn the tide of victory that was running so strongly in favor of the Swedish monarch. That man was Wallenstein; and to him the emperor now turned. This strange man had been watching with secret satisfaction the success of the Swedish arms, and had even offered to Gustavus his aid, promising " to

DEATH OF GUSTAVUS ADOLPHUS AT THE BATTLE OF LÜTZEN. (From an old print.)

chase the emperor and the House of Austria over the Alps."

To this proud subject of his, fresh from his dalliances with his enemies, the emperor now appealed for help. Wallenstein agreed to raise an army, provided his control of it should be absolute. Ferdinand was constrained to grant all that his old general demanded. Wallenstein now raised his standard, to which rallied the adventurers not only of Germany, but of all Europe as well. The array was a vast and heterogeneous host, bound together by no bonds of patriotism, loyalty, or convictions, but by the spell and prestige of the name of Wallenstein.

With an army of 40,000 men obedient to his commands, Wallenstein, after numerous marches and counter-marches attacked the Swedes in a terrible battle on the memorable field of Lützen, in Saxony. The Swedes won the day, but lost their leader and sovereign (1632).

Notwithstanding the death of their great king and commander, the Swedes did not withdraw from the war. Hence the struggle went on, the advantage being for the most part with the Protestant allies. Ferdinand, at just this time, was embarrassed by the suspicious movements of his general Wallenstein. Becoming convinced that he was meditating the betrayal of the Imperial cause, the emperor caused him to be assassinated (1634). This event marks very nearly the end of the Swedish period of the war.

The Swedish-French Period (1635–1648). — Had it not been for the selfish and ambitious interference of France, the woeful war which had now desolated Germany for half a century might here have come to an end, for both sides were weary of it and ready for negotiations of peace. But Richelieu was not willing that the war should end until the House of Austria was thoroughly crippled. Accordingly he encouraged Oxenstiern, the Swedish chancellor, to persevere in carrying on the war, promising him the aid of the French armies.

The war thus lost in large part its original character of a contest between the Catholic and the Protestant princes of Germany, and became a political struggle between the House of Austria and the House of Bourbon, in which the former was fighting for existence, the latter for national aggrandizement.

The Treaty of Westphalia (1648). — And so the miserable war dragged on. The earlier actors in the drama at length passed from the scene, but their parts were carried on by others. The year 1642, which marks the death of Richelieu, heard the first whisperings of peace. Everybody was inexpressibly weary of the war, and longed for the cessation of its horrors, yet each one wanted peace on terms advantageous to himself. The arrangement of the articles of peace was a matter of immense difficulty; for the affairs and boundaries of the states of Central Europe were in almost hopeless confusion. After five years of memorable discussion and negotiation, the articles of the celebrated Treaty of Westphalia, as it was called, were signed by the different European powers.

The chief articles of this important treaty may be made to fall under two heads : (1) those relating to territorial boundaries, and (2) those respecting religion.

As to the first, these cut short in three directions the actual or nominal limits of the Holy Roman Empire. Switzerland and the United Netherlands were severed from it ; for though both of these countries had been for a long time practically independent of the empire, this independence had never been acknowledged in any formal way. The claim of France to the three cities of Metz, Toul, and Verdun in Lorraine, which places she had held for about a century, was confirmed, and a great part of Alsace was given to her. Thus on the west, on the southwest, and on the northwest, the empire suffered loss.

Sweden was given cities and territories in Northern Germany which gave her control of a long strip of the Baltic shore, a most valuable possession. But these lands were not given to the Swedish king in full sovereignty ; they still remained a part of the Germanic body, and the king of Sweden as to them became a prince of the empire.

The changes within the empire were many, and some of them important. Brandenburg especially received considerable additions of territory.

The articles respecting religion were even more important than those which established the metes and bounds of the different states. Catholics, Lutherans, and Calvinists were all put upon the same footing. The Protestants were to retain all the benefices and Church property of which they had possession in 1624. Every prince was to have the right to make his religion the religion of his people, and to banish all who refused to adopt the established creed : but such non-conformists were to have three years in which to emigrate.

The different states of the empire were left almost independent of the emperor. They were given the right to form alliances with one another and with foreign princes ; but not, of course, against the empire or emperor. This provision made Germany nothing more than a lax confederation, and postponed to a distant future the nationalization of the German states.

Effects of the War upon Germany. — It is simply impossible to picture the wretched condition in which the Thirty Years' War left Germany. When the struggle began, the population of the country was 30,000,000; when it ended, 12,000,000. Many of the once large and flourishing cities were reduced to " mere shells." Two or three hundred ill-clad persons constituted the population of Berlin. The duchy of Würtemburg, which had half a million of inhabitants at the commencement of the war, at its close had barely 50,000. On every hand were the charred remains of the hovels of the peasants and the palaces of the nobility. The lines of commerce were broken, and some trades and industries were swept quite out of existence.

The effects upon the fine arts, upon science, learning, and morals were even more lamentable. Painting, sculpture, and architecture were driven out of the land. The cities which had been the home of all these arts lay in ruins. Education was entirely neglected. For the lifetime of a generation, men had been engaged in the business of war, and had allowed their children to grow up in absolute ignorance. Moral law was forgotten. Vice, nourished by the licentious atmosphere of the camp, reigned supreme. " In character, in intelligence, and in morality, the German people were set back two hundred years."

To all these evils were added those of political disunion and weakness. The title of emperor still continued to be borne by a member of the House of Austria, but it was only an empty name. By the Peace of Westphalia, the Germanic body lost even that little cohesion which had begun to manifest itself between its different parts, and became simply a loose assemblage of virtually independent states, of which there were now over two hundred. Thus weakened, Germany lost her independence as a nation, while the subjects of the numerous petty states became the slaves of their ambitious and tyrannical rulers. Worse than all, the overwhelming calamities that for the lifetime of a generation had been poured out upon the unfortunate land, had extinguished the last spark of German patriotism. Every sentiment of pride and hope in race and country seemed to have become extinct.

Conclusion. — The treaty of Westphalia is a prominent landmark in universal history. It stands at the dividing line of two great epochs. It marks the end of the Reformation Era and the beginning of that of the Political Revolution. Henceforth men will fight for constitutions, not creeds. We shall not often see one nation attacking another, or one party in a nation assaulting another party, on account of a difference in religious opinion.[1]

But in setting the Peace of Westphalia to mark the end of the religious wars occasioned by the Reformation, we do not mean to convey the idea that men had come to embrace the beneficent doctrine of religious toleration. As a matter of fact, no real toleration had yet been reached—nothing save the semblance of toleration. The long conflict of a century and more, and the vicissitudes of fortune, which to-day gave one party the power of the persecutor and to-morrow made the same sect the victims of persecution, had simply forced all to the practical conclusion that they must tolerate one another, — that one sect must not attempt to put another down by force. But it required the broadening and liberalizing lessons of another full century to bring men to see that the thing they *must* do is the very thing they *ought* to do, — to make men tolerant not only in outward conduct, but in spirit.

With this single word of caution, we now pass to the study of the Era of the Political Revolution, the period marked by the struggle between despotic and liberal principles of government. And first, we shall give a sketch of absolute monarchy as it exhibited itself in France under the autocrat Louis XIV.

---

[1] The Puritan Revolution in England may look like a religious war, but we shall learn that it was primarily a political contest, — a struggle against despotism in the state.

(FROM THE PEACE OF WESTPHALIA IN 1648 TO THE PRESENT TIME.)

CHAPTER LIV.

THE ASCENDENCY OF FRANCE UNDER THE ABSOLUTE GOVERNMENT OF LOUIS XIV.

(1643–1715.)

The Divine Right of Kings. — Louis XIV. stands as the representative of absolute monarchy. This indeed was no new thing in the world, but Louis was such an ideal autocrat that somehow he made autocratic government strangely attractive. Other kings imitated him, and it became the prevailing theory of government that kings have a " divine right " to rule, and that the people should have no part at all in government.

According to this theory, the nation is a great family with the king as its divinely appointed head. The duty of the king is to govern like a father ; the duty of the people is to obey their king even as children obey their parents. If the king does wrong, is harsh, cruel, unjust, this is simply the misfortune of his people : under no circumstances is it right for them to rebel against his authority, any more than for children to rise against their father. The king is responsible to God alone, and to God the people, quietly submissive, must leave the avenging of all their wrongs.

Before the close of the period upon which we here enter, we shall see how this theory of the divine right of kings worked out in practice, — how dear it cost both kings and people, and how the people by the strong logic of revolution demonstrated that they are not children but mature men, and have a divine and inalienable right to govern themselves.

The Basis of Louis XIV.'s Power. — The basis of the absolute power of Louis XIV. was laid by Cardinal Richelieu during the reign of Louis XIII. (see p. 580).   Besides crushing the political power of the Huguenots, and thereby vastly augmenting the security and strength of the royal authority, the Cardinal succeeded, by various means, — by annulling their privileges, by banishment, confiscations, and executions, — in almost extinguishing the expiring independence of the old feudal aristocracy, and in forcing the once haughty and refractory nobles to yield humble obedience to the crown.

In 1643, barely six months after the death of his great minister, Louis XIII. died, leaving the vast power which the Cardinal had done so much to consolidate, as an inheritance to his little son, a child of five years.

The Administration of Mazarin. — During the minority of Louis the government was in the hands of his mother, Anne of Austria, as regent.   She chose as her prime minister an Italian ecclesiastic, Cardinal Mazarin, who, in his administration of affairs, followed in the footsteps of his predecessor, Richelieu, carrying out with great ability the comprehensive policy of that minister. France was encouraged to maintain her part — and a very glorious part it was, as war goes — in the Thirty Years' War, until Austria was completely exhausted, and all Germany indeed almost ruined. Even after the Peace of Westphalia, which simply concluded the war in Germany, France carried on the war with Spain for ten years longer, until 1659, when the Treaty of the Pyrenees, which gave the French the two provinces of Artois and Roussillon, asserted the triumph of France over Spain.   Richelieu's plan had at last, though at terrible cost to France[1] and all Europe, been

---

[1] The heavy taxes laid to meet the expenses of the wars created great discontent, which during the struggle with Spain led to a series of conspiracies or revolts against the government, known as the *Wars of the Fronde* (1648–1652).   "Notwithstanding its peculiar character of levity and burlesque, the

crowned with success. The House of Austria in both its branches had been humiliated and crippled, and the House of Bourbon was ready to assume the lead in European affairs.

Louis XIV. assumes the Government. — Cardinal Mazarin died in 1661. Upon this event, Louis, who was now twenty-three years of age, became his own prime minister, and for more than half a century thereafter ruled France as an absolute and irresponsible monarch. He regarded France as his private estate, and seemed to be fully convinced that he had a divine commission to govern the French people. It is said that he declared, *L'État, c'est moi*, "I am the State," meaning that he alone was the rightful legislator, judge, and executive of the French nation. The States-General was not once convened during his long reign. Richelieu made Louis XIII. "the first man in Europe, but the second in his own kingdom." Louis XIV. was the first man at home as well as abroad. He had able men about him ; but they served instead of ruling him.

Colbert. — Mazarin when dying said to Louis, "Sire, I owe everything to you ; but I pay my debt to your majesty by giving you Colbert." During the first ten or twelve years of Louis's personal reign, this extraordinary man inspired and directed everything ; but he carefully avoided the appearance of doing so. His maxim seemed to be, Mine the labor, thine the praise. He did for the domestic affairs of France what Richelieu had done for the foreign. So long as Louis followed the policy of Colbert, he gave France a truly glorious reign ; but unfortunately he soon turned aside from the great minister's policy of peace, to seek glory for himself and greatness for France through new and unjust encroachments upon neighboring nations.

The Wars of Louis XIV. — During the period of his personal administration of the government, Louis XIV. was engaged in four

---

Fronde must be regarded as a memorable struggle of the aristocracy, supported by the judicial and municipal bodies, to control the despotism of the crown. . . . It failed; . . . nor was any farther effort made to resuscitate the dormant liberties of the nation until the dawning of the great Revolution."

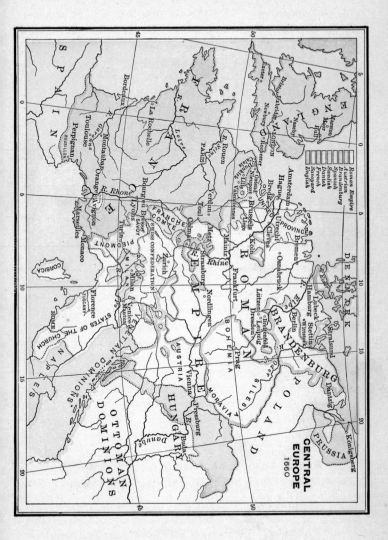

CENTRAL EUROPE
1660

great wars : (1) A war respecting the Spanish Netherlands (1667–1668 ; (2) a war with Holland (1672–1678) ; (3) the War of the Palatinate (1689–1697) ; and (4) the War of the Spanish Succession (1701–1714).

All these wars were, on the part of the French monarch, wars of conquest and aggression, or were wars provoked by his ambitious and encroaching policy. The most inveterate enemy of Louis during all this period was Holland, the representative and champion of liberal, constitutional government.

The War concerning the Spanish Netherlands (1667–1668). — Upon the death of Philip IV. of Spain (1665), Louis immediately claimed, in the name of his wife, portions of the Spanish Netherlands (see p. 568, n.). The Hollanders were naturally alarmed, fearing that Louis would also want to annex their country to his dominions. Accordingly they effected what was called the Triple Alliance with England and Sweden, checked the French king in his career of conquest, and, by the Treaty of Aix-la-Chapelle, forced him to give up much of the territory he had seized.

The War with Holland (1672–1678). — The second war of the French king was against Holland, whose interference with his plans in the Spanish Netherlands, as well as some uncomplimentary remarks of the Dutch humorists on his personal appearance, had stirred his resentment. Before entering upon the undertaking which had proved too great for Philip II. with the resources of two worlds at his command, Louis, by means of bribes and the employment of that skilful diplomacy of which he was so perfect a master, prudently drew from the side of Holland both her allies (Sweden and England), even inducing the English king, Charles II., to lend him active assistance. Money also secured the aid of several princes of Germany. Thus the little commonwealth was left alone to contend against fearful odds.

The brave Hollanders made a stout defence of their land. It was even seriously proposed in the States-General, that, rather than submit to the tyranny of this second Philip, they should open the dykes, bury the country and its invaders beneath the ocean, and taking their families and household goods in their ships, seek new homes in lands beyond the sea. The desperate resolve was in part executed; for with the French threatening Amsterdam, the dykes were cut, and all the surrounding fields were laid under water, and the invaders thus forced to retreat.

The heroic resistance to the intruders made by the Hollanders in their half-drowned land, the havoc wrought by the stout Dutch sailors among the fleets of the allies, and the diplomacy of the Dutch statesmen, who, through skilful negotiations, detached almost all of the allies of the French from that side, and brought them into alliance with the republic, — all these things soon put a very different face upon affairs, and Louis found himself confronted by the armies of half of Europe.

For several years the war now went on by land and sea, — in the Netherlands, all along the Rhine, upon the English Channel, in the Mediterranean, and on the coasts of the New World. At length an end was put to the struggle by the Treaty of Nimeguen (1678). Louis gave up his conquests in Holland, but kept a large number of towns and fortresses in the Spanish Netherlands, besides the province of Franche-Comté and several Imperial cities on his German frontier.

Thus Louis came out of this tremendous struggle, in which half of Europe was leagued against him, with enhanced reputation and fresh acquisitions of territory. People now began to call him the *Grand Monarch*.

The Revocation of the Edict of Nantes (1685). — Louis now committed an act the injustice of which was only equalled by its folly, — an act from which may be dated the decline of his power. This was the Revocation of the Edict of Nantes, the well-known decree by which Henry IV. secured religious freedom to the French Protestants (see p. 578). By this cruel measure all the Protestant churches were closed, and every Huguenot who refused to embrace the Roman Catholic faith was outlawed. The persecution which the Huguenots had been enduring and which was now greatly increased in violence, is known as the *Dragonnades,* from the circumstance that *dragoons* were quartered upon the Protestant families, with full permission to annoy and persecute them in every way "short of violation and death," to the end that the victims of these outrages might be constrained to recant, which multitudes did.

Under the fierce persecutions of the *Dragonnades*, probably as many as three hundred thousand of the most skilful and industrious of the subjects of Louis were driven out of the kingdom. Several of the most important and flourishing of the French industries were ruined, while the manufacturing interests of other countries, particularly those of Holland and England, were correspondingly benefited by the energy, skill, and capital which the exiles carried to them. Many of the fugitive Huguenots found ultimately a refuge in America; and no other class of emigrants, save the Puritans of England, cast

> "Such healthful leaven 'mid the elements
> That peopled the new world." [1]

The War of the Palatinate (1689–1697). — The indirect results of the Revocation of the Edict of Nantes were quite as calamitous to France as were the direct results. The indignation that the barbarous measure awakened among the Protestant nations of Europe enabled William of Orange to organize a formidable confederacy against Louis, known as the League of Augsburg (1686).

Louis resolved to attack the confederates. Seeking a pretext for beginning hostilities, he laid claim, in the name of his sister-in-law, to portions of the Palatinate, and hurried a large army into the country, which was quickly overrun. But being unable to hold the conquests he had made, Louis ordered that the country be turned into a desert. The Huns of an Attila could not have carried out more relentlessly the command than did the soldiers of Louis. Churches and abbeys, palaces and cottages, villas and cities, were all given to the flames.

[1] See Baird, *History of the Huguenot Emigration to America.*

This barbarous act of Louis almost frenzied Germany. Another and more formidable coalition, known as the "Grand Alliance," was now formed (1689). It embraced England, Holland, Sweden, Spain, the German emperor, the Elector Palatine, and the Electors of Bavaria and Saxony. For ten years almost all Europe was a great battle-field. Both sides at length becoming weary of the contest and almost exhausted in resources, the struggle was closed by the Treaty of Ryswick (1697). There was a mutual surrender of conquests made during the course of the war, and Louis had also to give up some of the places he had unjustly seized before the beginning of the conflict.

DUKE OF MARLBOROUGH.
(After a painting by F. Kneller.)

War of the Spanish Succession (1701–1714). — Barely three years passed after the Treaty of Ryswick before the great powers of Europe were involved in another war, known as the War of the Spanish Succession.

The circumstances out of which the war grew were these: In 1700 the king of Spain, Charles II., died, leaving his crown to Philip of Anjou, a grandson of Louis XIV. "There are no longer any Pyrenees," was Louis's exultant epigram, meaning of course that France and Spain were now practically one.

England and Holland particularly were alarmed at this virtual consolidation of these two powerful kingdoms. Consequently a second Grand Alliance was soon formed against France, the object of which was to dethrone Philip of Anjou and place upon the Spanish throne Charles, Archduke of Austria. The two greatest generals of the allies were the famous Duke of Marlborough (John

Churchill), the ablest commander, except Wellington perhaps, that England has ever produced, and the hardly less noted Prince Eugene of Savoy.

For thirteen years all Europe was shaken with war. During the progress of the struggle were fought some of the most memorable battles in European history, — Blenheim, Ramillies, Oudenarde, and Malplaquet, — in all of which the genius of Marlborough and the consummate skill of Prince Eugene won splendid victories for the allies.

Finally, changes wrought by death in the House of Austria brought the Archduke Charles to the imperial throne. This changed the whole aspect of the Spanish question, for now to place Charles upon the Spanish throne also would be to give him a dangerous preponderance of power, would be, in fact, to re-establish the great monarchy of Charles V. Consequently the Grand Alliance fell to pieces, and the war was ended by the treaties of Utrecht (1713) and Rastadt (1714).

By the provisions of these treaties the Bourbon prince of Anjou was left upon the Spanish throne, but his kingdom was pared away on every side. Gibraltar and the island of Minorca were ceded to England; while Milan, Naples, Sardinia, and the Netherlands (Spanish) were given to Austria. France was forced to surrender to England considerable portions of her possessions in the New World, — Newfoundland, Nova Scotia, and the Hudson Bay territory.

Death of the King. — Amidst troubles, perplexities, and afflictions, Louis XIV.'s long and eventful reign was now drawing to a close. The heavy and constant taxes necessary to meet the expenses of his numerous wars, and to maintain an extravagant court, had bankrupted the country, and the cries of his wretched subjects clamoring for bread could not be shut out of the royal chamber. Death, too, had invaded the palace, striking down the dauphin, the dauphiness, and two grandsons of Louis, leaving as the nearest heir to the throne his great-grandson, a mere child. On the morning of September 1st, 1715, the Grand Monarch breathed his last, bequeathing to this boy of five years a kingdom overwhelmed with debt, and filled with misery, with threatening vices and dangerous discontent.

The Court of Louis XIV. — The Court sustained by the Grand Monarch was the most extravagantly magnificent that Europe has

ever seen. Never since Nero erected his Golden House upon the burnt district of Rome, and ensconcing himself amid its luxurious appointments, exclaimed, "Now I am housed as a man ought to be," had prince or king so ostentatiously lavished upon himself the wealth of an empire. Louis had half a dozen palaces, the most costly of which was that at Versailles. Upon this and its surroundings he spent fabulous sums. The palace itself cost what would probably be equal to more than $100,000,000 with us. Here were gathered the beauty, wit, and learning of

LOUIS XIV.

France. The royal household numbered fifteen thousand persons, all living in costly and luxurious idleness at the expense of the people.

One element of this enormous family was the great lords of the old feudal aristocracy. Dispossessed of their ancient power and wealth, they were content now to fill a place in the royal household, to be the king's pensioners and the elegant embellishment of his court.

As we might well imagine, the life of the French court at this period was shamefully corrupt. Vice, however, was gilded. The scandalous immoralities of king and courtiers were made attractive by the glitter of superficial accomplishment and by exquisite suavity and polish of manner.

But notwithstanding its immorality, the brilliancy of the Court of Louis dazzled all Europe. The neighboring courts imitated its manners and emulated its extravagances. In all matters of taste and fashion France gave laws to the continent, and the French language became the court language of the civilized world.

Literature under Louis XIV. — Louis gave a most liberal encouragement to men of letters, thereby making his reign the Augustan Age of French literature. In this patronage Louis was not unselfish. He honored and befriended poets and writers of every class, because he thus extended the reputation of his court. These writers, pensioners of his bounty, filled all Europe with their praises of the Great King, and thus made the most ample and grateful return to Louis for his favor and liberality.

Almost every species of literature was cultivated by the French writers of this era, yet it was in the province of the Drama that the greatest number of eminent authors appeared. The three great names here are those of Corneille (1606–1684), Racine (1639–1699), and Molière (1622–1673).

Decline of the French Monarchy under Louis XV. — The ascendency of the House of Bourbon passed away forever with Louis XIV. In passing from the reign of the Grand Monarch to that of his successor, Louis XV. (1715–1774), we pass from the strongest and most brilliant reign in French history to the weakest and most humiliating.

France took part, but usually with injury to her military reputation, in all the wars of this period. The most important of these were the War of the Austrian Succession (see p. 644), and the Seven Years' War (see p. 631), known in America as the French and Indian War, which resulted in the loss to France of Canada in the New World and of her Indian possessions in the Old.

Though thus shorn of her colonial possessions in all quarters of the globe, France managed to hold in Europe the provinces won for her by the wars and the diplomacy of Louis XIV., and even made some fresh acquisitions of territory along the Rhenish frontier.

But taken all together, the period was one of great national humiliation: the French fleet was almost driven from the sea; the martial spirit of the nation visibly declined; and France, from the foremost place among the states of Europe, fell to the position of a third or fourth rate power.

CHAPTER LV.

ENGLAND UNDER THE STUARTS: THE ENGLISH REVOLUTION.

(1603–1714.)

I. THE FIRST TWO STUARTS.

1. *Reign of James the First* (1603–1625).

The "Divine Right" of Kings and the "Royal Touch." —
With the end of the Tudor line (see p. 561), James VI. of Scotland, son of Mary Stuart, came to the English throne, as James I.
of England. The accession of the House of Stuart brought England and Scotland under the same sovereign, though each country
still retained its own Parliament.

The Stuarts were firm believers in the doctrine of the " Divine
Right " of kings. They held that hereditary princes are the Lord's
anointed, and that their authority can in no way be questioned or
limited by people, priest, or Parliament. James I.'s own words
were, " As it is atheism and blasphemy to dispute what God can
do, so it is high contempt in a subject to dispute what a king can
do, or to say that the king cannot do this or that."

This doctrine found much support in the popular superstition
of the " Royal Touch." The king was believed to possess the
power — a gift transmitted through the royal line of England
from Edward the Confessor — of healing scrofulous persons by
the laying on of hands.[1] It is simply the bearing of this strange
superstition upon the doctrine of the divine right of kings that
concerns us now. "The political importance of this superstition,"

---

[1] Consult Lecky, *A History of England in the Eighteenth Century*, Vol. I.
p. 73. The French kings were also supposed to possess the same miraculous
power, inherited, as most believed, from Louis the Saint.

observes Lecky, "is very manifest. Educated laymen might deride it, but in the eyes of the English poor it was a visible, palpable attestation of the indefeasible sanctity of the royal line. It placed the sovereignty entirely apart from the categories of mere human institutions."

By bearing this superstition in mind, it will be easier for us to understand how so large a proportion of the people of England could support the Stuarts in their extravagant claims, and could sincerely maintain the doctrine of the sinfulness of resistance to the king.

The Gunpowder Plot (1605). — In the third year of James's reign was unearthed a plot to blow up with gunpowder the Parliament Building, upon the opening day of the Session, when king, lords, and commons would all be present, and thus to destroy at a single blow every branch of the English Government. This conspiracy, known as the Gunpowder Plot, was entered into by a few Roman Catholics, because they were disappointed in the course which the king had taken as regards their religion.[1] The leader of the conspiracy, Guy Fawkes, was arrested, and after being put to the rack, was executed. His chief accomplices were also seized and punished. The alarm created by the terrible plot led Parliament to enact some very severe laws against all the Roman Catholics of the realm.

Colonies and Trade Settlements. — The reign of James I. is signalized by the commencement of that system of colonization which has resulted in the establishment of the English race in almost every quarter of the globe.

In the year 1607 Jamestown, so named in honor of the king, was founded in Virginia. This was the first permanent English settlement within the limits of the United States. In 1620 some Separatists, or Pilgrims, who had found in Holland a temporary refuge from persecution, pushed across the Atlantic, and amidst heroic sufferings and hardships established the first settlement in

---

[1] Though son of the Catholic Mary Stuart, James had been educated as a Protestant.

New England, and laid the foundations of civil liberty in the New World.

Besides planting these settlements in the New World, the English during this same reign established themselves in the ancient country of India. In 1612 the East India Company, which had been chartered by Elizabeth in 1600, established their first trading-post at Surat. This was the humble beginning of the gigantic English empire in the East.

Contest between James and the Commons. — We have made mention of James's idea of the divine right of kingship. Such a view of royal authority and privileges was sure to bring him into conflict with Parliament, especially with the House of Commons. He was constantly dissolving Parliament and sending the members home, because they insisted upon considering subjects which he had told them they should let alone.

The chief matters of dispute between the king and the Commons were the limits of the authority of the former in matters touching legislation and taxation, and the nature and extent of the privileges and jurisdictions of the latter.

As to the limits of the royal power, James talked and acted as though his prerogatives were practically unbounded. He issued proclamations which in their scope were really laws, and then enforced these royal edicts by fines and imprisonment, as though they were regular statutes of Parliament. Moreover, taking advantage of some uncertainty in the law as regards the power of the king to collect customs at the ports of the realm, he laid new and unusual duties upon imports and exports. James's judges were servile enough to sustain him in this course, some of them going so far as to say that "the sea-ports are the king's gates, which he may open and shut to whom he pleases."

As to the privileges of the Commons, that body insisted, among other things, upon their right to determine all cases of contested election of their members, and to debate freely all questions concerning the common weal, without being liable to prosecution or imprisonment for words spoken in the House. James denied that these privileges were matters of right pertaining to the Commons, and repeatedly intimated to them that it was only through his own gracious permission and the favor of his ancestors that they were allowed to exercise these liberties at all, and that if their conduct was not more circumspect and reverential, he should take away their privileges entirely.

On one occasion, the Commons having ventured to debate certain matters of state which the king had forbidden them to meddle with, he, in reproving them, made a more express denial than ever of their rights and privileges, which caused them, in a burst of noble indignation, to enter upon their journal a brave protest, known as "The Great Protestation," which declared that "the liberties, franchises, privileges, and jurisdictions of Parliament are the ancient and undoubted birthright and inheritance of the subjects of England, and that the arduous and urgent affairs concerning the king, state, and defence of the realm . . . . are proper subjects and matter of council and debate in Parliament" (1621).

When intelligence of this action was carried to the king, he instantly sent for the journal of the House, and with his own hands tore out the leaf containing the obnoxious resolution. Then he angrily prorogued Parliament, and even went so far as to imprison several of the members of the Commons. In these high-handed measures we get a glimpse of the Stuart theory of government, and see the way paved for the final break between king and people in the following reign.

King James died in the year 1625, after a reign as sovereign of England and Scotland of twenty-two years.

Literature. —One of the most noteworthy literary labors of the reign under review was a new translation of the Bible, known as *King James's Version.* This royal version is the one in general use at the present day.

The most noted writers of James's reign were a bequest to it from the brilliant era of Elizabeth (see p. 560). Sir Walter Raleigh, the petted courtier of Elizabeth, fell on evil days after her death.   On the charge of taking part in a conspiracy against the crown, he was sent to the Tower, where he was kept a prisoner for thirteen years.   From the tedium of his long confinement, he found relief in the composition of a *History of the World*.   He was at last beheaded.

The close of the life of the great philosopher Francis Bacon was scarcely less sad than that of Sir Walter Raleigh.   He held the office of Lord Chancellor, and yielding to the temptations of

THE TOWER OF LONDON.

the corrupt times upon which he had fallen, accepted bribes from the suitors who brought cases before him.   He was impeached and brought to the bar of the House of Lords, where he confessed his guilt, pathetically appealing to his judges " to be merciful to a broken reed."   He was sentenced to pay a heavy fine, and to imprisonment in the Tower.   But the king in pity released him from all the penalty, and even conferred a pension upon him. He lived only five years after his fall and disgrace, dying in 1626.

Bacon must be given the first place among the philosophers of the English-speaking race.   His system is known as the *Inductive*

Method of Philosophy. It insists upon experiment and a careful observation of facts as the only true means of arriving at a knowledge of the laws of nature.

2. *Reign of Charles the First* (1625–1649).

The Petition of Right (1628). — Charles I. came to the throne with all his father's lofty notions about the divine right of kings.

CHARLES I. (After a painting by A. Vandyke.)

Consequently the old contest between king and Parliament was straightway renewed. The first two Parliaments of his reign Charles dissolved speedily, because instead of voting supplies they persisted in investigating public grievances. After the dissolution of his second Parliament Charles endeavored to raise the money he needed to carry on the government, by means of " benevolences " and forced loans. But all his expedients failed to meet his needs, and he was compelled to fall back upon Parliament. The Houses met, and promised to grant him generous subsidies, provided he would sign a certain *Petition of Right* which they had drawn up. Next after Magna Charta, this document up to this date is the most noted in the constitutional history of England. It simply reaffirmed the ancient rights and privileges of the English people as defined in the Great Charter and by the good laws of Edward I. and Edward III.

Four abuses were provided against : (1) the raising of money by loans, " benevolences," taxes, etc., without the consent of Parliament ; (2) arbitrary imprisonment ; (3) the quartering of soldiers in private houses — a very vexatious thing ; and (4) trial without jury.

Charles was as reluctant to assent to the Petition as King John was to affix his seal to the Magna Charta ; but he was at length forced to give sanction to it by the use of the usual formula, " Let it be law as desired " (1628).

Charles rules without Parliament (1629–1640). — It soon became evident that Charles was utterly insincere when he put his name to the Petition of Right.   He immediately violated its provisions in attempting to raise money by forbidden taxes and loans. For eleven years he ruled without Parliament, thus changing the government of England from a government by king, lords, and commons, to what was in effect an absolute and irresponsible monarchy, like that of France or Spain.

As is always the case under such circumstances, there were enough persons ready to aid the king in his schemes of usurpation.   Prominent among his unscrupulous agents were his ministers Thomas Wentworth (Earl of Strafford) and William Laud. Wentworth devoted himself to establishing the royal despotism in civil matters ; while Laud, who was made Archbishop of Canterbury, busied himself chiefly with exalting above all human interference the king's prerogatives in religious affairs as the supreme head of the English Church.

All these high-handed and tyrannical proceedings of Charles and his agents were enforced by certain courts that had been wrested from their original purpose and moulded into instruments of despotism.   These were known as the *Council of the North*, the *Star Chamber*, and the *High Commission Court*.[1]   All of these courts sat without jury, and being composed of the creatures of the king, were of course his subservient instruments.   Their decisions were unjust and arbitrary ; their punishments, harsh and cruel.

---

[1] The first was a tribunal established by Henry VIII., and was now employed by Wentworth as an instrument for enforcing the king's despotic authority in the turbulent northern counties of England.   The Star Chamber was a court of somewhat obscure origin, which at this time dealt chiefly with criminal cases affecting the government, such as riot, libel, and conspiracy. The High Commission Court was a tribunal of forty-four commissioners, created in Elizabeth's reign to enforce the acts of Supremacy and Uniformity.

John Hampden and Ship-Money. — Among the illegal taxes levied during this period of tyranny was a species known as ship-money, so called from the fact that in early times the kings, when the realm was in danger, called upon the sea-ports and maritime counties to contribute ships and ship-material for the public service. Charles and his agents, in looking this matter over, conceived the idea of extending this tax over the inland as well as the sea-board counties.

Among those who refused to pay the tax was a country gentleman, named John Hampden. The case was tried in the Exchequer Chamber, before all the twelve judges. All England watched the progress of the suit with the utmost solicitude. The question was argued by able counsel both on the side of Hampden and of the crown. Judgment was finally rendered in favor of the king, although five of the twelve judges stood for Hampden. The case was lost ; but the people, who had been following the arguments, were fully persuaded that it went against Hampden simply for the reason that the judges stood in fear of the royal displeasure, and that they did not dare to decide the case adversely to the crown.

The arbitrary and despotic character which the government had now assumed in both civil and religious matters, and the hopelessness of relief or protection from the courts, caused thousands to seek in the New World that freedom and security which was denied them in their own land.

The Covenanters. — England was almost ready to rise in open revolt against the unbearable tyranny. Events in Scotland hastened the crisis. The king was attempting to impose the English liturgy (slightly modified) upon the Scotch Presbyterians. At Edinburgh this led to a riot, one of the women worshippers throwing a stool at the bishop who attempted to read the service. The spirit of resistance spread. All classes, nobles and peasants alike, bound themselves by a solemn covenant to resist to the very last every attempt to make innovations in their religion. From this act they became known as Covenanters (1638).

The king resolved to crush the movement by force, but he soon found that war could not be carried on without money, and was constrained to summon Parliament in hopes of obtaining a vote of supplies. But instead of making the king a grant of money, the Commons first gave their attention to the matter of grievances, whereupon Charles dissolved the Parliament. The Scottish forces crossed the border, and the king, helpless, with an empty treasury and a seditious army, was forced again to summon the two Houses.

The Long Parliament. — Under this call met on November 3, 1640, that Parliament which, from the circumstance of its lasting over twelve years, became known as the Long Parliament. The members of the Commons of this Parliament were stern and determined men, who were resolved to put a check to the despotic course of the king.

Almost the first act of the Commons was the impeachment and trial of Strafford and Laud, as the most prominent instruments of the king's tyranny and usurpation. Both were finally brought to the block. The three iniquitous and illegal courts of which we have spoken (see p. 607) were abolished. And the Commons, to secure themselves against dissolution before their work was done, enacted a law which provided that they should not be adjourned or dissolved without their own consent.

Charles's Attempt to seize the Five Members. — An act of violence on the part of Charles now precipitated the nation into the gulf of civil war, towards which events had been so rapidly drifting. With the design of overawing the Commons, the king made a charge of treason against five of the leading members, among whom were Hampden and Pym, and sent officers to effect their arrest; but the accused were not to be found. The next day Charles himself, accompanied to the door of the chamber by armed attendants, went to the House, for the purpose of seizing the five members; but, having been forewarned of the king's intention, they had withdrawn from the hall. The king was not long in realizing the state of affairs, and with the observation, " I see the birds have flown," withdrew from the chamber.

Charles had taken a fatal step. The nation could not forgive the insult offered to its representatives.   All London rose in arms. The king, frightened by the storm which he had raised, fled from the city to York.   From this flight of Charles from London, may be dated the beginning of the Civil War (Jan. 10, 1642).

Having now traced the events which led up to this open strife between the king and his people, we shall pass very lightly over the incidents of the struggle itself, and hasten to speak of the Commonwealth, to the establishment of which the struggle led.

End of The Civil War (1642-1649).

The Beginning. — After the flight of the king, negotiations were entered into between him and Parliament with a view to a reconciliation.   The demands of Parliament were that the militia, the services of the Church, the education and marriage of the king's children, and many other matters should be subject to the control of the two Houses.   In making all these demands Parliament had manifestly gone to unreasonable and unconstitutional lengths ; but their distrust of Charles was so profound, that they were unwilling to leave in his hands any power or prerogative that might be perverted or abused.   Charles refused, as might have been and was expected, to accede to the propositions of Parliament, and unfurling the royal standard at Nottingham, called upon all loyal subjects to rally to the support of their king (Aug. 22, 1642).

The Two Parties. —The country was now divided into two great parties.   Those that enlisted under the king's standard — on whose side rallied, for the most part, the nobility, the gentry, and the clergy — were known as Royalists, or Cavaliers ; while those that gathered about the Parliamentary banner were called Parliamentarians, or Roundheads, the latter term being applied to them because many of their number cropped their hair close to the head, simply for the reason that the Cavaliers affected long and flowing locks.   The Cavaliers, in the main, favored the Established Church, while the Roundheads were, in general, Puritans.   During the progress of the struggle the Puritans split into two parties, or sects, known as Presbyterians and Independents.

For six years England now suffered even greater evils than those that marked that earlier civil strife known as the Wars of the Roses.

Oliver Cromwell and his "Ironsides." — The war had continued about three years when there came into prominence among the officers of the Parliamentary forces a man of destiny, one of the great characters of history, — Oliver Cromwell. During the early campaigns of the war, as colonel of a regiment of cavalry, he had exhibited his rare genius as an organizer and disciplinarian. His regiment became famous under the name of " Cromwell's Ironsides." It was composed entirely of " men of religion." Swearing, drinking, and the usual vices of the camp were unknown among them. They advanced to the charge singing psalms. During all the war the regiment was never once beaten.

The Self-Denying Ordinance (1645). — In the course of the war the Puritans, as has been said, became divided into two parties, the Presbyterians and the Independents. The former desired to reëstablish a limited monarchy; the latter wished to sweep aside the old constitution and form a republic.

In the third year of the war there arose a struggle as to which party should have control of the army. By means of what was called the "Self-denying Ordinance," which declared that no member of either House should hold a position in the army, the Independents effected the removal from their command of several conservative noblemen. Cromwell, as he was a member of the House of Commons, should also have given up his command; but the ordinance was suspended in his case, so that he might retain his place as lieutenant-general. Sir Thomas Fairfax was made commander-in-chief. Though Cromwell was nominally second in command, he was now really at the head of the army.

The "New Model." — Cromwell at once set about to effect the entire remodelling of the army on the plan of his favorite Ironsides. His idea was that " the chivalry of the Cavalier must be met by the religious enthusiasm of the Puritan." The army was reduced to 20,000 men — all honest, fervent, God-fearing, psalm-singing Puritans. When not fighting, they studied the Bible, prayed and sung hymns. Since Godfrey led his crusaders to the rescue of the Holy Sepulchre, the world had not beheld another such army of religious enthusiasts. From Cromwell down to the lowest soldier of the "New Model," every man felt called of the Lord to strike down all forms of tyranny in Church and State.

The Battle of Naseby (1645). — The temper of the "New Model" was soon tried in the battle of Naseby, the decisive engagement of the war. The Royalists were scattered to the winds, and their cause was irretrievably lost. Charles escaped from the field, and ultimately fled into Scotland, thinking that he might rely upon the loyalty of the Scots to the House of Stuart; but on his refusing to sign the Covenant and certain other articles, they gave him up to the English Parliament.

"Pride's Purge" (1648). — Now, there were many in the Parliament who were in favor of restoring the king unconditionally to his throne, that is, without requiring from him any guaranties that he would in the future rule in accordance with the constitution and the laws of the land. The Independents, which means Cromwell and the army, saw in this possibility the threatened ruin of all their hopes, and the loss of all the fruits of victory. A high-handed measure was resolved upon, — the exclusion from the House of Commons of all those members who favored the restoration of Charles.

Accordingly, an officer by the name of Pride was stationed at the door of the hall, to arrest the members obnoxious to the army. One hundred and forty members were thus kept from their seats, and the Commons thereby reduced to about fifty representatives, all of whom of course were Independents. This performance was appropriately called "Pride's Purge." It was simply an act of military usurpation.

Trial and Execution of the King. — The Commons thus "purged" of the king's friends now passed a resolution for the immediate trial of Charles for treason. A High Court of Justice, comprising 150 members, was organized, before which Charles was summoned. Before the close of a week he was condemned to be executed "as a tyrant, traitor, murderer, and enemy of his country."

II. THE COMMONWEALTH (1649–1660).

Establishment of the Commonwealth. — A few weeks after the execution of Charles, the Commons voted to abolish the Monarchy and the House of Lords, and to establish a republic, under the name of "The Commonwealth." The executive power was lodged in a Council of State, composed of forty-one persons. Of this body Bradshaw, an eminent lawyer, was the nominal, but Cromwell the real, head.

Troubles of the Commonwealth. — The republic thus born of mingled religious and political enthusiasm was beset with dangers from the very first. The execution of Charles had alarmed every sovereign in Europe. Russia, France, and Holland, all refused to have any communication with the ambassadors of the Commonwealth. The Scots, who too late repented of having surrendered their native sovereign into the hands of his enemies, now hastened to wipe out the stain of their disloyalty by proclaiming his son their king, with the title of Charles the Second. The impulsive Irish also declared for the Prince; while the Dutch began active preparations to assist him in regaining the throne of his unfortunate father. In England itself the Royalists were active and threatening.

War with Ireland. — The Commonwealth, like the ancient republic of Rome, seemed to gather strength and energy from the very multitude of surrounding dangers. Cromwell was made Lord-Lieutenant of Ireland, and sent into that country to crush a rising of the Royalists there. With his Ironsides he made quick and terrible work of the conquest of the island. Having taken by storm the town of Drogheda (1649), he massacred the entire garrison, consisting of three thousand men. About a thousand who had sought asylum in a church were butchered there without mercy. The capture of other towns was accompanied by massacres little less terrible. The conqueror's march through the island was the devastating march of an Attila or a Zinghis Khan. The following is his own account of the manner in which he dealt with the captured garrisons : " When they submitted, their officers were knocked on the head, and every tenth man of the soldiers killed, and the rest shipped for Barbadoes [to be sold into slavery]."

War with Scotland. — Cromwell was called out of Ireland by the Council to lead an army into Scotland. The terror of his name went before him, and the people fled as he approached. At Dunbar he met the Scotch army. Before the terrible onset of the fanatic Roundheads the Scots were scattered like chaff before the wind (1650).

The following year, on the anniversary of the Battle of Dunbar, Cromwell gained another great victory over the Scottish army at Worcester, and all Scotland was soon after forced to submit to the authority of the Commonwealth. Prince Charles, after many adventurous experiences, escaped across the Channel into Normandy.

Cromwell ejects the Long Parliament (1653). — The war in Scotland was followed by one with the Dutch. While this war was in progress Parliament came to an open quarrel with the army. Cromwell demanded of Parliament their dissolution, and the calling of a new body. This they refused ; whereupon, taking with him a body of soldiers, Cromwell went to the House, and after listening impatiently for a while to the debate, suddenly sprang to his feet, and, with bitter reproaches, exclaimed : " I will put an end to your prating. Get you gone ; give place to better men. You are no Parliament. The Lord has done with you." The soldiers rushing in at a preconcerted signal, the hall was cleared, and the doors locked (1653).

In such summary manner the Long Parliament, or the " Rump Parliament," as it was called in derision after Pride's Purge, was dissolved, after having sat for twelve years. So completely had the body lost the confidence and respect of all parties, that scarcely a murmur was heard against the illegal and arbitrary mode of its dissolution.

The Little Parliament. — Cromwell now called a new Parliament, or more properly a convention, summoning, so far as he might, only religious, God-fearing men. The "Little Parliament," as generally called, consisted of 156 members, mainly religious persons, who spent much of their time in Scripture exegesis, prayer, and exhortation. Among them was a London leather-merchant, named Praise-God Barebone, who was especially given to these exercises. The name amused the people, and they nicknamed the Convention the "Praise-God Barebone Parliament."

The Little Parliament sat only a few months, during which time, however, it really did some excellent work, particularly in the way of suggesting important reforms. It at length resigned all its powers into the hands of Cromwell; and shortly afterwards his council of army officers, fearing the country would fall into anarchy, persuaded him — though manifesting reluctance, he probably was quite willing to be persuaded — to accept the title of "Lord Protector of the Commonwealth."

OLIVER CROMWELL.

The Protectorate (1653–1659). — Cromwell's power was now almost unlimited. He was virtually a dictator. His administration was harsh and despotic. He summoned, prorogued, and dissolved parliaments. The nation was really under martial law. Royalists and active Roman Catholics were treated with the utmost rigor. A censorship of the Press was established. Scotland was overawed by strong garrisons. The Irish Royalists, rising against the "usurper," were crushed with remorseless severity.

Thousands were massacred, and thousands more were transported to the West Indies to be sold as slaves.

While the resolute and despotic character of Cromwell's government secured obedience at home, its strength and vigor awakened the fear as well as the admiration of foreign nations. He gave England the strongest, and in many respects the best, government she had had since the days of Henry VIII. and Elizabeth.

Cromwell's Death. — Nothwithstanding Cromwell was a man of immovable resolution and iron spirit, he felt sorely the burdens of his government, and was deeply troubled by the perplexities of his position. With his constitution undermined by overwork and anxiety, fever attacked him, and with gloomy apprehensions as to the terrible dangers into which England might drift after his hand had fallen from the helm of affairs, he lay down to die, passing away on the day which he had always called his "fortunate day" — the anniversary of his birth, and also the anniversary of his great victories of Dunbar and Worcester (Sept. 3, 1658).

Richard Cromwell (1658–1659). — Cromwell with his dying breath had designated his son Richard as his successor in the office of the Protectorate. Richard was exactly the opposite of his father, — timid, irresolute, and irreligious. The control of affairs that had taxed to the utmost the genius and resources of the father was altogether too great an undertaking for the incapacity and inexperience of the son. No one was quicker to realize this than Richard himself, and after a rule of a few months, yielding to the pressure of the army, whose displeasure he had incurred, he resigned the Protectorate. Had he possessed one-half the energy and practical genius that characterized his father, the crown would probably have become hereditary in the family of the Cromwells, and their house might have been numbered among the royal houses of England.

The Restoration (1660). — For some months after the fall of the Protectorate the country trembled on the verge of anarchy. The gloomy outlook into the future, and the unsatisfactory experiment of the Commonwealth, caused the great mass of the English people earnestly to desire the restoration of the Monarchy. Prince Charles, towards whom the tide of returning royalty was running, was now in Holland. A race was actually run between Monk, the leader of the army, and Parliament, to see which should first present him with the invitation to return to his people, and take his place upon the throne of his ancestors. Amid the wildest demonstrations of joy, Charles stepped ashore on the island from which he had been for nine years an exile. As he observed the preparations made for his reception, and received from all parties the warmest congratulations, he remarked with pleasant satire, "It is my own fault that I did not come back sooner, for I find nobody who does not tell me he has always longed for my return."

1. *Puritan Literature.*

It lights up the Religious Side of the English Revolution. — No epoch in history receives a fresher illustration from the study of its literature than that of the Puritan Commonwealth. To neglect this, and yet hope to gain a true conception of that wonderful episode in the life of the English people by an examination of its outer events and incidents alone, would, as Green declares, be like trying to form an idea of the life and work of ancient Israel from the *Kings* and the *Chronicles*, without the *Psalms* and the *Prophets*. The true character of the English Revolution, especially upon its religious side, must be sought in the magnificent Epic of Milton and the unequalled Allegory of Bunyan.

Both of these great works, it is true, were written after the Restoration, but they were both inspired by the same spirit that had struck down Despotism and set up the Commonwealth. The Epic was the work of a lonely, disappointed Republican; the Allegory, of a captive Puritan.

Milton (1608–1674) stands as the grandest representative of Puritanism. He was the greatest statesman of the Revolution, the stoutest champion of English liberties against the tyranny of the House of Stuart. After the beheading of Charles I. he wrote a famous work in Latin, entitled *The Defence of the English People*, in which he justified the execution of the king.

The Restoration forced Milton into retirement, and the last fourteen years of his life were passed apart from the world. It was during these years that, in loneliness and blindness, he composed the immortal poems *Paradise Lost* and *Paradise Regained*. The former is the " Epic of Puritanism." All that was truest and grandest in the Puritan character found expression in the moral elevation and religious fervor of this the greatest of Christian poems.

John Bunyan (1628–1688) was a Puritan non-conformist. After the Restoration, he was imprisoned for twelve years in Bedford jail, on account of non-conformity to the established worship. It was during this dreary confinement that he wrote his *Pilgrim's Progress*, the most admirable allegory in English literature. The habit of the Puritan, from constant study of the Bible, to employ in all forms of discourse its language and imagery, is best illustrated in the pages of this remarkable work.

III. The Restored Stuarts.

1. *Reign of Charles the Second* (1660–1685).

Punishment of the Regicides. — The monarchy having been restored in the person of Charles II., Parliament extended a general pardon to all who had taken part in the late rebellion, save most of the judges who had condemned Charles I. to the block. Thirteen of these were executed with the revolting cruelty with which treason was then punished, their hearts and bowels being cut out of their living bodies. Others of the regicides were condemned to imprisonment for life. Death had already removed the great leaders of the rebellion, Cromwell, Ireton, and Bradshaw, beyond the reach of Royalist hate ; so vengeance was taken upon their bodies. These were dragged from their tombs in Westminster Abbey, hauled to Tyburn in London, and there, on the anniversary of Charles's execution, were hanged, and afterwards beheaded (1661).

The "New Model" is disbanded. — This same Parliament, mindful of how the army had ruled preceding ones, took care to disband, as soon as possible, the " New Model." " With them," in the words of the historian Green, " Puritanism laid down the sword. It ceased from the long attempt to build up a kingdom of God by force and violence, and fell back on its truer work of building up a kingdom of righteousness in the hearts and consciences of men."

On the pretext, however, that the disturbed state of the realm demanded special precautions on the part of the government, Charles retained in his service three carefully chosen regiments, to which he gave the name of Guards. These, very soon augmented in number, formed the nucleus of the present standing army of England.

The Conventicle and Five-Mile Acts. — Early in the reign the services of the Anglican Church were restored by Parliament, and harsh laws were enacted against all non-conformists. Thus the Conventicle Act made it a crime punishable by imprisonment or transportation for more than five persons besides the household to gather in any house or in any place for worship, unless the service was conducted according to the forms of the Established Church.

The Five-Mile Act forbade any non-conformist minister who refused to swear that it is unlawful to take arms against the king *under any circumstances,* and that he never would attempt to make any change in Church or State government, to approach within five miles of any city, corporate town, or borough sending members to Parliament. This harsh act forced hundreds to give up their homes in the towns, and, with great inconvenience and loss, to seek new ones in out-of-the-way country places.

Persecution of the Covenanters. — In Scotland the attempt to suppress conventicles and introduce Episcopacy was stubbornly resisted by the Covenanters, who insisted on their right to worship God in their own way. They were therefore subjected to most cruel and unrelenting persecution. They were hunted by English troopers over their native moors and among the wild recesses of their mountains, whither they secretly retired for prayer and worship. The tales of the suffering of the Scotch Covenanters at the hands of the English Protestants form a most harrowing chapter of the records of the ages of religious persecution.

The Fire, the Plague, and the Dutch War. — The years from 1664 to 1667 were crowded with calamities, — with war, plague, and fire. The poet Dryden not inaptly calls the year 1666, in which the Great Fire at London added its horrors to those of pestilence and war, the *Annus Mirabilis*, or "Year of Wonders."

The war alluded to was a struggle between the English and the Dutch, which grew out of commercial rivalries (1664–1667). Just before the war began, the English treacherously seized the Dutch settlement of New Amsterdam in America, and changed its name to New York in honor of the king's brother, the Duke of York.

Early in the summer of 1665 the city of London was swept by a woeful plague, the most terrible visitation the city had known since the Black Death in the Middle Ages (see p. 485). Within six months 100,000 of the population perished.

The plague was followed, the next year, by the great fire, which destroyed 13,000 houses, and a vast number of churches and public buildings. The fire was afterwards acknowledged to be, like the Great Fire at Rome in Nero's reign, a blessing in disguise. The burnt districts were rebuilt in a more substantial way, with broader streets and more airy residences, so that London became a more beautiful and healthful city than would have been possible without the fire.

Charles's Intrigues with Louis XIV. — Charles inclined to the Catholic worship, and wished to reëstablish the Roman Catholic Church, because he thought it more favorable than the Anglican to such a scheme of government as he aimed to set up in England. In the year 1670 he made a secret treaty with the French king, the terms and objects of which were most scandalous. In return for aid which he was to render Louis in an attack upon Holland, he was to receive from him a large sum of money; and in case his proposed declaration in favor of the restoration of the Catholic Church produced any trouble in the island, the aid of French troops. The scheme was never consummated; but these clandestine negotiations, however, becoming an open secret, made the people very uneasy and suspicious. This state of the public mind led to a serious delusion and panic.

The "Popish Plot" (1678). — A rumor was started that the Catholics had planned for England a St. Bartholomew massacre. The king, the members of Parliament, and all Protestants were to be massacred, the Catholic Church was to be reëstablished, and the king's brother James, the Duke of York, a zealous Catholic, was to be placed on the throne. Each day the reports of the conspiracy grew more exaggerated and wild. Informers sprang up on every hand, each with a more terrifying story than the preceding. One of these witnesses, Titus Oates by name, a most infamous person, gained an extraordinary notoriety in exposing the imaginary plot. Many Catholics, convicted solely on the testimony of perjured witnesses, became victims of the delusion and fraud.

The excitement produced by the supposed plot led Parliament to pass what was called the Test Act, which excluded Catholics from the House of Lords. (They had already been shut out from the House of Commons by the oath of Supremacy, which was required of commoners, though not of peers.) The disability created by this statute was not removed from them until the present century, — in the reign of George the Fourth.

Origin of the Whig and Tory Parties. — Besides shutting Catholic peers out of Parliament, there were many in both houses who were determined to exclude the Duke of York from the throne. Those in favor of the measure of exclusion were called Whigs, those who opposed it Tories.[1] We cannot, perhaps, form a better general idea of the maxims and principles of these two parties than by calling the Whigs the political descendants of the Roundheads, and the Tories of the Cavaliers. Later, they became known respectively as Liberals and Conservatives.

The King's Death. — After a reign of just a quarter of a century, Charles died in 1685, and was followed by his brother James, whose rule was destined to be short and troubled.

----

[1] For the meaning of the names Whig and Tory, see *Glossary*.

2. *Reign of James the Second* (1685–1688).

James's Despotic Course.[1] — James, like all the other Stuarts, held exalted notions of the divine right of kings to rule as they please, and at once set about carrying out these ideas in a most imprudent and reckless manner. Notwithstanding he had given most solemn assurances that he would uphold the Anglican Church, he straightway set about the reëstablishment of the Roman Catholic worship. He arbitrarily prorogued and dissolved Parliament. The standing army, which Charles had raised to 10,000 men, he increased to 20,000, and placed Catholics in many of its most important offices. He formed a league against his own subjects with Louis XIV. The High Commission Court of Elizabeth, which had been abolished by Parliament, he practically restored in a new ecclesiastical tribunal presided over by the infamous Jeffries (see note, below).

The despotic course of the king raised up enemies on all sides. No party or sect, save the most zealous Catholics, stood by him. The Tory gentry were in favor of royalty, indeed, but not of tyranny. Thinking to make friends of the Protestant dissenters, James issued a decree known as the Declaration of Indulgence, whereby he suspended all the laws against non-conformists. This edict all the clergy were ordered to read from their pulpits. Almost to a man they refused to do so. Seven bishops even dared to send the king a petition and remonstrance against his unconstitutional proceedings.

The petitioners were thrust into the Tower, and soon brought

[1] James was barely seated upon the throne before the Duke of Monmouth, an illegitimate son of Charles II., who had been in exile in the Netherlands, asserted his right to the crown, and at the head of a hundred men invaded England. Thousands flocked to his standard, but in the battle of Sedgemoor (1685) he was utterly defeated by the royal troops. Terrible vengeance was wreaked upon all in any way connected with the rebellion. The notorious Chief Justice Jeffries, in what were called the "Bloody Assizes," condemned to death 320 persons, and sentenced 841 to transportation. Jeffries conducted the so-called trials with incredible brutality.

to trial on the charge of "seditious libel." The nation was now thoroughly aroused, and the greatest excitement prevailed while the trial was progressing. Judges and jury were overawed by the popular demonstration, and the bishops were acquitted. The news of the result of the trial was received not only by the people, but by the army as well, with shouts of joy, which did not fail to reach even the dull ears of the king.

The Revolution of 1688. — The crisis which it was easy to see was impending was hastened by the birth of a prince, as this cut off the hope of the nation that the crown upon James's death would descend to his daughter Mary, now wife of the Prince of Orange, Stadtholder of Holland. The prospect of the accession in the near future of a Protestant and freedom-loving Prince and Princess had reconciled the people to the misgovernment of their present despotic and Catholic sovereign. The appearance upon the stage of an infant prince gave a wholly different look to affairs, and, as we have said, destroyed all hope of matters being righted by the ordinary course of events.

This led the most active of the king's opponents to resolve to bring about at once what they had been inclined to wait to have accomplished by his death. They sent an invitation to the Prince of Orange to come over with such force as he could muster and take possession of the government, pledging him the united and hearty support of the English nation. William accepted the invitation, and straightway began to gather his fleet and army for the enterprise.

Meanwhile King James, in his blind and obstinate way, was rushing on headlong upon his own destruction. He seemed absolutely blind to the steady and rapid drift of the nation towards the point of open resistance and revolution. At last, when the sails of the Dutch fleet were spread for a descent upon the English shores, then the infatuated despot suddenly realized that absolute ruin was impending over his throne. He now adopted every expedient to avert the threatened evil. He restored to cities the charters he had wrongfully taken from them, reinstated magistrates in the positions from which they had been unjustly deposed, attempted to make friends with the bishops, and promised to sustain the Anglican Church and rule in accordance with the constitution of the realm.

All concessions and promises, however, were in vain. They came too late. The king was absolutely deserted; army and people went over in a body to the Prince of Orange, whose fleet had now touched the shores of the island. Flight alone was left him. The queen with her infant child secretly embarked for France, where the king soon after joined her. The last act of the king before leaving England was to disband the army, and fling the Great Seal into the Thames, in order that no parliament might be legally convened.

The first act of the Prince of Orange was to issue a call for a Convention to provide for the permanent settlement of the crown. This body met January 22, 1689, and after a violent debate declared the throne to be vacant through James's misconduct and flight. They then resolved to confer the royal dignity upon William and his wife Mary as joint sovereigns of the realm.

But this Convention did not repeat the error of the Parliament that restored Charles II., and give the crown to the Prince and Princess without proper safeguards and guaranties for the conduct of the government according to the ancient laws of the kingdom. They drew up the celebrated Declaration of Rights, which plainly rehearsed all the old rights and liberties of Englishmen; denied the right of the king to lay taxes or maintain an army without the consent of Parliament; and asserted that freedom of debate was the inviolable privilege of both the Lords and the Commons. William and Mary were required to accept this declaration, and to agree to rule in accordance with its provisions, whereupon they were declared King and Queen of England. In such manner was effected what is known in history as "the Revolution of 1688."

3. *Literature of the Restoration.*

It reflects the Immorality of the Age. — The reigns of the restored Stuarts mark the most corrupt period in the history of

English society. The low standard of morals, and the general profligacy in manners, especially among the higher classes, are in part attributable to the demoralizing example of a shockingly licentious and shameless court; but in a larger measure, perhaps, should be viewed as the natural reaction from the over-stern, repellent Puritanism of the preceding period. The Puritans undoubtedly erred in their indiscriminate and wholesale denunciation of all forms of harmless amusement and innocent pleasure. They not only rebuked gaming, drinking, and profanity, and stopped bear-baiting, but they closed all the theatres, forbade the Maypole dances of the people, condemned as paganish the observance of Christmas, frowned upon sculpture as idolatrous and indecent, and considered any bright color in dress as utterly incompatible with a proper sense of the seriousness of life.

Now all this was laying too heavy a burden upon human nature. The revolt and reaction came, as come they must. Upon the Restoration, society swung to the opposite extreme. In place of the solemn-visaged, psalm-singing Roundhead, we have the gay, roistering Cavalier. Faith gives place to infidelity, sobriety to drunkenness, purity to profligacy, economy to extravagance, Bible-study, psalm-singing and exhorting to theatre-going, profanity, and carousing.

The literature of the age is a perfect record of this revolt against the "sour severity" of Puritanism, and a faithful reflection of the unblushing immorality of the times.

The book most read and praised by Charles II. and his court, and the one that best represents the spirit of the victorious party, is the satirical poem of *Hudibras* by Samuel Butler. The object of the work is to satirize the cant and excesses of Puritanism, just as the *Don Quixote* of Cervantes burlesques the extravagances and follies of Chivalry.

So immoral and indecent are the works of the writers for the stage of this period that they have acquired the designation of "the corrupt dramatists." Among the authors of this species of literature was the poet Dryden.

IV. The Orange-Stuarts.

1. *Reign of William and Mary* (1689–1702).

The Bill of Rights. — The Revolution of 1688, and the new settlement of the crown upon William and Mary, marks an epoch in the constitutional history of England. It settled forever the long dispute between king and Parliament — and settled it in favor of the latter. The Bill of Rights, — the articles of the Declaration of Rights (see p. 624) framed into a law, — which was one of the earliest acts of the first Parliament under William and Mary, in effect "transferred sovereignty from the king to the House of Commons." It asserted plainly that the kings of England derive their right and title to rule, not from the accident of birth, but from the will of the people, and declared that Parliament might depose any king, exclude his heirs from the throne, and settle the crown anew in another family. This uprooted thoroughly the pernicious doctrine that princes have a divine and inalienable right to the throne of their ancestors, and when once seated on that throne rule simply as the vicegerents of God, above all human censure and control. We shall hear but little more in England of this monstrous theory, which for so long a time overshadowed and threatened the freedom of the English people.

Mindful of Charles's attempt to reëstablish the Roman Catholic worship, the framers of this same famous Bill of Rights further declared that all persons holding communion with the Church of Rome or uniting in marriage with a Roman Catholic, should be "forever incapable to possess, inherit, or enjoy the crown and government of the realm." Since the Revolution of 1688 no one of that faith has worn the English crown.

The other provisions of the bill, following closely the language of the Declaration, forbade the king to levy taxes or keep an army in time of peace without the consent of Parliament; demanded that Parliament should be frequently assembled; reaffirmed, as one of the ancient privileges of both Houses, perfect freedom of debate; and positively denied the dispensing power of the crown, that is, the authority claimed by the Stuarts of exempting certain persons from the penalty of the law by a royal edict.

All of these provisions now became inwrought into the English Constitution, and from this time forward were recognized as part of the fundamental law of the realm.

Settlement of the Revenue. — The articles of the Bill of Rights were made effectual by appropriate legislation. One thing which had enabled the Tudors and Stuarts to be so independent of Parliament was the custom which prevailed of granting to each king, at the beginning of his reign, the ordinary revenue of the kingdom during his life. This income, with what could be raised by gifts, benevolences, monopolies, and similar expedients, had enabled despotic sovereigns to administer the government, wage war, and engage in any wild enterprise just as his own individual caprice or passion might dictate. All this was now changed. Parliament, instead of granting William the revenue for life, restricted the grant to a single year, and made it a penal offence for the officers of the treasury to pay out money otherwise than ordered by Parliament.

We cannot overestimate the importance of this change in the English Constitution. It is this control of the purse of the nation which has made the Commons — for all money bills must originate in the Lower House — the actual seat of government, constituting them the arbiters of peace and war. By simply refusing to vote supplies, they can paralyze instantly the arm of the king.[1]

James attempts to recover the Throne : Battle of the Boyne (1690). — The first years of William's reign were disturbed by the efforts of James to regain the throne which he had abandoned. In these attempts he was aided by Louis XIV., and by the Jacobites (from *Jacobus*, Latin for James), the name given to the adherents of the exiled king. The Irish gave William the most trouble, but in the decisive battle of the Boyne he gained a great victory over them, and soon all Ireland acknowledged his authority.

Plans and Death of William. — The motive which had most

---

[1] For the *Mutiny Bill*, enacted at this time, see *Glossary*.

strongly urged William to respond to the invitation of the English revolutionists to assume the crown of England, was his desire to turn the arms and resources of that country against the great champion of despotism, and the dangerous neighbor of his own native country, Louis XIV. of France.

The conduct of Louis in lending aid to James in his attempts to regain his crown had so inflamed the English that they were quite ready to support William in his wars against him, and so the English and Dutch sailors fought side by side against the common enemy in the War of the Palatinate (see p. 595).

A short time after the Peace of Ryswick, broke out the War of the Spanish Succession (see p. 596). William, as the uncompromising foe of the ambitious French king, urged the English to enter the war against France. An insolent and perfidious act on the part of Louis caused the English people to support their king in this plan with great unanimity and heartiness. The matter to which we refer was this. James II. having died at just this juncture of affairs, Louis, disregarding his solemn promises, at once acknowledged his son, known in history as the " Pretender," as " King of Great Britain and Ireland."

Preparations were now made for the war thus provoked by the double sense of danger and insult. In the midst of these preparations William was fatally hurt by being thrown from his horse (1702). Mary had died in 1694, and as they left no children, the crown descended to the Princess Anne, Mary's sister, who had married Prince George of Denmark.

2. *Reign of Queen Anne* (1702–1714).

War of the Spanish Succession (1701–1714). — The War of the Spanish Succession covered the whole of the reign of Queen Anne. Of the causes and results of this war, and of England's part in it, we have spoken in connection with the reign of Louis XIV. (see p. 596) ; and so, referring the reader to the account of the contest there given, we shall pass to speak of another event of a domestic character which signalized the reign of Queen Anne.

Union of the Parliaments of England and Scotland (1707). —
We refer to the union of England and Scotland into a single kingdom, under the name of Great Britain (1707). It was only the
two *crowns* that were united when James I. came to the English
throne : now the two *Parliaments* were united. From this time
forward the two countries were represented by one Parliament,
and in time the name " British " becomes the common designation of the inhabitants of England, Wales, and Scotland. The
union was advantageous to both countries ; for it was a union not
simply of hands, but of hearts.

Death of Queen Anne: the Succession. — Queen Anne died
in the year 1714, leaving no heirs. In the reign of William a
statute known as the Act of Settlement had provided that the
crown, in default of heirs of William and Anne, should descend
to the Electress Sophia of Hanover (grandchild of James I.), or
her heirs, " being Protestants." The Electress died only a short
time before the death of Queen Anne ; so, upon that event, the
crown descended upon the head of the Electress's eldest son
George, who thus became the founder of a new line of English
sovereigns, the House of Hanover, or Brunswick, the family in
whose hands the royal sceptre still remains.

Literature under Queen Anne. — The reign of Queen Anne
is an illustrious one in English literature. Under her began to
write a group of brilliant authors, whose activity continued on into
the reign of her successor, George I. Their productions are, many
of them, of special interest to the historian, because during this
period there was an unusually close connection between literature
and politics. Literature was forced into the service of party. A
large portion of the writings of the era is in the form of political
pamphlets, wherein all the resources of wit, satire, and literary skill
are exhausted in defending or ridiculing the opposing principles
and policies of Whig and Tory.

The four most prominent and representative authors of the times
were Alexander Pope (1688–1744), Jonathan Swift (1667–1745),
Joseph Addison (1672–1719), and Daniel Defoe (1661–1731).

In the scientific annals of the period the name of Sir Isaac New-
ton (1642–1727) is most prominent. As the discoverer of the
law of gravitation and the author of the *Principia*, his name will
ever retain a high place among the few who belong through
their genius or achievements to no single nation or age, but to the
world.

End of gen History

V. ENGLAND UNDER THE EARLIER HANOVERIANS.[1]

The Sovereign's Loss of Political Influence. — The new Han-
overian king, George I. (1714–1727), was utterly ignorant of the
language and the affairs of the people over whom he had been
called to rule. He was not loved by the English, but he was
tolerated by them for the reason that he represented Protestantism
and those principles of political liberty for which they had so long
battled with their Stuart kings. On account of his ignorance of
English affairs the king was obliged to intrust to his ministers the
practical administration of the government. The same was true
in the case of George II. (1727–1760). George III. (1760–1820),
having been born and educated in England, regained some of the
old influence of former kings. But he was the last English sovereign
who had any large personal influence in shaping governmental
policies. Since his time the English government has been carried
on in the name of the king by a prime minister, dependent upon
the will of the House of Commons. This marks an important
step in the process by which sovereignty has been transferred from
the Crown to the People. (For later steps, see Chap. LXIII.)

England and Continental Affairs. — It must be borne in mind
that the Georges, while kings of England, were also Electors of
Hanover in Germany. These German dominions of theirs caused
England to become involved in continental quarrels which really
did not concern her. Thus she was drawn into the War of the

---

[1] The sovereigns of the House of Hanover are George I. (1714–1727);
George II. (1727–1760); George III. (1760–1820); George IV. (1820–
1830); William IV. (1830–1837); Victoria (1837–   ).

Austrian Succession (see p. 644) in which she had no national interest, and which resulted in no advantage to the English people. Hence these matters may be passed over by us without further notice here.

The Pretenders. — Several times during the eighteenth century the exiled Stuarts attempted to get back the throne they had lost. The last of these attempts was made in 1745, when the "Young Pretender" (grandson of James II.) landed in Scotland, effected a rising of the Scotch Highlanders, worsted the English at Preston Pans, and marched upon London. Forced to retreat into Scotland, he was pursued by the English, and utterly defeated at the battle of Culloden Moor, — and the Stuart cause was ruined forever.

Old French and Indian War (1756–1763). — Just after the middle of the eighteenth century there broke out between the French and the English colonists in America the so-called Old French and Indian War. The struggle became blended with what in Europe is known as the Seven Years' War (see p. 645). At first the war went disastrously against the English, — Braddock's attempt against Fort Du Quesne, upon the march to which he suffered his memorable defeat in the wilderness, being but one of several ill-starred English undertakings. But in the year 1757, the elder William Pitt (afterwards Earl of Chatham), known as "the Great Commoner," came to the head of affairs in England. Straightway every department of the government was infused with new vigor. His own indomitable will and persistent energy seemed to pass into every subordinate to whom he intrusted the execution of his plans. The war in America was brought to a speedy and triumphant close, the contest being virtually ended by the great victory gained by the English under the youthful Major-General Wolfe over the French under Montcalm upon the Heights of Quebec (1759). By the Treaty of Paris (1763) France ceded to England Canada and all her possessions in North America east of the Mississippi River, save New Orleans and a little adjoining land (which, along with the French territory west of the Mississippi, had already been given to Spain), and two little islands in the neighborhood of Newfoundland, which she was allowed to retain to dry fish on.

The American Revolution (1775–1783). — By a violation of one of the principles which the English people had so stoutly maintained against the Stuarts, the ruling powers in England now drove the American colonies to revolt. A majority in Parliament insisted upon taxing the colonists ; the colonists maintained that taxation without representation is tyranny, — that they could be justly taxed only through their own legislative assemblies. The Government refusing to acknowledge this principle, the colonists took up arms in defence of those liberties which their fathers had won with so hard a struggle from English kings on English soil. The result of the war was the separation from the mother-land of the thirteen colonies that had grown up along the Atlantic seaboard, — and a Greater England began its independent career in the New World.

Legislative Independence of Ireland (1782). — While the American War of Independence was going on, the Irish, taking advantage of the embarrassment of the English government, demanded legislative independence. Ireland had had a Parliament of her own since the time of the conquest of the island by the English, but this Irish Parliament was dependent upon the English Parliament, which claimed the power to bind Ireland by its laws. This the Irish patriots strenuously denied, and now, under the lead of the eloquent Henry Grattan, drew up a Declaration of Rights, wherein they demanded the legislative independence of Ireland. The principle here involved was the same as that for which the English colonists in America were at this time contending with arms in their hands. Fear of a revolt led England to grant the demands of the Irish, and to acknowledge the independence of the Irish Parliament.

Thus both in America and in Ireland the principles of the Political Revolution triumphed. In Ireland, however, the legislative independence gained was soon lost (see Chap. LXIII.).

CHAPTER LVI.

THE RISE OF RUSSIA: PETER THE GREAT.

(1682–1725.)

General Remarks. — The second great struggle between the principles of Liberalism and of Despotism, as represented by the opposing parties in the English Revolution, took place in France. But before proceeding to speak of the French Revolution, we shall first trace the rise of Russia and of Prussia, as these two great monarchies were destined to play prominent parts in that tremendous conflict. We left Russia at the close of the Middle Ages a semi-savage, semi-Asiatic power, so hemmed in by barbarian lands and hostile races as to be almost entirely cut off from intercourse with the civilized world (see p. 508). In the present chapter we wish to tell how she pushed her lines out to the seas on every side, — to the Caspian, the Euxine, and the Baltic. The main interest of our story gathers about Peter the Great, whose almost superhuman strength and energy lifted the great barbarian nation to a prominent place among the powers of Europe.

Accession of Peter the Great (1682). — The royal line established in Russia by the old Norseman Ruric (see p. 508), ended in 1589. Then followed a period of confusion and of foreign invasion, known as the Troublous Times, after which a prince of the celebrated house of Romanoff came to the throne. For more than half a century after the accession of the Romanoffs, there is little either in the genius or the deeds of any of the line calculated to draw our special attention. But towards the close of the seventeenth century there ascended the Russian throne a man whose capacity and energy and achievements instantly drew the gaze of his contemporaries, and who has elicited the admiration and wonder of all succeeding generations. This was Peter I., universally known as Peter the Great, one of the remarkable characters of history.   He was but seventeen years of age when he assumed the full responsibilities of government.

The Conquest of Azof (1696). — At this time Russia possessed only one sea-port, Archangel, on the White Sea, which harbor for a large part of the year was sealed against vessels by the extreme cold of that high latitude. Russia, consequently, had no marine commerce ; there was no word for *fleet* in the Russian language.   Peter saw clearly that the most urgent need of his empire was outlets upon the sea.   Hence, his first aim was to wrest the Baltic shore from the grasp of Sweden, and the Euxine from the hands of the Turks.

PETER THE GREAT.

In 1695 Peter sailed down the Don and made an attack upon Azof, the key to the Black Sea, but was unsuccessful.   The next year, however, repeating the attempt, he succeeded, and thus gained his first harbor on the south.

Peter's First Visit to the West (1697–1698). — With a view to advancing his naval projects, Peter about this time sent a large number of young Russian nobles to Italy, Holland, and England to acquire in those countries a knowledge of naval affairs, forbidding them to return before they had become good sailors.

Not satisfied with thus sending to foreign parts his young nobility, Peter formed the somewhat startling resolution of going abroad himself, and learning the art of ship-building by personal experience in the dockyards of Holland. Accordingly, in the year 1697, leaving the government in the hands of three nobles, he set out *incognito* for the Netherlands. Upon arriving there he proceeded to Zaandam, a place a short distance from Amsterdam, and there hired out as a common laborer to a Dutch ship-builder.

Notwithstanding his disguise it was well enough known who the stranger was. Indeed there was but little chance of Peter's being mistaken for a Dutchman. The way in which he flew about, and the terrible energy with which he did everything, set him quite apart from the easy-going, phlegmatic Hollanders.

To escape the annoyance of the crowds at Zaandam, Peter left the place, and went to the docks of the East India Company in Amsterdam, who set about building a frigate that he might see the whole process of constructing a vessel from the beginning. Here he worked for four months, being known among his fellow-workmen as Baas or Master Peter.

It was not alone the art of naval architecture in which Peter interested himself; he attended lectures on anatomy, studied surgery, gaining some skill in pulling teeth and bleeding, inspected paper-mills, flour-mills, printing-presses, and factories, and visited cabinets, hospitals, and museums, thus acquainting himself with every industry and art that he thought might be advantageously introduced into his own country.

From Holland Master Peter went to England to study her superior naval establishment. Here he was fittingly received by King William III., who had presented Peter while in Holland with a splendid yacht fully armed, and who now made his guest extremely happy by getting up for him a sham sea-fight.

Returning from England to Holland, Peter went thence to Vienna, intending to visit Italy; but hearing of an insurrection at home, he set out in haste for Moscow.

Peter's Reforms. — The revolt which had hastened Peter's return from the West was an uprising among the Strelitzes, a body of soldiers numbering 20,000 or 30,000, organized by Ivan the Terrible as a sort of imperial body-guard. In their ungovernable turbulence, they remind us of the Pretorians of Rome. The mutiny settled Peter in his determination to rid himself altogether of the insolent and refractory body. Its place was taken by a well-disciplined force trained according to the tactics of the Western nations.

The disbanding of the seditious guards was only one of the many reforms effected by Peter. So intent was he upon thoroughly Europeanizing his country, that he resolved that his subjects should literally clothe themselves in the "garments of Western Civilization." Accordingly he abolished the long-sleeved, long-skirted Oriental robes that were at this time worn, and decreed that everybody save the clergy should shave, or pay a tax on his beard. We are told that Peter stationed tailors and barbers at the gates of Moscow to cut off the skirts and to train the beards of those who had not conformed to the royal regulations, and that he himself sheared off with his own hands the offending sleeves and beards of his reluctant courtiers. The law was gradually relaxed, but the reform became so general that in the best society in Russia at the present day one sees only smooth faces and the Western style of dress.

As additional outgrowths of what he had seen, or heard, or had suggested to him on his foreign tour, Peter issued a new coinage, introduced schools, built factories, constructed roads and canals, established a postal system, opened mines, framed laws modelled after those of the West, and reformed the government of the towns in such a way as to give the citizens some voice in the management of their local affairs, as he had observed was done in the Netherlands and in England.

Charles XII. of Sweden. — Peter's history now becomes intertwined with that of a man quite as remarkable as himself, Charles XII. of Sweden, the "Madman of the North." Charles was but fifteen years of age when, in 1697, the death of his father called him to the Swedish throne. The dominions which came under his sway

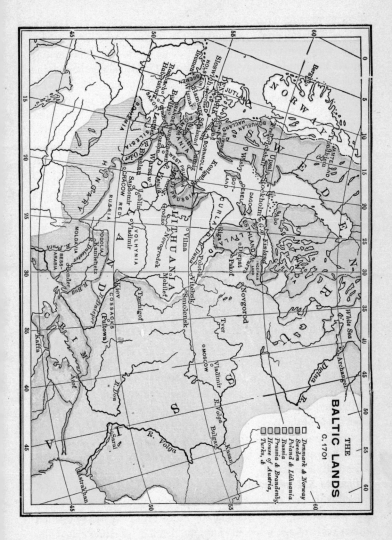

THE
BALTIC LANDS
c. 1701

Denmark & Norway
Sweden
Poland & Lithuania
Russia
Prussia & Brandenb.
House of Austria,
Turkey, &

embraced not only Sweden, but Finland, and large possessions along the Southern Baltic, — territory that had been won by the arms of his ancestors.

Taking advantage of Charles's extreme youth, three sovereigns, Frederick IV. of Denmark, Augustus the Strong, Elector of Saxony and King of Poland, and Peter the Great of Russia, leagued against him (1700), for the purpose of appropriating such portions of his dominions as they severally desired to annex to their own.

The Battle of Narva (1700). But the conspirators had formed a wrong estimate of the young Swedish monarch. Notwithstanding the insane follies in which he was accustomed to indulge, he possessed talent ; he had especially a remarkable aptitude for military affairs. With a well-trained force — a veteran army that had not yet forgotten the discipline of the hero Gustavus Adolphus — Charles now threw himself first upon the Danes, and in two weeks forced the Danish king to sue for peace ; then he turned his little army of 8,000 men upon the Russian forces of 20,000, which were besieging the city of Narva, on the Gulf of Finland, and inflicted upon them a most ignominious defeat. The only comment of the imperturbable Peter upon the disaster was, "The Swedes will have the advantage of us at first, but they will teach us how to beat them."

The Founding of St. Petersburg (1703). — After chastising the Czar[1] at Narva, the Swedish king turned south and marched into Poland to punish Augustus for the part he had taken in the conspiracy against him. While Charles was busied in this quarter, Peter was gradually making himself master of the Swedish lands on the Baltic, and upon a marshy island at the mouth of the Neva was laying the foundations of the great city of St. Petersburg, which he proposed to make the western gateway of his empire.

The spot selected by Peter as the site of his new capital was low and subject to inundation, so that the labor requisite to make it fit

---

[1] Czar is probably a contraction of *Cæsar*. The title was adopted by the rulers of Russia because they regarded themselves as the successors and heirs of the Cæsars of Rome and Constantinople.

for building purposes was simply enormous. But difficulties never dismayed Peter. In spite of difficulties the work was done, and the splendid city stands to-day one of the most impressive monuments of the indomitable and despotic energy of Peter.

Invasion of Russia by Charles XII. — Meanwhile Charles was doing very much as he pleased with the king of Poland. He defeated his forces, overran his dominions, and forced him to surrender the Polish crown in favor of Stanislaus Lesczinski (1706). With sufficient punishment meted out to Frederick Augustus, Charles was ready to turn his attention once more to the Czar. So marvellous had been the success attendant upon his arms for the past few years, nothing now seemed impossible to him. Deluded by this belief, he resolved to march into Russia and dethrone the Czar, even as he had dethroned the king of Poland.

In 1708, with an army of barely 40,000 men, Charles marched boldly across the Russian frontier. At Pultowa the two armies met in decisive combat (1709). It was Charles's Waterloo. The Swedish army was virtually annihilated. Escaping with a few soldiers from the field, Charles fled southward, and found an asylum in Turkey.[1]

Close of Peter's Reign. — In 1721 the Swedish wars which had so long disturbed Europe were brought to an end by the Peace of Nystadt, which confirmed Russia's title to all the Southern Baltic lands that Peter had wrested from the Swedes. The undisputed possession of so large a strip of the Baltic seaboard vastly increased the importance and influence of Russia, which now assumed a place among the leading European powers.

In 1723 troubles in Persia that resulted in the massacre of some Russians afforded Peter a pretext for sailing down the Volga and

---

[1] After spending five years in Turkey, Charles returned to Sweden, and shortly afterwards was killed at the siege of Frederickshall, in Norway (1718). At the moment of his death he was only thirty-six years of age. He was the strangest character of the eighteenth century. Perhaps we can understand him best by regarding him, as his biographer Voltaire says we must regard him, as an old Norse sea-king, born ten centuries after his time.

seizing the southern shore of the Caspian Sea, which now became virtually a Russian lake. This ended Peter's conquests. The Russian colossus now "stood astride, with one foot on the Baltic and the other upon the Caspian."

Two years later, being then in his fifty-fourth year, Peter died of a fever brought on by exposure while aiding in the rescue of some sailors in distress, in the Gulf of Finland (1725).

Peter's Character and Work. — Peter's character stands revealed in the light of his splendid achievements. Like Charlemagne he was a despotic reformer. His theory of government was a rough, brutal one, yet the exclamation which broke from him as he stood by the tomb of Richelieu[1] discloses his profound desire to rule well : "Thou great man," he exclaimed, " I would have given thee half of my dominion to have learned of thee how to govern the other half." He planted throughout his vast empire the seeds of Western civilization, and by his giant strength lifted the great nation which destiny had placed in his hands out of Asiatic barbarism into the society of the European peoples.

The influence of Peter's life and work upon the government of Russia was very different from what he intended. It is true that his aggressive, arbitrary rule strengthened temporarily autocratic government in Russia. He destroyed all checks, ecclesiastical and military, upon the absolute power of the crown. But in bringing into his dominions Western civilization, he introduced influences which were destined in time to neutralize all he had done in the way of strengthening the basis of despotism. He introduced a civilization which fosters popular liberties, and undermines personal, despotic government.

Reign of Catherine the Great (1762–1796). — From the death of Peter on to the close of the eighteenth century the Russian throne was held, the most of the time, by women, the most noted of whom was Catherine II., the Great, "the greatest woman probably," according to the admission of an English

---

[1] In 1716 Peter made a second journey to the West, visiting France, Denmark, and Holland.

historian (McCarthy), "who ever sat on a throne, Elizabeth of England not even excepted." But while a woman of great genius, she had most serious faults of character, being incredibly profligate and unscrupulous.

Carrying out ably the policy of Peter the Great, Catherine extended vastly the limits of Russian dominion, and opened the country even more thoroughly than he had done to the entrance of Western influences. The most noteworthy matters of her reign were the conquest of the Crimea and the dismemberment of Poland.

CATHERINE II. OF RUSSIA.

It was in the year 1783 that Catherine effected the subjugation of the Crimea. The possession of this peninsula gave Russia dominion on the Black Sea, which once virtually secured by Peter the Great had been again lost through his misfortunes. Catherine greatly extended the limits of her dominion on the west at the expense of Poland, the partition of which state she planned in connection with Frederick the Great of Prussia and Maria Theresa of Austria. On the first division, which was made in 1772, the imperial robbers each took a portion of the spoils. In 1793 a second partition was made, this time between Russia and Prussia;

and then, in 1795, after the suppression of a determined revolt of the Poles under the lead of the patriot Kosciusko, a third and final division among the three powers completed the dismemberment of the unhappy state, and erased its name from the roll of the nations. The territory gained by Russia in these transactions brought her western frontier close alongside the civilization of Central Europe. In Catherine's phrase, Poland had become her "door mat," upon which she stepped when visiting the West.

Besides thus widening her empire, Catherine labored to reform its institutions and to civilize her subjects. Her labors in bettering the laws and improving the administration of the government, have caused her to be likened to Solon and to Lycurgus; while her enthusiasm for learning and her patronage of letters led Voltaire to say, "Light now comes from the North."

By the close of Catherine's reign Russia was beyond question one of the foremost powers of Europe, the weight of her influence being quite equal to that of any other nation of the continent.

CHAPTER LVII.

THE RISE OF PRUSSIA: FREDERICK THE GREAT.

(1740—1786.)

The Beginnings of Prussia. — The foundation of the Prussian Kingdom was laid in the beginning of the seventeenth century (1611) by the union of two small states in the North of Germany. These were the Mark, or Electorate, of Brandenburg and the Duchy of Prussia. Brandenburg had been gradually growing into prominence since the tenth century. Its ruler at this time was a prince of the now noted House of Hohenzollern, and was one of the seven princes to whom belonged the right of electing the emperor.

The Great Elector, Frederick William (1640–1688). — Although this new Prussian power was destined to become the champion of German Protestantism, it acted a very unworthy and vacillating part in the Thirty Years' War. But just before the close of that struggle a strong man came to the throne, Frederick William, better known as the Great Elector. He infused new vigor into every department of the state, and acquired such a position for his government that at the Peace of Westphalia he was able to secure new territory, which greatly enhanced his power and prominence among the German princes.

The Great Elector ruled for nearly half a century. He laid the basis of the military power of Prussia by the formation of a standing army, and gave the world to understand that this rising power was to be the fearless champion of the cause of religious toleration, by defying the wrath of Louis XIV. and opening his dominions as an asylum to the Huguenots driven from France by the Revocation of the Edict of Nantes.   •

How the Elector of Brandenburg acquired the Title of King. — Frederick III. (1688–1713), son of the Great Elector, was ambitious for the title of king, a dignity that the weight and influence won for the Prussian state by his father fairly justified him in seeking. He saw about him other princes less powerful than himself enjoying this dignity, and he too " would be a king and wear a crown." The recent elevation of William of Orange, Stadt-holder of Holland, to royal honors in England (see p. 624), stim-ulated the Elector's ambition.

It was necessary of course for Frederick to secure the consent of the emperor, a matter of some difficulty, for the Catholic ad-visers of the Austrian court were bitterly opposed to having an heretical prince thus honored and advanced, while the emperor himself was not at all pleased with the idea. But the War of the Spanish Succession was just about to open, and the emperor was extremely anxious to secure Frederick's assistance in the coming struggle. Therefore, on condition of his furnishing him aid in the war, the emperor consented to Frederick's assuming the new title and dignity *in the Duchy of Prussia,* which, unlike Brandenburg, did not form part of the empire.

Accordingly, early in the year 1701, Frederick, amidst imposing ceremonies, was crowned and hailed as king at Königsberg. Hitherto he had been Elector of Brandenburg and Duke of Prussia ; now he is Elector of Brandenburg and King of Prussia.

Thus was a new king born among the kings of Europe. Thus did the house of Austria invest with royal dignity the rival house of Hohenzollern. The event is a landmark in German, and even in European history. The cue of German history from this on is the growth of the power of the Prussian kings, and their steady advance to imperial honors, and to the control of the affairs of the German race.

Frederick William I. (1713–1740). — The son and successor of the first Prussian king, known as Frederick William I., was one of the most extraordinary characters in history. He was a strong, violent, brutal man, full of the strangest freaks, yet in many re-spects just the man for the times. He would tolerate no idlers. He carried a heavy cane, which he laid upon the back of every unemployed person he chanced to find, whether man, woman, or child.

Frederick William had a mania for big soldiers. With infinite expense and trouble he gathered a regiment of the biggest men he could find, which was known as the " Potsdam Giants," — a regiment numbering 2400 men, some of whom were eight feet in height. Not only were the Goliaths of his own dominions impressed into the service, but big men in all parts of Europe were coaxed, bribed, or kidnapped by Frederick's recruiting officers. No present was so acceptable to him as a giant, and by the gift of a six-footer more than one prince bought his everlasting favor.

Rough, brutal tyrant though he was, Frederick William was an able and energetic ruler. He did much to consolidate the power of Prussia, and at his death in 1740 left to his successor a considerably extended dominion, and a splendid army of 80,000 men.

Frederick the Great (1740–1786). — Frederick William was followed by his son Frederick II., to whom the world has agreed to give the title of " Great." Frederick had a genius for war, and his father had prepared to his hand one of the most efficient instruments of the art since the time of the Roman legions. The two great wars in which he was engaged, and which raised Prussia to the first rank among the military powers of Europe, were the War of the Austrian Succession and the Seven Years' War.

War of the Austrian Succession (1740–1748). — Through the death of Charles VI. the Imperial office became vacant on the very year that Frederick II. ascended the Prussian throne. Charles was the last of the direct male line of the Hapsburgs, and disputes straightway arose respecting the possessions of the House of Austria, which resulted in the long struggle known as the War of the Austrian Succession.

Now, not long before the death of Charles, he had bound all the leading powers of Europe in a sort of agreement called the Pragmatic Sanction, by the terms of which, in case he should leave no son, all his hereditary dominions — that is, the kingdom of Hungary, the kingdom of Bohemia, the archduchy of Austria, and the other possessions of the House of Austria — should be bestowed upon his daughter Maria Theresa. But no sooner was Charles dead than a number of princes immediately laid claim to greater or lesser portions of these territories. Prominent among these claimants was Frederick of Prussia, who claimed Silesia.[1] Before Maria Theresa could arm in defence of her dominions, Frederick pushed his army into Silesia and took forcible possession of it.

Queen Theresa, thus stripped of a large part of her dominions, fled into Hungary, and with all of a beautiful woman's art of persuasion appealed to her Hungarian subjects to avenge her wrongs. Her unmerited sufferings, her beauty, her tears, the little prince in her arms, stirred the resentment and kindled the ardent loyalty of the Hungarian nobles, and with one voice, as they rang their swords in their scabbards, they swore to support the cause of their queen with their estates and their lives. England and Sardinia also threw themselves into the contest on Maria Theresa's side. The war lasted until 1748, when it was closed by the Peace of Aix-la-Chapelle, which left Silesia in the hands of Frederick.

The Seven Years' War (1756–1763). — The eight years of peace which followed the war of the Austrian Succession were improved by Frederick in developing the resources of his kingdom and perfecting the organization and discipline of his army, and by Maria Theresa in forming a league of the chief European powers against the unscrupulous despoiler of her dominions. France, Russia, Poland, Saxony, and Sweden, all entered into an alliance with the queen. Frederick could at first find no ally save England, — towards the close of the struggle Russia came to his side, — so that he was left almost alone to fight the combined armies of the Continent.

At first the fortunes of the war were all on Frederick's side. In the celebrated battles of Rossbach, Leuthen, and Zorndorf, he defeated successively the French, the Austrians, and the Russians,

---

[1] Charles Albert, Elector of Bavaria, set up a claim to the Austrian States. France, ever the sworn enemy of the House of Austria, lent her armies to aid the Elector in making good his pretensions.

and startled all Europe into an acknowledgment of the fact that the armies of Prussia had at their head one of the greatest commanders of the world. His name became a household word, and everybody coupled with it the admiring epithet of "Great."

But fortune finally deserted him. In sustaining the unequal contest, his dominions became drained of men. England withdrew her aid, and inevitable ruin seemed to impend over his throne and kingdom. A change by death in the government of Russia now put a new face upon Frederick's affairs. In 1762 Elizabeth of that country died, and Peter III., an ardent admirer of Frederick, came to the throne, and immediately transferred the armies of Russia from the side of the allies to that of Prussia. The alliance lasted only a few months, Peter being deposed and murdered by his wife, who now came to the throne as Catherine II. She reversed once more the policy of the Government; but the temporary alliance had given Frederick a decisive advantage, and the year following Peter's act, England and France were glad to give over the struggle and sign the Peace of Paris (1763). Shortly after this another peace (the Treaty of Hubertsburg) was arranged between Austria and Prussia, and one of the most terrible wars that had ever disturbed Europe was over. The most noteworthy result of the war was the exalting of the Prussian kingdom to a most commanding position among the European powers.

Frederick's Work: Prussia made a New Centre of German Crystallization. — The all-important result of Frederick the Great's strong reign was the making of Prussia the equal of Austria, and thereby the laying of the basis of German unity. Hitherto Germany had been trying unsuccessfully to concentrate about Austria; now there is a new centre of crystallization, one that will draw to itself all the various elements of German nationality. The history of Germany from this on is the story of the rivalry of these two powers, with the final triumph of the kingdom of the North, and the unification of Germany under her leadership, Austria being pushed out as entitled to no part in the affairs of the Fatherland. This story we shall tell in a subsequent chapter (see Chap. LXI.).

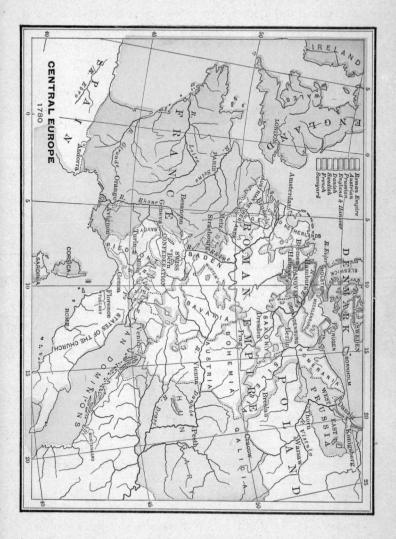

CENTRAL EUROPE

1780

Roman Empire
Austrian
Prussian
England & Hanover
Danish
Swedish
French
Savoyard

CHAPTER LVIII.

THE FRENCH REVOLUTION.

(1789-1799.)

1. CAUSES OF THE REVOLUTION : THE STATES-GENERAL OF 1789.

Introductory. — The French Revolution is in political what the German Reformation is in ecclesiastical history. It was the revolt of the French people against royal despotism and class privilege. "Liberty, Equality, Fraternity," was the motto of the Revolution. In the name of these principles the most atrocious crimes were indeed committed ; but these excesses of the Revolution are not to be confounded with its true spirit and aims. The French people in 1789 contended for those same principles that the English Puritans defended in 1640, and that our fathers maintained in 1776. It is only as we view them in this light that we can feel a sympathetic interest in the men and events of this tumultuous period of French history.

Causes of the Revolution. — Chief among the causes of the French Revolution were the abuses and extravagances of the Bourbon monarchy ; the unjust privileges enjoyed by the nobility and clergy ; the wretched condition of the great mass of the people ; and the revolutionary character and spirit of French philosophy and literature. To these must be added, as a proximate cause, the influence of the American Revolution. We shall speak briefly of these several matters.

The Bourbon Monarchy. — We simply repeat what we have already learned, when we say that the authority of the French crown under the Bourbons had become unbearably despotic and oppressive. The life of every person in the realm was at the arbitrary disposal of the king. Persons were thrown into prison without even knowing the offence for which they were arrested. The royal decrees were laws. The taxes imposed by the king were simply robberies and confiscations. The public money, thus gathered, was squandered in maintaining a court the scandalous extravagances and debaucheries of which would shame a Turkish Sultan.

The Nobility. — The French nobility, in the time of the Bourbons, numbered about 80,000 families. The order was simply the remains of the once powerful but now broken-down feudal aristocracy of the Middle Ages. Its members were chiefly the pensioners of the king, the ornaments of his court, living in riotous luxury at Paris or Versailles. Stripped of their ancient power, they still retained all the old pride and arrogance of their order, and clung tenaciously to all their feudal privileges. Although holding one-fifth of the lands of France, they paid scarcely any taxes.

The Clergy. — The clergy formed a decayed feudal hierarchy. They possessed enormous wealth, the gift of piety through many centuries. Over a third of the lands of the country was in their hands, and yet this immense property was almost wholly exempt from taxation. The bishops and abbots were usually drawn from the families of the nobles, being too often attracted to the service of the Church rather by its princely revenues and the social distinction conferred by its offices, than by the inducements of piety. These "patrician prelates" were hated alike by the humbler clergy and the people.

The Commons. — Below the two privileged orders of the State stood the commons, who constituted the chief bulk of the nation, and who numbered, at the commencement of the Revolution, probably about 25,000,000. It is quite impossible to give any adequate idea of the pitiable condition of the poorer classes of the commons throughout the century preceding the Revolution. The peasants particularly suffered the most intolerable wrongs. They were vexed by burdensome feudal regulations. Thus they were forbidden to fence their fields for the protection of their crops, as the fences interfered with the lord's progress in the hunt; and they were even prohibited from cultivating their fields at certain seasons, as this disturbed the partridges and other game. Being kept in a state of abject poverty, a failure of crops reduced them to absolute starvation. It was not an unusual thing to find women and children dead along the roadways. In a word, to use the language of one (Fénelon) who saw all this misery, France had become "simply a great hospital full of woe and empty of food."

Revolutionary Spirit of French Philosophy. — French philosophy in the eighteenth century was sceptical and revolutionary. The names of the great writers Rousseau (1712–1778) and Voltaire (1694–1778) suggest at once its prevalent tone and spirit. Rousseau declared that all the evils which afflict humanity arise from vicious, artificial arrangements, such as the Family, the Church, and the State. Accordingly he would do away with these things, and have men return to a state of nature — that is, to simplicity. Savages, he declared, were happier than civilized men.

The tendency and effect of this sceptical philosophy was to create hatred and contempt for the institutions of both State and Church, to foster discontent with the established order of things, to stir up an uncontrollable passion for innovation and change.

Influence of the American Revolution. — Not one of the least potent of the proximate causes of the French Revolution was the successful establishment of the American republic. The French people sympathized deeply with the English colonists in their struggle for independence. Many of the nobility, like Lafayette, offered to the patriots the service of their swords; and the popular feeling at length compelled Louis XVI. to extend to them openly the aid of the armies of France.

The final triumph of the cause of liberty awakened scarcely less enthusiasm and rejoicing in France than in America. In this young republic of the Western world the French people saw realized the Arcadia of their philosophers. It was no longer a dream. They themselves had helped to make it real. Here the Rights of Man had been recovered and vindicated. And now this liberty which the French people had helped the American colonists to secure, they were impatient to see France herself enjoy.

"**After us, the Deluge.**" — The long-gathering tempest is now ready to break over France. Louis XV. died in 1774. In the early part of his reign his subjects had affectionately called him the "Well-beloved," but long before he laid down the sceptre, all their early love and admiration had been turned into hatred and contempt. Besides being overbearing and despotic, the king was indolent, rapacious, and scandalously profligate. During twenty years of his reign the king was wholly under the influence of the notorious Madame de Pompadour.

The inevitable issue of this orgy of crime and folly seems to have been clearly enough perceived by the chief actors in it, as is shown by that reckless phrase so often on the lips of the king and his favorite — "After us, the Deluge." And after them, the Deluge indeed did come. The near thunders of the approaching tempest could already be heard when Louis XV. lay down to die.

Calling of the States-General (1789). — Louis XV. left the tottering throne to his grandson, Louis XVI., then only twenty years of age. He had recently been married to the fair and brilliant Marie Antoinette, archduchess of Austria.

The king called to his side successively the most eminent financiers and statesmen (Maurepas, Turgot, Necker, and Calonne) as his ministers and advisers; but their policies and remedies availed little or nothing. The disease which had fastened itself upon the nation was too deep-seated. The traditions of the court, the rigidity of long-established customs, and the heartless selfishness of the privileged classes, rendered reform and efficient retrenchment impossible.

In 1787 the king summoned the Notables, a body composed chiefly of great lords and prelates, who had not been called to advise with the king since the reign of Henry IV. But miserable counsellors were they all. Refusing to give up any of their feudal privileges, or to tax the property of their own orders that the enormous public burdens which were crushing the commons might be lightened, their coming together resulted in nothing.

As a last resort it was resolved to summon the united wisdom of the nation, — to call together the States-General, the almost-forgotten assembly, composed of representatives of the three estates, — the nobility, the clergy, and the commons, the latter being known as the Tiers État, or Third Estate. On the 5th of May, 1789, a memorable date, this assembly met at Versailles. It was the first time it had been summoned to deliberate upon the affairs of the nation in the space of 175 years. It was now composed of 1,200 representatives, more than one-half of whom were deputies of the commons. The eyes of the nation were turned in hope and expectancy towards Versailles. Surely if the redemption of France could be worked out by human wisdom, it would now be effected.

2. THE NATIONAL, OR CONSTITUENT ASSEMBLY
(June 17, 1789–Sept. 30, 1791).

The States-General changed into the National Assembly. — At the very outset a dispute arose in the States-General assembly between the privileged orders and the commons, respecting the manner of voting. It had been the ancient custom of the body to vote upon all questions by *orders ;* and thinking that this custom would prevail in the present assembly, the king and his counsellors had yielded to the popular demand and allowed the Third Estate to send to Versailles more representatives than both the other orders. The commons now demanded that the voting should be by individuals ; for, should the vote be taken by orders, the clergy and nobility by combining could always outvote them. For five weeks the quarrel kept everything at a standstill.

Finally the commons, emboldened by the tone of public opinion without, took a decisive, revolutionary step. They declared themselves the National Assembly, and then invited the other two orders to join them in their deliberations, giving them to understand that if they did not choose to do so, they should proceed to the consideration of public affairs without them.

Shut out from the palace, the Third Estate met in one of the churches of Versailles. Many of the clergy had already joined the body. Two days later the nobility came. The eloquent Bailly, President of the Assembly, in receiving them, exclaimed, "This day will be illustrious in our annals; it renders the family complete." The States-General had now become in reality the *National Assembly*.

Storming of the Bastile (July 14, 1789). — During the opening weeks of the National Assembly, Paris was in a state of great excitement. The Bastile was the old state prison, the emblem, in the eyes of the people, of despotism. A report came that its guns were trained on the city; that provoked a popular outbreak. "Let us storm the Bastile," rang through the streets. The mob straightway proceeded to lay siege to the grim old dungeon. In a few hours the prison fortress was in their hands. The walls of the hated state prison were razed to the ground, and the people danced on the spot. The key of the fortress was sent as a "trophy of the spoils of despotism" to Washington by Lafayette.

The destruction by the Paris mob of the Bastile is in the French Revolution what the burning of the papal bull by Luther was to the Reformation. It was the death-knell not only of Bourbon despotism in France, but of royal tyranny everywhere. When the news reached England, the great statesman Fox, perceiving its significance for liberty, exclaimed, "How much is this the greatest event that ever happened in the world, and how much the best!"

The Emigration of the Nobles. — The fall of the Bastile left Paris in the hands of a triumphant mob. Those suspected of sympathizing with the royal party were massacred without mercy. The peasantry in many districts, following the example set them by the capital, rose against the nobles, sacked and burned their castles, and either killed the occupants or dragged them off to prison. This terrorism caused the beginning of what is known as the emigration of the nobles, their flight beyond the frontiers of France.

"To Versailles." — An imprudent act on the part of the king and his friends at Versailles brought about the next episode in the progress of the Revolution. The arrival there of a body of troops was made the occasion of a banquet to the officers of the regiment. While heated with wine, the young nobles had trampled under foot the national tri-colored cockades, and substituted for them white cockades, the emblem of the Bourbons. The report of these proceedings caused in Paris the wildest excitement. Other rumors of the intended flight of the king to Metz, and of plots against the national cause, added fuel to the flames. Besides, bread had failed, and the poorer classes were savage from hunger.

October 5th a mob of desperate women, terrible in aspect as furies, and armed with clubs and knives, collected in the streets of Paris, determined upon going to Versailles, and demanding relief from the king himself. All efforts to dissuade them from their purpose were unavailing, and soon the Parisian rabble was in motion. A horrible multitude, savage as the hordes that followed Attila, streamed out of the city towards Versailles, about twelve miles distant. The National Guards, infected with the delirium of the moment, forced Lafayette to lead them in the same direction. Thus all day Paris emptied itself into the royal suburbs.

The mob encamped in the streets of Versailles for the night. Early the following morning they broke into the palace, killed two of the guards, and battering down doors with axes, forced their way to the chamber of the queen, who barely escaped with her life to the king's apartments. The timely arrival of Lafayette alone saved the entire royal family from being massacred.

The Royal Family taken to Paris. — The mob now demanded that the king should return with them to Paris. Their object in this was to have him under their eye, and prevent his conspiring with the privileged orders to thwart the plans of the revolutionists. Louis was forced to yield to the demands of the people.

The procession arrived at Paris in the evening. The royal family were placed in the Palace of the Tuileries, and Lafayette was charged with the duty of guarding the king, who was to be held as a sort of hostage for the good conduct of the nobles and for-

eign sovereigns while a constitution was being prepared by the
Assembly.

Such was what was called the "Joyous Entry" of October 6th.
The palace at Versailles, thus stripped of royalty and left bespat-
tered with blood, was never again to be occupied as the residence
of a king of France.

The Flight of the King (June 20, 1791). — For two years following the Joyous Entry there was a comparative lull in the storm
of the Revolution. The king was kept a sort of prisoner in the
Tuileries. The National Assembly were making sweeping reforms
both in Church and State, and busying themselves in framing a
new constitution. The emigrant nobles watched the course of
events from beyond the frontiers, not daring to make a move for
fear the excitable Parisian mob, upon any hostile step taken by
them, would massacre the entire royal family.

Could the king only escape from the hands of his captors and
make his way to the borders of France, then he could place
himself at the head of the emigrant nobles, and, with foreign aid,
overturn the National Assembly and crush the revolutionists. The
flight was resolved upon and carefully planned. Under cover of
night the entire royal family, in disguise, escaped from the Tuileries, and by post conveyance fled towards the frontier. When
just another hour would have placed the fugitives in safety among
friends, the Bourbon features of the king betrayed him, and the
entire party was arrested and carried back to Paris.

The attempted flight of the royal family was a fatal blow to the
Monarchy. Many affected to regard it as equivalent to an act of
abdication on the part of the king. The people now began to talk
of a republic.

The Clubs: Jacobins and Cordeliers. — In order to render
intelligible the further course of the Revolution we must here
speak of two clubs, or organizations, which came into prominence
about this time, and which were destined to become more powerful than the Assembly itself, and to be the chief instruments in
inaugurating the Reign of Terror. These were the societies of the

Jacobins and Cordeliers, so called from certain old convents in which they were accustomed to meet. The purpose of these clubs was to watch for conspiracies of the royalists, and by constant agitation to keep alive the flame of the Revolution.

The New Constitution. — The work of the National Assembly was now drawing to a close. On the 14th of September, 1791, the new constitution framed by that body, and which made the government of France a constitutional monarchy, was solemnly ratified by the king. The National Assembly, having sat nearly three years, then adjourned (Sept. 30, 1791). The first scene in the drama of the French Revolution was ended.

3. THE LEGISLATIVE ASSEMBLY (Oct. 1, 1791–Sept. 21, 1792).

The Three Parties. — The new constitution provided for a national legislature to be called the Legislative Assembly. This body, comprising 745 members, was divided into three parties : the Constitutionalists, the Girondists, and the Mountainists. The Constitutionalists of course supported the new constitution, being in favor of a limited monarchy. The Girondists, so called from the name (*La Gironde*) of the department whence came the most noted of its members, wished to establish in France such a republic as the American colonists had just set up in the New World. The Mountainists, who took their name from their lofty seats in the assembly, were radical republicans, or levellers. Many of them were members of the Jacobin club or that of the Cordeliers. The leaders of this faction were Marat, Danton, and Robespierre, — names of terror in the subsequent records of the Revolution.

War with the Old Monarchies. — The kings of Europe were watching with the utmost anxiety the course of events in France. They regarded the cause of Louis XVI. as their own. If the French people should be allowed to overturn the throne of their hereditary sovereign, who would then respect the divine rights of kings? The old monarchies of Europe therefore resolved that the revolutionary movement in France, a movement threatening all aristocratical and monarchical institutions, should be crushed, and that these heretical French doctrines respecting the Sovereignty of the People and the Rights of Man should be proved false by the power of royal armies.

The warlike preparations of Frederick William III. of Prussia and the Emperor Francis II., awakened the apprehensions of the revolutionists, and led the Legislative Assembly to declare war against them (April 20, 1792). A little later, the allied armies of the Austrians and Prussians, numbering more than 100,000 men, and made up in part of the French emigrant nobles, passed the frontiers of France. Thus were taken the first steps in a series of wars which were destined to last nearly a quarter of a century, and in which France almost single-handed was to struggle against the leagued powers of Europe, and to illustrate the miracles possible to enthusiasm and genius.

The Massacre of the Swiss Guards (Aug. 10, 1792). — The allies at first gained easy victories over the ill-disciplined forces of the Legislative Assembly, and the Duke of Brunswick, at the head of an immense army, advanced rapidly upon Paris. An insolent proclamation which this commander now issued, wherein he ordered the French nation to submit to their king, and threatened the Parisians with the destruction of their city should any harm be done the royal family, drove the French people frantic with indignation and rage. The Palace of the Tuileries, defended by a few hundred Swiss soldiers, the remnant of the royal guard, was assaulted. A terrible struggle followed in the corridors and upon the grand stairways of the palace. The Swiss stood "steadfast as the granite of their Alps." But they were overwhelmed at last, and all were murdered, either in the building itself or in the surrounding courts and streets.

The Massacre of September ("Jail Delivery"). — The army of the allies hurried on towards Paris to avenge the slaughter of the royal guards and to rescue the king. The capital was all excitement. "We must stop the enemy," cried Danton, "by striking terror into the royalists." To this end the most atrocious measures were now adopted by the Extremists. It was resolved that all

the royalists confined in the jails of the capital should be murdered. A hundred or more assassins were hired to butcher the
prisoners. The murderers first entered the churches of the city,
and the unfortunate priests who had refused to take oath to
support the new constitution, were butchered in heaps about the
altars. The jails were next visited, one after another, the persons
confined within slaughtered, and their bodies thrown out to the brutal hordes that followed the butchers to enjoy the carnival of blood.

The victims of this terrible "September Massacre," as it is
called, are estimated at from six to fourteen thousand. Europe
had never before known such a "jail delivery." It was the greatest
crime of the French Revolution.

Defeat of the Allies. — Meanwhile, in the open field, the fortunes
of war inclined to the side of the revolutionists. The French generals were successful in checking the advance of the allies, and
finally at Valmy (Sept. 20, 1792) succeeded in inflicting upon them
a decisive defeat, which caused their hasty retreat beyond the frontiers of France. The day after this victory the Legislative Assembly came to an end, and the following day the National Convention
assembled.

4. THE NATIONAL CONVENTION (Sept. 21, 1792–Oct. 26, 1795).

Parties in the Convention. — The Convention, consisting of
seven hundred and forty-nine deputies, among whom was the
celebrated freethinker, Thomas Paine, was divided into two parties,
the Girondists and the Mountainists. There were no monarchists;
all were republicans. No one dared to speak of a monarchy.

The Establishment of the Republic (Sept. 21, 1792). — The
very first act of the Convention on its opening day was to abolish
the Monarchy and proclaim France a Republic. The motion for
the abolition of Royalty was not even discussed. "What need is
there for discussion," exclaimed a delegate, "where all are agreed?
Courts are the hot-bed of crime, the focus of corruption; the history of kings is the martyrology of nations."

All titles of nobility were also abolished. Every one was to be addressed simply as *citizen*. In the debates of the Convention, the king was alluded to as Citizen Capet, and on the street the shoeblack was called Citizen Shoeblack.

The day following the Proclamation of the republic (Sept. 22, 1792) was made the beginning of a new era, the first day of the Year I. That was to be regarded as the natal day of Liberty. A little later, excited by the success of the French armies, — the Austrians and Prussians had been beaten, and Belgium had been overrun and occupied, — the Convention called upon all nations to rise against despotism, and pledged the aid of France to any people wishing to secure freedom.

Trial and Execution of the King (Jan. 21, 1793). — The next work of the Convention was the trial and execution of the king. On the 11th of December, 1792, he was brought before the bar of that body, charged with having conspired with the enemies of France, of having opposed the will of the people, and of having caused the massacre of the 10th of August. The sentence of the Convention was immediate death. On Jan. 21, 1793, the unfortunate monarch was conducted to the scaffold.

Coalition against France. — The regicide awakened the most bitter hostility against the French revolutionists, among all the old monarchies of Europe. The act was interpreted as a threat against all kings. A grand coalition, embracing Prussia, Austria, England, Sweden, Holland, Spain, Portugal, Piedmont, Naples, the Holy See, and later, Russia, was formed to crush the republican movement. Armies aggregating more than a quarter of a million of men threatened France at once on every frontier.

While thus beset with foes without, the republic was threatened with even more dangerous enemies within. The people of La Vendée, in Western France, who still retained their simple reverence for Royalty, Nobility, and the Church, rose in revolt against the sweeping innovations of the revolutionists.

To meet all these dangers which threatened the life of the new-born republic, the Convention ordered a levy, which placed 300,000 men in the field. The stirring Marseillaise Hymn, sung by the marching bands, awakened everywhere a martial fervor.

The Fall of the Girondists (June 2, 1793). — Gloomy tidings came from every quarter, — news of reverses to the armies of the republic in front of the allies, and of successes of the counter-revolutionists in La Vendée and other provinces. The Mountainists in the Convention, supported by the rabble of Paris, urged the most extreme measures. They proposed that the carriages of the wealthy should be seized and used for carrying soldiers to the seat of war, and that the expenses of the government should be met by forced contributions from the rich.

The Girondists opposing these communistic measures, a mob, 80,000 strong, it is asserted, surrounded the Convention, and demanded that the Girondists be given up as enemies of the Republic. They were surrendered and placed under arrest, a preliminary step to the speedy execution of many of them during the opening days of the Reign of Terror, which had now begun.

Thus did the Parisian mob purge the National Convention of France, as the army purged Parliament in the English Revolution (see p. 612). That mob were now masters, not only of the capital, but of France as well. There is nothing before France now but anarchy, and the dictator to whom anarchy always gives birth.

The Reign of Terror (June 2, 1793–July 27, 1794).

Opening of the Reign of Terror. — As soon as the expulsion of the Moderates had given the Extremists control of the Convention, they proceeded to carry out their policy of terrorism. Supreme power was vested in the so-called Committee of Public Safety, which became a terrific engine of tyranny and cruelty. Marat was president of the Committee, and Danton and Robespierre were both members.

The scenes which now followed are only feebly illustrated by the proscriptions of Sulla in ancient Rome (see p. 283). All aristocrats, all persons suspected of lukewarmness in the cause of liberty, were ordered to the guillotine. Hundreds were murdered simply because their wealth was wanted. Others fell, not because they were guilty of any political offence, but on account of having in some way incurred the personal displeasure of the dictators.

Charlotte Corday: Assassination of Marat (July 13, 1793). — At this moment appeared the Joan of Arc of the Revolution. A maiden of Normandy, Charlotte Corday by name, conceived the idea of delivering France from the terrors of proscription and civil war, by going to Paris and killing Marat, whom she regarded as the head of the tyranny. On pretence of wishing to reveal to him something of importance, she gained admission to his rooms and stabbed him to the heart. She atoned for the deed under the knife of the guillotine.

Events after the Death of Marat. — The enthusiasm of Charlotte Corday had led her to believe that the death of Marat would be a fatal blow to the power of the Mountainists. But it only served to drive them to still greater excesses, under the lead of Danton and Robespierre. She died to stanch the flow of her country's blood ; but, as Lamartine says, "her poniard appeared to have opened the veins of France." The flame of insurrection in the departments was quenched in deluges of blood. Some of the cities that had been prominent centres of the counter-revolution were made a terrible example of the vengeance of the revolutionists. Lyons was an object of special hatred to the tyrants. Respecting this place the Convention passed the following decree : "The city of Lyons shall be destroyed : every house occupied by a rich man shall be demolished ; only the dwellings of the poor shall remain, with edifices specially devoted to industry, and monuments consecrated to humanity and public education." So thousands of men were set to work to pull down the city. The Convention further decreed that a monument should be erected upon the ruins of Lyons with this inscription : "Lyons opposed Liberty ! Lyons is no more ! "

Execution of the Queen and of the Girondists. — The rage of the revolutionists was at this moment turned anew against the remaining members of the royal family, by the European powers proclaiming the Dauphin King of France. The queen, who had now borne nine months' imprisonment in a close dungeon, was brought before the terrible Revolutionary Tribunal, a sort of court organized to take cognizance of conspiracies against the republic, condemned to the guillotine, and straightway beheaded.

Two weeks after the execution of the queen, twenty-one of the chiefs of the Girondists, who had been kept in confinement since their arrest in the Convention, were pushed beneath the knife. Hundreds of others followed. Day after day the carnival of death went on. Seats were arranged for the people, who crowded to the spectacle as to a theatre. The women busied their hands with their knitting, while their eyes feasted upon the swiftly changing scenes of the horrid drama.

Most illustrious of all the victims after the queen was Madame Roland, who was accused of being the friend of the Girondists. Woman has always acted a prominent part in the great events of French history, because the grand ideas and sentiments which have worked so powerfully upon the imaginative and impulsive temperament of the men of France, have appealed with a still more fatal attraction to her more romantic and generously enthusiastic nature.

Sweeping Changes and Reforms. — While clearing away the enemies of France and of liberty, the revolutionists were also busy making the most sweeping changes in the ancient institutions and customs of the land. They hated these as having been established by kings and aristocrats to enhance their own importance and power, and to enthrall the masses. They proposed to sweep these things all aside, and give the world a fresh start.

A new system of weights and measures, known as the metrical, was planned, and a new mode of reckoning time was introduced. The names of the months were altered, titles being given them expressive of the character of each. Each month was divided into three periods of ten days each, called *decades*, and each day into ten parts. The tenth day of each decade took the place of Sunday. The five odd days not provided for in the arrangement were made festival days.

Abolition of Christianity. — With these reforms effected, the

revolutionists next proceeded to the more difficult task of subvert-
ing the ancient institutions of religion. Some of the chiefs of the
Commune of Paris declared that the Revolution should not rest
until it had "dethroned the King of Heaven as well as the kings
of earth."

An attempt was made by the Extremists to have Christianity
abolished by a decree of the National Convention; but that body,
fearing such an act might alienate many who were still attached to
the Church, resolved that all matters of creed
should be left to the decision of the people
themselves.

The atheistic chiefs of the Commune of
the capital now determined to effect their
purpose through the Church itself. They
persuaded the Bishop of Paris to abdicate his
office; and his example was followed by
many of the clergy throughout the country.
The churches of Paris and of other cities
were now closed, and the treasures of their
altars and shrines confiscated to the State.
Even the bells were melted down into cannon. The images of the Virgin and of the
Christ were torn down, and the busts of
Marat and other patriots set up in their
stead. And as the emancipation of the
world was now to be wrought, not by the
Cross, but by the guillotine, that instrument
took the place of the crucifix, and was called the Holy Guillotine.
All the visible symbols of the ancient religion were destroyed. All
emblems of hope in the cemeteries were obliterated, and over
their gates were inscribed the words, "Death is eternal sleep."

THE GUILLOTINE.

The madness of the Parisian people culminated in the worship
of what was called the Goddess of Reason. A celebrated beauty,
personating the Goddess, was set upon the altar of Notre Dame as
the object of homage and adoration. The example of Paris was

followed in many places throughout France. Churches were everywhere converted into temples of the new worship. The Sabbath
having been abolished, the services of the temple were held only
upon every tenth day. On that day the mayor or some popular
leader mounted the altar and harangued the people, dwelling upon
the news of the moment, the triumphs of the armies of the republic, the glorious achievements of the Revolution, and the privilege
of living in an era when one was oppressed neither by kings on
earth nor by a King in heaven.

Fall of Hébert and Danton (March and April, 1794). — Not
quite one year of the Reign of Terror had passed before the revolutionists, having destroyed or driven into obscurity their common
enemy, the Girondists, turned upon one another with the ferocity
of beasts whose appetite has been whetted by the taste of blood.

During the progress of events the Jacobins had become divided
into three factions, headed respectively by Danton, Robespierre,
and Hébert. Danton, though he had been a bold and audacious
leader, was now adopting a more conservative tone, and was condemning the extravagances and cruelties of the Committee of
Public Safety, of which he had ceased to be
a member.

Hébert was one of the worst demagogues
of the Commune, the chief and instigator
of the Parisian rabble. He and his followers, the sans-culottes of the capital,
would overturn everything and refound
society upon communism and atheism.

ROBESPIERRE.

Robespierre occupied a position mid-
way between these two, condemning alike the moderatism of
Danton and the atheistic communism of Hébert. To make his
own power supreme, he resolved to crush both.

Hébert and his party were the first to fall, Danton and his
adherents working with Robespierre to bring about their ruin, for
the Moderates and Anarchists were naturally at bitter enmity.

Danton and his friends were the next to follow. Little more

than a week had passed since the execution of Hébert before Robespierre had effected their destruction, on the charge of conspiring with and encouraging the counter-revolutionists.

With the Anarchists and Moderates both destroyed, Robespierre was now supreme. His ambition was attained. "He stood alone on the awful eminence of the Holy Mountain." But his turn was soon to come.

Worship of the Supreme Being. — One of the first acts of the dictator was to give France a new religion in place of the worship of Reason. Robespierre wished to sweep away Christianity as a superstition, but he would stop at deism. He did not believe that a state could be founded on atheism. "Atheism," said he, "is aristocratic. The idea of a great being who watches over oppressed innocence, and who punishes triumphant guilt, is and always will be popular. If God did not exist, it would behoove man to invent him." Accordingly Robespierre offered in the Convention the following resolution : "The French people acknowledge the existence of the Supreme Being and the immortality of the soul." The decree was adopted, and the churches that had been converted into temples of the Goddess of Reason were now consecrated to the worship of the Supreme Being.

The Terror at Paris. — At the very same time that Robespierre was establishing the new worship, he was desolating France with massacres of incredible atrocity, and ruling by a terrorism unparalleled since the most frightful days of Rome. With all power gathered in his hands, he overawed all opposition and dissent by the wholesale slaughters of the guillotine. The prisons of Paris and of the departments were filled with suspected persons, until 200,000 prisoners were crowded within these republican Bastiles. At Paris the dungeons were emptied of their victims and room made for fresh ones, by the swift processes of the Revolutionary Tribunal, which in mockery of justice caused the prisoners to be brought before its bar in companies of ten or fifty. Rank or talent was an inexpiable crime. "Were you not a noble?" asks the president of the court of one of the accused. "Yes," was the reply. "Enough ; another," was the judge's verdict. And so on through the long list each day brought before the tribunal.

The scenes about the guillotine were simply infernal. Benches were arranged around the scaffold and rented to spectators, like seats in a theatre. A special sewer had to be constructed to carry off the blood of the victims. In the space of a little over a month (from June 10th to July 17th) the number of persons guillotined at Paris was 1285, an average of 34 a day.

Massacres in the Provinces. — While such was the terrible state of things at the capital, matters were even worse in many of the other leading cities of France. The scenes at Nantes, Bordeaux, Marseilles, and Toulon suggested, in their varied elements of horror, the awful conceptions of the "Inferno" of Dante. At Nantes the victims were at first shot singly or guillotined ; but these methods being found too slow, more expeditious modes of execution were devised. To these were playfully given the names of "Republican Baptisms," "Republican Marriages," and "Battues."

The "Republican Baptism" consisted in crowding a hundred or more persons into a vessel, which was then towed out into the Loire and scuttled. In the "Republican Marriages" a man and woman were bound together, and then thrown into the river. The "Battues" consisted in ranging the victims in long ranks, and mowing them down with discharges of cannon and musket.

By these various methods fifteen thousand victims were destroyed in the course of a single month. The entire number massacred at Nantes during the Reign of Terror is estimated at thirty thousand. What renders these murders the more horrible is the fact that a considerable number of the victims were women and children. Nantes was at this time crowded with the orphaned children of the Vendéan counter-revolutionists. Upon a single night three hundred of these innocents were taken from the city prisons and drowned in the Loire.

The Fall of Robespierre (July, 1794). — By such terrorism did Robespierre and his creatures rule France for a little more than three months. The awful suspense and dread drove many into insanity and to suicide. The strain was too great for human nature to bear. A reaction came. The successes of the armies of the republic, and the establishment of the authority of the Convention throughout the departments, caused the people to look upon the massacres that were daily taking place as unnecessary and cruel. They began to turn with horror and pity from the scenes of the guillotine.

The first blow at the power of the dictator was struck in the Convention. A member dared to denounce him, upon the floor of the assembly, as a tyrant. The spell was broken. He was arrested and sent to the guillotine, with a large number of his confederates. The people greeted the fall of the tyrant's head with demonstrations of unbounded joy. The delirium was over. " France had awakened from the ghastly dream of the Reign of Terror (July 28, 1794)."

The Reaction. — The reaction which had swept away Robespierre and his associates continued after their ruin. The clubs of the Jacobins were closed, and that infamous society which had rallied and directed the hideous rabbles of the great cities was broken up. The deputies that had been driven from their seats in the Convention were invited to resume their places and the Christian worship was reëstablished.

Napoleon defends the Convention (Oct. 5, 1795). — These and other measures of the Convention did not fail of arousing the bitter opposition of the scattered forces of the Terrorists, as they were called ; and on the 5th of October, 1795, a mob of 40,000 men advanced to the attack of the Tuileries, where the Convention was sitting. As the mob came on they were met by a storm of grape shot, which sent them flying back in wild disorder. The man who trained the guns was a young artillery officer, a native of the island of Corsica, — Napoleon Bonaparte. The Revolution had at last brought forth a man of genius capable of controlling and directing its tremendous energies.

5. THE DIRECTORY (Oct. 27, 1795–Nov. 9, 1799).

The Republic becomes Aggressive. — A few weeks after the defence of the Convention by Napoleon, that body declaring its labors ended, closed its sessions, and immediately afterwards the Councils and the Board of Directors provided for by the new constitution[1] that had been framed by the Convention, assumed control of affairs.

Under the Directory the republic, which up to this time had been acting mainly on the defensive, entered upon an aggressive policy. The Revolution, having accomplished its work in France, having there destroyed royal despotism and abolished class privilege, now set itself about fulfilling its early promise of giving liberty to all peoples (see p. 658). In a word, the revolutionists became propagandists. France now exhibits what her historians call her social, her communicative genius. " Easily seduced herself," as Lamartine says, " she easily seduces others." She would make all Europe like unto herself. Herself a republic, she would make all nations republics.

Had not the minds of the people in all the neighboring countries been prepared to welcome the new order of things, the Revolution could never have spread itself as widely as it did. But everywhere irrepressible longings for social and political equality and freedom, born of long oppression, were stirring the souls of men. The French armies were everywhere welcomed as deliverers. Thus was France enabled to surround herself with a girdle of commonwealths. She conquered Europe not by her armies, but by her ideas. "An invasion of armies," says Victor Hugo, " can be resisted : an invasion of ideas cannot be resisted."

The republics established were, indeed, short-lived ; for the times were not yet ripe for the complete triumph of democratic

---

[1] There were to be two legislative bodies, — the Council of Five Hundred and the Council of the Ancients, the latter embracing two hundred and fifty persons, of whom no one could be under fifty years of age. The executive power was vested in a board of five persons, which was called the Directory.

ideas. But a great gain for freedom was made. The reëstablished monarchies never dared to make themselves as despotic as those which the Revolution had overturned.

The Plans of the Directory. — Austria and England were the only formidable powers that still persisted in their hostility to the republic. The Directors resolved to strike a decisive blow at the first of these implacable foes. To carry out their designs, two large armies, numbering about 70,000 each, were mustered upon the middle Rhine, and intrusted to the command of the two young and energetic generals Moreau and Jourdan, who were to make a direct invasion of Germany. A third army, numbering about 36,000 men, was assembled in the neighborhood of Nice, in South-eastern France, and placed in the hands of Napoleon, to whom was assigned the work of driving the Austrians out of Italy.

Napoleon's Italian Campaign (1796–1797). — Straightway upon receiving his command, Napoleon, now in his twenty-seventh year, animated by visions of military glory to be gathered on the fields of Italy, hastened to join his army at Nice. He found the discontented soldiers almost without food or clothes. He at once aroused all their latent enthusiasm by one of those short, stirring addresses for which he afterwards became so famous. Then before the mountain roads were yet free from snow, he set his army in motion, and forced the passage of the low Genoese, or Maritime Alps. The Carthaginian had been surpassed. " Hannibal," exclaimed Napoleon, " crossed the Alps ; as for us, we have turned them." Now followed a most astonishing series of French victories over the Austrians and their allies. As a result of the campaign a considerable part of Northern Italy was formed into a commonwealth under the name of the Cisalpine Republic. Genoa was also transformed into the Ligurian Republic.

Treaty of Campo Formio (1797). — While Napoleon had been gaining his surprising victories in Italy, Moreau and Jourdan had been meeting with severe reverses in Germany, their invading columns having been forced back upon the Rhine by the Archduke Charles. Napoleon, having effected the work assigned to the army of Italy, now climbed the Eastern Alps, and led his soldiers down upon the plains of Austria. The near approach of the French to Vienna induced the emperor, Francis II., to listen to proposals of peace. An armistice was agreed upon, and a few months afterwards the important treaty of Campo Formio was arranged. By the terms of this treaty Austria ceded her Belgian provinces to the French Republic, surrendered important provinces on the west side of the Rhine, and acknowledged the Cisalpine Republic.

With the treaty arranged, Napoleon set out for Paris, where a triumph and ovation such as Europe had not seen since the days of the old Roman conquerors, awaited him.

Napoleon's Campaign in Egypt (1798–1799). — The Directors had received Napoleon with apparent enthusiasm and affection; but at this very moment they were disquieted by fears lest the conqueror's ambition might lead him to play the part of a second Cæsar. They resolved to engage the young commander in an enterprise which would take him out of France. This undertaking was an attack upon England, which they were then meditating. Bonaparte opposed the plan of a direct descent upon the island as impracticable, declaring that England should be attacked through her Eastern possessions. He presented a scheme very characteristic of his bold, imaginative genius. This was nothing less than the conquest and colonization of Egypt, by which means France would be able to control the trade of the East, and cut England off from her East India possessions. The Directors assented to the plan, and with feelings of relief saw Napoleon embark from the port of Toulon to carry out the enterprise.

Escaping the vigilance of the British fleet that was patrolling the Mediterranean, Napoleon landed in Egypt July 1, 1798. Within sight of the Pyramids, the French army was checked in its march upon Cairo by a determined stand of the renowned Mameluke cavalry. Napoleon animated the spirits of his men for the inevitable fight by one of his happiest speeches. One of the sentences is memorable: "Soldiers," he exclaimed, pointing to the Pyramids, "forty centuries are looking down upon you." The terrific struggle that followed is known in history as the "Battle of the Pyramids." Napoleon gained a victory that opened the way for his advance. The French now entered Cairo in triumph, and all Lower Egypt fell into their hands.

Napoleon had barely made his entrance into Cairo, before the startling intelligence was borne to him that his fleet had been destroyed in the bay of Aboukir, at the mouth of the Nile, by the English admiral Nelson (Aug. 1, 1798).

In the spring of 1799, Napoleon led his army into Syria, the Porte having joined a new coalition against France. He captured Gaza and Jaffa, and finally invested Acre. The Turks were assisted in the defence of this place by the distinguished English admiral, Sir Sidney Smith.[1] All of Napoleon's attempts to carry the place by storm were defeated by the skill and bravery of the English commander. "That man Sidney," said Napoleon afterwards, "made me miss my destiny." Doubtless Napoleon's vision of conquests in the East embraced Persia and India. With the ports of Syria secured, he would have imitated Alexander, and led his soldiers to the foot of the Himalayas.

Bitterly disappointed, Napoleon abandoned the siege of Acre, and led his army back into Egypt. There his worn and thinned ranks were attacked near Aboukir by a fresh Turkish army, but the genius of Napoleon turned threatened defeat into a brilliant victory. The enthusiastic Kleber, one of Napoleon's lieutenants, clasping his general in his arms, exclaimed, "Sire, your greatness is like that of the universe."

Establishment of the Tiberine, Helvetic, and Parthenopæan Republics. — We must turn now to view affairs in Europe. The year 1798 was a favorable one for the republican cause represented by the Revolution. During that year and the opening month of the following one, the French set up three new republics. First, they incited an insurrection at Rome, made a prisoner

---

[1] The besieged were further assisted by a Turkish army outside. With these the French fought the noted Battle of Mount Tabor, in which they gained a complete victory.

of the Pope, and proclaimed the Roman, or Tiberine, Republic. Then they invaded the Swiss cantons and united them into a commonwealth under the name of the Helvetic Republic. A little later the French troops drove the king of Naples out of his kingdom, and transformed that state into the Parthenopæan Republic. Thus were three new republics added to the commonwealths which the Revolution had already created.

The Reaction: Napoleon overthrows the Directory (18th and 19th Brumaire). — Most of this work was quickly undone. Encouraged by the victory of Nelson over the French fleet in the battle of the Nile, the leading states of Europe had formed a new coalition against the French Republic. Early in 1799 the war began, and was waged in almost every part of Europe at the same time. The campaign was on the whole extremely disastrous to the French. They were driven out of Italy, and were barely able to keep the allies off the soil of France. The Tiberine and the Parthenopæan Republics were abolished.

The reverses suffered by the French armies caused the Directory to fall into great disfavor. They were charged with having through jealousy exiled Napoleon, the only man who could save the Republic. Confusion and division prevailed everywhere. The royalists had become so strong and bold that there was danger lest they should gain control of the government. On the other hand, the threats of the Jacobins began to create apprehensions of another Reign of Terror.

News of the desperate state of affairs at home reached Napoleon just after his victory in Egypt, following his return from Syria. He instantly formed a bold resolve. Confiding the command of the army in Egypt to Kleber, he set sail for France, disclosing his designs in the significant words, " The reign of the lawyers is over."

· Napoleon was welcomed in France with the wildest enthusiasm. A great majority of the people felt instinctively that the emergency demanded a dictator. Some of the Directors joined with Napoleon in a plot to overthrow the government. Meeting with opposition in the Council of Five Hundred, Napoleon with a body of grenadiers drove the deputies from their chamber (Nov. 9, 1799).

The French Revolution had at last brought forth its Cromwell (see p. 611). Napoleon was master of France. The first French Republic was at an end, and what is distinctively called the French Revolution was over. Now commences the history of the Consulate and the First Empire, — the story of that surprising career, the sun of which rose so brightly at Austerlitz and set forever at Waterloo.

CHAPTER LIX.

THE CONSULATE AND THE FIRST EMPIRE: FRANCE SINCE THE SECOND RESTORATION.

1. THE CONSULATE AND THE EMPIRE (1799-1815).

The Veiled Military Despotism. — After the overthrow of the Directorial government, a new constitution — the fourth since the year 1789 — was prepared, and having been submitted to the approval of the people, was heartily indorsed. This new instrument vested the executive power in three consuls, elected for a term of ten years, the first of whom really exercised all the authority of the Board. Napoleon, of course, became the First Consul.

The other functions of the government were carried on by a Council of State, a Tribunate, a Legislature, and a Senate. But the members of all these bodies were appointed either directly or indirectly by the consuls, so that the entire government was actually in their hands, or, rather, in the hands of the First Consul. France was still called a republic, but it was such a republic as Rome was under Julius Cæsar or Augustus. The republican names and forms merely veiled a government as absolute and personal as that of Louis XIV., — in a word, a military despotism.

Wars of the First Consul. — Neither Austria nor England would acknowledge the government of the First Consul as legitimate. In their view he was simply an upstart, a fortunate usurper. The throne of France belonged, by virtue of divine right, to the House of Bourbon.

Napoleon mustered his soldiers. His plan was to deal Austria, his worst continental enemy, a double blow. A large army was collected on the Rhine, for an invasion of Germany. This was intrusted to Moreau. Another, intended to operate against the

Austrians in Italy, was gathered at the foot of the Alps. Napoleon himself assumed command of this latter force.

In the spring of the year 1800 Napoleon made his memorable passage of the Alps, and astonished the Austrian generals by suddenly appearing, with an army of 40,000 men, on the plains of Italy. Upon the renowned field of Marengo the Austrian army, which outnumbered that of the French three to one, was completely overwhelmed, and Italy lay for a second time at the feet of Napoleon (June 14, 1800).

But at the moment Italy was regained, Egypt was lost. On the very day of the battle of Marengo, Kleber, whom Napoleon had left in charge of the army in Egypt, was assassinated by a Turkish fanatic, and shortly afterwards the entire French force was obliged to surrender to the English.

The French reverses in Egypt, however, were soon made up by fresh victories in Europe. A few months after the battle of Marengo, Moreau gained a decisive victory over the Austrians at Hohenlinden, which opened the way to Vienna. The Emperor Francis II. was now constrained to sign a treaty of peace at Lunéville, in which he allowed the Rhine to be made the eastern frontier of France (February, 1801). The emperor also recognized the Cisalpine, Ligurian, Helvetian, and Batavian republics. The following year England was also glad to sign a peace at Amiens (March, 1802).

His Works of Peace: the Code Napoleon. — Having wrung from both England and Austria an acknowledgment of his government, Napoleon was now free to devote his amazing energies to the reform and improvement of the internal affairs of France. So at this time were begun by him those great works of various character which were continued through all the fifteen years of his supremacy. His great military road over the Alps by the Simplon Pass, surpasses in bold engineering the most difficult of the Roman roads, while many of his architectural works are the pride of France at the present day.

Taking up the work of the Revolution, he caused the laws of

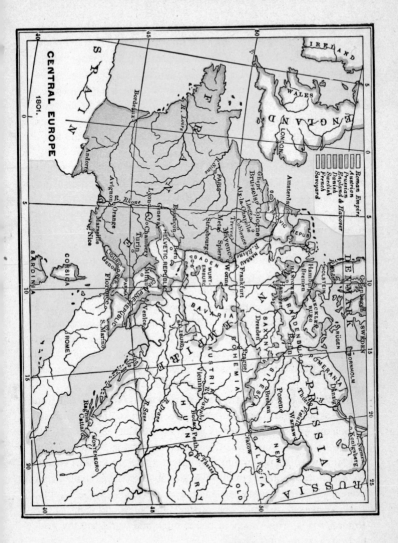

CENTRAL EUROPE
1801.

France to be revised and harmonized, producing the celebrated *Code Napoleon*, a work that is not unworthy of comparison with the *Corpus Juris Civilis* of the Emperor Justinian. The influence of this Code upon the development of Liberalism in Western Europe is simply incalculable. It secured the work of the Revolution. It swept away the unequal, iniquitous, oppressive customs, regulations, decrees, and laws that were an inheritance from the feudal ages. It recognized the equality in the eye of the law of noble and peasant. "It is to-day the frame-work of law in France, Holland, Belgium, Western Germany, Switzerland, and Italy." Had Napoleon done nothing else save to give this Code to Europe, he would have conferred an inestimable benefit upon mankind.

Napoleon made Consul for Life (1802). — As a reward for his vast services to France, and also in order that his magnificent schemes of reform and improvement might be pursued without fear of interruption, Napoleon was now, by a vote of the people, made Consul for Life, with the right to name his successor (August, 1802). Thus he moved a step nearer the coveted dignity of the Imperial title.

Napoleon proclaimed Emperor (1804). — A conspiracy against the life of the First Consul, and the increased activity of his enemies, caused the French people to resolve to increase his power, and secure his safety and the stability of his government, by placing him upon a throne. A decree conferring upon him the title of Emperor having been submitted to the people for approval was ratified by an almost unanimous vote, less than three thousand persons opposing the measure.

Surrounding Republics changed into Kingdoms. — Thus was the First French Republic metamorphosed into an unveiled empire. We may be sure that the cluster of republics which during the Revolution sprang up around the great original, will speedily undergo a like transformation; for Napoleon was right when he said that a revolution in France is sure to be followed by a revolution throughout Europe. As France, a republic, would make all states republics, so France, a monarchy, would make all nations monarchies. Within five years from the time that the government of France assumed an imperial form, all the surrounding republics raised up by the revolutionary ideas and armies of France, had been transformed into monarchies dependent upon France, or had become a component part of the French Empire.[1] Thus was the political work of the Revolution undone. Political *liberty* was taken away; the people were not yet ready for self-government. Social *Equality* was left.

The Wars of Napoleon I. — It will not be supposed that the powers of Europe were looking quietly on while France was thus metamorphosing herself and all the neighboring countries. The colossal power which the soldier of fortune was building up, was a menace to all Europe. The empire was more dreaded than the republic, because it was a military despotism, and as such, an instrument of irresistible power in the hands of a man of such genius and resources as Napoleon. Coalition after coalition, always headed by England, — who had sworn a Punic hatred to the Napoleonic empire, — was formed by the monarchies of Europe against the "usurper," with the object of pressing France back within her original boundaries and setting up again the subverted throne of the Bourbons.

From the coronation of Napoleon in 1804 until his final downfall in 1815, the tremendous struggle went on almost without intermission. It was the war of the giants. Europe was shaken from end to end by such armies as the world had not seen since the days of Xerxes. Napoleon, whose hands were upheld by a score of distinguished marshals, performed the miracles of genius. His brilliant achievements still dazzle, while they amaze, the world.

---

[1] The Cisalpine, or Italian Republic, was changed into a kingdom, and Napoleon, crowning himself at Milan with the iron crown of the Lombards, assumed the government of the state with the title of King of Italy (May 26, 1805). The Ligurian Republic, embracing Genoa and a portion of Sardinia, was made a part of France, while the Batavian Republic was changed into the Kingdom of Holland, and given by Napoleon to his brother Louis (June, 1806).

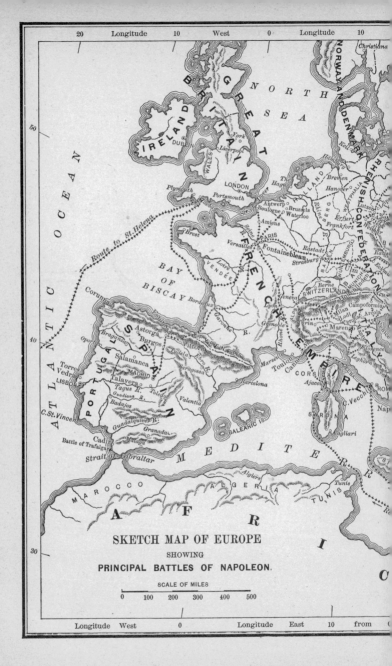

SKETCH MAP OF EUROPE

SHOWING

PRINCIPAL BATTLES OF NAPOLEON.

SCALE OF MILES

0   100   200   300   400   500

To relate in detail the campaigns of Napoleon from Austerlitz to Waterloo would require the space of volumes. We shall simply indicate in a few brief paragraphs the successive steps by which he mounted to the highest pitch of power and fame, and then trace rapidly the decline and fall of his astonishing fortunes.

Austerlitz (1805) : **End of the Holy Roman Empire** (1806). — The year following his coronation, Napoleon made a gigantic effort to break the coalition which England, Russia, Austria, and Sweden had formed against him. He massed an immense army at Boulogne, on the Channel, preparatory to an invasion of England ; but the failure of his fleet to carry out its part of the plan, and intelligence of the approach of the Austrians and Russians towards the Rhenish frontier, caused him suddenly to transfer his troops to the opposite side of France.

Without waiting for the attack of the allies, Napoleon flung his Grand Army, as it was called, across the Rhine, defeated the Austrians in the battle of Ulm, and marched in triumph through Vienna to the field of Austerlitz beyond, where he gained one of his most memorable victories over the combined armies of Austria and Russia, numbering more than 100,000 men (Dec. 2, 1805).

This battle completely changed the map of Europe. Austria was forced to give up Venetia and other provinces about the head of the Adriatic, this territory being now added to the kingdom of Italy. Sixteen of the German states, declaring themselves independent of the empire, were formed into a league, called the *Confederation of the Rhine*, with Napoleon as Protector. Furthermore, the Emperor Francis II. was obliged to surrender the crown of the *Holy Roman Empire*, and thereafter to content himself with the title of *Emperor of Austria*.

Thus did the Holy Roman Empire come to an end (1806), after having maintained an existence, since its revival by Otto the Great, of more than eight hundred years. The *Kingdom of Germany*, which was created by the partition of the empire of Charlemagne (see p. 408), now also passed out of existence, even in name.

Trafalgar (Oct. 21, 1805). — Napoleon's brilliant victories in Germany were clouded by an irretrievable disaster to his fleet, which occurred only two days after the engagement at Ulm. Lord Nelson having met, near Cape Trafalgar on the coast of Spain, the combined French and Spanish fleets, — Spain had become the ally of Napoleon, — almost completely destroyed the combined armaments. The gallant English admiral fell at the moment of victory. "Thank God, I have done my duty," were his last words.

This decisive battle gave England the control of the sea, and relieved her from all danger of a French invasion. Even the "wet ditch," as Napoleon was wont contemptuously to call the English Channel, was henceforth an impassable gulf to his ambition. He might rule the continent, but the sovereignty of the ocean and its islands was denied him.

Jena and Auerstadt (1806). — Prussia was the state next after Austria to feel the weight of Napoleon's power. Goaded by insult, the Prussian king, Frederick William III., very imprudently threw down the gauntlet to the French emperor. Moving with his usual swiftness, Napoleon overwhelmed the armies of Frederick in the battles of Jena and Auerstadt, which were both fought upon the same day (Oct. 14, 1806). Thus the great military power consolidated by the genius of Frederick the Great, was crushed and almost annihilated. What had proved too great an undertaking for the combined powers of Europe during the Seven Years' War, Napoleon had effected in less than a month.

Eylau and Friedland (1807). — The year following his victories over the Prussians, Napoleon led his Grand Army against the forces of the Czar, Alexander I., who had entered Prussia with aid for King Frederick. A fierce but indecisive battle at Eylau was followed, a little later in the same season, by the battle of Friedland, in which the Russians were completely overwhelmed (June 14, 1807). The Czar was forced to sue for peace.

By the terms of the Treaty of Tilsit Prussia was stripped of more than half of her former dominions, a part of which was made into a new state, called the Kingdom of Westphalia, with Napoleon's brother, Jerome, as its king, and added to the Confederation of the Rhine; while Prussian Poland, reorganized and clumsily christened the "Grand Duchy of Warsaw," was given to Saxony. What was left of Prussia became virtually a dependency of the French empire.

The Continental System: the Berlin and Milan Decrees. — While Napoleon was carrying on his campaigns against Prussia and Russia, he was all the time meditating vengeance upon England, his most uncompromising foe, and the leader or the instigator of the coalitions which were constantly being formed for the overthrow of his power. We have seen how the destruction of his fleet at Trafalgar dashed all his hopes of ever making a descent upon the British shores. Unable to reach his enemy directly with his arms, he resolved to strike her through her commerce. By two celebrated imperial edicts, called from the cities whence they were issued the Berlin and the Milan decree, he closed all the ports of the continent against English ships, and forbade any of the European nations from holding any intercourse with Great Britain, all of whose ports he declared in a state of blockade.

So completely was Europe under the domination of Napoleon, that England's trade was by these measures very seriously crippled, and great loss and suffering were inflicted upon her industrial classes. We shall have occasion a little later to speak of the disastrous effects of the system upon the French empire itself.

Beginning of the Peninsular Wars (1808). — One of the first consequences of Napoleon's "continental policy" was to bring him into conflict with Portugal. The prince regent of that country presuming to open its ports to English ships, Napoleon at once deposed him, and sent one of his marshals to take possession of the kingdom. The entire royal family, accompanied by many of the nobility, fled to Brazil, and made that country the seat of an empire which has endured to the present day.

Having thus gained a foothold in the Peninsula, Napoleon now resolved to possess himself of the whole of it. Insolently interfering in the affairs of Spain, he forced the weak-minded Bourbon king to resign to him, as his "dearly beloved friend and ally," his crown, which he bestowed at once upon his brother, Joseph Bonaparte (1808). The throne of Naples, which Joseph had been occupying,[1] was transferred to Murat, Napoleon's brother-in-law. Thus did this audacious man make and unmake kings, and give away thrones and kingdoms.

But the high-spirited Spaniards were not the people to submit tamely to such an indignity. The entire nation, from the Pyrenees to the Straits of Gibraltar, flew to arms. Portugal also arose, and England sent to her aid a force under Sir Arthur Wellesley, afterwards Duke of Wellington, and the hero of Waterloo. The French were soon driven out of Portugal, and pushed beyond the Ebro in Spain. Joseph fled in dismay from his throne, and Napoleon found it necessary to take the field himself, in order to restore the prestige of the French arms. He entered the Peninsula at the head of an army of 80,000 men, and scattering the Spaniards wherever he met them, entered Madrid in triumph, and reseated his brother upon the Spanish throne.

Threatening tidings from another quarter of Europe now caused Napoleon to hasten back to Paris.

Second Campaign against Austria (1809). — Taking advantage of Napoleon's troubles in the Peninsula, Francis I. of Austria, who had been watching for an opportunity to retrieve the disaster of Austerlitz, gathered an army of half a million of men, and declared war against the French emperor. But Austria was fated to suffer even a deeper humiliation than she had already endured. Napoleon swept across the Danube, and at the end of a short campaign, the most noted battles of which were those of Eckmühl and Wagram, Austria was again at his feet, and a second time he entered Vienna in triumph. Austria was now still farther dismembered, large tracts of her possessions being ceded directly to Napoleon or given to the various neighboring states (1809).

---

[1] Napoleon dethroned the Bourbons in Naples in 1805.

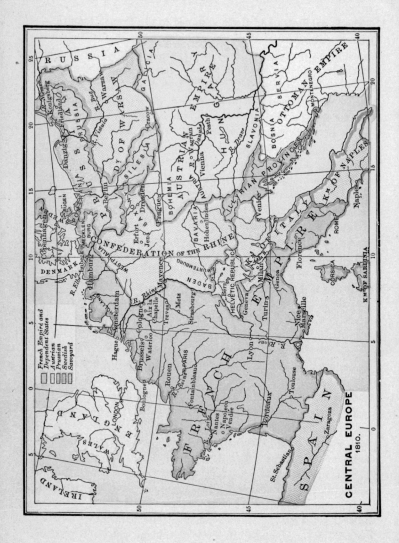

CENTRAL EUROPE
1810.

French Empire and
Dependent States
Austrian
Prussian
Swedish
Samogard

RUSSIA

DY OF WARSAW

PRUSSIA

GALICIA

AUSTRIAN EMPIRE

HUNGARY

OTTOMAN EMPIRE

BOSNA

SERVIA

MONTENEGRO

SLAVONA

ILLYRIAN PROVINCES

SILESIA

BOHEMIA

AUSTRIA

BAVARIA

CONFEDERATION OF THE RHINE

WESTPHALIA

DENMARK

MECKLE-BURG

HOLLAND

WURTEMBERG

BADEN

HELVETIC REPUBLIC

K M OF ITALY

K M OF NAPLES

Naples

ROME

CORSICA

K M OF SARDINIA

FRENCH EMPIRE

Rome

Florence

Genoa

Turin

Nice

Marseille

Geneva

Bern

Lyon

Rhone

Bordeaux

Toulouse

St Sebastian

Zaragoza

SPAIN

PARIS

Fontainebleau

Rouen

Boulogne

Nantes

Vendée

Metz

Treves

Strasbourg

Aix la Chapelle

Cologne

Mayence

Brussels

Waterloo

Amsterdam

Hague

Hamburg

Lubeck

Berlin

Erfurt

Jena

Dresden

Prague

Hohenlinden

Vienna

Wagram

Pesth

Venice

Drave

Save

Rugen

Copenhagen

Danzig

Königsberg

Friedland

Warsaw

Cracow

R Vistula

R Bug

R Drave

R Elbe

R Rhine

R Loire

ENGLAND

WALES

IRELAND

LONDON

The Papal States and Holland joined to the French Empire. — That Napoleon cared but little for the thunders of the Church is shown by his treatment of the Pope. Pius VII. opposing his continental system, the emperor incorporated the Papal States with the French empire (1809). The Pope thereupon excommunicated Napoleon, who straightway arrested the Pontiff, dragged him over the Alps into France, and held him in captivity for four years.

The year following the annexation of the Papal States to the French empire, Louis Bonaparte, king of Holland, who disapproved of his brother's continental system, which was ruining the trade of the Dutch, abdicated the crown. Thereupon Napoleon incorporated Holland with France, on the ground that it was simply "the sediment of the French rivers."

Napoleon's Second Marriage (1810). — The year following his triumph over Francis I. of Austria, Napoleon divorced his wife Josephine, in order to form a new alliance, with Maria Louisa, Archduchess of Austria. The fond and faithful Josephine bowed meekly to the will of her lord, and went into sorrowful exile from his palace. Napoleon's object in this matter was to cover the reproach of his own plebeian birth, by an alliance with one of the ancient royal families of Europe, and to secure the perpetuity of his government by leaving an heir who might be the inheritor of his throne and fortunes. His hope seemed realized when, the year following his marriage with the Archduchess, a son was born to them, who was given the title of "King of Rome."

Napoleon at the Summit of his Power (1811). — Napoleon was now at the height of his marvellous fortunes. Marengo, Austerlitz, Jena, Friedland, and Wagram were the successive steps by which he had mounted to the most dizzy heights of military power and glory. The empire which he had built up stretched from the Baltic to Southern Italy, embracing France proper, Belgium, Holland, Northwestern Germany, Italy west of the Apennines as far south as Naples, besides large possessions about the head of the Adriatic. On all sides were allied, vassal, or dependent states. Several of the ancient thrones of Europe were occupied by Napoleon's relatives or favorite marshals.   He himself was head of the kingdom of Italy, and Protector of the Confederation of the Rhine.   Austria and Prussia were completely subject to his will.   Russia and Denmark were his allies.

Elements of Weakness in the Empire. — But splendid and

imposing as at this moment appeared the external affairs of Napoleon, the sun of his fortunes, which had risen so brightly at Austerlitz, had already passed its meridian.   There were many things just now contributing to the weakness of the French empire and foreboding its speedy dissolution.   Founded and upheld by the genius of Napoleon,

NAPOLEON BONAPARTE.

it depended solely upon the life and fortunes of this single man. The diverse elements it embraced were as yet so loosely joined that there could be no hope or possibility of its surviving either the misfortune or the death of its founder.

Again, Napoleon's continental system, through the suffering and loss it inflicted upon all the maritime countries of Europe, had caused murmurs of discontent all around the circumference of the continent.   This ruinous policy had also involved the French emperor in a terribly wasteful war with Spain, which country was destined — more truly than Italy, of which the expression was first used — to become "the grave of the French."   Napoleon after his downfall himself admitted that his passage of the Pyrenees was the fatal misstep in his career.

Furthermore, the conscriptions of the emperor had drained France of men, and her armies were now recruited by mere boys, who were utterly unfit to bear the burden and fatigue of Napoleon's rapid campaigns.   The heavy taxes, also, which were necessary to meet the expenses of Napoleon's wars, and to carry on the splendid public works upon which he was constantly engaged, produced great suffering and discontent throughout the empire. And the crowd of deposed princes and dispossessed aristocrats in those states where Napoleon had promulgated his new code of equal rights (see p. 675), were naturally restless and resentful, and watchful for an opportunity to recover their ancient power and privileges. Even the large class in the surrounding countries that at first welcomed Napoleon as the representative of the French ideas of equality and liberty, and applauded while he overturned ancient thrones and aristocracies, which, like the monarchy and the feudal nobility in France swept away by the Revolution, had become unbearably proud, corrupt, and oppressive,—even these early adherents had been turned into bitter enemies through Napoleon's adoption of imperial manners, and especially by his setting aside his first wife, Josephine, in order that he might ally himself to one of the old royal houses of Europe, which act was looked upon as a betrayal of the cause of the people.

Nothing save the prestige of Napoleon's name and the dread of his vengeance keeps his enemies at bay. Let the lion be wounded and a hundred enemies will spring upon him from every side.

The Invasion of Russia (1812–1813).—The signal for the uprising of Europe was the terrible misfortune which befell Napoleon in his invasion of Russia. The Czar having cast aside the old ties of alliance and friendship, and entered a coalition against France, Napoleon crossed the frontiers of Russia, at the head of what was proudly called the Grand Army, numbering more than half a million of·men.

The Russians threw themselves across the path of the invaders at Borodino, but their lines were swept back by the strong columns of the Grand Army, although the victory cost the French dear. Following closely the retreating enemy, the French pushed on towards the ancient Russian capital, Moscow. This city Napoleon had thought would supply food for his army, and shelter from the severity of the northern winter, which was now approaching. But to his astonishment he found the city deserted by its inhabitants ; and scarcely had he established himself in the empty palace of the Czar (the Kremlin), before the city, probably fired by persons whom the Russians had left behind for this purpose, burst into flames. After waiting about the ruins until the middle of October, in hopes that the Czar would accept proposals of peace, Napoleon was forced to give the command for the return of the army to France.

The retreat was attended with incredible sufferings and horrors. The Russian winter setting in earlier than usual and with terrible severity, thousands of the French soldiers were frozen to death, and falling upon the snow traced with a long black line the trail of the retreating army. The spot of each bivouac was marked by the circles of dead around the watch-fires. Thousands more were slain by the wild Cossacks, who surrounded the retreating columns and harassed them day and night. The passage of the river Beresina was attended with appalling losses.

Soon after the passage of this stream, Napoleon, conscious that the fate of his empire depended upon his presence in Paris, left the remnant of the army in charge of his marshals, and hurried by post to his capital. Marshal Ney, "the bravest of the brave," performed miracles in covering the retreat of the broken and dispirited columns. He was the last man, it is said, to cross the Niemen. His face was so haggard from care and so begrimed with powder, that no one recognized him. Being asked who he was, he replied, " I am the rear guard of the Grand Army."

The loss by death of the French and their allies in this disastrous campaign is reckoned at about 300,000 men,[1] while that of the Russians is estimated to have been almost as large.

"**The Battle of the Nations**" (Leipsic, 1813). — Napoleon's fortunes were buried with his Grand Army in the snows of Russia. His woeful losses emboldened the surrounding powers to think that now they could crush him. A sixth coalition was formed, embracing Russia, Prussia, England, and Sweden. Napoleon made gigantic efforts to prepare France for the struggle. By the spring of 1813 he was at the head of a new army, numbering over 300,000 men.

[1] The Russians took 100,000 prisoners, and about 100,000 recrossed the Niemen.

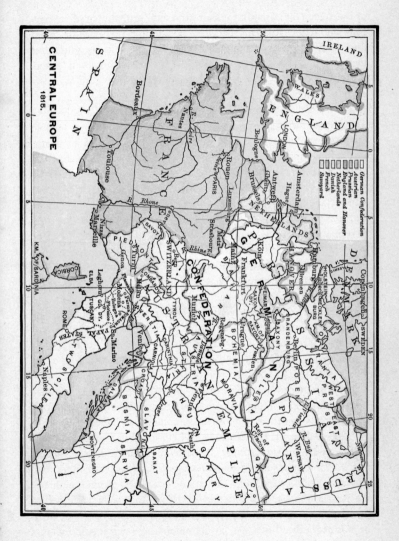

CENTRAL EUROPE
1815.

German Confederation
Austrian
Prussian
Netherlands
England and Hanover
Danish
French
Savoyard

Falling upon the allied armies of the Russians and Prussians, first at Lutzen and then at Bautzen, he gained a decisive victory upon both fields. Austria now appeared in the lists, and at Leipsic the French were met by the leagued armies of Europe. So many were the powers represented upon the renowned field, that it is known in history as the "Battle of the Nations." The combat lasted three days. Napoleon was defeated, and forced to retreat into France.

The Abdication of Napoleon (1814). — The armies of the allies now poured over all the French frontiers. Napoleon's tremendous efforts to roll back the tide of invasion were all in vain. As the struggle became manifestly hopeless, his most trusted officers deserted and betrayed him. Paris surrendered to the allies. Napoleon was forced to abdicate, and the ancient House of the Bourbons was reëstablished in the person of a brother of Louis XVI., who took the title of Louis XVIII. Napoleon was banished to the little island of Elba in the Mediterranean, being permitted to retain his title of Emperor, and to keep about him a few hundred of his old guards. But Elba was a very diminutive empire for one to whom the half of Europe seemed too small, and we shall not be surprised to learn that Napoleon was not content with it.

The Congress of Vienna (Sept., 1814–June, 1815). — After the overthrow of Napoleon, commissioners of the different European states met at Vienna to readjust the map of Europe. It was a great task to harmonize the conflicting claims that came before the convention, and to effect a settlement of the continent that should satisfy all parties. But after nearly a year of negotiations and debate, an agreement respecting the boundaries and relations of the various states was reached. As we shall hereafter, in connection with the history of the separate countries, have occasion to say something respecting the relations of each to the Congress, we shall here say but a word regarding the temper of the assembly and the general character of its work.

The Vienna commissioners seemed to have had but one thought and aim — to put everything back as near as possible in the shape that it was in before the Revolution. They had no care for the people; the princes were their only concern. The crowd of thrones that Napoleon had overturned were righted, and the old despots were invited to remount them. Italy and Germany were divided among a horde of petty tyrants. In Spain and Naples the old Bourbon families were re-instated, and the former despotisms renewed. In short, the clock was set back to the hour when the Bastile was attacked. Everything that had happened since was utterly ignored.

But the Revolution had destroyed privilege as expressed in the effete feudal aristocracies of Europe, and impaired beyond restoration the monstrous doctrine of the divine right of kings. An attempt to bring these things back again was an attempt to restore life to the dead, — to set up again the fallen Dagon in his place.

Notwithstanding, the commissioners at Vienna, blind to the spirit and tendencies of the times, did set up once more the broken idol, — only, however, to see it flung down again by the memorable social upheavals of the next half century. The kings had had their Congress : the people were to have theirs, — in 1820 and '30 and '48.

The Hundred Days (March 20–June 29, 1815). — The allies who placed Louis XVIII. upon the French throne set back the boundaries of France as nearly as possible to the lines they occupied in 1792. In like manner the king himself, seemingly utterly oblivious to the spirit and tendencies of the times, as soon as he was in possession of the ancient inheritance of his family, began to put back everything just as it was before the reforms of the Revolution. He always alluded to the year he began to rule as the nineteenth of his reign, thus affecting to ignore entirely the government of the republic and of the empire.

The result of this reactionary policy was widespread dissatisfaction throughout France. Many began to desire the return of Napoleon, and the wish was perhaps what gave rise to the report which was spread about that he would come back with the spring violets.

In the month of March, 1815, as the commissioners of the various powers were sitting at Vienna rearranging the landmarks and boundaries obliterated by the French inundation, news was brought to them that Napoleon had escaped from Elba and was in France. At first the members of the Congress were incredulous, regarding the thing as a jest, and were with difficulty convinced of the truth of the report.

Taking advantage of the general dissatisfaction with the rule of the restored Bourbons, Napoleon had resolved upon a bold push for the recovery of his crown. Landing with a few followers at one of the southern ports of France, he aroused all the country with one of his stirring addresses, and then immediately pushed on towards Paris. Never was the changeable, impulsive character of the French people better illustrated than now ; and never was better exhibited the wonderful personal magnetism of Napoleon. His journey to the capital was one continuous ovation. One regiment after another, forgetting their recent oath of loyalty to the Bourbons, hastened to join his train. His old generals and soldiers embraced him with transports of joy. Louis XVIII., deserted by his army, was left helpless, and, as Napoleon approached the gates of Paris, fled from his throne.

Napoleon desired peace with the sovereigns of Europe ; but they did not think the peace of the continent could be maintained so long as he sat upon the French throne. For the seventh and last time the allies leagued their armies to crush the man of destiny. A million of men poured over the frontiers of France.

Hoping to overwhelm the armies of the allies by striking them one after another before they had time to unite, Napoleon moved swiftly into Belgium with an army of 130,000, in order to crush there the English and Prussians. He first fell in with and defeated the Prussian army under Blücher, and then faced the English at Waterloo (June 18, 1815).

The story of Waterloo need not be told, — how all day the French broke their columns in vain on the English squares ; how, at the critical moment at the close of the day, Blücher with a fresh force of 30,000 Prussians turned the tide of battle ; and how the famous Old Guard, that knew how to die but not how to surrender, made its last charge, and left its hitherto invincible squares upon the lost field.

A second time Napoleon was forced to abdicate, and a second time Louis XVIII. was lifted by the allies upon his unstable throne. Bonaparte desired to be allowed to retire to America, but his enemies believed that his presence there would not be consistent with the safety of Europe. Consequently he was banished to the island of St. Helena, in the South Atlantic, and there closely guarded by the British until his death, in 1821.

2. FRANCE SINCE THE SECOND RESTORATION (1815–   ).

Character of the Period. — The history of France since the second restoration of the Bourbons may be characterized briefly. It has been simply a continuation of the Revolution, of the struggle between democratic and monarchical tendencies. The aim of the Revolution was to abolish privileges and establish rights, — to give every man lot and part in shaping the government under which he lives. These republican ideas and principles have, on the whole, notwithstanding repeated reverses, gained ground ; for revolutions never move backward. There may be eddies and counter-currents in a river, but the steady and powerful sweep of the stream is ever onward towards the sea. Not otherwise is it with the great political and intellectual movements of history.

The Revolution of 1830. — Profiting by the lessons of The Hundred Days, Louis XVIII. ruled after the second restoration with reasonable heed to the results and changes effected by the Revolution. But upon the death of Louis in 1824 and the accession of Charles X., a reactionary policy was adopted. The new king seemed utterly incapable of profiting by the teachings of the Revolution. His blind, stubborn course gave rise to the saying, " A Bourbon learns nothing and forgets nothing." The result might have been foreseen. The people rose in revolt, and by one of those sudden movements for which Paris is so noted, the despot was driven into exile, and Louis Philippe, Duke of Orleans, was placed on the throne (1830).

A new constitution was now given to France, and as Louis Philippe had travelled about the world considerably, and had experienced various vicissitudes of fortune, — having at one time been obliged to support himself by teaching mathematics, — the people regarded him as one of themselves, and anticipated much from their " Citizen King " and their reformed constitution.

The French " July Revolution," as it is called, lighted the signal fires of liberty throughout Europe. In almost every country there were uprisings of the Liberals. Existing constitutions were so changed as to give the people a larger share in the government; and where there were no constitutions, original charters were granted. In some instances, indeed, the uprisings had no other result than that of rendering the despotic governments against which they were directed more cruel and tyrannical than they were before; yet, on the whole, a decided impulse was given to the cause of constitutional, republican government.[1]

Establishment of the Second Republic (1848). — The reign of Louis Philippe up to 1848 was very unquiet, yet was not marked by any disturbance of great importance. But during all this time the ideas of the Revolution were working among the people, and the republican party was constantly gaining strength. Finally, in 1848, some unpopular measures of the government caused an uprising similar to that of 1830. Louis Philippe, under the assumed name of Mr. Smith, fled into England. The Second Republic was now established. An election being ordered, Louis Napoleon Bonaparte, nephew of the great Napoleon, was chosen president of the new republic (Dec. 20, 1848).

[1] It was at this time that Belgium became an independent state; for upon the downfall of Napoleon Bonaparte in 1815, the Congress of Vienna had made the Low Countries into a single kingdom, and given the crown to a prince of the House of Orange. The Belgians now arose and declared themselves independent of Holland, adopted a liberal constitution, and elected Leopold I., of Saxe-Coburg, as their king (1831).

The truth of the first Napoleon's declaration, which we have before quoted, that a revolution in France is sure to be followed by a revolution throughout Europe, was now illustrated anew. Almost every throne upon the continent felt the shock of the French Revolution of 1848. The constitutions of many of the surrounding states again underwent great changes in the interest of the people and of liberty. " It is scarcely an exaggeration to say that during the month of March, 1848, not a single day passed without a constitution being granted somewhere." France had made another of her irresistible invasions of the states of Europe — " an invasion of ideas."

The Second Empire (1852–1870). — The life of the Second Republic spanned only three years. By almost exactly the same steps as those by which his uncle had mounted the French throne, Louis Napoleon now also ascended to the imperial dignity, crushing the republic as he rose.

Dissensions having arisen between the President and the Legislative Assembly, he suddenly dissolved that body, placed its leaders under arrest, and then appealed to the country to indorse what he had done. By a most extraordinary vote of 7,437,216 to 640,737 the nation approved of the President's *coup d'état*, and rewarded him for it by electing him President for ten years, which was virtually making him dictator. The next year he was made emperor, and took the title of Napoleon III. (1852).

The important political events of the reign of Napoleon III. were the Crimean War (1853–1856), the Austro-Sardinian War (1859), and the Franco-Prussian War (1870–1871). The first and second of these wars need not detain us at this time, as we shall speak of them hereafter in connection with Russian and Italian affairs.

The third war was with Prussia. The real causes of this war were French jealousy of the growing power of Prussia, and the Emperor's anxiety to strengthen his government in the affections of the French people by reviving the military glory of the reign of his great-uncle. The pretext upon which the war was actually declared was that Prussia was scheming to augment her influence by allowing a Prussian prince (Leopold of Hohenzollern) to become a candidate for the vacant throne of Spain (see p. 705).

The French armies invaded Germany, but were pushed back by the Prussians and their allies, who followed the retreating enemy across the frontier, defeated one large French army at Gravelotte (Aug. 18, 1870) and imprisoned it in Metz, captured the strong fortress of Sedan, — making a prisoner here of the emperor himself,[1] — and then advancing upon Paris, forced that city, after an investment of a few months, to capitulate (Jan. 28, 1871).

The terms of the treaty that followed were that France should surrender to Germany the greater portion of the Rhenish provinces of Alsace and Lorraine, pay an indemnity of 5,000,000,000 francs (about $1,000,000,000), and consent to the occupation of certain portions of French territory until the fine was paid.

The Red Republicans, or Communists, of Paris, indignant at the terms of the treaty, shut the gates of the city, and called the population to arms, declaring that the capital would never submit to see France thus dismembered and humiliated. A second reign of terror was now set up. The Tuileries, the Hotel de Ville, and many other public buildings were burned. The government at length succeeded in suppressing the Anarchists, and restoring order.

The Third Republic (1871). — The organization of the Third Republic was now completed. M. Thiers, the historian, was made its first president[2] (Aug. 31, 1871). Since the establishment of the republic, its enemies have been busy and vigilant, hoping to see democratic institutions discredited and the monarchy revived. But it is believed that each succeeding year of republican government in France strengthens the faith of the French people in their ability to govern themselves, and that the history of France as a monarchy is ended.

[1] After the war Louis Napoleon found an asylum in England (at Chiselhurst), where he died January 9, 1873.

[2] The successors of M. Thiers have been Marshal MacMahon (1873-1879), M. Grévy (1879-1887), and M. Carnot (1887).

CHAPTER LX.

RUSSIA SINCE THE CONGRESS OF VIENNA.

Alexander I. and the Holy Alliance. — Upon the downfall of Napoleon, Alexander I. (1801–1825) of Russia organized the celebrated union known as the *Holy Alliance*. This was a league embracing as its chief members Russia, Austria, and Prussia, the ostensible object of which was the maintenance of religion, peace, and order in Europe, and the reduction to practice in politics of the maxims of Christ. The several sovereigns entering into the union promised to be fathers to their people, to rule in love and with reference solely to the promotion of the welfare of their subjects, and to help one another as brothers to maintain just government and prevent wrong.

All this had a very millennial look. But the " Holy Alliance " very soon became practically a league for the maintenance of absolute principles of government, in opposition to the liberal tendencies of the age. Under the pretext of maintaining religion, justice, and order, the sovereigns of the union acted in concert to suppress every aspiration among their subjects for political liberty. Yet, when Alexander founded the alliance, he meant all that he said. But conspiracies among his own subjects, and popular uprisings throughout Europe, all tended to create in him a revulsion of feeling. From an ardent apostle of liberal ideas, such as he was during all the earlier part of his reign, he was transformed into a violent absolutist, and spent all his later years in aiding the despotic rulers of Spain, Italy, and Germany to crush every uprising among their subjects for political freedom.

This reactionary policy of Alexander caused bitter disappointment among the Liberals in Russia, the number of whom was large, for the Russian armies that helped to crush Napoleon came back from the West with many new and liberal ideas awakened by what they had seen and heard and experienced.

The Russo-Turkish War of 1828-1829. — In 1825 Alexander I. was succeeded by his brother Nicholas I. (1825-1855), "a terrible incarnation of autocracy." He carried out the later policy of his predecessor, and strove to shut out from his empire all the liberalizing influences of Western Europe.

In 1828, taking advantage of the embarrassment of the Sultan through a stubborn insurrection in Greece,[1] Nicholas declared war against the Ottoman Porte. The Balkans were quickly passed, and the victorious armies of the Czar were in full march upon Constantinople, when their advance was checked by the jealous interference of England and Austria, through whose mediation the war was brought to a close by the Peace of Adrianople (1829). Nicholas restored all his conquests in Europe, but held some provinces in Asia which gave him control of the eastern shore of the Euxine. Greece was liberated, and Servia became virtually independent of the Sultan. Thus the result of the contest was greatly to diminish the strength and influence of Turkey, and correspondingly to increase the power and prestige of Russia.

Revolution in Poland (1830-1832). — The Congress of Vienna (1815) re-established Poland as a constitutional kingdom dependent upon Russia. But the rule of the Czar over the Poles was tyrannical, and they were impatient of an opportunity to throw off the Russian yoke. The revolutionary movements of the year 1830 sent a wave of hope through Poland; the people arose and drove out the Russian garrisons. But the armies of the Czar quickly poured over the frontiers of the revolted state, and before

---

[1] This was the struggle known as the "War of Grecian Independence." It was characterized by the most frightful barbarities on the part of the Turks. Lord Byron enlisted on the side of the Greeks. The result of the war was the freeing of Greece from Turkish rule. England, France, and Russia became the guardians of the little state, the crown of which was given to Prince Otto of Bavaria (Otto I., 1832-1862).

.the close of the year 1831 the Polish patriots were once more under the foot of their Russian master.

It was a hard fate that awaited the unhappy nation. Their constitution was taken away, and Poland was made a province of the Russian empire (1832). Multitudes were banished to Siberia, while thousands more expatriated themselves, seeking an asylum in England, America, and other countries. Of all the peoples that rose for freedom in 1830 none suffered so cruel and complete an extinguishment of their hopes as did the patriot Poles.[1]

The Crimean War (1853–1856). — A celebrated phrase applied to the Ottoman Porte by the Czar Nicholas casts a good deal of light upon the circumstances that led to the Crimean War. "We have on our hands," said the Czar, "a sick man — a very sick man; I tell you frankly it would be a great misfortune if he should give us the slip some of these days, especially if it happened before all the necessary arrangements were made."

Nicholas had cultivated friendly relations with the English government, and he now proposed that England and Russia, as the parties most directly interested, should divide the estate of the "sick man." England was to be allowed to take Egypt and Crete, while the Turkish provinces in Europe were to be taken under the protection of the Czar, which meant of course the complete absorption, in due time, of all Southeastern Europe into the Russian empire.

A pretence for hastening the dissolution of the sick man was not long wanting. A quarrel between the Greek and Latin Christians at Jerusalem about the holy places was made the ground by Nicholas for demanding of the Sultan the admission and recognition of a Russian protectorate over all Greek Christians in the Ottoman dominions. The demand was rejected, and Nicholas prepared for war.

The Sultan appealed to the Western powers for help. England and France responded to the appeal, and later Sardinia joined her

[1] For Russia's part in the affairs of the revolutionary years 1848–49, see p. 702.

forces to theirs. England, rejecting the Czar's proposal of a division of the dying man's estate, fought to prevent Russia from getting through the Bosporus to the Mediterranean, and thus endangering her route to her Eastern possessions. The French emperor fought to avenge Moscow, and to render his new imperial throne attractive to his people by surrounding it with the glamour of successful war. Sardinia was led to join England and France through the policy of the far-sighted Cavour, who would thus have the Sardinians win the gratitude of these powers, so that in the next conflict with Austria the Italian patriots might have some strong friends to help them.

The main interest of the struggle centred about Sebastopol, in the Crimea, Russia's great naval and military depot, and the key to the Euxine. Around this strongly fortified place were finally gathered 175,000 soldiers of the allies. The siege, which lasted eleven months, was one of the most memorable and destructive in history. The Russian engineer Todleben earned a great fame through his masterly defence of the works. The English " Light Brigade " earned immortality in their memorable charge at Balaklava. The French troops, through their dashing bravery, brought great fame to the emperor who had sent them to gather glory for his throne.

The Russians were at length forced to evacuate the place. They left it, however, a "second Moscow." The war was now soon brought to an end by the Treaty of Paris (1856). Every provision of the treaty had in view the maintenance of the integrity of the empire of the Sultan, and the restraining of the ambition of the Czar. Russia was given back Sebastopol, but was required to give up some territory at the mouth of the Danube, whereby her frontier was pushed back from that river ; to abandon all claims to a protectorate over any of the subjects of the Porte ; to agree not to raise any more fortresses on the Euxine nor keep upon that sea any armed ships, save what might be needed for police service. The Christian population of the Turkish dominions were placed under the guardianship of the great powers, who were to see that the Sublime Porte fulfilled its promise of granting perfect civil and religious equality and protection to all its subjects.

Emancipation of the Serfs (1858–1863). — Alexander II. (1855–1881), who came to the Russian throne in the midst of the Crimean War, abandoned the narrow and intolerant system of his predecessor Nicholas, and reverting as it were to the policy of Peter the Great, labored for popular reform, and for the introduction into his dominions of the ideas and civilization of Western Europe. The reform which will ever give his name a place in the list of those rulers who have conferred singular benefits upon their subjects, was the emancipation, by a series of imperial edicts, of the Russian serfs, who made up more than 45,000,000 of the population of the empire. More than half of these serfs belonged to the Crown, and were known as Crown peasants.

The Crown serfs were only *nominal* bondsmen, their servitude consisting in scarcely more than the payment of a light rent. The serfs of individual proprietors, however, might be designated as semi-slaves. Thus, their owners could flog them in case of disobedience, but could not sell them individually as slaves are sold ; yet when a proprietor sold his estate, the whole community of serfs living upon it passed with it to the purchaser.

Besides the emancipation measure, Alexander's name is associated with other reforms, the earlier part of his reign especially being characterized by a very liberal spirit. This liberal policy was followed until the revolt of the Poles in 1863, when Alexander was led to adopt a more reactionary policy, a policy which persistently pursued has yielded bitter fruit in Nihilism.

The Russo-Turkish War of 1877–1878. — Anxiously as the Treaty of Paris had provided for the permanent settlement of the Eastern Question, barely twenty-two years had passed before it was again up before Europe, and Russia and Turkey were again in arms. The Sultan could not or would not give to his Christian subjects that equal protection of the laws which he had solemnly promised should be given. The Moslem hatred of the Christians was constantly leading to disturbance and outrage. In 1860 there

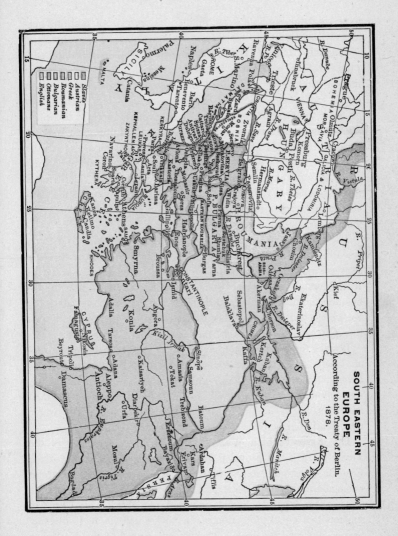

SOUTH EASTERN
EUROPE.
According to the Treaty of Berlin.
1878.

Slaves
Austrian
Greek
Roumanian
Bulgarian
Ottomans
English

was a great massacre of Syrian Christians by the Druses and Turks, and in 1876 occurred in Bulgaria the so-called "Bulgarian atrocities," massacres of Christian men, women, and children, more revolting perhaps than any others of which history tells. The greatest indignation was kindled throughout Europe. The Russian armies were set in motion (1877). Kars in Asia Minor and

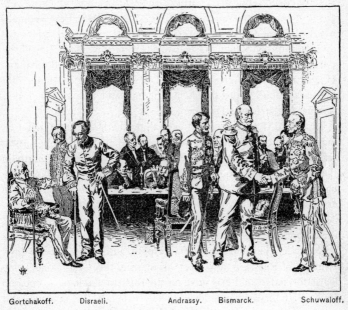

| Gortchakoff. | Disraeli. | | Andrassy. | Bismarck. | | Schuwaloff. |

THE CONGRESS OF BERLIN.
(After Anton von Werner, Prussian Court Painter.)

Plevna in European Turkey fell into the hands of the Russians, and the armies of the Czar were once more in full march upon Constantinople, with the prospect of soon ending forever Turkish rule on European soil, when England, as in 1829, interfered, and by the movements of her iron-clads in the Bosporus again arrested the triumphant march of the Russians.

The Treaty of Berlin (1878) adjusted once more the disorganized affairs of the Sublime Porte, and bolstered as well as was possible the "sick man." But he lost a good part of his estate. Out of those provinces of his dominions in Europe in which the Christian population was most numerous, there was created a group of wholly independent or half-independent states. The absolute independence of Roumania, Servia, and Montenegro was formally acknowledged ; Bulgaria, north of the Balkans, was to enjoy self-government, but was to pay a tribute to the Porte ; East Roumelia was to have a Christian governor, but was to remain under the dominion of the Sultan. The Balkans were thus made the northern boundary of the Turkish empire in Europe. Bosnia and Herzegovina were given to the Austro-Hungarian monarchy. Russia acquired some places in Armenia, and also received Bessarabia on the Lower Danube.

In a word, Russia regained everything she had lost in the Crimean struggle, while Turkey was shorn of half her European possessions. There were left in Europe under the direct authority of the Sultan barely 5,000,000 subjects, of which number about one-half are Christians. England alone is responsible for the work of emancipation not having been made complete.

Nihilism and the Exile System. — Russian Nihilism is a smothered French Revolution. It is the form which Liberalism has taken under the repressions of a despotic autocracy ; for the government of Russia is a perfect absolutism, the Czar alone being legislator, judge, and executive for the Russian nation of 85,000,000 souls. He makes laws, levies taxes, expends the revenue, and condemns his subjects to exile or death, according to his own will, without let or hindrance. The terrible character of the repressive measures of the government is revealed by the fact that during the years 1879 and 1880 sixty thousand persons were, *without trial,* sent into exile in Siberia.[1]

It is a principle of the extreme Nihilists, that assassination is a righteous means of reform. Within the last few years many at-

---

[1] On the Exile System of Russia read the excellent series of articles by George Kennan in *The Century Magazine* for 1888-9.

tempts have been made upon the life of the reigning Czar. On March 13, 1881, Alexander II. was killed by means of a bomb filled with dynamite.

The son of the murdered Czar who now came to the throne as Alexander III., immediately instituted a still more sternly repressive system than that pursued by his father, whom he seemed to regard as the victim of the over-liberal policy of the earlier years of his reign. It appears to be his determination to close his empire against the entrance of all liberal or progressive ideas, political, religious, and scientific, of Western Europe. A rigid censorship of the press is being maintained (1889), and the writings of such authors as Huxley, Spencer, Agassiz, Lyell, and Adam Smith, are forbidden circulation.

There can be but one outcome to this contest between the " Autocrat of all the Russias " and his subjects. Either through wise concessions on the part of its rulers, or through the throes of a terrible revolution, like that of 1789 in France, the Russian empire will sooner or later come to possess a constitutional representative government. The Czar of Russia is simply fighting the hopeless battle that has been fought and lost by the despotic sovereigns of every other European country — a battle which has the same invariable issue, the triumph of liberal principles and the admission of the people to a participation in the government.

CHAPTER LXI.

GERMAN FREEDOM AND UNITY.

Formation of the German Confederation (1815). — The German states, thirty-nine in number, were reorganized by the Congress of Vienna as a Confederation, with the emperor of Austria President of the league. A Diet formed of representatives of the several states was to settle all questions of dispute between the members of the Confederation, and determine matters of general concern. In all affairs concerning itself alone, each state was to retain its independence. It might carry on war with foreign states, or enter into alliance with them, but it must do nothing to harm any member of the Confederation. The articles of union, in a spirit of concession to the growing sentiment of the times, provided that all sects of Christians should enjoy equal toleration, and that every state should establish a constitutional form of government.

Under this scheme of union Germany was to rest half a century — until 1866. Though Austria was nominally head of the Confederation, Prussia was actually the most powerful member of the league.

The Uprisings of 1830 : First Step towards Freedom. — For a long time previous to the French Revolution there had been gradually forming among the German people a double sentiment — a longing for freedom and for unity. It was the influence of the rising patriotic party that had secured the provision in the act of confederation which required that all the princes of the union should give their states a representative form of government. But the faces of these rulers, like those of the restored Bourbons in France, were turned towards the past. They opposed all changes that should give the people any part in the government, and clung to the old order of things.

We have seen what was the consequence of the reactionary policy of the Bourbons in France, — how in 1830 the people arose, drove out Charles X., and set upon the throne the "Citizen King," Louis Philippe. Events ran exactly the same course in Germany. The princes refused or neglected to carry out in good faith that article of the act of confederation which provided for representative governments in all the German states. The natural result was widespread discontent among the people. Consequently, when the French Revolution of 1830 occurred, a sympathetic thrill shot through Germany, and in places the popular party made threatening demonstrations against their tyrannical rulers. The princes of several of the smaller states were forced to give to their peoples the liberal constitutions that were demanded. Thus a little was gained for freedom, though after the flutter of the revolutionary year the princes again took up their retrograde policy, and did all in their power to check the popular movement and keep governmental matters out of the hands of the people.

The Customs Union: First Step towards Unity. — Just about this time the first step was taken towards the real union of the German states through the formation of what is known as the *Customs Union*. This was a sort of commercial treaty binding those states that became parties to it, and eventually all the states save Austria acceded to the arrangement, to adopt among themselves the policy of free trade ; that is, there were to be no duties levied on goods passing from one state of the Union to another belonging to it. The greatest good resulting from the Union was, that it taught the people to think of a more perfect national union. And as Prussia was a prominent promoter and the centre of the trade confederation, it accustomed the Germans to look to her as their head and chief.

Uprising of 1848: a Second Step towards Freedom. — The history of Germany from the uprising of 1830 to that of 1848 may be summarized by saying that during all these years the people were steadily growing more and more earnest in their demands for liberal forms of government, while the princes, strangely blind to the spirit and tendency of the times, were stubbornly refusing all concessions that should take from themselves any of their power as absolute rulers.   In some instances the constitutions already granted were annulled, or their articles were disregarded.

Finally, in 1848, news flew across the Rhine of the uprising in France against the reactionary government of Louis Philippe, and the establishment by the French people of a new republic (see p. 689).   The intelligence kindled a flame of excitement throughout Germany.   The liberal party everywhere arose and demanded constitutional government.

Almost all of the princes of the minor states yielded to the popular clamor, and straightway adopted the liberal measures and instituted the reforms demanded.   In Austria and Prussia, however, the popular party carried their point only after demonstrations that issued in bloodshed.   Prince Metternich, the celebrated prime minister of the Emperor of Austria, was forced to flee the country, because he had opposed so obstinately all the demands of the Liberals.

The Revolution of 1848 thus effected much for the cause of liberal government in Germany.   The movements of that revolutionary year brought into the hands of the people much more power than they had ever before exercised.

Hungary: Kossuth. — Meanwhile the Austrian emperor was having serious trouble with his Hungarian subjects.   Led by the distinguished orator Louis Kossuth, they had revolted, and declared their independence.   A memorable struggle now followed (1848–1849), in which the patriotic Hungarians made a noble fight for freedom, but were at last overpowered and crushed by the combined Austrian and Russian armies.   Hungary was made a second Poland (see p. 693).

Rivalry between Austria and Prussia. — While the attention of Austria was directed to the suppression of the Hungarian rebels, Prussia proposed a plan for the unification of Germany, with herself as the head of the body, Austria being excluded from the confederation.   Several of the states joined Prussia in this move, and an alliance called the "German Union" was formed. Austria watched with the greatest concern this bold move of her rival for leadership in German affairs, a move whereby she was to be pushed aside entirely, and just as soon as the Hungarian trouble was composed, she made a counter-move to that of Prussia, by forming a confederation of all those states which she could persuade to accept her leadership.

The state of Germany at this moment, divided between the allies of Austria and those of Prussia, may be likened to the condition of Greece at the outbreak of the Peloponnesian War, when the Hellenic states had grouped themselves, according to their sympathies, about Athens and Sparta. It does not require a second Pericles to see war lowering in the horizon.

The Seven Weeks' War between Austria and Prussia (1866). — The inevitable war which was to decide whether Austria or Prussia should be leader in German affairs came on apace. In the year 1861, Frederick William IV. of Prussia died, and his brother, already an old man of sixty, yet destined to be for more than a score of years the central figure in the movement for German unity, came to the Prussian throne as William I. (1861–1888). He soon called to his side the now distinguished Otto von Bismarck as his prime minister, a man of wonderful energy and decision, whose policies have shaped German affairs for a quarter of a century. He saw clearly enough how the vexed question between Austria and Prussia was to be settled — "by blood and iron." His appearance at the head of Prussian affairs marks an epoch in history. He was in disposition a conservative and despot, and the liberal party distrusted and hated him.

Early in 1866 the war opened, the occasion of it being a dispute in regard to some petty Danish provinces (Schleswig and Holstein). Almost all of the lesser states grouped themselves about Austria. Prussia, however, found a ready ally in Italy (see p. 713), which served to divert a part of the Austrian forces. Yet it seemed an unequal contest, the population of Prussia at this time not being more than one-third (19,000,000) that of the states arrayed against her. But Bismarck had been preparing Prussia for the struggle which he had long foreseen, and now the little kingdom, with the best disciplined army in the world, headed by the great commander Von Moltke, was to astonish the world by a repetition of her achievements under the inspiration of Frederick the Great.

The Prussian armies, numbering more than a quarter of a million of men, began to move about the middle of June. Battle followed battle in rapid succession. Almost every encounter proved a victory for the Prussians. On the third of July was fought the great battle of Sadowa, in Bohemia. It was Austria's Waterloo. The emperor was forced to sue for peace, and on the twenty-third day of August the Peace of Prague was signed.

The long debate between Austria and Prussia was over. By the terms of the treaty Austria was shut out from participation in German affairs. Prussia was now without a rival in Germany.

Establishment of the North-German Union (1867). — Now quickly followed the reorganization of the northern states of Germany into what was called the North-German Union, under the leadership of Prussia. Prussia was to have command of the entire military force of the several states composing the league, the Prussian king being President of the Union. A constitution was adopted which provided that the affairs of the confederation should be managed by a Diet, the members of which were to be chosen by the different states.

Thus was a long step taken towards German unity. Bismarck's policy of "blood and iron," though seemingly rough and brutal, now promised to prove a cure indeed for all of Germany's troubles. Though so much had been effected, there was still remaining much to be desired. The states to the south of the Main — Baden, Bavaria, and Würtemberg — were yet wanting to complete the unification of the Fatherland. Many patriots both north and south of the dividing line earnestly desired the perfect union of North and South. But the Catholics of the southern states were bitterly opposed to Prussia's being exalted to the chief place in Germany,

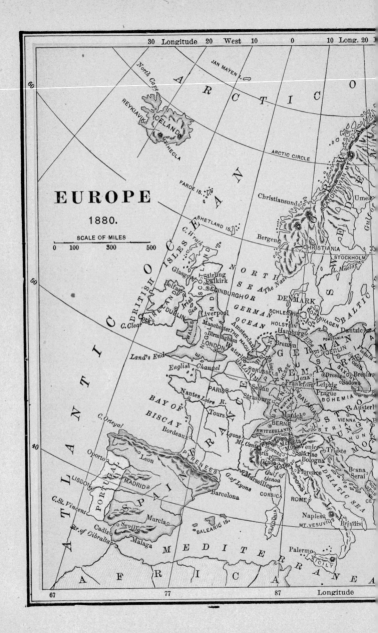

EUROPE

1880.

SCALE OF MILES

0   100   300   500

OCEAN

North Cape

Varanger fiord

Kola

Tornea

LAPLAND

KOLGUEV I.

VIAGAT'S I.

Archangel

Petchora R.

Obi R. B

URAL

Tobolsk

Dwina R.

L. Onega

Vlatka

Kunga

MOUNTAINS

SIBERIA

G. of Finland

Cronstadt

ST. PETERSBURG

Pskov

Moscow

RUSSIA

Orsk

50

gsburg

Minsk

Bolkhev

Saratov

R. Volga

Orenburg

Grodno

Koursk

arsaw

Kharkov

R. Dnieper

R. Don

Astrakhan

CASPIAN SEA

N. Alexandrovsk

Odessa

Sea of Azov

Stavropol

Petrovsk

Krasnovodsk

40

Sebastopol

CAUCASUS MTS.

TRANSCAUCASIA

BLACK SEA

GALICIA

TRANSYLVANIA

ROUMANIA

BULGARIA

BALKAN MTS.

E. ROUMELIA

Adrianople

Constantinople

Sinope

Kars

ASIA MINOR

ARMENIA

PERSIA

Hamadan

TURKEY

Smyrna

Diarbekir

AL JEZIRAH

GREECE

Athens

Sparta

RHODES

SEA

MESOPOTAMIA

Bagdad

because she was Protestant, while many of the democratic party were loth to see Germany reconstructed under the supremacy of Prussia on account of the repressive and despotic character of her government. But the fervid enthusiasm awakened by another successful war serves to weld the states of both North and South into a firm and close union, and complete the work of Germany's unification.

The Franco-Prussian War (1870–1871). — It will be recalled with what jealousy France viewed the rise to power of the House of Hohenzollern (see p. 691). All of her old bitter hostility to the House of Austria seems to have been transferred to her successful rival in the North. So when in 1870 the vacant throne of Spain was offered to Leopold, a member of the Hohenzollern family, the Emperor Napoleon III. affected to see in this a scheme on the part of the House of Hohenzollern to unite the interests of Prussia and of Spain, just as Austria and Spain were united, with such disastrous consequences to the peace of Europe, under the princes of the House of Hapsburg. Even after Leopold, to avoid displeasing France, had declined the proffered crown, the Emperor Napoleon demanded of King William assurance that no member of the House of Hohenzollern should ever become a candidate for the Spanish throne. The demand was rudely made, was refused, and the two nations rushed together in a struggle which was destined to prove terribly disastrous to France, and memorable to Germany for the glory and unity it won for her.

The important thing for us to notice here is the enthusiasm that the war awakened not only throughout the states of the North-German Confederation, but among the states of the South as well, which placed their armies at the disposal of King William. The cause was looked upon as a national one, and a patriotic fervor stirred the hearts of all Germans alike.

Establishment of the New German Empire (1871). — The astonishing successes of the German armies on French soil (see p. 691) created among Germans everywhere such patriotic pride in the Fatherland, that all the obstacles which had hitherto prevented anything more than a partial union of the members of the Germanic body were now swept out of the way by an irresistible tide of national sentiment. While the siege of Paris was progressing, commissioners were sent by the southern states to Versailles, the headquarters of King William, to represent to him that they

STATUE OF EMPEROR WILLIAM I., IN BERLIN.

were ready and anxious to enter the North-German Union. Thus in rapid succession Baden, Bavaria, and Würtemberg were received into the Confederation, the name of which was now changed to that of the German Confederation.

Scarcely was this accomplished, when, upon the suggestion of the king of Bavaria, King William, who now bore the title of *President* of the Confederation, was given the title of *German Emperor*, which honor was to be hereditary in his family. On the 18th of January, 1871, within the Palace of Versailles, — the siege of Paris being still in progress, — amidst indescribable enthusiasm, the Imperial dignity was formally conferred upon King William, and Germany became a constitutional Empire.

Thus amidst the throes of war the free German *nation* was born. The German people, after long centuries of division and servitude, had at last found Freedom and Unity.

CHAPTER LXII.

LIBERATION AND UNIFICATION OF ITALY.

Italy at the Downfall of Napoleon. — The Italian people, as being the most dangerously infected with the ideas of the Revolution, were, by the reactionary Congress of Vienna, condemned to the most strict and ignominious slavery. The former commonwealths were forbidden to restore their ancient institutions, while the petty principalities were handed over in almost every case to the tyrants or the heirs of the tyrants who had ruled them before the Revolution. Austria appropriated Venetia and Lombardy, and from Northern Italy assumed to direct the affairs of the whole peninsula. Tuscany, Modena, Parma, and Piacenza were given to princes of the House of Hapsburg. Naples was restored to its old Bourbon rulers. The Pope and Victor Emmanuel I., king of Sardinia, were the only native rulers.

"Italy was divided on the map, but she had made up her mind to be one." The Revolution had sown the seeds of Liberty, and time only was needed for their maturing. The Cisalpine, the Ligurian, the Parthenopæan, the Tiberine republics (see pp. 668, 670), short-lived though they were, had awakened in the people an aspiration for self-government; while Napoleon's kingdom of Italy (see p. 676, n.), though equally delusive, had nevertheless inspired thousands of Italian patriots with the sentiment of national unity. Thus the French Revolution, disappointing as seemed its issue, really imparted to Italy her first impulse in the direction of freedom and of national organization.

Arbitrary Rule of the Restored Princes. — The setting up of the overturned thrones meant, of course, the re-instating of the old tyrannies. The restored despots came back with an implacable hatred of everything French. They swept away all French institutions that were supposed to tend in the least to Liberalism. At Rome even vaccination and street-lamps, French innovations, were abolished. In Sardinia, nothing that bore the French stamp, nothing that had been set up by French hands, was allowed to remain. Even the French furniture in the royal palace at Turin was thrown out of the windows, and the French plants in the royal gardens were pulled up root and branch.

The Carbonari: Uprising of 1820–1821. — The natural results of the arbitrary rule and retrogressive policy of the restored princes was deep and widespread discontent. The French Revolution, as we have said, had sown broadcast in Italy the seeds of liberty, and their growth could not be checked by the repressions of tyranny. An old secret organization, the members of which were known as the *Carbonari* (charcoal-burners), formed the nucleus about which gathered the elements of disaffection.

In 1820, incited by a revolution in Spain, the *Carbonari* raised an insurrection in Naples, and forced King Ferdinand, who was ruler of both Naples and Sicily, now united under the name of the Kingdom of the Two Sicilies, to grant his Neapolitan subjects what was known as the Spanish Constitution of 1812. But Prince Metternich (see p. 702), who had been watching the doings of the Liberal party in Naples, interfered to mar their plans. He reasoned that Lombardy and Venetia could be kept free from the contagion of Liberalism only by the stamping out of the infection wherever else in Italy it might show itself. Hence 60,000 Austrian troops were sent to crush the revolutionists. Ferdinand was re-instated in his former absolute authority, and everything was put back on the old footing.

Meanwhile a similar revolution was running its course in Piedmont. King Victor Emmanuel I., rather than yield to the demands of his people for a constitutional government, gave up his crown, and was succeeded by his brother Charles Felix, who, by threatening to call to his aid the Austrian army, compelled his subjects to cease their clamor about kings ruling, not by the grace of God, but by the will of the people.

The Revolution of 1830–1831. — For just ten years all Italy lay in sullen vassalage to Austria.   Then the revolutionary years of 1830–31 witnessed a repetition of the scenes of 1820–21.   The revolution in France which placed Louis Philippe upon the French throne (see p. 688) sent a tremor of excitement and hope through all Italy.   The centre of the revolution was the Papal States.   But the presence of Austrian troops, who, " true to their old principle of hurrying with their extinguishers to any spot in Italy where a crater opened," had poured into Central Italy, resulted in the speedy quenching of the flames of the insurrection.

The Three Parties: Plans for National Organization. — Twice now had Austrian armies crushed the aspirations of the Italians after national unity and freedom.   Italian hatred of these foreign intermeddlers who were causing them to miss their destiny, grew ever more intense, and " death to the Germans " became the watch-cry that united all the peoples of the peninsula.

But while united in their deadly hatred of the Austrians, the Italians were divided in their views respecting the best plan for national organization.   One party, known as "Young Italy," founded and inspired by the patriot Joseph Mazzini, wanted a republic ; another party wanted a confederation of the various states, with the Pope as chief; while still a third wished to see Italy a constitutional monarchy, with the king of Sardinia at its head.

The Revolution of 1848–1849. — After the suppression of the uprising of 1830, until the approach of the momentous year of 1848, Italy lay restless under the heel of her oppressor.   The republican movements throughout the continent of Europe which characterized that year of revolutions, inspired the Italian patriots to make another attempt to achieve independence and nationality. Everywhere throughout the peninsula they rose against their despotic rulers, and forced them to grant constitutions and institute reforms.   But through the intervention of the Austrians and the French [1] the third Italian revolution was thwarted.   By the autumn

---

[1] This interference by the French in Italian affairs was instigated by their jealousy of Austria, and by the anxious desire of Louis Napoleon to win the good-will of the Catholic clergy in France.

of the year 1849 the Liberals were everywhere crushed, their leaders executed, imprisoned, or driven into exile, and the dream of Italy's unity and freedom dispelled by the hard present fact of renewed tyranny and foreign domination.

Much, however, had been gained. The patriotic party had had revealed to itself its strength, and at the same time the necessity of united action, — of the adoption of a single policy. Henceforth the Republicans and Federalists were more inclined to give up as impracticable their plans of national organization, and with the Constitutionalists to look upon the kingdom of Sardinia as the only possible basis and nucleus of a free and united Italy.

Victor Emmanuel II., Count Cavour, and Garibaldi. — Sardinia was a state which had gradually grown into power in the northwest corner of the peninsula. The throne was at this time held by Victor Emmanuel II. (1849–1878). To him it was that the hopes of the Italian patriots now turned. Nor were these hopes to be disappointed. Victor Emmanuel was the destined liberator of Italy, or perhaps it would be more correct to say that his was the name in which the achievement was to be effected by the wise policy of his great minister Count Cavour, and the reckless daring of the hero Garibaldi.

Count Cavour was a man of large hopes and large plans. His single aim and purpose was the independence and unification of Italy. He was the genius of Italian liberty. Garibaldi, "the hero of the red shirt," was the knight-errant of Italian independence. Though yet barely past middle life, he had led a career singularly crowded with varied experiences and romantic adventures. Because of his violent republicanism, he had already been twice exiled from Italy.

The Austro-Sardinian War (1859–1860). — The hour for striking another blow for the freedom of Italy had now arrived. In 1859 Count Cavour, in the pursuance of his national policy for Italy, having first made a secret arrangement with the French emperor, gave Austria to understand that unless she granted Lombardy and Venetia free government and ceased to interfere in the affairs of the rest of Italy, Sardinia would declare war against her. Of course the Austrian government refused to accede to the demand, and almost immediately war followed. The French emperor, actuated probably less by gratitude for the aid of the Sardinian contingent in the Crimean struggle (see p. 726) than by jealousy of Austria and the promise of Savoy and Nice in case of a successful issue of the war, supported the Sardinians with the armies of France. The two great victories of Magenta and Solferino seemed to promise to the allies a triumphant march to the Adriatic. But just now the threatening attitude of Prussia and other German states, in connection with other considerations, led Napoleon to enter upon negotiations of peace with the Austrian emperor at Villafranca.

The outcome was that Austria retained Venice, but gave up to Sardinia the larger part of Lombardy. The Sardinians were bitterly disappointed that they did not get Venetia, and loudly accused the French emperor of having betrayed their cause, since at the outset he had promised them that he would free Italy from the mountains to the sea. But Sardinia found compensation for Venice in the accession of Tuscany, Modena, Parma, and Romagna, the peoples of which states, having discarded their old rulers, besought Victor Emmanuel to permit them to unite themselves to his kingdom. Thus, as the result of the war, the king of Sardinia had added to his subjects a population of 9,000,000. One long step was taken in the way of Italian unity and freedom.

Sicily and Naples added to Victor Emmanuel's Kingdom (1860). — The romantic and adventurous daring of the hero Garibaldi now added Sicily and Naples to the possessions of Victor Emmanuel, and changed the kingdom of Sardinia into the kingdom of Italy.

The king of Naples and Sicily, Francis II., was by nature a despot. In 1860 his subjects rose in revolt. Victor Emmanuel and his minister Cavour were in sympathy with the movement, yet dared not send the insurgents aid through fear of arousing the jealousy of Austria and of France. But Garibaldi, untrammelled by any such considerations, having gathered a band of a thousand or more volunteers, set sail from Genoa for Sicily, where upon landing he assumed the title of Dictator of Sicily for Victor Emmanuel, King of Italy, and quickly drove the troops of King Francis out of the island. Then crossing to the mainland, he marched triumphantly to Naples, whose inhabitants hailed him tumultuously as their Deliverer.

The Neapolitans and Sicilians now voted almost unanimously for annexation to the Sardinian kingdom. The hero Garibaldi, having first met and hailed his Sovereign " King of Italy," surrendered his dictatorship. He had earned the lasting gratitude of his country.

Thus was another great step taken in the unification of Italy. Nine millions more of Italians had become the subjects of Victor Emmanuel. There was now wanting to the complete union of Italy only Venetia and the Papal territories.

Venetia added to the Kingdom (1866). — The Seven Weeks' War which broke out between Prussia and Austria in 1866 afforded the Italian patriots the opportunity for which they were watching to make Venetia a part of the kingdom of Italy. Victor Emmanuel formed an alliance with the king of Prussia, one of the conditions of which was that no peace should be made with Austria until she had surrendered Venetia to Italy. The speedy issue of the war added the coveted territory to the dominions of Victor Emmanuel. Rome alone was now lacking to the complete unification of Italy.

Rome becomes the Capital (1870). — After the liberation of Naples and Sicily the city of Turin, the old capital of the Sardinian kingdom, was made the capital of the new kingdom of Italy. In 1865 the seat of government was transferred to Florence. But the Italians looked forward to the time when Rome, the ancient mistress of the peninsula and of the world, should be their capital. The power of the Pope, however, was upheld by the French, and this made it impossible for the Italians to have their will in this matter without a conflict with France.

But events soon gave the coveted capital to the Italian government. In 1870 came the sharp, quick war between France and

Prussia, and the French troops at Rome were hastily summoned home. Upon the overthrow of the French Monarchy and the establishment of the Republic, Victor Emmanuel was informed that France would no longer sustain the Papal power. The Italian government at once gave notice to the Pope that Rome would henceforth be considered a portion of the kingdom of Italy, and forthwith an Italian army entered the city, which by a vote of 133,681 to 1,507 joined itself to the Italian nation. The family was now complete. Rome was the capital of a free and united Italy. July 2, 1871, Victor Emmanuel[1] himself entered the city and took up his residence there.

End of the Temporal Power of the Pope. — Through the extension of the authority of the Italian government over the Papal states, the Pope was despoiled of the last vestige of that temporal power wherewith Pepin and Charlemagne had invested the Bishops of Rome more than a thousand years before (see p. 404). The Papal troops were disbanded, but the Pope, Pius IX., still retained all his spiritual authority, the Vatican with its 11,000 chambers being reserved to him as a place of residence. Just a few months before the loss of his temporal sovereignty a great Ecumenical Council of the Roman Catholic Church had proclaimed the doctrine of Papal Infallibility, which declares decrees of the Pope "on questions of faith and morals" to be infallible.

Conclusion. — Although there has been much antagonism between the Vatican and the Quirinal, that is, between the Pope and the Italian government, still reform and progress have marked Italian affairs since the events of 1870. A public system of education has been established; brigandage has been suppressed; agriculture has been encouraged; while the naval and military resources of the peninsula have been developed to such an extent that Italy, so recently the prey of foreign sovereigns, of petty native tyrants, and of adventurers, is now justly regarded as one of the great powers of Europe.

---

[1] In the early part of the year 1878 Victor Emmanuel died, and his son came to the throne, with the title of Humbert I., the second king of Italy.

QUEEN VICTORIA AS A YOUNG WOMAN.

CHAPTER LXIII.

ENGLAND SINCE THE CONGRESS OF VIENNA.

The Three Chief Matters. — English history since the close of the Napoleonic wars embraces a multitude of events. A short chapter covering the entire period will possess no instructive value unless it reduces the heterogeneous mass of facts to some sort of unity by placing events in relation with their causes, and thus showing how they are connected with a few broad national movements or tendencies. Studying the period in this way, we shall find that very many of its leading events may be summed up under the three following heads: 1. Progress towards democracy; 2. Expansion of the principle of religious equality; 3. Growth of the British Empire in the East.

1. PROGRESS TOWARDS DEMOCRACY.

Effects of the French Revolution upon Liberalism in England. — The French Revolution at first gave a fresh impulse to liberal tendencies in England. The English Liberals watched the course of the French Republicans with the deepest interest and sympathy. It will be recalled how the statesman Fox rejoiced at the fall of the Bastile, and what auguries of hope he saw in the event (see p. 652). The young writers Coleridge, Wordsworth, and Southey were all in sympathy with democratic sentiments, and inspired with a generous enthusiasm for political liberty and equality. But the wild excesses of the French Levellers terrified the English Liberals. There was a sudden revulsion of feeling. Liberal sentiments were denounced as dangerous and revolutionary.

But in a few years after the downfall of Napoleon, the terrors of the French Revolution were forgotten. Liberal sentiments began to spread among the masses. The people very justly complained that, while the English government claimed to be a government of the people, they had no part in it.[1]

Now, it is instructive to note the different ways in which Liberalism was dealt with by the English government and by the rulers on the continent. In the continental countries the rising spirit of democracy was met by cruel and despotic repressions. The people were denied by their rulers all participation in the affairs of government. We have seen the result. Liberalism triumphed indeed at last, but triumphed only through Revolution.

In England, the government did not resist the popular demands to the point of Revolution. It made timely concessions to the growing spirit of democracy. Hence here, instead of a series of revolutions, we have a series of reform measures, which, gradually popularizing the House of Commons, at last renders the English nation not alone in name, but in reality, a self-governing people.

The Reform Bill of 1832. — The first Parliamentary step in

---

[1] The English Revolution of 1688 transferred authority from the king to the Parliament. The elective branch of that body, however, rested upon a very narrow electoral basis. Out of 5,000,000 Englishmen who should have had a voice in the government, not more than 160,000 were voters, and these were chiefly of the rich upper classes. At the opening of the nineteenth century the number of electors in Scotland did not exceed 3000.

reform was taken in 1832. To understand this important act, a retrospective glance becomes necessary.

When, in 1265, the Commons were first admitted to Parliament (see p. 480), members were called only from those cities and boroughs whose wealth and population fairly entitled them to representation. In the course of time some of these places dwindled in population, and new towns sprang up : yet the decayed boroughs retained their ancient privilege of sending members to Parliament, while the new towns were left entirely without representation. Thus Old Sarum, an ancient town now utterly decayed and without a single inhabitant, was represented in the Commons by two members. Furthermore, the sovereign, for the purpose of gaining influence in the Commons, had, from time to time, given unimportant places the right of returning members to the Lower House. In 1793 less than 200 electors, or voters, sent to the Commons 197 members. Of course, elections in these small or " pocket boroughs," as they were called, were almost always determined by the corrupt influence of the crown or of the resident lords. The Lower House of Parliament was thus filled with the nominees of the king, or of some great lord, or with persons who had bought the office, often with little effort at concealment. At the same time, such large, recently grown manufacturing towns as Birmingham and Manchester had no representation at all in the Commons.

Agitation was begun for the reform of this corrupt and farcical system of representation. The contest between the Whigs and the Tories, or Liberals and Conservatives, was long and bitter. The Conservatives of course opposed all reform. Bill after bill was introduced into Parliament to correct the evil, but most of these, after having passed the Commons, were lost in the House of Lords. At last the public feeling became so strong and violent that the lords were forced to yield, and the Reform Bill of 1832 became a law.[1]

By this act the electoral system of the kingdom was radically

[1] The popularizing of the House of Commons led to a series of acts of a popular character. Among them was an act (in 1833) for the abolition of

changed. Fifty-six of the " rotten boroughs " were disfranchised,
and the 143 seats in the Lower House which they had filled were
given to different counties and large towns. The bill also greatly
increased the number of electors by extending the right of voting
to all persons owning or leasing property of a certain value. We
can scarcely exaggerate the importance of this Reform Bill.

Chartism: the Revolutionary Year of 1848. — But while the
Reform bill of 1832 was almost revolutionary in the principle it
established, it went only a little way in the application of the
principle. It admitted to the franchise the middle classes only.
The great laboring class were given no part in the government.
They now began an agitation, — characterized by much bitterness,
— known as Chartism, from a document called the " People's
Charter," which embodied the reforms they desired. These were
" universal suffrage, vote by ballot, annual parliaments, the division
of the country into equal electoral districts, the abolition of the
property qualifications of members, and payment for their services."

The agitation for these changes in the constitution went on with
more or less violence until 1848. That year the Chartists, encouraged by the revolutions then shaking almost every throne
on the European continent, indulged in riotous demonstrations
which frightened the law-abiding citizens, and brought discredit
upon themselves. Their organization now fell to pieces. The
reforms, however, which they had labored to secure, were, in the
main, desirable and just, and the most important of them have
since been adopted and made a part of the English Constitution.

The Reform Bill of 1867. — The Reform Bill of 1867 was simply another step taken by the English government in the direction
of the Reform Bill of 1832. Like that measure, it was passed only
after long and violent agitation and discussion both without and
within the walls of Parliament. Its main effect was the extension
of the right of voting, — the enfranchisement of the great " fourth
estate, or the masses." By it also a few small boroughs in Eng-

slavery throughout the British colonies. 780,993 slaves in the British West
Indies were freed at a cost to the English nation of £20,000,000.

land — for the bill did not concern either Ireland or Scotland, separate bills of somewhat similar provisions being framed for them — were disfranchised, and several new ones created.

The Reform Bill of 1884. — One of the conservative leaders, the Earl of Derby, in the discussions upon the Reform Bill of 1867, said, "No doubt we are making a great experiment, and taking a leap in the dark." Just seventeen years after the passage of that bill, the English people were ready to take another leap. But they were not now leaping in the dark. The wisdom and safety of admitting the lower classes to a participation in the government had been demonstrated.

In 1884 Mr. Gladstone, then prime minister, introduced and pushed to a successful vote a new reform bill, more radical and sweeping in its provisions than any preceding one. It increased the number of voters from about 3,000,000 to about 5,000,000. The qualification of voters in the counties was made the same as that required of voters in the boroughs. Hence its effect was to enfranchise the great agricultural classes.

Only the Forms of Monarchy remain. — The English government is now in reality as democratic as our own. Only the forms of monarchy remain. It does not seem probable that these can long withstand the encroachments of democracy. Hereditary privilege, as represented by the House of Lords and the Crown, is likely soon to be abolished.

Home Rule for Ireland. — In connection with the above outline of the democratic movement in England, a word must be said about the so-called Home Rule movement in Ireland.

The legislative independence secured by Ireland in 1782 (see p. 632), was maintained only a short time. In 1798, England being then engaged in war with the revolutionists of France, the Irish rose in revolt, with the purpose of setting up an Irish republic. The uprising was quelled, and then as a measure of security the Irish Parliament was abolished (1801) and Ireland given representation in the English Parliament, just as had been done in the case of Scotland at the time of the legislative union of England and Scotland (see p. 629).

The Irish patriots bitterly resented this extinction of the legis-lative independence of Ireland, and denounced as traitors those members of the last Irish Parliament who, corrupted by the English minister, William Pitt (the younger), had voted away Irish liberties. Consequently from the day of the Union to the present, there has been more or less agitation for its repeal and the re-establishment of the old Irish Parliament. In 1841, under the inspiration of the eloquent Daniel O'Connell, Ireland was brought to the verge of insurrection, but the movement was suppressed. In 1886 Mr. Gladstone, then prime minister, introduced a bill in Parliament, granting a separate legislature to Ireland. This led to bitter debate both within and without the walls of Parliament, and at the present time (1889), the question of Home Rule for Ireland is the leading issue in English politics.[1]

2. Expansion of the Principle of Religious Equality.

Religious Freedom and Religious Equality. — Alongside the political movement traced in the preceding section has run a similar one in the religious realm. This is a growing recognition by the English people of the true principle of religious toleration.

At the opening of the nineteenth century there was in England religious freedom, but no religious equality. That is to say, one might be a Catholic or a dissenter, if he chose to be, without fear of persecution. Dissent from the Established Church was not unlawful. But one's being a dissenter disqualified him from holding certain public offices. Where there exists such discrimi-nation against any religious sect, or where any one sect is favored or sustained by the government, there of course is no religious equality, although there may be religious freedom. Progress in this direction, then, has consisted in the growth of a really tolerant spirit, which has led to the removal of all civil disabilities from

[1] Closely connected with this political question of Home Rule for Ireland, is the agrarian, or land trouble. At bottom, this is a matter that involves the right of private property in land, and touches questions that belong to the In-dustrial Age (see p. 729) rather than to that of the Political Revolution.

Catholics, Protestant dissenters and Jews, and the placing of all sects on an absolute equality before the law. This is but a completion of the work of the Protestant Reformation.

Methodism and its Effects upon Toleration. — One thing that helped to bring prominently forward the question of emancipating non-conformists from the civil disabilities under which they were placed, was the great religious movement known as Methodism, which during the latter part of the eighteenth and the beginning of the nineteenth century revolutionized the religious life of England.[1] By vastly increasing the body of Protestant dissenters, Methodism gave new strength to the agitation for the repeal of the laws which bore so heavily upon them.

Disabilities removed from Protestant Dissenters (1828). — One of the earliest and most important of the acts of Parliament in this century in recognition of the principle of religious equality, was the repeal of the Corporation and Test Acts, in so far as they bore upon Protestant dissenters. These were acts passed in the reign of Charles II., which required every officer of a corporation, and all persons holding civil and military positions, to take certain oaths, and partake of the communion according to the rites of the Anglican Church. It is true that these laws were not now strictly enforced ; nevertheless, the laws were invidious and vexatious, and the Protestant dissenters demanded their repeal. The result of the debate in Parliament was the repeal of such parts of the ancient acts as it was necessary to rescind in order to relieve Protestant dissenters, — that is, the provision requiring persons holding office to be communicants of the Anglican Church.

---

[1] The leaders of the movement were George Whitefield (1714–1770) and John Wesley (1703–1791). Whitefield became the leader of the *Calvinistic* Methodists, and Wesley the founder of the sect known as *Wesleyans*. The Methodists at first had no thought of establishing a church distinct from the Anglican, but simply aimed to form within the Established Church a society of earnest, devout laymen, somewhat like that of the Young Men's Christian Association in our present churches. Petty persecution, however, eventually constrained them to go out from the established organization and form a Church of their own. This of course constituted them dissenters.

Disabilities removed from the Catholics (1829).— The bill of 1828 gave no relief to Catholics. They were still excluded from Parliament and various civil offices by the declarations of belief and the oaths required of office-holders, — declarations and oaths which no good Catholic could conscientiously make. They now demanded that the same concessions be made them that had been granted Protestant dissenters. The ablest champion of Catholic emancipation was the eloquent Daniel O'Connell, an Irish patriot.

A threatened revolt on the part of the Irish Catholics hurried the progress of what was known as the *Catholic Emancipation Act* through Parliament. This law opened all the offices of the kingdom, below the crown, — save that of Lord Chancellor of England and Ireland, the Viceroyalty of Ireland, and a few others, — to the Catholic subjects of the realm.

Disabilities removed from the Jews. — The Jews were still laboring under all the disabilities which had now been removed from Protestant dissenters and Catholics. In 1845 an act was passed by Parliament which so changed the oath required for admission to corporate offices — the oath contained the words " on the faith of a Christian " — as to open them to Jews.

In 1858, after a long and unseemly struggle, the House of Commons was opened to the long-proscribed race ; and about a quarter of a century later, the House of Lords admitted to a seat Baron Rothschild, the first peer of Hebrew faith that had ever sat in that body.

Disestablishment of the Irish Church (1869). — Forty years after the Catholic Emancipation Act, the English government took another great step in the direction of religious equality, by the disestablishment of the State Church in Ireland.

The Irish have always and steadily refused to accept the religion which their English conquerors have somehow felt constrained to force upon them. The vast majority of the people are to-day and ever have been Catholics ; yet up to the time where we have now arrived these Irish Catholics had been compelled to pay tithes and fees for the maintenance among them of the Anglican Church worship. Meanwhile their own churches, in which the great masses were instructed and cared for spiritually, had to be kept up by voluntary contributions. The proposition to do away with this grievance by the disestablishment of the State Church in Ireland was bitterly opposed by the Conservatives; but at length, after a memorable debate, the Liberals, under the lead of Bright and Gladstone, the latter then prime minister, carried the measure. This was in 1869, but the actual disestablishment was not to take place until the year 1871, at which time the Irish State Church, ceasing to exist as a state institution, became a free Episcopal Church. The historian May pronounces this "the most important ecclesiastical matter since the Reformation."

Proposed Disestablishment of the State Church in England and in Scotland. — The perfect application of the principle of religious equality demands, in the opinion of many English Liberals, the disestablishment of the State Church in England and in Scotland.[1] They feel that for the government to maintain any particular sect, is to give the State a monopoly in religion. They would have the churches of all denominations placed on an absolute equality. Especially in Scotland is the sentiment in favor of disestablishment very strong.

3. GROWTH OF THE BRITISH EMPIRE IN THE EAST.

The Clew to England's Foreign Policy in the Nineteenth Century. — Seeking the main fact of modern English history, Professor Seeley[2] finds it in the expansion of England. He says, in substance, that the expansion of England in the New World and in Asia is the formula which sums up for England the history of the last three centuries. As the outgrowth of this extension into remote lands of English population or influence, England has come successively into sharp rivalry with three of the leading powers of Europe, her competitors in the field of colonization or in the race for empire. The seventeenth century stands out as an age of in-

[1] The Established Church in Scotland is the Presbyterian.
[2] J. R. Seeley, in his work entitled *The Expansion of England.*

tense rivalry between England and Spain; the eighteenth was a period of gigantic competition between England and France; while the nineteenth has been an age of jealous rivalry between England and Russia.

England triumphed over Spain and France; it remains to be seen whether she will in like manner triumph over Russia.

We have space simply to indicate how England's foreign policies and wars during the present century have grown out of her Eastern connections, and her fear of the overshadowing influence of the Colossus of the North.

Rise of the English Power in India. — And first, we must say a word respecting the establishment of English authority in India. By the close of the seventeenth century the East India Company (see p. 603) had founded establishments at Bombay, Calcutta, and Madras, the three most important centres of English population and influence in India at the present time. The company's efforts to extend its authority in India were favored by the decayed state into which the Great Mogul Empire — founded in Northern India by the Tartar conquerors (see p. 461) — had fallen, and by the contentions of the independent native princes among themselves.

For a long time it was a matter of doubt whether the empire to be erected upon the ruins of the Great Mogul Empire and of the contending native states should be French or English. About the middle of the eighteenth century the former had the stronger foothold in the peninsula, just as previous to the French and Indian War in the New World they had the stronger hold upon the North American continent.

A terrible crime committed by the Nabob Surajah Dowlah of Bengal, a province lying along the lower courses of the Ganges, determined the fate not only of that native state, but of all India. Moved by jealousy of the growing power of the English, and encouraged by the French, the Nabob attacked and captured the English post at Calcutta. His one hundred and forty-six prisoners he crowded into a close dungeon, called the Black Hole. In the course of a sultry night the larger part of the unfortunate prisoners were suffocated.

The crime was avenged by Robert Clive, the English commander at Madras. With only 100 English soldiers and 2000 sepoys (native soldiers in European employ), he sailed for Calcutta, recaptured that place, and on the memorable field of Plassey, scattered to the winds the Nabob's army of 60,000 (1757).

The victory of Plassey established upon a firm basis the growing power of the Company. During the next one hundred years it extended its authority throughout almost every part of the peninsula. Many of the native princes were, and still are, allowed to retain their thrones, only they must now acknowledge the suzerainty or paramount authority of the English government.

We will now speak briefly of the most important wars and troubles in which England has been involved through her interests in India.

The Afghan War of 1838-1842. — One of the first serious wars into which England was drawn through her jealousy of Russia was what was known as the Afghan War. It was England's policy to maintain the Afghan state as a barrier between her East India possessions and Russia. Persuaded that the ruler of the Afghans, a usurper named Dost Mahommed, was inclined to a Russian alliance, the English determined to dethrone him, and put in his place the legitimate prince. This was done. The Afghans, however, resented this interference in their affairs. They arose in revolt, and forced the English army to retreat from the country. In the wild mountain passes leading from Afghanistan into India, the fleeing army, 16,000 in number, counting camp-followers, was cut off almost to a man. The English took signal vengeance. They again invaded the country, defeated the Afghans, punished some of their leaders, burned the chief bazaar of Cabul, and then withdrawing from the country, left the Afghans to themselves.

Opium War with China (1840-1842). — The next war incited by British interest in India was the so-called Opium War with China.

During the first half of the present century the opium traffic between India and China grew into gigantic proportions, and became an important source of wealth to the British merchants, and of revenue to the Indian government. The Chinese government, however, awake to the enormous evils of the growing use of the narcotic, forbade the importation of the drug; but the British merchants, notwithstanding the imperial prohibition, persisted in the trade, and succeeded in smuggling large quantities of the article into the Chinese market. Finally, the government seized and destroyed all the opium stored in the warehouses of the British traders at Canton. This act, together with other "outrages," led to a declaration of war on the part of England. British troops now took possession of Canton, and the Chinese government, whose troops were as helpless as children before European soldiers, was soon forced to agree to the treaty of Nanking, by which the island of Hong-Kong was ceded to the English, several important ports were opened to British traders, and the perpetuation of the nefarious traffic in opium was secured.

The Crimean War (1854–1856). — Scarcely was the Opium War ended before England was involved in a gigantic struggle with Russia, — the Crimean War, already spoken of in connection with Russian history (see p. 694). From our present standpoint we can better understand why England threw herself into the conflict on the side of Turkey. She fought to maintain the integrity of the Ottoman Empire, in order that her own great rival, Russia, might be prevented from seizing Constantinople and the Bosporus, and from that point controlling the affairs of Asia through the command of the Eastern Mediterranean.

The Sepoy Mutiny (1857–1858). — The echoes of the Crimean War had barely died away before England was startled by the most alarming intelligence from the country for the secure possession of which English soldiers had borne their part in the fierce struggle before Sebastopol.

In 1857 there broke out in the armies of the East India Company what is known as the Sepoy Mutiny. The causes of the uprising were various. The crowd of deposed princes was one element of discontent. A widespread conviction among the natives, awakened by different acts of the English, that their religion was in danger, was another of the causes that led to the rebellion. There were also military grievances of which the native soldiers complained.

The mutiny broke out at Bengal. At different points, by pre-concerted signals, the native regiments arose against their English officers and put them to death.[1] Delhi and Cawnpore were seized, and the English residents and garrisons butchered in cold blood. Fortunately many of the native regiments stood firm in their allegiance to the English, and with their aid the revolt was speedily quelled.

At the close of the war, the government of India, by act of Parliament, was taken out of the hands of the East India Company and vested in the English crown. Since this transfer, the Indian government has been conducted on the principle that " English rule in India should be for India."[2]

Later events: The English in Egypt. — It only remains for us to refer to some later matters which are more or less intimately connected with England's Eastern policy.

In 1874 Mr. Disraeli, who had then just succeeded Mr. Gladstone as prime minister, purchased, for $20,000,000, the 176,000 shares which the Khedive of Egypt held in the Suez Canal. This was to give England more perfect control of this all-important gateway to her East India possessions.

[1] The East India Company at this time had an army of nearly 300,000, of which number not more than 45,000 were English troops. The chief positions in the native regiments were held by English officers.

[2] Within the last two or three decades the country has undergone in every respect a surprising transformation. Life and property are now as secure in India as in England. The railways begun by the East India Company have been extended in every direction, and now bind together the most distant provinces of the empire. All the chief cities are united by telegraph. Lines of steamers are established on the Indus and the Ganges. Public schools have been opened, and colleges founded. Several hundred newspapers, about half published in the native dialects, are sowing Western ideas broadcast among the people. The introduction of European science and civilization is rapidly undermining many of the old superstitions, particularly the ancient system of caste.

In 1878, towards the close of the Russo-Turkish War, England, it will be recalled, interfered in behalf of the Turks, and, by the presence of her iron-clads in the Bosporus, prevented the Russians from occupying Constantinople. In the treaty negotiations which followed, England received from Turkey the island of Cyprus.

In the year 1882 political and financial reasons combined led the English government, now conducted by Gladstone, to interfere in the affairs of Egypt. A mutinous uprising against the authority of the Khedive having taken place in the Egyptian army, an expedition was sent out under the command of Lord Wolseley for the purpose of suppressing the revolt, and by the restoration of the authority of the Khedive to render secure the Suez Canal, and protect the interest of English bondholders in Egyptian securities.

Three years later, in 1885, a second expedition had to be sent out to the same country. The Soudanese, subjects of the Khedive, encouraged by the disorganized condition of the Egyptian

government, had revolted, and were threatening the Egyptian garrisons in the Soudan with destruction. Lord Wolseley was sent out a second time, to lead an expedition up the Nile to the relief of Khartoum, where General Gordon, a representative of the English government, was commanding the Egyptian troops, and trying — to use his own phrase — to "smash the Mahdi," the military prophet and leader of the Soudanese Arabs.

The expedition arrived too late, Khartoum having fallen just before the advance relief party reached the town. The English troops were now recalled, and the greater part of the Soudan abandoned to the rebel Arabs. Further complications seem likely to grow out of England's presence in Egypt.

CONCLUSION: THE NEW AGE.

The Age of Material Progress, or the Industrial Age. — History has been well likened to a grand dissolving view. While one age is passing away another is coming into prominence.

During the last fifty years the distinctive features of society have wholly changed. The battles now being waged in the religious and the political world are only faint echoes of the great battles of the sixteenth, seventeenth, and eighteenth centuries. A new movement of human society has begun. Civilization has entered upon what may be called the Industrial Age, or the Age of Material Progress.

The decade between 1830 and 1840 was, in the phrase of Herzog, "the cradle of the new epoch." In that decade several of the greatest inventions that have marked human progress were first brought to practical perfection. Prominent among these were ocean steam navigation, railroads, and telegraphs.[1] In the year 1830 Stephenson exhibited the first really successful locomotive. In 1836 Morse perfected the telegraph. In 1838 ocean steamship navigation was first practically solved.

The rapidity with which these inventions have been introduced into almost all parts of the world, partakes of the marvellous.

Within the last fifty years the continents have been covered with a perfect network of railroads, constructed at an enormous cost of labor and capital. The aggregate length of the world's steam railways in 1883 was about 275,000 miles, sufficient, to use Mul-

---

[1] Ploetz in his *Epitome of History*, instructively compares these inventions to the three great inventions or discoveries — the magnetic needle, gunpowder, and printing — that ushered in the Modern Age.

hall's illustration, to girdle the earth eleven times at the equator, or more than sufficient to reach from the earth to the moon. The continental lines of railways are made virtually continuous round the world by connecting lines of ocean steamers. Telegraph wires traverse the continents in all directions, and cables run beneath all the oceans of the globe.

By these inventions the most remote parts of the earth have been brought near together. A solidarity of commercial interests has been created. Thought has been made virtually cosmopolitan : a new and helpful idea or discovery becomes immediately the common possession of the world. Facilities for travel, by bringing men together, and familiarizing them with new scenes and different forms of society and belief, have made them more liberal and tolerant. Mind has been broadened and quickened. And by the virtual annihilation of time and space, governmental problems have been solved. The chief difficulties in maintaining a confederation of states widely separated have been removed, and such extended territories as those of the United States made practically as compact as the most closely consolidated European state. England, with her scattered colonies, may now, Professor Seeley thinks, well enough become a World-Venice, with the oceans for streets. Furthermore, the steps of human progress have been accelerated a hundred-fold. The work of years, and of centuries even, is crowded into a day. Thus Japan, on the outskirts of the world, has been modified more by our civilization within the last decade or two, than Britain was modified by the civilization of Rome during the four hundred years that the island was connected with the empire.

But a still more important feature of the new epoch is the use of steam engines, electric motors, and machinery in the manufactures and the various other industries of mankind. At the beginning of the nineteenth century the great manufactures of the world were in their infancy. Under the impulse of modern inventions they have been carried to seeming perfection at a bound. New motors and improved machinery have increased incalculably the productive forces of society. This enormous augmentation of the power of production is one of the most significant features of the age.

The history of this wonderful age, so different from any preceding age, cannot yet be written, for no one can tell whether the epoch is just opening or is already well advanced. It may well be that we have already seen the greatest surprises of the age, and that the epoch is nearing its culmination,[1] and that other than material development — let us hope intellectual and moral development — will characterize future epochs.

[1] "It is probable," says Professor Ely, "that as we, after more than two thousand years, look back upon the time of Pericles with wonder and astonishment, as an epoch great in art and literature, posterity two thousand years hence will regard our era as forming an admirable and unparalleled epoch in the history of industrial invention." — *French and German Socialism in Modern Times.*

INDEX, PRONOUNCING VOCABULARY, AND GLOSSARY.

NOTE.— In the case of words whose correct pronunciation has not seemed to be clearly indicated by their accentuation and syllabication, the sounds of the letters have been denoted thus: ā, like *a* in *grāy ;* ă like ā, only less prolonged; ă, like *a* in *hăve ;* ä, like *a* in *fär ;* ē, like *ee* in *fēet ;* ĕ, like *e* in *ĕnd ;* ẹ and ẹh, like *k ;* ç, like *s ;* g̣, like *j ;* ô like *o* in *for ;* s̟, like *z.*

Gi-ron′dists, the name, 655; party in the national convention, 657; fall of, 659.

Gladiatorial combats, 361–363; suppression of, 339, 340.

Gladiators, war of the, 285, 286.

Gladstone, prime minister, 719, 728.

Godfrey of Bouillon (god′fri boo-yŏn′), 442, 443.

Godwin, earl of Wessex, 434.

Golden Candlestick, 347, n.

Go-ma′tes, 78.

Gordon, General, 728.

Gor′gi-as, 205.

Gor′gons, 104.

Goths, the, 336, 337; conversion of, 377.

Grac′chi, reforms of, 276, 277.

Grac′chus, Caius, 276, 277.
Tiberius, 276.

Grace, edict of, 581.

Græco-Persian War, 125–135.

Gra-nä′da, 398; conquest of, 499, 500.

Grand Alliance, the, 596.

Gra-ni′cus, battle of the, 162.

Gra′ti-an, Roman emp., 336, 337, 338.

Grăt′tan, Henry, 632.

Great Britain, the name, 629. See *England.*

Great Fire in Rome, 312.

Great Schism, the, 468.

Great Seal of England, 624.

Grecian architecture, 176–182.
sculpture, 187–189.
temples as banks of deposit, 178, n.

Greece, divisions of, 87; mountains of, 87, 88; islands about, 88; influence of country upon inhabitants, 89.

Greek Church, the, 417.

Greek Empire. See *Eastern Empire.*

Greek Fire, 398.

Greeks, local patriotism of, 92; myths and legends of, 93–97; society of, in the Heroic Age, 98–108; piracy among, 99; religion of, 101–108; colonies, 110, 111; literature, 190–202; philosophy and science, 203–214; social life, 215–222.

Gregory. For this name see *Popes.*

Grey, Lady Jane, 552.

Guē′bers, 401, n. See *Fire-worshippers.*

Guelphs (gwĕlfs), 504.

Guillotine (gĭl′lo-teen′), the, 662.

Guiscard (gēs-kar′), Robert, 433.

Guise (gweez), family of, 573.

Gunpowder, effect of use in war, 427.

Gunpowder Plot, the, 602.

Gŭs-tā′vŭs Vasa, 512.

Gutenberg (goo′ten-berg′), John, 476.

Gy-lip′pus, Spartan commander, 152.

Ha′des, realm of, 101; the god, 103.

Ha′dri-an, Roman emp., 320.

Hal′i-car-nas′sus, mausoleum at, 182.

Ha′lys, the, 75.

Ha-mil′car Bar′cas, 252, 256.

Hamites, 3.

Hampden, John, 608, 609.

Hanging Gardens of Babylon, 62.

Han′ni-bal, his vow, 257; attacks Saguntum, 257; crosses the Alps, 258, 259; in Italy, 259–264; his death, 265, n.

Han′no, Carthaginian admiral, 253.

Hanover, house of, 630; sovereigns of, 630, n.

Hanseatic League, 468, 469.

Harold I. (son of Godwin), k. of England, 434, 435.

Harold Hardrada, k. of Norway, 434.

Haroun-al-Raschid (hä-roon′äl-rash′-id), 400.

Has′dru-bal, Hannibal's brother, 264.

Has′dru-bal, son-in-law of Hamilcar, 256.

Hastings, battle of, 434, 435.

Hébert (ā′bêr′), 663.

Hebrew monarchy, founding of, 63, 64; division of, 66.

Hebrew Temple, robbed by Titus, 314.

Hebrews, enter Egypt, 21; history of, 63–68; their religion and literature, 68, 69.

Hector, 95.

He-gi′ra, the, 393.

Helen, 95.

He-le′na, St., 688.

Hel′i-con, Mount, 88.

Hellas, the name, 91, n.

Hel-le′nēs, the, 89–91. See *Greeks.*

Lu'beck, peace of, 583.

Lu'can, 313.

Lu-ca'ni-a, 222.

Lu'ce-res, 224.

Lu-cil'i-us, 354.

Lu'ci-us, grandson of Augustus, 308.

Lu-cre'ti-us, 354.

Luneville (lu'ne-vil), treaty of, 674.

Lu'si-ta'ni-ans, the, 272.

Luther, Martin, opposes Tetzel, 522; his ninety-five theses, 522, 523; burns the papal bull, 523; at the Diet of Worms, 523, 524; his death, 525.

Lützen (loot'sen), battle of, 585.

Lux'or, temple of, 33.

Ly-ce'um, the Athenian, 122.

Lyc'i-a, 75, 268.

Ly-cur'gus, legend of, 112, 113.

Lydia, 75.

Lydians, the, 75.

Lyons, 660.

Ly-san'der, Spartan general, 154.

Ly-sim'a-chus, kingdom of, 171.

Ly-sip'pus, 186, 187.

Mac'ca-bees, the, 68.

Macchiavelli (mäk-ke-ä-vel'lee), 468, n.

Macedonia, population of, 159; under Philip II., 159–161; after the death of Alexander, 173–175.

Macedonian supremacy, p. of, 159–168.

Mad-rid', peace of, 532.

Mæ-ce'nas, minister of Augustus, 307.

Mag'de-burg, sack of, 584.

Magellan (ma-jel'lan), 515, 516.

Magenta (ma-jĕn'ta), battle of, 712.

Magi, 78, n., 84.

Ma'gi-an-ism, 78, n.

Magna Charta, 479, 480.

Magna Græcia, 111.

Mag-ne'si-a, battle of, 268.

Ma'go, brother of Hannibal, 261.

Magyars (mŏd'yors'). See *Hungarians*.

Ma-har'bal, Carthaginian general, 262.

Malplaquet (mäl'plä'kä'), battle of, 597.

Man'de-ville, Sir John, 451.

Man'e-tho, 19.

Manlius, M., 240, 241, 242.

Man'ti-ne'a, battle of, 158.

Marat (mä-rä'), 655; his assassination, 660.

Mar'a-thon, battle of, 126, 127.

Mar-cel'lus, Marcus Claudius, 262.

Mar-cel'lus, nephew of Augustus, 308.

Mar'co Po'lo, 451.

Mar-do'ni-us, Persian general, 80, 135.

Margaret, Duchess of Parma, 564.

Ma-ren'go, battle of, 674.

Marie Antoinette (mä're'on'twä'nĕt'), her execution, 660.

Marie Theresa (ma-rē'a te-ree'sä), of Austria, 645.

Mariette (mä're-ett'), 29.

Marlborough (mawl'b'ro), d. of, 596, 597.

Ma'ri-us, Caius (ka'yus), in the Jugurthine war, 278; defeats the Cimbri and Teutones, 278, 279; contest with Sulla, 281; wanderings of, 281, 282; his death, 282.

Mars, 228.

Marseillaise (mär'säl-yäz') hymn, 658.

Marsic War. See *Social War*.

Mary Stuart, q. of Scots, 557, 558.

Mary Tudor, q. of England, reign, 552–554.

Mary, wife of William III. of England, 624–628.

Mas'i-nis'sa, k. of Numidia, 269, 270.

Maspero, Professor, quoted, 39.

Mas-sa'li-a, 111.

Maurepas (mōr'pä'), 650.

Maurice (maw'riss), of Nassau, 569.

Mau-so'lus, 182.

Max-en'ti-us, 353.

Max'i-min, 328.

Max-im'i-an, Roman emp., 330, 331.

Maximilian I., emp. H. R. E., 507.

Mazarin (mäz-a-reen'), Cardinal, 591, 592.

Mazzini (mät-see'nee), Joseph, 710.

Mec'ca, 392.

Medes, 4, 74.

Medici (med'e-chee), Catherine de, her character, 573; her part in the massacre of St. Bartholomew, 576; Mary de, 579.

Spanish Succession, war of the, 596, 597, 628.

Sparta, early history of, 112–117; opposes the Athenian democracy, 124.

Spar'ta-cus, 285, 286.

Spartan supremacy, 155, 156.

Spartans, the. See *Sparta.*

Spar'ti-a'tæ. See *Spartans.*

Spenser, Edmund, 562, n.

Sphac-te'ri-a, 150.

Sphinx, great Egyptian, 34.

Spires, second diet of, 525.

Spor'a-dēs, the, 88.

Spu-rin'na, Roman astrologer, 299.

Sta-ği'ra, 209.

Stamford Bridge, battle of, 434.

Stăn-is-la'ŭs Lesczinski (lĕsh-chin'skee), 638.

Star Chamber, the, 607, n.

States-General of France, first meeting of, 494; no meeting under Louis XIV., 592; meeting of, in 1789, 650, 651; changed into the National Assembly, 651.

Steamship, ocean, navigation, 729.

Stephen of Blois (blwä), 436, n.

Stil'i-cho, 339, 341.

Stoics, the, 210, 211.

Strĕl'it-zes, 635.

Stuart, house of. See *Table of Contents.*

Stuart, Henry (Lord Darnley), 557.

Stuart, Mary, 557, 558.

Sū'dras, 8, 11.

Sue'vi, 341; conversion of, 378.

Suez Canal, 727, 728.

Suf'fe-tes̨, Carthaginian magistrates, 247.

Sulla, fights under Marius in Africa, 278; secures command of Mithridatic expedition, 281; brings war to a close, 282, 283; proscriptions of, 283, 284.

Su'ni-um, 179, n.

Sŭn'nītes, 395, n.

Supremacy, act of, 546, 555.

Supreme Being, worship of, set up by Robespierre, 664.

Surajah Dowlah (sŭr-ä'jah dow'lah), 724.

Surat (soo-rat'), 603.

Su'sa, 42, 78.

Sut-tee', 12, n.

Sweden, in Thirty Years' War, 583–586; receives lands in Germany, 587; under Charles XII., 636, 637, 638.

Swift, Jonathan, 629.

Swiss Guards, massacre of the, 656.

Sy-a'gri-us, 374.

Syb'a-ris, 111.

Syracuse, 111, 152, 262.

Tabor, Mount, battle of, 670, n.

Tac'i-tus, the historian, 356.

Tac'i-tus, Roman emp., 329.

Tā'gus, the, 400.

Tal'mud, 69.

Tăm'er-lane, 461.

Tancred, 442, 443.

Tao, 17.

Taoism (tä'o-ism), 17.

Ta-ren'tum, 111, 244, 245.

Tar-pe'i-a (-ya), 242, n.

Tar-pe'i-an Rock, 242, n.

Tar-quin'i-us Priscus, 225; Superbus, 225, 227.

Tarquins, the, Rome under, 226; expulsion from Rome, 227.

Tar'ta-rus, 101.

Te'ğe-a, 117.

Tel'a-mon, battle near, 255.

Telegraph, 729, 730.

Te-lem'a-ehus, 340.

Tell, William, 506.

Tem'pe, vale of, 87.

Templars, order of the, origin, 443, n.

Ten Thousand Greeks, the, expedition of, 156.

Ten Tribes, the, captivity of, 48.

Ter'ence, 354.

Test Act, 621.

Tetzel, 521, 522.

Teu'to-nēs, the, 278, 279.

Teutonic knights, order of, origin, 443.

Teutons, the, their character, 368, 369; kingdoms established by, 371–376; conversion of, 377–384; fusion with the Latins, 385–388; legislation of, 386; ordeals among, 387, 388.

Tha'lēs, 203, n.

Disc of America, causes of same

Vasco Do Homna

Protestant Reformation
Political
causes of

Martin Luther

Pope Leo X

Pesants war

Division of Protestant

Jesuits

Outcome of the Revolt

Parson

TEXT-BOOKS ON HISTORY

FOR HIGHER SCHOOLS AND COLLEGES

By PHILIP VAN NESS MYERS, recently Professor of History and
Political Economy in the University of Cincinnati, and
WILLIAM F. ALLEN, late Professor of History
in the University of Wisconsin

Myers' General History. Half morocco. 759 pages. Illustrated. List price,
$1.50; mailing price, $1.65.

Myers' Ancient History. (Part I is Myers' Eastern Nations and Greece.
Part II is Myers' Rome.) Half morocco. 617 pages. Illustrated. List
price, $1.50; mailing price, $1.65.

Myers' Outlines of Mediaeval and Modern History. Half morocco. 740 pages.
Illustrated. List price, $1.50; mailing price, $1.65.

Myers' Mediaeval and Modern History (Revised Edition)
Part I. **The Middle Ages.** Cloth. 454 pages. With maps. Illustrated.
List price, $1.10; mailing price, $1.20.
Part II. **The Modern Age.** Cloth. 650 pages. With maps. List price,
$1.25; mailing price, $1.40.

Myers' Eastern Nations and Greece. (Part I of Myers' and of Myers and
Allen's Ancient History.) Cloth. 369 pages. Illustrated. List price,
$1.00; mailing price, $1.10.

Myers' History of Rome. (Part II of Myers' Ancient History.) Cloth. 230
pages. Illustrated. List price, $1.00; mailing price, $1.10.

Myers' History of Greece. Cloth. 577 pages. Illustrated. List price, $1.25;
mailing price, $1.40.

Myers' Rome : Its Rise and Fall. Cloth. xiii + 626 pages. With maps.
Illustrated. List price, $1.25; mailing price, $1.40.

Allen's Short History of the Roman People. (Part II of Myers and Allen's
Ancient History.) Cloth. 370 pages. Illustrated. List price, $1.00;
mailing price, $1.10.

Myers and Allen's Ancient History. (Part I is Myers' Eastern Nations and
Greece. Part II is Allen's Short History of the Roman People.) Half
morocco. 763 pages. Illustrated. List price, $1.50; mailing price, $1.65.

PROFESSOR MYERS' histories have a national use and a national reputation. They are among the few American text-books which command
the enthusiastic approval of both secondary teachers and university
professors.

The author sees the world's history from all its sides, — social, political, literary, intellectual, and religious. The great movements of civilization are clearly before him in their due order and relative importance.
No single topic or period receives more attention than its worth to the
world justifies. This sense of proportion is of the utmost importance
in books which attempt to cover such sweeps of time and prolonged
activities.

GINN & COMPANY Publishers

TEXT-BOOKS ON HISTORY